TOCQUEVILLE IN AMERICA

ALEXIS CHARLES HENRI CLEREL DE TOCQUEVILLE

# Tocqueville in America

By GEORGE WILSON PIERSON

The Johns Hopkins University Press

Baltimore and London

Originally published as *Tocqueville and Beaumont in America* in a hardcover edition by
Oxford University Press, 1938
Johns Hopkins Paperbacks edition, 1996
05 04 03 02 01 00 99 98 97      5 4 3 2


The Johns Hopkins University Press
2715 North Charles Street
Baltimore, Maryland 21218-4319
The Johns Hopkins Press Ltd., London

**Library of Congress Cataloging-in-Publication Data**

Pierson, George Wilson, 1904–
  [Tocqueville and Beaumont in America]
  Tocqueville in America / by George Wilson Pierson.
    p.   cm.
  Includes bibliographical references (p.   ) and index.
  ISBN 0-8018-5506-3 (pbk. : alk. paper)
    1. United States—Description and travel.   2. Tocqueville, Alexis de, 1805–1859—
Journeys—United States.   3. Beaumont, Gustave de, 1802–1866—Journeys—United
States.   4. United States—Social life and customs—1783–1865.   I. Title.
E165.P65   1996
973.5´6—dc20
                                                                        96-27754
                                                                        CIP

A catalog record for this book is available from the British Library.

*Frontispiece:* Alexis Charles Henri Clerel de Tocqueville, from a portrait by Chassériau
in the possession of Baron Bernard de Tocqueville.

This is the narrative of an intellectual adventure: the story of how two ambitious French aristocrats of 1831 risked honour, comfort, and career in quest of an understanding of democratic government in the modern world. Alexis de Tocqueville and Gustave de Beaumont were extraordinarily young and inexperienced when they set sail. They had no very great command of the English language. They were supposed to devote their time to an inspection of American prisons for the government of Louis Philippe. And they were recalled after only nine months. Yet out of their American experiences later emerged a book that was to affect the thinking of the western world:

## TOCQUEVILLE'S
### *DE LA DÉMOCRATIE EN AMÉRIQUE*

Why, precisely, Tocqueville and Beaumont decided to escape from France, how they secured their official mission, where they went in the United States and Canada, what they saw, whom they talked to, and how gradually there took shape in Tocqueville's mind the outline of his commentary and the substance of his striking political philosophy will here for the first time be set forth. The account has been reconstructed from a few published writings of Alexis de Tocqueville, and from a mass of newly discovered letters, diaries, sketches, and other unpublished manuscripts: the whole pieced together into a story that is at the same time a personal biography, a panorama of the United States in 1831–1832, and a coherent history of Tocqueville's thought up to the publication of his book.

IN MEMORY OF

PAUL LAMBERT WHITE

1890–1922

HISTORIAN

WHOSE ENTHUSIASM AND

PERSEVERANCE MADE

POSSIBLE THE

DISCOVERY OF THE

TOCQUEVILLE

MANUSCRIPTS

# TABLE OF CONTENTS

ix

# PART III

## *New York to Buffalo*

# PART IV

## *Great Lakes and Canada*

# PART V

## *New England: The Heart of the Experience*

# PART VI

## *Philadelphia and Baltimore*

# PART VII

## *Ohio and Mississippi*

# PART VIII

## *New Orleans to Washington*

# CONTENTS

## PART IX

### *The Interpretation of an Experience*

## APPENDIX

# ILLUSTRATIONS

*Following page 354*

## NOTE ON BEAUMONT'S SKETCHES

Beaumont carried two sketching albums with him: the first for his rapid impressions, his rough pencil sketches on the spot, and his paintings of birds; the second for pen-and-ink reproductions of these scenes, and for his more pretentious pieces. On his return home, he then presented these pictorial note-books to his two brothers; and the first has come down, apparently untouched, in the Beaumont branch of the family, while the album now in the possession of the Romanets purports to be the second of these documents. Whether this Romanet album is absolutely authentic, however, is still not certain. Despite Beaumont's initials and an unusual fidelity in detail, these ink sketches may be merely extraordinarily careful copies from an original second album since lost. Unfortunately, the Beaumont Album of original pencil drawings—which are often quite charming and close to the scene—were sketched so lightly, and have now so faded into the paper, as sometimes to defy reproduction. The second—or Romanet Album—on the contrary, is still vivid. As a consequence, the illustrations here reproduced have deliberately been taken in some part from the second and occasionally less reliable source (Photo, R.Guilleminot, reduced from an original size of $10\frac{3}{4}'' \times 8\frac{1}{2}''$).

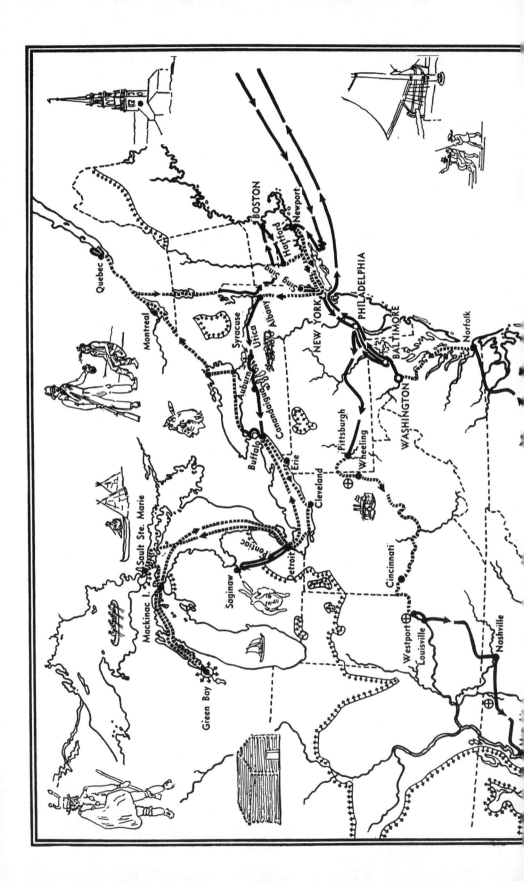

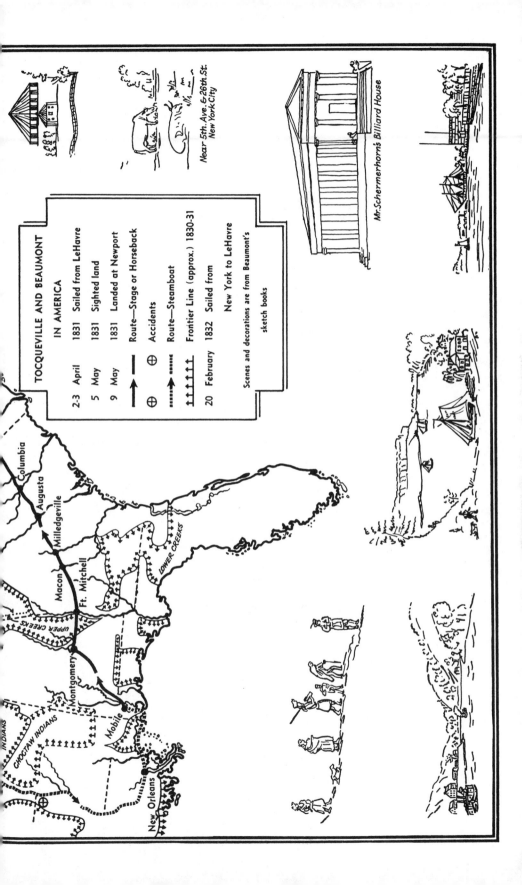

TOCQUEVILLE AND BEAUMONT
IN AMERICA

| | | |
|---|---|---|
| 2-3 April | 1831 | Sailed from LeHavre |
| 5 May | 1831 | Sighted land |
| 9 May | 1831 | Landed at Newport |
| ↑ | | Route—Stage or Horseback |
| ⊕ | | Accidents |
| ┅┅┅⟶ | | Route—Steamboat |
| ↑↑↑↑↑ | | Frontier Line (approx.) 1830-31 |
| 20 February | 1832 | Sailed from New York to LeHavre |

Scenes and decorations are from Beaumont's sketch books

Near 5th.Ave.&26th.St.
New York City

Mr.Schermerhorn's Billiard House

Columbia

Augusta

Milledgeville

Macon

Ft. Mitchell

LOWER CREEKS

UPPER CREEKS

Montgomery

Mobile

CHOCTAW INDIANS

INDIANS

New Orleans

# TOCQUEVILLE IN AMERICA

I

## A CELEBRATED BOOK

In January 1835, midway through the second administration of President Andrew Jackson, there issued from the press in Paris a treatise on the government of the United States that was to be known, and read with admiration, in all the countries of the civilized world. This treatise combined a description of the American political system with philosophical essays, or commentaries, thereon. Its two small volumes bore the ambitious yet modest title, *De la Démocratie en Amérique*: Of (or Concerning) Democracy in America.*

The author of this work was practically unknown to his fellow-citizens of the July Monarchy. They found him, when they came to call, almost diminutive in stature; a dignified, reserved, shy little gentleman, delicate of feature and restrained in gesture. Proud, dark, troubled eyes arrested the glance and fitfully illumined his pale and serious face. A sensitive mouth and lightly-cleft chin, below a strong aquiline nose, betrayed his breeding and bespoke a more than ordinary determination. The finely shaped head was darkly framed in his long black hair, which he wore falling in locks to his shoulders, in the proud fashion of the day. When receiving, or conversing, he waved his narrow hands with grace and distinction. And, when he spoke, a resonant and moving voice, surprising in so small and frail a body, made his listeners forget all but the intense conviction and innate sincerity of the man. He seemed dignity and honour personified. His name was Alexis de Tocqueville.

At once the journals took notice of the unusual *ouvrage* of M. de Tocqueville. The two small volumes were *extraordinaires*: what a clear picture of American government—what a masterful analysis of democracy in the modern world—what a striking essay in political

---

* For the sources and materials on which this study is based, see the Bibliography (Appendix E) and the special chapter notes (Appendix D). A table of the abbreviations used in citation will be found in Appendix C.

philosophy! * But it was Royer-Collard who set the seal of greatness on the work (Royer-Collard, the battle-scarred veteran of the *Doctrinaires*, the grand old champion of constitutional government in France). After having stood like Horatius at the bridge in defence of his country's liberties during the long, feverish years of the Restoration, the noble Roman was at last looking for someone on whom he could cast his warrior's mantle. He seized on the work, read it, sent for the author. Honoured beyond his expectations, M. de Tocqueville called. He had never met the great man. Royer-Collard gazed at him. *De la Démocratie en Amérique* was 'the most remarkable political work which had appeared in thirty years,' he said. And to his followers, and to all and sundry he repeated, 'Since Montesquieu, there has been nothing like it.' [1]

'Since Montesquieu. . . .' It was the unanimous verdict. Statesmen, students, politicians—and in those days few of the elite were not preoccupied with politics—all joined in the chorus of praise. Royalists, moderates, republicans, ultra-conservatives, and radicals, without distinction of party the great of France honoured themselves in doing honour to the author of this new masterpiece of political science. Louis Blanc, the socialist, and Salvandy, the royalist, wrote most appreciative reviews. Lamartine and Barrot, the republicans of '48, expressed their pleasure. Even *le petit bonhomme* M. Thiers, the ambitious little mischief-maker of the July Revolution, felt called upon to twinkle at M. de Tocqueville from behind his enormously thick glasses, and to shower him with compliments.[2]

The most polite society in the world craved to see the new literary celebrity. A man who could speak with such knowledge and understanding of the land of Washington and Franklin was worth adding to one's circle of habitués. M. de Tocqueville was sought by the *salons*. Proud of his cousin, the Vicomte de Chateaubriand soon found an opportunity to show him off. It is well known that this illustrious genius held court in the library of Mme Récamier. Heavy blinds made the sacred room dark; for she had lost her beauty, though not her charm. Each afternoon when the lesser suns—the writers, philosophers, and thinkers, most eminent and most in vogue—were admitted, they would find Chateaubriand already established. Short, stoop-shouldered, but

---

* I have recovered the trace of twenty-three articles in no less than sixteen different periodicals within a year of the publication of *De la Démocratie en Amérique*. Of those still available for examination, only the review in the ultra-royalist *Gazette de France* (3 Feb., 13 Feb. 1835) could have been regarded as in the least unfriendly to the author.

with a mighty head, the dictator of their circle would be enthroned like a demigod in his special armchair. Someone would have brought a newly composed manuscript to read. Conversation—brilliant, mordant, *spirituelle*—would follow. Mme Récamier would listen. Chateaubriand would be the judge.

One day, about two months after the appearance of M. de Tocqueville's book, the invitation came. 'Madame Récamier,' the honoured author confided to his old travelling companion, Gustave de Beaumont, 'Madame Récamier invited me to come at three o'clock, to hear the great man [Chateaubriand] read a portion of his memoirs. I went. I found there a parcel of celebrities, in bud or already in full bloom, a small *salon* very well composed. Chateaubriand first, Ampère, Ballanche, Sainte-Beuve, the Duc de Noailles and the Duc de Laval. . . .'[3] Chateaubriand, who had his own rather lordly way of doing things, undertook to introduce his embarrassed cousin to the distinguished company. 'He presented me to all those people,' the victim wryly confessed, 'in a way to make friends for me of some of them, sincere enemies of most. One and all paid me many compliments.'

This ceremony performed, the society proceeded to the afternoon's business. 'After having played the curtain-raiser [*procédé à la petite pièce* was the author's modest phrase] the real performers came on the stage. . . . It was the First Restoration and the Hundred Days. Bad taste sometimes, occasionally also very bitter bile . . . verve throughout . . . Napoleon's march on Paris after the return from the isle of Elba painted as Homer and Tacitus together might have done, the battle of Waterloo described in a way to make your nerves tremble. . . .' The *séance* at length ended, the honoured initiate returned home still vibrating from the experience, his spirit borne, as he put it, on that airy medium which is somewhere between heaven and earth.

A very few days had sufficed to make *De la Démocratie en Amérique* known, and by this time the first edition of five hundred copies was completely exhausted. Gosselin, the publisher, otherwise an intelligent fellow, is said not to have read the manuscript. At all events, he had only accepted it after an heroic resistance (*à son corps défendu*), and he had declined to publish the thousand copies originally asked.[4] Now the man was talking about getting out an 'unlimited' second edition. Before going to Mme Récamier's *salon,* therefore, the diffident author had dropped in to discuss arrangements.

'I went yesterday morning,' he wrote his friend Beaumont,* 'to the house of Gosselin, who received me with the world's most beaming face, saying: "*Ah ca!* But it appears that you have made a *chef-d'œuvre.*" Don't you find a full-length portrait of the man of business in this exclamation! I sat down. We chatted about a second edition. It was necessary to talk business, which I did clumsily enough and with the air of a small boy in the presence of his teacher. In short, I found nothing to object to in all his propositions; and, having put on my head the hat which I had been turning in my hands the past quarter-hour, I left, convinced of two things: 1. That Gosselin had the best intentions in the world; 2. that I was certainly a great fool in business matters, the which does not prevent my being an insignificant fellow.'

Certainly, if anyone had been astonished at the reception of his work, it had been M. de Tocqueville himself. A month after its publication he wrote to one of his boyhood friends:[5] 'The book up to the present goes marvellously. I am confounded by its success; for I feared, if not failure, at least a cold reception. . . . I am at present therefore on the crest of the tide, much bewildered by what is happening to me and altogether stupefied by the praises which buzz in my ears.' Whimsically, he thought of Mme Sans-Gêne. 'There was,' he recalled, 'a woman of Napoleon's court whom the Emperor one day took it into his head to make a duchess. In the evening, on entering a great *salon* and hearing herself announced by her new title, she forgot who she was, and stepped aside to let pass the lady whose name had just been pronounced. I assure you that something of the sort is happening to me. I ask myself if it is really of me they speak, and when there is no longer room for doubt, I conclude that the world must be composed of very poor people that a book, which has issued from my brain and whose limitations I know so well, should create the sensation that this one appears to produce in it.'

The modest author was already receiving letters of congratulation and praise from England. His friend Henry Reeve, later editor of the *Edinburgh Review,* was making a translation of his book and would soon get out an English edition, under the title, *Democracy in America.*† But already the London world of politics and letters was aroused

* 1 April 1835, *O.C.*,VI,28. '*De la Démocratie en Amérique* . . . had, at the time, the unbelievable success of an issue of 4000 copies. Redier, *Comme disait Monsieur de Tocqueville...,*' p.109.

† Though only twenty-two at the time, Reeve had been well educated, and his translation was long to remain the standard translation in English. Perhaps this was a misfortune. For if later American editors were to show themselves a little hypercritical

to enthusiasm. New friends like Nassau William Senior, the economist, and John Stuart Mill, the political philosopher, wrote of their interest and admiration.[6] And even the pontifical reviews accepted the new French commentary as the most illuminating work on America then extant.[7] It came to pass that M. de Tocqueville made a journey to England in June of the year. No sooner had he arrived in London than he was invited to attend a meeting of a select committee of the House of Commons on bribery at elections. There ensued, then, the spectacle of the dignitaries of the realm, in council assembled, soliciting and receiving the advice of this small Frenchman.[8] Six months later, the great Lord Peel cited his work in a famous speech.[9] The following year John Stuart Mill, in whom Tocqueville was finding a sympathetic spirit and a kindred intelligence, asked him to write an article for the *London Review*.[10] And thereafter (and for the remaining years of his life) the author of *Democracy in America* was to find in Englishmen his second audience, in England his second spiritual home.

In due course of time, if more slowly, *Democracy in America* next found its way across the water to Boston and New York; and so came to the eyes of the very democrats whose government and civilization it purported to describe. M. de Tocqueville had hoped that this would happen. But it had not occurred to Monsieur to provide against so searching a test. Writing for his fellow-countrymen rather than for Americans, he had been frank without reservations, as severe in his judgments as open in his praise. Should some of his comments fall a little gratingly on sensitive Yankee ears, so much the worse. Assuredly, thought he, his American friends would do him the justice to observe his impartiality.

The event proved the Frenchman right. Only, he had been too pessimistic. In America his book was hailed with amazement and delight, and the success that followed was beyond expectation. The story need hardly detain us long. If few to-day remember the astonishment with which our great-grandfathers learned that a foreigner could so clearly comprehend and portray the peculiar political institutions of our country, something of the commentary's character and extraordinary influence, something of its role in the political education of their descendants has long been known to every cultivated citizen. Suffice it

---

in their attacks on the accuracy of the original rendering, the writer is convinced that the young Englishman did make one capital error. In transliterating the French title, he came close to misconstruing Tocqueville's meaning both for himself and for posterity. The true sense of the original demanded rather some such title as: 'Concerning Equality in America.' For elucidation on this point, see below, ch.XIII, pp.158,165.

then to recall that, once issued in an American edition, with an able introduction by John Canfield Spencer,* *Democracy in America* soon won for itself an almost unique place in the literature of our country. Immediately sought for the libraries of scholars and statesmen, it early achieved the distinction of a special edition for use in the schools.[11] The result was that, for generations, both fathers and children were to study the government of the United States in 'De Tocqueville's' † pages. For scholars and travellers, the understanding Frenchman became an oracle and friend; among publicists and historians his name was long to be one with which to conjure. And when, finally, another foreigner—James, Viscount Bryce—was to come to supplant the celebrated treatise with his own, more modern survey, the Englishman could not refrain from paying his predecessor the high compliment of a careful and approving analysis. Wrote Bryce: 'There is perhaps no book of the generation to which he [Tocqueville] belonged which contains more solid wisdom in a more attractive dress.'[12]

For those on this side of the water who are less familiar with the story, it may, finally, be recalled that abroad the success of *De la Démocratie en Amérique* proved fully as persistent and lasting. In France, particularly, M. de Tocqueville's little volumes, so enthusiastically received in 1835, were destined to a long and glorious career. One year after the magnificent Chateaubriand had claimed his relationship, the Academy awarded the author an 'extraordinary' prize of 8000 francs for a work which, according to the reporter M.Villemain, 'did not leave the Academy the hope of often crowning its equals.'[13] Soon M. de Tocqueville was elected to the Academy of Moral and Political Sciences, finally to the *Académie française* itself.‡ Already the government of

---

* New York, 1838. Spencer took Reeve's translation, and added a new preface and some notes. The absence of a copyright agreement with England, rather than ignorance or lack of interest, seems to have been responsible for the delay in getting out an American edition.

† The name should be either Monsieur de Tocqueville, Alexis de Tocqueville, or—simply—Tocqueville. Americans, however, have used the 'De' without the title or Christian name from the very beginning, their error arising, apparently, out of the very human dislike of being misunderstood. The 'Monsieur,' obviously, would have made the name too long and ceremonious. On the other hand, the naked word 'Tocqueville' smote the American ear with too suddenly strange a sound. So the happy compromise was hit upon of calling this gentleman 'De Tocqueville,' the 'De' serving as a sort of red flag to warn the listener and reader that a French name was on the way. That the full aristocratic flavour of the name was thus brought out at the same time simply made the temptation irresistible.

‡ This was after Tocqueville had continued his commentary with two further volumes (1840) discussing the influence of '*démocratie*' on the social and cultural civilization of the Americans.

Louis Philippe, not to be outdone, had claimed him for its own, a *Chevalier de la Légion d'Honneur.* And before long, some of the younger liberals began to look to him and to his work for guidance, so that finally a school of political philosophy was to be formed, to carry on his thought long after he was dead.

Distinguished alike for its lucid descriptions of the American political system and for its thoughtful philosophical comments—to Americans a great text, to Englishmen a storehouse of wisdom, to Frenchmen a bible of political precepts and a prophecy of change—*De la Démocratie en Amérique* in the course of time became known to men the world over. To few out-of-the-way corners of the earth did its name, at least, not penetrate. One day not long before the American Civil War, it is recorded,[14] two ships were caught together in the ice in Baffin's Bay, off the shores of Greenland. The French officer from the one and the American doctor from the other fell into conversation. The circumstances in which they found themselves were soon forgotten, and their talk turned to topics of more permanent interest. Afterwards the Frenchman noted in his journal: 'Doctor Kane tells me that M. de Tocqueville's book is considered so exact that it is taken as a text-book in the United States, and given to serious persons to read.'

By serious and discerning persons, here and abroad, it has now been read with pleasure and profit for just over a hundred years.

*

* *

Yet on that now distant day when *De la Démocratie en Amérique* first issued from the Paris press, its author—*ce tout petit homme,* reserved, shy, proud—was discovered to be an obscure member of the French nobility, and exactly six months short of being thirty years old !

He was, it developed, the son of Comte Hervé de Tocqueville, a Norman aristocrat of ultra-conservative connections. And the society of Versailles knew that the Comte had served as prefect in the Restoration and had even been raised to the peerage by the reactionary Charles X, just two years before the collapse of the ill-fated House of Bourbon. Perhaps Tocqueville's mother, then . . . ? But his mother, too, belonged to the *noblesse,* and had as a matter of course brought him up in the traditions and ideals of the *ancien régime.* In his boyhood, therefore, he had enjoyed but little schooling, never attended a university, for example, or had what might be called a scholar's education. In particular, he had never been given any training in government or political science!

What manner of man, then, was M. Alexis de Tocqueville? How had he come to write—how had he been able to write his commentary? Was it not strange that a youth with his family background should have chosen to write about democracy? And what mysterious studies and experiences could he have known that he should be able to write so learnedly?

Certain additional facts, indeed, soon came to the attention of the curious public. How had so youthful and inexperienced an aristocrat been able to write so masterful a treatise of political philosophy? M. de Tocqueville was not inclined to say much about himself. But his great-grandfather, it was pointed out, had been none other than the statesman Lamoignon de Malesherbes. Hence, doubtless, his unusual ability. Furthermore, young as he seemed, Tocqueville had already visited North America and spent a short time in the country whose strange political system he so lucidly described. Four years before, together with his friend, Gustave de Beaumont, he had been sent to the United States by the French government for the purpose of making a study of the novel penitentiaries and prison reforms recently developed there. From this nine-months' prison expedition, no doubt, had come his knowledge of American institutions.

The explanation was accepted as complete and satisfactory. Mystery? Tocqueville's contemporaries saw no mystery. Inexperienced and comparatively uneducated, a scion of the aristocracy, Alexis de Tocqueville had glimpsed America at 25. Now, at 29, still unknown and unheralded, he was the author of a book on American democracy that they had to acknowledge nothing less than a masterpiece. Yet Frenchmen of 1835 were aware of no riddle to be solved.

Nor were later students of *De la Démocratie en Amérique* any more curious or critical. Extraordinary though it seems, the problem of the origins of his classic was not only ignored by Tocqueville's contemporaries: it has been neglected ever since.

First, then, of Alexis de Tocqueville, of whence he had come, of what manner of man he was, of why, in the fall of 1830, he decided to visit America.

PART I: BEHIND THE JOURNEY OF
A PROPHET

## II

## THE EDUCATION OF AN ARISTOCRAT

THERE is a device dear to the hearts of all philosophic young Frenchmen: the *idée mère,* or general remark.

Let us begin with the remark, then, that all human beings are the product of three elements. Their characters are shaped and their careers directed by the impact and interplay of three major forces, these forces being: first, their race and inheritance; secondly, their environment, the times and *milieu* in which they find themselves; thirdly, the individualizing element of personal character—the fortuitous variant that is born and grows, no one knows how, in each individual—the twist or spark that gives to each a spirit, idiosyncrasies, personal and peculiar to himself. Tocqueville, at least, was such a man. Unfortunately, with him the unanswerable forces, the elemental currents of his being that would mould his character and shape his career, were singularly powerful and singularly inharmonious, rendering his every decision difficult, making of his whole existence a problem.

By inheritance, by instinct, by many traits of character, Alexis Charles Henri Clerel de Tocqueville belonged—first of all—to the nobility. To steal away his singleness of mind, however, an invincible unselfishness and a strong idealism made him acknowledge a higher duty than the service of his class; spurred him to dedicate his career to the welfare of his fellow-men. Unhappily, he had been born in Paris on the tenth day of Thermidor in the year XIII, or—as we now write it—on 29 July 1805. That is to say, an aristocrat to his very marrow, but a crusader by instinct, he found himself in seething, embittered, nineteenth-century France.

Wrestling with contrary impulses, his spirit torn by opposing loyalties, his career was to be one long, never-ending struggle to reconcile the powerful forces clashing for mastery within him. In the end, it was only as a crier in the wilderness, only as the solemn, foreboding prophet of equality that he was to achieve some measure of spiritual peace.

\*

\*    \*

Tocqueville's father, Hervé Louis François Jean Bonaventure Clerel de Tocqueville,\* was the last of the old Norman family of Clerel, a race of provincial seigneurs—devout, conservative and loyal to their king—who through nine good generations had handed on the traditions and the proud code of the *petite noblesse*.

By the time of the Revolution, both Hervé de Tocqueville's soldier father and the gentle, honourable lady Catherine Antoinette de Damas-Crux, his mother, were dead ; though he, himself, was but seventeen. In the first joyous emigration, the Damas and other relatives of the family left the country. Reluctantly, Hervé de Tocqueville joined them. Soon, however, disgusted by the frivolity of life in Brussels, he returned to continue his education in Paris, enroll among the King's defenders, and marry Louise Marie Le Peletier de Rosambo.

This lady was one of the three daughters of the Marquis de Rosambo of the *Parlement de Paris,* and so, through her mother the Marquise, granddaughter of the aged Lamoignon de Malesherbes. The ceremony took place in 1793, just after the venerable man had defended his former master, Louis XVI, before the Convention. Hervé joined the devoted family group at the Malesherbes château. A few months of domestic happiness, and commissioners arrived from Paris, carried them all to prison.

The rest was horrible. The Marquis de Rosambo, Hervé de Tocqueville's father-in-law, was executed for the Parlement's protest against a revolutionary decree. On 24 April 1794, a keeper of the most ferocious mien entered the chamber in the Porte-Libre where the others were: 'Citizen Malesherbes, citizeness Rosambo, Chateaubriand husband and wife, you are wanted at the tribunal.' † A few hours, and delegates of the section came to take possession of their effects; they had all been

---

\* Born, château de Menou, 3 Aug. 1772, died 9 June 1856, author of: *De la Charte provinciale*, 1829; *Histoire Philosophique du Règne de Louis XV*, 2 v., 1847; *Coup d'Oeil sur le Règne de Louis XVI*, 1850; *Épisodes de la Terreur*, reprinted from *Le Contemporain*, Jan. 1867.

† *Épisodes de la Terreur*, p.27. M. de Chateaubriand was the brother of the Vicomte de Chateaubriand; his wife was the eldest daughter of M. de Rosambo and sister of Mme de Tocqueville.

guillotined. Only the fall of Robespierre saved the stricken Hervé de Tocqueville and his wife from the same fate. Finally, they were released. Ten months. Mme de Tocqueville's nerves and health had been permanently shattered, and, though he was but twenty-one when they came out, Hervé de Tocqueville's hair was white.

Twelve years afterwards, in Paris on 29 July 1805, Alexis was born, a third son * to the unhappy couple. Napoleon was just mobilizing the forces of France for Austerlitz; and Hervé de Tocqueville took his family a short distance to Verneuil, where, obscurely, the days of Tocqueville's infancy and childhood stole by. The future author of *Démocratie* had begun life, therefore, under a dictatorship and almost, as it were, in the very shadow of the Emperor. But it was some years before the contact and influence of the outside world reached him, before the strong, troubled current of nineteenth-century France poured in upon his consciousness.

From his first days, on the other hand, the infant Tocqueville sensed the family tragedy and was steeped in the traditions of his race. In the fine Verneuil château, which Hervé de Tocqueville had acquired on the settlement of the Rosambo estate, his parents lived in retirement, drawing what consolation they could from the society of other noble families, from the constant visits of relatives and friends who also had suffered during the Revolution. One family scene, typical of those days, made a deep impression on the young Tocqueville.

'I remember to-day as if it were yesterday'—fifty years later the recollection would still be vivid in his mind [1]—'a certain evening in a château where my father then dwelt, and where a family celebration had gathered to us a large number of our near relatives. The domestics had been sent out ; the whole family had collected about the hearth. My mother, who had a voice sweet and penetrating, began to sing an air which had been famous in our civil troubles, and whose words told of the misfortunes of King Louis XVI and of his death. When she ceased, every one was weeping; not over the many private misfortunes they had suffered, not even over the many relatives lost in the civil war and on the scaffold, but over the fate of this man who had died more than fifteen years before and whom most of those who were weeping over him had never seen. But this man'—was it necessary to add?—'this man had been the King.'

---

* His brothers were Hippolyte and Édouard; from the latter the present Tocquevilles are descended.

Though Hervé de Tocqueville had taken the oath to Napoleon and become mayor of Verneuil, his children were raised according to aristocratic traditions. As playmates the young Tocqueville had none others than his cousins the Chateaubriands, sons of the guillotined aunt whom he had never seen. His father, in the moment of parting, had sworn to care for them. Madame de Tocqueville was often ill, always sad at the memory of old times; and Tocqueville with his brothers (as became children of the *noblesse*) had been entrusted to the care of the family priest, to have their characters formed, to be taught the difference between right and wrong, and to be given their first introduction to religion, their first rude education. The good abbé Lesueur —a venerable, kindly man—had performed the same office for Hervé de Tocqueville in the days of Catherine Antoinette de Damas-Crux, before being forced to flee Paris during the Revolution. Now he had returned, to live again with the Tocquevilles and perform once more his patient, necessary task. With infinite care and touching devotion, he tended his new charges, teaching them chiefly, it has been well said,* hatred of the Revolution and love of those freed by it.

Finally, in 1814, for the Tocquevilles as for so many others in France, relief arrived and prosperity returned: Napoleon had fallen. For a moment the Hundred Days intervened, but with Waterloo and the second return of the Bourbons, the years without annals had been left behind and a period of activity and power opened for the family. Their relatives being influential at court, particularly with the faction of Artois (later Charles X), Hervé de Tocqueville secured appointment as prefect of the department of the Oise. His first task was to evacuate the Prussian troops from Beauvais. And thereafter, for so long as the Bourbons continued on the throne, he remained a prefect, moving about from department to department as the court desired. A tall, distinguished-looking man and an able and conservative administrator, though not a great governor, he served his masters and the cause of monarchy faithfully.† Madame de Tocqueville, meanwhile, had not followed her husband. Always ailing, she stayed behind, first at Paris, then on the Côte d'Or. And her children, ever under the

* Redier, *Comme disait Monsieur de Tocqueville...*, p.36. Among the Tocqueville manuscripts is a bundle of Lesueur's letters—affectionate, humorous, and utterly charming—which should be published some day. They were written to Édouard and to Alexis, largely in the years 1820–1823.

† His letters and reports to the government, in the *Archives Nationales*, were to be valued highly by Taine (see footnotes in Section V, 'Le Peuple,' *Les Origines de la France contemporaine*).

gentle and imaginative tutelage of abbé Lesueur, spent much of their time with her, but later more and more with their father. Gradually the influence of the rather stern but straightforward prefect increased. Édouard showed signs of becoming a cultured and conservative seigneur, fit scion of his line; and the impulsive Hippolyte entered the army, as for generations the eldest son had had the honour to do.

At length the youngest himself was allowed to go away to school. The *Lycée* at Metz, whither Hervé de Tocqueville had been transferred as prefect of the Moselle, was chosen; and Alexis plunged into his first formal studies. Under a curriculum still largely Napoleonic in character, he studied a little Greek, more Latin and mathematics, and a good deal of history and French composition. The rather narrow instruction did not develop in him much interest in books or much curiosity for knowledge; and he showed but moderate aptitude in his classes, failing in the classics and excelling only in the field in which the devoted Lesueur had especially trained him, the art of rhetoric and French composition. Later these deficiencies in his education were to prove a handicap to him.

He lived with his father, and even on occasion acted as his secretary; but often the prefect was busy and left him to his own devices. With few friends or diversions, the lonely young boy spent much time dreaming about his future. One day, wandering the corridors of the prefecture, he happened to explore his father's library. There, to the profound sorrow of the good abbé, and his own life-long regret, he came upon some sceptical or agnostic works, probably those of the eighteenth-century philosophers (whom, it is interesting to note, his great-grandfather Malesherbes had at first befriended). These books, without making an atheist of the fifteen-year-old student, shook his Catholic faith irreparably.* With the result that, as the reader will have occasion to notice, a torturing fire of intense and anxious interest in the whole subject of religion was kindled in him.

At eighteen, the year before the death of Louis XVIII and the accession of Charles X, the partially educated young man returned to Paris to take up the study of the law. Three years of legal preparation, an interval of travel, and in 1827 he embarked upon a career in the magistracy. As soon as he reached his majority and the age of eligibility,

* 'Je crois; mais je ne puis pratiquer,' Tocqueville wrote his grief-stricken 'Bébé.' Lesueur to Toc., 8 September 1824 (TT).

his father secured his appointment as *juge auditeur* * in the government court at Versailles. At once he entered upon his duties. Though finding himself unprepared and the work exacting and somewhat uncongenial, he took an active part in the business of the court from the first and conscientiously endeavoured to perfect himself in his chosen profession.

Meanwhile Hervé de Tocqueville, now a Comte, had been transferred once more, but this time to the court itself, to Versailles: and the whole family found itself reunited. Sundays, it was the duty of the white-haired prefect to accompany his King to mass. Afterwards, his privilege allowed him to watch the Dauphin at a game of chess, hear Charles X scold his partner at whist, take two good meals in the palace. Alexis de Tocqueville's parents moved in the best of society. He himself was able to count the sons of the nobility, then thronging the ranks of the magistracy, among his friends and daily associates. In 1828, finally, the Comte his father was rewarded by elevation to the peerage; and by 1830 his own increasing eloquence was beginning to win for him compliments in which the name of his great-grandfather, Malesherbes, was adroitly recalled. To his relatives and friends, the young man's future seemed assured. With his promise, his family influence, a great judicial career was freely predicted for him.

*

*     *

Tocqueville himself, however, was sure neither of his fitness nor of his desire for such a life. He still felt awkward and ill at ease on his feet, and his spirit was often stifled by the pedantry and exacting intricacies of the law. Sometimes, he wrote, he was afraid of becoming a *machine à droit.*[2] Secretly, he was ambitious to be something more than a jurist —a statesman, perhaps, though just how he did not know. Politics, at all events, was beginning to absorb his most earnest attention. Fascinated

---

* *Juges Auditeurs* were, so to speak, apprentice magistrates, assigned to the courts of first instance but retained under the direct control of the Minister of Justice (*Garde des Sceaux*). Their functions were voluntary and consultative, unless (like Tocqueville) they asked to be allowed to participate in the labours of the court, when they were given cases to investigate and report on, with the privilege of a deliberative voice. Among Tocqueville's papers are notes of eighteen cases on which he spoke. It is interesting to discover that one of Tocqueville's elderly relatives considered even the '*noblesse* of the robe' beneath the family dignity. 'Souvenez vous, Monsieur, que votre famille a toujours été de la noblesse de l'épée,' Mme de Blangy reproached him. Quoted in *Edinburgh Review*, CXIII,432–433.

by what was going on in the Chambers, the keen young man had for some time past been watching the rise and fall of ministries, the increasing exasperation of the parties, the struggles of the liberals with the ultra-conservatives, and the reactionary tendencies of Charles X. Unlike his family and their friends, he was troubled by the obstinacy of the King; and more and more strongly the conviction was growing in him that all was not well with France, that grave convulsions threatened unless the monarchy yielded to the liberal movement of the times. With this movement, strange to say, he even found himself in reluctant sympathy.

The truth was, in several ways Alexis de Tocqueville had quite grown away from his family; and in politics, particularly, he now disagreed so thoroughly with them, and the conservative aristocracy whom they represented, that he could no longer even discuss the subject with them. For this rift, two things had been responsible: his own imperious idealism and the strong influence of his times.

Ever since going away to school, apparently, he had been practising the habit, first developed in childhood, of thinking for himself. By nature strong-willed and restive under authority, he had—even in early boyhood—wanted to form his own opinions and be the best judge of his own conduct, as became a man of intelligence and character. After reading the philosophers, accordingly, not even his love for Lesueur and his reluctance to hurt the kind old man had been strong enough to smother his nascent doubts, or persuade him to continue a faithful and practising Catholic. Naturally, therefore, on coming to Paris to study law, he had followed the same procedure and turned his strong and inquiring mind toward the most important questions of the day: toward politics. With his fellow-students he had watched the struggles over the Charter,* and followed the efforts, first of Louis XVIII, then of Charles X, to govern constitutionally but at the same time royally, to reimpose the *ancien régime*, so far as they could, on modern, nineteenth-century France. What others had believed was not enough for him; he would have to form his own opinions. Gradually but inevitably, then, as he read the debates and listened to the discussions going on all about him, the thoughtful young Tocqueville was beginning to sympathize with many of the ideals of the *Doctrinaires*,

* Tocqueville's law papers indicate that he was a member, and for a time secretary, of a students' debating society which discussed politics and the new laws, when not listening to essays on legal history written by its members.

to discard many of the prejudices and dogmas of the royalists and aristocrats from whom he had sprung. In his hopes and fears, in other words, he was coming to have much in common with the younger liberals: with his contemporaries of the romantic and generous younger generation who, schooled in the speeches of Royer-Collard, were just preparing to enter the political arena as the friends of 'liberty' and better government, the champions of a more liberal and progressive regime.

From the first, however, Tocqueville's liberalism was moderate, hesitating, intellectual, rather than positive and radical. A thinker rather than an actor, a student rather than a politician or manipulator of men, an aristocrat in the liberal fold, he was puzzled and full of doubts. What had been done before, or elsewhere? he asked himself. What did he know about history or political science? about the institutions not only of foreign countries but of his own? Little, or nothing. Yet he would have to know much before he could have an intelligent opinion—before he could help formulate a reasonable program for France.[3] Program? The thought was suggestive. A decision was taking shape in his mind. Only half consciously at first, yet with all the generous enthusiasm of a crusader, the young man was slowly coming to the conclusion that only in the service of his country could he be happy. For a statesman in nineteenth-century France, for a man of character brought up to the duty of serving his kind, particularly for a man of his intelligence, of his blood and family tradition, Tocqueville was beginning to see no other honourable role.* The sturdy, liberty-loving independence of the Norman Clerels was reasserting itself in him. Often, too, he thought of his great-grandfather, who had first, he proudly remembered, defended his people before the King, then defended his King before the people. Almost he could feel the hand of Malesherbes, the statesman, on his shoulder.

With characteristic thoroughness, therefore, the young idealist set about remedying the defects in his education. On his travels in Italy and Sicily, after finishing his law course, he had tried to obtain an insight into the institutions and customs of a foreign people, taken many notes, made several remarks, even attempted to deduce some

---

* In 1833 Tocqueville was to sum up his ideal in a characteristic phrase: 'There is only one great goal in this world which merits the efforts of man: that is the good of humanity.' Toc. to Kergolay, Paris, 13 Nov. 1833 (O.C.,V,320).

general philosophic principles.* Later, on looking his records over, he was to think them mediocre; to the student to-day there is even something comic in the spectacle of the twenty-year-old Frenchman, reasoning like an ancient professor on the ruins of Rome and the graves of vanquished peoples. But it had been valuable training. And the training had continued. In the intervals of his court duties after his return, he began to read.

He then made the acquaintance of another young magistrate, generous, idealistic, and ambitious like himself, a young noble by the name of Beaumont.† Coming from the pleasant, rolling country of the Sarthe, where the châteaux were smaller, humbler than along the Loire, but where the *petite noblesse* knew and practised all the code of their loyal race, Gustave de Beaumont had been brought up to honour his kind. But he had also been taught to stand firmly and with dignity

---

* See *O.C.*,V,127–159, where fragments from these notes are published. The effects of tyranny and oppression in Sicily seem particularly to have stirred the young traveller's indignation.

† Of Gustave Auguste de la Bonninière de Beaumont (1802–1866)—lifelong friend, political associate, and literary executor of Alexis de Tocqueville—but little has as yet been written.

Born at Beaumont-la-Chartre (Sarthe) in February 1802, a few months after the Concordat with Rome, a few months before Napoleon's election as First Consul for life, Gustave de Beaumont was destined to take a larger part in national affairs than the other members of his immediate family. He was the youngest son of Cte. Jules de Beaumont (1777–1851) and Rose Préau de la Baraudière (1778–1848), and so grandson of the aged Anne Claude de Beaumont, who had lived through the days of the Revolution. Together with his brothers and sister—Jules, Eugénie, Achille— he had been brought up on the small tree-shaded farm of the Château de la Borde, which stood, overlooking the meadows, on the hillside edge of the commune of Beaumont-la-Chartre, over which their father, the Comte, presided as Mayor.

The Sarthe, in general, was a backward, unsettled, and discontented province. The Vendéans had been defeated there by Marceau in 1793, the royalists massacred in the streets of the towns; and in the 1820s the region was still afflicted with exceptional laws, still torn between loyalty to the old families and to the clergy, two loyalties which died hard, and the new influence of the liberal politicians Benjamin Constant and Lafayette.

In this struggle, however, Beaumont's family—conservative, good-natured, and joying in their small, sunny countryside—seem to have taken no part. While visiting Gustave at the Château de la Borde in 1834, Tocqueville was thus to describe the Beaumonts: 'To come back to my hosts, there is one thing that strikes me and that I find it hard to understand, which is: the interest they take in all the small things they do. This throws on the human heart a new light, hitherto unfamiliar to me. These *braves gens*, calm of imagination and tranquil of heart, find pleasures where I should never have been able to imagine that any existed. They take the liveliest interest in the growth of a tree, in the raising of a crop, in the hatching of a brood. They continue interested in such things for years and desire nothing more, while men who have shaken the world have often died of chagrin at being unable to do more.' Toc. to Marie Mottley, 23 Aug. 1833 (copy in TT).

on his own feet, and so had followed the promptings of his heart into the camp of the young liberals. He was three years older than Tocqueville, less wracked by doubts and self-questionings and so more calm and cheerful, but on all the essentials the two were in complete agreement. It did not take Tocqueville long to decide that here was a man after his own heart. Soon they were confiding to each other all their own idealistic ambitions, all their hopes for France; the friendship that was to last unbroken through their lives had begun.

With kindling enthusiasm they plunged together into an intense course of studies. Some of the more radical liberals were preaching to Frenchmen the necessity of a revolution such as had liberated England from the Stuarts in 1688 ; so English history at once attracted their attention. Some years before, when Tocqueville had been only nineteen, this constant praise of England had irritated the high-spirited law student into a scheme for making a flying visit to London with a dashing young comrade, named Kergolay. 'I should be more than satisfied to see just once those rascally English who, we are told, are so strong and so flourishing,' he had written.[4] The project had come to nothing, for lack of parental consent and money. Now he and Beaumont read Lingard's history, inwardly digesting it and drawing from what they read certain general opinions and philosophical conclusions, much as one of Tocqueville's professors at Metz had taught him to do.* Next they bought J.B.Say's work on political economy.†

More important still to the development of their thought, however,

---

* John Lingard's *History of England from the First Invasion by the Romans*, 8 v. (1819–1830), was the sober, political narrative of a moderate Catholic, soon to be continued to the flight of James II to France in 1688—hence, doubtless, its appeal to the two students. Tocqueville had been trained by a certain Mougin, Professor of Rhetoric at Metz, to write down his own observations and reflections while reading, instead of taking extracts or factual notes; and he now exercised his talent for reasoning and for concise analysis by writing to his '*cher futur collègue*' (Beaumont) a twenty-five page essay on the main tendencies of English development from the Normans down through Elizabeth. In this paper, he expressed sympathy with the common people. But he likened the lot of the English clergy under Henry VIII to that of the priests of France during the Revolution; and, on the whole, he found that he disliked the English, and had little faith in the 1688 parallel for France. Toc. to Bt., Tocqueville, 5 Oct. 1828; Mougin to Toc., 4 Sept. (?) 1823, 4 Jan. 1829 (TT); Bt. notes (BB).

† 'Notes sur l'économie Politique—J.B.Say, 1828–1829 (TT), probably from the *Cours complet d'Économie politique pratique*, 6 v., 1828. Say was an optimistic follower of Adam Smith. At the same time Tocqueville and Beaumont were studying English together, and Tocqueville was reading a history of the Dukes of Burgundy, whose author (Barante?) he thought too sympathetic to the people, too hostile to the '*grands*.' Toc. to Bt., 7 Dec. 1828, 19 Sept. 1829 (copies in TT).

they were together attending a stimulating course of lectures given by one of the greatest of the *Doctrinaires,* a man who had a role ahead of him in France. Six years before, Professor Guizot had delivered a series of talks, or *Essays on the History of France,* that, for those who could understand covert allusions and disguised suggestions for modern France, had been explosive with the dynamite of new ideas. Thereupon he had been dismissed from the Sorbonne. Now, back again in his chair, he was confining himself strictly to his subject, the early civilization of Europe and of the French,* and was outlining the development of the people with such consummate ability and apparent precision as to draw large and enthusiastic audiences. But his lectures were none the less suggestive, Tocqueville and Beaumont found. Particularly interesting were the Professor's insistence on the *enchaînement* of events, and his theory that history was governed by certain inexorable laws. The young men listened with avidity and took many notes. But there was one idea that was too big to be put on paper. Guizot believed in progress, in the gradual, inevitable forward march of society through the slow growth and rise to power of the Middle Class. In the course of its advance, Guizot pointed out, the 'Third Estate' had humbled feudal lords and aristocracy, levelled class distinctions and churchly privilege; now it was attacking the monarchy. All history bore witness to this progress, apparently. That meant, reasoned Tocqueville, that all inequalities would disappear, that the nations were being swept toward a more equal distribution of rights and privileges, as on an irresistible tide; in short, that the tendency of the age was toward democracy. Of course it was to be some time yet before the full implications of the *Doctrinaire* premise would be clear to this apprentice philosopher. Other thinkers would have to add the weight of their testimony, the experience of the last months of the Restoration its arguments, and the July Revolution its stentorian, decisive voice, before the logical deductions would seem justified. But already the idea that was to dominate Tocqueville's thinking for the rest of his life had been born.

Meanwhile, the political situation under the ill-advised Polignac administration continuing to go from bad to worse, Tocqueville grew

---

* Guizot's course on the *Histoire générale de la Civilisation en Europe* (1828) was much expanded and deepened in his *Histoire de la Civilisation en France* (1829–1830). Tocqueville attended the latter lectures between the dates of 11 April 1829 and 29 May 1830 (Toc. notes, TT). For a good discussion of Guizot as an historian and political philosopher, see Flint, *Philosophy of History,* pp.492ff., particularly pp.508–509.

more and more restless.* Finally, swallowing his shyness and his pride, and taking his courage in both hands, he went to interview one or two of the politicians. Somehow, somewhere, he must get the assurance that the leaders really had a plan, that France was not helplessly sliding into revolution and chaos. Their professions sent him away discouraged and disillusioned. There was no program, the leaders were blind and pulling at cross-purposes, the rank and file of the politicians selfish, dishonest, untruthful. On paper Tocqueville set it down that truth and virtue were to be found only in private life.†

As the year 1830 dawned, therefore, the two seemingly settled young magistrates were in reality approaching a point where some sort of decision would have to be made. Tocqueville, in particular, was in a state of excitement and nervous tension. His mind wrestling with the uncertainties of the future, his spirit perpetually on the stretch, he was being driven more and more to seek relief in passionate movement.‡ Some sort of planned activity, whether mental or physical, was gradually becoming a necessity for him, no matter how hard the action or difficult the self-imposed task. Looking backward more than a quarter of a century later, he would be satisfied that for indecision there had been no other remedy. 'Success is impossible, especially in youth,' he was to urge a young protégé,[5] 'if you haven't *un peu le diable au corps.* At your age I should have undertaken to jump over the towers of Notre Dame if I had thought to find what I was looking for on the other side.' In 1830, the twenty-four year old Tocqueville had not yet vaulted the towers of Notre Dame, but he was preparing to do, naturally, things that would be impossible for ordinary men.

Momentarily, there was no alternative but to attend the approaching crisis, watching the thunder-clouds roll up in the sky and hoping the storm would clear the air and show him what to do. Without much

---

* 'God grant that the House of Bourbon may not one day repent what has just been done!' Toc. to his brother Édouard, 9 Aug. 1829 (*O.C.*,VI,6) apropos of the calling of the Polignac Ministry to power by Charles X. See also, Toc. to Édouard, 6 April 1830 (*O.C.*,VI,19–20).

† 'Conversations assez curieuses avec MM. Guizot et Boinvilliers' (in TT). Boinvilliers was a member of *Aide-toi et le Ciel t'Aidera*, and the conversations are dated, June–Sept. 1830.

Tocqueville then wrote an essay which he labelled '*Idées sur la Vérité dans la vie politique*,' June 1830 (TT).

‡ A frail, nervous constitution and miserable ill-health, inherited apparently from his mother, made Tocqueville tire easily. In fact, he had already begun the unceasing silent struggle against illness that he was to have to sustain throughout his life. But his relentless, unquenchable spirit only spurred him to try to forget his bodily sufferings, too, in feverish activity.

faith in British precedents, studying each new development anxiously in the darkening light, restless, discouraged, a prey to doubts and disillusionment, he and Beaumont waited for the catastrophe that they and many others were sure was coming. Either France would be deluged by fresh revolution, or constitutional government would be suppressed. Things could not proceed much longer as they were going.

*

\*    \*

Suddenly, the storm broke. On 25 July 1830, Charles X, failing of support in the Chamber of Deputies, issued his fatal decrees. The journals protested, the barricades sprang up, Paris rose. Three 'Glorious Days'—and the Bourbons had lost. Charles X took carriage for England.

To Tocqueville's ageing parents, as to the ultra-conservatives and to so many others of the upper classes, this revolution meant disaster. In the instant they saw prosperity for themselves and rightful government for France go up in the smoke from the barricades. An anxious interval ensued, while Lafayette tried to force the adoption of his favourite scheme, an American-style republic. Then an active group of industrialists, bankers and journalists succeeded in establishing the head of the House of Orléans, Louis Philippe, on the throne. France still continued a monarchy; but that was about all that could be said. Like other families in high or official station, and in common with the great majority of the royalist nobility, the Tocquevilles were appalled at the idea of having *Égalité*'s son on the throne, and deeply offended by the personal treachery of Louis Philippe to the Bourbon cause. A king whose father had betrayed Louis XVI and who had himself usurped the throne of the rightful line and compromised with demagogues and money-greedy bourgeoisie, a king whose sceptre was a green umbrella, seemed to them almost intolerable. Many of their friends resigned from office rather than take the oath of allegiance, and —the Comte himself being no longer prefect—the Tocquevilles retired from the court. In the fall of 1830, the world seemed dark indeed. All that was left to protect the ancient heritage was the Chamber of Peers: and even this was not safe. The late appointees of Charles X, Comte Hervé de Tocqueville among them, were already under attack; the Chamber itself in jeopardy.

Meanwhile, what of Alexis de Tocqueville and Gustave de Beaumont? At the first signs of trouble, apparently, the young Tocqueville had thought of his father, and sent him a message urgently pressing him to lie low and avoid the perils of conspicuous resistance. The grim but understanding Comte, however, had seen revolutions before, and was more afraid for his forthright and passionate son. 'Whatever your opinions on the measures taken, I urge you to express them with moderation and restraint,' he had replied. Young men of talent needed to be especially careful, so as not to compromise their future careers, he thought.* Tocqueville obeyed as best he could. With many others he protested against the unconstitutionality of the King's ordinances. But when the tocsin sounded in the night and the fusillading began in the streets, he made his escape from Paris somehow and reached Versailles. There he enrolled in the National Guard, and carried arms on patrol, but otherwise constrained himself to inactivity. So it happened that on the thirtieth of July, at dawn, he met the slow, mournful carriages of the departing Charles X on the outer boulevards of Versailles—and was unable to restrain his tears.[6] But that was all.

As for Beaumont, in the thick of things at Paris, his curiosity and anxiety had been so strong that he had been unable to keep from traversing the city several times at the height of the battle.[7] But when it was over he, too, found himself still alive. Moreover, France once again had a government and a king; the courts still existed; and he and Tocqueville were still magistrates. What, then, did the revolution of July 1830 mean to the two earnest young friends?

Nothing less than the turning point in their lives. For it was the July Revolution that drove Tocqueville and Beaumont to the United States and so set Tocqueville on the road to writing his *De la Démocratie en Amérique.*

* Hervé de Tocqueville to Toc. at Versailles, Paris, 27 July 1830 (TT). Though the world was at the moment crashing down about his ears, the firm and honourable Comte knew his own loyalty unshaken. And a quarter of a century later, after Louis Philippe had yielded to the Republic, and that in turn to Napoleon III, the one-time peer was to end his memoirs with the proud thought he himself had no right to complain, since he had had the rare happiness of serving only the same master and the same cause throughout his eighty years.

## III

## THE DECISION TO VISIT AMERICA—
## AND A GOOD EXCUSE

WHY, it would sometimes in later years be asked, why had Tocqueville left France, to visit America? Even his readers would not know precisely; and no adequate explanation was ever to be given.* Yet the real answer was not so far to seek.

For Alexis de Tocqueville, almost in the very instant that dawn at Versailles, must have guessed his hour of decision come. It made no difference that he had foretold the catastrophe. The heavens had flashed and the earth been shaken. Helpless, trembling with anxiety, for one fearful instant he had glimpsed the great Bourbon edifice still standing. Then it had crumbled, to pitch headlong past his very feet. And in the August morning strangers were already building a new House . . . where only ruins stared at him accusingly.

A bystander, he knew at once, he could remain no longer. Even yet the ground rocked, and the thunder of revolution, the muttering of the still unsatisfied masses, disturbed the air. No peace any more (if only in his own soul the tocsin would cease ringing!): the future was on the way, an unhappy future for all France. What, then, would he do? Perhaps he did not know. Perhaps at first he did not even have any clear thought of leaving France, or any idea of visiting America. Yet gradually, as the days passed and the new monarchy rose into view, both of these solutions would suggest themselves to him. By the autumn, at all events, the young Versailles magistrate would be acutely aware of a number of good reasons for visiting the United States; and of these reasons, three, he would feel, were of particular urgency. It was necessary to cross the Atlantic: first of all, because he was exceed-

* An analysis of some of the reasons commonly advanced to explain Tocqueville's visit to America will be found in Appendix D, at the head of the notes to this chapter.

ingly uncomfortable in France; secondly, because he was ambitious to make a name for himself; thirdly, because he wanted to qualify himself to be of service to his country. And each of these reasons would have its background, and its own insistent motivation.

*

*      *

The courts might continue, but almost immediately after the July Days Tocqueville discovered himself in a false position. Disinterested though he had always tried to be, he was now suddenly caught between the requirements of the new monarchy, his loyalty to the Bourbon dynasty and the class from which he had sprung, and the exacting demands of his own idealistic conscience.

Early in August he was asked to take the oath to Louis Philippe. This was not a personal demand. Quite naturally, as soon as the stout bourgeois King had been installed, his counsellors wished to assure themselves of the loyalty of the permanent administration, of the bureaucracy and officialdom holding over from the Restoration. The new government therefore dismissed its known enemies and required oaths of allegiance from the rest—particularly from the judges and prosecutors in the government courts on whom, of course, it depended both for the enforcement of the law and the success of many of its policies.

The requirement put Tocqueville, Beaumont, and a great many others of their class in a quandary. Like most of the nobility, Tocqueville regretted the July Revolution and despised Louis Philippe. As his early morning encounter with the fleeing King had demonstrated, the instinctive loyalty of his race to the Bourbons still persisted in him. In spite of the recent actions of Charles X, he could not so easily root out an age-old faith in divine-right monarchy. Furthermore the daily proceedings of the Orleanists but confirmed him in his dislike of revolution, of demagogues whether royal or republican, of bargains with rich shop-keepers. On the other hand, the young man could not escape his high sense of duty toward his country and toward the wishes of the majority of his countrymen. And to him an Orleans King seemed the best that France, for the moment, could hope for. Did not Louis Philippe represent her last chance for a constitutional monarchy? Clearly, in the present state of opinion, a return to the Bourbons was out of the question. 'If Louis Philippe were overturned, it would certainly not be in favour of Henry V, but of the republic and of anarchy. Those who love their country ought therefore to rally frankly to the new power, since it alone can now save France from herself,' he argued.* With Frenchmen still so inexperienced in self-government, no true patriot at least could possibly desire the republic.

Tocqueville and Beaumont both took the oath. 'In acting thus I thought to fulfil the strict duty of a Frenchman,' Tocqueville wrote. But even so, it had not been easy. He had brought himself to it only after hours of torment and self-questioning, only because there was no other way. 'I have finally sworn it, this oath!' he confided to the woman he was later to marry.[3] 'My conscience has nothing to reproach me, but I am no less profoundly wounded and I shall number this day among the most unhappy of my life. Since coming into the world, this is the first time that I must avoid the presence of people whom I esteem at the same time that I disapprove of them. Oh! Marie, this idea rends me . . . I am at war with myself. It's a new state, frightful for me. . . .' The unhappy young man was touching the very depths of wretchedness and despair. For in taking the oath he had mortally offended most of his relatives and nearly all the friends of his family, in short, the great majority of those whose opinion and approval he was accustomed to value.

Furthermore, even at the moment of swearing he was thinking that he would be classed with the turncoats, with the office-holders of no principle who were showing themselves so anxious to barter their oath and honour for a job. And here again his fears proved only too well founded. Unable to understand his reasons for so swiftly abandoning the cause of his ancestors, his best friends promptly accused him of cowardice and self-interest. Even Louis de Kergolay, with whom Tocqueville had been on terms of the most affectionate intimacy since earliest boyhood, wrote him an excoriating letter, referring to the incorruptible Malesherbes, and using the words 'dishonour'—'perjury'—'traitor'—'cupidity'—'subterfuge'—and 'degradation' of anyone so miserable as to take the oath. Tocqueville was deeply wounded and repelled the accusations with heat. As for his great-grandfather, 'rightly or wrongly,' he wrote,[4] 'I am profoundly convinced that he would have acted exactly as I in my place, just as I have the presumption to hope

---

* Toc. to Charles Stoffels, Versailles, 26 Aug. 1830 (from copy in possession of Mlle Stoffels d'Hautefort). He took the oath on 16 August, as *juge auditeur* at the tribunal at Versailles.

that I should have done as he did, in his.' The thought was comforting. But, none the less, the July Revolution had made his position in society almost intolerable. And Beaumont shared the feeling. In his case, too, the revolution had set father against son, brother against brother. For his older brothers had refused to take the oath and had resigned, to range themselves with the rest of his tolerant but reproachful family, on the side of the banished Bourbons.

Worse still, even the government was not long in showing itself suspicious of their proffered loyalty. The whole body of magistrates was under a cloud. Before the revolution, Tocqueville, in common with many of his fellows, had been regarded by his superiors as too liberal. Now their new chiefs, alarmed by the indifference of the public and the weakness of the government, suspected every one of reactionary tendencies.[5] Toward the end of October, Tocqueville was even required a second time to take the oath.

This was too much for the sensitive young man. He took the oath;[*] but already he was planning some means of escape from his position. For it was now clear that his ambitions would never be gratified if he remained where he was. Already demoted to *juge suppléant* without pay, he would always be regarded with suspicion by his superiors of the July Monarchy, for ever held back, never allowed to rise to a position in the magistracy where he could be of some real service to his country. Obviously, his only hope for a career lay in some profession where he could make a fresh start and not have his old services held against him—in politics, perhaps. Another thought suggested itself. The disorders were becoming serious, throughout the whole country, and the very stability and future of the new regime seemed every day more dubious. If he stayed on, therefore, and the government of Louis Philippe fell, he would only have compromised himself hopelessly with its successor. Would it not be far better to dissociate himself while still there was time, perhaps even get out of the country altogether, for a while?[6] On 31 October, just six days after taking the oath for a second time, he and Beaumont acted. They submitted to the government a request for a mission to go and study the new American prison reforms.[7]

* 25 Oct. 1830, as *juge suppléant* before the *Chambre des Vacations de la Cour Royale de Paris* ('*Extraits de deux procès-verbaux du tribunal . . . à Versailles,*' TT). On 10 Dec. 1830 the office of *juge auditeur* was abolished by law, and thenceforth apprentice magistrates began as *juges suppléants*.

Who first had the inspiration, they did not record. Personal experience had given Tocqueville's father an interest in prisons; and the two young magistrates had themselves, in the course of their duties in the courts, had numerous opportunities to observe the vices and defects of the almost medieval prisons and houses of arrest in the neighbourhood of Paris. The source of their inspiration, however, was of no consequence. What was important was the fact that the revolution had brought reforms of all sorts into vogue, and that, among others, the reform of the country's penal institutions was beginning to excite the attention of all France. The Chamber was demanding a renovation of the administration of justice and a revision of the criminal code; and the government had just appointed Lucas, the prominent philanthropist, inspector of prisons. A proposal to study the two novel penitentiary systems just developed in the United States could not, therefore, have come at a more propitious moment.[8]

Such a mission would, at least, suit the purposes of the two young friends admirably. It would, in the first place, provide a graceful way out of a difficult situation, and give them a chance to abandon their jobs without antagonizing the government. Again, and this appealed strongly to them, the mission would give them the opportunity to master thoroughly the subject of prison reform. As a result, on their return, not only would the political skies have cleared, not only would the July Monarchy either have fallen or established itself on solid foundations, but they themselves would be able to enter politics with a claim to the nation's attention.[9] Uncompromised by participation in the settlement of the government question, they would enter the Chamber as masters of one of the new liberal reforms, leaders in the cause that had not yet become involved in party politics, but appealed to the sympathies of all. In short, the prison mission would be for them the ladder to a new career, the first step toward influence and fame.[10]

Finally, there was one other consideration that seemed of the greatest importance and promise to the two young men. This prison mission would enable them to see—to explore—to study—the famed republic on the other side of the Atlantic!

'I have long had the greatest desire to visit North America: I shall go see there what a great republic is like; my only fear is lest, during that time, they establish one in France,' Tocqueville had written to a young friend toward the end of August.[11] The idea had, apparently, just occurred to him. And his friend didn't approve of it, tried, in fact, to dissuade him from leaving France. But the more he considered the possibilities of such a visit, the better Tocqueville liked them. The knowledge 'acquired among so celebrated a people' would raise him above the crowd, he argued.[12] 'You know just exactly what a vast republic is like, why it is practicable here, impracticable there! All the points of public administration have been examined successively. On returning to France, you certainly know yourself possessor of a talent that you did not have on leaving. If the moment is favourable, some sort of publication may let the public know of your existence and fix on you the attention of the parties. If that doesn't happen, well and good! Your voyage at least has not injured you. . . .'

That was at the beginning of November. By the middle of February (1831), the plans of the two young magistrates were even more definite. 'We are leaving,' wrote Tocqueville,[13] 'with the intention of examining, in detail and as scientifically as possible, all the mechanism (*ressorts*) of that vast American society which every one talks of and no one knows. And if events leave us the time, we are counting on bringing back the elements of a fine work or, at the very least, of a new work; for there is nothing on this subject.'

A book on America! Sometime during the dismal months following the July Revolution, then, was born the resolution that was to influence the whole course of their lives, the plan that was eventually to produce the first classic commentary on American government to be written by a foreigner: Tocqueville's *De la Démocratie en Amérique*. Who first thought of the idea, Tocqueville did not say. Probably the future author himself (though one cannot to-day be sure). Certainly Beaumont shared his friend's enthusiasm.[14] And to neither of the ambitious young pair did it even occur, apparently, that such a study and investigation might be beyond their powers. Together they had read the history of England; together they would master the American constitution and the nature of a republican society. Then, once back from their mission, they would make themselves known. And, whether or not they published a book, their knowledge would be invaluable to themselves and to France.

Why a book on the United States should interest Frenchmen, or an exact and scientific knowledge of American institutions be of value to France, Tocqueville and Beaumont did not specify; for they had not at all made up their minds just how they would present their findings. Certain indications, however, already foreshadowed the line their thought would take. By Guizot's lectures, now in retrospect so dismally prophetic, Tocqueville had been impregnated with the idea that conditions were everywhere becoming more and more equal, that the whole tendency of the age was toward more democratic forms of government. Certainly, everything that the two young men had since seen and heard had confirmed this view. The very revolution of the preceding July, introducing, as it had, a monarchy founded on the support of the middle class, seemed to the anxious young students significant, indicative of a strong trend toward the democracy they dreaded. Nor did it escape their notice that a number of respectable men were already discussing the probability of a republic.* Might not a work on the United States prove illuminating, therefore, might it not reveal to Frenchmen the destiny toward which they themselves were blindly stumbling?

Tocqueville and Beaumont meant, at least, to find out.

* Needless to say Tocqueville—though he later became the greatest—was not the first exponent of the theory that the tendency of modern times was toward equality and complete self-government. The '1688 school' of historians, in urging the English example, were themselves advocating a moderate step toward representative government as necessary and beneficial. And, as early as the winter of 1822, de Serre and Royer-Collard had foreshadowed Tocqueville's thesis. 'With us *la démocratie*,' said de Serre on presenting the law for further restrictions on the press, 'is everywhere full of sap and energy; it is in industry, in the land, in the laws, in men, in things. The torrent is flowing up to the banks in the feeble dikes which scarce contain it.' And Royer-Collard had replied: 'I agree that *la démocratie coule à pleins bords* in the France that the centuries and the circumstances have made . . . as for me, I render thanks to Providence that she has called to the benefits of civilization an increasing (*plus grand*) number of her creatures.' (Quoted in Ch. de Rémusat, 'De l'Esprit de Réaction, Royer-Collard et Tocqueville,' *Revue des deux Mondes*, 15 Oct. 1861.) Naturally, the July Revolution had added to the group of thinkers who, joyful or apprehensive, were proclaiming the democratic destiny of France. See especially, A.d'Herbelot to Léon Cornudet, 31 Aug. 1830, quoted in *La Jeunesse Libérale de 1830* . . . (1908), pp.269–271; also Chateaubriand's defence of his refusal to serve Louis Philippe, in his *De la Restauration et de la Monarchie élective*.

IV

## PREPARATIONS FOR ESCAPE

THE first thing to do, of course, was to secure the mission, the all-important means of reaching America. Their request, it seemed to the two friends, had been rather astutely put. After pointing out the general demand for the reform of the prison administration, and the interest that the government itself was taking in the question, the young magistrates had submitted a memoir which should have convinced even an unenthusiastic Minister of Justice that the conditions in the prisons in France were, to say the least, backward, and really could not go unreformed any longer. Would it not therefore be useful to gather some exact information as to what had been done elsewhere along this line? In the United States, the Ministry had been told, the two most advanced and liberal methods in the treatment of criminals—called penitentiary systems—had just been perfected; and only in the United States themselves could precise data be gathered on the relative merits of the two new systems for application in France.*

The Minister of the Interior, it seemed, was willing to give the two magistrates the mission requested, provided the Ministry of Justice would grant them the necessary eighteen-months' leave of absence from their duties in the government courts. But here the friends encountered

---

* BB¹⁸1323. Early in August Tocqueville had seen the *maison d'arrêt* at Versailles, where all classes of criminals—thieves, murderers, debtors—were mixed in together; and in the course of duty both he and Beaumont had had frequent occasion to visit the *maison centrale* at Poissy. Furthermore, on 26 September they had made a special trip to Poissy to study the evils of the cantine system there (Draft of request for mission, TT). These first-hand experiences, and a consultation of some documents and books, enabled the two magistrates to take the first step toward bringing themselves and their mission to the attention of their fellow-countrymen. In February 1831, they published an appeal for sympathy and for aid in reforming the prisons of France: *Note sur le Système pénitentiaire et sur la Mission confiée par M. le Ministre de l'Intérieur à MM. Gustave de Beaumont et Alexis de Tocqueville*, 48pp., Paris, Fournier.

an obstacle. Their superiors proved suspicious, and exceedingly reluctant to grant the leaves, especially Beaumont's,* at a time when the court calendars were so crowded. The Tocqueville family brought to bear all the influence that it could muster, and the Minister of the Interior interested himself in their cause. But it was not until 6 February 1831, and only after three months of the most obstinate negotiation, that the coveted leave was at last secured. And when Tocqueville and Beaumont tried to get one or the other of the two Ministries to defray the cost of the proposed trip, they failed utterly. This was, perhaps, partly their own fault. For, in their eagerness, they had made a tactical blunder at the very start. In their first request they had been so generous as to offer to pay the expenses of the mission themselves, if necessary. Naturally, the two Ministries had taken these philanthropic young men at their own word. It even occurred to the Minister of Justice that they could stop Beaumont's pay while he was away.† One senses from this, that the authorities were not altogether blind to some of the real motives underlying the proposed prison investigation. If these young magistrates insisted on looking out for themselves first, just when the going was roughest, they could pay for the privilege, the government seemed to say. Fortunately, their families now came to the rescue. Unsympathetic though the Tocquevilles and Beaumonts had sometimes felt, they were glad to underwrite the future of their determined offspring to the extent of making the American trip financially possible. So, at last, the two young friends were free to go.

That decision reached, it remained to get ready for the momentous expedition. The preparations were thoughtful, and characteristically

---

* Beaumont's Christmas vacation was cancelled, owing to the press of work. *Substitut du Procureur du Roi* successively at Arcis-sur-Aube, Versailles, and now at Paris, he evidently enjoyed a reputation for sense and ability. In particular, a memoir that he had just written, pointing out the impolitic and impractical nature of the political prosecutions that the government was instituting after the July Revolution, had attracted the favourable notice of his chiefs, the *Procureur Général* of his court and the *Garde des Sceaux*; and the former had arranged for him a very pleasant interview with the King. (14 Sept. 1830. Notes in BB.) Altogether, Beaumont seemed to the ministry too valuable a man to lose.

† It was proposed to make him amenable to the law governing the pay of magistrates absent without leave. The announcement drew forth repeated protests from the Ministry of the Interior, but it is impossible to make out, from the documents available, whether these were effective. For eighteen months Beaumont's pay would have been 10,500 francs. In a final effort to reduce the cost of the expedition, Tocqueville, induced the Minister of the Interior to inquire of Admiral de Rigny about letting them ship free on a government vessel. But there was no vessel going to the United States, it appeared.

thorough. Theirs was to be no idle tourists' visit. They meant to go as students and serious observers, both of American prisons and of America itself. First of all, therefore, they wanted to be sure to be well received on the other side of the Atlantic, and to meet the most important and worthwhile people in the United States. So they canvassed everybody within reach, without distinction of relationship or prejudice, for letters of introduction to distinguished Americans. Among others, Hyde de Neuville, former minister to the United States, proved that he had not forgotten his pleasant years, or his friends, in Philadelphia.* And the Duc de Montebello and the Baron de Gerando did their best, as did perhaps also Tocqueville's brilliant but egotistical cousin, the Vicomte de Chateaubriand, who had once visited America himself, seen Washington, and later fashioned a classic romance out of his shadowy wanderings among the Indians. The young Tocqueville was not very fond of his overbearing relative; but in an emergency like this, the famous man undoubtedly presented a resource. Finally, the two young aristocrats even pocketed their pride and solicited letters from Lafayette, who was a cousin of Beaumont, but none the less a vain and dangerous demagogue in their opinion.† And David Bailie Warden, the American ex-consul, received them,‡ doubtless to give them advice, letters, and his book on the antiquities of North America.

---

* In particular, Neuville confided a letter for William Short of Philadelphia to Tocqueville, whom he introduced as 'an excellent young man, son of the Cte. de toqueville [*sic*], Peer of france, he goes to Your country to Examine the Prisons there, with Views Full of Benevolence. . . .' Hyde de Neuville to W.Short 'chesnut Street,' Paris, 25 March 1831, in William Short Papers, Library of Congress.

† Whether Lafayette ever gave them any introductions, we do not know. 'At eleven o'clock I returned to La Fayette's. He had gone out again without leaving anything for me. The Devil take him. I shall not return there any more. I am going to write him and tranquilly await his reply.' (Toc. to Bt., 14 March 1831. Fragment, BB.) Apparently Lafayette at least tried to get them some introductions for America from James Fenimore Cooper, as indicated by the following letter, dated 'Tuesday evening': 'General Lafayette presents his affectionate compliments to Mr. Cooper and begs him to send him the letters for M.M. de Tocqueville & de Beaumont, as they leave town to day before 3 o'clock.' This note, now in the Yale University Library, is not in Lafayette's own hand, however. The indication is perhaps that some member of his household was moved by Tocqueville's evident chagrin and tried to make up for the 'Hero's' absence of mind. See Yale Univ. Library *Gazette*, April 1934, pp.126–127.

Charles Lucas, the new inspector of prisons, gave Tocqueville and Beaumont notes to Edward Livingston and to (James J. ?) Barclay of Philadelphia, Montebello one to H.D.Gilpin of the same city; and altogether they managed to collect about seventy letters of introduction before they sailed (see below, ch.VII). Unfortunately, no list seems ever to have been made, so the names of the writers and addresses have for the most part been lost.

‡ D.B.Warden's 'Visitors' Book' (Warden Papers, Library of Congress) shows that Tocqueville and Beaumont called twice during the winter; his book on America

It also occurred to them, as serious students, to get Cooper's and Volney's works on the United States,\* and to take along the text-book of the liberal economist J.B.Say, for they wanted to be able to understand the strange things they were going to see on the other side of the earth. Some of their friends, however, proved more anxious to protect them from moral harm, and from the spiritual danger of exposure to the world, and flesh (and Protestant America). For among the books which they were to carry with them were two works designed to strengthen them in the faith.

One, a book of prayer, touched the young Tocqueville deeply. It was a farewell gift from his 'Bébé,' the kindly, loving old abbé Lesueur. With sorrow this tender guardian had seen his youngest charge fall under the influence of anti-clerical literature and cease to be a practising Catholic; but he knew that Alexis was deeply religious by nature, and he seemed always to hope by kindness and example to win his beloved son back to the single faith. When Alexis had decided to spend a year in America, however, the eighty-year-old priest had realized that he would not live to see his son return to France. So he had done all he could. And Tocqueville, on opening the prayer book, was to find in the front leaf, written in the trembling and upright hand of the good old man, a letter.† It was his blessing—a testament of love and a legacy of comfort and Christian counsel. It began :

'We are nearing, my friend, the moment of your departure. The unhappy circumstances in which we find ourselves require this painful separation, which is going to cost us many tears, especially as I may not hope for more than a few days longer on earth. I should be inconsolable if, on bidding you good-bye, I said to myself: *It is for always!* But no, dear friend, you shall follow me there where, by the grace of God, I hope to go. . . .

'The sky is the goal toward which we are both tending. I have well studied the road; and as we cannot long travel together, and as I should

---

had been translated from the English edition under the title *Description statistique, historique, et politique des États-Unis.* . . . 5 v., 1820. Beaumont was in touch with W.C.Rives as well. W.C.Rives to Bt., 5 Nov. 1830 (BB).

\* Cte. de Volney, *Tableau du Climat et du Sol des États-Unis d'Amérique,* 2 v., 1803. 'Cooper' may have been James Fenimore Cooper, then touring Europe, whose *Notices of the Americans, picked up by a travelling Bachelor,* in two volumes, had been published in London in 1828. More probably, however, Tocqueville was referring to Thomas Cooper's *Renseignments sur l'Amérique,* translated in 1795 from his well-known *Some Information respecting Americans* (1793–1794).

† '*A mon cher Alexis,*' signed '*Ton bien sincère ami, L. Le Sueur, prêtre*' (TT).

arrive well before you at the *rendez-vous*, I am going briefly to trace the path for you. I shall indicate the provisions to be made for the journey, and the encounters to be avoided. . . .'

. . . Faith . . . Hope . . . Charity . . . Truth . . . Patience. Then the things to be avoided: . . . Pride . . . Incontinence . . . 'The Philosophers' . . . finally the close:

'Adieu once more. I commit you and your kind companion to the care of the Divine Providence. My wishes, my prayers and my blessing will go with you, everywhere. . . .'

The idealistic young Beaumont was likewise presented by a member of his family with a package, but in this case the package was sealed and marked: *à Gustave embarqué*—not to be opened before sailing. On unwrapping it he was to find that it contained two little volumes of moral and religious thoughts, in the shape of a precept for each day of the year. He was to be amused and a little annoyed, but not greatly surprised. Being a young liberal in a family which was steeped in the conservative traditions of the provincial nobility and which had neither understood nor wholly forgiven his rejection of their code and his conversion to liberal ideas, he had to expect such gifts. 'Liberals,' to these good people, were Jacobins: atheists or Deists at the very least. Hence these books—given more in sorrow than in anger certainly, because one had to admit that Gustave was good-hearted—but nevertheless marked *à Gustave embarqué*. As Beaumont was indulgently to observe,[1] 'It's obvious that she only sealed the package in this way because she was convinced that I wouldn't take it along if I knew that it was a book of piety. The means adopted, if necessary, were certainly ingenious, but it must be admitted that they reveal small confidence on her part in my religious sentiments. Really, I am less bad than she thinks me. . . .' And he would later be found reading in the little volumes and looking through Lesueur's book of prayer. 'Unhappily, it isn't my own convictions in the matter that determine what others will believe.'

Then, of course, there was the final pleasant task of getting clothes together for a year and a half of travel. In February and March Tocqueville laid out 162 francs for the following:[2] Leather trunk from Colin (40fr.), with engraved name plate (3fr.); from Joly, 52 r. du Bac, a *chapeau rond* (25fr.), a silk hat recovered (5fr.); and from Gastene, bootmaker, r. Vivienne, one pair of *bottines* or half-boots (25fr.), a pair of *pied en tirant* (17fr.), another pair of half-boots

(25fr.), a pair of *de fort lasé* (laced shoes?) (12fr.), and a pair re-soled (10fr.). If this list was any indication, the ambitious Tocque-ville had a rather pedestrian vision of his future tour in America. But doubtless both young lawyers had also prepared themselves with clothes to be worn between the ear and the ankle: with a great coat, with stocks, with linen, and with culottes and hose, as became members of the most fashionable society in the world. Naturally, also, a fine gun or fowling piece was carefully added to the equipment of each. And Beaumont (who came of a family that even to this day is amateur of the arts) had also provided himself with two sketchbooks, water-colours, brushes, pen and ink, and—for he was also musical—his flute.

At last, the end of March approached. Letters, books, boots and linen, and quantities of blank note-paper for taking notes on American pris-ons, all were packed in the smallest compass possible. Unquestionably Tocqueville even tried to squeeze all his belongings into his new leather trunk, as he knew that whatever could not be carried on a stage-coach would eventually have to be left behind. Finally, the day itself arrived. Supplied with money and a letter of credit* by their families, and armed with the credentials of their appointment as gov-ernment commissioners—but with no other mark of their country's interest or favour—Tocqueville and Beaumont set forth from Paris.

Young, obscure, and unregarded, they were off on the most impor-tant adventure of their lives.

* Beaumont had a bill on Hottinguer Cie. for 2000 francs, Tocqueville one for 5000 francs (TT).

PART II: KNICKERBOCKER AMERICA

# V

## HAVRE TO NEW YORK—38 DAYS

I<small>F</small> Tocqueville and Beaumont had imagined that the Atlantic crossing would be comfortable, or in any way commonplace or dull, they were immediately disillusioned. The *Havre*, which had been due to sail at noon on the second of April, was delayed in getting off, missed the turn of the tide, and promptly ran hard aground in Havre harbour. To their anxiety and despair, the two commissioners therefore were set ashore, to pass a disconsolate afternoon on a deserted waterfront, chewing on the bitter rumour that it might be six days before their vessel could be got off. In the evening they re-embarked, to sleep on board. Shortly after midnight, hearing a noise on deck, Tocqueville went up to find that they were proceeding under full sail. On the horizon the jetty lantern still twinkled; but that was the last land that he was to see for more than a long month.*

He went below in the expectation of sea-sickness. As the *Havre*, though an able packet 'copper sheeted and riveted,' [2] boasted only 300 tons, they were soon being tossed about appallingly (*à rendre l'âme*) in the windy Channel. 'For two days I was sick and depressed,' Tocqueville wrote his family, 'Beaumont well and cheerful as usual. It was the natural order of things. The third day I took some interest in the things of this world and the fourth I was cured. Altogether I was one of those least upset. . . .' And he noted with amusement the 'fine collection of faces' that finally appeared one by one out of the cabins: 'pale, yellow and green, enough to make all the colours of the rainbow.'

Almost immediately the inquisitive young commissioners began looking over their fellow-passengers with a discerning eye. ' . . . aside from a cow and a donkey,' Tocqueville gravely noted, 'we number 181 souls

---

* Neither of the two friends could await their arrival in New York to begin describing their adventures. The following story of their crossing is therefore condensed from the shipboard letters which they began while still two weeks from land. See Note 1.

43

on board, neither more nor less, to wit: 30 in the cabin, 13 'tween decks, 120 in the bow and 18 sailors.' And he and Beaumont enlivened their first letters home with thumb-nail sketches of some of these odd voyagers. 'Noah's Ark did not contain animals more diverse,' they were certain. In addition to a Swiss family, there were several Frenchmen, a son of a Napoleonic general, a ludicrous wine merchant of St. Malo, a Cuban, an M.P., an American naval officer, a New York merchant with his family, and a Protestant minister. Almost at once, it is interesting to observe, the two friends had rejected most of their own countrymen— at least to the extent that such a course was possible in so small and intimate a company—and begun instead to cultivate the friendship of the well-informed and distinguished little group of Americans and English on board.

'You cannot imagine, dear Mother, what a droll life one lives in this great stage-coach called a ship,' Tocqueville was soon writing from mid-Atlantic. 'The necessity of living on top of each other and of look-ing each other in the eye all the time establishes an informality and a freedom of which one has no conception on terra firma.* Here each one carries on in the middle of the crowd as if he were alone: some read aloud, others play, others sing, there are those who write as I do for in-stance at this moment, while close by a neighbour is supping. Each one drinks, laughs, eats or cries as his fancy suggests. Our cabins are so narrow that one goes outside them to dress; and but for publicly putting on one's pants, I know not what part of one's toilet doesn't take place in the face of Israel. In a word, we live on the forum like the ancients. This is the true land of liberty. But it can only be practised between four wooden planks, there's the difficulty. Thus the majority of our com-panions pass the greater part of their time in the most miserable way. One may call it distilling boredom drop by drop.

'As for us, we have not been touched by it. So far as the ocean al-lows it, we follow our land habits: we get up before day, work till breakfast . . . at noon we begin again till dinner. After dinner we chat in English with whatever gentlemen or ladies are willing to listen to us, and at 9 we go to bed in order to begin again. . . .'

As a matter of fact, one gathers that these busy and attractive young

---

* In translating from the Tocqueville and Beaumont manuscripts, accuracy has been preferred to elegance. I have tried to retain the original sentence structure, spelling, and capitalization, wherever the form of the document has not conflicted too violently with the English idiom, or stood in the way of a reasonable understanding of the author's meaning.

Frenchmen, with their government mission and their curiosity, were soon the centre of the ship's life. The bored were diverted and the intelligent were interested by their daily questions and their dogged attempts to improve their command of English. 'There are in our company some really distinguished men,' wrote Beaumont in his faithful and illuminating account of their daily occupations. 'We have among others an Englishman who has been a member of the House of Commons and who combines with a broad education a character the soul of honour. He thinks the mission with which we are charged very fine, and does everything he can to facilitate our work.

'Our most urgent need at present is to speak English well. This same man of whom I was speaking, and whose name is Mr. Palmer, loses not a single opportunity of giving us useful suggestions and of correcting us when we make mistakes. In general we speak only English, the English and Americans being in the majority on the packet. Although I was already able to ask for bread in this tongue, I now realize the difference between a superficial acquaintance with a language and a thorough study of it. It is of the last importance for us to have English on the tips of our fingers, to understand its idiom, to be aware of all its fine distinctions; and to appreciate all its shades of expression; otherwise we shall not be certain to understand what we are told.' They had supposed they knew English at Paris (like people who believe themselves wise on graduating from school, as Tocqueville put it);[3] but they had not been slow to undeceive themselves.

'There is also in the vessel a most agreeable and gracious American girl, Miss Edwards, who is most useful for our purpose, and who gives us our English lesson with great regularity. This lesson consists ordinarily of long and more or less insignificant conversations, during which she corrects all the errors and mistakes we make. In spite of her 18 years, her fresh complexion, her kindness, and all the charms of her person, our relations are altogether brotherly. The expression is apt for she is really a sister to me. [No use alarming the family!] She is not in the least flirtatious, which is not without its fortunate side, as she is really pretty and very *spirituelle*. The other Americans with us are in general very worth while, particularly the Scarmehorn [Schermerhorn] family, whose name I have not yet been able to catch exactly and do not promise to reproduce correctly.

'We meet with a great deal of kindness from everybody and are treated with real distinction. Every one volunteers to help us in some way. As we are busy, the time flies; [but] all of those who surround us are not in the same position and the majority are bored to death. Here is how we fill our days: At 5½ we are aroused by an infernal charivari which drowns out both the wash of the sea and the whistling of the wind—I am speaking of Jules' alarm clock, inestimable treasure, of whose beneficent services we become daily more appreciative. One gets up as best one can, midst the tossing of the ship, that is to say in nautical language, in spite of the *pitching* and *rolling*, which from time to time cause one to bump one's head or elbow in dressing in a narrow cabin. We work till 9. . . . At that time we are interrupted by the breakfast bell. . . .

'After *déjeuner* one generally goes on deck. The lazy even stay there all day making observations on the rain and the fair weather. Less put to it than they to kill time, we take up our studies again at 11. At this moment we are making a translation of an English work, on the prisons of America, which it is so important for a certain French administration to know that our translation may interest them. We will present it to them on our return. As such a study is by its very nature quite fatiguing, we mix in with it readings which are exceedingly interesting and even more useful. We have already read a complete history of the United States.* Now with all our energies we are doing political economy with the work of J.B.Say. This study has an extreme attraction; and it is a real happiness for us when, enclosed in our little cell, we put our ideas in common in an honest search after the truth. Tocqueville is a really distinguished man. He has high-minded ideas and great nobility of soul; the better I know him, the more I like him. Here are our two lives linked together. It is evident that our destinies are, and will be, always the same. That is a tie which makes friendship livelier and closer. . . .'

Tocqueville returned the feeling. He had realized for some time past how much Gustave's friendship could mean to him, and how valuable to them both was to be this gradually forming habit of mutual assistance and co-operative endeavour. A year before they thus found themselves setting out on a voyage of discovery together, he had written to his tall friend, with the frankness and feeling characteristic of all his friendships:[4] 'You are the only man in the world on whose judgment I can lean with confidence . . . you alone have the qualities

* Unfortunately, it has not been possible to identify these two works.

of mind and the necessary experience. When I reflect on that, my dear friend, I know that it is a happiness for which we are not sufficiently grateful to have thus tied up to each other in the middle of the crowd.'

Drawn together by birth and education, animated by kindred interests, a common outlook, and like political opinions, these two young liberals were beginning to derive great benefit and satisfaction from their comradeship. Though they had known each other only three years, they already knew that they agreed absolutely on the fundamentals, and they were fast finding out how effectively they could work together. Their letters already showed Tocqueville, his curiosity as to the fact satisfied, quickly attempting a general description or diving down to the underlying idea; while Beaumont, idealistic himself, gave a longer attention and a larger notice to the actual and particular appearance of things. Thus, when they came to put their heads together in their narrow little cabin, there took place a stimulating exchange of thought.

At the same time, neither was exclusively interested in a single aspect of their surroundings. Both were careful observers and industrious readers; and each was in the habit of drawing general inferences from his observations. Consequently, when they talked over their ideas and developed their thoughts in their daily *tête-à-têtes*, they would time and again reach identical conclusions, if, indeed, they had not found themselves in perfect agreement from the start. So characteristic was this process with them that it is often impossible to ascertain which of them originated a given idea. All that can sometimes be said is that the thought had its genesis in their co-operative studies, and was fashioned in one or more of the friendly and intimate discussions that took place between them every day that they were together. As Beaumont went on to tell his father about their American plans, therefore, he naturally fell into the first person plural:

'We are meditating great projects. First of all we will accomplish to the best of our ability the mission given us; it is a rigorous duty which we ought to perform conscientiously. But while working on the penitentiary system we shall see America; in visiting its prisons we shall be visiting its inhabitants, its cities, its institutions, its customs; we shall come to know the mechanism of its republican government. . . . This government is not understood in Europe. People speak of it endlessly, for the sake of making false comparisons between it and countries which do not in any way resemble it. Would not that be a fine book which would give an exact conception of the American people, would paint its character in bold strokes, would analyse its social conditions and would rectify so many opinions which are erroneous on this point?—What do you, dear Father, think on this subject? I beg you to tell me your feeling in this matter. . . .'

Evidently, the once vague plan for a book on America was rapidly crystallizing in the minds of the youthful magistrates. For nearly a year past, the two friends had been considering the possibility of drawing political object lessons for themselves and for France from a first-hand examination of republican government in the United States. And Tocqueville, for one, had even thought of publishing something on the subject after his return. But there on shipboard, somewhere out on the Atlantic, for the first time emerged a definite resolve and a succinct, workmanlike program. If Tocqueville had originated the scheme, therefore, without question the ambitious and idealistic Beaumont was finding the voyage a wonderful opportunity to instil something of his own resolution into his friend, the while contributing also his own ideas to the plan.* This much, at least, was settled: it would be from then on, definitely, a joint enterprise.

From the day of Beaumont's letter in that little 300-ton packet, also the idea was never to be absent from their minds. It came to dominate their thoughts and to direct their occupations. As they read up on American history in the daylight hours, they were really trying to get outside the preconceptions and prejudices of their race and caste and preparing themselves to grasp the true character of the new world civilization they were going to visit.

They were a courageous pair. They would gather materials for their book. They would read, ask questions and, above all, observe. Every experience, every conversation, every new bit of information encountered from then on was to be seized on and carefully analysed for its contribution to their knowledge and understanding. In fact, the nine months to follow would never be justly appreciated until studied in the light of this intention. The story of their American experiences would be a tale of travels and adventures. But it would be also, and designedly, the story of the gradual shaping of Tocqueville's and Beaumont's thoughts, of the slow ripening of their plans

* The fact that Beaumont had not previously confided in his family indicates the tentative nature of the original proposal; while his request for his father's opinion suggests that he and Tocqueville were anxious for advice as to the best course to pursue.

for a book on the society and government of America that should perhaps some day be of use and guidance to harassed France.

Tocqueville's first diary notes showed that this process of vivisecting
a foreign society had already begun. He and Beaumont had for some
time been listening to tales by the Americans on board of what the
United States was like. He now began to question them and to note
down the most significant of their replies. He particularly valued the
opinions of Mr. Peter Schermerhorn,* a distinguished merchant, descended from a long line of New Yorkers, who was just returning with
his family from two years of residence and travel in Europe. Mr.
Schermerhorn had become interested in his young French acquaintances, and was evidently more than willing to talk with them about
the character and prospects of American society. Tocqueville's first
notes were :

### PARTY SPIRIT IN AMERICA

Mr. Schermerhorn told me that there were no parties in America as
with us; the nation is no longer divided in two by contrary principles,
serving as barriers.

This state of affairs came to an end with the extinction of the Federalists and the non-Federalists. Now one knows only those who support
and those who attack the measures of the administration, in order to obtain
jobs and win public opinion over to their side. April 1831.

### NATIONAL CHARACTER OF THE AMERICANS

Mr. Schermerhorn (who is however much infatuated with his country)
told me that the greatest blot on the national character was the avidity
to get rich and to do it by any means whatever. There are in the United
States a great number of business failures, and these do not sufficiently
injure those who are responsible. 24 April 1831.

After further conversations on prisons and crime with Mr. Schermerhorn and their English friend, Mr. Palmer,† Tocqueville ventured
an important question:

---

* Peter Schermerhorn ('The Younger,' 1781–1852) had made a fortune, first with
his father, then with his brothers, in the Ship Chandler business in New York; and
was the owner of valuable real estate, a bank director, and one of the vestry of
Grace Church in that city. With him on the *Havre* were his wife, and three sons:
John Jones (1806–1876) who was but nine months younger than Tocqueville; Peter
Augustus (1811–1845) who had graduated from Columbia with honour in 1829;
and the ten-year-old William Colford, who was to live on into the twentieth century.
† The shipboard conversations here given are to be found among the miscellaneous
American notes, at Tocqueville (TT, YT). Mr. Palmer was not certain whether the

*DIVISION OF AMERICAN EMPIRE*

When I spoke to Mr. Schermerhorn of the possible division that might take place between the united provinces [States], he did not seem to believe that it was the least in the world to be feared in the near future, but thinks that it would come some day, *by and by*. April 1831.

That is, just how long would this seemingly successful federal republic in America last? Some of their friends back home believed that in the United States the perfect government, the government of the future, had been found. Most, though, could not conceive of a permanently successful republic, believed, in fact, that the democratic form of government was contrary to nature. Tocqueville and Beaumont wanted to know.

\*

\*     \*

The *Havre* sailed on, and the peaceful monotony of the sea settled on the small community as the weeks slipped by. One lonely day Beaumont felt the pangs of homesickness. Tocqueville, for his part, was more affected by impatience, especially when to the fair weather off Ireland succeeded the headwinds and rolling calms of mid-ocean. He tried hard to bring a little of good abbé Lesueur's philosophy to bear. But probably it was his consuming interest in everything that went on about him that more often diverted and reconciled him.

One day a barrel was sighted in the water. There was a commotion, pistols were brought, and it was Tocqueville who had the honour to hit it. Another day of good omen a little bird from America, 'blue as the sky,' was carried by a squall into the rigging. One delicious spring evening a dance was proposed, Beaumont got out his flute, 'and we skipped about with the greatest gaiety in the world.' And one stormy night 'the sea set itself to sparkling like the electric machine. The night

---

number of crimes was increasing in England. 'The opinion of Mr. Schermerhorn,' wrote Tocqueville, 'is that the number of crimes is augmenting in the United States. This argument would be almost decisive against the penitentiary system, if the fact were true. But he who reports it to us did not seem to have studied the question seriously.' On the other hand, on the subject of 'Commerce,' this merchant's opinions had to be given more weight. 'Mr. Schermerhorn pretended that the construction of ships, the pay of the sailors, and the different expenses of navigation, cost the Americans more than the French. He attributed the superiority of the former simply to their extreme activity, constantly stimulated by the passion to get rich, also to the almost total absence of restrictions. *It is accepted in France that the Americans are the cheapest carriers in the world.*'

was very black, and the prow of the vessel in cutting the water set boiling up for twenty paces about a foam of fire. The better to observe I went and placed myself on the forward mast, called the bowsprit . . . from there at some distance I could see the prow, which seemed to rush upon me with the sparkling wave which it spurned before it. The spectacle was more admirable and sublime than I can paint it.'

It was very stormy and so dark one could hardly see the rigging against the sky. How long his love of the sublime had kept him on that cold and dangerous perch on the raking bowsprit, after his insatiable curiosity had lured him out there, Tocqueville did not say. But the spectacle of the dark ship ploughing through the seas as through a crucible of incandescent metal made a deep impression on him. When he climbed back he found that the *Havre* 'left behind it a long flaming trail . . . it was a scene of beauty defying description.'[5]

It began to blow up. Mrs. Schermerhorn later noted in her diary that it had been 'a most boisterous passage.'[6] '. . . On approaching the bank of Newfoundland we experienced two pretty strong blows. One of them lasted 36 hours without interruption,' and Tocqueville was reminded of the fact that there was no doctor on board—200 people for weeks on end without a doctor! What happened when one smashed an arm or a leg in a storm at sea? Both Tocqueville and Beaumont were careful not to tell their families that the broken bones would have to be set by the mate or the carpenter, if at all!

Shipboard life, they discovered, was peculiar in one other respect: its table. Beaumont was particularly impressed by the character of the food supply. 'Each one takes his place at the common table and begins to eat, without worrying too much about the breaking glasses, the falling bottles, the sauces which are spilled, etc., etc. We have fresh bread every day, excellent wine, Bordeaux, as much Madeira as we want, and often champagne. Our food would also be good if we had a good cook, but he is so bad he spoils everything he touches. Still, we live ordinarily on ducks, chickens, turkeys, which are crossing with us and diminishing in number every day. I've forgotten to tell you that among our travelling companions are a cow, some sheep, a donkey . . . all of whom, with the exception of Mylord *Aliboron* [Ass], arrive opportunely at the word *lunch*, for these animals will figure one after the other on our table. . . .'

As this was before the days of canning and refrigeration, the *Havre*, like its sister packets, was carrying its fresh food alive and on the hoof.

These pigs, sheep, goats, chickens, turkeys, and ducks which were making the voyage with the commissioners of the French government, had their quarters—till their turn came to join the cabin passengers—in pens and coops 'tween decks or in the long boat. There was also a special cowhouse somewhere on deck for the Alderney and mylord the donkey. Tocqueville had come across this little community—known as the 'ship farm'—when, like the inquisitive Moses, he had been numbering the host: 'Aside from a cow and a donkey,' he had gravely reported, 'we number 181 souls.' But in general he and Beaumont were too busy with studies worthier the attention of two serious young men to take the time more than to mention these inhabitants of their ocean-going ark as they appeared on the table. Besides, they were not (like milk-drinking Americans) concerned for the health of the cow in rough weather. And they did not visualize the food supply as a possible source of danger. So long as they did not have to eat donkey, Tocqueville's delicate stomach would apparently stand the bad cooking wonderfully well. And if they were appalled by the heavy eating that was going on around them, they did not have to participate.

*

* *

The two exiles, straining their eyes toward America by day, but at night dreaming back to their families and the disturbed country they had left behind them, suddenly awoke to more immediate concerns. A week after first sitting down to tell his family how the crossing was going, Tocqueville took up his letter again and wrote:

'To-day, 4 May . . . we find ourselves on the 66th degree of longitude; we have only about 130 leagues to cover to reach New-York. That is nothing if we have good wind, but we can put eight days more into getting there. However, here we have been 32 days at sea. A great part of our fresh provisions are exhausted, and they are already giving us sugar only by rations! . . .'

Rations! What happened when the stocking of the larder and of the 'ship farm' had been mismanaged, and the food ran short ? In a little sailing vessel held back by head winds there was not much one could do. Try as he might, Tocqueville could not completely conceal from his family his own anxiety over the predicament in which their careless captain had placed them. If the *Havre* had not made an exceedingly fast run the first week out, they would have been facing starvation far at sea. As it was, they were lucky. When the shortage was discovered they were rapidly nearing New York.

'*9 May.* Yesterday morning the first cry of land was heard but it took a glass to see the coast. To-day the rising sun has just revealed *Long Island* to us. We are approaching the shore rapidly, one already sees grass and trees in leaf; it's a delicious sight. I leave you to go join all those who are rejoicing on deck. The sea makes no one uncomfortable to-day.

'*New-York 14 May.* I scarcely anticipated, dear Mother, when we were in view of *Long Island,* what was going to happen to us. Upon going on deck I noticed that the wind, which had been blowing from the east since morning, was veering to the west. An hour later it became gusty and contrary; and we had to start to tack, that is to say, to zigzag without advancing. In the *mâture (matinée?)* the west wind became settled, as the sailors say. In other words the weather took on an appearance of stability which promised to last several days. Now we had some sick people * on board and our provisions were giving out. Even the wood and the flour were beginning to dwindle in a disquieting way. All the passengers therefore got together and asked that, with the aid of the west wind, we gain the little town of Newport, which is situated 60 leagues to the north of New-York. The captain consented. . . .' So all day they ran down the south shore of Long Island till they passed by the wild, bare point of Montauk and Block Island.

'At eight o'clock in the evening we dropped anchor in the outer harbour of Newport. A fishing dory soon came to reconnoitre us. We were so happy to find ourselves at land that all the young people and the captain himself immediately embarked in the dory, and a half hour afterwards we arrived, not without wetting our seats a little, at the wharf of Newport. Never, I guess, were people so glad to be alive.' Night had fallen and there was nothing to be seen, but they were all so happy they embraced each other.

'We jumped ashore and each of us made more than a dozen awkward gambols before we got ourselves solidly on our feet. In this way we went to an inn where the captain treated us to supper. What I for one liked best about this meal was something that has no merit in your eyes, water. Ours hadn't been drinkable for several days. (I must tell you *à propos* of that, that the captain, an excellent man and a good

---

* 'Several 'tween decks and one in the cabin down with fever,' Toc. to his brother Édouard, New-York, 20 June 1831 (YT).

sailor, had horribly mismanaged the provisioning, and that nothing was less comfortable than our ship.) * To come back to our story, we supped then *à estomac renversé* (my companions at least), after which we re-collected our *galanterie française* and, having bought a great number of fresh provisions, we re-embarked and came to the vessel at midnight. No one had gone to bed. The provisions which we brought were carried in triumph down to the ladies' saloon, and we sat down to supper again. I ask you to believe that when I say we *supped*, I only speak for myself of the intellectual part of dining. . . .'

It had been a narrow escape.

The following morning Tocqueville and Beaumont were up with the sun.

' . . . We went to visit the town, which seemed to us very attractive. It's true we weren't difficult. It's a collection of small houses, the size of chicken coops, but distinguished by a cleanness that is a pleasure to see and that we have no conception of in France. Beyond that, the inhabitants differ but little superficially from the French. They wear the same clothes, and their physiognomies are so varied that it would be hard to say from what races they have derived their features. I think it must be thus in all the United States.'

Beaumont had been particularly receptive to new impressions that morning. 'Very early next day 10 May,' he wrote,[7] 'we went to the Collector (receiver of customs duties) to get permission to take off our baggage; which was granted us. They made us swear on the Bible that we had nothing dutiable, and in consideration of the light tax of a dollar (5fr. 30c.), we obtained a pass from the customs. Beyond that they examined our trunks with but slight care; and it appears that in this respect the inspectors of Newport bear no resemblance whatever to the French customs agents. This formality fulfilled, we wandered about the town. It has 16,000 inhabitants, a magnificent harbour, newly fortified, tiny houses modelled one would say on the kitchen of Beaumont-la-Chartre, but so clean they resemble opera scenery. They are all painted. There is also a church whose bell tower is in a rather remarkable architectural style. I sketched it on Jules' album. We had been told that the women of Newport were noteworthy for their beauty; we found them extraordinarily ugly. This new race of people we saw bears

---

* The captain was either transferred or cashiered for his mismanagement, for (in spite of generous efforts on the part of his passengers, in the shape of a testimonial in the papers) when next the *Havre* sailed, it was under a different officer.

no clear mark of its origin (*n'a aucun caractère original*); it's neither English, nor French, nor German; it's a mixture of all the nations. This race is entirely commercial. In the small city of Newport there are 4 or 5 banks; the same is true in all the cities in the Union. . . .'

Mr. Schermerhorn had remarked that the greatest blot on the American character was cupidity and the overweening desire to get rich. Tocqueville had noted this opinion down. And Beaumont was already testing it by actual observation. . . . Four or five banks in each. . . . Then it was true that the Americans were a commercial people !

But there was no time for philosophizing yet. Here at last was the dreamed-of, longed-for, legendary country of the Americans, awaiting their inspection. The two eager observers felt their very hearts in their eyes as they strained for their first glimpses at Newport and coasting down to New York in a Sound steamer, those late spring days.

'After having for three hours savoured the pleasure of being on land,' Tocqueville pursued his description,[8] 'we embarked on a tremendous steamship which, coming down from Providence, was making for New-York.* It is impossible to picture to oneself the interior of this immense machine. Let it suffice you to know that it contains three great saloons, two for men, one for women, where four, five, and often eight hundred people eat and sleep comfortably. You can judge of its speed, since in spite of a contrary sea and wind we covered in 18 hours the 60 leagues which separated us from New-York.

'All this coast of America is low and little picturesque. In this country, covered by impenetrable forests two centuries ago, one has trouble finding a tree. Yet land was on either hand; for we were passing between *Long Island* and the shores of *Connecticut*. At sunrise we approached New-York, entering its harbour, consequently, from the back. I don't know whether the rather unattractive aspect of the country we had already seen, and our 35 days at sea, subjected us to an illusion; but what's certain is that we uttered cries of admiration on glimpsing the environs of the city. Picture to yourself an attractively varied shore-

---

* 'Of all the inhabitants of the vessel, we are, without comparison, those who have best supported the crossing. I was sick only two days, and Beaumont wasn't a single instant,' Tocqueville later boasted (Toc. to E.Chabrol, New-York, 18 May 1831, YT). Nevertheless the two young men were so tired of the sea, 'and especially of the inconstancy of the winds,' that instead of staying by the *Havre*, they joined the other passengers who had decided to complete the journey by Sound steamer. The *President*, of the New York and Boston Steam Boat Line, took them down.

line, the slopes covered by lawns and trees in bloom right down to the water, and more than all that, an unbelievable multitude of country houses, big as boxes of candy, but showing careful workmanship,— add to this if you can—a sea covered with sails, and you will have the entrance to New-York from the *Sound*. I have been so struck by how convenient these little houses must be, and by the attractive air they gave the countryside, that I shall try to have the sketch or the plan of one or two of the prettiest. Emily might perhaps profit by them for Nacqueville. I already know that they are not expensive. We have nothing like them in France. . . .'

Beaumont also found this little voyage 'in an immense house' full of 'almost magical occurrences.' To him there was 'something prodigious in the navigation of such a vessel, and especially in the means employed to run it.' To describe the houses set amidst their trees by the narrowing shores of the Sound, as they drew near to New York, he used the same word 'candy-box.' 'At each instant one glimpses great bays which cut into the shores and which form the most picturesque sites. We were in real admiration; doubtless we have things as beautiful in France, but we haven't anything of the same kind. What struck us particularly was the animation given this majestic tableau by the immense number of vessels, brigs, gondolas, and boats of all sizes which crossed [and recrossed] in every direction.'

A peculiar interest attaches to these first impressions, for they were the impressions of utter strangers at the first encounter:—clear, sharp, photographic almost, and at the same time self-revealing. Tocqueville's and Beaumont's descriptions were pictures both of the American scene and of their own minds. They were disillusioned—enchanted—surprised. Chiefly they were surprised. Their shipboard friends had evidently warned them not to expect on the Atlantic coast those vast impenetrable forests alive with redmen, immemorially associated in the French mind with the word America. But for the neatness of a New England town, for the quiet charm of the wooden churches and Georgian country houses, for the vast bulk and power of the American steamboat, they were totally unprepared.

The *President* swung in and docked at the foot of Manhattan, at Courtlandt Street, the morning of the eleventh of May. It was exactly thirty-eight and a half days since the group of travellers lining the rails on its forward deck had slid out of Havre in the darkness and set sail down the English Channel in a badly provisioned ship. New York!

But as they stepped on the pier the two young French magistrates suddenly realized that they were tired out. In the excitement of the landing at Newport and of seeing the Sound, they had hardly slept a wink in three days. So they 'went to a kind of hotel called boarding house. It's nothing but a *pension* into which we were introduced and where we are very well off. This doesn't cost us too dear. Thereupon we went to bed, though in plain daylight. We were so tired, so tossed about, so bruised that a good bed seemed to us the most desirable of all things. We lay down at 4 and the morrow at 8 we were still in bed. . . .'

# VI

## RECEPTION IN NEW YORK

When Tocqueville and Beaumont arose from bed next morning, 12 May, prepared to face their first day in America, they were startled to find that the news of their arrival was abroad in the city. They were being talked about in the newspapers. In that day's *Mercantile Advertiser*, New York read:

'We understand that two magistrates, Messrs. de Beaumont and de Tonqueville [*sic*], have arrived in the ship *Havre*, sent here by order of the Minister of the Interior, to examine the various prisons in our country, and make a report on their return to France. To other countries, especially in Europe, a commission has also been sent, as the French Government have it in contemplation to improve their Penitentiary system, and take this means of obtaining all proper information. In our country, we have no doubt that every facility will be extended to the gentlemen who have arrived.'

That same evening this ponderous and somewhat obscure announcement was reprinted verbatim in William Cullen Bryant's *New-York Evening Post*. Thereupon it was promptly echoed by the rest of the New York City press. From New York the issues went out in the mail. Two days later the *Newport Mercury* carried the item; five days later Boston was reading about the prison commission sent out by the government of France; and soon the citizens of Philadelphia, Baltimore, and Annapolis were aware that two worthy French dignitaries had landed in America.

As would appear in their letters, Tocqueville and Beaumont were taken completely by surprise. It was pleasing that the newspapers of the city should speak of them and of their mission in such a friendly way; but they were bewildered at being noticed at all by the press of a foreign country in which they had only just landed. Certainly the American editors could have very little to talk about if they considered the arrival of two unknown prison investigators as news that would interest their readers.

The fact was, Tocqueville and Beaumont did not in the least understand the significance of this unsolicited and unexpected publicity. The first thing they did, therefore, was to make elaborate preparations to bring themselves and their mission to the attention of the American authorities. In spite of their government credentials and in spite of the articles in the newspapers, the two commissioners felt entirely too young and unimpressive to be venturing on a difficult investigation in a strange country without further introduction. During the last six months in France, it had been made painfully clear to them that the question of prison reform was of but slight political and social importance, while they themselves were unheard-of beginners of no dignity or consequence whatever. Governments, they had learned, listened only to influential people, not to youths still in their twenties. It followed that in so large a country as the United States, they would need all the influence that could be mustered for them, if the officials in charge were to be persuaded to give them a friendly reception and to facilitate their investigation. So Tocqueville and Beaumont spent their first hours in New York enlisting the aid of the accredited representatives of the French government in the United States. They wrote to Serurier, Minister of France at Washington, asking him to get them letters from the American Secretary of State (Edward Livingston) to the wardens of the prisons they wished to visit. They got into touch with the French consuls in New York and Philadelphia. And they also presented the first of their letters of introduction to influential Americans residing in the city.

They were wrong; and they knew it even before the shrewd Serurier could write to tell them so. After only two days Beaumont wrote to his mother:[1] 'Every one here overwhelms us with courtesy and services. . . . We have a thousand letters of introduction we could do without entirely, to such an extent are our wishes anticipated. We shall soon be obliged to forbid our door. Our arrival in America has *created a sensation. . . .*'

It had. Seemingly all New York was interested in them. No sooner had the newspapers published the notice of their arrival than they were besieged by friendly strangers. Prison officials came to see them, or wrote inviting them to visit their institutions. The city authorities, far from having to be importuned, came forward of their own accord to offer their services ; and the doors of society swung open as if by magic. Of course, this was nothing compared to the triumphal reception New

York had given another Frenchman they knew, six years before. But that had been Lafayette, and the occasion had been the old general's return to the United States to see how the country he had helped to independence was getting on. So there had been a reason for the interest and gratitude of the Americans. Now there was none. The warmth of this welcome therefore surpassed Tocqueville's and Beaumont's wildest imaginings. It was, to them, incredible.

Yet the explanation was, after all, quite simple. The experienced Serurier down in Washington, the moment he heard of their mission, guessed what was going to happen. The federal government, he wrote them, had nothing to do with the prisons; but they would be shown every courtesy without the letters they asked. 'Your mission,' he said,[2] 'will flatter the natural pride of a young nation which sees travellers from the old societies of Europe coming to learn something from it.'

That was it exactly: the Americans were feeling extraordinarily flattered. The appointment by the French government of a commission to study prison reforms in some foreign country was, after all, a compliment to the people of that country. It implied that they ordered those things better there than in France. Any nation, therefore, would have had cause to be pleased on discovering itself the object of such a mission. But to the Americans the honour meant a great deal more. The United States was, Serurier had said, a young nation. That is, its people were not used to being paid such compliments. Since their origins the Americans had occupied the position of younger brother to the societies of Europe. The older governments had tyrannized, patronized, insulted, or ignored—but very rarely flattered. And their nationals had been doing the same. In fact, it seemed to be fast becoming the custom of travellers from the old world, particularly of Englishmen and Englishwomen, to visit the United States for the sole purpose of writing a book criticizing Americans and American ways.* Inevitably the people of New York found themselves tickled and gratified at the news that Tocqueville and Beaumont had actually been sent by the French gov-

---

* Beaumont himself was to be struck by the unreasonableness of the performance: 'Full of his national prejudices, and able, moreover, without partiality, to find America inferior to his own country, the Englishman on his return home writes his *transatlantic* voyage, which is nothing but a satire continued in one or two volumes. Sometimes he doesn't even respect proper names and delivers over to the ridicule of his fellow-citizens the worthy stranger whose hospitality he has received. Those whose style is most reserved are still unjust and wounding. The work published in England soon arrives in the United States, where its appearance is a thunderbolt to American vanity.' *Marie*, I,351.

ernment to study and admire an American institution. And as a matter of course they wanted to make such worthy visitors welcome.

There was also another reason why the Americans of 1831 were at once interested in their latest visitors. Serurier did not mention this second reason, and Tocqueville and Beaumont were apparently for some time unaware of its force. But on 18 May the *New York Daily Advertiser*, under the heading PRISON DISCIPLINE, stated it clearly: 'It is gratifying to learn that the French government are engaged in extensive examinations on the important subject of prison discipline. Commissioners, it is stated, have already gone to the different countries of Europe, and two have arrived here in the packet ship Havre, who are to visit our principal prisons and penitentiaries, and report on their return to France. They are Messrs. De Beaumont and Tonqueville. As humanity is deeply interested in the improvement of the prisons of France and of all Europe, we hope our philanthropists will afford the gentlemen all desirable facilities.'

The two words 'humanity' and 'philanthropists' in the last sentence supplied the clue. They suggested that the New Yorkers were interested, not only as Americans whose institutions were being complimented, but as members of the larger brotherhood of all human kind.

The truth was, Tocqueville and Beaumont had unwittingly come to the United States at the very moment when a great humanitarian movement was just gathering way. It was not without significance, for instance, that in New England, in that very year 1831, Garrison had started his abolition crusade. At the same time, as the two unsuspecting young commissioners were fated often to be reminded, enlightened citizens all over the country were beginning to be aroused over the notorious abuse of spirituous liquors. In a number of the communities and States which they were to visit, Temperance societies had already been formed; and a national convention was in prospect. Much in the same spirit, the Pennsylvanians whom they would meet were busily discussing free education through tax-supported public schools; while in New York, as in Boston, people were actively advocating the abolition of imprisonment for debt.

Unquestionably, the conscience of America was awake; philanthropy was in the air. And unmistakably, the two rival penitentiary systems—one perfected by the New Yorkers themselves at Auburn in 1826, the other instituted with the building of the Eastern State Penitentiary near Philadelphia only two years before—were among the most popular, as they had been among the earliest, of the new reforms. From the newspapers, even the man in the street knew something about the novel prison theories which seemed to be yielding such promising results. And for the intelligent reader, there had already been issued a considerable pamphlet literature on the subject, to say nothing of the publicity given it by two very active prison societies.

Since 1826, it was well known, a certain Massachusetts philanthropic association called the Boston Prison Discipline Society had, in a series of striking and widely-read annual reports, reviewed the whole history of the penitentiary movement, from its beginnings down to its most recent developments.[3] And in Philadelphia, as the two French travellers were by and by to discover, there lived and wrote an amiable and enthusiastic group of Quakers, who called themselves a 'Society for the Alleviation of the Miseries of the Public Prisons,' and who took the liveliest interest in the success of the new Pennsylvania experiments. As for New York City, Sing Sing lay only a few miles up the Hudson; and on an island in the East River an Auburn-style prison was at the very moment in process of construction. The *New York Daily Advertiser* was not overestimating the interest of its subscribers, therefore, when it referred to prison discipline as an 'important subject.' The fact was, if Tocqueville and Beaumont had deliberately set out to enlist the aid of Americans in an enterprise, they could hardly have chosen a more appropriate question for their investigation, or a much better year.

So no sooner had they settled themselves in their boarding house at 66 Broadway, not far from the American Hotel on the most fashionable cobblestone street of that busy and fast growing city, than visitors and invitations began to pour in. The architect of the new penitentiary at Sing Sing sent a letter enclosing a sketch of the prison and offering the services of himself, the warden, and the State agent in their investigation.[4] The chaplain of Connecticut's prison at Wethersfield, who happened to be in town, got in touch with them and suggested they come to Wethersfield.[5] Every one else seemed to be interested in prisons and houses of correction, too, particularly the lawyers.

Tocqueville and Beaumont's papers showed, for instance, that they were fairly being pursued by William W. Campbell,* an earnest young man who had just finished studying law under Chancellor Kent and writing a *History of Tryon County*. One day this future jurist

---

* Wm.W.Campbell, 1806–1861, in his career jurist, historian, Congressman, member of Native American party.

(who was, incidentally, interested in the Temperance movement) called their attention to some almshouse and hospital statistics in the evening paper; on another he sent them an article just published on the penitentiary system in Pennsylvania, and offered to be their guide to the almshouse and penitentiary in New York.[6] In the same spirit, a resident of Cherry Valley, Judge J.O.Morse,* at once volunteered his services in introducing Tocqueville and Beaumont to important people, and before they had been five days in the country was listing the statesmen they should call on if they went to Albany. This paper he proudly entitled: *'Memo for our French Friends.'*[7] Other lawyers also took an interest in their investigation into the treatment of criminals; and it was not long before they had made the acquaintance of two vigorous personalities, the Scotchman Hugh Maxwell † and his partner Ogden Hoffman,‡ who between them had held the office of District Attorney and handled most of the criminal cases of the city for more than eleven years.

Meanwhile, almost before they could get their leather trunks unpacked, the young Frenchmen were being introduced to New York society. Their shipboard friends and their bankers were seeing to that. The Englishman Palmer, who had put up at the same boarding house, was searching the city for people who could help them in their study of prison reforms; and, at 21 Park Place, substantial Peter Schermerhorn was soon presenting them to his relations and friends. As they had a letter of credit on Prime, Ward & King, the great banking house of the day, they also met the dark and rather stern Nathaniel Prime § of 1 Broadway, a self-made man who was reputed as wealthy as any in New York. Almost immediately they were on intimate terms with him. In the same way they made the acquaintance of his travelled and agreeable partner, James Gore King,¶ Rufus King's third son, who was before long to entertain them at dinner at his home.

---

* James Otis Morse, 1788–1837.

† Hugh Maxwell, 1787–1873, had been District Attorney for New York County, 1819–29, Prosecutor in the 'Conspiracy trials.'

‡ Ogden Hoffman, 1793–1856, had served under Decatur, who is said to have expressed regret that he should have 'exchanged an honorable profession for that of the law.' He was to be District Attorney 1829–35, Congressman, State Attorney General, and reputed perhaps the outstanding criminal lawyer of his generation.

§ Nathaniel Prime, 1786–1840, had come to New York from an old Rowley (Mass.) family. He became, 'next to Astor, the wealthiest man in New York,' and was worth $800,000 when he died.

¶ James Gore King, 1791–1853, was later head of James G. King & Sons, President of the New York & Erie R.R., Congressman.

Their acquaintance widened. New York's distinguished Professor of Medicine, Dr. David Hosack,* who was noted for his mastery of medicine, surgery, botany, philanthropy, and society, proved to be interested as well in the great question of the solitary confinement of criminals. They were soon being hospitably received by John R. Livingston Jr. and his charming wife. And their letters showed that they came to be at home in the house of 'the very lofty, learned, and accomplished John Duer,'† joint author of the Revised Statutes. There they must also have met his brother, William Alexander Duer,‡ President of Columbia College, then situated on Park Place. In a city of about 230,000, occupying only the very lower end of Manhattan island, from the Battery north to Canal Street, the socially prominent were not so numerous or scattered but that Tocqueville and Beaumont might hope to meet them all. Every one seemed to live either on or near Broadway, and a surprising number were to prove interested in their government mission.

'One of our first visits,' Beaumont wrote to his father on 16 May, 'was to the consul of France, Baron de St. André,§ for whom we had a letter from the Minister of Foreign Affairs. He has a wife and children. They are likeable people ; and he immediately asked us to dinner. But there is nothing to be gained from their conversation. They don't know the country they are in at all and they are entirely without the faculty of observation. We dine there again to-day, which bores us, because we have much better things to do.

'Mr. Palmer, that Englishman of whom I spoke before, continues to overwhelm us with attentions and with care. He is on the hunt for all the persons who can be useful to us, so as to put us into touch with them. We have been presented to the Governor of the State of New-York, to the Mayor of the city, to the Recorder, to the Aldermen, and to nearly all the magistrates ; several among them even anticipate us and offer us their services. . . .'

---

* Dr. David Hosack, 1769–1835. In addition to being one of the greatest medical and botanical authorities of his day in America, he was founder and first president of the New York Historical Society, president of numerous philanthropic and social organizations, and the owner of a fine library. Distinguished visitors often were asked to his famous Saturday evening parties.

† Judge Silliman on John Duer, 1782–1858 (quoted in *D.A.B.*). Duer was noted as an insurance lawyer. Later he became Chief Justice of the Superior Court.

‡ William Alexander Duer, 1780–1858, Judge, friend of Edward Livingston, President of Columbia College, 1829–1842.

§ Durant (de) St. André, Consul-General at New York since September 1829.

So they had also met the politicians of the city. And from Mayor Bowne and his welcoming committee they were going to hear a good deal more later. But already they were on friendly terms with the famous Recorder of New York, the lame and genial Richard Riker.* This remarkable man had held the office of Recorder for so long that he had almost become one of the historical monuments of the city, and Fitz-Greene Halleck had made him the subject of his poem, *The Recorder.* He was a Princeton graduate of engaging manners and easy-going ways, who sometimes signed papers without reading them, for he was reputed once to have signed his own jail *mittimus* obligingly prepared for him by a friend. But there was also a story of how he had quelled a riot at the Five Points with Father O'Brien.[8] At all events, long service and experience had made him a 'most notable man to preserve order and administer justice'; and he knew a great deal about criminal law. Before Tocqueville and Beaumont went back to France, they were to be deeply indebted to this amiable gentleman for many services.

For the moment, however, it was their visit to the governor of New York State that most impressed the bewildered young Frenchmen, and became the subject of the first diary note Tocqueville made in America. The introduction took place on 13 May, through the kind offices of their friend Judge Morse. The latter knew that the Hon. Enos T. Throop,† Martin Van Buren's friend and successor in the governorship, had come down to New York to attend the forty-second anniversary dinner of the Tammany Society the evening before. So, only two days after his new acquaintances had landed, the indefatigable judge took them to call on the first official of the state. The French commissioners approached this ceremony with some trepidation. And afterwards Tocqueville jotted down on paper :

### AMERICAN USAGES

The greatest equality seems to reign, even among those who occupy very different positions in society.

The authorities seem extraordinarily approachable.

The thirteenth of May *Mr. Morse,* judge at Cherry Valley, presented

---

* Richard Riker, 1773–1842, Recorder with two short intermissions, 1815–38.

† Enos Thompson Throop, 1784–1874, as circuit judge had tried the kidnappers of William Morgan. He had become acting governor when Van Buren resigned to be Secretary of State, and had then been elected for the term 1831–33. 'He was a sturdy democrat and he gave a turn to thought within the family which even in collateral branches still tends to be, more or less enthusiastically, democratic.'

us to the governor of New-York, who was staying at a *boarding house* and who received us in the parlor without any ceremony whatever. Mr. Morse assured us that anyone could at any time do as we had done.

This was their introduction to American democratic equality. It evidently shocked their French sense of the fitness of things that the most important dignitary of one of the greatest territorial and political units in the United States should put up at a *boarding house*—as humble visitors did—and should be accessible to anybody and everybody all day long. No soldiers, no guards, no doormen, no formalities. In their astonishment they had almost assaulted Judge Morse with incredulous questions. The fact was there, however; it was a custom in the United States. So Tocqueville noted down the experience and put it away with the other documents he was beginning to collect on the ways and character of the American people.

Impressions came crowding fast. In three days on dry land they had found lodgings, appeared in the newspapers, been presented to the governor, the Mayor, Recorder and Aldermen, and been almost overwhelmed with offers of assistance from the hospitable people of New York. The announcement of their mission had created a sensation in official and prison circles, and it had made them many friends among the philanthropists. As a result they already had a wide acquaintance among the political and social rulers of the city. At the same time, living in an American boarding house, keeping the hours, going about with volunteer guides, they had at once plunged into the rushing current of life in the city and were fast learning American ways. The strange and new was all about them. They had come to observe: theirs was a matchless opportunity.

## VII

## FIRST IMPRESSIONS OF THE AMERICANS

'So here we are in New-York,' wrote Tocqueville to his mother at the end of their third day.[1] 'To a Frenchman the aspect of the city is bizarre and not very agreeable. One sees neither dome, nor bell tower, nor great edifice, with the result that one has the constant impression of being in a suburb. In its centre the city is built of brick, which gives it a most monotonous appearance. The houses have neither cornices, nor balustrades, nor *portes-cochères*. The streets are very badly paved, but sidewalks for pedestrians are to be found in all of them. We had all the trouble in the world getting lodgings because at this time of year strangers abound; and we wanted to find a *pension* rather than an inn. At length we succeeded in establishing ourselves admirably in the most fashionable street, called Broadway.* By an accident, which we bless every day, Mr. Palmer, that Englishman of whom I spoke at the beginning of the letter, had already taken lodgings in the same house. The friendship which bound him to us during the crossing, and above all the interest which he takes in the result of our trip, lead him to render us all the services in his power; and he has already been extremely useful to us. In addition, and this is the finest part of all, you have no conception of the facilities and *agréments* we find in this country for the accomplishment of our mission. All the Americans of all the classes seem to rival each other as to who will be the most useful and agreeable to us. It is true that the newspapers, which concern themselves with everything, have announced our arrival and expressed the hope that we would find active assistance everywhere. The result is that all doors are opened to us and that everywhere we receive the most flattering reception. I, who have always lived in coaches and inns while travelling, find this new manner of life most agreeable.

---

* 'We are lodged in the prettiest quarter, which is not very fine.' Bt. to his mother, New-York, 14 May 1831 (BBlb).

'One great difficulty, which we encountered the moment we left France and which we are now beginning to surmount, is the language. We thought we knew English at Paris. . . . We had only the equipment needed for learning it fast. On shipboard we made unbelievable efforts in that direction; it so happened that we made translations from the English in the midst of a storm which scarce permitted us to write. Unfortunately, we had too many French-speaking people on the vessel. However we made great progress. But once here, it became necessary to give up our language entirely; no one speaks it. So we express ourselves only in English. Often it's pitiful to hear us; but we at length make ourselves understood, and we understand everything. They assure us that we will end by speaking remarkably well. We shall then have made an excellent acquisition. . . .

'You no doubt want to know, my dear mother, what is our present manner of life. It is this: We get up at five or six and we work till eight. At eight o'clock the bell announces breakfast. Every one goes in promptly. After that we go out to visit a few establishments or to get into touch with certain men who are interesting to listen to. We return to dine at three o'clock. At five we usually go home to put our notes in order till seven, the hour at which we go out into society to take tea. This style of life is very agreeable and, I believe, very healthy. But it upsets all our settled habits. For instance, we were utterly astounded the first day to see the women come to breakfast at eight o'clock in the morning carefully dressed for the whole day. It's the same, we are told, in all the private houses. One can with great propriety call on a lady at nine o'clock in the morning.

'The absence of wine at our meals at first struck us as very disagreeable; and we still can't understand the multitude of things that they succeed in introducing into their stomachs here. You see, in addition to breakfast, dinner, and tea with which the Americans eat ham, they also eat a very copious supper, and often a *gouter*. That up to now is the only indisputable superiority that I grant them over us. But they see in themselves many others. These people seem to me stinking with national conceit; it pierces through all their courtesy.

'Sunday 15. I take up my letter, dear mother, on returning from a mass that we have just heard in a Catholic church which is situated at five minutes from here. . . . I can't tell you what a strange feeling it is to find so far from home all the religious ceremonies that one has witnessed since childhood. The illusion of being in France was so complete that I spoke to my neighbours in French. But all the worshipers were Americans. The church, which is a large one, was entirely full, and the meditation was more profound than in the churches of France. We heard a good sermon on *grace* in English, and were delighted to discover that we understood perfectly everything the preacher said. . . .

'The Catholics have a considerable establishment in New-York. They have five churches and more than twenty thousand faithful. I have heard Americans say that the number of converts is very large. The church is also growing in the different provinces of the union; and I should not be surprised if the religious faith which is so attacked in Europe made great conquests in this country. Each year brings nearly fifteen to twenty thousand European Catholics here, who spread into the wildernesses of the west. The need of a religion is felt there more than anywhere else. They become fervent if they are not so already, or at least their children become so. The necessity of having some religious doctrine is so deeply felt on this side of the Atlantic that it seems to me that the Protestants themselves look down on Catholics who appear to neglect their cult. . . .'

That same day, 15 May, Tocqueville made a long and interesting entry in his diary, which he entitled: 'First Impressions.'

'Thus far,' wrote the young traveller, 'the Americans seem to us to carry national pride altogether too far. I doubt whether it is possible to draw from them the least truth unfavourable to their country. Most of them boast about it without discernment and with an assertiveness that is disagreeable to strangers and that shows but little intelligence. In general it seems to me that there is much of the *small town* in their attitude and that they magnify objects like people who are not accustomed to seeing great things. But we haven't yet seen a truly remarkable man.

'Taken altogether they seem a religious people. It's evident that no one thinks of ridiculing the practice, and that the goodness and even the truth of religion are admitted *in theory*. To what point does their life conform to their doctrine? What is the true power of the religious principle on their soul? How is it the diversity of sects does not engender indifference, if not on the surface at least within? There's what remains to be discovered.

'What seems clear to me at present is that this country shows the attainment of outward perfection by the middle classes, or rather the whole society seems to have melted into a middle class. No one seems to have the elegant manners and the refined courtesy of the high classes in Europe. On the contrary, one is srtuck at first by something both vulgar and disagreeably uncultivated. But at the same time no one is what in France one might call *ill bred*. All the Americans whom we have encountered up to now, even to the simplest *shop salesman*, seem to have received, or wish to appear to have received, a good education. Their manners are grave, deliberate, reserved, and they all wear the same clothes.

'All the customs of life show this mingling of the two classes which in Europe take so much trouble to keep apart. The women dress for the whole day at seven in the morning. At nine o'clock one can already make calls. At noon one is received everywhere. Everything bears the stamp of a very busy existence. We have not yet seen any *fashionables*. I even have the notion that good morals are here the result less of the severity of principles than of the impossibility in which all the young people find themselves of thinking of love or busying themselves seriously with it.'

These were 'First Impressions' only, of course, but the future author of *Democracy in America* was perfectly definite about them. And apparently the other French prison commissioner found himself at least equally startled by the strange, new-world people with whom he now had to do. As a matter of fact, Beaumont was fairly bursting with his observations and new ideas.

' . . . I want, *mon petit père*, to inform you at once of the position in which I find myself here,' the ebullient young man wrote home next day.[2] '. . . The new society in which we are does not at all resemble our European societies. It has no prototype anywhere. It has also some primary conditions of existence that no other possesses, which makes it dangerous for any other society to imitate it:—It's quite a remarkable phenomenon, a great people which has no army, a country full of activity and vigour where the action of the government is hardly perceived! But what conclusion to draw from it for the states of Europe? The United States have no ambitious neighbours to fear; they are more powerful than the peoples who surround them, so of what use would an army be?

'In the United States political parties are almost unknown. There are sometimes personal disputes for places and public office; but never is the basis of things in question. The sole interest which absorbs the attention of every mind, is *trade*. It's the *national passion*, and it's not necessary to have all the arms of the Guard and of the Troops of the Line for the merchants to do their business. But is it the same in the states where for a long time past interior dissensions divide the people, and where the administration is unceasingly forced to have recourse to the public force to disarm the factions?

'The American people is, I said, a *merchant* people. That is to say that it is devoured by the thirst for riches, which brings in its train many hardly honourable passions, such as cupidity, fraud, and bad faith. Thus they appear to have but one single thought here, but one single purpose, that of getting rich. In addition, they consider the bankruptcies which are very frequent in all the cities as of no importance or of very little account.* Undoubtedly this is a very vicious side. Yet it is impossible not to admit that there is much morality in this people. (This at first glance seems hard to reconcile with what precedes) but I explain. Morals there are extremely pure. A woman who does not conduct herself well is cited as an extreme rarity. To tell the truth, you meet only happy households. People get together often in winter; but everything in the last analysis comes down to family life. Unmarried men pay attention only to girls; these once married think only of their husbands. So long as they are not *engaged*, they exercise an extreme freedom in their relations. One sees them out walking alone, for example. A young man accosts them, goes to the country with them, and this is considered quite natural. They receive at home without their parents finding fault. But this life of freedom ends for them the day they get married. In short, the happiness which seems to reign in their families has something tempting in it. Doubtless I should never want to marry in a foreign country, because such a union entails a host of unpleasant consequences. But Tocqueville and I, glimpsing the happiness so common here and so rare in other countries, were unable to keep from saying that, if we should ever be victimized by political

---

* For the preceding, see Tocqueville's shipboard diary notes on conversations with Peter Schermerhorn, ch.V. Beaumont long remained convinced that in no other country in the world were there so many bankruptcies, the reason being that the Americans tried to get rich too quickly. Four years later he was to write: 'Shortly after my arrival in America, as I was entering a *salon* where were gathered the elite of society of one of the greatest cities of the Union, a Frenchman, long resident in that country, said to me: "Above all, don't go and speak ill of bankrupts." I followed his advice and did well; for among all the rich persons to whom I was presented, there was not a single one who had not failed once or twice in his life before making his fortune.' *Marie*, I,362.

circumstances in France, we would come to live here with our wives and children.'

Having carefully assured his family that he really was not contemplating matrimony with *une américaine*, however faithful such a charmer might be, Beaumont was probably exaggerating his willingness to live in New York. True Frenchman that he was, only the most acute emergency, in all likelihood, would ever reconcile him to expatriation. His interest in the relations of the sexes and in the family life of his hosts, however, was perfectly natural and genuine. Obviously he was astonished by what seemed the extraordinary purity of American morals; and, like Tocqueville, was troubled to account for what he saw.

'Whence comes this morality so powerful in the habits of a people which, as we have seen, is not always a virtuous people?' he pursued. 'I believe that by and by I will be in a better position to answer this question than I am now. I already see however some causes which seem of a character to explain this fact. The first seems to me to be the religious spirit which dominates society. Nowhere are religious ideas more in honour. All the cults here are free and are honoured; but he would be looked on as a *Brute* who did not belong to any religion. This general opinion spread throughout society arises out of some first causes which *some day* we will develop.

'In the second place, there is here as I said only a single class of *Merchants*, all concerned with the same one interest, and competing against each other for one thing, *riches*. There is not, as in France, a certain number of individuals who, if they didn't busy themselves seducing women, would have nothing to do. Why are garrison towns more immoral than the others? Because a regiment in a city increases the number of unoccupied whose only pastime is to corrupt and seduce. Here commerce and industry take up all the time. One must add that the Americans have a colder temperament than we. Thus this people has an interest in being moral; it believes besides in a religion which commands morality, and the nature of its blood, instead of being an obstacle, favours this disposition and leaning in it.

'I am going to study with care the divers religious sects which exist here, and inform myself of the reasons for there being such perfect harmony between them. It seems that each day catholicism makes numerous converts.

'There are several Roman Catholic churches and a cathedral here;

we visited them yesterday. The Bishop, Mr. Dubois, is absent at the moment. We learned that at his home where we went to see him. We asked for his grand vicar, who was also out. We heard mass, and a Catholic priest delivered a sermon in English which we understood very well (we are making great progress in English, as we speak it all day long). We found Mme de St. André * at the Catholic church, and she had us sit in her pew. Sunday is observed here with the greatest rigour. Not a single person works; the shops are closed otherwise than at Paris; one allows oneself no other reading than the Bible. I am not describing New-York to you because I don't know the city yet. However, Saturday evening Tocqueville and I, while out walking, perceived a church that was open. Within were only a few pious souls wrapped in prayer. We found the door of the stairway leading to the steeple open. There we were climbing from attic to attic, by little staircases dark and steep. At last, after many tribulations, we got all the way to the top, and we enjoyed an admirable spectacle: that of a city of 240,000 inhabitants built in an island, surrounded on one side by the ocean and on the other by immense rivers, on which are to be seen an unending multitude of vessels and small boats. Its harbour is immensely wide. Its public buildings are few and as a rule of undistinguished construction.

'The fine arts are here in their infancy. The commerce and industry which are the source of riches do not at the same time produce good taste. As for the *political notions* which the Americans entertain about France, you must not believe that they are as enthusiastic about our revolutionists as it is thought. In general they consider the hero of two worlds † as a fine man who lacks judgment and who wants to apply political theories to a people whom they don't suit.

'What's more, the aristocracy of fortune aims at distinctions here as elsewhere. Much is made of the oldness of families. I was astonished to hear these proud champions of equality call themselves *honourable esquires*. They put heraldic arms on their carriages and on their seals. The taste for superiority crops up everywhere. They are besides excessively vain. This results from the eulogies of their government which are made in Europe. As a consequence, to be on good terms with them, you have to praise them a great deal. I do it with all my heart, without its affecting my manner of seeing. This national pride induces

* Wife of the French consul.
† Lafayette.

them to do everything they can to fascinate our eyes and to show us only the fine side of things; but I hope that we will manage to find out the truth.

'You can have no conception of the activity of our existence. We haven't the time to breathe. It's a rolling fire of agreeable invitations, of useful occupations, of official presentations, etc., etc. *They tear us away from each other*, and each one does all in his power to make our stay in New-York pleasant for us. The Sharmerhall [Schermerhorn] family with whom we crossed is one of the richest and most esteemed of the city; it overwhelms us with friendship. Mr. Prime, our banker, who is the wealthiest man in this country, also puts himself out to be nice to us.

'There's where we stand, and as yet we have presented only two of our letters of recommendation. According to calculation, we still have seventy to present, and we realize now that we could have done without them. . . .'

There was another kind of assistance, however, of which Beaumont was already beginning to feel the need.

'When you answer, *mon petit père*,' he concluded, 'please tell me what you think of the ideas I hazard in this letter on what I have already seen, and especially what you think of the country where I am? Do you believe that this people is called to a great destiny among the civilized nations; do you think that its institutions have solid foundations? Do you believe that it will long conserve its territorial unity?' And the young commissioner went on to ask his father what he thought would happen to American republicanism in that case. Would not the result of interstate war be a 'dictatorial and soon a monarchical authority? What is your opinion on the character of the Americans? To what cause, think you, must the purity of their morals be attributed?'

There were, it seemed to Beaumont, 'a thousand other questions to ask'; and he proceeded to convoke a regular 'family council.'

This was the fifth day. By the end of their first week in New York, curiously enough, Tocqueville, too, was feeling the need of asking questions. And his queries were, if anything, even more comprehensive.

'You must,' he wrote their mutual friend Chabrol,[3] 'do Beaumont and me another [service], which is, you are going to laugh perhaps, to write us at the greatest possible length what they think of this country at home. Since leaving France we have lived with Americans, either on the boat that brought us or since our arrival here. As a result, we have accustomed ourselves by degrees and without brusque transitions to the new order of things midst which we are now living. We have already largely lost our national prejudices in regard to this people. Nevertheless, you appreciate how necessary it is for us to know the opinions prevalent among us if we wish to modify them, and even if we desire to study here particularly what can serve to enlighten general opinion.

'Gather together then as much as you can your thoughts and those of others on this question, and send them to us. For example, what idea do people in France form of the political institutions of the United States? of the national character, of the different classes of society, of the state of commerce, of the future of this country, of its religious situation?

'I have a mind while I am on the subject to ask you a series of questions which you will answer if you wish:

'What idea do you hold as to the power of Congress over the Union in general and over each state in particular? To what cause do you attribute the prosperity of this nation? Is it to political institutions or to material and industrial causes?

'What degree of civilization do you suppose this people has reached, and precisely what forms does this civilization take? At what point are they, do you believe, in the matter of *esprit de Société*, of literary tastes, of the pleasures of the imagination, of the fine arts?

'Do you think there are political parties in the United States? How far do you think they carry the spirit of equality here? Is it in the customs or in the laws? What form do you imagine it takes?

'What do you understand to be the liberty of the press in the United States, the freedom of commerce, the right of suffrage or of eligibility?

'Chat, prattle, wander on about all that in your reply. This is not everything yet. You must give us your ideas as to what would be the most useful to examine in this country, the points which may most pique public attention or be the most useful to our present society.

'I must count greatly on your friendship, my dear Chabrol, to load you with so ungrateful a task. This letter will seem to you the more tiresome because I have not wished to speak to you of America, fearing to produce on you the same impressions that our travel companions made on me. But I promise to make up amply in my first letter, which will not be long in following. . . .'

Meanwhile it would be well, before his opinions insensibly suffered any further modification, to set down on paper exactly what he now did think of the whole American experiment. So the young Tocqueville made haste to record in his diary some important 'General Remarks.' * It was 18 May, just one week after their arrival in New York harbour:

'Up to now all I have seen doesn't enchant me, because I attribute it more to accidental circumstances than to the will of man. That's the sum of my present impressions. But the sight before my eyes is none the less an immense spectacle. Never before has a people found for itself such a happy and fruitful basis of life. Here freedom is unrestrained, and subsists by being useful to every one without injuring anybody. There is undeniably something *feverish* in the activity it imparts to industry and to the human spirit. But up to now that fever seems only to increase man's power without affecting his reason. In spite of this activity, nature's resources are inexhaustible. What remains to be done seems to increase in proportion to what has already been done. New-York, which had 20,000 souls at the moment of the American Revolution, has 200,000 now, and each year adds immense developments to its greatness. We are assured that the wildernesses of the Mississippi are being populated still more rapidly. Every one tells us that the most fertile soil in America is to be found there, and that it stretches almost indefinitely. Amid this unbelievable physical activity, political agitation seems very accessory to me. It's on the surface and doesn't profoundly excite the masses. We are told that it is hard to get men to take public offices that would take them out of private business. The fact is that this society is proceeding all alone and is lucky (*marche tout seul et bien lui prend*) to encounter no obstacles. The art of government seems to me to be in its infancy here. . . .'

*

*   *

At first glance, as Tocqueville himself would have admitted, his letters and diary notes of 11–18 May seemed almost hopelessly confused and meaningless. They covered such a wide range of topics in such a fragmentary way as to yield no clear picture of the writer's mind. Obviously, they contained neither a connected narrative of the activities of that week nor a comprehensive description of Tocqueville and

* YT (dated 20 May, *O.C.*,VIII,227–228).

Beaumont's new surroundings. Instead, a few incidents and a chaotic mass of impressions, the latter a strange mixture of fact and surmise, had been recorded side by side. A stranger might have been tempted to dismiss such half-formed thoughts and ill-assorted fragments of information as unimportant.

Yet these records of Tocqueville and Beaumont's first week in America were actually of tremendous significance. They were the key to the trip, they were the clue to the character of Tocqueville and Beaumont's investigation, they prophesied the book that one day would result.

First of all, these letters and diary notes at least made it plain that Tocqueville and Beaumont were not tourists or visitors in the ordinary sense of the words. It was worthy of remark that they had not bothered to describe New York City. They were impressed by its natural surroundings, its rivers and harbour, its trade. They noticed that the houses were of homely brick and the streets had sidewalks. They were surprised at seeing no large dominating public edifices, and confessed to having 'the constant impression of being in a suburb.' Later Tocqueville was to sum up the city by saying, 'It does not in the least resemble our capital cities in Europe.'[4] That was all.

Their manuscripts could have been searched in vain for a picture of the many-spired town, or even for the description of one house or church. Nothing was said of the furnishings of their boarding house, or of the haircloth furniture, the marble mantelpieces and the mahogany sideboards in the homes of their wealthy friends. The plumbing, the meagre water supply, and the public bathing establishments had been passed by in silence. So had the Park and Bowery theatres, the public libraries, and the numerous charitable and philanthropic institutions (such as hospitals, asylums, and societies for the relief of the poor) which distinguished the city. They had attempted no description of the strange 'Canal' Street, with its underground sewers and its new houses, where ended the area of dense settlement on the north side of the city. Nor did they mention driving in the two muddy country lanes (Third and Eighth Avenues) which struck out from there up the island toward the distant villages of Harlem and Manhattanville. They did not speak of the rows of fine steamboats tied at the North River wharves down near the battery, nor did they exclaim on the 'triple lines of beautiful merchantmen' which stood proudly in their East River docks and made of the waterfront streets one enormous warehouse.* They remarked that every New Yorker was engaged in business, but neglected to specify the trade by which he was kept so busy and made so prosperous.

The same was true of their descriptions of people. Tocqueville and Beaumont had neither the biographer's nor yet the cartoonist's instinct. 'We are all eyes and ears,' wrote Tocqueville,[5] but no thumb-nail sketches of their enthusiastic lawyer friends enlivened their letters home. One learned nothing of the personal appearance or idiosyncrasies of Peter Schermerhorn or Nathaniel Prime or Judge Morse. They were interested in Governor Throop, but only as a symbol of equality, not as a man or even as an American politician. They observed with astonishment that American women appeared at seven or eight in the morning, dressed for the whole day; but not a word did they write about the puffed sleeves and shawls, the coal-scuttle bonnets and fringed parasols adorning the happy ladies as they so early went sailing down Broadway. The two young friends were even indifferent to preserving the story of their own doings. The daily record of their adventures and activities had sometimes been kept, but only when it served an ulterior purpose or when there was nothing better to do. In short, they were not interested in individuals, they were not story-tellers, they were not sight-seeing tourists. These things were on the surface and did not seem important enough.

What did interest them was the real character of the American people. They had but little time to describe the 'domestic manners of the Americans' because they were intent on discovering the inward qualities of the race. The obvious features of life in an American city might be deceptive; they were the flesh and cartilage that concealed the structure of society. Tocqueville and Beaumont were probing for the bone. They wanted to know where the strength of the political organism lay, what were its enduring elements, how it was knit together. In other words, they were not tourists nor yet historians but political scientists, analysing the force and weakness of a nation organized along federal and republican lines.

There was also another side to their investigation. They were trying to determine what were the fundamental instincts of a democratic society, what was its motive power and, consequently, what were the permanent tendencies of a self-governing people. And then they wanted

* As did, for example, the Englishman, G.T.Vigne, with whom they were later to tour the Great Lakes. *Six Months in America*, I,9ff.

to know how far such a society was a product of its environment, how well it would be adapted to other environments. Later scholars would but have to change their terminology to see that the two young Frenchmen were sociologists before their day. When they discovered the dollar-chasing proclivities and the religious tendencies of the Americans, they were but saying that the acquisitive and superstitious instincts dominated man in the western hemisphere. From their analysis it would be but a short step to the 'folkways' of William Sumner, or the 'traits' and 'culture patterns' of the modern anthropologist. Only their task was harder. Instead of dealing with a primitive and relatively simple society, they were tackling an advanced civilization and vivisecting it.

This explained their method. They wanted to get beneath the surface, to pierce the outer layer of appearances. So they used the X-ray of the mind more than the camera of the eye. They began with a number of observed phenomena. From these, by inductive reasoning, they inferred a general principle governing American society. The general law ascertained, they then began to deduce from it all its consequences for similarly organized societies. As the reader follows Tocqueville and Beaumont's intellectual progress through the inner structure of the American nation a hundred years ago, he will find them applying this method time and again. Occasionally they were, like many of their contemporaries, perhaps a little too quick to jump to the general law. They inferred it on too little evidence and without sufficient examination of the facts: they had, for instance, already made the error of mistaking New Yorkers for average Americans. Or they took ideas conceived before they ever set foot in the United States for demonstrated fact. As a result of thus emphasizing the *a priori* method, the two young scientists would sometimes come to lay too much stress on unsound philosophic principles and to attribute too many of the phenomena observed to the same assumed cause.

For the moment, however, it was this preoccupation with the internal fabric of American society that gave such peculiar shape and character to their manuscripts. Both letters and diaries were being used by Tocqueville and Beaumont primarily as storehouses for the data they were accumulating. Each bit of information, each idea was 'thrown' on paper at the earliest moment so it would not be lost. Thus, for want of a card filing system, facts, inferences, conclusions, and anecdotes to illustrate, all came to be jumbled together. Their letters were to be saved for them by their families so that when they got home these diverse materials could be disentangled and sorted out. And Tocqueville divided his diaries topically, rather than chronologically, so that each new thought was at once entered under its appropriate alphabetical heading. But at the moment the main idea was to preserve their discoveries till the day when they could be singled out and marshalled for use in their book.

The reader is now led to notice once more that a very particular purpose directed this sociological investigation. Tocqueville and Beaumont were not analysing American society in order to write a treatise on man as a social animal or add to the world's knowledge about the basic elements of human nature. They were studying the laws and conditions of humanity in the United States for the specific purpose of comparing them with those obtaining in the older societies of Europe, more particularly in France. They wanted to determine for their fellow-countrymen, once and for all, what were the lessons that France could safely draw from the example of the United States. They wished to inform French thinking on America, and replace both the enthusiastic illusions fostered by republican idealists like Lafayette, and the ignorant prejudices that swayed the conservatives, with a scientific and dispassionate knowledge of the real character of democratic institutions in the United States. Consequently, the thought of France was always present in their minds. Its needs directed their inquiries, its image stood before their eyes in perpetual apposition to the spectacle of American society.

For Tocqueville and Beaumont it now remained to deduce, with the aid of their own records, the first important results of this purposeful and scientifically conducted investigation. In seven days, what data had they stored for the future in their letters and diaries? After one week in New York what were their clearest impressions? What were their earliest reactions to a country which would one day adopt Tocqueville's future commentary as a text-book in many of its schools?

The answer was: Tocqueville and Beaumont's impressions were anything but favourable to America. In the first place, they found the Americans personally a little distasteful, because so conceited and materialistic. In spite of the warmth of the welcome, in spite of the many kindnesses received at the hands of these friendly strangers, the two newly-arrived commissioners were oppressed by the feeling that the distinguishing quality of New Yorkers was conceit. 'The people seem to me stinking with national conceit,' Tocqueville had written, while even the charitable Beaumont found them 'excessively vain.' Their other peculiarity was no better. When they were not talking about their own superior virtues, the Americans were all engaged in business, all chasing the almighty dollar. Just as Mr. Schermerhorn had said on shipboard, their vice was to be interested only in money. Naturally Tocqueville and Beaumont missed the leisured refinement, the culture, and the gentle amenities of the best society of Paris.

Their observations had also a second and a far more important result: to convince them that France and the United States had nothing in common. Everything in America seemed just the opposite of things at home. The two peoples had different traditions, a different training; the nations were not made up of the same elements,* they did not have the same resources and opportunities, nor the same neighbours. In America—to state their conclusions briefly—a religious tradition, a mercantile bent, and unlimited natural resources were the basic factors of civilization. These made the people busy, moral, prosperous, and contented with a minimum of government democratically organized. Of France none of these things could be said. Tocqueville and Beaumont were therefore struck by the futility of drawing analogies between the two countries; and imitation of the American example by France seemed to them even more foolish than it had before. Democratic institutions might go with American conditions; they were not suited to the European environment.

It followed, then, that it would be their duty to warn France that the United States could not safely be imitated; and this would be one of the major ideas of their future book—unless of course they changed their opinions in the meantime. Curiously enough, for some time no such modification of their views occurred. Ten days later, for instance, the conclusion was still the same. For on 28 May, after thinking about the question a good deal, Tocqueville stated his conviction as follows: [6]

' . . . We are most certainly in another world here. Political passions here are only on the surface. The profound passion, the only one which profoundly stirs the human heart, the passion of all the days, is the acquisition of riches; and there are a thousand ways of acquiring them without troubling the state. One has to be exceedingly blind in my opinion to want to compare this country to Europe and adapt to one

---

* Even the average, middle-class American seemed so different from a member of the French middle class that it apparently never occurred to either Tocqueville or Beaumont to use the word 'bourgeois' in their descriptions.

what suits the other. I believed this before leaving France; I believe it more and more on examining the society midst which I now live. They are a race of merchants, who busy themselves with public affairs when their business leaves them the leisure. I hope that on our return to Europe we shall be in a position to make some helpful observations on this subject. No one perhaps has found himself better placed to study a people than we. Our mission and our letters give us access everywhere. We are continuously in touch with all classes; all the available documents are furnished us *à l'envie*. Lastly, we come here only with a serious purpose; our energy is unceasingly directed toward the acquisition of useful information. It's an immense undertaking, but not a disagreeable one, because in a way we absorb ideas through all our pores and we learn as much in a *salon* or in a promenade as closeted in our study.'

As a matter of fact Tocqueville and Beaumont were absorbing more than ideas and useful information. Their first letters showed them beginning to absorb an attitude. Through living in constant association with 'all classes' of Americans they were being so thoroughly steeped in the atmosphere of American life that they found themselves fast getting used to their strange surroundings, and even beginning to take American ideas as a matter of course. Queer though the customs of these people had at first seemed, and peculiar though their institutions were, there was something so reasonable about the American attitude, something so agreeable in the free and contented air of the New Yorkers, that the two young Frenchmen found themselves being attracted almost in spite of themselves.

This was the other important revelation made by their first letters home. When Tocqueville, one week after landing, wrote to a friend in France: 'We have already lost our national prejudices in regard to this people. . . .' 'You must . . . write us at the greatest possible length what they think of this country at home,' he was confessing that he was already largely converted to certain features of American civilization. Things that were considered preposterous in Paris—practices like the intermingling of all classes, and the absence of an army—worked so well in New York that he and Beaumont were no longer able to dismiss them with a smile. In fact, in many cases the American way of doing things was already beginning to seem the natural, the desirable way.

Of course, different conditions in France made imitation out of the question. But it would have to be acknowledged that American institutions had some unsuspected merits. So gradually had this knowledge come to Tocqueville and Beaumont, however, so imperceptibly had this free, co-operative society grown on them, that they had not realized what was going on in their own minds until suddenly one day they awoke to the realization that they no longer thought as Frenchmen thought, in fact, no longer knew just what Frenchmen thought. Yet they would have to know what the prejudices of their fellow-countrymen were if their book was to be a corrective and was to present an effective argument for a new attitude toward the United States. Hence the long lists of questions home, on every phase of the political, intellectual, and material civilization of America.

In one week in New York it had come to this: Americans individually were conceited, materialistic, middle-class people. Americans collectively had no government and no intellectual culture worthy the name. But in the social philosophy and the democratic practice of these people there was, undeniably, a strange seductive charm.

## VIII

## SOCIETY AND THE CITY AUTHORITIES

'I HAVE been in New-York two weeks.' It was 26 May, and Beaumont had much to tell his family. 'Tocqueville and I,' he wrote,[1] 'are leading here the most active agitated life it is possible to imagine. Our great difficulty is to keep from getting confused between all the engagements and invitations that we have each day. We are overwhelmed by courtesies, burdened with visits, etc., etc. In the midst of all that one has to find time to work, and above all to reflect, and in truth it's not easy. We always get up very early, thanks to what *beneficient instrument* you well know.

'We breakfast at eight, according to the custom. We then go to the Athenaeum,* which is a sort of public library, where French, English, and American newspapers are to be found. This establishment has been opened to us free, as has also another library of the same kind where are to be had an even greater number of interesting works. We pass as much time as we can there making statistical investigations on the state of the population, on the public institutions, and on all the political questions which occupy us.

'If we can escape *the pursuit of our numerous friends*, we throw on paper our ideas on what we have seen, we set ourselves problems to solve and we lay the foundations of a great work which ought some day to make our reputation. We have never done half of all that we had to do when dinner rings.

'We take our places at a table always served with meats more solid than well prepared, and around which are seated some very pretty persons, occasionally accompanied by some very ugly ones. The great merit of women here is to be very fresh complexioned. Beyond that they have very few, or rather they have none at all of those exterior charms which

---

* The Athenaeum had been founded in 1824 to make the standard works of science and literature available to the public. Monthly lectures by distinguished men were a feature of its program.

contribute so powerfully to elegance of figure, and whose rounded form so agreeably flatters the eye.

'I don't know why I speak of their physical qualities, for they are above all remarkable for their moral virtues. I said in one of my letters that in general they are of very severe principle and irreproachable conduct. All the people who have made observations on this point confirm me in this opinion.

'Evenings we go out into society. We see several American families fairly often, particularly that of Mr. Prime, our banker. He is the richest business man in New-York. He has a tall daughter, dry and homely, an excellent person, who is a good musician.* We play charming duos of flute and piano, which amuses me a good deal. We are entirely at our ease in this house. They left yesterday for the country, which is on the shore of the Sound (East River) and we are much pressed to go see them. We also see the Jones family† allied to the Shermerhall [Schermerhorns] with whom we were on the vessel which brought us to America. There are also in this house some very attractive girls, but without beauty, and rich rather than seductive.

'We are received with infinite kindness in the Livingston family. Mr. Edward Livingston is at this moment Prime Minister of the United States. His family is very numerous. I see particularly his nephew John Livingston‡ for whom Montebello had given me a letter. Mrs. John Livingston is a charming woman, as attractive as can be, and flirtatious as well. But I do not know and shall never know myself if her coquetry goes further. We are to go together in several days to visit the military school of West-Point, which is only a few miles from New-York.

'There are, finally, some very attractive women in the *cruyère* [Schuyler? Grier?], Duer families, etc., etc., where we go when we have the time.

'If we went into society with intentions of *pleasure* or *seduction*, we could regard as lost the time we pass in these families. But as our resolutions are entirely opposed to this result, we find only profit in it. In the first place we inevitably learn the English language, for although many women know and speak French, nevertheless among twenty people there are always at least fifteen with whom we have to speak English.

* Mathilda Prime, who was shortly to marry Gerard Coster.
† Mrs. Peter (Sarah Jones) Schermerhorn was the daughter of John and Eleanor (Colford) Jones.
‡ John R. Livingston, Jr.

'In the second place, to acquire information about institutions and public establishments, etc., etc., we really have to see people, and the most enlightened are in the best society.

'In the third place, it's in society that one learns the morals, the usages, the spirit, and the character of a nation. Finally, one improves oneself in seeing the world, and one learns to know men of all kinds.

'All the while we busy ourselves with such interests, we do not lose sight of the special object of our public mission: we had expressed the wish to be presented to the guardians of the various prisons which are to be found in the city and neighbourhood of New-York. The city authorities wished to treat us with distinction, so we were invited in the name of the municipal body, and of all the officials occupying a high position in the city, to make a solemn visit to the prisons and establishments of beneficient character. This visit was to be followed by a grand dinner. It was yesterday, 25 May, that this ceremony took place.

'We left the city hall at ten o'clock in the morning in carriages prepared for us and in which they gave us the places of honour. First of all we visited the House of Refuge for delinquent minors,* an establishment already known in Europe, on whose plan is being constructed at this moment a similar institution at Melun. We passed in review everything there was to be seen. My report on the prisons of France has already bored you enough without my making you another on those of America. I shall not enter into any detail, then; you will read later on the work we shall write for the government, in which we shall give the fullest developments. The same carriages which had brought us to the House of Refuge carried us to Bloomingdale, hospital for the insane. . . . There is also in the hospital a charming young girl, only fifteen years old, whose religious ideas have unbalanced her mind. This effect is quite frequent in the United States where the religious spirit is very ardent. In general the majority of derangements here are the result of strong spirits drunk with excess.

'There is at the very top of the building for the insane a kind of Belvedere,† to which they had us climb, and from which I saw the most beautiful view I have yet found. I discovered to my left the North

* On Bloomingdale Road, on about what is now the northwest corner of Madison Square, Fifth Avenue and 25th–26th Streets.

† Bloomingdale asylum was a severe, red sandstone structure, surmounted by a round, truncated tower, whose top was a platform. It was located in Manhattanville, seven miles from the city, and stood on an eminence (now occupied by Columbia University) one hundred and fifty feet above the Hudson. The place was supposed to be run so as to make the inmates, who were paying guests, cheerful.

River (the Hudson) whose shores unfolded before my eyes to a distance of thirty miles. The banks of this river whose width is immense are very lofty; they are more than 300 feet high. This stream has a really majestic course; it is covered with vessels and small boats; and a better place to see it from than the one where we were could not be imagined. On leaving Bloomingdale we went to the establishment for the deaf and mute, then to the poorhouse.* We hadn't enough time for all our tour, so that this visit was very superficial.

'In the poorhouse which resembles a palace, we found a very fine dinner prepared for 25 persons. If you had seen Tocqueville and me treated with the greatest distinction by all the first officials of the largest city of the United States, if you had seen us occupying the places of honour, receiving all the courtesies, being the object of all the attentions, in a word really playing *a great role,* you would certainly have felt your brotherly pride agreeably flattered. Perhaps also you would have thought that the Americans have mighty few political interests to occupy them, since small persons like us loom so large in their eyes! There is one thing that we were afraid of and that happily did not take place. It is the custom at this kind of banquet to *faire du patriotisme* and to propose toasts of a more or less political character. Very fortunately for us, we still had a tour to make after dinner; we were hurried; they therefore limited themselves to personal compliments, and no mention was made of the hero of two worlds nor of any personages of like character.

'We kept up our end as best we could; speaking English indifferently and responding with modesty to the honours with which we saw ourselves surrounded.

'Our tour ended with a visit to Blackwell's Island, a penitentiary prison in which are shut up three or four hundred prisoners, who are busied building another house beside the one that holds them. This edifice is constructed with so much care and zeal, one would never believe that they are working in order to imprison themselves in it. Finally, after having made two or three charming promenades on the East River (the Sound) in boats made ready for us, we were brought back to New-York by all *the honourable Gentlemens* [*sic*] accompanying us, the whole group of whom filled five carriages.

---

* The Deaf and Dumb asylum lay on Fifth Avenue, about three and a half miles out of town. Bellevue Almshouse and Penitentiary, a large establishment on First Avenue between 27th and 28th Streets, overlooked the East River.

'In a few days we shall return to all these establishments. We shall visit them alone. Yesterday it was only a ceremony, later it will be a useful labour. To-morrow we are going to Sing-Sing (Mount Pleasant) where the most perfect penitentiary in the United States is to be found. It is about 25 miles from New-York on the Hudson, on the right bank as you look at the map. We have several letters of introduction, and the best lawyer of New-York is going there expressly to introduce us.

'This is already a long letter, my dear Jules, but I haven't yet spoken of what interests me the most deeply. I received a week ago my first letter from France. . . . *Mon Dieu*, my friend, how happy we will be when we find ourselves together again! Perhaps this voyage will be useful to me. It will help, I think, to increase my knowledge, to form my judgment, and perhaps also it will put me in a position to be useful to my country. That, all things considered, is the best or rather the only ambition that one should have. . . .'

The tone of resignation with which this letter closed showed that the ambitious young man was finding the way of the patriot hard. To be useful to his country, he was having to endure not only daily homesickness but also, every now and again, a situation of acute discomfort. The public dinner in the poorhouse had been such an occasion.

It had all come about very innocently. Mayor Bowne * and the aldermen had been unwilling to allow the honourable French Commissioners to begin their investigation of American prisons in any piecemeal or unceremonious fashion. So after some negotiation † a day had been agreed on, Mayor Browne and the aldermen had hired carriages, and the official visits and formal dinner above described had taken place. The Mayor and his welcoming committee had performed their part with dignity and with evident satisfaction. But during the most agreeable part of the ceremonies the two young guests had been quite unhappy. Beaumont's letter hinted at one reason.

It was 'the custom at this kind of dinner,' he believed, 'to *faire du patriotisme* and to propose toasts of a more or less political character.' In this he was correct. Political and patriotic toasts were the fashion of the day in America. At holiday celebrations and at party banquets

---

* Walter Bowne, d.1846, had entered politics from the hardware business, become Grand Sachem of the Tammany Society in 1820, and been appointed Mayor by the Common Council of the city in 1827.

† Jno. R. Livingston Jr. to Beaumont and 'Tokeville,' 21 May; J.W.Smith to Beaumont and 'Tockeville,' 22 May 1831 (BB).

there were always thirteen regular toasts, to correspond to the thirteen original States of the Union. These were announced in advance and each was drunk to an appropriate tune from the band.* Then the floor would be thrown open to an unlimited number of voluntary toasts, and the different members of the company would propose sentiments until they could no longer rise to the occasion. Other affairs had no music, and did not usually last so long. But at the end of any formal dinner a liberal mixture of alcohol, politics, and patriotism was to be expected. People thought it a harmless and elevating custom.

Not so Tocqueville and Beaumont. They had watched their dinner drawing to its close in an agony of apprehension, afraid—that a toast to Lafayette would be proposed. Afraid, because they came of the conservative provincial aristocracy of France who regarded republicans as criminals against society, and the so-called 'hero of two worlds' as a traitor to their class. They themselves were liberals, but even French liberals were anything but republican in sentiment, and fought Lafayette and his friends as dangerous demagogues in the same way that they fought the ultra-conservatives as dangerous reactionaries. Besides, Tocqueville and Beaumont were at that moment the official servants of the constitutional monarchy of Louis Philippe, a monarchy to which the aged Lafayette had consented in the July Revolution a year before—but only with the greatest reluctance and only when it became clear that there was no hope for an American-style republic. *Bref*, the two young commissioners did not approve of Monsieur de Lafayette.

On the other hand, the Americans emphatically did. Only a few days before, at the Tammany celebration which Governor Throop had attended, one of the voluntary toasts had been: 'The Friend of Washington, the Champion of the Rights of Man—General Lafayette. Nine Cheers.'[2] The toast was a natural one at any time, and when a group of serious-minded Americans were endeavouring to honour visitors from France. . . . ! Tocqueville and Beaumont had felt it coming. The

---

* When the 'ancient, respectable, and patriotic' Tammany Society and Columbian Order had celebrated its forty-second aniversary on 12 May, among the toasts had been: '7th. Democracy—its citadel, firm to its basis, has stood unmoved by the shocks and whirlwinds of party, and dreads not the unprincipled attack now directed against it. Tune—Jefferson's March. . . . 9th. Education—The extension of our public schools a national blessing—a means afforded whereby the rising generation can properly appreciate our free institutions. Tune—Praise Ye The Lord. . . . 13th. The Press—The channel of public opinion. Who would not submit to its occasional abuse rather than forego the blessings of its freedom? Tune—Yankee Doodle. . . .' *New-York Evening Post*, 14 May 1831. See also below.

association of ideas would be irresistible: France—the United States—their friendship—Lafayette! Instantaneously, the toast . . . with a smile and a bow to each of them in turn.

It would be bad enough, they had realized, to have to appear pleased. Unfortunately, more would be required. It was the custom, after the drinking of such a toast, for the representative of the country thus honoured to rise and acknowledge the courtesy with a few well-chosen remarks. Serurier, down in Washington, had long been familiar with the situation and liked it as little as they. '*Je me suis alors levé,*' he was to report to his government after the Fourth of July, '*Je me suis alors levé, selon le terrible usage du Pays, et j'ai répondu 2 mots de politesse. . . .*'[3] Tocqueville and Beaumont had wondered whether they could bring themselves to make the necessary response.

Then, just when the series of after-dinner toasts had been due to begin, every one had risen from the table and they had been hurried on to finish their tour of inspection. For this time the crisis had been avoided. It had been a lucky escape.

They had not got through the ordeal by dinner, however, without a scare of another sort. Fortunately, some quick thinking on Tocqueville's part had averted the danger.

'The other day,' he began his account of the ceremony,[4] 'the mayor of New-York and the Aldermen . . . to the number of 25 or 30 conducted us with great ceremony to all the prisons or houses of charity of the city. After which they invited us to an immense dinner, the first of this kind we have attended. I should like to describe it to you, but the thing is difficult. Picture to yourself, however, a long table like a refectory table at the high end of which the mayor flanked by your two servants was seated. Next came all the *convives, tous grands personnages à faire pleurer*, for they laugh mighty little on this side of the Atlantic.

'As for the dinner itself, it represented the infancy of art: the vegetables and fish before the meat, the oysters for dessert. In a word, complete barbarism. My first glance around the table relieved me of a great weight; I didn't see any wine but only, as usual, water and brandy. So I seated myself with becoming gravity at the right of Mr. Mayor and awaited developments. Unfortunately, as soon as the soup was removed, they brought wine. The mayor drank to our health in the English manner, which consists in filling a small glass, in raising it while looking at you, and in drinking it, the whole performed with great solemnity. The person to whom this civility is addressed has to respond to it by doing exactly the same thing. We each, then, drank our glass, always with befitting dignity. Up to that point everything was going well.

'But we began to tremble on perceiving that each of our table companions was getting ready to do us the same honour. We had the appearance of hares with a pack of dogs on their trail, and the fact is they would soon have had us in distress if we had allowed them to. But at the third glass I took the step of only swallowing a mouthful, and I thus very happily gained what we in France call the end of the dinner, but which is here only the end of the first act. Most of the dishes being then taken off, they bring lighted candles and serve you very neatly a certain number of cigars on a plate. Each one takes possession of one and, the society enveloping itself in a cloud of smoke, the toasts begin, muscles relax the least little bit, and they give themselves to the heaviest gaiety in the world.

'Now you have a fair idea of a formal dinner in America. I confess that during this august ceremony I couldn't keep from laughing in my beard on thinking of the difference 1500 leagues of sea make in the position of men. I thought of the more than subordinate role that I played in France two months ago and of the comparatively elevated situation in which we were finding ourselves here, the little noise that our mission has made at home and that which it makes here, all because of this little bit of sea-water I just spoke of.

'I assure you, though, that we do not give ourselves the airs of a great seigneur. We are on the contrary the best princes in the world, and we are far from receiving as a debt the courtesies they show us. But these people, who have no great political questions to debate and who see nothing more worthy the attention of a government than the state of the prisons and penal legislation, insist on regarding us as young men of high merit charged with a mission of extreme importance. The French agents themselves treat us with much distinction, and as they know that we are of the nobility, they give out on this head details which are of service to us. For you shall know that in this republican country they are a thousand times more fond of nobility, of titles, of crosses, and of all the inconsequential distinctions of Europe than we are in France. The greatest equality reigns here in the laws. It is even in appearance in the customs. But I tell you the Devil loses nothing by it. And the pride which cannot come out in public finds at the very

bottom of the soul a fine corner in which to install itself. We sometimes laugh heartily to ourselves at the way some of our acquaintances
affect to link themselves to the families of Europe and at the industry
with which they seize on the smallest social distinctions to which they
may attain.

'We are going to-morrow morning to Sing-Sing, a village ten leagues
distant from New-York and situated on the North River. We shall
stay there a week to study the discipline of a vast penitentiary recently
built there. What we have seen up to now suffices to prove to us that
prisons attract general attention here and that in several respects they
are much better than those of France.

'But that's still only a very superficial view. We are delighted to go
to Sing-Sing. It is impossible to imagine anything more beautiful than
the North or Hudson River. The great width of the stream, the admirable richness of the north bank and the steep mountains which
border its eastern [!] margins make it one of the most admirable sights
in the world. But that still isn't the America I should like to see. We
are envying every day the first Europeans who two hundred years ago
discovered for the first time the mouth of the Hudson and mounted
its current, then when its two banks were covered with numberless
forests and only the smoke of the savages was to be seen above the place
where now buzz the two hundred thousand inhabitants of New-York.

'Man has so much that he is never content. . . .'

## IX

## SING SING—THE PRISON

ON the twenty-ninth of May, the two very social Frenchmen took leave of their assiduous friends, the 'honourable esquires' of New York, bundled together a few clothes and the sheaves of note-paper they would need, and set out up the Hudson. They were merely off to visit a prison in the country, and were to be gone only a week. But it was their first expedition out from New York since landing in America; and they were so excited that they quite forgot to take along the fine fowling pieces which—as nobles and sportsmen—they had brought with them all the way from France to do execution on the American birds. What stupidity thus to have thrown away their first opportunity for sport! The disgust and disappointment of the keen young commissioners were matched only by their blissful ignorance of what lay ahead of them, a few miles up the river.

Originally, Tocqueville and Beaumont had intended to begin their penitentiary studies by going first to the Massachusetts and Connecticut state prisons at Charlestown and Wethersfield. But recently their plans had changed. Perhaps the irrepressible investigators were finally coming to realize the gigantic size of America, and to appreciate that even New England was not so small as it looked on the map. More probably, it had been their introduction to the interesting House of Refuge on Bloomingdale Road that had induced the commissioners to begin with the penitentiaries and reformatories in the vicinity of New York. At all events, they had now decided to spend a few days at Mount Pleasant investigating the famous though still unfinished prison located there, then return to the city, to make a detailed study of the House of Refuge and the other institutions to which the mayor and his solemn committee had taken them. After that, they would visit Auburn and the New England prisons.

In short, the two French magistrates had, in their innocence, arranged

93

an extraordinary experience for themselves: they were off to see Sing Sing as their first American penitentiary!

*

* *

Before following Tocqueville and Beaumont into the prison itself, a word on the character of Sing Sing and a glance at the history of penal reform in the United States are necessary.

In 1831, Sing Sing was one of the most highly organized institutions of its kind in the world. It represented the climax of a long development in the handling of criminals: the extreme application, to the problem of punishment and reform, of a certain group of idealistic American theories that had finally been evolved after more than a century and a half of adjustment and experiment.

In the beginning, of course, the early colonists had brought with them to America the rigorous criminal code and harsh practices of England in the time of her Stuart kings. Under this code, as enforced in the mother country, a multitude (if not the majority) of offences, major and minor, had been punishable by death—a simple and expeditious way of getting rid of the individuals whom society found obnoxious. The other offenders had been 'treated with pitiless publicity combined with bodily pain,'[1] that is, by flogging, mutilation, branding, or exposure in the stocks, after which they were turned loose. In the land of the Stuarts there had been, then, no prison problem. Cruel and unfeeling though the gallows and whipping post might be, at least they disposed of criminals without locking them up. The mutilated being sent about their business, and the dead requiring no confinement, it had followed that the so-called prisons were simply boarding-houses reserved for the safe lodging of the impecunious and the unfortunate: places where debtors and those awaiting trial could be confined, in privacy or crowded filth, according to their means. With England already feeling the pressure of population, neither the hanged nor the residents in the Fleet had been missed.

In America, however, this system had not proved altogether satisfactory. Many of the death penalties, it was true, had been retained in the laws; and at the same time regular resort had been had to the whipping post and to the stocks for punishing both religious and civil offenders. As in the mother country, therefore, prisons had not figured to any large extent in the administration of justice. On the other hand, certain changes in the point of view of society had eventually become perceptible. In particular, certain religious influences, and long exposure to conditions in the new world had not been without their effects on the colonials; and the first of these effects had been an increased consideration for human life. Out of religious and moral scruples, the kindly and intelligent Quakers had from the first opposed the brutal punishments of the Anglican code. And with so much land calling for settlement and exploitation, the colonists in general had early begun to feel that man-power was too precious to waste: the frontier had created, as it were, an interest in the conservation of human life. Under the pressure of moral conviction and economic circumstance, therefore, the settlers had more than once been led to consider modifying the old English rules for the treatment of crime. In fact, between 1682 and 1717 the Quakers of Pennsylvania and West Jersey actually succeeded in substituting imprisonment at hard labour for the barbarous code of the mother country.[2] But this enlightened piece of legislation had proved too far ahead of its times and had been repealed: with the result that, as the colonies had swung into their rapid development in the eighteenth century, the whole movement for new codes of justice had lagged behind. At best, then, the progress of the reform in the colonial period had been hesitating, its gain in adherents and momentum discouragingly slow.

Happily, the American Revolution had promptly accelerated the movement, and in the end given it a new direction as well. With the infiltration of humanitarian ideas from Europe and the liberal impulse imparted by the cause of freedom, a radical reduction had first been made in the number of capital crimes. Next—and this was an important development—the standard punishment for other offences had been changed from pain and public humiliation to imprisonment. That is, the prison had been erected to take the place of the stocks and the whipping post as 'the instrument of punishment and of hoped-for reformation,' quite as the Pennsylvania Quakers had once tried to do. As should perhaps have been expected, this alteration in the criminal code had at once created new and serious difficulties. With the condemned of whatever age, sex, colour, or criminal experience all herded indiscriminately together in large, unventilated, uncleaned rooms, the new prisons had rapidly become unhealthy. Worse still, they had degenerated into schools of crime and seminaries of vice. The end of the eighteenth century, therefore, had seen the sudden emergence of an acute prison problem. Something more, the public spirited had told themselves, would certainly have to be done.

The logical solution had been the development of the 'cellular' idea. The movement had started in the 1780s,[3] with the inauguration by the Pennsylvania Quakers of the first so-called 'penitentiary system' in the United States. This pacific and philanthropic sect had agreed that it was the duty of Christians to try to reform criminals—rather than punish or kill them. When the harsh English laws of the state were amended, therefore, they succeeded in getting the death penalty for all offences but first degree murder replaced by a sentence to solitary confinement in the single cells that were built into the Walnut Street prison in Philadelphia.* The theory had been that strict solitary confinement, day and night, would of itself reform the average criminal. The enforced loneliness and idleness of the confinement would leave him nothing to do but think. He would reflect on his misdeeds, fall a prey to his own conscience, and repent. While he was thus overcoming his own evil inclinations, isolation from his fellow convicts would protect him from contamination or reinfection by them. At the expiration of his sentence the prisoner would therefore return into a world a chastened and a contrite man. Logically, the new kind of prison with the solitary cells had been called a 'penitentiary' or house of penitence and reform. And, not unreasonably, people at home and abroad had seen great promise in it. Franklin had talked about it to the liberal philosophers of France of the late eighteenth century. Mirabeau had been interested; and liberal young nobles like La Rochefoucauld-Liancourt had visited the Walnut Street jail, while on their travels in America after the War of Independence, and had then written about the new reform in the treatment of criminals on their return to France.[4]

In France nothing had changed. And in the United States, owing to crowded conditions and an insufficient number of cells, it was a long time before the 'penitentiary system' had a fair trial. Then, in 1821, an experiment with eighty selected convicts at Auburn in New York had established the fact that the solitary system did not accomplish all that was hoped from it. Lonely reflection did not always result in the victory of the criminal's better self and—what was more

---

* After sundry petitions to the legislature and the revision of the penal code in 1786, the Philadelphia Society for the Alleviation of the Miseries of the Public Prisons was organized in 1787. In 1790, the appointment of prison inspectors was secured; and shortly afterwards the solitary cells were built. Barnes, *Evolution of Penology in Pennsylvania*, pp.72ff.

serious—solitary confinement in idleness often broke the health and the mind as well as the spirit of the offender, so that insanity and death resulted instead of reform. In this particular instance, within three years the convicts had either died, or become insane, or so declined in health that the governor had to pardon the survivors.[5] The necessity of giving the prisoner work to occupy his hands, and education and religious instruction to form and direct his mind, had therefore been proven beyond reasonable doubt. Consequently, as the penitentiary movement had evolved into its second phase, the ideas of work and instruction had been added to the original principle of solitary confinement.

At this point the States of New York and Pennsylvania, which were pioneering the development, had adopted different methods of applying the same body of principles, and two rival schools of penitentiary practice had sprung up.

At Auburn in western New York, where the absolute necessity of giving work to the convicts had first been demonstrated, it was found difficult to supply prisoners with work in their cells and it was believed that continuous confinement day and night, even with occupation during the day, was dangerous to the mental and bodily health of the inmates. So the prisoners had been brought out to work together in the daytime. To protect them from corruption by their fellows, and to preserve the principle of isolation, a rule of silence was imposed. While at work, the inmates were not allowed to speak to each other or to communicate in any way; and this rule was enforced by the old-fashioned whip. At the same time, a new style of multiple-story building had been developed to house them at night and to eliminate the communication commonly, if surreptitiously, practised by the inmates of the old-style solitary cells. This was known as the Auburn cell-block. By making the cells smaller (since they were used only for sleeping) and by placing them back to back in rows and tiers, with an area-way all around and above them, and with the walls and roof of the building acting simply as an outer shell about this area-way, the danger of undetected communication had been much reduced, and the germ of the modern cell-block had been developed. The Auburn system, also known as the 'congregate' system, was therefore one of solitary confinement in the new cell-block at night, and work in common but in silence by day.

The Pennsylvanians, on the other hand, had stuck more closely to the original model. The Quakers considered the expedient of work in common by day a violation of the essential 'penitentiary' principle, and the use of the whip to enforce the rule of silence an ineffective and brutalizing punishment. When, in 1829, therefore, they had finally come to the conclusion that work was essential to the prisoners, they had supplied it to each man in his cell, and given each cell a little walled backyard where the inmate could take his daily exercise. These features had been incorporated into the new Eastern State Penitentiary completed in that very year outside of Philadelphia. The model cell-block, Pennsylvania style, was therefore a single-story building housing two rows of rather large cells, which faced each other across an inner corridor and opened behind into individual walled yards. For purposes of surveillance, the six cell-blocks had been so placed in relation to each other that their corridors radiated outward like the spokes of a wheel from a common hub or observation station; and this wheel-like prison had then been enclosed in a high, rectangular outer wall. The Pennsylvania system, thus finally perfected, was therefore one of solitary confinement night and day, with work, in large cells.

A sincere difference of opinion and also some State jealousy had gone into the development of these two penitentiary systems. So no sooner had they emerged into practical shape than an intense struggle for popular favour had begun between them. Up to 1831, the adherents of the Auburn plan had had distinctly the better of the argument, as both Massachusetts and Connecticut had modelled their prisons after Auburn, and other States were considering doing the same. This was partly because the New York penitentiary had been the first in the field, partly because it appeared to be the more economical, and partly also because there was an element of the spectacular in the results it had achieved, especially in the building of Sing Sing prison.

When, in 1825, the State of New York had decided to construct another and larger prison near New York City, Elam Lynds, the man who as warden at Auburn had had as much to do as any other man with the development of the 'congregate' system, had taken with him 100 convicts from Auburn and had built the first cell-block at Sing Sing. There had been no walls around them, the men had laboured unmanacled and almost unguarded, and at night they had slept in tents—yet none had tried to escape. And in a short space of time convicts had built their own penitentiary!

The achievement had created a sensation. Some said it had been possible only because of the extraordinary hold that the iron ex-soldier had on the convicts. He dominated them by sheer force of character. A story was told of how once, on hearing that a certain inmate was out to 'get' him, he sent for the man to his bedroom and, without appearing to notice his uneasiness, ordered the would-be murderer to shave him. The man had lost his nerve, and obeyed. Afterwards, Lynds had dismissed him, saying: 'I knew that you wanted to kill me; but I despised you too much to believe that you would ever have the courage to execute your design. Alone and without arms, I am always stronger than all of you.'[6] Unquestionably, to his convicts, Lynds was a terrible figure. Yet the man's system counted for something, too. As late as 1831, when Lynds was no longer warden and when the unfinished prison already housed nearly a thousand desperate criminals, there were still no attempts at revolt and very few evasions, though there were even yet no walls, and many of the convicts worked unfettered and lightly guarded in the open quarries above the prison. Such was the discipline possible with the Auburn system of silence and the whip, such the penitentiary Tocqueville and Beaumont had chosen for their first visit.

Needless to say, the two young French commissioners were not quite prepared for the spectacle. It was not that they had never been in a prison before: they had seen the insides of the prisons of France. For some years past, as assistant prosecutors in the government courts, they had known what the houses of detention of Paris and Versailles were like. And only recently, as applicants for their mission, they had made a first-hand study of one or two of the larger prisons of the vicinity. They knew the beaten coarseness of the criminal's face; the gray, bestial hopelessness of his glance; the dark and filthy grimness of the places where he was kept. They had whiffed the fetid odour of his damp and unclean clothes, and known the nauseating smell that taints the cells, the corridor walls, the unfresh food—the searching inescapable 'institutional' smell. They had seen one or two of the dread *maisons centrales* of France, where criminals of all kinds and of all ages were thrown in together under lock and key in a common dormitory, to quarrel and to plot and to teach each other unclean things. Sing Sing was by no means to be their first prison.

Nor was it that Tocqueville and Beaumont were altogether unfamiliar with American theories of prison management. They stood in direct

descent from the La Rochefoucauld-Liancourts of the preceding century
who had first brought the American 'penitentiary' idea to the attention
of France. They were the heirs in spirit of the philanthropic French
travellers of the 1780s and 1790s, had read some of their books, and
were now following in their footsteps. They were also aware of the
progress that had been made in the United States while France had
been busy with Napoleon and the Restoration, and their reading had
made them familiar with the reforms that had once again made American prisons the talk of the world. They had heard that solitary confinement, work, and moral education were the principles of the revised penitentiary system, just as the reform of the criminal was still
its goal; and they knew something of the individual characteristics of
the two rival schools at Auburn and Philadelphia.*

There was one thing, however, they knew nothing about. And that
was: how the idealistic theories worked in practice.

*

*   *

Tocqueville and Beaumont, minus their guns, arrived at Mount
Pleasant on 29 May, just as the weather was turning hot after a cold,
late spring. They found Elam Lynds' famous prison down by the
river. A long, grim, four-story cell-block first caught the eye, but as
they approached they became acutely conscious of the swarms of convicts who were working together in the open, or labouring in the quarries above, in apparent freedom and in perfect silence. For Frenchmen,
accustomed to the fortress-like houses of detention and the old-fashioned
walled prisons of France, it was an extraordinary sight.

'It is certain that the system of discipline established in the penitentiary of Sing-Sing is very remarkable,' Beaumont soberly observed to
his mother.[7] 'This prison contains 900 inmates, condemned for terms
of varying length. They are made to work, either in the prison court

---

* During the autumn of 1830, Tocqueville and Beaumont had been at particular pains
to procure themselves a bibliography of English and American prison literature
(Theophile Barrois to Bt., 30 Oct. 1830; W.C.Rives to Bt., 5 Nov. 1830. BB). Their
request for the prison mission (31 Oct. 1830, *Archives Nationales*, BB[18]1323) showed
that they were also familiar with developments in Switzerland and the Netherlands.
Much of their information had doubtless been derived from Ch. Lucas, *Du Système
Pénitentiare en Europe et aux États-Unis*, 2 v., 1828–1830, the first volume of which
gave a translation of Livingston's Louisiana Code. Cf. also Ferdinand-Dreyfus, 'Un
prédécesseur d'Alexis de Tocqueville—La Rochefoucauld-Liancourt aux États-Unis,
1794–1797,' *Revue Parlementaire*, XXXVII, 133–149; and Robert G. Mahieu, *Les
Enquêteurs français aux États-Unis de 1830 à 1837* . . . , Paris, 1934.

which isn't shut, or in the quarries a short distance away. They are at complete liberty, carrying irons neither on hands nor feet, and yet they labour assiduously at the hardest tasks. Nothing is rarer than an evasion. That appears so unbelievable that one sees the fact a long time without being able to explain it.*

'Nevertheless one manages to discover the secret of this marvellous discipline. It reposes on certain essential principles. The first is the *absolute silence* to which the prisoners are condemned. They aren't free to offer a single word, and the truth is that during all the time I passed in their midst, I did not hear a single one let a word escape.

'The second capital rule is an unexampled severity in the application of bodily punishments. One is certain that this rigour is exercised in all its fulness because the discipline of the prison belongs to the *principal officer*, who has the entire *responsibility*.

'On the other hand, the guardians well appreciate their numerical weakness, and as they are 30 against 900, they must at each instant fear to see a revolt break out. It's that which generally makes them just in the punishments they inflict; they understand that every oppression of theirs might bring on a rebellion. In spite of the various elements of order it is hard enough to understand the results that are obtained.'

The bluff young Frenchman was mystified, and obviously floundering. 'There is, however,' he suggested, 'a general reason which dominates all the others and which serves to resolve the problem.

'It is undeniable that 900 condemned men, 900 bandits, are stronger, more powerful than 30 individuals charged with their keeping. And when these 900 criminals, who have everything to gain from fleeing, find themselves at liberty, it is evident that nothing would be easier for them than to do it and to overcome the resistance that might be offered. But if they are materially the stronger, have they the same moral force as the small number of individuals charged with watching them? No, because they are isolated, one from the other. All strength is born of association; and 30 individuals united through perpetual communication, by ideas, by plans in common, by concerted schemes, have more real power than 900 whose isolation makes them weak. . . .'

Their first astonishment over, the young commissioners decided that

* 'We have seen 250 prisoners working under a shed, cutting stone. These men, subjected to a very special surveillance, had all committed acts of violence indicating a dangerous character. Each, at his right and at his left, had a stone-cutter's *hache*. Three unarmed guards walked up and down in the shed. Their eyes were in continuous agitation.' Toc. diary note, 30 May 1831 (Alph.A, TT).

moral as well as physical force went into the discipline of the Auburn system. Nothing else could explain its extraordinary hold over the convicts. Still, even this explanation was unsatisfactory, and Tocqueville and Beaumont were uneasy. The unfinished penitentiary seemed to be clean and economical as well as exceedingly well ordered. Moreover, as they analysed the construction and observed the operation of their first American prison, they could discern the influence of idealistic principles, in fact could actually see the philanthropic ideas of which they had read taking shape in stone, and discipline, and solitary cell. But the place was bathed in heat and an unnatural silence, and there was an unmistakable undercurrent of terror in the silence. Mingling with the handful of guards and watching the inmates at work, the French commissioners themselves became afraid. The prison seemed to them a sleeping volcano which might at any moment erupt under their feet. Or, as Tocqueville whimsically expressed it,[8] 'The system at Sing-Sing seems in many particulars to resemble the steamboats of which the Americans make such great use. Nothing is more comfortable, more swift, more perfect, in short, in the normal course of things. But if some part of the machinery happens to go wrong, the vessel, the passengers and the cargo jump in the air.' Even the prison chaplain, Mr. Prince, 'likened the warden of the establishment to a man who has tamed a tiger that one day may devour him.' *

More than a year later, when they came to make their moderate and thoughtful report to their government, the impression was still so vivid in their memories that Tocqueville wrote:[9] 'One cannot see the prison of Sing-Sing and the system of labour which is there established without being struck by astonishment and fear. Although the discipline is perfect, one feels that it rests on fragile foundations: it is due to a *tour de force* which is reborn unceasingly and which has to be reproduced each day, under penalty of compromising the whole system of discipline. The safety of the keepers is constantly menaced. In the presence of such dangers, avoided with such skill but with difficulty, it seems to us impossible not to fear some sort of catastrophe in the fu-

---

* Toc. diary note, Sing Sing, 31 May 1831 (Alph.A, TT). 'Mr. Prince seemed to me intelligent and in a position to have an opinion.' By way of 'factual observation' Tocqueville also noted: 'Three years ago a man, who was pointed out to us, rushed suddenly axe in hand from the shop calling his fellow-workers to revolt. They hesitated and he was arrested. It is obvious that that day the life of the Sing-Sing guards hung by a thread. If by the negligence of one of them five or six inmates had been able to agree on a plot, without doubt they would have formed a nucleus and carried the others with them.'

ture. . . .' * And again Tocqueville wrote: [10] 'Will they never be frightened by the danger of allowing a thousand condemned criminals to work in liberty outside the walls of the prison?' Silence and the whip were being counted on too heavily; the discipline was miraculous, but it was also precarious. Such was their first impression of an Auburn-style penitentiary.

Yet Tocqueville and Beaumont did not let their feeling of insecurity interfere with their investigation of the prison. 'Scarcely had we arrived at Sing-Sing, conducted by a very distinguished lawyer of New-York, when they came to offer us all imaginable services,' Beaumont informed his mother.[11] 'The principal officer of the prison, the guardians, in a word all the employees have been at great pains on our behalf.† They delivered us all the registers, opened all the doors. We installed ourselves in a room meant for the inspectors and there we worked all day as if at home. We've made many observations and important researches.'

During nine days they buried themselves in the grim cell-block of the silent prison and devoted themselves to the task of understanding it. They had come to find out precisely how the system worked, both in theory and in practice, how the prison was administered, how much the keepers were paid, what the hours were, what the food was like, what kind of work was done. They had come to make a study of the unusual methods of discipline, and their records show them asking how many whippings there were a day,‡ and how many deaths resulted from it. They wanted to know by what methods and with what success the reform of the criminals was effected. They sought to find out how much it cost to build and to run an Auburn-style penitentiary, and what returns the labour of the convicts in shop and quarry brought in. Finally, of course, they were anxious to make up their minds how well the Auburn system would suit France.

It is less interesting to review the results they obtained than to notice how thorough and how specific were the inquiries which they made at Sing Sing and were prepared to repeat in all the major prisons of the country. They studied the warden's records and the architect's plans,

---

* Sing Sing's freedom from revolts Tocqueville and Beaumont took to be a proof that the silence had been perfectly observed.
† It has not been possible to identify the distinguished lawyer who accompanied Tocqueville and Beaumont to Sing Sing. The warden of the prison was Robert Wiltse, the architect and engineer George W. Cartwright, the chaplain the aforementioned Mr. Prince.
‡ Du Syst. Pén., p.75 note. 'They told us there are about five or six a day.'

collected all the State documents and the Sing Sing statistics available, and laid every member of the staff, from the warden to the prison chaplain, under contribution. When they came to examine into the moral influences brought to bear on the convicts to reclaim them for society, they personally attended the prison school and even went to divine service on Sunday.

' . . . We ought to say that at Sing-Sing,' Tocqueville was to report,[12] 'the school, though carefully conducted, seems to us restricted to too limited a number of inmates. The number of convicts admitted to Sunday school varies from 60 to 80, feeble proportion on 1000 (see the report of 1832 on Sing Sing). The direction of this establishment is too materialistic, a condition resulting doubtless from the fact that the warden and the under officers are wholly preoccupied with the maintenance of the outward discipline, whose existence is unceasingly threatened. We were witnesses of an incident which proves what might be the success of the school at Sing-Sing if it were to receive a larger development. A poor negro, who had learned to read in the prison, recited by heart in front of us two pages of the Bible, which he had studied in his leisure hours of the week, and he did not make the slightest mistake in memory.'

Naturally, this constant display of patience and thoroughness by the visiting commissioners was not lost on the officers of the prison. The warden and his staff were flattered and no little pleased, especially when the Frenchmen were discovered to be as enthusiastic as they were industrious. For Tocqueville and Beaumont, with a tact that would have done credit to a Chinese diplomat, had suppressed their doubts and expressed nothing but admiration for what they saw in Sing Sing. As a result, the prison authorities could hardly contain themselves for satisfaction. And no sooner did the two friends leave than the following inspired article appeared in the *Westchester Herald*:[13]

' . . . M. de Beaumont and M. de Tocqueville, the distinguished gentlemen composing the [French Prison] Commission, have spent the last two weeks in this place, and after a most laborious and careful inspection of the prison here, its construction, its order, cleanliness, discipline and regularity, together with a strict investigation into all the minutiae of its government and its operation, we are gratified with the opportunity of stating that they are highly pleased with the institution, and do not hesitate to pronounce it superior, in many of its branches, to any which they have ever visited in Europe. They are gentlemen of engaging manners, of first rate talents and acquirements, and have been repeatedly honored with distinguished offices by their country. We trust that the attention and kindness of the American people, who cannot but feel flattered with the object of their mission, will render their visit throughout the Union both pleasant and profitable.*'

The two tactful young men who had been 'repeatedly honored with distinguished offices by their country' were so amused and pleased by this notice, when it was reprinted in the New York papers, that each of them promptly sent a copy of it to his family. But they did not let the flattery 'interfere with their manner of seeing,' as Beaumont was fond of saying.

' . . . In spite of the tribute of admiration we pay to what we have seen, we still have many doubts on the solidity and effectiveness of the system,' the young man confided to his family.[14] 'The discipline established seems to us a slippery terrain on which clever and firm men maintain themselves with skill and success, but on which it might easily happen to them to fall. In the second place, imitation of a serious people is grave and dangerous for a nation whose principal characteristic is to be *vive et légère*.†

'Thirdly, there are enormous expenditures to be made, and their result is not sufficiently clear (at least up to the present) for them to be undertaken without ripe reflections.‡ I have just begun a long report which we are going to address to the Minister of the Interior on the establishment of Sing-Sing. I am presenting vast developments without saying anything [final]: the object of the report is to inform the govern-

---

* Francis Lieber's interleaved copy of his own translation of Beaumont and Tocqueville's report shows that the English prison commissioners who came over two years later were also tremendously impressed by Tocqueville and Beaumont's industry at Sing Sing. 'On August 19, 1833 I went to town (N.Y.) and saw Mr. Crawford and Newman, who had returned from Sing-Sing, where they had spent a whole week in making out statistical accounts from the books. They said: The French Commissioners must have been exceedingly industrious whilst they were here, & shunned no labor. We can judge now of their immense labor. They have done as much as they possibly could do, etc.' Note in Lieber's hand, Lieber papers, Johns Hopkins University Library.

† Tocqueville's statistical notes show that he perhaps exaggerated this difficulty, for in the state of New York one prisoner out of every three was either a negro or an Irishman! *Du Syst. Pén.*, pp.399–403.

‡ In his diary note of 29 May (Alph.A, TT), Tocqueville summed up the achievements of Sing Sing as follows: '1. The health of the inmates, 2. Their extreme application to work, 3. Income for the state from this labour, 4. Perhaps the moral reform of a certain number.'

ment that we are busying ourselves with the mission confided to us. It is necessary that he take an interest and that he be in suspense over the advantages to be drawn from it; lastly we want to attract his attention without as yet expressing a definite opinion on our subject. In spite of my good intention to put aside the prison and speak of other things, it is absolutely necessary that I say a word about something which is connected with it and which seems strange to me.

'Moral and religious instruction is one of the means employed in the establishment. Every Sunday the inmates attend a religious service and they never fail to hear a sermon. Thus far that's very fine. But what is less natural is that the office in question is said turn by turn by a Presbyterian minister, or by an anabaptist, or, etc. In a word, ministers belonging to different Christian communions celebrate Sundays alternately, and all the prisoners attend the service together, without perhaps knowing the difference between the sects to which their preachers belong. If they don't, so much the better. But if they do know the difference, they must find themselves much embarrassed to choose between the various cults the best and only true one. As a matter of fact, nothing is commoner in the United States than this indifference toward the nature of religions, which doesn't however eliminate the religious fervour of each for the cult he has chosen. Actually, this extreme tolerance on the one hand toward religions in general—on the other this considerable zeal of each individual for his own religion, is a phenomenon I can't yet explain to myself. I would gladly know how a lively and sincere faith can get on with such a perfect toleration; how one can have equal respect for religions whose dogmas differ; and finally what real influence on the moral conduct of the Americans can be exercised by their religious spirit, whose outward manifestations, at least, are undeniable. Would it not be from their outward show of religion that there is more breadth than depth in it? Does not the multiplicity of sects existing in the United States cause each one to try to surpass the others in the observance of the cult and of the moral principles which religion commands? If that were so, one would perhaps have to attribute some of their virtues to conceit and emulation rather than to conviction and consciousness of the truth. . . .'

## X

## SING SING—REFLECTIONS ON AMERICAN SOCIETY

DURING Sunday worship at Sing Sing, Beaumont's mind had stumbled against one of the riddles of Protestant America.

He and Tocqueville had gone to the service to study the moral education of criminals in a penitentiary. As his letter showed, however, he had soon ceased to follow the minister's sermon on morality. In the faces of the inmates, quietly, uneasily intent on what the preacher was saying, the young commissioner had caught a glimpse of a religious attitude that puzzled him. Apparently it made no difference to the directors of the prison or to the prisoners themselves what branch of the Christian church the minister of the day belonged to. So long as he preached the common body of Christian morality and abstained from pressing the dogmas peculiar to his sect, the convicts could participate in the service with fervour and listen to his teaching of the gospel with benefit. To criminals, then, there was no one church which alone taught the true faith! Beaumont's thoughts soared beyond prison walls. In the practice of such 'extreme tolerance' was not the little prison community the image of all Protestant America? 'I would gladly know,' he had reflected, 'how a lively and sincere faith can get on with such a perfect toleration, how one can have equal respect for religions whose dogmas differ, and finally what real influence on the moral conduct of the Americans their religious spirit can have. . . .'

It would not have been just to accuse Gustave de Beaumont of letting his mind wander, in thus for the moment sinking his prison investigation in the larger riddle of religious toleration. For it was no accident that he and Tocqueville should have been thinking about America in general while they were engaged in the specific task of analysing the moral influence of their first penitentiary. On the contrary, their letters and notes showed that they spent a good part of their nine days at Sing Sing doing just that. Apparently they were able to combine an almost infinite care in their prison inspection with a constant and consuming interest in the whole of American civilization. As a result, in their brief stay at Mount Pleasant the two young friends not only made one of the most thorough studies of Sing Sing ever attempted, but also succeeded in adding very considerably to their knowledge and understanding of American society.

It was partly a process of acquiring new information, partly a process of digesting what their eyes and ears had already taken in. Their first fortnight in New York, as their own manuscripts showed, had introduced Tocqueville and Beaumont to the range of life in an American city, and had brought to their astonished attention certain distinctive features (such as the 'money-mindedness' of their hosts) that seemed to indicate the existence of fundamental peculiarities in the American people. The instantaneous effect had been to convince the young Frenchmen that the United States was so different from the older societies of Europe that it could not safely be imitated. Starting, then, with this basic concept, they had begun to analyse the social and political constitution of the nation. But they had at once been so overwhelmed by the friendly attentions of the hospitable New Yorkers, that they had found the time too short for more than a feverish glance around and a few summary and superficial judgments. When they arrived at Sing Sing, therefore, the whole work of dissecting, examining and describing American civilization still remained to be done, and to this study they at once addressed themselves.

In the comparative quiet of the long warm days at Mount Pleasant they pursued their reflections. If the United States was radically different, wherein did the differences lie? Of what racial elements was this people composed? What instincts governed Americans? What moral influences and material interests held them together in a nation: harmonious, moral, law-abiding? What was the character of the American continent, the influence of the American environment? These were the questions that they now began to try to answer in Tocqueville's pithy diary notes and in their letters home.

First, however, there was the matter of getting established at Sing Sing, and the story of their daily activities and adventures.

\*

\*    \*

'You would never guess, my dear Father,'—Tocqueville was in high spirits [1]—'in what situation I am placed in order to write to you. I am going to begin my letter by describing it to you. I am on the summit of a fairly high hill which borders the course of the Hudson. A hundred paces away a country house where we are lodging forms the foreground of the landscape. At the foot of the hill flows the river, which is five quarter-leagues wide and covered with sails. It penetrates to the north and disappears between high blue mountains. There is no more delicious sight than the spectacle offered by its banks. There reigns an air of prosperity, activity, and industry that rejoices the sight. The whole is lit up by an admirable sun which, striking its rays through the damp atmosphere of this country, throws over everything a soft and transparent colouring.

'You may judge by the length of this description that he who makes it is comfortably placed to observe the countryside. In fact, at the top of the highest hill is an enormous plane tree; I am perched in the branches to avoid the heat, and it's from there that I write you. Beaumont, who is at the foot, is sketching what I am trying to describe. We make, as you see, a perfect composition. Now it must be explained where we are, and why and how we are there. Sing-Sing, so called after an Indian chief who inhabited the place sixty years ago but whose tribe has since retired into the interior, is situated on the Hudson eleven leagues to the north of New-York. It's a town of 1000 to 1200 souls which has been rendered famous by its prison . . . the most vast in the United States. . . . We have come here with the intention of examining it from top to bottom; we have already been here a week, and we experience a well-being that you can't conceive. The extreme agitation in which we were obliged to live in New-York, the number of visits we had to make and receive each day began to weary us a little. Here we have the best employed and most peaceful existence. We live with a very decent American family which holds us in great consideration. We have made the acquaintance in the village of several persons whom we go to see when we are free. . . .'

'At two or three hundred paces from the small town of Sing-Sing,' Beaumont was later to supplement this description,[2] 'there is on the summit of the hill forming the bank of the Hudson a charming country house, occupied by a lady who takes in the people who wish to stay there as pensioners by the week or month. There we established ourselves. Several people were already before us in this house, among others an Englishwoman, Mme Maceheidge [?] and her daughter, whose society we found very agreeable.

'We always took a short walk at five in the morning. At half past eight after breakfast we took a second. And in the evening at seven we went swimming in the Hudson. I am beginning to swim passably. Tocqueville is giving me lessons with all the fierce energy of a friend who realizes how unfortunate would be my position if I by chance fell into the middle of a great American river. Where we were the Hudson is one and a quarter leagues wide. In the evening on leaving the prison we went to call on the people of the village and the neighbourhood; everywhere we were overwhelmed with civilities and invitations. The clear profit I've found in these calls in society has been to speak much English. We are making progress. Nevertheless, it happens to us every day to confuse things strangely. We are never entirely certain of what we are told. When it's a matter of a banal conversation, the mistake is of no consequence; but it's not the same when they give us an invitation which we do not understand. We sometimes mistake the day on which we are invited to tea, and very recently a great landholder of the neighbourhood, a member of the Livingston family, had made great preparations to receive us. He had prepared a splendid dinner and gathered together a number of people in our honour. His dinner was for three o'clock. He waited till five, and we did not come. Alas! We were at the moment quietly at home, completely ignorant that they were waiting for us.

'You conclude from that that we are not yet very strong in English; I readily agree. Nevertheless, in France we would have the reputation of speaking it like Londoners, we are so nonchalant in saying the clumsiest things.

'We saw several attractive persons in Sing-Sing society.'—And Beaumont was reminded of an error in judgment of which he and Tocqueville had been guilty, to their sorrow. 'American women,' he wrote, 'have a fault we cannot pardon them, which is that of being detestable musicians and of always playing music.'

It seems that two evenings before—but there is a curious document in Beaumont's hand that throws an interesting light on their misadventure. This paper is in the form of a legal certificate, or affidavit.

Beaumont, it will be remembered, was a lawyer by profession. The certificate begins: *

I, the undersigned, doctor of politeness and courtesy, and frank friend of Sir Alexis de Tocqueville, that is to say more prompt to tell him his faults than his good qualities, certify the following facts:

'The said Sir Alexis, formerly reproachable for too cool and reserved an air of society, too much indifference toward those he didn't like, and a silent and calm attitude too near to dignity, has accomplished a complete reform in his manners. He is now seen to be affable and agreeable toward every one, kind to old ladies as to young, and putting himself out to entertain even those whose face he doesn't like. Is an example of this necessary? The fifth of June in an overwhelming heat, we found ourselves at Sing-Sing in the parlour of a *respectable* woman (more respectable perhaps than she of whom Brantôme spoke and Descessars reminded us on the eve of our departure). This lady, who numbers about 45 springs, is passionately fond of music, an unhappy passion if ever there was one. To our misfortune, she sits down at the piano, she begins an infernal music which she continues two mortal hours, singing, crying, howling as if she were possessed of the devil. Traitor to my habits, I was in a corner succumbing to *ennui* and without strength to dissimulate.

'What was Alexis doing at this moment? Seated near the piano with a smiling face, he was approving, applauding each tirade, and pouring the balm of *satisfaction* on the soul of our *virtuosa*, avid for praise without measure. He really had the air of enjoying himself, and the expression of happiness was painted on his face! And yet that woman was ugly, old, and a detestable musician!! There's the man! *Ab uno disce omnes.*'

I owe so many salutary reforms to the said Alexis, I daily receive from him so many services, that I should like to be able to say that I have rendered him one, in urging him to correct the little fault he had. But as I hadn't spoken of it again to him since our departure from Havre, I am forced to recognize that paternal advice has had more effect than mine. However that may be, I certify the fact to be true, and since I am giving certificates, I attest that the said Alexis is the best friend one could find on earth, and this friend being mine, I am happy to have him.

Made and given at Sing-Sing
6 June 1831

G. DE BEAUMONT

* This is one of the few American trip notes, in Beaumont's hand, that still survive. It was discovered among the Tocqueville papers (TT).

Whether the impulsive Beaumont wrote this affidavit purely for his own amusement or not, there was no question of his admiration for Tocqueville—or of his feelings about American women when they ran and plumped themselves down at the piano. 'They haven't the taste for it,' his letter pursued; 'it's only a matter of fashion; they sing in a priceless (*impayable*) way. There is in their throat a certain gentle cooing that has a particular character which I could never render, but which has nothing in common with the laws of harmony. If one says to them: you sing wonderfully, they reply with rare ingenuousness: *it's very true*. They study piano for three months, then they play, without the least reluctance, admitting always with good grace that they are mad about music and that they have real talent. There are of course certain exceptions to the rule; but the women are in general as I describe them.

'What's more, this love of praise crops up everywhere with the Americans, and one could never praise them so as to satisfy them. We draw considerable profit from the principle that every flatterer aims to profit from him who listens; we do not spare our eulogies. So they conduct themselves with us in a way to spoil us. They hold us in such consideration that it's an honour to serve us. Do we need written documents? They give us books, they send us notes written out in longhand. The other day I gave an engineer (Mr. Cartwright), a man of much talent, two pages of questions of diverse nature, to which I asked him to make a written reply. He hastens to do as I suggest; he gave us at the same time some plans which he had made and which we needed. We really make useful servants of all our friends. . . .'

'Time has a thousand different uses for us here,' Tocqueville assured his father;[3] 'because of that, perhaps, it seems to slip through our fingers with frightening rapidity. I believe that, even if we should not succeed in writing something passable on the United States, we would not have wasted our time in giving ourselves to the studies which occupy us without intermission. We have, in truth, but one single idea since our arrival here; that idea is to know the country we are travelling through. To succeed in that, we are obliged to decompose society *a priori*, and search out the elements of which it is composed at home, in order to be able to ask useful questions and forget nothing here. This study, very difficult but full of attraction, makes us perceive a great number of details which lose themselves in the mass when one does not have recourse to analysis, and it suggests a great number of remarks and practical ideas of which we never should have thought. The result of this work has been a series of questions which we are all the time trying to answer. Knowing exactly what we want to ask, the smallest conversations are instructive, and we can say that there is not a man, on whatever rung of society he finds himself, who cannot teach us something. . . .'

*

*   *

'Not a man' who could not teach Tocqueville and Beaumont 'something'! The statement casts a sudden flood of light on the two young visitors. One wonders a little what Mrs. Trollope, or Matthew Arnold of a later day, would have thought of such industry and humility on the part of travellers. One hardly dares imagine what Mr. Thomas Carlyle, or the often scarcely less choleric aristocrats of England, would have said of such an attitude toward things American. To Tocqueville and Beaumont, however, this method seemed the only safe and really instructive one for two sincere investigators to adopt. They were to pursue it throughout their travels in the United States.

Meanwhile, fragments of information—and the germs of the ideas that they suggested—were already beginning to accumulate in Tocqueville's notes. On 29 May, the evening of their arrival at Sing Sing, Tocqueville had been speculating on the ultimate purpose of modern democracies. Like all cultivated Frenchmen, he had in the course of his schooling been introduced to the republics of ancient Greece and Rome. The comparison could hardly be avoided.

'The theory of the ancient Republics,' he had jotted down to start with,[4] 'was the sacrifice of the interest of the individual to the general good; in this respect one can say that it was virtuous. The theory of this one seems to be to include the interest of the individual in that of the whole. A sort of refined and intelligent egoism seems to be the pivot on which the whole machine turns. These people don't bother to find out if public virtue is good, but they claim to be able to prove that it is useful. If this last point is true, as I in part believe, this society can pass for enlightened, but not virtuous. But how far can the two principles of the good of the individual and the good of the whole really coincide? How long will a conscience, that one might call a reflective and calculating conscience, master the political passions which are not yet born, but which will not fail to appear? That only the future will show us.'

Two days later, Tocqueville thought he saw a gleam of light: 'When one reflects on the nature of this society, one sees up to a certain point the explanation of the preceding: American society is composed of a thousand different elements newly brought together. The men who live under these laws are still English, French, German, Dutch. They have neither religion, nor morals, nor ideas in common. Up to the present it can't be said that the Americans have a national character, unless it's that of having none. Here there are no common memories, no national roots. What can be then the only tie which unites the different parts of this vast body? *L'intérêt?*'

That same day, 1 June, Tocqueville summed up the results of a number of conversations in a note that he entitled 'Public Instruction.' A better example of his cumulative method it would be hard to find. The entry began:

'All the people I've seen up to now, to whatever rank of society they belong, have seemed incapable of conceiving that the advantages of education might be doubted. They never fail to smile when told that this opinion is not universal in Europe. They all agree that the spreading of education, which is useful to all peoples, is an absolute necessity for a free people like theirs, where there is no money qualification required for voting or holding office. That's an idea which seemed alive in every mind. Thus the great expenditure of these states has been for institutions for the education of the people (Beaumont has the actual figures). I don't yet know what is thought here of the inconveniences of a partial education, so great with us. However, it seems to me that the greatest arguments advanced in Europe against the excessive diffusion of education, do not apply here. Thus:

'(1) Religious morale is less hurt by it here than anywhere else. There is no hostility between religion and science.

'(2) Here less than anywhere else is to be feared the disquiet caused a state by the large number of people whom their education raises above their fortune, and whose restlessness torments society. Here the resources presented by nature are still so far beyond the efforts of man to exhaust them that there is no moral energy or intellectual activity which does not find a ready outlet.'

Besides, in America, to attack 'the state' would be difficult. For where was the government? 'In the matter of administration,' Tocqueville observed to his father,[5] 'this country seems to me fallen into the opposite excess from that of France. With us the government concerns itself with everything; [here] there is, or appears to be, no government. All the good in centralization seems to be as unknown as all the bad; no central idea seems to govern the movement of the machine. Thence a mass of general results defying enumeration. . . .

'You will perhaps ask me, my dear Father, since we are now *examining machines*, what most strikes me in this country. But it would take a volume to tell you everything, and perhaps I would no longer believe it to-morrow. For I assure you that we are not people of dogma. There are, however, two or three impressions which strike me and in which I should like you to participate. Up to now I am full of two ideas: the first, that this people is one of the happiest in the world; the second, that it owes its immense prosperity much less to its peculiar virtues, less to a form of government of itself superior to other forms, than to the particular circumstances in which it finds itself, which are peculiar to it and which make its political constitution to be perfectly in accord with its needs and its social condition. This is perhaps a trifle metaphysical, but you will understand very well what I want to say when you know, for instance, that nature here offers a sustenance so immense to human industry that the class of theoretical speculators is absolutely unknown. Everybody works, and the mine is still so rich that all those who work rapidly succeed in acquiring that which renders existence happy. The most active spirits, like the most tranquil, find enough to fill their life here without busying themselves troubling the state. The restlessness which so wracks our European societies seems to co-operate toward the prosperity of this one. It aims only at wealth, and finds a thousand roads which lead there. Thus politics only occupies a small corner of the picture here. I have no doubt it agitates more profoundly the most peaceful appearing European state than the whole American confederation. There is not a newspaper, among those we read every day, in which the price of cotton does not take up more room than general questions relative to government. The rest passes off with discussions of local questions, which feed the public curiosity without in the least disturbing society.

'To sum up: the more I see this country the more I admit myself penetrated with this truth: that there is nothing absolute in the theoretical value of political institutions, and that their efficiency depends almost always on the original circumstances and the social condition of the people to whom they are applied. I see institutions succeed here which would infallibly turn France upside down; others which suit us would obviously do harm in America; and yet, either I am much mistaken, or man is neither other nor better here than with us. Only he is otherwise placed. I shall tell you another time what strikes me in American character. Do you not find that at the moment I rather resemble *Maître corbeau sur un arbre perché*? I am going to finish my oration there. I am so well on my branch, *so comfortable* in every respect that I am really afraid of going to sleep; in which event it might happen to me, as to my old friend Robinson Crusoe, to cry: "My dear parents!" and to wake up below. I therefore take the step of climbing down. I shall finish my letter to-morrow. . . .'

Four days later, on their arrival in New York, Beaumont took up the thread of Tocqueville's argument.[6] '. . . We are living in a country which for a long time past has not known civil and political dissensions. To tell the truth, there is only one party in America. The quarrels which are carried on in the newspapers or in society concern persons rather than things. It is to be noted that the highest public offices are little sought; there is but one thing which keenly arouses ambitions, that is riches. Wealth alone gives credit, consideration, power. Public offices which are little paid yield neither consideration, nor power, nor credit; thus they are not sought after except by those who have nothing better to do. This indifference in this matter is a great element for peace and order in a society, as the passion for place, for honours, and for public office is with us a principle of discord and agitation. The more we consider this American society, the more we realize it to be composed of peculiar elements which render imitation very dangerous if not impossible.

'We pass the half of our time taking notes. I've forgotten to tell you an incident of our return from Sing-Sing which I am going to relate since I still have half a page.

'Desolated to have been impolite to Mr. Livingston in spite of ourselves, we wanted to make a courtesy call on him. His country house is situated between Sing-Sing and New-York. It was therefore on our road, on returning, to pass by his house. We knew that he dined at two o'clock. Consequently we arrived at his house at three. But by misfortune we had been mistaken and we arrived at the moment of family dinner. There we were then at table with everybody, but resolved not to eat, because the visit would have lost its character of civility. Judge of our position. We were dying of hunger and the dishes passed under our noses. They pressed us to eat some excellent ices prepared in haste for us. We had to accept; we devoured them. But at four o'clock the steamboat was to pass and we were to go on board. It was for us the only method of getting away. Four o'clock rings; no steamboat. Someone says it has passed, so that we were in mortal embarrassment. For if we stayed at the house, how dine after having said that we had already dined? We saw ourselves in the plight of having eaten an ice for a meal. We couldn't help laughing at the comical in our situation. Happily the steamboat which was late came to deliver us.

'We saw enough of the Livingston house to desire deeply to return there. Adieu. . . .'

As a matter of fact, in spite of their embarrassment, Tocqueville had seized the opportunity to angle for Mr. Livingston's opinion on some of the questions that were bothering them. And the gentle cross-examination had been a success. Or, at least, their host's answers had been so striking that Tocqueville had made a careful record of the whole conversation. It went, apparently, as follows: [7]

'*I.* One of the drawbacks of American society in my opinion is its want of intellectual tone.

'*He.* I think as you do. Instead of making progress in this direction we are receding every day.

'*I.* To what do you attribute this?

'*He.* Principally to the inheritance law. I can still remember when I was young having seen this country peopled with rich proprietors who lived on their lands like English gentry, cultivated the mind, and followed certain traditions of thought and manners. High morals and distinction of mind then existed among a certain class of the nation. The law equalizing the portions [of the heirs] has constantly worked to destroy and redistribute the fortunes; those morals and those ideas became lost and are now finally disappearing. Lands change hands with unbelievable rapidity, no one has time to become attached to a place. Every one has to resort to practical work to sustain himself in the position his father occupied. Families almost all disappear at the second or third generation.

'*I.* Is there anything resembling the influence of landed proprietors? of *patronage*?

'*He.* No. A man only counts for what he himself is worth.

'*I.* How do the wealthy classes take such a state of affairs?

'*He.* They bear it like one of the necessities of existence to which one has to submit, since there is no way to prevent it.

'*I.* But is there some animosity between them and the people?

'*He.* None. All classes co-operated in the revolution. Since then the power of democracy has been so invincible that no one has undertaken to struggle against it. In general the people have no repugnance to electing the wealthiest and best educated.

'*I.* What strikes me in American society is the extreme equality in the social relationships. The plutocrat and the lowly worker shake hands in the street.

'*He.* The equality is very great, less however than a stranger supposes. The manners which strike you are often a formality which has no more meaning than the *very humble servant* at the end of letters. Here you must be polite toward everybody, since they all have political rights. In New-York there is much financial pride among the newly rich. We know, as they do everywhere, the aristocracy of money, if one can use the word aristocracy of a class that changes all the time and that has pretensions but no power.

'*I.* What kind of men generally fill public office?

'*He.* Ordinarily the offices are held by men whose capacity and character place them in the second rank. Public positions yield neither enough money nor enough consideration nor enough power to attract the energies of distinguished men. It was not so at the beginning of the Republic. To-day we no longer see great statesmen. One's energy and means are employed in other careers.'

'Mr. Livingston has been to Europe,' Tocqueville wound up his note. 'He belongs to a very old family and seems a man of *esprit*.'

All of which could hardly, it seemed to Tocqueville, be said of the average American. The young Frenchman had been doing a good deal of thinking about what he called the 'National Character of the Americans'; and now had finally singled out two important qualities or peculiarities that seemed to distinguish the citizens of the United States from all Europeans.

'A restless temper,' Tocqueville's diary note of 7 June began,[8] 'seems to me one of the distinctive traits of this people. . . . We have been told that the same man has often tried ten estates. He has appeared successively as merchant, lawyer, doctor, minister of the gospel. He has lived in twenty different places and nowhere found ties to detain him. And how should it be otherwise? In a word, here man has no settled habits, and the scene before his eyes prevents his adopting any. (1) Many have come from Europe, leaving their customs and traditions behind. (2) Even those long established in the country have preserved this difference. There are no American *mœurs* as yet. Each accepts what he likes from the group, but remains a law unto himself. Here the laws vary continuously, magistrates succeed each other, different systems of administration triumph one after the other, nature itself changes more rapidly than man. Through a singular inversion of the usual order of things, it's nature that appears to change, while man stays immovable. The same man has given his name to a wilderness that none before him had traversed, has seen the first forest tree fall and the first planter's house rise in the solitude, where a community came to group itself, a village grew, and to-day a vast city stretches. In the short space between death and birth he has been present at all these changes, and a thousand others have been able to do the same. In his youth he has lived among nations which no longer exist except in history. In his life-time rivers have changed their courses or diminished their flow, the very climate is other than he knew it, and all that is to him but the first step in a limitless career.

'However powerful and impetuous the flow of time here, imagination anticipates it and is already taking possession of a new universe. The tableau is not big enough for it. There is not a country in the world where man more confidently seizes the future, where he so proudly feels that his intelligence makes him master of the universe, that he can fashion it to his liking. It's an intellectual movement which can only be compared to that which led to the discovery of the new world three centuries ago; and one can really say that America has been discovered a second time. And let it not be supposed that such thoughts rise only in the minds of philosophers. They are as present to the artisan as to the speculator, to the farmer as to the city dweller. They inhere in all objects, they are a part of every sensation. They are palpable, visible, in a way felt; perceived by all the senses.

'Born often under another sky, placed in the middle of an always moving scene, himself driven by the irresistible torrent which draws all about him, the American has no time to tie himself to anything, he grows accustomed only to change, and ends by regarding it as the natural state of man. He feels the need of it, more, he loves it; for the instability, instead of meaning disaster to him, seems to give birth only to miracles all about him. (The idea of perfection, of a continuous and endless amelioration of social conditions, this idea is presented to him unceasingly, in all its aspects.)'

## XI

## FINDING A PHILOSOPHY—AND LOSING IT

WHEN the student of to-day analyses these documents, and stops to realize that they were penned by two untrained French youths more than a century ago, he cannot but be struck with admiration. For it is clear that, after only a few weeks of study and reflection, Tocqueville and Beaumont were stating a philosophy of sociology that was so far ahead of their times that its full implications for politics, social science, and history have only been realized within very recent years. At the same time, and in a few short pages, they were applying the principle thus discovered to the living body of American society with a skill and an insight that command attention. One follows their essay in descriptive anatomy with a growing awareness of the keenness of their intuition, however clumsy and confused this first expression of their thought.

Toqueville perhaps best defined their new attitude toward social and political science when, sitting in the branches of his tree on a hill above the wide Hudson, he wrote to his father; 'The more I see this country the more I admit myself penetrated with this truth: that there is nothing absolute in the theoretical value of political institutions, and that their efficiency depends almost always on the original circumstances and the social condition of the people to whom they are applied.'

It would have been hard for him to have said anything more revolutionary. For, in proposing that there was nothing absolute in the value of political institutions, he and Beaumont were repudiating the accepted political thought of their time. They were denying the doctrine, so fiercely believed in and so religiously propagated by their hosts the Americans, that republican self-government is always the best of all possible governments. They were going against the teachings of their fellow-liberals in France, who for generations had been looking toward England and preaching the gospel according to the British constitution. Of course they were repudiating the 'divine right' of conservative governments, as well. (Whether such governments were adapted to the needs of particular peoples was another matter.) In other words, the two young students professed to know of no absolute standards of government toward which all peoples should tend. Like the sociologists of a hundred years later, they were talking about the 'relativity of culture.' There could be no single standard of judgment; cultures and governments could only be compared.

Simultaneously, Tocqueville and Beaumont were unwittingly making a great advance in the study and writing of history; for they were emphatically denying that history is just past politics, and politics present history. Without apparently ever having read Hume or Robertson or Gibbon they were expanding the eighteenth-century theories of natural cause and climatic influence. They had but to go one step further to originate at least two of the modern schools of historical interpretation. They had but to say that political institutions were secondary to—as well as dependent upon—material and social forces, and they would have been suggesting the economic interpretation of history and the influence of the American frontier.

A glance at the foregoing extracts from Tocqueville's and Beaumont's manuscripts will clarify their theory and illustrate its implications.

The efficiency of political institutions depends, Tocqueville said, 'on the original circumstances and the social condition of the people to whom they are applied,'—that is, on the two factors of environment and tradition: on the material and social *surroundings* of the nation on the one hand, and on the social, political and spiritual *inheritance* of the people themselves on the other. Applying this principle to their analysis of the United States, Tocqueville and Beaumont were led to some startling ideas.

The situation or environment in which the Americans found themselves was, it appeared, a peculiarly happy one, for they had no enemies to fear and a wide unsettled continent of unlimited natural resources into which to expand. These circumstances had been fruitful of consequences for the ex-colonials, the consequences being (1) political, (2) industrial, and (3) social.

(1) Politically, the absence of powerful neighbours and the existence of unexploited lands and resources in the West had made a strong centralized government entirely unnecessary. With no outside enemies to resist and no large unsatisfied factions within to suppress, a highly

efficient, all-regulating central authority had not been required. In the United States, therefore, no such central authority had been created. And the Americans, making a virtue of ability, had even come to glory in their ungoverned condition. Of the facts and of the argument Tocqueville and Beaumont were equally certain. It had not needed a visit to Washington nor a profound study of the Bill of Rights in the Constitution to demonstrate how lightly governed the people really were. The very absence of a show of federal authority in New York, and the independent self-reliant attitude of the New Yorkers, had said perfectly plainly that American citizens were unfamiliar with the discouraging bureaucratic tyranny of a domineering national administration. No less certainly, the calmness of their interest in party politics and their preoccupation with business betrayed the relative unimportance of the former. In the United States office-holders were evidently neither so respected nor so influential as they were—say—in France; for Americans did not, like Frenchmen, all struggle bitterly against each other for official position and political power. The 'indifference in this matter is a great element for peace and order in a society,' Beaumont ventured to declare. In short, natural causes had led the Americans to organize themselves under a federal and republican government which was decentralized, weak, and actually of far smaller importance to them than they pretended.

Incidentally, the very satisfaction of the Americans with the federal and republican principle of their government demonstrated rather how well it was adapted to the necessities of their situation, than its absolute value under all circumstances. They had simply rationalized a fortunate situation into a political doctrine. Though Tocqueville and Beaumont had never read the writings of Thomas Jefferson, there were still many left to echo the famous philosopher's belief that that government is best which governs least. Given the American continent, this was perhaps so, Tocqueville and Beaumont were now ready to acknowledge. But only, given the American continent. In other words, the basic cause, the one factor that accounted for and explained the whole development, had been the American environment.

(2) The industrial or material consequences of this environment were, in their opinion, no less striking. The continent of unlimited space and natural resources, the land of opportunity, had naturally turned the European settlers to farming, industry, and trade, and directed western civilization into commercial channels. And the economic neces-

sities of their situation had held the diverse settlements together in one nation. American society, Tocqueville and Beaumont had noted, was 'composed of a thousand different elements newly brought together . . . English, French, German, Dutch,' with no single heritage, 'no common memories, no national roots.' But the interests of trade and the profits of association had cemented the conglomerate materials into one nation.

(3) At the same time, the alteration in the appearance of the country and the mastering of the forces of nature in the course of settlement and exploitation had accustomed the Americans to change and made them dissatisfied with standing still. 'The same man,' in Tocqueville's eloquent words, 'has given his name to a wilderness which none before him had traversed, has seen the first forest tree fall and the first planter's house rise in the solitude, where a community came to group itself, a village grew, and to-day a vast city stretches. In the short space between death and birth he has been present at all these changes.' Inevitably, such a life had its effect on American character. 'A restless temper seems to me one of the distinctive traits of this people,' Tocqueville concluded. His whole diary note on the 'National Character of the Americans' was a challenge to accepted thought, a frank proclamation of the influence of the American frontier.

Another consequence of the unusual environment had been to make the American a practising optimist. Fifty years of independence, of change, and of material success, had indoctrinated him with the philosophy of progress. He believed in progress and in himself in a way that a Frenchman did not. Tocqueville had caught the spirit of this attitude. There was not a country in the world where men were so confident of their future or certain of their ability to master the forces of nature, he wrote. 'It's an intellectual movement which can only be compared to that which led to the discovery of the new world three centuries ago; and one can really say that America has been discovered a second time.'

Finally, since the nature of the environment had stimulated the American to the achievement of practical success, he believed in practical success. He was a utilitarian, who estimated the value of things by their usefulness. In the business of life he was a materialist.

At this point Tocqueville and Beaumont turned away from the first factor of circumstance to the second, the American social heritage, for it was in the 'social condition' of the Americans that they thought they perceived the moralizing influences that had made of these restless and independent traders one harmonious, law-abiding people. If the frontier had made the Americans energetic and optimistic, and if a rich unsettled continent had provided them with a safe outlet for their energies and with wealth for the taking, what had kept them orderly and moral? Granting that economic necessity and the hope of prosperity (*l'intérêt*) was holding the divers racial strains together in one nation, what was keeping this untutored, self-governing nation from running amuck?

On examining the code of American society, Tocqueville and Beaumont thought they discovered the spiritual safeguards for which they were seeking in two traditions: the traditions of religion and education.

Education, they were given to understand, had been part of the Puritan program from the very beginning. Faith in its beneficence for all peoples and a specific belief in its indispensable usefulness in democracies were salient features of the American creed. Certainly the New Yorkers of their acquaintance seemed wholeheartedly convinced of the necessity of popular instruction, especially now that universal suffrage had come.

Almost in spite of themselves, the two young Frenchmen were considerably impressed. Without knowing the [disappointing] history of American education, or even investigating the present [dilapidated] * state of the schools, the future was plain. The United States would have universal public education. With American energy and enthusiasm, anything was possible if seriously undertaken; and there could be little doubt of the purpose of their New York hosts. Characteristically, almost every one seemed confident, too. Education would make democracy work. A people could educate itself to govern itself, New Yorkers thought, and 'never failed to smile' at the doubts of the young Frenchmen.

The latter, it is plain, could not but still harbour a few doubts. With their European training and their experience of the danger of educating the propertyless in a stratified and semi-rigid society, they naturally were not so easily or quickly won to a complete faith. As a consequence, in their study of the moralizing forces in American civi-

---

* Needless to say, had Tocqueville and Beaumont made an investigation in detail, they would have been astonished at the chaotic and backward conditions actually obtaining in American education. No matter how deplorable the gap between practice and theory, however, the future probabilities would remain the same.

lization, they were inclined to attach a greater importance to the influence of the second tradition: the tradition of religion.

The devout quiet in the churches, the deserted Sunday streets, the religious spirit obvious in the conduct and conversation of their acquaintances, deeply impressed the two friends. When, a month later at Auburn, a Presbyterian minister was to say to Tocqueville, 'I don't believe a people can be moral if it isn't religious, I therefore judge the maintenance of the religious spirit one of our greatest political interests,' * he was to put into words a truth of which his questioner had already become convinced. 'Mama and Bébé seemed to fear that I would fall into irreligious ways,' Tocqueville was soon to write his brother.[1] 'I assure you we are far from that. Never have I been so conscious of the influence of religion on the morals and the social and political state of a people as since my arrival in America. It is impossible not to recognize here the necessity of this motivator and regulator of human actions. That's an impression my companion himself is keenly conscious of.'

With the thought of the importance of religion, therefore, Tocqueville and Beaumont rounded out their first general analysis of the United States. Environment and custom, the frontier, the school and the church, these had been the great causative influences in the making of the country.

*

*   *

The implications of Tocqueville and Beaumont's reflections have been stressed, and their statement of a revolutionary interpretation of American civilization has been insisted on, because, with the development of their 'sociological theory' and its application to the United States, their study of American society in many respects reached its high point. Two days after returning to New York Tocqueville summed up his conclusions as to the material side of American civilization in a letter (given below) that well shows the value of the data they had

* See below, pp.214–215. It is amusing to compare Tocqueville's reactions with those of a fellow-countryman and forerunner in the same field of exploration. Brissot de Warville had adorned the title-page of his *Nouveau voyage dans les États-Unis . . . 1788* (3 vol.,1791) with the following declaration of faith: *On peut conquérir la liberté, sans mœurs; on ne peut la conserver, sans mœurs.* As for the United States, he wrote (p.xii), 'if the Americans have such pure morals, it's that nine tenths of them live scattered in the country,' i.e., farmers were moral, and therefore independent. 'The potato, there's the aliment of the man who wishes, and knows how to be free.' (p.xv, note.)

been collecting and the promise of their method. But thereafter came a change. The promise was never to be fulfilled. Tocqueville's latest French biographer sees in this letter the root and substance of the famous commentary he was to write.[2] But it was rather the germ of a book that never was written, of a sociological study of the United States that Tocqueville and Beaumont might have made had they gone on as they started. For actually, just at the moment when they had thus begun to lay the foundations for an analysis of the character of American society in the light of its heritage and environment, they turned aside to take up the second side of their study: American political institutions.

The pioneering investigators apparently reasoned as follows: If the efficiency of political institutions depended 'almost always on the original circumstances and the social condition of the people to whom they were applied,' and if they themselves, therefore, had occasionally to turn social scientists and analyse the character of American circumstances and traditions, the fact remained that American government was the important question for France, and political science was their own primary study. Granted that the Americans could well afford a weak kind of government, how had they come to have complete self-government, instead of a weak form of constitutional monarchy or of empire? What was it that had made their federal republic so democratic, so equalitarian in its operation? In short, what were the origins of American democracy?

Their conversation with Mr. Livingston, over the specially prepared ices, had started this train of thought in their minds. Mr. Livingston had called their attention to the change in the inheritance laws that had occurred during and after the American Revolution; and he had apparently given Tocqueville to understand that equal distribution of property between the heirs had been made compulsory. Hence a forced subdivision of land that had very soon reduced the Lords of the Manor and the old patroon families to the level of the small property-holders, with equality in government and society the inevitable consequence.

This was, according to our present way of thinking, a very partial view. And certainly it was an unfortunate thing for Tocqueville and Beaumont to have heard. Mr. Livingston was no doubt right in suggesting that the abolition of entail in New York had removed one of the greatest aids to the creation and perpetuation of a landed aristocracy along the banks of the Hudson. The repeal of primogeniture, too, had made it possible for the heirs of a man, who had neglected to make a will, to share equally in his property. Possibly Mr. Livingston had also said something about the wholesale confiscation of loyalist estates under Governor Clinton in 1779, which had thrown large areas of land, held up to then in an almost feudal proprietorship, open to purchase and settlement by independent, small farmers—with far-reaching consequences. In any case, as a descendant of a famous family, Mr. Livingston unquestionably knew whereof he spoke when he pointed out that the old aristocratic oligarchy, that so long had ruled the State, was now in 1831 almost gone; while even their manners and ways of life were fast disappearing. Thus far his remarks were intelligent and just.

The fact remains, however, that the causes of the social and political revolution, which he so soberly regretted, lay far deeper than any change in the laws of inheritance. The American trend toward complete democracy, it is now recognized, was much older than the war for independence. And the inheritance laws of that revolutionary period had been symptomatic of an increasing emphasis rather than causal in themselves; permissive, not compulsory; * the flowering of an old colonial tendency rather than the root of a new idea. In the case of primogeniture, furthermore, only the property of those dying intestate had been made subject to distribution among the heirs in a ratio prescribed by law. And the abolition of entail, whatever had been expected of it, had not in practice resulted in the complete disappearance of large estates. On the contrary, in 1831, a number of large holdings were being formed and exploited in the western part of the State; while along the Hudson more than one of the old manors still survived. The Patroon (Stephen Van Rensselaer) was even yet a man of power and great influence in the region of Albany. And the Livingstons themselves were still collecting rents from the Manor tenants. If the family had some time since lost the paternal influence over their lease-holders that of old they had been accustomed to exercise, the loss had probably been

* The relation of the land and inheritance laws to the extension of the suffrage, the growth of equality, and the decline of aristocracy in New York (and national) politics, is a thorny and as yet unsettled problem. Dixon Ryan Fox has described the symptoms of the change for the years 1800–1840 in his 'Decline of Aristocracy in the Politics of New York' (Columbia University, *Studies in History* . . . vol.86); but the writer has relied chiefly for his facts and interpretation on E. Wilder Spaulding, 'New York in the Critical Period, 1783–1789' (New York State Historical Association *Series,* 1932), the first part of which (pp.30–114) yields a stimulating insight into conditions along the Hudson and the politics of the landlords in the post-revolutionary decade.

due to long-standing dissatisfaction with the rental system, and more particularly to the substitution of the secret ballot for *viva voce* voting, just after the Revolution.

In short, whosesoever the fault, Tocqueville and Beaumont had been misled. If they had but doubted Mr. Livingston, if only their host had not been to Europe and spoken with such apparent authority, an investigation would have convinced the French visitors of their mistake. Evidence was readily available to prove to them that they had received a very one-sided interpretation of the American property laws, and a very inadequate explanation of the origins of social equality and political democracy in the United States. Unfortunately, they entertained no doubts and made no investigation. As a result, before the two friends were to discover their error, the thought about the influence of the inheritance laws had obtained such a grip on their minds that they could not shake it off. The conviction thus implanted by Mr. Livingston was therefore to warp their judgment, again and again to lead their interpretations astray, and finally one day to reappear in the pages of Tocqueville's book.*

\*

\*    \*

Since the reader will have no trouble in following this development, it is enough here to call attention once more to the origin of the misconception in an otherwise instructive conversation with a descendant of an old New York family, as the young Frenchmen were on their way back to the city. For the moment—if for the moment only—the thought remained on the surface of their minds, a new and as yet undigested concept, working no disturbance in the Sing Sing ideas and sociological interpretations in which they were still utterly absorbed, and which they were now anxious to put in order.

No sooner had they arrived at their New York lodgings, therefore, than Tocqueville sat down to organize, in essay form, all their hard-won conclusions as to the influence of the American environment. His ideas were in 'confusion' and he felt 'stunned' by all he had seen and

---

* See particularly Tocqueville's introductory discussion of the 'Social Conditions of the Anglo-Americans,' *Dém. en Am.*, I,48–58; and the note (G), at the end of his work, in which he makes the very tardy acknowledgment that the French inheritance laws were infinitely more equalitarian in their tendencies because, in spite of the abolition of primogeniture, the Americans were still allowed to distribute their property as they chose in their wills.

heard. But he owed his friend Chabrol, at Versailles, some sort of description of the United States as compensation for the long list of questions sent him three weeks before; and a long letter seemed the best means, both of paying his debt and of disentangling his thoughts. His topic, it appears, was the material civilization of the Americans, his method a skilful synthesizing of all the fragments of thought on the subject that he and Beaumont had painfully been collecting.

In more than one respect, then, this letter to Chabrol proves an interesting and illuminating document. To compare it, paragraph by paragraph, with the notes that they had taken during the preceding weeks, is to see where Tocqueville had obtained his ideas and how completely he had been able to make them his own. Furthermore, one has but to examine its conclusions to find the results of their sociological investigations to that date epitomized. This letter-essay, in other words, not only stands as Tocqueville and Beaumont's first comprehensive interpretation of American society, but it reveals as well, in striking fashion, the promise of their newly developed sociological method, unfortunately so soon to be abandoned.

'. . . Picture to yourself if you can, my dear friend,' wrote Tocqueville,[3] 'a society formed of all the nations of the earth: English, French, German . . . all people having different languages, beliefs, and opinions: in a word a society without roots, without memories, without prejudices, without habits, without common ideas, without national character; a hundred times happier than ours; more virtuous? I doubt it. There's the starting point. What serves as a tie to these diverse elements? What makes of them a people? *L'intérêt*. That's the secret. Individual *intérêt* which sticks through at each instant, *l'intérêt* which, moreover, comes out in the open and calls itself a social theory.

'We are a long way from the ancient republics, it must be admitted, and yet this people is republican and I don't doubt will long remain so. And the Republic is for it the best of governments.

'I can only explain this phenomenon in thinking that America finds itself, for the present, in a physical situation so happy that the interest of the individual is never opposed to the interest of the whole, which is certainly not the case in Europe.

'What is it that in general leads men to trouble the state? On one side, the desire to attain to power; on the other, the difficulty of creating for himself a happy existence by ordinary means.

'Here there is no public power and, to tell the truth, there is no need of it. The territorial boundaries are very limited; the states have no enemies, consequently no armies, no tax, no central government; the power of the executive is nothing, it gives neither money nor power. So long as things stay thus, who will torment his life to attain it?

'Now, on examining the other half of the proposition, you reach the same result. For if a career in politics is almost closed, a thousand, ten thousand others are open to human activity. The whole world here seems a malleable substance that man turns and fashions to his pleasure; an immense field, whose smallest part only has yet been traversed, is here open to industry. Not a man but may reasonably hope to gain the comforts of life; not one who does not know that with love of work his future is certain.

'Thus, in this happy country nothing draws the restless human spirit toward political passions; everything, on the contrary, draws it toward an activity that has nothing dangerous for the state. I wish that all those who, in the name of America, dream of a republic for France, might come to see for themselves what it is here.

'This last reason I have just given you, in my estimation fundamental, explains equally the only two salient characteristics which distinguish this people here: the industrial turn of mind, and the instability of character.

'Nothing is easier than to enrich oneself in America. Naturally the human spirit, which needs a dominating passion, ends by turning all its thoughts toward gain. It results from this that at first appearance this people seems to be a company of merchants gathered together for trade; and as one digs further into the national character of the Americans, one sees that they have sought the value of all things in this world only in the answer to this one question: how much money will it bring in?

'As for the instability of character, that crops up in a thousand places. An American takes up, leaves, goes back to ten occupations in this life; he is constantly changing his domicile and is continually forming new enterprises. Less than any other man in the world does he fear to compromise an acquired fortune, because he knows with what facility he can gain a new one.

'Besides, change seems to him the natural state of man; and how would it be otherwise? Everything about him is in constant movement: laws, opinions, public officials, fortunes, the very land here changes in appearance from day to day. In the midst of this universal movement which surrounds him, the American couldn't keep still.

'Therefore, one must not look here for the family spirit, nor those ancient traditions of honour and virtue which so eminently distinguish several of our old societies of Europe. A people which seems to live only to get rich would not know how to be virtuous, in the strict meaning of the word. But it is ordered. *Tous les riens qui tiennent à la richesse oisive,* it does not have. Its habits are regular. One has little or no time to sacrifice to women and seems to esteem them only as mothers of children and housekeepers. Morals are pure; that is undeniable. The European roué is absolutely unknown in America. The passion to get rich leads and dominates all the others.

'You perceive that all the things I tell you there, my dear friend, are only approximate statements. I have been here only a very short time, but I have already had a multitude of occasions to instruct myself. . . .

'. . . Take everything I've just told you as first impressions only, which I shall perhaps myself modify some day. . . .'

# XII

## JUNE IN NEW YORK

WHEN Tocqueville and Beaumont were rescued by their steamboat and brought down the Hudson to the foot of Manhattan, it was the evening of the seventh of June. The warm weather was setting in, the summer was beginning, and the fast-growing, river-mouth town was enjoying the pleasantest season of its year.

Established once more in their Broadway lodgings, the young commissioners proceeded to confine themselves to New York for the rest of the month of June. For three industrious weeks they studied the prisons and houses of detention in the immediate vicinity of the city. They inspected the new short term prison going up on Blackwell's Island, to which they had already been introduced by the Mayor and Aldermen;—also the Bridewell, and the hospital of Bellevue, institutions which for the most part represented the old order of carelessness and neglect in the handling of the city's charges, and for that reason seemed quite unsatisfactory.

Most of their days, however, were spent in the famous House of Refuge directed by the able N.C.Hart.* This was a reformatory or school for juvenile delinquents, one of the earliest of its kind in the world and one destined to exert a far-reaching influence. Founded by private philanthropy in New York six years before, it had immediately attracted attention as representing a new development in penal institutions. And such had been its prospects of success that it had already been copied in Boston and Philadelphia, and was exciting the interest of foreign governments, as well.

The House of Refuge was a prison, Tocqueville and Beaumont found, but a prison whose purpose was largely preventive. As its name implied, it was a place where those particularly subject to temptation or

---

* For an excellent account of the House of Refuge and of the zeal, firmness, and kindness of its superintendent, see *Du Syst. Pén.*, Pt.3, 'Des Maisons de Refuge,' pp.189ff. The keeper at Blackwell's Island was John O. Woodruff.

apt to be led astray could find asylum. Devised exclusively for the young, and especially designed to take care of the vagrants and juvenile delinquents of the crowded quarters, a class of actual and potential offenders that had suddenly begun to multiply alarmingly with the recent rapid growth of the city, it was being much used by the local magistrates. When sentenced to the Refuge, the boys and girls were housed separately, classified according to industry and improvement, stimulated to reform themselves by a scheme of rewards and punishments, and finally discharged when they were thought fit to return into society. The youthful inmates slept in solitary cells; but in the day time went to school together and were also taught trades by which it was hoped they would later be able to support themselves. On release they were apprenticed out, preferably to some farmer of the vicinity, and a docket was kept on their later records. If they relapsed into wrongdoing, they were resentenced; and they could be kept at the House until they came of age.

Tocqueville and Beaumont were much struck by the possibilities of this institution, as were also a number of the magistrates and practical penologists of the city. A conversation that the commissioners had toward the end of the month with the former district attorney Hugh Maxwell underlined one reason for their interest.*

'*I*. What do you think of the penitentiary regime?

'*He*. One must distinguish between penitentiaries, properly so called, and the house of refuge. As for the penitentiaries, I believe their discipline excellent in that it maintains admirable order in the prison and renders the labour of the inmates productive; but I do not believe in its power to alter a man's tendencies and habits. In general, I do not believe that the adult criminal reforms, however one goes about it. My opinion is that he comes out of our penitentiaries hardened. As for the houses of refuge, my way of thinking is different: I believe in the reform of the young delinquents and I think that the only means of diminishing the number of crimes in a country is to multiply and improve institutions of this sort. When I was *district attorney*, the number of young delinquents had become very alarming. It was increasing every day with frightful rapidity. Several persons conceived the idea of establishing a house of refuge to remedy this evil. This idea had un-

---

* 'Conversation with Mr. Maxwell, 27 June 1831. Mr. Maxwell was for ten years District Attorney. He is one of the founders of the House of Refuge and has the reputation of being very capable ("broad but very able man").' Toc. diary note (Non-Alph.I, TT). For Hugh Maxwell, see above, ch.VI.

believable difficulty in taking root in public opinion. Now success has made it popular. There are now five or six times fewer juvenile delinquents than five years ago.—

'*I*. Have you an authentic document which proves this last fact?

'*He*. No. But it is a matter of personal knowledge and I can affirm it. I think that the houses of refuge will multiply not only in the different States but in the districts of the same State. . . .

'Note. This belief in the ineffectiveness of the penitentiary system for moral reform has appeared up to now to be shared by a great number of other very capable men, among others by the practical men. . . .'

As a matter of fact, in one of his diaries the meticulous Tocqueville had made a table in three columns, wherein he could record the opinions of the persons whom he had consulted on the question whether penitentiaries worked the reform of the convicts incarcerated in them. In the first column—'those who believe in the moral reform of adult prisoners'—there were still no names. In the second—'those who do not believe in it'—appeared Maxwell, Rob. Wiltse, warden at Sing Sing, and the warden at Blackwell's Island; in the third—'those who doubt it'— were listed Duer, Hart of the House of Refuge, and Riker the Recorder. It was beginning to appear to the young commissioners that the American penitentiaries might after all be less effective in making the adult criminal penitent than they had supposed. In that case, the chief hope of the future might lie rather in such preventive and curative institutions as reformatories for juvenile delinquents.*

There was also a special reason for making a careful study of the New York House of Refuge. The French government was at the very moment engaged in building a prison along similar lines at Melun, and wanted full information on the New York experiment. So Tocqueville and Beaumont spent many days working in the reformatory out toward the country by the road called Bloomingdale. As their chief interest lay in the question whether the institution really did reform young delinquents or not, they had to find out if possible what the records had been of those who had been released from the Refuge,

* Speaking of the New York House of Refuge, Beaumont wrote: 'It's perhaps of all the prisons the only one whose advantages are not balanced by some disadvantages. I believe that there is little to be hoped from a man hardened in crime and inveterately corrupt. The same is not true of the evil tendencies which may be cured in childhood, when early combatted.' Bt. to his brother Achille, New-York, 18 June 1831 (BBlb, corrected from original in possession of Mme de Langavant of St. Malo.)

after having been educated and taught a trade within its walls. This was a tremendous task; for as usual no general statistics had been kept, and Tocqueville and Beaumont had to study the dockets on each of the more than 500 boys and girls who had gone through the House of Refuge since its founding.* This they did, 'in the sweat of our brow' as the conscientious Tocqueville put it.[1] Once Beaumont took a moment off to sketch the quiet and peaceful countryside, but day after day they kept steadily at their job until it was done.

\*

\* \*

In the late afternoons and evenings, however, the two friends were free and went out into society, where they were received even more warmly than before. Those who concerned themselves with philanthropy had read the newspaper reports of the careful and approving study the French Commissioners had made at Sing Sing, and were delighted to honour such intelligent guests. Society people, on the other hand, were pleased to entertain two attractive and presentable young foreigners who proved to be members of the nobility of France. And the substantial men of the community were evidently interested by the questions their visitors were asking about American law and government.†

So no sooner were Tocqueville and Beaumont back from their Sing Sing excursion than the round of introductions and invitations began all over again. At three o'clock each day, first of all, they returned from the House of Refuge to their lodgings for dinner. In this particular, as in many others, the two Frenchmen were now living the lives of New Yorkers. Beaumont was even drinking tea 'like an American. This change in habits was indispensable; wine is unobtainable except for its weight in gold,' he wrote.[2] Besides, the beverage seemed to agree with him. 'In spite of the heat which prostrates us . . . our health remains good, never have I felt better. . . .'

---

\* Tocqueville and Beaumont were able to get data on 364 of the 513 who had re-entered society from the House of Refuge in the period 1825–1829. Of these, some had relapsed, some inspired doubts, and 201 (about 55%) had 'abandoned a life of disorders and crimes for an honourable and regular existence.' *Du Syst. Pén.*, pp.215–216.

† This interest was natural, as Americans commonly believed that in the matter of government and political science, at least, the new world could teach the old a good deal. An apt statement of this conviction, with gratified reference to 'Commissioners from France,' appeared in the *New York Mercury for the Country* for 10 June 1831, three days after Tocqueville and Beaumont's return from Sing Sing.

'The company with whom we eat,' he continued, 'is always composed of attractive people. Evenings we make calls; and each day we make new acquaintances.' As a matter of fact, sought after as he and Tocqueville had been on first landing in the city, they were now enjoying what might almost be called a vogue. Hardly had they returned when·they were presented to the Rev. Jonathan Mayhew Wainwright, who, as Rector of Grace Church, was reputed one of the foremost pulpit orators of the day, a scholar, a lover of music, and a power in society.* Next they made the acquaintance of the celebrated jurist, Chancellor James Kent,† joint author of the Revised Statutes and fashioner of the equity jurisprudence of the State. The Chancellor was just in town for a day or two between excursions—though almost seventy he loved to spend his summers travelling about—but the moment sufficed. Apparently his friends saw to it that the distinguished foreigners were introduced to the lively, kind old man; and he, discovering in the course of the interview the interest of the young Frenchmen in American government, wished to help them in their investigation. For a few days later they received from the Chancellor a copy of his famous *Commentaries*, 'which he accompanied with a very kind letter.' How important his book was to be to them they would only discover later.

On 10 June, at some club in the city, they were introduced to the former Secretary of the Treasury, the third member of Jefferson's famous triumvirate, the distinguished Albert Gallatin.‡ That evening they attended a dance at James Gore King's. The night before they had been to a 'sort of ball' at the house of the old soldier of the Revolution, Col. Nicholas Fish,§ whose son Hamilton, three years younger than

---

* Wainwright, 1792–1854, named after his grandfather Jonathan Mayhew, was a graduate of Harvard, one of the founders of New York University, and a prolific writer. For many years secretary of the Protestant Episcopal House of Bishops, he became, in 1852, fifth Bishop of the Diocese of New York.

† 1763–1847. Kent, a graduate of Yale in 1781, had been one of the founders of Phi Beta Kappa, and was to deliver the Phi Beta Kappa address in September at the fiftieth reunion of his class at New Haven. After a long and distinguished career as Recorder, Chief Justice of the Supreme Court of New York, and law lecturer at Columbia, he had retired and was revising his *Commentaries,* the fruit of those lectures, for a new edition.

‡ Albert Gallatin, 1761–1849, statesman, diplomat, and financier, was living in New York. In 1831, as President of the National (later the Gallatin) Bank, he published *Considerations on the Currency and Banking System of the United States,* a pamphlet that was to be used by Biddle in the United States Bank campaign.

§ 1758–1833. After the Revolution, Lieut. Col. Fish had led a regiment out into the Ohio country. He had been a friend of Alexander Hamilton, and had become President of the New York Cincinnati, later also Alderman of the city.

Tocqueville, was to live to be Secretary of State after the Civil War. A few evenings later, they ventured out into the country for the first of two very amusing parties on the banks of the East River. And a week after that, Robert Emmet,* the well-known son of the famous Irish patriot Thomas Addis Emmet, asked them to dinner and introduced them to New York's most distinguished social leader, the courtly Philip Hone.

Altogether, Tocqueville and Beaumont were soon enjoying themselves hugely. With their studies in the morning, with the amusements and stimulating contacts that their social engagements afforded them in the evenings, the hours began to succeed each other like the slides of a 'magic lantern.' The best part of it all was that some of the men they met proved so interesting.

They finally found the Rev. John Power,† for instance. Father Power was the vicar of the Catholic Church in New York, an Irish-born priest and professor who had helped found the *Truthteller*, said to be the first Catholic weekly in the United States owned and managed by laymen. Naturally, Tocqueville and Beaumont were curious to know what he could tell them about Catholicism in America; and he rewarded them with the story of the growth of the Church, and fascinated them with tales of the French in Canada.

'There are 95,000‡ Catholics in New York,' Tocqueville recorded in his diary the second day after their return from Sing Sing. 'There weren't as many as 30 fifty years ago. Mr. Powers (grand vicar) says that their number increases daily through conversions. They already form the most numerous *communion*.

'What struck me most in Mr. Powers' conversation is: 1. That he appears to have no prejudice against republican institutions, 2. That he regards education as favourable to morality and religion.'

This was also the day, apparently, on which the French commissioners were presented to Jonathan Mayhew Wainright. To Tocqueville, Dr. Wainwright seemed 'a man of *esprit*. He has (a rare thing in America) the manners of the best company.'[3] Of Catholic sympathies, the two young men were instinctively reluctant to discuss religion with an

---

* 1792–1873. Born in Ireland, Emmet was himself to be noted for his championship of the Irish cause in 1848. He became Justice of the Superior Court of New York.

† 1792–1849. Power had come to New York in 1819 at the invitation of the trustees of St. Peter's, the mother church of the state, and was in 1831 'one of the leading personalities of the Church in the United States.' Thomas F. Meehan.

‡ Perhaps 15,000? The number recorded by Tocqueville seems excessive. Cf.p.69.

Anglican minister; but perhaps this courteous gentlemen might be able to give them some information on the relation of the Protestant churches to the republican government?

'Is there some point of conflict between religious ideas and political doctrines?' they asked.

'*A*. None. They are two entirely separate worlds in each of which one lives in peace.

'*Q*. From what comes this state of things?

'*A*. From the fact that the ministers of the different sects have never entered into politics and have never been or pretended to be a political power. We should think that we were injuring our standing if we were to concern ourselves with a political matter. A great number among us even abstain from voting at the elections; that's what I myself am always careful to do.'

In this manner the evenings passed. 'We continue,' wrote Beaumont,[4] 'to gather materials for our great work.' Bravely, in the midst of social diversions, the two popular young men pursued their studious investigations. Only so would they waste no time; only so could their presence in America be justified, they felt. That a reasonable person could spend whole months travelling for the mere idle pleasure of it had not occurred to them, apparently. At James Gore King's *soirée dansante,* however, they met two French noblemen who proclaimed that they were indeed travelling simply 'for their pleasure.' Yet these gentlemen professed to have a 'horror of society' and had deliberated all day as to whether or not they would come to Mr. King's! It was incomprehensible. The very idea of such folly appalled the serious-minded commissioners. 'I should like to know what purpose their voyage will serve,' Beaumont indignantly observed. 'They are going to traverse all the states one after the other. I conclude from that that they will know the roads and inns marvellously well. We wanted to make them talk. I don't believe there are more worthless fellows anywhere in the world.'

With Tocqueville and himself, fortunately, things were different. 'We are always questioning those whom we meet; we *squeeze* whoever falls in our hands.' That very morning, for example, they had pumped no less a personage than Albert Gallatin. 'He is a remarkable man,' Beaumont informed his family. 'Though I speak English like a true lion, I am not displeased to meet persons to whom I can speak French, because then I can explain myself even more clearly. Mr. Galatin [*sic*] knows French marvellously; we had some conversations with him which were very interesting and which have thrown much light on a number of points which were obscure for us.' Tocqueville, of course, had noted them down.*

'*He*. We have no villages in America, that is to say, no centres peopled by farmers. The landowner lives on his land, and the houses are all scattered through the countryside. What you call villages deserve rather the name of town, since the population is composed of merchants, artisans, and lawyers.

'*I*. I interrupt you at the last word. Lawyers are then very common with you?

'*He*. Much more so, I think, than in any part of Europe.

'*I*. What is their position in society and their character?

'*He*. One is explained by the other. Lawyers occupy the first ranks in society; they exert a great influence. It results that, instead of being restless disturbers as in Europe, they are rather conservative. But for the lawyers we should already have revised our civil laws, but they defend the abuses and obscurities by which they profit.

'*I*. Do they play a great role in the legislatures?

'*He*. They compose the majority of the members of those bodies; but it has been remarked that the most distinguished orators and above all the greatest statesmen were not lawyers.

'*I*. What is the composition, the position, and the character of your bench?

'*He*. The magistrates are all taken from among the lawyers and, but for the discipline of the court room, remain on a footing of equality with them. Our bench is extremely respected. Sustained only by public opinion, it has to make continual efforts to retain it. Its integrity is beyond question. I regard the bench, upheld as it is on every occasion by the body of lawyers, as the regulator of the irregular movements of our democracy, and the part that maintains the balance of the whole machine. Notice that, being able to refuse to apply an unconstitutional law, it is in a sense a political body.

'*I*. Is it true, as I am told, that morals are pure?

'*He*. Conjugal fidelity is admirably kept. It's not always thus with virtue before marriage. It very often happens in the country (not in

* Toc. diary note, New-York, 10 June 1831 (Non-Alph.I., TT, quoted, *O.C.*,VIII,230–231,234). The rather artificial flavour of this conversation, as quoted, demonstrates that it was not recorded on the spot but, as with some other interviews, recollected in tranquillity. In such cases Tocqueville's records were only approximately accurate.

our cities) that the extreme liberty enjoyed by the young people of both sexes has its drawbacks. The savage peoples who surround us carry disregard for chastity before marriage even further. They do not regard it as a moral obligation.'

'The same day at a club where I was,' Tocqueville concluded, 'it was argued that the Americans in penetrating into the interior of the continent would see their navy diminish. Mr. Gallatin estimated at about 60,000 the sailors who are at present navigating under the American flag. He added: As we have neither the English press gang, nor the *inscription maritime* of the French, I predict that at the first war we won't be able to find enough sailors to man twelve vessels.'

Here, indeed, was food for thought. 'We already have a pretty good provision of documents,' wrote Beaumont eight days later. '[But] when our day is ended, we are so tired that the mere thought of the repose that the night will bring us is a real happiness. Thus we sleep like the blessed on beds as hard as rock (a good bed is unheard of in America). . . .'

\*

\*    \*

Busy as Tocqueville and Beaumont were, June in New York was undeniably agreeable. And pleasantest of all were the long, warm evenings in the countryside. Many of their acquaintances were now leaving town for their summer places; but this customary exodus did not take them far. For the city was still so small that the country was right at hand.\* One had but to follow Third and Eighth Avenues northward, till they dwindled into lanes. Only the southern tip of Manhattan was, in effect, densely populated. The rest of the island, including the upland centre and much of both shores, was covered with farms. To the west, an occasional village looked across the Hudson toward the green heights of Weehawken. But on the other hand, along the banks of the

---

\* 'At present,' wrote Beaumont, 'the most fashionable and widespread diversion seems to be riding. No one owns his own horses. You rent them. Very handsome and good ones are to be found, and for seven or eight francs you can have them for half a day. Every evening in the city and the neighbouring countryside you meet a multitude of amazons and of cavaliers escorting them.

'There were in the house where I lodged in New-York two women, the very pretty daughters of the proprietor. On account of that they were forced to serve us from morning to evening, supplying linen, preparing the table, etc., etc. In the evening complete metamorphosis, change of scene. They donned very pretty riding costumes, put on fine feathered hats, rode through the city with an air of triumph; and at night on their return it was they who prepared us a glass of sugared water.' Bt. to his brother Jules, Albany, 4 July 1831 (BBlb).

East River, the pleasant countryside was divided into small farms and rural estates, each with its shore frontage, its trees, and its country-house looking out over the water. When, therefore, the hospitable New Yorkers asked the French commissioners to come to see them for the evening, it was possible to go, even if the rendezvous were for the family's country estate.

Tocqueville was much struck by these summer houses of his friends, first glimpsed from the deck of the steamboat which had brought them down from Newport a month before. 'There are no *châteaux* in this country,' he now wrote.[5] 'Fortunes are too limited; the division of the estate at the death of the father is too great to permit them to think of building anything very vast or very durable.* Instead of that, the Americans put up, at small expense, houses whose form and location are extremely picturesque and elegant. They set them in the most favourable spot, in sight of the sea when the thing is possible. Nothing is more gracious or fresh than these habitations. . . . All the rich families of this country have one, where they pass the summer. . . .'

On 15 June, their friend Peter Schermerhorn asked Tocqueville and Beaumont to dinner at his place, Belmont Farm, and they had their first opportunity to inspect one of these seashore establishments. The cottage, which they found charming, stood on the bank of the East River (at the foot of what is now 64th Street). Adjoining it, a tiny Greek temple housed the billiard room; and to the north and south stretched the farms of the well-to-do. The billiard room—an amusing illustration of how indiscriminate Americans could be in their use of the fashionable Greek Revival Style—caught Beaumont's eye, and he sketched it hastily in his album. 'Mr. Schermerhorn,' wrote Beaumont,[6] 'had got together all our old companions of the crossing (on the *Havre*). There we found Miss Edwards again; we jumped, danced, gamboled; only music was lacking. But to make up we had a little mechanical music box which served as orchestra the whole time.

'Our evening yesterday was even finer. Mr. Prime has just married off one of his daughters.† For this occasion he gave a charming party at his country place. He is a neighbour of Mr. Schermerhorn, but his house is without comparison more beautiful and agreeable than the latter's. There was a howling mob; all the fashionable women of New-

---

* Cf. comment on Livingston conversation, above, ch.XI.
† Mathilda Prime married Gerard Coster, 9 June 1831. It was with her that Beaumont had played his enjoyable flute and piano duets.

York were gathered there. That's the first time we've seen many women together. It seemed to me that several of them were very pretty. I am not certain because one alone occupied me during the evening. Miss Fulton * rightly passes for the most beautiful woman of New-York; it's to her that I continuously paid the tribute of my admiration. We took some charming walks by the light of the moon. . . . Alas! It's a hundred to one that I shall never see her again. She is the daughter of the famous Fulton, inventor of the *steamboat*. It seems that this great man did not apply his process to the creation of children, for she hasn't at all the air of being filled with vapour. . . .'

'They have here a good custom,' Tocqueville began his report of the occasion: [7] 'a few days after a young woman is married she has it announced that she wants to see all her friends and that she will be at home or at her parents' at such and such a day. That being known, every one who has any relations with the family comes, and all the wedding visits are made at once. It's to an assemblage of that kind that we have been. The reunion place is at two leagues from New-York, in a charming country house situated on the edge of the water. The evening was magnificent, the ocean breeze freshened the air, the lawn on which the house was placed sloped right down to the shore, great trees surrounded it on all sides. They have flies in this country which give as much light as glow worms. The trees are filled with these little animals, one would have said a million sparks leaping in the air. It was really a very extraordinary scene.

'The only thing overdone was the music. Don't take me for a barbarian. It was *de trop* because it resembled what one hears in the booths at a fair.† This people is, without contradiction, the most unhappily organized, *in matter of harmony*, that it's possible to imagine. If only they realized the truth. But they are a hundred leagues from suspecting it. We spend our life enduring howling of which one has no conception in the old world. What the young ladies who regale us with this *musique miaulante* ‡ affect most are its difficult passages. And I

---

* Probably Julia Fulton, who was a noted beauty.

† Philip Hone, one of the guests, described in his diary the 'brilliant company' and the 'beautiful grounds,' and mentioned 'leaving the bridal party dancing to the music of a fine Band [!].' Hone Diary, New York Historical Society.

‡ Thirty years later, when Beaumont came to publish some of Tocqueville's American letters, he thought it owing to diplomacy to tone down a few of his friend's more critical remarks. I am inclined to believe that Beaumont did not intentionally alter the meaning or character of Tocqueville's comments, in his editorial tampering, but in this instance the passage above quoted appeared as follows (*O.C.*,VII,30–31, italics

answer for it that if their object is to produce contrasting and discordant sounds, it would be impossible to succeed better and very hard to carry the thing any further. Aside from the fact that one is never sure that the air is finished, it ends always like a book whose last page has been torn out. At first I used to think the singer had stopped short, and I would always listen instead of applauding. You must think that I speak of this subject with a sort of indignation; but note that besides the displeasure which detestable music causes, however little one has heard of good, there is always the feeling of moral violence to which one is subjected in being forced to listen, willy-nilly, and to appear pleased as well.

'The other day, à propos of that, I had an amusing misadventure. We were at the house of a lady who set out to sing us a national song whose air and words are comical.* After the first couplet they laughed, myself with the rest of them. It was a way of applauding. The second couplet begins and I start thinking of something else, so profoundly that I soon am a total stranger to my surroundings. In the middle of my aerial voyage I hear the tune ending. I remember that one must laugh and I laugh, quite loudly even. At this explosion of gaiety every one looks at me, and I am confounded to learn that the comic song whose beginning I had heard had ended five minutes before, and that the song which had just put me into such a cheerful mood was the most plaintive, the most tearful, in short the most chromatic, of the whole American repertory. . . .'

Altogether, the good ladies of New York were a source of never-ending amusement and stupefaction to their courteous, if absent-minded guest.

---

mine): 'The only thing overdone was the music: don't take me for a barbarian. The Americans, *otherwise so well endowed*, are, in all that touches harmony, the most unhappily organized that it's possible to imagine. We spend our life *hearing harmonies* of which one has no conception in the old world, *unless it be in England among the ancestors of the Americans.* What are affected most by the young ladies who *draw from their throat this singular "melody" (au demeurant, de ravissantes, jeunes filles, presque toutes d'une beauté remarquable)* are the difficult passages; and I answer for it that if their object is to produce contrasting and discordant sounds, it would be impossible to succeed better. Note that one is never sure that the air is finished; it ends always like a book whose last page has been torn out. At first I used to think the singer had stopped short, and I would always listen instead of applauding. You must think that I speak of this subject with a sort of "indignation"; *that's because the other day there happened to me an adventure which, putting me apparently in the wrong, authorizes me, I think, to recriminate a little.* We were at the house. . . .'

* Yankee Doodle? This anecdote, among others, was quoted by Paul L. White in 'American Manners in 1830; de Tocqueville's letters and diary,' *Yale Review*, Oct.1922.

'We are living, dear sister, in the most singular country in the world,' Tocqueville had announced in his letter of 9 June. 'You have certainly heard it said that in England the married women lead a sedentary life, and that the young ladies enjoyed, on the contrary, a great liberty. Very well! Know that here they are as far [advanced] over England as England is over us. When a woman marries, it's as if she entered a convent, except however that it is not taken ill that she have children, and even many of them. Otherwise, it's the life of a nun; no more balls; hardly any more society; a husband as estimable as cold for all company; and that to the life eternal. I ventured the other day to ask one of these charming recluses just how, exactly, a wife could pass her time in America. She answered me, with great *sang-froid*: in admiring her husband. I'm very sorry: but that's the literal translation of the English. I tell you this so that, should you happen to be bored at home, you may know what you have to do.

'So much for the married women: you will comprehend the young ladies even less. Imagine the daughters of the first families, slim and elegant, from one o'clock in the afternoon on, tripping all the streets of New-York, doing their shopping, riding horseback, without father or mother, uncle or aunt, without even a servant. You are not at the end. A young man—and this has already happened to us several times—encounters on his path one of these *travellers*. If one is already acquainted, one stops, one chats in quite friendly fashion a quarter of an hour at the corner curb-stone, and at the end of the conversation the young lady invites you to come to see her and indicates the hour at which you will find her at home. At the said hour, in effect, [one goes calling on] Mademoiselle So-and-so, and one finds her often alone in her father's parlour, of which she does you the honours. Everybody tells us that this order of things has none of the inconveniences that one might foresee. Perhaps. If, as they also assure us, the *tête-à-tête* is ordinarily spent in discussing the value of wool and the price of cotton. We often see in society what are called *accordés*. They are a young man and a young woman who are to be married in several months and who are constantly together meanwhile, paying court to each other most respectfully. The fact is, there is not the least question here of playing the butterfly. *Peste!* One would speedily get burnt at the candle. These people here are very straightforward. They take words in the most literal meaning; and if one did not turn one's tongue seven times before speaking, as counsels the sage, one might find oneself much embarrassed. . . .'

\*

\*   \*

'Yesterday,' wrote Tocqueville, 'we were at the Court of Assizes to see a famous thief tried.' It was 20 June, and Tocqueville had something he thought would interest his magistrate friend Chabrol.[8] 'The District Attorney had invited us to come and had saved seats for us; it was the finest affair of the session. Unfortunately the accused had not had time to have an important witness summoned: great disappointment on the part of the Attorney and the Court, who wished to show us a fine specimen of criminal trial. They tried to find a thousand difficulties for the poor devil to oblige him to allow himself to be judged immediately. I believed that for the love of us they would condemn him without a hearing. They were forced, however, at the end of an hour and a quarter to put his trial over to the next session.

'You see that men on this side of the Atlantic resemble closely enough those on our side.

'The big affair falling through, they hurried over three or four small ones in our presence. The foundation is the same as in France, but the formalities are much simpler. They draw the jurors for all the trials on the same day, unless the accused challenges some of them. There is neither *acute d'accusation* nor *examen*; everything greatly resembles the *Police Correctionnelle*. The attorney and the public prosecutor have exactly the same instincts as in France. It is indeed two causes that they defend, of impartiality not a word. The President (presiding officer) sums up in a few words, expresses his opinion, counsels the jurors. The latter deliberate without going into a council chamber, and in two minutes the man is condemned. The judgment is only pronounced at the end of the session.

'There is good and bad in these forms. I think that ours are better for big affairs, but I am convinced that if trial by jury is ever applied to small cases, which cannot fail to happen sooner or later, we shall be forced to do like the Americans.

'I hope, however, that we shall never adopt the carelessness that reigns here. The public prosecutor speaks with his hands in his pockets, the Court chews, and the lawyer picks his teeth while interrogating witnesses.

'I doubt whether these ways of acting are absolutely inherent in the good administration of justice. Moreover it is evident that the magistrates and the bar form one and the same thing. Properly speaking, there is no *Magistrature*, only lawyer-magistrates. This state of affairs does not produce, according to what I believe I see, the bad results which we naturally expect from it in France. In general, the position of lawyers here is quite different from what you might imagine it.

'I have no time to tell you why. Let it suffice you to-day to know that they form the *résistance*, in other words the *stationary* class.* I shall throw light on this another time. Adieu. . . .'

Of 'the great dinner at Mr. Emmet's' to which Beaumont had looked forward so uneasily,† his own letters failed to say the first word. Yet the solemn affair, after one postponement, was held on the twenty-third, and Tocqueville and Beaumont were among the guests. As the somewhat sensitive commissioners had, after their experience at the Mayor's dinner, highly resolved to remain silent in the event of '*republican healths*,' it is perhaps a fair inference that no such toasts were proposed and that the whole banquet passed off very smoothly.

Apparently the conservative New York lawyers respected their '*political line*' with exemplary tact, and even agreed that self-government would not be suitable for a powerful nation like the French. For a note of pleased surprise could be detected in their next letters. Writing a week after the dinner, Beaumont threw out a significant remark:[9] 'The country where I am, altogether republican though it is, is much more *sage* than it is thought in the matter of monarchy. All the men I meet proclaim with all their might that a republic would not in the least suit France.' Tocqueville had the same report to make, though he substituted 'great nation' for the word 'France,' thereby broadening the significance of the admission. 'The Americans,' he said, 'I mean the enlightened people, have more reasonable opinions than I thought about the state of France. I assure you that, though republicans at home, they do not believe any more than we do that a republic can *s'établir chez une grande nation*.'[10] . . . 'Opinion on Lafayette is also much more divided than I thought. In general the upper classes judge him as we do. . . .'[11]

* Cf. Gallatin conversation, above, p.139.
† He was afraid a toast to Lafayette would be offered.

Was it New York's great diarist, Philip Hone,* who at the banquet told Tocqueville and Beaumont what, secretly, they most wanted to hear? Neither of the two mentioned any names. But this much was certain. The wealthy and cultivated gentleman, who for years had been a leader in all the social activities of the city, and entertained many well-known foreigners in his home with its fine library, was one of the guests at the dinner and there met both the French commissioners. For in his famous diary for that day he made the following entry:

'Thursday June 23d. Dined with Mr. Robert Emmet where I met Messrs. Tocqueville and Bourmont [*sic*] Commissioners sent out by the french Government to examine the State of our Prisons and Prison discipline. the latter Gentleman with whom I had most conversation is intelligent, ardent and inquisitive. and well calculated, I think, for the business in which he is employed. I must see more of them.'

Unfortunately, Beaumont and Tocqueville were leaving town within the week, to be gone seven months, so Hone apparently saw no more of them until early the next year. At the moment of the Emmet dinner, as a matter of fact, the commissioners were rapidly finishing their examination of the House of Refuge and were just getting ready to go to Auburn prison in western New York for their next penitentiary visit—after which they intended to study the other Auburn-style prisons in Massachusetts and Connecticut.

Before following the penitentiary reform to New England, however, the young Frenchmen were also planning to visit Niagara Falls† and Canada. 'Canada piques our curiosity keenly,' Tocqueville wrote to his mother,[12] 'the French nation has kept itself intact there. They have the customs and language of the century of Louis XIV. It's Mr. Powers, the grand vicar of New-York of whom I think I spoke, who above all has counselled us this trip. He has lived a long time in Canada and has offered us letters of introduction for that country.'

Apparently Mr. Power had also warned Tocqueville about the fevers that one sometimes caught in the Ohio valley in summer. Lured

---

* Of German-French ancestry, Philip Hone (1780–1851) had made a fortune in the auction business, which enabled him to retire at forty and devote himself to literary and philanthropic pursuits. After touring Europe, he had built up a library and an art collection. He was a patron of the stage, the friend of Webster, Clay, Adams, and Seward, and a trustee of Columbia College. He had served as mayor with great distinction in 1825, the year of Lafayette's visit to the city, and of the Erie Canal celebration.

† 'We shall not have been in America without seeing the thing they say is the most extraordinary in the whole country.' Beaumont.

therefore by curiosity, and guided by the medical advice of a priest, Tocqueville and Beaumont were anxious to be off. Especially as they had now received a number of reassuring letters from home and were therefore less homesick than before.[13] Having taken some time to say good-bye to their New York friends, they were also looking forward to a vacation from social obligations.

The tour to Niagara and Canada 'will be a little pleasure tour which will recompense us for the boredom of the towns,' was Beaumont's explanation. 'After having suffered all that civilization can produce that is most fatiguing and boring, we shall find a certain charm in this excursion into lands which are still wild and where nature has preserved her primitive beauty. I am tired of men, and above all of Americans. I have kept too far away from American women to know if they are attractive, so it's with a true feeling of happiness that I leave them and their cities behind to go into parts where I have many *chances* of not meeting them. I say chances because I am not certain of my fact. Niagara draws a great crowd, especially at this season, and there are a few of our *devoted friends* who threaten to rejoin us. We should even be certain to find ourselves among them if we hadn't taken the course of misleading them as to our route. . . .'

# XIII

## TAKING STOCK OF IMPRESSIONS

BEAUMONT exaggerated. The two lionized commissioners were not quite so world-weary as he pretended.

For no sooner had they embarked on the little sloop which was to carry them as far as Yonkers on their way to Albany: in fact no sooner had they shaken off the heat and feverishness of New York and begun to enjoy the rest and change which were after all what they needed, than they returned to their consideration of the United States. The two long essays that they promptly composed were the proof. Both were written within five days of the moment when they lost Manhattan Island in the distance.

Tocqueville began his long letter-essay almost at once and completed it in the intervals of their journey to Albany, a journey whose natural distractions were enhanced by their first exciting experience with an American steamboat and a wild ride up the Hudson in the dark. And as for the disenchanted Beaumont, he wrote his sketch but two or three days after, while waiting for the Fourth of July parade and celebration in Albany to start. Before the colours should fade and the freshness of the impression be blurred, each was anxious to organize their experiences on shipboard and in New York into an intelligible composition. Only New York implied so much, behind the steepled town the American scene opened so wide and swept so far into the distance, that it was impossible for the young observers to comprehend the whole field of vision at a glance. Beaumont therefore chose to sketch the tableau of the business habits and social customs of the Americans, while Tocqueville looked deeper and sought to grasp the inner feelings of the people, the religious and political movement of their thought.

A word about Beaumont's essay, first.

He made it into a sort of tableau of American manners.[1] The industry of New Yorkers, and their feverish pursuit after money, received under his hand a fresh and pungent analysis. Next in order, if not indeed first in importance, came the topic: American women. How early they rose in the mornings, how nonchalantly they went promenading all alone, how white they were of skin, and how attentive to strangers: all these beguiling and interesting details were made to contribute their colours to his sketch. Finally, he came to the subject of amusements.

New Yorkers, it was now his opinion, were too busy for diversions; and the few they had were of small importance. In the winter, society had its balls. In the summer, one went cantering in the countryside. 'Shows are a small resource for society. It's not the fashion to go there. The theatres are bad, and in none is passable music to be heard.'

'The Fine Arts are in their infancy here. Nature has refused them a constitution adapted to music. You ask me if there is a museum in New-York? No doubt, there are even several. But do you know what is to be seen there? The magic lantern and some stuffed birds. Toqueville and I laughed like the blessed when, seeing *American Museum** written on a building and having gone in, we found things like that in it, instead of the paintings we expected to see.

'There are several public libraries; but they do not contain more than 20,000 volumes, and one sees no one there. Moreover, literature is little cultivated; every one learns to read, to write, and to calculate. In a word, they want enough knowledge to do business, but as for *belles lettres*, they hardly bother about them. We are told that in Boston and Philadelphia it is different. We shall see.'

There was one literature, of course, that even the servants all read: the newspaper. But these sheets, huge as they were, seemed to be devoted almost entirely to advertisements. 'In everything and for everything one sees the commercial and mercantile spirit dominate,' was Beaumont's unflattering conclusion.

\*

\* \*

* This museum, housed in a five-story marble building standing in Broadway opposite St. Paul's Church, was one of the noted institutions of the city. It contained four 'halls' or showrooms, the first exhibiting stuffed birds; the second, quadrupeds; and 'the best collection of Fish ever known'; the third, 'miscellaneous curiosities'; and the fourth, a 'Grand Cosmorama, which contains Views of most of the principal cities in the world.' Peale's Museum, opposite the Park, was at the moment specializing in wax figures, and the 'Canadian Giant,' said to be 6' 4½" and to weigh 619 lbs. Advs. in *New-York Evening Post*, 24 May 1831.

It was plain that Tocqueville and Beaumont had a low opinion of the literary and artistic capacity of the New Yorkers. The museums were a mockery, the theatres not worth visiting, and their literary productions were such that even the New Yorkers themselves seemed to hold a low opinion of them. Boston and Philadelphia might be more cultivated, but Beaumont was evidently sceptical. 'We shall see.'

These views were interesting as conclusions independently arrived at. At the same time, even the more intelligent and modest of Beaumont's New York friends would have found them deeply disappointing, for they merely duplicated the superficial criticisms of the other European travellers and writers of the day, when so much more might have been said.*

Far more original, and of an altogether different character, were Tocqueville's newly-developed theories. Ten days before leaving New York he had written to his brother Édouard,[2] 'We have not yet written a line but we are amassing some magnificent materials and if we should discover in ourselves the talent to put them to use, *nous ferions incontestablement quelquechose de neuf.*'

The 'magnificent materials' referred to were of course the experiences of their last weeks in New York and the whole stuff of their thought since landing, re-examined and reappraised. To Tocqueville, evidently, two aspects of American civilization stood out in importance beyond all the others. The first was the religious organization and attitude of these law-abiding republicans. Deprived since boyhood of the comfort of a firm and unquestioning faith, he had always felt a burning concern in religious questions, and had therefore given a special attention to the problem as it presented itself in the United States—with the result that he was becoming conscious of what seemed to him a most curious and interesting situation. In particular, a visit that he and Beaumont had made to a Unitarian service in New York the preceding Sunday had so astonished them, and their conversations with the optimistic Catholic priest John Power had so stimulated their imaginations, that new thoughts on the religious peculiarities of the

* After writing out a detailed criticism and explanation of the commissioners' opinion, I have decided to abandon Tocqueville and Beaumont, in this particular, to the mercies of historians of American literature. Whatever the mitigating circumstances that might be mentioned in their defence, the plain fact of the matter is that Tocqueville and Beaumont were ignorant. And they were ignorant because they were not interested in American literature. In Tocqueville's fourteen diaries there is only one (undated) note, listing as 'Living American authors: Verplank—Paulding—Hall—Stone—Neal—Barker—Willis—Miss Sedgwick.'

Americans were now seething in their heads and demanding expression. To this topic, therefore, would be devoted a considerable portion of Tocqueville's essay.

His other absorbing interest, of course, was the problem of democratic self-government. And here again their continuing studies, and such experiences as their day in criminal court, had now so matured their reflections, that they were fast achieving an understanding of democratic practice and a very nice appreciation of American political philosophy.

As a result, while seeking to give expression to their new concept or religious and political beliefs in the United States, Tocqueville found himself being forced to revise his whole estimate of civil society. After seven weeks in New York, it seemed, his opinion of Americans was not at all what it had been on first landing. The full significance of this change of heart would not appear until later. But already a startling light was beginning to play on his greatest problem: the problem of what to say in his book. Having reconsidered America, Tocqueville saw in a flash what his great thesis was to be.

### TOCQUEVILLE'S ESSAY ON AMERICAN GOVERNMENT AND RELIGION *

'. . . You ask me in your last letter if there are any *croyances* here? I don't know exactly what meaning you attach to that word. What strikes me is that the immense majority of spirits join together in certain *common opinions*. Up to now that's what I envy America most.

'Thus, 1st, I haven't yet been able to surprise in the conversation of anyone, no matter to what rank he belongs, the thought that the republic is not the best possible government, and that the people haven't the right to give themselves the government that pleases them. The great majority understand republican principles in the most democratic sense. With a few a certain aristocratic tendency, which I shall try to explain to you later on, shows through perceptibly. But that the republican is a good form of government, that it is natural to human societies, those are things no one seems to doubt, priests, magistrates, merchants, artisans. It's an opinion so general and so little disputed, even in a country where the freedom of speech is unlimited, that one might almost call it a faith.

* Extracted from letter, Toc. to L. de Kergolay, Yonkers, 29 June 1831, 20 miles from New-York (YT, quoted in part, *O.C.*,V,312–319). By this time Tocqueville and Kergolay were again on terms of friendship.

'There is a second idea which seems to have the same character. The immense majority have *faith* in the wisdom and good sense of human kind, faith in the doctrine of human perfectibility. That's another thought that finds few or no denials. That the majority may be mistaken once, no one denies; but they think that necessarily in the long run it will be right; that it is not only the sole judge of its interests, but also the surest and most infallible judge.

'The consequence of this idea is that enlightenment ought to be spread in profusion among the people, that one cannot enlighten it too much. You know how many times in France we (we and a thousand others) have tormented ourselves to know whether it was to be desired or to be feared that instruction should penetrate into all ranks of society. This question, so hard for France to solve, doesn't seem even to have presented itself to minds here. A hundred times already it's happened to me to propose it to the most thoughtful men; I saw by the positive way in which they decided it that they had never stopped to consider it, and that the very statement of it seemed to them in a way shocking and absurd. Education, said they, is the only guarantee we have against the aberrations of the masses.

'There, my dear frined, are what I should call the faiths of this country. They honestly believe in the excellence of the government which rules them; they believe in the wisdom of the masses provided they are enlightened, and don't seem to suspect that there is a certain instruction which can never be the lot of the masses and which may nevertheless be necessary to govern a state.

'As for what we generally understand as faiths, such as customs, ancient traditions, the strength of memories, up to the present I don't see a trace of them. I even doubt whether religious opinions have as much influence as one at first thinks. The religious state of this people is perhaps the most curious thing to examine here. I shall try to tell you what I know of it when I resume my letter, which I must interrupt perhaps for several days.

*Calwell* [?], *45 miles from New-York*

'My mind has been so aroused since this morning by the beginning of my letter that I feel the need of continuing it, without however knowing exactly what I am going to say.

'I was speaking of religion. Sunday is rigorously observed. I have seen streets barred off before churches during divine service; the law commands these things imperiously, and public opinion, much stronger than the law, obliges every one to show himself at church and to abstain from all diversion. And yet, either I am much mistaken or there is a great depth of doubt and indifference hidden under these external forms. No political passion mixes in with irreligion as with us, but for all that religion has no more power. It's a very strong impulsion which was given in former times and which is now diminishing every day. Faith is evidently inert. Go into the churches (I mean the Protestant ones) you will hear morality preached, of dogma not a word. Nothing which can at all shock the neighbour; nothing which can arouse the idea of dissent. The abstractions of dogma, the discussions especially appropriate to a religious doctrine, that's however what the human spirit loves to plunge into when a belief has seized it strongly. Of this character were the Americans themselves in former times.

'This pretended toleration, which, in my opinion, is nothing else than good round indifference, is pushed so far that in the public institutions such as the prisons, the houses of education for juvenile delinquents, etc. . . . seven or eight different ministers in succession come to preach to the same congregation. But, said I, how do these men and children, who are communicants of one sect, like hearing the minister of another? The infallible response is this: The different preachers, treating only the common grounds of morality, cannot do each other any harm.

'Besides, it's evident that here, generally speaking, religion does not profoundly stir the souls. In France those who believe manifest this belief by sacrifices of time, of effort, of fortune. One feels they are acting under the sway of a passion which dominates them and whose agents they have become. It's true that at their side is a sort of brute who has a horror of the very name of religion and who does not even very easily discern the good from the bad. Neither one nor the other of these classes seems to exist here in the Protestant mass. One follows a religion as our fathers took medicine in the month of May. If it doesn't do any good, one seems to say, at least it can do no harm.

'And besides, it is proper to conform to the common rule. In the last analysis, how should it be otherwise? The reformers of the sixteenth century made in the matter of religion the same compromise that one is trying to make to-day in the matter of politics. They said: such and such a principle is bad up to a given result; from there on we find it good, and you must find it good with us, and vice versa. But there have been some ardent and logical spirits who have not been able to suffer being stopped half way. The result has been that an immense field has been opened to the mind of man, and he has profited from it, I assure you.

'It's incredible to see the infinite number of subdivisions into which the sects in America have split. Like circles traced successively about the same point, each new one a little farther away than the next. The Catholic faith is the immovable point from which each new sect separates a little further, while nearing pure Deism. You realize that such a spectacle can't fail to throw the mind of a thinking Protestant into inextricable doubt; and that's the emotion that I think I see in visible control at the bottom of nearly every soul. It seems clear to me that the reformed religion is a sort of compromise, a kind of *representative* Monarchy, a kind of religion that may well fill an epoch, serve as transition from one state to another, but which could never constitute a definitive state, and which is nearing its end.

'By what will it be replaced? Here, doubt begins for me. This country presents for the solution of that question, which is moreover a question of all mankind, some very precious premises. The religious and anti-religious instincts which can exist in man are developing here in perfect liberty. I should like to have you witness this curious show. You would find the struggle of the two principles there which divide the political world elsewhere. Protestants of all communions, Anglicans, Lutherans, Calvinists, Presbyterians, Anabaptists, Quakers, and a hundred other Christian sects, there's the basis of the population. A practising but indifferent population, which lives from day to day, accustoms itself to surroundings that are hardly satisfying but tranquil, and whose *appearances* are satisfied. Those people live and die *dans des à peu près*, without ever bothering to get to the bottom of things. They no longer replenish themselves.

'Above them are a handful of Catholics, taking advantage of the tolerance of their former adversaries, but still at bottom as intolerant as they have ever been, as intolerant in a word as people who believe. For them, there is no truth except in a single point, a line on this or that side of the point, eternal damnation. They live in the midst of civil society, but they forbid themselves all relations with the religious societies which surround them. I even suspect that their dogma on the liberty of conscience is about the same as in Europe; and I am not sure that they would not persecute if they found themselves the strongest. These people are in general poor, but full of zeal, their priests are entirely devoted to the cult of sacrifice which they have embraced; they are not business men of religion, like the Protestant ministers.*

'The Catholics are increasing in numbers in a prodigious way. Many arriving Europeans come to recruit them; but the conversions are numerous. New England, the basin of the Mississip[p]i begin to be filled with them. It is evident that all the naturally religious minds among the Protestants, the grave and proud souls whom the Protestant vogue wearies and who at the same time deeply feel the need of religion, are abandoning the search for truth in despair and throwing themselves again under the sway of *authority*. Their reason is a burden which weighs on them and which they sacrifice with joy. They become Catholics.

'Catholicism also appeals vividly to the senses and the soul and suits the masses better than the reformed religion; thus the majority of the converts belong to the working classes of society. There's one end of the chain. We are now going to pass to the other end.

'On the confines of Protestantism is a sect which is Christian only in name, the *Unitarians*. Among the Unitarians, that is to say among those who deny the Trinity and recognize only one God, there are some who see in Jesus Christ only an angel, others a prophet, others, lastly, a philosopher like Socrates. They are pure Deists. They speak of the Bible because they do not wish to shock public opinion, still entirely *Christian*, too deeply. They have a service Sundays; I was there.† There they read verses of Dryden or other English poets on the existence of God and the immortality of the soul. A discourse is made on some point of morality, and it's done. This sect gains proselytes in about the same proportion as Catholicism, but it converts in the high ranks of society. Like Catholicism it gains from the losses of Protestantism.

'It's evident that the Protestants whose minds are cold and logical, the *argumentative* classes, the men whose habits are intellectual and scientific, are grasping the occasion to embrace an entirely philosophic faith which allows them to make almost public profession of pure Deism. Otherwise this sect does not resemble in any way the St.

---

* 'The evangelical mission appears to us to be here an industrial enterprise rather than an affair of zeal and conviction. Mr. Cartwright told us that it was almost impossible to have chaplains of talent in the penitentiaries because they were paid too little.' Toc. diary, Sing-Sing, 30 May 1831 (TT).
† Beaumont, who had also attended the service, shared Tocqueville's views. His letter to his father of 29 June (BBlb) was full of the subject.

Simonians of France. Aside from the point of departure, which is entirely different, the Unitarians mix nothing gross, nothing clownish with their doctrine and their cult. On the contrary, they aim so far as possible to resemble on the surface the Christian sects. So no kind of ridicule attaches to them; no party spirit pushes them or arrests them. Their ways are naturally grave, and their forms simple.

'Thus, you see, Protestantism, mixture of authority and reason, is attacked at the same time by the two absolutes, *reason* and *authority*.* This spectacle is to be glimpsed a little everywhere by him who is willing to look; but here it hits you between the eyes; because in America no power, no opinion interferes with the progress of human thought and passions. In this respect they follow their natural inclinations.

'At a time which does not seem to me very far off I am convinced that the two extremes will find themselves face to face. What will then be the final outcome? Here I lose myself in conjecture and no longer see the way marked.

'Will Deism ever be able to satisfy all classes, especially those which most need the rein of religion? I can't persuade myself of that. I admit that what I see here makes me more disposed than I was before to believe that what one calls Natural Religion may suffice the higher classes of society, provided that the belief in the two or three great truths that it teaches is real and some sort of external cult is added, visibly to unite men in the public profession of those truths. But either the people will become other than they have been and still are in all parts of the world, or they will see in this natural religion only the absence of all belief in the other life and will fall headlong into the single doctrine of *intérêt*.

'But to get back to the actual situation of the United States, you mustn't give what I have just said too absolute an interpretation. I have spoken of mental disposition and not of accomplished facts. It's obvious there still remains here a greater foundation of Christianity than in any other country of the world to my knowledge, and I don't doubt but that this disposition still influences the political regime. It gives a moral and orderly turn to ideas, it arrests the wanderings of the innovating spirit; especially does it make very rare that moral disposition, so com-

---

* No apology is in order for so long a quotation on the topic: religion. Whatever Tocqueville's prejudices, few more penetrating (or prophetic) criticisms of American Protestantism from the authoritarian point of view will be found in print.

mon with us, to launch oneself through all obstacles, *per fas et nefas,* toward the chosen goal.

'It is certain that a party, however anxious to obtain a result, would still think itself obliged to attain it only by means which would have an appearance of morality and would not openly shock the religious beliefs, always more or less moral, even when they are false.

'Don't you marvel at the smallness of our nature? One religion has a great influence over the desires, it dominates the imagination, it inspires real and profound beliefs; but it divides the human race into blessed and damned, creates divisions on earth which should exist only in the other life, breeds intolerance and fanaticism. The other preaches toleration, appeals to the reason, makes of reason its symbol; it obtains no power, it is an inert thing, without influence and almost without life.

'That's enough on this subject, toward which my imagination draws me continuously and which would end by making me mad if I plumbed it often. Besides, I seem to have a lot of other things to tell you.

'Do you know what in the way of politics strikes me most in this country? The effects of the inheritance laws. . . .' And Tocqueville went into his peculiar but by now firmly rooted convictions as to the origins of American equalitarianism.* To Kergolay he insisted that he was only repeating 'the recitals of the Americans themselves'; but actually he was beginning to build a sort of mythology around the repeal of primogeniture and entail in the Revolutionary period. 'A change that partook of the magical resulted. The domains split up and passed into other hands, the family traditions disappeared, the aristocratic spirit which had distinguished the early times of the republic was replaced by an irresistible tendency toward equality, against which one can no longer have the least hope of struggling. . . .'

'I have heard it said in Europe that there was an aristocratic tendency in America. Those who say that are mistaken; that's one of the things I should affirm most willingly. *Démocratie* (the levelling tendency),†

---

* Cf. conversation with Mr. Livingston, and comment, above, chs.X,XI.
† Herewith Tocqueville began his inexact and confusing use of the word *démocratie.* As employed in these letters and notes—and later in his book—the term has a great many different connotations. Sometimes Tocqueville gave it its literal meaning; the rule of the people, political self-government. But more often he meant to speak of equality: of political equality in its narrowest sense; or of civil, or social, or economic equality; of equality as a trend or levelling tendency; or of equality as a general condition. Occasionally he even used *démocratie* for the word *peuple,* to connote the masses and their supposedly disorderly instincts. This unconscious lack of precision

on the contrary, is either in full progress in some states or in its fullest possible development in others. It is in the customs, in the laws, in the opinions of the majority. Those who are opposed to it hide themselves and are reduced to adopting its own colours in order to advance. In New-York only vagabonds are deprived of electoral rights.

'The effects of a "democratic" government are visible, besides. They are a perpetual instability in the men and in the laws,* an outward equality pushed to the highest point, a kind of manners and a turn of thought uniformly shared by all. One could not doubt that the law of inheritance is one of the principal causes of this complete triumph of "democratic" principles. The Americans realize it themselves, whether they complain of it or are glad because of it. It's the inheritance law which has made us what we are, it's the foundation of our republic, such is the language we hear every day.

'This has made me reflect seriously. If it is true that the equal partition of goods leads more or less rapidly, but infallibly, to the destruction of families and family traditions and to the complete nullification of aristocratic principles (a thing which now seems to me evident), does it not necessarily result that all the peoples with whom a like civil law is established are rapidly approaching either absolute government or the republic, and that the attempts that are being made to arrest them permanently on one or the other of these two routes are chimerical?

'Applying these ideas to France I can't keep from thinking that the Charter of Louis XVIII was a work necessarily without duration; it had created aristocratic institutions in the political laws, and left in the civil laws a "democratic" principle so active that it was shortly to destroy the foundations of the edifice that he was raising. The faults of Charles X without doubt greatly accelerated the movement, but we were going in that direction without him.

'We are ourselves going, my dear friend, toward a *démocratie* (an equality) without limits. I don't say that it is a good thing, what I

---

was unfortunate, for it came to cloud much of Tocqueville's thinking about America and to vitiate for American readers certain parts of his great commentary. For the sake of clarity in this volume the editor will reproduce the word in French and attempt to give the English equivalent whenever 'democracy' in its strict sense is not intended.

* Note that the instability in men and laws and the turn of thought shared by all, once attributed to the influence of the frontier and of the unlimited opportunities provided by a rich, unsettled continent (see above, pp.119,123), are now put forward as the effects of popular self-government.

see in this country convinces me on the contrary that France will ill stomach it; but we are going there pushed by an irresistible force. All the efforts that will be made to arrest the movement will only procure temporary halts; since the human force does not exist which can change the inheritance law, our families will disappear, the goods will pass into other hands, wealth will tend more and more to be equalized, the high class to melt into the middle, that to become immense and to impose its equality on all.

'To refuse to embrace these consequences appears to me a weakness, and I am perforce led to think that the Bourbons, instead of obviously trying to strengthen an aristocratic principle that is dying with us, ought to have worked with all their might to give an interest in order and stability to *démocratie* (the masses).

'In my opinion, the communal and departmental system should from the first have drawn all their attention. Instead of living carelessly on with the local institutions of Bonaparte, they should have hastened to modify them, initiate the inhabitants little by little into running them, interest the people with time, create local interests and above all found, if it is possible, *those habits and legal ideas* which are in my opinion the only possible counterweight to *démocratie* (the aberrations of the masses). Perhaps they would then have rendered the movement which is going on less dangerous for themselves and for the state.

'In a word, *démocratie* (the progress of equality) appears to me from now on to be a fact which a government may have the pretension to *regulate*, but to arrest, no. It's not without pain, I assure you, that I have come to this idea. What I see in this country does not prove to me that even in the most favourable circumstances, and they exist here, government by the multitude is an excellent thing. They are just about agreed that in the early days of the republic the statesmen, the members of the chambers, were much more distinguished than they are to-day. They were almost all of that class of proprietors whose race is daily dying. Now the country no longer has *the happy touch*. The choice falls generally on those who flatter the passions and put themselves at its command.

'This effect of *démocratie* (popular government), joined to the extreme instability of everything, to the total absence of that spirit of continuity and permanence that one remarks here, convinces me more every day that the most rational government is not that in which *all*

the interested participate, but that directed by the most enlighened
and moral classes of society.

'One can't disguise from oneself, however, that on the whole this
country presents an admirable spectacle. It impresses me, I tell you
frankly, with the superiority of free governments over all others. I
feel myself more than ever convinced that all the peoples are not made
to enjoy it to the same extent, but also I am more than ever disposed
to think that it is to be regretted that it is so. Here, there reigns a
universal satisfaction with the existing government that is incon-
ceivable. The people are undoubtedly placed higher on the moral ladder
than we. Each man has a consciousness of his independent position
and of his individual dignity which doesn't always make him very
agreeable to approach, but which in the last analysis leads him to
respect himself and to respect others.

'I especially admire two things here: the first is the extreme respect
they have for the law; alone and without public force it commands in
an irresistible way. I think in truth that the principal reason is that they
make it themselves and can change it. One constantly sees thieves who
have violated all the laws of their country scrupulously obey those
they have made for themselves. I think something of the same sort
goes on in the mind of peoples.

'The second thing I envy this people is the ease with which they do
without government. Each man here regards himself as interested in
public security and in the functioning of the laws. Instead of counting
on the police, he counts only on himself. It results that, on the whole,
public force is everywhere without ever showing itself. It's really an
incredible thing, I assure you, to see how this people keeps itself in
order through the single conviction that its only safeguard against
itself lies in itself.

'You see that I render you as fully as possible all the impressions I
receive. On the whole they are more favourable to America than they
were the first days after my arrival. There are a mass of faulty details
in the tableau, but the ensemble seizes the imagination. I can understand especially that it has an irresistible attraction for minds that are
logical and superficial, a combination that is not rare. The principles
of the government are so simple, the consequences result with such
perfect regularity, that the mind is subjugated and led captive if one
does not take care. One has to return into oneself, struggle against
the current to perceive that such simple and logical institutions would

not suit a great nation which needs a strong internal government and a fixed foreign policy; that it isn't durable of itself; that it demands of the people who adopt it a long practice in freedom and a mass of *true* enlightenment that is only acquired rarely and after a long time. And after one has said all that, one comes back again to say that it is a fine thing nevertheless, and it is to be regretted that the moral and physical constitution of man forbids him to obtain it everywhere and for always.'

\*

\*     \*

In this frank confession of an honest young man three things of great importance stood out.

The first was Tocqueville's avowal that 'on the whole' the country he was visiting presented 'an admirable spectacle.' So far as the present writer is aware, it was in the above essay that the future commentator on American democracy for the first time in his life expressed a general approval of America. He had not been won over to that point of view without a struggle. Before setting sail from France his attitude toward the United States had been one of somewhat apprehensive disapproval; and on their arrival in New York he and Beaumont clearly had been more antagonized than attracted by the vulgar and boastful habits of their middle-class hosts. Contrary to the impression of some of Tocqueville's later critics, therefore, the two young men had not been swept off their feet by enthusiasm at their first glimpse of a democratic country. It was only in this essay, after nearly two months of study on American soil,—only gradually, in other words, as he came to understand and to appreciate the American point of view \* toward self-government—that Tocqueville came to give the Americans his (almost grudging) admiration. It was only when he had learned that intelligence, training, respect for the law were considered prerequisite to a republic, only when he had himself witnessed the self-restrained and orderly character that 'long practice in freedom' had given the people, that Tocqueville for the first time 'regretted that the moral and physical constitution of man' forbade him to obtain the American type of self-government 'everywhere and for always.'

\* This point of view was, of course, not that of Jacksonian democrats. The lawyers and merchants and landed families of New York were more conservative. They seem to have held a sort of *old-American* point of view, compounded in part of Federalist theory, in part of Jeffersonian idealism.

Tocqueville and Beaumont were never to accept the American theory in its entirety, never to give the rule of the people their unqualified approval. Furthermore, as Tocqueville's long letter showed, they found it hard to approve, or even to understand, the Protestant temper of mind which was obviously so important and necessary an ingredient in American civilization. Emancipated though they considered themselves, the two liberal young men could not altogether abandon the Catholic point of view, or rid themselves of an instinctive prejudice against the Protestant rationale. Nevertheless, from this moment on they felt much less hostile to the American example and distinctly less apprehensive of its consequences for France. As a result they at once revised their original conclusion that the United States could serve only as a warning to Europe and began to analyse American society for customs and institutions that might be worth copying or imitating. Needless to say, this was an important decision, destined to exert a far-reaching influence on their study. Its first effects could be discerned in this very essay: Participation by the people in local affairs had evidently already suggested itself to Tocqueville's mind; the American habits of self-respect and obedience to the law were admirable; something might even be done through mass education along American lines.

In the second place, Tocqueville's letter-essay betrayed the fact that he and Beaumont had developed some ideas as to the origins and the effects of American democracy—some very unfortunate ideas, as it later turned out. Briefly restated, their conception was that the political and social conditions they had been observing in the United States were the result of 'démocratie,' that is, of a providential levelling tendency (which itself had come in with the revision of the laws on the inheritance of property).

This was striking out in a new direction and abandoning a very promising line of thought. Less than a month before Tocqueville had laid it down* 'that there is nothing absolute in the theoretical value of political institutions and that their efficiency depends almost always on the original circumstances and the social conditions of the people to whom they are applied.' At that point he and Beaumont had been on the verge of a great discovery. Almost they had proclaimed the truth that was not fully to be recognized until many years later: that democratic government in America had resulted from a multitude of

* See above, ch.X,p.115.

causes but chiefly from environment and tradition—from the colonists' English training in local self-government, from their Protestant habit of independence, from the isolation of the new world, from the influence of the all-encompassing frontier, from economic necessity.

Now, however, Tocqueville and Beaumont had receded from their position and were narrowly limiting the application of their great sociological principle. Environment and inherited custom were henceforth to be considered merely as conditions that had made a given political institution either possible or impossible, they were not to be considered as causal, as having in any way originated or shaped the institution. Apparently they were not even to be thought of as having given rise to the temperament and social philosophy of the Americans; to their restlessness, their self-reliance, their habit of co-operation. They were the conditioning factors, that was all. The true cause was to be found in American *démocratie*, which had entered America in the form of some laws on property.

Where had two such fair-minded students and acute observers picked up this curious idea? What had led them to place their interpretation of America on such a narrow base? The answer, apparently, was that they were in the grip of a preconceived idea, that they were fitting the facts observed in the United States to a conviction about America brought with them from France.

Apparently their thought had developed along the following lines: In France liberal statesmen like Royer-Collard and *doctrinaire* professors like Guizot had for some years been suggesting that the tendency of modern nations was toward the more democratic forms of organization. That is, the peoples had long been demanding—and were gradually in spite of all obstacles obtaining—a larger share of control in their governments (and a better portion of the goods of life in general). This tendency had been observable everywhere in Europe and was undeniable in post-Revolution France. The idea had begun to spread that this trend was one of the laws of modern civilization, and Tocqueville and Beaumont had, almost unconsciously,* become indoctrinated. Then in 1830 the July Revolution of the bourgeois against restored absolutism had arrived, *à point* to demonstrate the theory. Apparently France was destined to an ever more democratic and equalitarian future. There where the United States had already arrived (Tocqueville and Beau-

* See above, ch.II,p.23.

mont had said to themselves in consternation) the French were slowly but surely going. Unprepared though she was, France was blindly driving toward a republic. At some future day her political institutions would approach American democracy as a limit. Thereupon the thought had come to Tocqueville and Beaumont that in America as it was they might catch a glimpse of the France that was to be, and from American mistakes in self-government they might be able to write a guide book for France. When they had sailed from France, therefore, it had been under the empire of an idea: that idea being that the United States represented the type of '*démocratie.*' It was the country where all kinds of equality were to be found and where, in particular, political equality—democratic self-government—existed in its unmixed purity.

Three months later, on considering what they had seen in New York, Tocqueville and Beaumont were reminded of this concept. For when they came to analyse American society, all the most striking phenomena seemed to be permeated by a certain universal equality. In manhood suffrage, in the practically unrestricted privilege of office-holding, in the unlimited business opportunities and the wide distribution of wealth, and in the absence of social distinctions, in every feature of American life in fact, the thing that dominated was equality, the same equality that was even then stealing into France. Tocqueville and Beaumont were deeply impressed. And when they were told that equality was but a recent development even in the United States, the case seemed to be proved.

Equality was obviously not a chance condition, it was a natural law. It was not an ordinary ingredient resulting from economic and social and political causes, it was an irresistible force, a great natural law of civilized peoples. In the guise of inheritance and property laws it entered into the political institutions of a country, no matter what their past history and actual organization; and once installed, it levelled all before it. . . .

Unfortunately, Tocqueville and Beaumont confused themselves, and later their readers, by continuing to use the word *démocratie* when they were no longer referring to democracy (the rule of the people) at all but to *la loi de l'égalité et ses conséquences*, if the expression may be coined for them. Instead of developing Tocqueville's promising sociological interpretation, the two young political scientists had invented (and misnamed) a 'natural law': a 'law' that had seemed, indeed, to correspond to real conditions, but that actually existed—if one may make bold to say so—only in their own minds.

The circle was therefore complete, and they were right back where they had started from—with this difference: that they were now more than ever convinced that they had found the key to the future.

At least, and this was the third revelation made by Tocqueville's essay, they had made up their minds what they wanted to say in their book. In fact, the reader has but to compare the last pages of Tocqueville's letter with the famous introduction of his *De la Démocratie en Amérique* to see that here, almost at the beginning of his travels in America, he was stating the proposition that was to make his name an influence in France for generations to come.

Tocqueville's thesis, which was later to be developed and elaborated not only in the introduction but throughout his commentary, was here stated in its simplest terms. It had four parts. The first was: * 'We are ourselves going, my dear friend, toward a *démocratie* (an equality) without limits. . . .' The second followed at the head of the next paragraph: 'To refuse to embrace these consequences appears to me a weakness. . . .' The third was a logical development of the preceding: 'In a word, *démocratie* (the progress of equality) appears to me from now on to be a fact which a government may have the pretension to regulate, but to arrest, no.' How to regulate? Tocqueville stated the fourth part of his proposition only indirectly, but what he meant was perfectly clear. France must profit by the experiences of others, France must study the American example. 'The Bourbons,' Tocqueville put it, 'instead of obviously trying to strengthen an aristocratic principle that is dying with us, ought to have worked with all their might to give an interest in order and stability to *démocratie* (the masses). In my opinion, the communal and departmental system should from the first have drawn all their attention. Instead of living carelessly on with the local institutions of Bonaparte, they should have hastened to modify them, initiate the inhabitants little by little into running them, interest them with time, create local interests, and above all found, if it is possible, *those habits and legal ideas* which are in my opinion the only possible counterweight to *démocratie* (the aberrations of the masses). Perhaps they would then have rendered the movement which is going on less dangerous for themselves and for the state.'

Where had Tocqueville and Beaumont seen people who managed

* See above, pp.159–162.

their own local affairs, were interested in 'order and stability,' and had been trained by their responsibilities in *'those habits and legal ideas'* which are the only possible counterweight to the aberrations of the populace? In the United States. What the Bourbons had failed to see, Tocqueville and Beaumont hoped to bring home to France. The body of their book was therefore to be devoted to a description of equality in America, particularly to its character, its weaknesses, its safeguards. Their purpose would be to warn France that equality was surely coming, to show France how the worst features of popular government might be mitigated. They hoped to temper the levelling wind sweeping the modern world to a France shorn of her aristocratic institutions.

They would make *démocratie* safe for the world.

PART III: NEW YORK TO BUFFALO

## XIV

## TO ALBANY BY SLOOP AND STEAM

THEY had left the island of Manhattan on the last day of June.

'We had,' related Beaumont, 'a visit to make to Mr. Livingston who lives at Younker.[1] Our intention was to go on board a steamboat; but that day the service was interrupted, so we were obliged to resort to another means of transport. By chance we found in the harbour a sloop (small vessel with one mast) making for the place where we wished to go. We took it on the spot, and after two or three hours of delightful sailing we arrived at Younker, a village near the residence of Mr. Livingston. But, lo and behold, the Livingstons were not at home. We therefore had to return to Younker. But what to do next? Where to go? We would have liked to continue our voyage up the Hudson and on our way up to Albany stop at different places worth inspecting more closely, such as West-point where the military school of the United States is, and Caskill [*sic*] whose heights present a noted view. But we have no means of transport and so are retained at Younker without any way of leaving it.

'We spent our afternoon as well as possible. After a modest repast Tocqueville took his gun, I my portfolio and album, and while I, seated on the summit of a hill, sketched a view of the Hudson, at the side of which I was careful to place Younker and the sloop which brought us, Tocqueville was carrying on a war to the death against the American birds.

'The birds are most of them charming. Many are entirely blue; others, whose body is black, have a small yellow collar which is very pretty. Those of whom I speak are very common here. We haven't had much opportunity to shoot them yet; we had forgotten to take our guns to Sing-Sing. Besides, for us in our position that's a very incidental occupation. To return to Younker, daylight having yielded to the shades of night, I had to close my album. We climbed down the bank and, arrived at water's edge, we plunged into the Hudson, where we took a very agreeable bath. I swim fairly well now, thanks to the lessons of friend Tocqueville, who has put a lot of perseverance into procuring me this talent which is so useful to travellers.

'That night we found in our inn two bad beds prepared in a kind of attic, so well warmed by the last rays of the setting sun that I thought we should suffocate during the night. Finally the steamboat from New-York to Preskill [Peekskill?] came next morning to draw us from our hole. In taking this boat we were counting on having it carry us to Calwell [*sic*], a small very picturesque village on the left bank of the Hudson, and, after passing the necessary time there, we intended to board another steamboat which should take us to West-point. We did in fact arrive at Calwell. There we took a charming promenade through woods and over rocks; and we sweat blood and water to get to the summit of a very high mountain from the top of which we saw one of the most beautiful spectacles and one of the most imposing tableaus that the north river (the Hudson) presents.

'On all sides we see chains of mountains stretching out before us. There was near us especially a bay called *Antony's nose*, whose shape is all that is most picturesque.* We waited until evening for a steamboat. At nine o'clock it arrived with its ordinary precipitation. It did not land where we were because that would have taken too much time, but it sent us off a boat into which we were thrown like packages with our trunks, and we found ourselves being towed by the steamboat until we caught up with it. All this happened so quickly, in such darkness and on such a vast sheet of water that there was something magical in our taking off. An instant after we were to experience a new surprise. Just as we were arriving at New-burgh, which is several leagues from Calwell, we suddenly see shooting up from the steamboat fireworks, skyrockets, and soon, by the aid of a certain combustible matter that I believe to be sulphur and resin, the ship is so lit up and throws on all the surroundings so strong a light that it seemed like midday.

'Imagine 500 people on the steamboat watching this unexpected

---

* The scene explored and admired by Beaumont is to-day familiar to motorists, as well as to steamboat excursionists, as the site of the Bear Mountain Bridge. To reach this bridge and the west shore of the Hudson, the motorist approaching from New York City or the lower part of New England knows that he must first negotiate a winding trail that quarters across the precipitous face of a rock mountain. Actually, in so doing, he is crawling over the arch of Antony's Nose.

spectacle, in the middle of a river a league wide, flowing between steep banks which are like two walls from 1000 to 1500 feet high enclosing it. Add to that the effect produced by the little town of New-burgh, opposite which we were, and which was so well lit up by our fireworks that one could distinguish the houses and the inhabitants crowded on the shore to watch us pass. From New-burgh we were answered by rockets and *boites*. We were ignorant of the cause of this rejoicing. It was the first of July. We thought at first that they were celebrating the anniversary of the Declaration of Independence of the United States, which took place the fourth of July, four days ahead of time.

'We finally learned that our steamboat the *North-America* had left New-York at the same time as another, and that they were racing. The *North-America,* which was ahead, was everywhere celebrating its victory; and, as this race had been announced, the shore was covered with people who wished to witness it.*

'Furthermore, this circumstance, which provided us with several very interesting episodes, was also the cause of a real disappointment. Scarcely had we boarded the steamboat than we said to the Capt'n that we were going as far as West-point.—He answered that he was unable to stop at that place . . . so that we were forced to continue our journey. Consequently we arrived on 2 July at Albany, which is about 50 leagues from New-York (144 miles). . . .'

Tocqueville and Beaumont were not pleased. Their letters did not specify whether or not their boat, the *North America,* reached Albany first and won its race. No doubt, if it did, their triumphant arrival was celebrated by all hands, perhaps even by a few of the passengers. But certainly not by Tocqueville and Beaumont. The two Frenchmen had missed West Point, America's military establishment, and would not be consoled.

Yet Tocqueville and Beaumont might, all things considered, have been profoundly thankful. For steamboat racing was perhaps the most dangerous pastime in all of reckless North America; and they were lucky to have reached Albany at all, without serious accident. More-

* The *North America*, of the North River Steamboat Line, was apparently on its last night run to Albany, and was about to inaugurate a 'through-by-daylight' service between the two cities. It has not been possible to find any mention of this race in the papers. But from the advertisements it seems probable that its rival was the *Constellation*, of the Hudson River Steamboat Line. On both lines, passage to Albany cost two dollars, meals extra.

over, their wild ride up the Hudson in the dark, besides being an exciting experience in itself, had given them an unusual opportunity to
see into the future of travel and industry on the American continent.
Had they not begun their journey up-river on an old-fashioned sailing
sloop, and finished it on the magnificent *North America*?

Certainly, an investigator with Tocqueville's gift for prophetic insight ought to have paused a little over these American steamboats.
After all, an engine which permitted a vessel to carry the population of a
small village from New York to Albany in one night might well have
conjured up visions.

To a foreseeing man, for instance, these load-carrying skimming-
dish vessels should have made plain the destiny of the unsettled but
navigable portions of North America. Clearly, with vehicles like these
at their disposal, the citizens of the United States could not fail to
expand throughout the vast valley and watershed of the Mississippi.
The very existence of steamboats, also, would tend to keep the various
sections of the growing country united, and prevent the (otherwise
probable) * breaking up of the nation, through sheer size, into distinct and independent fragments. Again—and this was important—
the application of steam power to transportation was a prophecy (to
him who could read such signs) that soon the same power would be
applied, on an ever expanding scale, to manufacture. Thence, inevitably,
the industrialization of the United States. In other words, the country
that to Tocqueville was a commercial and agricultural republic would
before long be an altogether different land.

In the wake of the steamboat, the smoky railroads would stretch
their iron net-work through the hills. And meanwhile—as was already
happening in England—power-driven factories would be built, cities
would grow, capital would accumulate, labour would organize. The
mast-fringed port of the trader, the lonely glade of the mountaineer,
would alike become the stone and iron cities of the wage-earner. The
future civilization of the ex-colonials would be fuel-burning, mech-
anized, 'citified.' Seeing these steamboats, harbingers of what was to
come, the inquiring Tocqueville might even have visioned the day
when the very farmer-democrats themselves would suddenly awake,
to find they were dependent on the machine—and no longer important.

It may be objected that such prophecies were too much to ask of
the young travellers of a hundred years ago. Yet only four years after-

* Cf. Tocqueville's opinion, *Dém. en Am.*, II,ch.10.

wards another Frenchman touring the United States, one Michel Chevalier, was to be struck with great force by the character of the new transportation and by its significance for the future of the civilized world. As a result, he was to make an economic study and a factual survey of America * as valuable and as prophetic in its way as was Tocqueville's more institutional and more philosophic description. Nor was this because he was to see things that had not been there for Tocqueville and Beaumont to see. He was simply to view the same sights with different eyes. As had already been betrayed by their every letter home, the truth was Tocqueville and Beaumont were not interested in machines—or even in material progress. Frankly, steam engines, and the great vessels they propelled, meant very little to the two young friends. They were explorers, prophets of a special sort: political philosophers and social idealists rather than practical men of business. By instinct and by training their interest lay, not in economics or in mechanical devices to material prosperity: but in what seemed to them the superior field of politics and statecraft, and in the less material but even more important world of ideas, traditions, laws, and social theories. It might have been predicted, therefore, from the very first, that they would fail to appreciate the real importance of some of the sights they would encounter in the United States.

In this instance, the long and the short of it was that Tocqueville and Beaumont saw in their midnight steamboat race up the Hudson only a spectacular adventure, which had deprived them of an anticipated pleasure.†

'We were,' Tocqueville humorously conceded,[2] 'in the position of a man who, mistaking his stage, should go to Rouen instead of to Compiègne: with this difference, that one can jump down from a stage but not from a steamboat. We therefore had to resign ourselves to our fate. Not only did we not go to West-point, but we sailed all the way up the north river, the most picturesque spot in the world, in the middle of the night, and we arrived *fraîchement* at five in the morning in the city of Albany.'

\*

\* \*

* Michel Chevalier, *Lettres sur l'Amérique du Nord* . . . , 2 v., Paris, 1836.
† The reader will forgive the foregoing digression by the editor when it is emphasized that this failure on the part of Tocqueville and Beaumont to interest themselves in the material progress of the American people constituted perhaps their chief weakness as observers, and later caused an obvious disproportion in Tocqueville's book.

'Albany counts 2500 inhabitants,' Beaumont next reported.[3] 'It's a fairly pretty city, well situated. It much resembles Amiens. The Hudson, which at this point has lost all its grandeur and majesty, quite recalled to me *the Somme*.

'Albany is the political capital of the state of New-York. It owes this advantage to its central position. In the last ten years it has doubled its population, and according to every indication its growth should not slow down. The Hudson gives it the easiest means of communication with New-York, which is the intermediary between it and Europe; and there is a canal which joins the waters of the Hudson with those of Lake Erie and which by this means makes Albany the market of all the peoples of that part of the west. These communications are soon to be rendered even more easy by a road in iron which is being built at this moment and which will go from Albany to Schenectady.*

'On arriving here we found a man for whom we had letters, Mr. Cambreleng, member of Congress.† He is a positive and practical man. He received us with much distinction and at once presented us to the Secretary of State. (That's the minister of the Interior of the State of New-York. This Secretary of State is a small man, whose face is very intellectual. He has the air of a clerk and wears blue stockings; the rest of his toilet is no less neglected; he lodges always at the inn and his minister's pay does not exceed seven to eight thousand francs. One might almost as well be *substitut* at Paris as Minister in America. Mr. Flagg (for that is his name) ‡ has given us a multitude of very precious documents: pamphlets, memoirs, books, plans. He sends us of all those at every hour of the day, and it's so many presents that he makes to the commissioners of the French government (as he calls us). . . .'

'Here, as elsewhere,' Tocqueville agreed,[4] 'the authorities show us

---

* The Albany and Schenectady Railroad. The people of Albany were much excited over this new 'improvement,' but failed to interest the French commissioners in it. Beaumont would certainly have been astonished could he have foreseen that he would devote a large part of his political career to the cause of railroads in France!

† C.C.Cambreleng, 1776–1862, a former associate of John Jacob Astor, and Congressman from 1821 to 1839, was one of the administration leaders for Jackson and Van Buren in the House of Representatives. Being an expert on commerce and navigation, he was at various times chairman of the Committees on Commerce, Ways and Means, and Foreign Affairs. Strong for a sound currency, he was also an industrious and astute politician. The unfriendly W'm Lyon Mackenzie described him as 'very short made & very stout—no great orator but well acquainted with business & politics.'

‡ Azariah Cutting Flagg, 1790–1873, had been appointed Secretary of State in 1826 by De Witt Clinton, whom he had assisted in the latter's canal policy. As Comptroller, after 1834, he was to be reputed one of the ablest financiers in his party. Tocqueville and Beaumont were to send him their prison report.

the most extreme kindness. All the printed documents in existence are given us. (We shall bring back a trunk full of them to France.)' *

From the diminutive but influential Flagg, besides the annual reports on the State prisons over a period of years, they acquired a mass of printed information of more general interest. Some of the pamphlets thus received as free gifts were even of considerable potential value to students of American government: they took the form of reports to the legislature of New York State, and the subjects covered in them ranged from education to finance and public policy, from the report of the Superintendent of the Common Schools of the State to that of the Commissioners of the Canal Fund for that year.

In addition to Flagg and the downright Congressman, Cambreleng, Tocqueville and Beaumont were presented to the suave and genial Chancellor, Reuben H. Walworth,† the friend of many of the distinguished men of his country and known to his profession as one of the ablest equity jurists then living. On the fourth of July they were likewise to meet the Lieutenant Governor, Edward P. Livingston, together with other notabilities participating in the ceremonies. As they had already been introduced to Governor Throop, they could therefore soon boast a wide acquaintance among the democrats of the 'Empire State.' Van Buren, it was true, they did not see; and Silas Wright, likewise, was apparently away from Albany at the moment. Otherwise they had met most of the leaders of that great and dreaded school of party politicians, then known and since remembered as the 'Albany Regency.' What use Tocqueville made of this circumstance will presently appear.

Meanwhile, one other acquaintance caught their attention. Tocqueville and Beaumont met the famous temperance reformer, E.C.Delavan.‡

---

* The Albany newspapers, which had announced the arrival of the French Prison Commissioners almost at once, had let it be known that they were staying at the Eagle Tavern. Thanks to this publicity, and to their letters of introduction, they immediately made the acquaintance of a number of the more important residents and sojourners in the city. Among these, the members of the democratic party, then in control of the State government, were evidently at particular pains to make themselves of service to the distinguished arrivals from France.

† Walworth, 1788–1867, appointed in 1828, was to be the last Chancellor of the State. Of him it was to be said that he was 'the great artisan of our equity laws.' He was a Presbyterian, and interested in temperance reform. Tocqueville and Beaumont marched with him in the Fourth of July parade.

‡ Edward Cornelius Delavan, 1793–1871. With Dr. Eliphalet Nott he had founded the New York Temperance Society two years before; and he was already the owner of a temperance journal which exerted considerable influence and aroused no little opposition.

This was the man who, after building up a fortune, largely in the wine business, had been persuaded that alcohol was evil, and had therefore begun to spend his fortune in the temperance cause. Such was his zeal that nine years later, at an expense of $7000, he was to circulate as propaganda 150,000 copies of some gruesomely coloured drawings, which purported to show the human stomach as it appeared when diseased by alcohol. And after that, Delavan was even to publish a work entitled: *Temperance in Wine Countries.*

Naturally, so sincere and indefatigable a crusader against drink saw no reason why he should not carry his appeal to the commissioners of the King of France. Perhaps he hoped that the light of truth would thus reach the land where much of the world's most tempting wine was made. At all events, Tocqueville and Beaumont, already familiar with the American prison philanthropists, in Delavan now met quite another kind of reformer. And in their leather trunk they dutifully placed the pamphlet which this strange gentleman gave them. It was none other than the *Second Annual Report of the New York Temperance Society,* inscribed on the title page with 'E.C.Delavan's Respects.'

*
*    *

The unusual and the surprising seemed now to be greeting the travellers at every step. On their second and third days in Albany they witnessed two of the queerest and most provocative spectacles to be met with anywhere in America.

The first was a full-dress Shaker meeting. Beaumont had heard about these 'Quakers Shakers,' as he called them, and his curiosity had been thoroughly aroused. Why a community of religious men and women should live practically under the same roof, and yet be vowed to celibacy—or how a society could be founded on 'the most anti-social principle in the world': the community of goods—passed his comprehension. Being offered the chance to inspect the Shakers of Niskayuna [now Watervliet], he and Tocqueville thought it too good an occasion to be missed.

They found the establishment about twelve miles from Albany 'in a perfectly isolated place, in the middle of the woods.' And at 10:30, in 'a large room, very clean, without altar or anything which recalls the idea of a cult,' the ceremony began. Beaumont was dumbfounded. He later, in great detail,[5] described how first the women in their special costumes, then the men, filed in. All arose—there were about a hundred present—and a silence of five minutes ensued. Then a Shaker spoke, briefly. This was followed by a religious chant, repeated over and over for 'twenty minutes.' Another orator was promptly followed by the 'really burlesque' part of the ceremony: they began to dance. As Tocqueville remembered it, 'they placed themselves two by two in a curving line, so that the men and women made but a single circle. They then held their elbows against the body, stretched out their forearms and let their hands hang, which gave them the air of trained dogs who are forced to walk on their hind legs. Thus prepared, they intoned an air more lamentable than all the others, and began to turn about the room, an exercise which they continued during a good quarter hour.' More Shakers spoke to the effect that the doctrine of the Quakers was the only true faith. After which the worship ended with a dance of a special character: 'men and women set themselves to jumping one after the other,' and danced around about fifteen or twenty Shakers who remained immobile. 'Great agitation in the arms, disjointed movements . . . songs more violent than the preceding. . . . From time to time they stopped to clap their hands,' which quite reminded Beaumont of the *contredanse de la boulangère* or of the *Carillon de Dunkerque*. He didn't understand the Shakers at all. He thought they must be mad.

'We had with us,' Tocqueville concluded his own account of their strange experience, 'a young American Protestant, who said to us on leaving: "two more spectacles like that, and I become a Catholic." '

\*

\*    \*

At daybreak next morning Tocqueville and Beaumont were awakened by an artillery explosion, which was followed by the further firing of guns (in a 'federal salute') and the ringing of all the church bells. Looking out, the commissioners discovered all the houses decorated with flags: the people of Albany were preparing to celebrate the Fourth of July.

At nine the parade began to assemble, and suddenly the two interested onlookers found themselves included. Their friend Azariah Flagg, with Lieutenant Governor Edward P. Livingston in tow, came to their hotel and insisted that they march with the dignitaries near the head of the procession.[6]

When the parade started at ten o'clock they found themselves preceded by what the *Albany Argus* proudly called the 'militia escort . . . all fine corps, well disciplined and equipped, and exhibiting on this occasion their usual soldier-like appearance.' * Next, drawn in a carriage, came a handful of veterans. Then, in considerable pomp, paraded the orator of the day, the Lieutenant Governor and the Chancellor with Tocqueville and Beaumont walking between them, the Secretary of State, the Comptroller, and the other civil authorities.

Following came the deputations of all the trades or associations of the city, each manned by local citizens, triumphantly turned out, and bearing aloft the emblems of their professions. If the two French visitors were astonished by such participation, the Americans seemed to look on with considerable pride. First in line, according to the solemn and circumstancial report of the *Argus,* came the Fire Department, nine companies strong, with a new banner and a miniature engine. Then the Sons of St. Andrews, and the Association of Printers and Albany Typographical Society, with a float on which were to be seen a printing press and a gilt bust of Benjamin Franklin. At this press printers were actually at work, turning off copies of the Declaration of Independence, which a boy distributed to the crowd along the way.

'On a flagstaff in the centre of the car, was displayed the U.S. colors, and in the several corners were the national banners of France, Belgium, Poland, and Columbia. . . . They displayed a very large and finely executed silk banner of the N.Y. association of morning and evening journals, politely sent up for the occasion by their brethren in New-York. . . . The design of the painting was a Clymer printing-press, over which soared, with extended wings, the American eagle, holding in its talons a bust of Franklin, and in its beak a scroll, with the motto, *vérité sans peur*—truth without fear. On the right was the Goddess of Liberty, supporting the American flag; on the left a full-sized figure of a slave, bound in chains, who having burst the shackles from one arm, was in the act of grasping or reaching towards the press for emancipation. Behind him was a crown reversed, and a sceptre broken in pieces. The whole presenting an imposing and animating spectacle. . . .

'Next came the Mechanics Benefit Society, Carpenters' Architectural

---

* Such was hardly Tocqueville's opinion of the militia. 'It's the national guard of the country,' he wrote, 'but of a country where the military spirit is absolutely unknown. You may judge what kind of *pigeons* these honest citizens made; their martial appearance was really comic to see.' Throughout the ensuing ceremonies, the views of the commissioners and the attitude of the Americans make an amusing contrast.

and Benevolent Association, Painters' Association, Apprentices Society, and other societies, with their various badges, banners, and implements of art. . . . The Carmen, about 60 in number, were well mounted, and all in snow white frocks, tied at the neck and wrist with green ribbons. . . .

'The Procession moved through South Market, Ferry, and South and North Pearl Streets to the second Methodist church. . . . It extended nearly the entire distance from Ferry street to the Methodist church.'

Two things about this parade bothered Beaumont considerably. The first was the order of precedence, which was not at all what he was used to.* And the other was the jovial participation of the industries and trades. 'Nothing would be easier than to ridicule these standards on which one sees written: *Association of Butchers, Association of Apprentices*, etc., etc. But, when one reflects, these emblems seem very natural among a people which owes its prosperity to commerce and industry.' Of course, the absence of real military splendour rather robbed the occasion of the brilliance that he had expected. Yet he was broad-minded enough to concede that there was 'something great in its simplicity. You must not look in this procession for fine uniforms and broidered habits; you must think of the great event which the day recalls and see under what emblems this recollection has engraved itself in the memory of the people. Here you see carried in great pomp an old American flag, bullet torn, which has come down from the war of independence. There, in a carriage at the head of the procession, are 3 or 4 old soldiers, who fought with Washington, whom the city preserves like precious relics, and whom all the citizens honour. . . .'

'The Declaration of Independence was read in the Methodist church by a magistrate who in America performs functions analogous to those of a *Procureur du Roi*. Into this reading he put much warmth and dignity. It's truly an admirable piece, and the sentiments which the reading excited in the breasts of the auditors were not feigned.

'This reading had been preceded by a religious prayer made by a Protestant minister. I recall this fact because it is characteristic of this country, where they never do anything without the assistance of religion. I don't believe things go any the worse for it.

---

* 'What's more, precedence here is not determined by any law. The eve of the celebration the citizens or their representatives get together to determine the order; and the next year they can establish a new one.'

'A young lawyer then pronounced a political oration very much resembling an exercise in rhetoric in which he spoke of all the countries in the world.* The master idea of his discourse was this: All countries are coming back, and will return, to liberty. To prove to you that he spoke of everything in his oration, it will suffice to tell you that he found a means of speaking of our mission in America. Finally the ceremony ended by a hymn to liberty, sung to the tune of the Marseillaise.† Each couplet was more or less well sung by different amateurs who in turn lifted their voice, and the refrain was repeated by everybody. This episode in the ceremony was quite original. The sense of the song was absolutely the same as that of the oration I just spoke of. I almost laughed once or twice on hearing the orchestra, which after each couplet played a *rétournelle*.

* The orator was John B. Van Schaik. His remarks on the July Revolution and the struggling Poles 'excited much feeling.' To his credit he courteously declined to allow his speech to be published.

† 'The execution' of this Ode was described as 'masterly.' It went:

### THE PROGRESS OF LIBERTY
#### Tune—'Marseilles Hymn'

Child of the skies—Jove's peerless daughter—
Birthright of men—soul of the free!
Through seas of blood, o'er fields of slaughter
Thy march has been, must ever be.
Though tyrants aye that march impeded,
And superstition spread o'er all
Thy cheerful smiles, her midnight pall,
Still from thy path thou'st ne'er receded.
(*Chorus*) Then onward be thy way,
Unstayed thy progress be,
Empires and thrones shall own thy sway
Triumphant Liberty!

There followed five other stanzas, tracing the progress of Liberty, as Beaumont said, from the beginning down to the present. From 'ancient Greece,' where it had been wiped out by tyrants, Liberty had fled to Rome, only to be smothered there by ambition. Came the Dark Ages. At length 'The Press arose—man hailed its birth—Bright guide to freedom never veering.' Then followed the rise of science, and the spread of freedom to America;—which brought the assemblage to the last triumphant stanza:

In this proud land, where freemen cherish
Untrammelled thought and action free,
Where tyranny but breathes to perish,
Thy chosen home must ever be:
Hence o'er the world thy light is streaming,
And radiating every land,
Cheering every heart, nerving each hand,
The west, the east, mankind redeeming.
Then onward be thy way. . . . etc.

'This orchestra was composed of a single flute. One could not imagine a sound *plus maigre* than that of this poor instrument, reduced to itself in a great chamber, and making itself heard all alone after a great tumult of voices singing together. Once more, however, it is not good taste and distinction that one must look for in these popular celebrations. Taken altogether, this ceremony with its parade *en habit Bourgeois*, with its commercial signs and its music with flute *en rétournelle*, has made a deeper impression on me than our great celebrations in France, such as reviews, *messe du St. Esprit*, Procession, birth of a Prince, anniversaries, etc., etc. There is more brilliance in our ceremonies; in those of the United States there is more truth. . . .'

With this verdict, Tocqueville was in pretty general agreement. The procession had struck him as remarkably taciturn and solemn, more like a funeral than a celebration. He liked the honour and respect accorded to the veterans of the Revolution, however. And he was particularly struck by the reading of the Declaration of Independence. 'That was really a fine spectacle: a profound silence reigned in the meeting. When in its eloquent plea Congress reviewed the injustices and the tyranny of England we heard a murmur of indignation and anger circulate about us in the auditorium. When it appealed to the justice of its cause and expressed the generous resolution to succumb or free America, it seemed that an electric current made the hearts vibrate.

'This was not, I assure you, a theatrical performance. There was in the reading of these promises of independence so well kept, in this return of an entire people toward the memories of its birth, in this union of the present generation to that which is no longer, sharing for the moment all its generous passions, there was in all that something deeply felt and truly great.

'They should have stopped there; but after the reading of the Declaration of Rights a lawyer stepped up to make us a long rhetorical harangue, in which he pompously passed the entire universe in review to get to the United States which, in all respects, he made the centre of the world.

'This had all the appearance of a *farce*. We see such things as that in France at the burial of our *great men*.

'I came out cursing the orator whose flow of words and stupid national pride had succeeded in destroying a part of the profound impression that the rest of the spectacle had made on me. . . .'

Whether Tocqueville and Beaumont were restored to good spirits by participating in any of the great banquets that followed these ceremonies, their letters did not say. If so, however, they encountered the inevitable 'republican healths.' For the day did not close without the symbolic thirteen toasts, not omitting Washington, or Lafayette 'The Great—The Good,' or, for the inevitable thirteenth: 'The Fair Sex—Always entitled to our protection—.' Finally the voluntary toasts began. At the military banquet, the author of the hymn of the day arose, and after him a major of militia. Probably the toasts that they gave could have been duplicated nowhere except in America. Yet the *Argus* saw nothing ludicrous to report:

By C. F. Ames. The memory of Percy Bysche Shelly [*sic*]—Unequalled as a poet, unswerving as a philosopher. Accident made him an aristocrat at birth—his innate honesty and good sense made him a Democrat for life. 3 cheers. . . .

By Segt. Maj. Winne. Railroads and canals . . . 6 cheers.

## XV

## A STATE WITHOUT A GOVERNMENT?

THEY had now witnessed the national holiday of the Americans, and at bottom the performance was not ludicrous. If neither of the visiting guests could regard the ceremonies with quite the uncritical enthusiasm of the average American, taken all together there still was something genuinely moving, something that spoke to the deepest feelings of liberal Frenchmen, in this spectacle of a free people honouring its ancient captains and celebrating so proudly its first birth of liberty, fifty-five years before.

But where, in Albany, was the State government? Where were the administration and departmental buildings of New York's capital, where the executive officials and their staffs, or where the permanent bureaucracy and the standing troops to carry out and enforce the State's will? Where, in fact, was the centralizing, controlling authority that could govern and regulate such a vast political territory as the great State of New York?

'We wished to stay several days at Albany because that city is the capital of the state of New-York,' wrote Tocqueville in some bewilderment.[1] 'The administration is installed and the legislature holds its sessions there. We wanted to gather there some precious information on whatever central government there might be in this country. All the bureaus as all the registers were opened to us, but, as for the *Government*, we are still seeking it. It really does not exist at all. The legislature regulates everything of general interest; the municipalities have the rest. . . .'

In a previous letter,[2] Tocqueville had already remarked on this disturbing discovery. 'The central government,' said he, 'amounts to very little here. It occupies itself only with what concerns the whole state, the localities managing their affairs all by themselves; it's thus that they have made the republic practicable. Individual ambition finds every-

185

where within reach a small centre of action where his activity is carried on without danger for the state. . . .'

As in the Fourth of July parade, for instance. There the people of
Albany had seemed to be acting on their own initiative, '*de marcher
tout seul*,' as he had expressed it. Surely, he thought, that would have
been the occasion for the display of whatever governmental authority
there was.

There existed, then, no governments of any great consequence or
importance in the States which composed the American Union. Tocqueville could see no other possible explanation.

Thus, in one of the largest and most important of the once sovereign
States, Tocqueville and Beaumont failed to find sovereignty. In the
very State which Alexander Hamilton had experienced such difficulty
in persuading to abdicate part of its independence and ratify the Federal Constitution, the same State which had but recently planned and,
at the cost of immense effort and expense, built the great canal linking
the Hudson to Lake Erie, the young French visitors encountered no
unified power, no effective government. In the city which gave its
name to the Albany Regency, and in actual association with
some of the members of that notably effective political machine,
these sharp-eyed investigators could discover no organization, no
central administration, that merited the name or was worthy their
attention.

Perhaps it was because they had come from France, where the hand
of the *gouvernement* was, and had long been, so plain and so unmistakably active in the lives of the people. Doubtless, they missed the
pomp and circumstance of their own Emperors and Kings;—to say
nothing of the daily contact with the *fonctionnaire*, that omnipresent
representative of the state. Unquestionably, the governor and the whole
executive branch in New York seemed to exercise but a shadow of that
power which, since time out of mind, had been wielded, first by the
intendants in the provinces, then by the vigilant prefects in the departments of France.

Be that, however, as it may. Their conclusion was as given: with
the result that when Tocqueville later came to write his commentary,
he was to say much about the township and units of local government, more still about the Federal government, but practically nothing
about the States which composed the American Union. Out of the
brief twenty-five pages he was to give the States, five only were to be

devoted to a description of their structure and political organization, the remaining twenty all to a discussion of the merits and disadvantages of the extreme decentralization that, to his mind, was their most striking characteristic. Fifty years afterwards, Bryce was to comment on this strange omission. And doubtless many readers, before and since, have wondered at the cause. Apparently it lay here: apparently the omission resulted directly from the experiences of Tocqueville and Beaumont during their three days in the capital of New York, participating in the Fourth of July parade and conversing with the democrats of Albany.

At all events, even as early as this, their curiosity was already being attracted by the American habit of local self-government. 'The advantage of this order of things,' reasoned Tocqueville,[3] 'is to interest each locality very keenly in its own affairs and to supply a great aliment to political activity. But the inconvenience, even in America, appears to me to be to remove all uniformity from the administration, to render general measures impossible and to give to all useful enterprises a character of instability of which you can give yourself no idea. . . .

'The United States should render thanks to heaven for having so placed them up to now that they have need neither of standing armies, nor public force, nor a skilful and sustained foreign policy. If ever one of these three necessities presents itself one can predict, without being a prophet, that they will lose their liberty or will concentrate power further. . . .'

With this thought Beaumont was in thorough agreement. 'Don't go and believe,' he wrote,[4] 'that I feel much enthusiasm for the government of the United States. I believe it very good for them and each day I recognize still more the impossibility of putting into practice with us their political institutions. I am making on this point many observations which you will read *some day* in our great work. But for the present, it is certain that the government established in North America is favourable to the prosperity of this country and to the well-being of its inhabitants. When in the same territory there will be forty million more inhabitants, when the opportunities of every kind to make one's fortune will be diminished; when that moral energy to be found in every man which now in America is spent in commerce, in industry, no longer finds the same outlet in the state of things (which will necessarily happen when the land is more crowded); finally, when that activity, instead of being industrial, becomes intellectual and transfers itself to political interests.

'Then I ask myself if we shall not see political quarrels beginning, parties with their divisions, etc., etc., and I don't know what will happen to a government in which the central authority has no power. . . .'

## XVI

## WHERE ONCE THE IROQUOIS . . .

Tocqueville and Beaumont left Albany for Schenectady, Utica, and the West—that is to say, for the penitentiary at Auburn—in the night of 4-5 July.

As the two friends had not had any real experience of American stages or taverns before, this was an adventure. At once they were filled with consternation. The trouble was, neither of them had even remotely imagined what this mode of travel could be like, particularly in the more recently settled portions of the United States. 'Trail infernal,' Tocqueville jotted in his little pocket note-book the first day,* 'carriage without springs and with blinds. Tranquillity of the Americans over all these inconveniences. They seem to bear them as necessary and passing evils.'

Whether either of them slept at all that first night, the two surprised young Frenchmen neglected to record. In any case, it seemingly was not long before they both became, if not as tranquil as their American companions, at least as oblivious of the discomforts of their journey.

'We left Albany in the *diligences* of this country, which are called stages,' Tocqueville later wrote his mother.[1] 'These are carriages suspended only on leather, and drawn at full trot on roads as detestable as those of lower Brittany. Thus one is *rompu* at the end of a few miles. But we didn't think of complaining, being altogether given over to curiosity at the novel spectacle which struck our eyes. It was the first

* These pocket note-books, or *cahiers portatifs* as Tocqueville called them, were made by folding eight or a dozen sheets of paper, six and a half inches square, once down the centre and binding them together with two pins. Such a diary Tocqueville could easily carry on his person and use as a receptacle for the thoughts and data of his travels. He seems to have manufactured his first *cahier portatif* on leaving New York. Before his return to France, four more were needed for his travels, and fourteen in all for his conversations, reflections and alphabetical notes. As all these diaries are to be found in the Tocqueville manuscript collection (TT, copies in YT), the location references will hereafter be omitted.

time that we were penetrating into the interior. Hitherto we had only seen the shores of the sea or the banks of the Hudson. Here everything was different. I think that in one of my letters I complained that one hardly found any more woods in America. I must now make honourable amends. Not only are woods to be found in America, but actually the entire country is still nothing but one vast forest, in the middle of which they have carved out some clearings. When you climb a steeple, as far as you can see you perceive only the tops of trees, which the wind is agitating like the waves of the sea. Everything is witness to the newness of the country. What one calls *clearing the land* here is cutting a tree at three feet from the ground. That operation completed, they work the ground and sow it. It results that in the midst of the finest harvests one perceives by hundreds the dead trunks of the trees which formerly beautified the land. That's not all. You well realize that a field cleared in that fashion still contains the germs of a thousand wild plants. It follows that in the same plot you see young shoots, big weeds, climbing vines, and wheat. All of that grows pell-mell. It's a confusion where everything vegetates with vigour, a sort of struggle between man and the forest in which the former does not always carry away the victory.

'But if the country is new, one sees at each step that it is an old people which has come to inhabit it. When by a fearful trail through a kind of wilderness you have succeeded in reaching a dwelling, you are astonished to meet with a civilization more advanced than in any of our villages. The proprietor is carefully dressed, his house is perfectly clean; usually he has his newspaper beside him, and his first concern is to talk politics with you. I could not say in what obscure and unknown corner of the Universe we have been asked how we left France: what was the relative strength of the parties, etc., etc., what questions I know not—questions I could hardly answer without a smile when I considered those who were asking them and the locality where we heard them.*

'All the region which we have just covered was formerly occupied by the famous confederation of the Iroquois, which has made such a noise in the world. We encountered the last of them on our way. They were begging, and are as harmless as their fathers were redoubtable. . . .'

* For the influence of this experience on the development of Tocqueville's interpretation of the American frontier, see below, pp.286–287.

'Arrival at Utica,' Tocqueville next day scribbled in his note-book. 'Charming city of 10,000 souls. Very pretty shops, founded since the war of the revolution, in the middle of an attractive plain.'

From an hotel in this town Beaumont sent home the following description of their journey:[2] 'Here I am now, penetrating into the west. You will probably find Utica on the map. . . . It's on the banks of the Mohawks [*sic*] that Cooper places *The Last of the Mohicans*.

'This country is very beautiful. From Schenectady to here it's one vast forest in which are to be found only a few clearings occupied by houses. The banks of the Mohawks are as picturesque as they could possibly be. This river often flows between cliffs that are perpendicular and prodigiously high. You frequently meet with cascades falling from mountain heights. Nature is everywhere rich, and often it presents scenes altogether wild.

'The land wherever it is cultivated appears very fertile; and there are certain valleys we crossed which quite recalled the idea of *Normandie* (in respect to the richness of the soil and the vigour of the vegetation). I put in that restriction because the said French province offers nothing so picturesque as the country where we are. We have, as you see, deviated from our first plans; on leaving Albany we intended to go first to Saratoga, but we have put off that excursion.

'I haven't time to tell you what emotions we experience in traversing this half-wild, half-civilized country, in which fifty years ago were to be found numerous and powerful nations who have disappeared from the earth, or who have been pushed back into still more distant forests; a country where are to be seen, rising with prodigious rapidity, new peoples and brilliant cities which pitilessly take the place of the unhappy Indians too feeble to resist them. Half a century ago the name of the Iroquois, of the Mohawks, their tribes, their power filled these regions, and now hardly the memory of them remains. Their majestic forests are falling every day; civilized nations are established on the ruins until the day when other peoples make them undergo the same destiny. . . .'

At Utica Tocqueville was under the influence of the same thought. 'One would say,' he sadly wrote in his diary,[3] 'One would say that the European is to the other races of men what man in general is to all animated nature. When he cannot bend them to his use or make them indirectly serve his well-being, he destroys them and makes them little by little disappear before him. The Indian races melt away in

the presence of European civilization as the snow before the rays of
the sun. The efforts they make to struggle against their destiny only
accelerate the destructive march of time. Every ten years, about, the
Indian tribes which have been pushed back into the wilderness of the
west perceive that they have not gained by recoiling, and that the
white race advances even faster than they withdraw. Irritated by the
very feeling of powerlessness, or inflamed by some new injustice, they
gather together and pour impetuously into the regions which they
formerly inhabited and where now rise the dwellings of the Europeans,
the rustic cabins of the pioneers and further back the first villages.
They overrun the country, burn the houses, kill the cattle, lift a few
scalps. Civilization then recoils, but it recoils like the wave of the
rising tide. The United States take up the cause of the last of their
colonists, the American federation declares war on these miserable
peoples (that these miserable peoples have violated the law of nations),
a regular army then marches to meet them, not only the American
territory is reconquered but the whites, pushing the savages before
them, destroying their villages and taking their cattle, push the extreme
limit of their possessions a hundred leagues farther than they were
placed. Deprived of their newly-adopted country by what it has pleased
wise and enlightened Europe to call the law (*droit*) of war, the Indians take up their march toward the west, until they halt in some new
solitudes where the axe of the white will not be long in making itself
heard again. In the region which they have just arrogated to themselves and which from then on is safe from invasion, smiling villages
arise, which soon (one inhabitant at least realizes it) will form populous
cities. Marching before the immense European family whose advance-
guard as it were he is, the pioneer takes possession of forests recently
inhabited by the savages. He there builds his rustic cabin, and waits
for the first war to open the road for him toward new wildernesses.'

Meanwhile, the roads already opened, the very roads used by the fast
mail coaches as they spanned the distance from Albany to Buffalo in
two and one half days of furious travel, remained certainly almost beyond words bad.

'. . . If ever the taste for travelling takes you,' Beaumont advised his
sister,[4] 'I do not counsel you to choose the part of America where I am
now. The roads are fearful, detestable, the carriages are so rough that
it's enough to break the toughest bones. I told Jules in my last letter the
places we passed through as far as Utica, where I finished my letter to

him. At the risk of repeating the same thing, I must try to give you an idea of the country I have traversed. I was saying to Jules that I seemed, in travelling, to be passing through a forest in which there was but one single road; as a matter of fact I should not know how to convey my thought more clearly. It is certain that here the natural state of the earth is to be covered with woods; that's the state of wild nature, and this untamed wilderness, as sovereign, still dominates the regions into which civilization has only penetrated in the last forty or fifty years. The woods are the emblem of this *sauvagerie*. (We have no word to render the idea that the English express by the word wilderness.) Thus it's against the woods that all the energy of civilized man seems to be directed. With us one cuts wood to use it; here it's but to destroy it. Prodigious efforts are made to annihilate it, and often these efforts are powerless. The growth of vegetation is so rapid that it eludes man's attack. The country-dwelling Americans spend half their lives cutting trees, and their children learn already at an early age to use the axe against the trees, their enemies. There is therefore in America a general feeling of hatred against trees. The prettiest country houses sometimes lack shade on this account. They believe that the absence of woods is the sign of civilization; nothing seems uglier than a forest; on the contrary, they are charmed by a field of wheat. . . .

'I was saying that the whole country is but a forest. I might add that everywhere where a clearing is to be seen, which is rare enough, the clearing is a village. They give to these villages the most celebrated names of ancient or modern cities, such as Troy, Rome, Liverpool, etc., etc. Besides, these burgs need only eight or ten years to become cities, wherever there is a collection of men and a certain number of buildings. The construction of the houses, which are generally of wood, is not lacking in elegance; their style is often imitated from the Greek. The inns are especially remarkable in this respect. As for the small isolated dwellings that one encounters here and there in the midst of the woods, they are made with a few logs placed one on top of the other; it's what is called a *Loghouse.*

'Beyond this there is nothing extraordinary in the aspect of the country. It much resembles France; no high mountains are to be seen. The only very picturesque thing I saw on the road from Albany to Utica was the bank of the Mohawk, which in certain places presents cliffs and waterfalls that are altogether remarkable.

'The verdure of the trees is not the same as in France. With us it is uniform and monotonous; here the foliage is much more varied; the pines form in all the woods a sombre background which brings out all the other foliages. I, who do not share the enthusiasm of the Americans for wheat fields, regret the fine trees they have cut. How beautiful these forests must have been before the hand of man had dishonoured them! Now they can be compared to a beautiful woman shorn of part of her hair.

'From Utica we have come to Syracuse where we were to see Mr. Elam Lynds, the founder of the penitentiary system. It's between Syracuse and Utica that I saw the first Indian women. There is a small village, called *Oneida Castle,* entirely peopled by an Indian tribe which remains nearly savage in the midst of the civilization which surrounds it. Furthermore, it is left in peace, it submits to the laws of the country, and if one of its members commits an offence against American law, he is judged by the American courts.

'I did not stop at Oneida Castle but while passing I saw on the road two Indian women walking barefoot. Their hair is black and dirty, their skin coppery, their faces extremely ugly. They wear on their backs a linen covering, although we are in the month of July. I seemed to be seeing our *French* poor, taken among those reduced to the greatest misery. These savages in their barbarism did at least have dignity, there was something noble and great in this wholly natural life. Now we see them degraded and degenerate; they no longer know how to get on without clothes, they have to have liquor which makes them drunk; moreover they take but the vices of civilization and the rags of Europe.

'Their *mœurs,* their mixed state, between savagery and a civilization not yet in existence, their relations with the Americans who push them further and further back into their forests, these will be the object of all my attention when I shall have advanced further west, that is to say, nearer the region whither the majority of their tribes have retired. It seems to me that nothing is more interesting to study. . . .'

Beaumont was baffled, disappointed—and immensely intrigued.

In sober truth, neither he nor Tocqueville quite knew what to make of the Mohawk valley. On leaving Albany to plunge into the dense woods, they had most certainly expected at last to see the American redskin in his native habitat. Was it not in the very forests they were traversing that Chateaubriand, Tocqueville's famous uncle, had encountered his first Indians—a magnificent group of savages bounding and circling to the sound of a flute played by a little French cook, whom, so it seemed, the braves had hired as a dancing master? Was it not on the banks of the Niagara, only two days' journey to the west, that Chateaubriand had been cared for by a wandering tribe of red-skins, after he had broken his arm climbing down into the gorge? [5] And was it not on the banks of the Mohawk River itself that Cooper's last Mohicans (Beaumont's memory was inaccurate here) had so nobly fought and died? Yet where, now, were the Indians?

Gone! In the valley of the Mohawk, along the Finger Lake trails evidently too, were now dotted, not the villages of the dread Six Nations, but the cabins and clearings of the civilized whites. Where once the fierce Iroquois stalked, Tocqueville and Beaumont now overtook . . . a few dirty, rag-clad women, ugly and disgusting, begging for whiskey.

The two young Frenchmen were shocked. Did these belong to the race of Indians of whom they had read? It hardly seemed possible. The Indians they had pictured, the Indians of Cooper's tales, the Indians whom they and their fellow-countrymen had hailed with such delight in Chateaubriand's stories of René and Atala, were red of skin, erect of carriage, magnificent specimens of savage manhood, proud, dignified, fierce. Untutored in the arts of civilized life, and apparently doomed to tragic extinction, they yet behaved with poetic courage and an instinctive nobility. Which could hardly be said, it seemed to Beaumont, of these specimens from Oneida Castle.

The real Indians were, therefore, just as the settlers said, further west. Exiled from these, the hunting grounds of their fathers, and driven ever further away by the irresistible wave of advancing pioneers, they naturally eluded his search. Touched by their fate, and his interest thoroughly aroused, Beaumont therefore made a resolve. If ever the opportunity presented itself, he would go to seek them out. He would study them. Their customs, their civilization, their relations with the whites—nothing could be more interesting.

A thought was evidently taking shape in Beaumont's mind. And it was a thought of no small importance. For out of it was one day to develop nothing less than Beaumont's own book on the United States.

Three months before, on their voyage over from Havre, Beaumont and Tocqueville had talked over the possibility of together writing a work on the United States, basing it on their observations while in this country. Apparently the scheme had appealed to both of them. At least, so far as the present writer is able to determine, a joint book on American customs and political institutions had at once become, and had thereafter remained, the goal of their studies; all their investigations had been directed toward this common end, and all their ideas and information pooled.

At this point, however, as Beaumont jounced and careened along in the stage from Utica, there started to life in his mind the germ of a great plan. Or, rather, it was the germ of an interest: an interest in the American Indian that was to grow and grow until it began to overshadow other aspects of their joint inquiry. Eventually, as the documents will show, Beaumont was to be led from studying the Indians to writing about them: in other words, to making his own book about America. And it would be Tocqueville, alone, who would assemble and publish the results of their political researches. But of that, more was to be revealed later. Here was simply the origin, or first prophetic sign, of Beaumont's interest in the American aborigines.

Shortly the two friends drove into another town with a Greek name. In Tocqueville's diary was written: 'Arrival at Syracuse, situated in the middle of a plain, quite unhealthy and yet very populous. Branching of the Erie and Oswego canals. . . .'

# XVII

## THE EXILE OF LAKE ONEIDA

In the afternoon Tocqueville and Beaumont did not go on with the stage, but set out from Syracuse alone, on horseback. They were off on an excursion to the north, on a pilgrimage to an island in Lake Oneida. On a sudden they had been captured by a romantic idea.*

'I feel,' Tocqueville began a description of their adventure not long after, 'I feel in such an excessively sentimental mood to-day, dear sister, that for nothing at all I would send you an idyll. Reassure yourself, however, I shall do nothing of the sort, but I do at least want to tell you the story of the visit we made the other day to Lake Oneida. If you don't dream of it for a week, I say dream wide awake, I no longer know you.

'You shall know then, for one must begin at the beginning, that about forty years ago a Frenchman, whose name they couldn't tell me but who belonged to a noble and rich family, landed in America after having been forced to leave his country in revolution. Our *émigré* was young, healthy (he never suffered from stomach trouble, note this point);† he had also a wife whom he loved with all his heart; beyond that he lacked the first penny on which to live.

'A friend to whom he addressed himself offered to lend him some money by means of which he could procure himself the necessities of life and establish himself in some corner where land was not dear.

'At that time western New York was still uncultivated; the woods

---

* Eventually, Tocqueville composed two descriptions of this odd expedition: the first in his letter to Alexandrine, Batavia, 25 [18] July 1831 (*O.C.*,VII,39–45) here quoted; and the second in a special sketch, entitled *Cours au lac Oneida*, which he polished into final form but then for some reason decided not to publish. Eventually Beaumont included *Cours au lac Oneida*, also, in his edition of his deceased friend's works (*O.C.*,V,161–171).

An unpublished diary note makes it plain that Tocqueville and Beaumont rented horses and rode to Fort Brewerton, where they spent the night at a 'detestable inn.'
† Tocqueville did.

which covered it were inhabited only by Indian tribes of the confederation of Iroquois. The *émigré* thought he saw his chance there. He confided his plan to his young wife, who had the courage to want to follow him into the wilderness.

'There were our two on the road and going forward so eagerly that they finally arrived on the banks of Lake Oneida. For a little powder and lead they bought from the Indians the island in the midst of its waters.*

'Never had a European, or perhaps any man, thought to make it his abode. He had to cut trees a hundred years old, clear with a spade ground that was honeycombed with roots of all sizes, finally build a cabin and struggle against all the needs of life.

'The first days were hard to pass, especially for people habituated like the Frenchman and his wife to all the pursuits of a regulated society. The second year their task became easier; little by little they became so perfectly accustomed to their lot that, if one may believe the story, they had never found themselves more content with each other nor more completely happy.

'The book which apprised me of these details said no more as to their fate, and I should doubtless never have known more if our route had not led us within four leagues of Lake Oneida. It was, if I mistake not, the ninth of July. We mounted our horses to go look for our Frenchman. At first, for several hours, we traversed one of those profound American forests that I hope to describe for you some day, and we finally found ourselves without suspecting it at the door of a fisherman's cabin on the very shore of the lake.

'Imagine a surface several leagues wide, water transparent and still, everywhere surrounded by thick woods whose roots it bathes, not a sail on the lake, not a house on its banks, not a wisp of smoke above the forest; perfect calm, a tranquillity as utter and complete as it should be at the beginning of the world. A mile from shore we discovered our island, it was only a tufted thicket in which it was impossible to perceive the least trace of a clearing.

'I began to fear that the traveller who had preceded us had amused himself inventing a romance, when we encountered the wife of the fisherman to whose hut we had come. We asked her the name of the

---

* 'At that time Lake Oneida was still surrounded by Indians, and the Frenchman was careful to make his way to his island without their knowledge.' Bt. to his sister Eugénie, 14 July 1831 (BBlb).

island before us. She replied that in the vicinity it was known as Frenchman's Island. We wanted to know why, and she told us that many years ago a Frenchman and his wife had come to stay in this island.

' "Bad speculation," she added, "for they were then too far from the market to be able to carry their produce there. Nevertheless they settled there and they were still there when we ourselves came twenty-two years ago to live in this corner. That year the Frenchman's wife died. Thereafter her husband disappeared, and no one knows how he crossed the lake nor where he went. About that time I was curious to go see the Frenchman's Island. I can still remember their small cabin; it was built at one end of the island under the branches of a great apple tree. The French couple had covered it with a vine and had planted all about, I don't really know for what purpose, a multitude of flowers. It was pitiful to see how the fields were already in disorder and how the weeds were beginning to grow. I never went back."

'You will readily believe me, dear sister, when I tell you that in spite of the good woman's tale we wanted to go see the island. But it was harder to make her understand that such was our desire. She opened her inflamed little eyes as wide as possible and assured us again that if we wished to settle in this island we should be making a bad speculation, considering that it was still very far from market.

'When she saw that we had made up our minds, however, she pointed out the boat of her husband (then sick) and allowed us to use it. We therefore began to row like the devil, and we scarce had acquired half a dozen blisters on each hand when our small craft grounded on the island.

'To penetrate into it was not easy, however, for our Frenchman, to make the approach more difficult and to hide himself more completely from the world, had been careful to clear nothing on the shore. We therefore had to pierce an enclosure through which a wild boar would with difficulty have made his way. That done, we came upon a curious but at the same time melancholy spectacle.

'The whole centre of the island obviously bore the profound trace of the work of man. One saw at first that the trees had been carefully removed, but time had already almost effaced these vestiges of incomplete civilization. The surrounding forest had rapidly pushed out its new shoots right into the middle of the Frenchman's fields. Climbing plants and parasites had already taken possession of the soil and were beginning to knit together in a tangle the new trees which were everywhere growing up.

'It's in the midst of that kind of chaos that for two hours we vainly searched for our man's house; there was no more of it to be seen than of his lawns and flowers. We were about to leave when Beau. spied the apple tree of which our aged hostess had spoken. Beside it an enormous vine which we at first took for a liana twisted up to the tops of the trees. We realized then that we were on the site of the house and, having parted the plants which covered the ground even there, we did in fact recover its traces.

'You others, dear sister, you suppose that because one has a *bonnet carré* and sends his man to the galleys one is a reasoning machine, a kind of syllogism incarnate. I am glad to inform you that you are mistaken, and that when a magistrate starts thinking of something other than law, one doesn't quite know how far that will lead.*

'So much so that we left Frenchman's island, our hearts wrung and each more full of pity than the other over the lot of this man whom we had never seen and whose name we didn't even know. But have you ever really heard of a fate like this poor devil's? Men drive him out from their society like a leper; he accepts his lot, creates a world for himself all alone. There he is, tranquil, happy. He stays there just long enough to be completely forgotten by his European friends; then his wife dies and leaves him alone in the wilderness, as incapable of living the life of a savage as of a civilized man.†

'And in spite of everything, I say it between ourselves and quite low so that the parents, people excessively reasonable by nature, do not treat us as mad, is there not something which captivates the imagination in the life hidden and cut off from the entire world which this poor couple led for so many years? Unfortunately, there is no doctor in the wilderness and one must have the health of a peasant or not think of going. . . .'

'After having explored the island in every direction,' Tocqueville

---

* 'We passed two hours there in veritable ecstasy.' (Bt.). 'We write our names on a *platane.*' Toc. diary note, 7–8 July.

† 'He is no longer made, either for solitude or for the world. He would no longer know how to live either with men or without them. He's neither a savage nor a civilized man; he's nothing but a ruin like these American forest trees which the wind has had the strength to uproot but not to fell. He stands, but no longer lives.' *Cours au lac Oneida.*

added in his more solemn sketch, 'after having visited all its remains and listened to the frozen silence which now reigns in its shade, we went back to our mainland road.

'It was not without regret that I saw disappearing in the distance that vast rampart of verdure which had known during so many years how to defend the two exiles from the lead of the European and the arrow of the savage, but which had not been able to protect their roof from the invisible stroke of death.'

*

*     *

One is tempted to terminate this episode here. It seems unfeeling to lay a sceptical hand on so delicately romantic a tale.

Yet, so far as it is possible to ascertain, the most appealing parts of Tocqueville's story of his exiled compatriots had small foundation in fact. Several local historians, and not a few other visitors to Frenchman's Island, both before and after Tocqueville's pilgrimage, have told the tale of these first settlers of the island; [1] and the accounts differ widely among themselves. It is, therefore, impossible to reconstruct with certainty the whole history of the French couple.

It seems,[2] however, that in 1786 one Monsieur de Vatine (or Desvatines), who claimed to have been a *seigneur* near Lille, France, came to America with his newly-wedded wife, 'a daughter of the noble house of Clermont.' After wasting a considerable portion of his already depleted fortune in travelling and unfortunate speculations, he became disgusted with civilization, particularly as he found it in the new world, and determined to make his home in the wilderness. With his wife and two children he followed the old Oswego trail to Oneida Lake. This, it appears, was in the spring or summer of 1791. The island upon which he settled, the westernmost of two lying along the southwestern shore of the lake, has ever since been known as Frenchman's Island. It seems that Vatine retained his library and some of his silver, portions of which he disposed of from time to time for the support of his family. He left the island about 1793 and moved to the mainland, purchasing 100 acres of land at Rotterdam (since Constantia) from George Scriba, the chief land-owner in a settlement largely composed of Dutch emigrants. Tradition has it that a few years later a sudden turn of fortune permitted Vatine and his family to return to France.

By the many travellers who, in the meantime, had visited this couple at Lake Oneida, certain additional observations have been recorded. Van der Kemp, who saw them on their island in 1792, was charmed by the beauty of the spot. It seemed a paradise. Much in the spirit of Tocqueville, he reported[3] that 'Mr. and Madame de Wattines . . . lived there without servants, without neighbours, without a cow; they lived, as it were, separated from the world.' They had three children, the last, Camille, having been born on the island (perhaps 'the first white child to be born in Oswego county'). Van der Kemp was struck by the thought that the wife and children had often to be alone.

Other travellers were less impressed by the sadness of the fate of the Vatines. Elkanah Watson, who had visited the island the year before, had found the Frenchman 'with no society but his dogs, gun and library, yet he appeared happy and contented.' Two years later, Baron de Zeng discovered them in Rotterdam, their house not yet roofed, yet 'jovial as cupids.'[4] And in 1795 that other great French traveller, La Roche-foucauld-Liancourt, had gathered their tale at first hand.[5]

On his road from Canada to Albany, by way of Oswego and Oneida Lake, the future French philanthropist had stopped at Rotterdam, on the north shore of the lake. There he was told of a French settler who was a clever gardener. He went to see the man, whom he found grubbing for potatoes and onions, which occupation, however, did not altogether disguise a certain distinction of face and manners. 'Vatine' soon told his story, much as given above. It seemed, also, that before settling on the island he had lived for a while with the Indians, of which he was quite proud. 'The instability of M. de Vatine's character,' wrote La Rochefoucauld-Liancourt, 'has, even according to his own admission, had more to do with his changes of domicile than any reasoned calculation. He is a man of thirty years, gay, well-disposed (*dispos*), always laughing, used to work, uncomplaining, but with a grudge against Americans because, says he, there is no good faith in their transactions, and especially because they are glum. Yet he lives on good terms with all the inhabitants of Rotterdam, though considering them even worse than the others. He aids them in their labours, and is helped in his, and he sells them as dear as he can the produce of a small garden which he skilfully cultivates in vegetables.'

Madame de Vatine proved young and pretty, and seemed more in love with her husband than he with her. She, too, did not love the Americans, and wanted to go live in some French settlement. Like her husband, though perhaps to a lesser degree, she appeared to have her foibles.

It seems, then, that Tocqueville and Beaumont were misinformed. Vatine had not been a poverty-stricken revolutionary exile, but an improvident *seigneur* who had wasted his substance and had only himself to blame for his misfortunes. Instead of stealing unseen through the country of the Indians, he had lived with them awhile; instead of dwelling on the island, solitary and unknown, over a period of years, he and his wife had had with them their three children (one of them half-grown), had been much visited, and had stayed only two years, when they had moved to Rotterdam, evidently to be nearer a market. As for the fishwife's tale of the death of the bride and the mysterious disappearance of the poor abandoned husband, that seems to have been simply . . . a fishwife's tale. The estimable lady cannot have known what she was talking about, for, according to the best evidence, the jolly couple had returned safely to France, many years before her own arrival on Oneida Lake.

To be short with Tocqueville and Beaumont, they had wasted their sympathy. One is even impelled to remark that, if it was for exiled Frenchmen they were looking, they had wasted their opportunity. For in Jefferson county, in the Black River country along the shores of Lake Ontario only a few short miles to the north, still in 1831 resided a large colony of exiled Bonapartists, with their retainers.[6] James D. Le Ray de Chaumont, the chief land-owner among them, was then living 'in his great mansion at Le Raysville, which he had constructed six years before. On every side for miles stretched his estate, including village, town and farm. At Cape Vincent, not far from Le Raysville, were Count Real and his friends. At Lake Diana, the present Lake Bonaparte, just over the line in Lewis county, was the summer camp of Joseph Bonaparte (known in the United States as the Count de Survilliers); and there he entertained many of those prominent in the France of the Empire.' Many of the more humble folk were also to be found, the village of Rosiere having been settled by Le Ray's tenants from France.

Of all these Frenchmen of northern New York, Tocqueville and Beaumont seem to have been completely ignorant. Not, one surmises, that knowledge would have made much difference. The two young aristocrats would certainly not have gone far out of their way to call on the sympathizers of the fallen Emperor. Whether exiles or not, Bonapartists hardly exercised the appeal of their lone victims of the French Revolution.

Open-minded in politics though they might pride themselves on being, and much as they might scorn the new Romanticism that was sweeping the literature of France, the two friends obviously could not altogether escape the influence of their age. And in this instance they had been acting under the spell of an extravagantly romantic idea. The tale * of their noble countryman had been singularly tragic and beautiful. Tocqueville had been but a boy when first he had come upon it, belief had been instinctive. The temptation to visit Frenchman's Island, therefore, on passing so close by, had been irresistible.

'. . . This book had left a profound and durable impression in my mind,' Tocqueville explained.[7] 'Whether this effect was due to the talent of the author, the real charm of the incidents or the influence of the age, I could not say, but the memory of the French couple of Lake Oneida had not been able to efface itself from my mind. How many times had I not envied them the tranquil delights of their solitude! Domestic happiness; the charms of conjugal union, love itself became associated in my mind with the image of the solitary island where my imagination had created a new Eden. This story, related to my travel companion, had in turn deeply moved him. We came to speak of it often, and we used always to end by repeating, whether laughing or with sadness: There is no happiness in the world but on the banks of Lake Oneida. When unforeseeable events had driven both of us to America, this memory came back to us with new force.† We promised ourselves that we would go visit our two Frenchmen, if they still lived, or at least explore their dwelling place. Admire here the strange power of the imagination on the mind of man: those wild surroundings, this lake silent and still, these islands covered with verdure did not strike us as new sights; on the contrary, we seemed to be revisiting a place where we had passed a part of our youth. . . .'

Ignorant of Vatine's true story, and of his cheerful, shiftless character, unmindful of the rather unromantic presence of three children in this

---

* The name of the story that he had read, Tocqueville said, was *Voyage to Lake Oneida*. I have not been able to identify this book.

† 'We were curious to see the solitary retreat of our compatriot. Who knows if some day we shall not be glad to find asylum there. . . .' Bt. to his sister Eugénie, 14 July 1831 (BBlb).

The possibility gained such a hold on Beaumont's mind that four years later the story of the exiled Frenchman, and the idea of an island refuge in America, reappeared in his *Marie* (II,46,329).

new garden of Eden, to say nothing of a colony of stolid Dutchmen at its very gate, the inquisitive young prison commissioners were in the transports of happiness.

Again Tocqueville wrote: 'This journey is the one that has the most interested and moved me, not only since I have been in America but since I began to travel.'

# XVIII

## AUBURN—WHERE HUMANITY MEANT THE WHIP

'ON leaving Lake Oneida,' wrote Tocqueville, 'we betook ourselves to Auburn prison. There's what I call a fall.'

As a matter of fact, while still at Syracuse, they had sought out the famous Elam Lynds and spent a fascinating hour conversing with the noted disciplinarian. Lynds, it will be recalled, had been warden at Auburn prison during the period in which the so-called 'Auburn system' had been developed; and it had been he who had built Sing Sing prison, with convict labour, six years before.* What Lynds told them, both in this first interview and later in Auburn prison itself, Tocqueville recorded in a long note (under the date: Syracuse, 7 July). And when he had finished writing, both he and Beaumont realized that they had collected perhaps the most extraordinary prison document of their investigation.[1]

'We were very curious,' Tocqueville began, 'to see Mr. Elam Lynds whose practical abilities are universally recognized, even by his enemies, and who can pass for the father of the present penitentiary system, which he has succeeded in bringing into vigorous existence by dint of perseverance and energy.

'We were ready early therefore to pay him a visit. We found him in a hardware store belonging to him. He was dressed like a salesman and performed the duties of one. Mr. Elam Lynds has a very common appearance, and I believe that his language has the same vulgar character. We saw by a note he left us that he does not know how to spell. Except for that he seems very intelligent and singularly energetic. We couldn't converse with him at once because there was no one to watch the shop, but half an hour afterward he joined us at our inn and we had the following conversation:

'*He.* I have spent ten years of my life in administering prisons. For a long time I was a witness of the abuses which reigned in the old sys-

* See above, ch.IX,pp.98–99.

tem. They were frightful. The prisons cost the state a great deal. The prisoners there lost the last vestiges of morality; all sorts of disorders ruled. I believe that this state of affairs would have ended by bringing us back to the barbarous laws of the old codes. At least, the majority were becoming disgusted with all the philanthropic ideas whose effect experience had shown to be nil or harmful. I undertook the reform of Auburn, but in the legislature and even in public opinion I at first found great obstacles to overcome. People cried tyranny. Nevertheless I achieved my ends. When it became a question of establishing Sing Sing, and when I offered to undertake it with convicts working in the open fields, they refused to believe it practicable. Now that I have succeeded many people are still ill-disposed or jealous toward me. A year ago I retired. I thought that I had done enough for the common weal, and that it was time to busy myself with my own fortune.

'*Q*. Do you believe that the system of discipline established by you could succeed elsewhere than in America?

'*A*. I am convinced that it will succeed everywhere that it is undertaken as I have undertaken it. I even think that in France it has more chance of success than with us. The prisons in France are under the immediate direction of the government, which can lend solid and durable support to its agents. Here we are slaves of a ceaselessly changing public opinion. Now, in my estimation, it is necessary that a prison director, especially when he is innovating, be clothed with an absolute and assured authority. He can't count on that in a democratic republic like ours. He must labour to captivate public opinion at the same time that he carries out his enterprise, two things which are often irreconcilable. In France the position is less difficult.

'*Q*. We have heard Americans say, and we should not be far from believing it, that the success of the penitentiary system should be in part attributed to the habit which your people has contracted of scrupulously obeying the law.

'*A*. I am persuaded of the reverse. At Sing Sing a quarter of the inmates are foreigners. I bent them all to the discipline as I did the Americans. Those who gave me the most trouble were the Spaniards of South America, a race of men who have more of the wild beast in them than of civilized man. The easiest to govern were the French. It was they who submitted the quickest to their lot. If I had the choice I should rather direct a French prison than an American.

'*Q.* What, then, is the secret of this powerful discipline of which you speak and whose effects we have ourselves remarked at Sing Sing?

'*A.* It would be difficult to tell you. It is the result of a daily succession of efforts, of which one ought to be a witness. The general rule may be indicated. It is a question of maintaining labour and perpetual silence, and to succeed one has to attend to business all the time, watch the keepers as well as the inmates, be pitiless and just. Once the machine is built, it runs with great ease. If I were in the government's place and wanted to change the state of the prisons, I should try to select an intelligent and capable man. It would be desirable that he should have seen with his own eyes a prison like ours, or at least that he should have as exact an idea as possible of them. This man found, I should give him entire authority to make changes. My principle has always been that for such a task it was necessary to concentrate in the same man both all the power and the entire responsibility. In this manner, the state actually has a better chance of success and of a real guarantee. When the inspectors wanted to torment my management, I used to say to them: you are perfectly free to dismiss me, I am dependent upon you. But so long as you keep me, I shall follow only my own plan. It's up to you to choose.

'*Q.* Do you believe that it is possible to get on without corporal punishment?

'*A.* I am absolutely convinced of the contrary. I regard whipping as the most effective and at the same time the most humane punishment, for it never injures the health and forces the inmates to live an essentially healthy life. Solitary imprisonment, on the contrary, is often powerless and always dangerous. I have seen many inmates whom it was impossible to reduce by this means, and who left the solitary cell only to go to the hospital. I believe it impossible to govern a large prison without using the whip, whatever the opinion of those who have seen human nature only in books.

'*Q.* Don't you think that they are committing an imprudence at Sing Sing in allowing the inmates to work in the open fields?

'*A.* I should rather direct a prison where such a state of affairs exists than one where it does not. It is impossible in a closed prison to obtain from the guards the same watchfulness or care. Once one has succeeded in completely subjugating the prisoners to the yoke of discipline, they can be employed on work that one judges most useful and in the place one wishes to choose. Thus the state can utilize criminals in several ways, once it has ameliorated the discipline of its prisons.

'*Q.* Do you believe it absolutely impossible to establish good discipline in a prison where the cellular system does not exist?

'*A.* I think one could maintain fine order in such a prison and render the labour productive, but it would be impossible to prevent a mass of abuses whose consequences would be very grave.

'*Q.* Do you believe that cells can be put into an old prison?

'*A.* That depends on the place. I have no doubt that this change can be introduced into most of the old prisons. It is very easy and cheap to make wooden cells. But they have the inconvenience of retaining the bad smell and, consequently, of occasionally becoming unhealthy.

'*Q.* Do you at bottom believe in the *reform* of a great number of the inmates?

'*A.* We must understand each other. I do not believe in complete reform (except for juvenile delinquents), that is to say that I do not think that one has often seen a mature criminal become a religious and virtuous man. I don't have any faith in the saintliness of those who leave prison, and I don't believe that the exhortations of the chaplain or the private reflections of the inmate ever make a good Christian of him.* But my opinion is that a great number of former convicts do not relapse into crime, and they even become useful citizens, having learned a trade in prison and acquired the habit of steady work. There's the only reform that I have ever hoped to produce, and I think it's the only one which society can demand.

'*Q.* What do you think of the contract system of labour? (*de l'entreprise?*)

'*A.* I think it very useful to rent the labour of the prisoners to contractors, *provided* however that the prison director remains absolute master of their persons and their time.

'*Q.* In France the value of the prisoners' labour is held very low.

'*A.* It would increase proportionately with the improvement of discipline. That is what we have observed here. The prisons were very expensive; they now show a profit. The well-disciplined inmate works more and better; he never spoils the raw material confided to him, as sometimes happened in the badly run prisons.

---

* The chaplain at Auburn, the Rev.B.C.Smith, was to tell Tocqueville and Beaumont that 'of the 650 inmates of the prison, there were already at least fifty who were radically reformed, and whom he considered *good Christians.*' *Du Syst. Pén.*, pp.101–102.

'*Q*. What, in your opinion, is the quality most to be sought for in a prison director?

'*A*. The practical art of managing men. He must above all be profoundly convinced, as I have always been, that a dishonest man is always a coward. This conviction, which he will not fail to communicate soon to those he must govern, will give him an irresistible ascendancy over them, and will render easy a number of things which may appear dangerous at first sight.

'During the whole course of this conversation which, often resumed, lasted several hours, Mr. Elam Lynds returned constantly to this idea that it was above all necessary to bend the prisoner to a *passive obedience*. That point obtained, everything became easy, whatever was the situation of the prison, the kind or place of work. . . .'

Tocqueville and Beaumont were profoundly impressed.*

They hastened on to Auburn. On their arrival they found that the warden, Judge Gershom Powers, had died two weeks before. But the agent in charge gave them free entry into the prison, and even supplied them with an essay in his own hand on the order and discipline of the penitentiary. The chaplain also proved eager to converse with them and furnish them with any documents they might need; and on every hand their investigation was facilitated.† They therefore were able to spend an industrious and profitable week in the very New York penitentiary which, more than any other, they had crossed the Atlantic to see.

It was fascinating to be able to study the famous 'Auburn system' at first hand; to see how its component elements of isolation, labour, and silence were in practice combined; to try to estimate its benefits both for the criminal and for society. Especially were Tocqueville and Beaumont interested in verifying what Elam Lynds had told them about the necessity of corporal punishment, and the possibility of making such expensive prisons bring in profits to the State. To this end, they not only made a thorough survey of the cells and prison quarters but visited all the shops within the walls, where the convicts were employed during the day. In each shop they approached the keeper in

---

* In fact, the French prison commissioners were so struck by the value of Lynds' experience and opinions that they were to publish these conversations, almost *in toto*, in their prison report; and were to base many of their own conclusions upon it. *Du Syst. Pén.*, pp.336–341, *et passim*.

† With Clark, the agent, and the Rev.B.C.Smith, Tocqueville and Beaumont seem to have had a number of conversations; and from the annual reports of the deceased Gershom Powers they derived a great deal of valuable statistical information.

charge, or the contractor whose materials the prisoners were silently engaged in turning into finished products, and endeavoured to ascertain exactly what results were being obtained. How patiently and methodically they pursued this phase of their inquiry is shown by the fact that in his notes Tocqueville soon had a minute record of conversations with the different individuals in charge of: the comb shop, the stone-cutting shop, the tool shop, the shoe-maker's shop, the cooper's shop, the weaver's shop, and the blacksmith's shop. In other words, what Tocqueville and Beaumont wanted was not a general impression, but exact, first-hand information, information on which they could base some definite recommendations when it should come time to make their report to the French government. One quotation will serve to illustrate the character of these conversations:

'*Tool Shop*. 30 prisoners, one contractor's man.

'*Q*. How much do you pay the prisoner a day?

'*A*. An average of 30 cents.

'*Q*. How much would you pay the same man at liberty?

'*A*. At least $20 a month.

'*Q*. What is the reason for the difference?

'*A*. First, the contractor was very much favoured because at the moment he made his bargain the state needed him. I think that he could give 50 cents without doing bad business. 2nd. The contractor is obliged to employ the inmates even when the product of their labour cannot be sold. He cannot dismiss his workers in proportion to the demand, so must make up this handicap on the daily wage.

'*Q*. Besides, the inmate does less work than the free labourer.

'*A*. That is true for a few days, not for a year. I am convinced that in the course of a year more work is obtained from a prisoner than from a free labourer.

'The keeper seems to be above the average.

'*Q*. How do you obtain this continual labour from the inmates?

'*A*. Through the fear inspired in them by the whip. I regard the punishment of whipping (the only one used at Auburn) as the only way of maintaining the discipline of the prison and as the most humane punishment.'

Tocqueville and Beaumont had to admit that the labour obtained from the convicts seemed good, and the discipline excellent. 'There is at Auburn,' Beaumont was later to write in their joint report,[2] 'an arrangement which singularly facilitates the discovery of all the contraventions of discipline. Each of the shops where the inmates work is encircled by a gallery, from which one can see them without being seen by them. We have often, by means of this gallery, spied on the prisoners' conduct, which we did not find at fault a single time.'

In the midst of these minute researches, Elam Lynds appeared at the prison. Apparently the stern disciplinarian had been much interested by the French commissioners, for he had submitted a memoir to them before they left Syracuse, and was now come to see how they were getting along.

'What,' they asked him, 'do you think the conduct of the inmate in prison proves about his future reform?'

'Nothing,' was Lynds' decisive answer. 'If I had to bet, I should even say that the inmate who behaves perfectly in prison will probably return to his old habits on coming out. I have always found that the worst characters made excellent inmates; they generally are more clever and intelligent than the others. They perceive more quickly and completely that the only way to make their lot less intolerable is to avoid the painful and repeated punishments which would be the infallible consequence of bad conduct. They therefore conduct themselves well, without being any better. The conclusion from this observation is: that one should never grant a pardon to an inmate for his good conduct in prison. The other method has no certainty, and only makes hypocrites. . . .'

There was no gainsaying Elam Lynds. When it came to prisons, this hard soldier seemed to know what he was talking about.* After weighing all the merits and demerits of the Auburn system, therefore, and after looking thoroughly into the economic and moral difficulties which any imitation of it would involve, the two commissioners of the government of France finally made up their minds.

'Here I am at last at Auburn,' Tocqueville wrote his friend Chabrol,[3] 'at this famous Auburn of which we have spoken so often and about which all those who live on the Penitentiary System in France have said things so fine and so false. Not that the institution is not really very fine, but it is other than it is imagined by our excellent friends, the philanthropists of France.

'Thus, it is very true, as they point out, that the health of the pris-

* How highly Tocqueville and Beaumont came to value Lynds' judgment in penitentiary matters, the merest glance at their report reveals. See especially *Du Syst. Pén.*, pp.11–56,63,83,100–104, etc.

oners is incredibly good, that the discipline there is admirable, and finally that the labour of the convicts covers the expenses of the establishment and more: all that is very true. But they forget to say that all that is obtained not through conviction but by the aid of an instrument which the Americans call the *Cat*, and we the *fouet*, if I mistake not. The whip, there's what Mr. Lucas * has been canonizing for ten years, what he tenderly demands in the name of philanthropy. . . .

'. . . Leaving aside our makers of theories, I shall tell you that we have here under our eyes an admirable penitentiary. It would take too long to give you the reasons for my opinion, but I shall generalize by saying that what we see rather surpasses than disappoints our hopes.'

'We are,' concluded Tocqueville, 'about decided on this point (after two months of work) that the American system is practicable in France. Keep this to yourself: we don't want to appear to have an opinion. . . .'

Beaumont agreed. 'We have,' he wrote Chabrol,[4] 'made many observations on the prison of this town, which is, I believe, the most complete of the penitentiary system. It is truly an admirable establishment, and it would be desirable that a just idea of it were had in France; for it could not fail to be imitated. . . .'

'You will tell me,' Beaumont continued, 'that it is up to us to enlighten the government in this respect. I answer that we will do all we can to accomplish that. I'll add that it will be little to have shown the government what good can be done, if the same conviction is not simultaneously communicated to the public. There's the difficulty, and I don't yet know how we should go about raising that obstacle. . . .'

Eventually, they would be led to publish their governmental report. For the moment, it was comforting that they themselves finally knew what to think of the Auburn penitentiary system.

---

* Charles Lucas, author of *Du Système Pénitentiaire en Europe et aux États-Unis* (2 v., Paris, 1828–30), and organizer of the petition of the Chamber for the reform of the prisons, after the July Revolution, was probably the leading prison reformer of his day in France. As this letter shows, Tocqueville disliked Lucas heartily. In later years, the inability of the two men to work together was to prove a serious handicap to the cause of prison reform in France.

## XIX

## ENCOUNTER WITH A GOVERNOR, A SQUIRREL, AND A JURIST

WITH their customary curiosity, the two young men had been exploring the town of their enforced confinement.

'At Auburn here,' Tocqueville wrote his mother,[1] 'we are in a magnificent hotel placed in the middle of a small town of 2000 souls, all of whose houses have well furnished shops. Auburn is to-day the centre of an immense commerce. Twenty years ago they hunted deer and bear here at their ease. I begin to habituate myself to this so rapid vegetation of society. I already surprise myself finding this quite simple, and saying with the Americans that an establishment is very old when it counts thirty years of existence. . . .'

Tocqueville and Beaumont next discovered the Presbyterian Theological Seminary, where they soon made the acquaintance of one of the older professors, the Rev. James Richards.* Mr. Richards was a man of education and wide experience in the ministry. While not a college graduate, he had studied at Yale and received degrees from that noted institution; and since 1807 he had been a trustee of the hardly less religious College of New Jersey. After their interview on 13 July, Tocqueville jotted down a note on:[2]

'*Religion*. I don't believe that a Republic can exist without *morals* and I do not believe that a people can have morals when it isn't religious. I therefore judge the maintenance of the religious spirit one of our greatest political interests.

'This is textually the *résumé* of a conversation we have just had with Mr. Richard [*sic*], superior of the Auburn Presbyterian Seminary,' Tocqueville wrote. As a matter of fact it was also a *résumé* of what was coming to be one of the young Frenchman's own profoundest convic-

---

* James Richards, 1767–1843, had been a pupil of Timothy Dwight's at Greenfield, Conn., and was characterized by 'deep, sober-minded, and cheerful piety.'

tions. 'Mr. Richard,' he continued, 'is an old man whose piety seemed to us sincere and even *ardent* (a rare thing in America). We asked him if in his opinion the religious principle was not losing its force: "perhaps in the large cities, not in the small ones and in the country. I believe that in the last thirty years, on the contrary, we have made some progress." (I am much afraid that he is mistaken.)'

'A few days ago,' wrote Beaumont to his sister on 14 July, 'we went to pay a visit to Mr. Troop [Throop] Governor of the state of New York,* who at this moment is living on a small country place a league from Auburn. He is a man of very simple manners. He has little money; the state gives him only twenty thousand francs as salary, which is very little for a man in his position. Therefore he spends only five or six months of the year at Albany (capital of the state), the time during which the legislature is in session. He passes the rest of the time in the country. This country place is but a farm which he cultivates. The house he lives in with his wife hardly appears sufficient to lodge them, so tiny is it. It stands, however, on a charming site. Owasco Lake touches its garden, and on the other side it is surrounded by great high trees. He took us for a walk in his woods. While admiring the beauty of the trees we caught sight of a squirrel. At that the governor began to run as fast as his legs would carry him to get his gun at the house. He soon came back, all out of breath, with his murderous weapon. The small animal had had the patience to wait for him, but the big man had the clumsiness to miss him four times in succession.†

'This governor is a fine fellow, but undistinguished. Mr. Elam Lynds, who came to see us at Auburn and to whom I confided my opinion of Mr. Troop, replied that he thought as I did. Why then, I said to him, did the people of New York choose him for governor? Because, answered Mr. Lynds, the men of great talent would not accept such employ; they prefer trade and business in which one makes *more money.* There in two words you have the American character. . . .'

* For Enos T. Throop, see above, ch.VI,p.63. His salary was $5,000.
† Perhaps it was on this occasion that Beaumont made the absent-minded remark that is still quoted with relish by his descendants at Beaumont-la-Chartre. It seems that before leaving France for the United States, he and Tocqueville had agreed never to contradict each other in public. Now it happened one day, so the story is told, that an American asked Beaumont: 'Have you any squirrels in France?' 'Squirrels? No,' replied Beaumont. 'They are unknown in France.' Tocqueville said nothing. But later, when they were alone: '*Ah! mon cher*, you say there are no squirrels in France, and what about those that gambol through the trees of Beaumont-la-Chartre, even up to your windows?' Both burst out laughing. Beaumont had clean forgotten —but Tocqueville had scrupulously kept his word.

But not the character of all Americans. For they had just met the man who was one day to get out the first American edition of Tocqueville's *Democracy*. His name was John Canfield Spencer,* and he was staying, it appeared, at his summer place near Canandaigua, thirty-odd miles to the west.

'From Auburn,' Beaumont wrote home,[3] when finally their investigation of its penitentiary was finished, 'we have come in a straight line to Canandagua [*sic*] and during this journey of ten to twelve leagues we saw nothing which merits particular mention unless it be the three charming lakes near which we passed. The first is *Lake Seneca* which is not far from Auburn; the second is *Lake Geneva* situated a little farther on. It lies at the foot of a hill on which a charming little town, which bears its name, is being built. To reach the town you have to cross the lake on a bridge which is half a league long. This bridge is rudely constructed and has nothing remarkable about it except its length. My third lake is *Lake Cananda[i]gua,* which has given its name to a small town near by where I am at this moment. This last lake is the prettiest of the three; perhaps even above all those I have seen to date, not excepting Lake Oneida. You see here and there on its banks country houses placed on the most picturesque sites, and three mountain ranges at varying distances forming a fine background for the rest of the picture. Cananda[i]gua is on the road from Auburn to Buffalo, whither we wish to go in order then to betake ourselves to Niagara, whose famous falls must necessarily have our visit.

'Now you must know why we have stopped here on our way. There is at Cananda[i]gua a Mr. Spencer, member of the New York legislature, who wanted us to come spend some days with him and to whose wishes we have yielded. He is the most distinguished man whom I have yet met in America. He is well versed in all the political questions which interest his country and possesses the most precise understanding of the judiciary institutions of the United States. He is one of the three

---

* J.C.Spencer, 1788–1855, son of Judge Ambrose Spencer, was a man of no little distinction and experience. A graduate of Union College, he had successively been secretary to Governor Tompkins, lawyer, Canandaigua postmaster, district attorney, congressman, Speaker of the New York Assembly (1821), and leader of the Clinton party in the State Senate. In 1826 he had been appointed by Van Buren special attorney general to prosecute the masons implicated in the abduction of Morgan; and in 1827, by appointment from Clinton, he had, with John Duer and B.F.Butler, begun the revision of the Statutes of New York. Later he was to be Superintendent of the Common Schools and Secretary of State; and in 1841–44 he was to serve in President Tyler's cabinet, first as Secretary of War, then as Secretary of the Treasury, until his scruples over the annexation of Texas led him to resign.

commissioners to whom the New York legislature has confided the trust of revising the laws of the state.

'We spend all our time with him in conversations from which we have everything to gain; as soon as we are alone we write down what he has said. I have not yet seen a single person from whom we have drawn as much as from him. There are at his house two charming women, his daughters Mary and Catherine, who would give us terrible distractions if once and for all we hadn't made up our minds to have none. Mary is the prettier of the two; she has that white and rose complexion, occasionally to be found with Englishwomen but almost unknown in France. I have not yet seen in the United States such pretty eyes as hers, they have a velvet softness it is impossible to describe. But why talk so long about her? Were I to continue you would think me in love, and the truth is that I am not. A long sojourn with her might be unhealthy, but in three or four days I shall quit Cananda[i]gua never to come back. After all, a woman, perfectly beautiful and possessing that *bonté* which is almost banal with American women, is a thing so rare that it is altogether natural to speak of it.

'Mr. Spencer puts himself out (*se met en quatre*) to render our stay in Cananda[i]gua agreeable. To-morrow we are to make an excursion by boat on the lake. . . .'

Since landing in America, so far as the present writer can ascertain, this was the first time that Tocqueville and Beaumont had slept in a private house. Hitherto all their nights had been spent either at a boarding house or tavern, or in a steamboat or stage. Apparently Mr. Spencer's summer home proved somewhat small—on their arrival Tocqueville noted an *embarras pour le coucher et le dîner*—but soon they were comfortably established and were broaching the most fundamental problems of government and public policy with their host.

'Mr. Spencer,' Tocqueville began his record of their conversations,[4] 'is a very distinguished jurist. . . . The nature of his mind seems to be clearness and perspicacity.

'*Q*. Are the members of the two chambers of the different legislatures elected by the same people and under the same conditions of eligibility?

'*A*. Yes. In the state of New York in particular the two chambers are filled by the same kind of men.

'*Q*. But what then is the use of having two chambers?

'*A*. The use is immense and so deeply felt that it is an axiom recog-

nized by all in America that a single-chambered legislative body is a
detestable institution. Pennsylvania, which had in its constitution made
the mistake of allowing only one chamber, has been forced to renounce
it. The great advantages of a legislative body of two branches are
these: The first and the greatest is to submit a resolution to two tests.
Between the two discussions an interval passes, by which good sense
and moderation profit; and it constantly happens that the *Senate*, though
composed of the same elements and moved by the same spirit as the
house, sees a question in a different light and corrects what the latter,
committed as it is by a first vote, cannot correct. The second advantage
I see in the institution of our Senate is that the members who compose it, staying in office longer than the Representatives and being renewed progressively, form always in the heart of the legislature a mass
of men who are instructed by precedent and who have already achieved
their political education. They give to our legislative assemblies a practical skill and a spirit of continuity which otherwise they would often
lack.

'*Q*. What in general is the spirit of the body of lawyers?

'*A*. People complain because it is stationary. I know that quite another
reproach is made against it in France. Here, in my opinion, are the
reasons for this difference: The first is that the body of lawyers in
America has no interest in change. The social order as it is organized
with us presents to it the most favourable combination. I believe, moreover, that there is in our civil laws a general principle, which differs
from yours and which should give the minds of our lawyers contrary
habits. Our civil law is entirely founded on *precedents*. A magistrate is
absolutely bound by what another has already judged. Thence it results that there is, so to speak, no discussion of the law with us. Everything is reduced as it were to a matter of fact; it is a question of knowing what has already been decided in a like case and of discussing the
greater or smaller applicability of the example. You appreciate that
such a study is not adapted to give one a taste for theories. Often it
even narrows the spirit. Your lawyers on the other hand, so far at least
as I can judge of them by the *comptes rendus*, believe themselves
obliged to sound to the foundations of society *à propos* of a ditch of ma-
nure.

'*Q*. Have the judges disciplinary power over them?

'*A*. Yes, they can reprimand them, fine them, strike them off the roll
or even send them to prison in extreme instances. Beyond that the

magistrates enjoy no superiority. Outside of court they are absolutely on the same footing.

'*Q*. What reproach is made against your magistracy?

'*A*. I could reproach it only with being a little too fond of flattering the people and not struggling with courage against an opinion believed to be shared by the masses. We have had examples of this in several cases of political interest. Habitually, in ordinary cases they can be moved [?] to indulgence through this motive more than through their own conviction.'

Tocqueville and Beaumont approached another problem of fundamental interest. 'What is the influence of the press on public opinion?' they asked.

'*A*. It has a great influence, but it does not exercise it in the same manner as in France. Thus we attach very little value to the opinions of the journalist. He obtains influence only through the facts which he makes known and the turn he gives them. It's in this way that he sometimes succeeds in misleading opinion about a man or a measure. In short, in all countries and under all governments the press will always be a redoubtable instrument.

'*Q*. What are the limits that you put on its liberty?

'*A*. Our principle in this matter is very simple. Everything in the realm of opinion is perfectly free. In America one could every day print that a monarchy is the best of all governments. But when a journal publishes calumnies, when it gratuitously attributes culpable intentions, then it is sued and ordinarily punished with a heavy fine. Not long ago I had a case of this. At the time of the trial instituted because of the disappearance of Morgan (the masonic affair), a journal published the charge, that the jury had rendered their verdict of guilty because of *party spirit*. I sued the author of the article and had him punished.

'*Q*. What is, in your opinion, the way to diminish the influence of the periodical press?

'*A*. I am completely convinced that the most effective of all is to multiply the number of newspapers as far as possible and sue them only in extreme cases. Their power diminishes as they become more numerous; our experience has shown this to be undeniable. I have heard it said that in France that there were only two or three great newspapers in repute; I can understand the press becoming a destructive agent in such a situation. Furthermore, I believe that your social situation will always make the action of the press more redoubtable for you than for us. Paris always exercises an immense influence over the rest of the kingdom. With us interests are divided in a thousand ways, there are no great centres of action. It is almost impossible to agitate public opinion over a large area. The New York City newspapers have no more influence on us than those of the neighbouring village. Another reason for the small influence obtained by journalists through the expression of their personal opinions is the ill use they put them to in the first years of the Republic. At that time it was proved that most of them were in the pay of England. From that time on public confidence was taken away from them.

'*Q.* Have you any influential men who write in the newspapers?

'*A.* The party chiefs do it often, but without signing their name.'

At this point the two commissioners revealed the confidence that they were coming to have in their host by venturing on a topic of real delicacy.

'*Q.* To what do you attribute the religious tolerance which reigns in the United States?

'*A.* Principally to the extreme division of sects (which is almost without limits). If there were but two religions, we should cut each other's throats. But no sect having the majority, all have need of tolerance. Moreover, it's a generally accepted opinion, in which I concur, that some sort of religion is necessary to man in society, the more so the freer he is. I have heard it said that in France the temptation was strong to abandon all positive religion. If that is true you are not, even with your spirit of liberty, near to seeing free institutions establish themselves among you, and you cannot hope before the next generation.

'*Q.* In your opinion, what would be the best way to render to religion its natural empire?

'*A.* I believe the Catholic religion less apt than the reformed to accord with ideas of liberty. However, if the clergy were entirely separated from all temporal power, I cannot but believe that with time it would regain the intellectual influence which naturally belongs to it. I think that to appear to forget the church, without being unfriendly to it, is the best way and even the only way to serve it. Pursuing this policy you will see public education little by little falling into its hands, and the youth will with time adopt a different attitude.

'*Q.* Does the clergy direct your public education?

'*A*. Absolutely. I know of only two exceptions in the state of New York. This state of affairs seems to me quite natural.

'*Q*. What are your poor laws?

'*A*. In this, as in many other things, we long followed the example of England. We finally renounced her system, which seemed to us too costly. Here is what the new system, introduced within a few years in the state of New York, is like: Each county has an almshouse, to which vagabonds are sent *de force et en vertu de jugements*, and where, furthermore, an officer called the overseer of the poor has the power to send those who have not the means of existence. To the almshouse is attached a reserve of land which the vagabonds and the poor therein housed are to cultivate. The object of the law is to have this farming, with time, cover the expenses of the establishment. We have great hopes of succeeding in it. It's not the place of birth but that of residence which determines where the pauper is to be sent.

'*Q*. How is your public education organized?

'*A*. The state has a special fund set aside for this use. Portions of this fund are accorded to counties which need it, in proportion to the efforts which the latter are willing to make themselves. For it is generally admitted with us that the state should always *help* and never *do the job all itself*. It is thought that the individuals, who give their money and who are on the spot, are by interest and situation in a position to give to the application of the fund a watchful attention of which a great administration would be incapable. Besides, we want as far as possible to create local interests. This combination of state and township money (*commune*) attains both objectives admirably. Education awakes here the solicitude of all. The people being really King, everyone feels the need of enlightening it.

'*Q*. Have you found that the last law abolishing all money qualifications for voting has had unfortunate results?

'*A*. No. On the contrary. Entirely satisfied, the people is escaping from the wiles of the agitators.'

*
*   *

It would be almost impossible to overestimate the influence on Tocqueville's thought of this conversation. Albert Gallatin, of course, had already commented in much the same terms as Mr. Spencer on the functions and rank of the bench and bar in American society. In like fashion, the necessity of religious beliefs in a republic had already been stated in the most formal language by the Rev. James Richards of the Auburn Theological Seminary. Similarly, the benefit of the separation of church and state, both to religion and government, had already been mentioned by Jonathan Mayhew Wainwright in New York City and by the chaplain of Auburn prison, to mention only two; and this question, like the suffrage problem, was to be the subject of considerable further research by the young Frenchmen. In certain respects, then, what Mr. Spencer said on these topics did not then have, or long retain, the freshness of an original point of view. The fact remained, however, that Spencer's remarks were so cleverly expressed, seemed so reasonable in themselves, and altogether revealed such a wide knowledge of the workings of American government, that they soon came to exercise an almost decisive influence on Tocqueville and Beaumont's thinking.

Particularly was this true when Mr. Spencer came to speak of the press, and of the necessity for bicameral legislatures in a republic. Future readers would but have to turn to the sections in Tocqueville's *Democracy* dealing with these subjects, to find Mr. Spencer's opinions reproduced almost verbatim as Tocqueville's own. All the reasons for two chambers, all the information about the character of the American press, even the suggestions as to how the evil effects of a free press could best be mitigated, Tocqueville was later to parade as his own. In fact, by the time he was to come to write his commentary, these principles were to seem so self-evident to him that he was unhesitatingly to speak of them as: 'axioms of political science.'[5] Of course he was not to acknowledge his indebtedness to his Canandaigua host, for he was resolved to keep his *Democracy*, his guide to political philosophy, as impersonal and as scientific as was humanly possible. But that he had great confidence in the New York jurist was to be revealed when the American edition came out. To-day, with the first complete publication of Tocqueville's notes, the influence of Mr. Spencer's thought can no longer be disguised. These conversations, indeed, make it no exaggeration to say that, in several important branches of constitutional theory and practice, the source of Tocqueville's knowledge, of his wisdom and intelligence, was none other than this learned and luminous lawyer.

The next day, the future Secretary of War and the Treasury took his young visitors to the almshouse, to verify what he had told them about the principles of American poor relief.* And there were other conversations. Mr. Spencer did much, for example, to make clear to Tocqueville the essential differences between the judiciary systems of France and the United States. In answer to the latter's questions, he described ordinary criminal procedure, and was particularly careful to define the functions of the American district attorney:

'*Q*. Is there a public prosecutor?

'*A*. Yes, in criminal matters. There is none for civil cases. The district attorney can plead on his own account in civil cases, after having fulfilled the functions of public prosecutor in criminal trials. The district attorneys are so badly paid that they would not have enough to live on but for the resource which civil cases give them. In the towns they receive only 200 dollars a year; in New York he receives 2000 dollars, but that's because all his time is absorbed by the exercise of his public functions. A good lawyer gains more in one case at civil law than the district attorney during the whole year.

'(This already tends to explain the perfect equality of position between the lawyers and the district attorneys.) This equality is complete (says Mr. Spencer) and nothing in their relations betrays any superiority of one over the other.

'In criminal trails, the public prosecutor always speaks last, and the judge (*Président*) expresses his opinion very clearly.

'*Q*. Is there a judge who orders arrests, then collects and presents the evidence?†

'*A*. None. There is no other presentation of evidence than that made before the grand jury.

'*Q*. Is there a general policy imparted to the administration of justice?

'*A*. No.

'*Q*. Who determines the qualifications of the juror?

'*A*. The Corporation.

'*Q*. What is the language of the public prosecutor to the jury?

'*A*. He sues with ardour (he is the accuser, and does not seem to aim at that impartiality to which the prosecutor in France pretends).

'*Q*. What is the language of the defence?

'*A*. The same.

---

* '17 July. Anglican church. Visit to the county almshouse. Promenade. Very agreeable evening.' Toc. diary note.

† In his diary, Tocqueville used the official French title: *juge d'instruction*.

'*Q*. What latitude has the defence?

'*A*. Great latitude. The lawyer himself addresses questions to the witnesses. If, however, he asks a question which is not "proper," the judge can rule it out; he is judge in the matter.

'*Q*. Has the public prosecutor any disciplinary rights over the defence?

'*A*. No.'

One of the two sharp young investigators—perhaps it was Beaumont—next revealed a curiosity about the American Indian. So Mr. Spencer told them some illuminating anecdotes of one of the great Indians he had known. These tales of the famous *Red Jacket* seemed worthy of record, and Tocqueville made haste to set them down.

Altogether, the two young Frenchmen found their host not only cultivated and well informed, but full of '*esprit*.' With him, wrote Tocqueville,[6] 'we spent the most interesting mornings, and besides a very fine library he had also two daughters with whom we *cordions* very well, as the lower classes say. Although they knew not the smallest word of French they had among other charms four blue eyes, not the same but two apiece. As I am certain that you have scarce seen their like on the other side of the water I would describe them to you, were I not afraid of being insipid. Let it suffice you to know that we gazed on them even more willingly than on the books of the father.

'Having confided this discovery to each other, Beau. and I resolved, with all the sagacity which characterizes us, to be on our way as soon as possible, resolution which we executed the next morning by crossing the lake, not by swimming as Mentor and Telemachus might have done, but in a steamboat, which is much more certain and comfortable. Here we are to-day at Batavia, anything to be no longer at Canandaigua, and all things considered glad to have left. . . . We shall leave to-morrow for Buffalo, whence we intend to visit the Falls of Niagara and, crossing Lake Ontario, return through Canada.'

'18. Departure from Canandaigua,' Tocqueville jotted in his pocket note-book. 'Settled aspect of country as far as Batavia. Scattered houses, then marshes. Rooms built of tree trunks. Arrival at Buffalo. Walk in the town. A multitude of savages in the streets (day of a payment), new ideas that they suggest. Their ugliness, their strange air, their bronzed and oily hide, their long hair black and stiff, their European clothes that they wear like savages. . . . Population brutalized by our wines and our liquors. More horrible than the equally brutalized peoples of Europe. Something of the wild beast besides. Contrast with the moral and civilized population all about.

'19. Second walk in Buffalo; pretty shops, French goods. The refinement of European luxuries. Second glimpse of the Indians. Less disagreeable impression than the evening before. Several of them resembling our peasants in feature (with savage colour, however) the skin of Sicilians. Not one Indian woman passable.'

PART IV: GREAT LAKES AND CANADA

## XX

# FORTNIGHT IN THE WILDERNESS

TWENTY-FOUR hours after their arrival in the Indian-infested little town of Buffalo, Tocqueville and Beaumont found themselves out on Lake Erie: cabin passengers in a steamboat bound for far-western Detroit, three hundred miles away. Curious, eager, almost feverishly excited— their plans for the 'grand tour' to Niagara Falls and Canada all postponed—the two friends were off to explore the frontier communities of Michigan Territory.

This was, they admitted, not at all what they had intended to do. They had had trouble enough overcoming a conscience-stricken feeling over taking even a few days off from their mission; and the opportunity that Buffalo would represent had obviously not been foreseen by either of them.[1] Apparently they had not fully realized that this strangely-named place, on their route to the celebrated Falls, lay also on the very shore of Lake Erie—that they would find it, consequently, the gateway to the whole Northwest. At all events, when, behind and beyond the steeples and low roofs of the port, they had caught sight of Lake Erie, the first of the huge inland lakes of America of which they had heard so much, a sudden inspiration had come to them. Insensibly allowing their eyes to follow its vast sheet of water westward to the horizon, the two inquisitive young men were already lost. The moment the stage drew up, they jumped out and began asking a thousand questions.

At the western end of Lake Erie, they learned, lay the old French frontier post—now the town—of Detroit; and behind it the Territory of Michigan. Yes, they were told, Michigan was still wild and but thinly settled. The white population could be counted 'in the hundreds,' and the large numbers of Indians in the surrounding regions were 'quite uncivilized.' At that very moment there were a number of English and Irish immigrants in town on their way to buy cheap lands, and settle. Tocqueville and Beaumont looked at each other.

'We were curious [the understatement was Beaumont's] to see an altogether savage region, to reach the last limits of civilization; we thought to find there Indian tribes entirely barbaric; finally, we wanted to see how those newly arrived in the remote regions go about establishing themselves.'

Theirs was, then, no idle curiosity, no simple desire to go where so few had ever penetrated. Convinced, as Beaumont said, that one of the primary causes of American prosperity was its vast area of unoccupied lands, they wanted also 'to explore at least once' this potent resource.

But how were they to get to Detroit, and how long would such an expedition to the far West take? Doubtless, so long that it would, happily, be quite out of the question. But no. There was, it appeared, a line of steamboats with daily sailings for Detroit, and the 300-mile trip generally took but two days and a night. As a matter of fact, if they were interested, the *Ohio* was casting off the next afternoon at four o'clock. 'Staunch built,' the notice read, 'in the best state of repair, and handsomely fitted up for the accommodation both of cabin and steerage passengers,' it would stop en route, 'wind and weather permitting, at the ports of Erie, Salem, Ashtabula, Grand River, Cleaveland and Sandusky.'[2] After this, further resistance was obviously impossible.

Yet it appears that Beaumont made one last effort to hold back. Much as he wanted to go, he was afraid the trip would be too much for the frail constitution of his friend. So far, Tocqueville's health had stood up extraordinarily well under the heavy demands put upon it by their travels and the man's ardent and unresting spirit. But Beaumont—as he was later to testify in his appealing memoir of his friend—was none the less apprehensive. 'Doubtless for his robust young travelling companion [Beaumont], such an enterprise offered nothing perilous; it was a danger for so fragile health as his. This expedition could not be accomplished without very long journeys made without stop, almost always on horseback; whole days would have to be spent without rest, nights without sleep, perhaps without shelter; no more regular meals, no inns, no roads. These were obviously good enough reasons for not undertaking such a campaign.' Especially as Beaumont knew that repose would be impossible for Tocqueville. It was antipathetic to his nature. Once off, he would never voluntarily rest from travel. So Beaumont tried to dissuade his friend. 'Not one of these arguments was not presented to him in the most pressing terms. But the struggle was impossible against the current of his passion. It was impossible to imagine, when he wanted something, how ingenious he was in proving to others and to himself that it was the most reasonable wish in the world.'[3] At last, Beaumont was forced to capitulate. 'We were unable to resist the desire to make this excursion,' he afterwards admitted: 'we therefore at once reserved our places on the steamboat for the next day.'

Thus began their expedition to the frontier region of northern Michigan. It was to be filled with hardship and adventure, was to carry the conscientious friends many hundreds of miles out of their way, to consume two precious weeks of their time, and finally to lead them into fresh and still longer travels on the Great Lakes, before they could get back. But never was Tocqueville's fragile physique to let him down; and never after the first moment were they able to regret their decision. In fact, no sooner was this unforeseen tour over, than Tocqueville sat down to record its history. And so interesting and important did their experiences in Michigan seem to him, that he took a great deal of pains with his story. The result was the account given below: a narrative of which Tocqueville was quite proud, and which remains to-day one of the striking literary achievements of his nine months in America. This story Tocqueville called:

*QUINZE JOURS AU DÉSERT*

Written on the steamboat the *Superior*, begun 1 August 1831.*

'One of the things which most piqued our curiosity in coming to America was [the thought of] travelling along the frontier of European civilization and even, if time allowed, of visiting some of the Indian tribes which have preferred to flee into the most savage soli-

---

* *Quinze Jours au Désert*, never before fully published from the original, has had an interesting history. When Tocqueville was finishing the second part of *De la Démocratie en Amérique*, toward 1840, he had the thought of inserting this manuscript in the appendix. But when he read it to Beaumont, whom he always consulted, the latter 'had the imprudence' to predict for it a greater success than would fall to the lot of *Marie. . . . Marie, ou l'Esclavage aux États-Unis*, it will develop, was Beaumont's own book on the United States: a treatise on American manners and race problems cast in the form of a novel, which he had written and published in 1835 as a companion piece to Tocqueville's political commentary. Many of its scenes were laid in the very forests and wilderness of Michigan that *Quinze Jours au Désert* would describe. 'At that moment,' Beaumont tells us, 'Toqueville said nothing; but his mind was made up. And nothing could ever move him to a publication which might appear to compete in the field and with the work of his friend. He had a refinement and delicacy in friendship that made necessary [the exercise of] great circumspection.' *O.C.*,V,27.

As a result, Tocqueville's manuscript was not published until after his death, when Beaumont himself got out an only moderately accurate transcription of it in his

tudes rather than bend themselves to what the whites call the delights
of social life. But it is to-day more difficult than one thinks to find the
wilderness. On leaving New York, and in measure as we advanced toward the northwest, the goal of our voyage seemed to flee before us.
We passed through places celebrated in the history of the Indians, we
encountered valleys they have named, we crossed streams which still
bear the name of their tribes; but everywhere the hut of the savage had
given place to the house of civilized man, the forests had fallen, the
solitude was coming to life.

'However, we seemed to be marching on the trail of the indigenies.
Ten years ago, we were told, they were here; there, five years ago;
there two years ago. On the spot where you see the most beautiful
church of the village, one man told us, I chopped down the first tree
of the forest. Here, another related, was held the great council of
the Iroquois confederation.—And what has happened to the Indians?
said I.—The. Indians, answered our host, have gone I don't know
exactly where, beyond the Great Lakes. Their race is dying. They are
not made for civilization; it kills them.

'Man accustoms himself to everything: to death on the battlefield,
to death in the hospitals, to killing and suffering. He trains himself
to every spectacle. An ancient people, the first and legitimate master
of the American continent, is melting away each day like snow in the
rays of the sun, and is visibly disappearing from the surface of the
earth. In the same regions and in its place another race is growing up
with an even more astonishing speed. By its agency the forests fall,
the swamps dry up. Lakes as large as seas, immense rivers, vainly oppose its triumphal progress. The wildernesses become villages; the villages, towns. A daily witness of all these marvels, the American sees
nothing astonishing in them. This unbelievable destruction, this still
more surprising growth seem to him the usual procedure of the events
of this world. He accustoms himself to them as to the immovable order
of nature.

'It's thus that, always in quest of the savages and the wilderness, we
covered the three hundred and sixty miles separating New-York from
Buffalo.

---

edition of his friend's works. Since then, Beaumont's version has been republished
in this country as a text and reader for students of French (R. Clyde Ford, *De
Tocqueville's Voyage en Amérique, Heath's Modern Language Series,* 1909). It is
now for the first time given in a complete and literal translation; and is here supplemented in the notes by excerpts from Tocqueville's own letters and diary, and
from Beaumont's letters describing the trip.

'The first object which struck our sight was a great number of Indians gathered that day at Buffalo to receive payment for the lands which they have ceded to the United States.

'I don't believe I've ever experienced a more complete disappointment than at the sight of those Indians.* I was full of memories of M. de Chateaubriand and of Cooper, and in the indigenies of North America I was expecting to see savages on whose faces nature would have left the trace of some of those proud virtues which the spirit of liberty produces. I thought to find in them men whose bodies had been developed by hunting and war and who would lose nothing by being seen in their nakedness. One can imagine my astonishment on comparing this portrait with what follows.

'The Indians I saw that day were small in stature. Their limbs, so far as it was possible to judge under their clothes, were thin and unmuscular; their skin, instead of being copper-red in colour, as commonly believed, was deep bronze, so that at first sight it seemed much like the skin of mulattoes. Their hair, black and gleaming, fell singularly straight to their neck and shoulders. Their mouths were generally beyond measure large, the expression of their faces ignoble and bad. Their physiognomy betrayed that profound depravity that only a long abuse of the benefits of civilization can produce. One would have said men belonging to the very lowest classes in our great European cities, and yet they were still savages. To the vices got from us was added something barbarous and uncivilized which made them still a hundred times more repulsive. These Indians did not carry arms; they were covered with European clothes, but did not wear them as we do. One saw that they were not accustomed to their use, and that they still felt imprisoned in their folds. To the adornments of Europe they joined the products of savage luxury, feathers, enormous ear rings, and collars of shells. Their movements were quick and disjointed, their voices shrill and discordant, their eyes restless and wild. At first one would have been tempted to see in each of them only a beast of the forest, who had been educated to look like a man but who remained none the less an animal. Yet these feeble and depraved beings belonged to one of the most celebrated tribes of the ancient American world. We had before us, and pity it is to say so, the last remains of that famous confederation of the Iroquois, which was known for its forceful intelligence no less than for its courage, and which

* Cf. p.224 above.

long held the balance between the two greatest nations of Europe.

'One would be wrong, however, to judge the Indian race by this unpleasant sample, this offshoot of a wild tree which has grown in the
mud of our towns. That would be to repeat the mistake that we made
ourselves and that we had the opportunity to recognize as such later on.

'That evening we went outside the town and, not far from the last
houses, we perceived an Indian lying on the edge of the road. It was
a young man. He lay without movement, and we thought him dead.
Some stifled groans which escaped painfully from his chest told us
that he was still living and was struggling against one of those dangerous drunkennesses caused by brandy. The sun had already gone down;
the earth was becoming more and more damp. Everything indicated
that this unfortunate man would breathe his last sigh there unless he
were succoured. It was the hour that the Indians were leaving Buffalo
to regain their village; from time to time a group of them came to
pass near us. They approached, brutally turned the body of their compatriot over so as to know who it was, and then resumed their march
without even deigning to reply to our observations. Most of these men
were themselves drunk. There came finally a young Indian woman
who at first seemed to draw near with a certain interest. I believed her
the wife or the sister of the dying man. She considered him attentively,
called him by name in a loud voice, felt of his heart and, being assured
that he was alive, tried to draw him from his lethargy. But as her
efforts were without effect, we saw her enter into a fury against the
inanimate body lying before her. She struck his head, twisted his face
with her fingers, stamped on him with her feet. In yielding to these
acts of ferocity she gave utterance to some wild and inarticulate cries
that seem to ring in my ears to this hour. We finally felt we ought to
intervene and we peremptorily ordered her away. She obeyed, but as
she disappeared we heard her give a shout of barbarous laughter.*

'Back in town, we spoke to several persons about the young Indian.
We spoke of the imminent danger to which he was exposed; we even
offered to pay his expenses at an inn. All that was useless. We couldn't
persuade anyone to budge. Some said to us: these men are used to
drinking to excess and to lying on the ground; they don't die from

* 'An Indian woman, said to be his wife, approached, shook his head violently, banging
it against the ground. As the unhappy man gave no sign of life, she uttered a cry
and began laughing stupidly. A little further on we saw an Indian woman, completely
drunk, being carried along by two or three Indians leaving town to regain their
forests.' Bt. to Chabrol, on board the *Ohio* on Lake Erie. 24 [?] July 1831 (BBlb).

such accidents. Others admitted that the Indian would probably die, but one read on their lips this half-expressed thought: What is the life of an Indian? That was the general sentiment. In the heart of this society, so policed, so prudish, so sententiously moral and virtuous, one encounters a complete insensibility, a sort of cold and implacable egoism when it's a question of the American indigenies. The inhabitants of the United States do not hunt the Indians with hue and cry as did the Spaniards in Mexico. But it's the same pitiless instinct which animates the European race here as everywhere else.

'How many times, in the course of our travels, have we not encountered honest citizens who, in the evening tranquilly seated by the fireside, said to us: Each day the number of the Indians grows less and less! It is not that we often make war on them, however; the brandy which we sell them cheap kills more of them every year than could our most deadly weapons.* This world belongs to us, add they. God, in denying its first inhabitants the faculty of civilizing themselves, has predestined them to inevitable destruction. The true proprietors of this continent are those who know how to take advantage of its riches.

'Satisfied with his reasoning, the American goes to the temple where he hears a minister of the gospel repeat to him that men are brothers and that the Eternal Being, who has made them all on the same model, has given all the duty to succour each other.

*
* *

'The nineteenth of July, at ten in the morning, we go on board the steamboat *Ohio*, heading for Detroit.† A very strong breeze was blowing from the northwest and gave to the waters of Lake Erie the appearance of ocean waves.‡ To the right stretched a boundless horizon;

---

* 'It would be too difficult to destroy them by war, that would cost men and money. A little time and much perfidy, there's something more certain and economical.' Bt. to Chabrol, 24 [?] July 1831 (BBlb).

† 'Departure for Detroit. Small steamboat. No one knows us. Notable change in the conduct of the Americans toward us.' Toc. diary note, 19 July.
   On board they met John Tanner, who presented [?] them with a copy of his book: *A Narrative of the Captivity and Adventures of John Tanner (U. S. Interpreter at Sault de Ste. Marie.) during thirty years residence among the Indians in the interior of North America* (1830).

‡ 'It's a *veritable* sea (but for the sweetness of the water): frequently the shores are lost to sight. Those who are exposed to seasickness experience it as on the ocean; I did not suffer from it at all. Our navigation was not very happy. Instead of the day and a half which should suffice to bring us to port, we were three days en route; and

on the left we hugged the southern shores of the lake, often within shouting distance. These shores were perfectly flat, and differed from those of all the lakes that I had had occasion to visit in Europe. They didn't resemble the seashore either. Immense forests shadowed them and made about the lake a thick and rarely broken belt. From time to time, however, the aspect of the country suddenly changes. On turning a wood one sights the elegant spire of a steeple, some houses shining white and neat, some shops. Two paces further on, the forest, primitive and apparently impenetrable, resumes its sway and once more reflects its foliage in the waters of the lake.

'Those who have travelled through the United States will find in this tableau a striking emblem of American society. Everything is in violent contrast, unforeseen. Everywhere extreme civilization and nature abandoned to herself find themselves together and as it were face to face. This is not imagined in France. As for me, with my traveller's illusions,—and what class of man has not his?—I anticipated something quite different. I had noticed that in Europe the situation more or less remote in which a province or a city lay, its wealth or poverty, its smallness or extent, exercised an immense influence on the ideas, the customs, the entire civilization of its inhabitants, and placed often the difference of several centuries between the diverse parts of the same territory.

'I imagined it was thus, and with all the more reason, in the new world, and that a country like America, peopled in an incomplete and partial way, ought to offer all the conditions of existence and present the image of society in all its ages. America was then, in my opinion, the only country where one could step by step follow all the transformations which the social state makes man undergo, and see as it were a vast chain falling link by link from the opulent city patrician all the way to the wilderness savage. It's there, in short, between a few degrees of longitude, that I hoped to find framed the history of all humanity.

'Nothing in this tableau is true. Of all the countries of the world America is the least fitted to furnish the spectacle I came there to seek. In America, even more than in Europe, there is only one society. It may

we were exposed almost without let-up to a beating rain.' Bt. to his father, Detroit, 1 August 1831 (Michigan) (BBlb).
'We traversed the whole of Lake Erie, which so perfectly resembles the ocean that I was a little seasick the first day. . . .' Toc. to Lesueur, Detroit (Michigan), 3 August 1831 (*O.C.*,VII,46).

be either rich or poor, humble or brilliant, trading or agricultural; but it is composed everywhere of the same elements. The plane of a uniform civilization has passed over it. The man you left in New-York you find again in almost impenetrable solitudes: same clothes, same attitude, same language, same habits, same pleasures. Nothing rustic, nothing naïve, nothing which smells of the wilderness, nothing even resembling our villages. The reason for this singular state of affairs is easy to understand. The portion of the territories longest and most completely settled has reached a high degree of civilization. Education has been profusely disseminated; the spirit of equality has spread a singularly even colouring over the inner habits of life. Now, note this well, it's precisely these same men who each year go to people the wilderness. In Europe, every one lives and dies on the soil which has seen him born; but in America you nowhere meet the representatives of a race which has multiplied in the solitude after having long lived ignored by the world and thrown upon its own resources. Those who inhabit these isolated places have arrived there since yesterday; they have come with the customs, the ideas, the needs of civilization. They only yield to savagery that which the imperious necessity of things exacts from them; thence the most bizarre contrasts. Without transition you pass from a wilderness into the streets of a city, from the wildest scenes to the most smiling pictures of civilized life. If, night coming on you unawares, you are not forced to take shelter at the foot of a tree, you have every prospect of arriving in a village where you will find everything, even to French fashions, the almanac of modes, and the caricatures of the boulevards. The merchant of Buffalo and of Detroit is as well stocked with them as he of New-York. The factories of Lyon work for one as for the other. You quit the large roads, you penetrate paths scarcely cleared, you perceive finally a cleared field, a cabin composed of half-squared logs, into which daylight enters only through one narrow window, you believe yourself at last come to the dwelling of an American peasant: *erreur*. You enter this cabin which seems the asylum of all the miseries, but the owner wears the same clothes as you, he speaks the language of the cities. On his rude table are books and newspapers; he himself hastens to take you aside to learn just what is going on in old Europe and to ask you what has most struck you in his own country. He will trace out for you on paper a plan of campaign for the Belgians, and will gravely inform you what remains to be done for the prosperity of France. One would believe oneself seeing a rich proprietor who has momentarily come to live for several nights in his hunting lodge. And in fact the wood cabin is only a temporary refuge for the American, a temporary concession made to the exigencies of the situation. When the surrounding fields are all under cultivation and the new proprietor has the time to concern himself with the comforts of life, a house more spacious and better adapted to his needs will replace the log house, and will serve to shelter numerous children who will also one day go to create for themselves a dwelling in the wilderness.

'But to come back to our voyage, we then navigated painfully all day in sight of the shores of Pennsylvania, and later of Ohio. We stopped an instant at *Presqu'Ile*, to-day Erie. It's there that the canal from Pittsburg[h] will end. By means of this work, whose completion is, they say, easy and from now on assured, the Mississip[p]i will communicate with the North river, and the riches of Europe will circulate freely across the five hundred leagues of land which separate the Gulf of Mexico from the Atlantic ocean.*

'In the evening, the weather having become favourable, we stood rapidly toward Detroit, crossing the middle of the lake. In the morning we were in sight of the small island called *Middle Sister*, near which commodore Perry in 1814 gained a celebrated naval victory over the English.

'Soon after the shores of Canada seemed to approach rapidly, and we saw the Detroit river opening before us and the walls of Fort Malden appearing in the distance. This place, founded by the French, still bears numerous traces of its origin. The houses there are shaped and placed like the houses of our peasants; in the centre of the hamlet rises the Catholic steeple surmounted by a cock. One would say a village near Caen or Evreux. While, not without emotion, we were considering this image of France, our attention was distracted by a singular spectacle. At our right, on the bank, a Scotch soldier stood on guard in full uniform. He wore that costume made famous by the field of Waterloo: the feathered bonnet, the jacket, nothing was missing, the sun made his uniform and arms sparkle. On our left, and as if to furnish a contrast, two Indians, entirely naked, their bodies streaked with paint, their noses pierced by rings, put off at the same moment from the opposite bank. They were in a small bark canoe, with a blanket

---

* '21 July. Quarrel with the captain. Arrival at Cleveland at six in the evening.' Toc. diary note.

for a sail. Abandoning this frail bark to the force of wind and current, they shot like an arrow toward our vessel, which in an instant they had circled; then they quietly went fishing near the English soldier who, still shining and motionless, seemed placed there as the representative of the brilliant and armed civilization of Europe.

*

\*    \*

'We arrived at Detroit at three o'clock. Detroit is a small town of two or three thousand souls, which was founded in the middle of the woods by the Jesuits in 1710, and which still contains a very great number of French families.

'We had traversed the entire state of New-York and done a hundred leagues on Lake Erie; we were approaching, this time, the limits of civilization, but we didn't know at all toward what place we should set out. To inform ourselves was not as easy as one might suppose. To cross almost impenetrable forests, pass deep rivers, brave pestilential swamps, sleep exposed to the damp of the woods: these are efforts the American has no difficulty understanding if it's a question of gaining a dollar, for that's the point. But that one should do such things through curiosity, that's something that doesn't reach his intelligence. Add that, living in a wilderness, he only esteems the works of man. He will willingly send you to visit a road, a bridge, a fine village; but that one has a high regard for great trees and a beautiful solitude, that's entirely incomprehensible to him.

'Nothing therefore more difficult than to find someone in a position to understand you.—You wish to see some woods, our hosts said to us smiling, go straight ahead, you will find enough to satisfy you. As it happens there are in the neighbourhood some new roads and some well defined trails. As for Indians, you will see but too many of them on our public places and in our streets; you don't need to go far for that. These at least are beginning to civilize themselves and are less savage in looks.—It didn't take us long to realize that it was impossible to get the truth from them by frontal attack, and that we should have to *manœuvre*.

'We therefore betook ourselves to the official entrusted by the United States with the sale of the unsettled lands which cover the district of Michigan. We introduce ourselves as people who, without having made up their minds to found a settlement in the country, might still have a distant interest in knowing the price of lands and their situation. Major Biddle,* it was the name of the official, understood perfectly this time what we wished to do, and immediately entered upon a mass of details to which we listened with avidity.†—This section here, said he, showing us on the map the river Saint Joseph which, after long twistings and turnings, discharges into Lake Michigan, seems to me to meet your purposes best. The land is good, some fine villages have already been built, and the road there is so well kept up that stages pass on it every day.—Good! say we to ourselves, we already know where we must not go, unless we want to visit the wilderness in the mail coach.—We thank Mr. Biddle for his information, and we ask with an air of indifference and a sort of scorn what was the portion of the district where to date the current of immigration had made itself the least felt.—Here, said he, without attaching more importance to his words than we appeared to attach to our question, here toward the northwest. As far as Pontiac, and in the neighbourhood of that village, some pretty fair establishments have lately been founded. But you mustn't think of settling further on. The country is covered with almost impenetrable forest which stretches on toward the northwest,

---

* John Biddle, 1789–1859, was the newly appointed register of the land office of Detroit. He had been Indian agent at Green Bay, and for two years Territorial Delegate from Michigan to Congress. Later, he was to write a number of papers on Michigan history.

† 'At Detroit I went to see the public official in charge of the sale of lands, or of the land office, and he gave me the following details:

'From the melting of the ice, that is to say from the month of May last, when the lake became navigable, up to the first of July there arrived in Michigan about five thousand new settlers (that's the English word, we have no exact equivalent). The largeness of this number surprised me, as you may believe, the more so as I thought, as we generally suppose, that all these *new settlers* were Europeans.

'The land agent informed me that among these 5000 there were not 200 immigrants from Europe. Even so the proportion of them is larger than usual. But, said I, to the agent, what is it that can induce this great number of Americans to leave their birthplace and come to dwell in the wilderness? Nothing is easier to understand, answered he: the law dividing the goods of the father equally among the children. From this it results that each generation finds itself poorer than the preceding. But as soon as the small proprietor of our peopled states perceives that he is beginning to find it hard to get a livelihood, he sells his field, comes with his whole family to the line of the frontier, buys with the small capital he has just created a very large property and makes his fortune in a few years.

'At his death, if this fortunes does not suffice his children, they will go like him to build another in a new wilderness. We have, thank God, the room to expand to the Pacific ocean.

'Don't you find, my dear friend, that there is a large book contained in this one reply? How imagine a revolution in a country where such a career is open to the needs and passions of man, and how compare the political institutions of such a people with those of any other?' Toc. to Chabrol, Buffalo, 17 August 1831 (YT).

where only wild beasts and Indians are to be found. The United States is planning to open a road there in the near future, but it's only just been begun and stops at Pontiac: I repeat, that's a section you mustn't think of. We again thanked Mr. Biddle for his good advice, and we knew ourselves determined to go just contrary to it. We couldn't possess ourselves for joy, at finally knowing a place not yet reached by the torrent of European civilization.

'The next day, 23 July, we hastened to rent two horses. As we were planning to keep them about ten days, we wanted to leave a certain payment in the hands of the proprietor; but he refused to take it, saying that we should pay him on our return. The fact is, he was not worried. Michigan is surrounded on all sides by lakes and wildernesses. He was letting us into a kind of corral to which he had the key. After then having purchased a compass as well as munitions, we set out, gun on shoulder, as carefree and lighthearted as two students leaving school to spend their vacation under the paternal roof.*

'As a matter of fact, if we had but wanted to see some trees, our Detroit hosts would have been right in saying that we didn't need to go far; for a mile from the town the road enters the forest for good. The terrain on which the forest grows is perfectly flat and often marshy. On your way you encounter new clearings from time to time. As these establishments bear a perfect resemblance to each other, whether they are to be found in the depths of Michigan or at the gate of New-York, I am going to describe them here once and for all.

'The bell the pioneer is careful to hang around the necks of his cattle in order to be able to find them in the thick woods announces from afar the approach to the clearing. Soon you hear the ringing of the axe cutting the forest trees and, as you approach, traces of destruction proclaim with even greater certainty the presence of man. Chopped branches cover the road. Trunks half consumed by fire or mutilated by iron nevertheless continue to stand upright in your way. You proceed and come into a wood all of whose trees seem to have been struck by sudden death; in midsummer their branches still present only the image of winter. On examining them more closely you perceive that they have been circled by a deep trench cut in the bark, which, arresting the flow of sap, has not been slow to make them die. It's really

---

* 'We set out on our dry hackneys [?], gun and game bag over our shoulders, straw hats on our heads, with each a dufflebag slung over the horse's back.' Bt. to Chabrol, 2 August, on board the *Superior* on Lake Huron (BBlb).

with this that the planter usually begins. Being incapable the first year of cutting all the trees which garnish his new property he sows corn under their branches and, by killing them, prevents their shading his crop.

'After this field, the rough sketch, the first step of civilization in the wilderness, you suddenly perceive the cabin of the proprietor. It is generally placed in the centre of a piece of land more carefully cultivated than the rest but where man still sustains an unequal struggle against nature. There the trees have been cut but not yet uprooted; their trunks still garnish and clutter up the land which formerly they shaded; about this dried debris, wheat, oak shoots, plants of all kinds, herbs of every sort, are tangled and grow together on an indocile and still half-savage soil. It's in the centre of this vigorous and varied vegetation that rises the planter's house, or, as it is called in this country, the *log house*.

'Like the surrounding field this rustic dwelling betrays recent and hasty work. Its length rarely exceeds thirty feet. It is twenty wide, fifteen high. The walls, like the roof, are formed of unsquared tree trunks, between which moss and earth have been placed to prevent the cold and rain penetrating into the interior of the house. As the traveller approaches, the scene becomes more animated. Warned by the sound of his footfall the children who were rolling in the surrounding debris get up precipitately and flee toward the paternal refuge as if frightened at the sight of a man, while two large half-savage dogs, with straight ears and long muzzles, come out of the cabin growling to cover the retreat of their young masters.

'At this point the pioneer himself appears at the door of his dwelling. He throws a scrutinizing glance at the new arrival, signs to the dogs to go back inside, and hastens himself to give them the example without betraying either curiosity or uneasiness.

'Arrived at the doorway of the *log house*, the European cannot keep from throwing an astonished glance around at the spectacle it presents.

'Generally this cabin has only one single window, on which is sometimes hung a muslin curtain; for in these places, where it isn't unusual to see necessaries missing, the superfluous is often found. On the hearth of trodden earth flames a resinous fire which better than daylight illuminates the interior of the building. Above this rustic hearth trophies of war or the hunt are to be seen: a long rifle, a deerskin, eagle feathers. On the right of the chimney is stretched a map of the United States which the wind, coming in through the cracks in the wall, ceaselessly lifts and agitates. Near it, on a solitary shelf of badly squared boards, are placed some ill-assorted books; there you find a Bible whose cover and edges are already worn by the piety of two generations, a book of prayers, and sometimes a song of Milton or a tragedy of Shakespeare. Along the wall are ranged some rude benches, fruit of the proprietor's industry: trunks instead of clothes cupboards, farming tools, and some samples of the harvest. In the centre of the room stands a table whose uneven legs, still garnished with foliage, seem to have grown from the soil where it stands. It's there that the whole family comes together every day for meals. A teapot of English porcelain, spoons most often of wood, a few chipped cups, and some newspapers are there to be seen.

'The appearance of the master of this house is no less remarkable than the place that serves him as asylum. The angular muscles and long thin arms and legs make you recognize at first glance the native of New England. This man was not born in the solitude where he dwells: his constitution alone proclaims that. His first years were passed in the bosom of an intellectual and reasoning society. It's his own desire that has thrown him into the labours of the wilderness for which he does not seem made. But if his physical forces seem beneath his enterprise, in his face, lined by the cares of life, reigns an air of practical intelligence, of cold and persevering energy, which strikes one at once. His step is slow and very regular, his word measured and his face austere. Habit, and pride even more, have imparted to his face that stoic rigidity which his actions belie. The pioneer, it is true, scorns what often most violently moves the heart of man; his goods and his life will never be staked on the throw of the dice or the destinies of a woman; but to become well-to-do he has braved exile, the loneliness and the numberless miseries of the savage life, he has slept on the bare ground, he has exposed himself to the forest fevers and the tomahawk of the Indian. He made this effort one day, he has been renewing it for years, he will continue it twenty years more perhaps without becoming discouraged or complaining. Is a man, capable of such sacrifices, a cold and insensible being? Ought not one on the contrary to recognize in him one of those mental passions, so burning, so tenacious, so implacable?

'Intent on the one goal of making his fortune, the emigrant has finally created for himself an altogether individual existence. Family sentiments have come to fuse themselves in a vast egoism, and it is doubtful if in his wife and children he sees anything else than a detached portion of himself. Deprived of habitual contacts with his fellows, he has learned to take a delight in solitude. When you present yourself on the sill of his isolated dwelling, the pioneer comes forward to meet you, he holds out his hand according to custom, but his face expresses neither benevolence nor joy. He only speaks to ask questions of you. It's an intellectual not an emotional need he is satisfying, and as soon as he has drawn from you the news he wished to learn he falls silent again. One would suppose oneself in the presence of a man who in the evening has retired to his dwelling, tired of the demands and the noise of the world. There is no cordiality in your reception. Interrogate him yourself, he will give you the information you need with intelligence; he will even see to your necessities, watch over your safety so long as you are under his roof; but there reigns in all his actions so much constraint, pride; you perceive in them such a profound indifference even for the results of your efforts, that you feel your gratitude freezing. Yet the pioneer is hospitable in his way, but his hospitality has nothing which touches you because in exercising it he seems to submit himself to a painful necessity of the wilderness; he sees in it a duty which his position imposes on him, not a pleasure. This unknown man is the representative of a race to which belongs the future of the new world: a restless, reasoning, adventurous race which does coldly what only the ardour of passion can explain; race cold and passionate, which traffics in everything, not excepting morality and religion; nation of conquerors who submit themselves to the savage life without ever allowing themselves to be seduced by it, who in civilization and enlightenment love only what is useful to well-being, and who shut themselves in the American solitudes with an axe and some newspapers.

'A people which, like all great peoples, has but one thought, and which is advancing toward the acquisition of riches, sole goal of its efforts, with a perseverance and a scorn for life that one might call heroic, if that name fitted other than virtuous things.

'It's this nomad people which the rivers and lakes do not stop, before which the forests fall and the prairies are covered with shade, and which, after having reached the Pacific ocean, will reverse its steps to trouble and destroy the societies which it will have formed behind it.

'In speaking of the pioneer one cannot forget the companion of his miseries and dangers. Look across the hearth at the young woman, who, while seeing to the preparation of the meal, rocks her youngest son on her knees. Like the emigrant, this woman is in her prime; like him, she can recall the ease of her first years. Her clothes even yet proclaim a taste for adornment ill extinguished. But time has weighed heavily on her: in her prematurely pale face and her shrunken limbs it is easy to see that existence has been a heavy burden for her. In fact, this frail creature has already found herself exposed to unbelievable miseries. Scarce entered upon life, she had to tear herself away from the mother's tenderness and from those sweet fraternal ties that a young girl never abandons without shedding tears, even when going to share the rich dwelling of a new husband. The wife of the pioneer has torn herself in one instant and without hope of returning from that innocent cradle of her youth. It's against the solitude of the forests that she has exchanged the charms of society and the joys of the home. It's on the bare ground of the wilderness that her nuptial couch was placed. To devote herself to austere duties, submit herself to privations which were unknown to her, embrace an existence for which she was not made, such was the occupation of the finest years of her life, such have been for her the delights of marriage. Want, suffering, and loneliness have affected her constitution but not bowed her courage. 'Mid the profound sadness painted on her delicate features, you easily remark a religious resignation and profound peace and I know not what natural and tranquil firmness confronting all the miseries of life without fearing or scorning them.

'Around this woman crowd half naked children, shining with health, careless of the morrow, veritable sons of the wilderness. From time to time their mother throws on them a look of melancholy and joy. To see their strength and her weakness one would say that she has exhausted herself giving them life and that she does not regret what they have cost her.

'The house inhabited by these emigrants has no interior partitions or attic. In the single apartment which it contains the entire family comes in the evening to seek refuge: this dwelling forms of itself a small world. It's the ark of civilization lost in the midst of an ocean of leaves. It's a sort of oasis in the desert. A hundred feet beyond, the eternal forest stretches about it its shade and the solitude begins again.*

\*
\* \*

* For an early reproduction of this description, see *Dém. en Am.*, IV,347–351.

'It was only in the evening after sundown that we reached Pontiac.*
Twenty very neat and pretty houses, forming so many well furnished
shops, a transparent stream, a clearing a quarter of a league square,
and the eternal forest about: there is the faithful tableau of Pontiac
which, in twenty years perhaps, will be a city. The sight of this place
recalled to me what Mr. Gallatin had said in New York a month before: "There are no villages in America, at least in the sense you give
this word." Here the houses of the farmers are all scattered through
their fields. One assembles in a place only to establish a market for the
use of the surrounding population. You see in these so-called villages
only men of law, printers, and merchants.

'We had ourselves taken to the finest inn of Pontiac (for there are
two), and we were introduced, as usual, into what is called the *bar-
room*; it's a room where you are given to drink and where the simplest
as well as the richest traders of the place come to smoke, drink, and
talk politics together, on the footing of the most perfect exterior equality. The master of the shop, or the landlord, was—I shall not call him
a huge peasant, there are no peasants in America—but at least a very
large man whose face wore that expression of candour and simplicity
which distinguishes the Normandy horse traders. He was a man who,
for fear of intimidating you, never looked you in the face while talking
to you but waited, to consider you at his ease, until you were busy
talking elsewhere; moreover, a deep politician and, according to American custom, a pitiless questioner. This estimable citizen, with the rest
of the company, regarded us at first with astonishment. Our travelling
clothes and our guns hardly proclaimed us business men, and to travel
to sightsee was something absolutely unusual. In order to cut the explanations short, we declared at once that we came to buy land. No
sooner had the word been pronounced than we perceived that in seeking to avoid one evil we had thrown ourselves into another much
more redoubtable.

'It is true they stopped treating us like extraordinary beings, but
each one wanted to bargain with us. To disembarrass ourselves of them
and of their farms we told our host that before deciding anything we
wanted to get from him some useful information about the price of
lands and the method of cultivating them. He immediately led us into

---

* 'Air of plenty near Troy. At the door of a log house a family taking tea. The houses
become more and more infrequent. We cross some delightful swamps, glimpse of
English gardens which nature alone has made. Dinner at Troy. We reach Pontiac
at eight in the evening.' Toc. diary note, 23 July.

another room, spread with appropriate deliberation a map of Michigan on the oak table in the middle of the room and, putting the candle between us three, waited in impassive silence for what we had to communicate to him. The reader, without having with us the intention of establishing himself in one of the American solitudes, may yet be curious to know how so many thousands of Europeans and Americans who come there each year in search of a refuge go about it. I shall therefore here transcribe the information furnished us by our Pontiac host. Often since we have been in a position to verify its perfect exactness.

' "It is not here as in France," said our host after having calmly listened to all our questions and snuffed the candle. "With you, labour is cheap and land is dear. Here the cost of land is nothing and the labour of man beyond price: which I say to you so you may realize that to establish oneself in America one needs capital just as in Europe, even though it is differently employed. For my part, I should not advise any one to seek his fortune in our wildernesses unless he has at his disposition from one hundred fifty to two hundred dollars (800 to 1000 francs). In Michigan the acre never costs more than ten shillings (about 6f. 50 cent.) when the land is still uncultivated.* That's about the price of a day's work. A labourer can therefore earn in one day enough to buy an acre of land. But, the purchase made, the difficulties begin. Here is how they generally go about surmounting them.

' "The pioneer betakes himself to the place he has just acquired with some cattle, a salted pig, two barrels of meal and some tea. If a cabin is to be found near there he goes and receives temporary hospitality. If not, he sets up a tent in the midst of the wood which is to become his field. His first care is to fell the nearest trees with which in haste he builds the rude hut whose construction you have perhaps already been able to examine. With us, the keeping of cattle hardly costs anything. The emigrant lets them run in the forest after having tied an iron bell about their necks. It is very rare for these animals, thus abandoned to themselves, to leave the vicinity of their home.

' "The greatest expense is the clearing. If the pioneer arrives in the wilderness with a family in a state to aid him in his first labours his task is easy enough. But it is rarely thus. In general the emigrant is young and, if he has children already, they are very young. Then he

* In his edition, Beaumont altered this to read 'never more than 4 to 5 shillings (from 5 to 6 francs).'

must himself all alone provide for the first needs of his family, or hire the services of his neighbours. It costs from three to four dollars (from 15 to 20 francs) * to have an acre cleared. The ground prepared, the new proprietor puts an acre into potatoes, the rest into wheat and corn. Corn is the providence of these wildernesses; it grows in the water of our swamps and under the forest foliage better than in the rays of the sun. It's the corn which saves the family of the emigrant from inevitable destruction when poverty, sickness, or carelessness has prevented its making a large enough clearing the first year. There is nothing harder than the first years after the clearing. Later come ease and then wealth." †

'Thus spoke our host. For our part, we listened to these simple details with almost as much interest as if we wished to profit from them ourselves,‡ and when he was silent we said to him:—The soil of all the woods left to themselves is generally marshy and unhealthy;

* '4 to 5 dollars (from 20 to 25 francs).' Beaumont.
† 'The revenue from an acre of cultivated land can be valued at two dollars or even more. The cost of the land is nothing, the real expense is its preparation, the price of labour. Here is how one must go about it when not cultivating the land personally (which is rare). I had a man clear twenty acres. I give him five dollars an acre, and I furnish him with the plow and the oxen for the work. I furnish him as well half the seed, and we then share the harvest of the first year. If the crop is good, my half more than repays the five dollars spent. The following crops belong entirely to me.
'Information furnished 26 July 1831 at Pontiac by our host.' Toc. diary note.
‡ It is notable that Tocqueville and Beaumont collected data on the methods and costs of settlement from a number of sources. From Doctor Burns, a new Scotch settler near Pontiac, Tocqueville learned that 'help costs a dollar when he is not fed, six shillings (75¢) when he gets his meals also. Plowing is done with oxen, which cost twelve shillings a day.' Diary, 30 July 1831.
'. . . In the neighbourhood of Syracuse and Lake Oneida uncultivated land sells for from five to six dollars an acre, and cultivated for from fifteen to twenty dollars (8 July 1831).
'At Canadaigua cultivated land sells for from eighteen to twenty dollars, the best for twenty-five dollars an acre. Same value at Buffalo.
'In Michigan Territory an acre of uncultivated land sells uniformly for ten shillings. One has to pay the total price on the spot. It's the same for all lands sold by the *state*. (It's a general measure adopted because of the difficulty of collecting the money due. The state finds its own interest and that of the public served by selling cheaper but for cash [*sans remise*].)
'They regard the purchase of the land as the easiest part of the enterprise of settling. The real expense is that of cultivating. This costs from five to ten dollars per acre (cutting and removing the trees, fencing, clearing the ground). The annual revenue of an acre thus prepared is from two to four dollars. The price of a day's labour is fifty cents, food not included. If you don't feed your help, it is six shillings (this is in contradiction with a number of statistics, according to which the cost of a day's labour without food is eight shillings or a dollar).
'Information obtained 22 July on Lake Erie from an inhabitant of Detroit.' Toc. diary note.

does the emigrant, who exposes himself to the miseries of solitude, have nothing to fear for his life?—All clearing is a dangerous enterprise, resumed the American, and it is almost without example that the pioneer and his family escape the woods fever during the first year. Often, when you travel in the fall, you find all the inhabitants of a cabin down with fever, from the emigrant to his youngest son.— And what becomes of these unfortunates when Providence strikes them in this way?—They resign themselves and await a better future. —But have they some assistance to hope for from their fellows?— Hardly any.—Can they at least procure the aid of a doctor?—The nearest doctor often lives sixty miles from their house. They do like the Indians: they die or get well, as it pleases God.

'We resumed:—Does the voice of religion sometimes reach them? —Very rarely. It has not yet been possible to do anything to assure the public observation of a cult in our woods. Almost every summer, it is true, some Methodist preachers come to make a tour of the new settlements. The noise of their arrival spreads with unbelievable rapidity from cabin to cabin: it's the great news of the day. At the date set, the emigrant, his wife and children set out by scarcely cleared forest trails toward the indicated meeting-place. They come from fifty miles around. It's not in a church that the faithful gather, but in the open air, under the forest foliage. A pulpit of badly squared logs, great trees felled for seats, such are the ornaments of this rustic temple. The pioneers and their families camp in the surrounding woods. It's there that, during three days and three nights, the crowd gives itself over to almost uninterrupted religious exercises. You must see with what ardour these men surrender themselves to prayer, with what attention they listen to the solemn voice of the preacher. It's in the wilderness that people show themselves almost starved for religion.—One last question: it is generally believed by us that the wildernesses of America are peopled by the aid of the European emigration; whence comes it then that since we have been traversing your forests we have not happened to encounter a single European?

'A smile of superiority and of satisfied pride painted itself on the features of our host on hearing this question.

'—It's only Americans, answered he with emphasis, who can have the courage to submit themselves to such miseries and who know how to buy prosperity at such a price. The European emigrant stops in the great cities along the coast or in the neighbouring districts. There he becomes an artisan, farm hand, or servant. He lives an easier life than in Europe and, satisfied to leave his children the same heritage, he is content. It's to the American that the land belongs, it's to him that it is given to take possession of the solitudes of the new world, to make them yield to man and to create for himself thus an immense future.

'After having pronounced these last words, our host stopped. He allowed an immense column of smoke to escape from his mouth and appeared ready to listen to what we had to tell him about our projects.

'We thanked him first of all for his valuable advice and his wise counsels, by which we assured him we should profit some day, and we added:—Before settling in your district, my dear host, we intend to go to Saginaw and we want to consult you on this point.

'At this word Saginaw, a singular revolution took place in the expression of the American. It was as if he were being violently drawn from the real world to be thrust into the realm of the imagination. His eyes dilated, his mouth opened, and the most profound astonishment painted itself on his features.

'—You want to go to Saginaw! cried he, to Saginaw Bay! Two reasonable men, two well educated foreigners want to go to Saginaw Bay! The thing is hardly credible.—And why not? answered we.—But do you realize, retorted our host, what you are undertaking? Do you know that Saginaw is the last inhabited place till the Pacific Ocean; that from here to Saginaw hardly anything but wilderness and pathless solitudes are to be found? Have you thought that the woods are full of Indians and mosquitoes; that you will have to sleep at least one night in the dampness of their shade? Have you thought of the fever? Would you know how to get yourself out of difficulties in the wilderness, and find your way in the labyrinth of our forests?

'After this tirade, he paused the better to judge the impression he had made. We replied:—all that may be very true, but we shall leave to-morrow morning for Saginaw Bay.

'Our host reflected an instant, lifted his head, and said slowly in a measured and positive tone:—Only a great interest can induce two foreigners to such an enterprise. You have doubtless imagined, quite wrongly, that it was advantageous to settle in places the furthest removed from all competition?

'We did not answer.

'He went on:—Perhaps too you are charged by the Canadian fur company to establish relations with the frontier Indians.

'Same silence.

'Our host was at the end of his conjectures, and he fell silent; but he continued to reflect deeply on the strangeness of our design.

'—Have you never been to Saginaw? we said.—I, he answered, I unhappily have been there five or six times, but I had an interest in going, and it is impossible to discover that you have any.—But don't forget, my worthy host, that we do not ask you if one should go to Saginaw, but only what are the means to get there with ease.

'Thus brought back to the question, our American recovered all his self-possession and all the clearness of his ideas. He explained to us in few words and with admirable practical sense how we should set about to cross the wilderness, he entered into the smallest details and foresaw the most fortuitous circumstances. At the end of his prescriptions he paused anew to see if we would not finally reach the mystery of our trip, and, perceiving that neither of us had anything more to say, he took the candle, led us to a room and, having shaken our hands very democratically, went to finish the evening in the common room.

'The next day we got up with the light and prepared to start. Our host was himself soon afoot: the night had not enabled him to discover what made us stick to a conduct so extraordinary in his eyes. However, as we appeared absolutely resolved to act contrary to his advice, he did not dare return to the charge; but he turned constantly about us. From time to time he muttered:—I can with difficulty understand what can induce two foreigners to go to Saginaw . . . and he repeated this phrase several times until finally I said to him, putting my foot in the stirrup:—There are many reasons which carry us there, my dear host!

'He brought up short on hearing these words and, looking me in the face for the first time, he seemed to prepare himself to hear the revelation of the great mystery. But I, calmly forking my horse, for my conclusion made a friendly gesture and went off at full trot.

'When after fifty yards I turned my head, I saw him still planted like a hay stack before his door. Shortly he went in, shaking his head. I imagine he was still saying: I understand with difficulty what two foreigners are going to do at Saginaw.*

*
*    *

* 'The finest inn of Pontiac,' where the scenes above related took place, was known as the 'yellow tavern'; its inquisitive proprietor was (Judge) Amasa Bagley, one of the early pioneers of the territory. Fifty years later, the inn-keeper's daughter wrote:

'It had been suggested to us that we apply to a Mr. Williams who, having long traded with the Chippewa Indians and having a son established at Saginaw, might furnish us with useful information.

'After having made some miles in the woods and as we were beginning to fear that we had already missed our man's house, we encountered an old man busy working a small garden; we approached him, it was Mr. Williams himself.*

'He received us with great benevolence and gave us a letter for his son. We asked him if we did not have anything to fear from the Indian tribes whose territory we were going to cross. Mr. Williams rejected this idea with a sort of indignation:—No, no, said he; you can proceed without fear. For my part, I should sleep more calmly among the Indians than among the whites.

'I note this as the first favourable impression about the Indians that I have received since my arrival in America. In the thickly settled regions they are spoken of only with a mixture of fear and scorn, and I believe that there, in fact, they deserve these two sentiments. It has already been possible to see what I thought of them myself when I encountered the first of them at Buffalo. As one advances in this diary and follows me among the Europeans of the frontier and the Indian tribes themselves, one will conceive an idea at the same time more honourable and more just of the first inhabitants of America.

'After having left Mr. Williams, we pursued our way in the woods. From time to time a small lake (this district is full of them) appears like a sheet of silver under the forest foliage. It is difficult to imagine the charm which surrounds these pretty places where man has not fixed his dwelling and where still reign a profound peace and an uninterrupted silence.

'In the Alps I have visited some fearful solitudes, where nature refused to yield to cultivation but where it deploys, even to the point of horror, a grandeur that transports and impassions the soul. Here the solitude is no less profound, but it does not give rise to the same impressions. The only feelings one experiences in journeying through

---

'His [Tocqueville's] visit to our house is very fresh in my mind. He came during a severe storm, remaining several days. There was a great mystery surrounding him and his servant, (the most important of the two in appearance). They took their meals alone and claimed a good share of my father's attention, seeking from him information on the new territory of Michigan. . . .' Nancy G. Davis, in *Pioneer Society of Michigan Collections*, III,600.[5]

* This seems to have been Major Oliver Williams.

these flowered wildernesses where, as in Milton's *Paradise,* all is prepared to receive man, are a tranquil admiration, a vague distaste for civilized life, a sweet and melancholy emotion, a sort of wild instinct which makes one reflect with sadness that soon this delightful solitude will be completely altered. In fact, the white race is already advancing through the surrounding woods, and in a few years the European will have cut the trees reflected in the limpid waters of the lake and forced the animals peopling its banks to retire to new wildernesses.

'Always progressing, we came into a region of a different appearance. The soil was no longer even, but cut by hills and valleys. Several of these hills were most savage in appearance.

'It was on one of these picturesque trails that, having suddenly turned around to contemplate the imposing spectacle we were leaving behind us, to our great surprise we saw near the crupper of our horses an Indian who seemed to be following us step by step.*

'He was a man about thirty years of age, tall and admirably proportioned as almost all of them are. His black gleaming hair fell to his shoulders except for two tresses attached on the top of his head. His face was daubed with black and red. He was covered by a kind of blue blouse, very short. He wore some red *mittas*: these are a kind of trouser which only go to the upper thigh; and his feet were garnished with moccasins. By his side hung a knife. In his right hand he held a long carbine, and in his left two birds which he had just killed.

'The first sight of this Indian made a rather disagreeable impression on us. The place was ill chosen to resist an attack. On our right a forest of pines rose to an immense height in the air; on our left stretched a deep ravine at the bottom of which tumbled a rocky stream which the thick foliage hid from our view and toward which we were blindly descending! To put our hands on our guns, turn about, and face the Indian in the path was the work of an instant. He himself stopped; we stood for a half minute in silence.

'His face presented all the characteristic traits which distinguish the Indian race from all the others. In his perfectly black eyes burned the wild fire which still animates the glance of the half-breed and is only lost with the second or third generation of white blood. His nose was arched in the middle, lightly flattened at the point; his cheekbones,

* 'At five miles from Little Spring an admirable valley. Hillsides covered with immense pines, torrent which makes itself heard at the bottom of a ravine. We turn to admire this spectacle. We perceive an Indian. . . .' Toc. diary note, 24 July.

very high; and his mouth, deeply cut, revealed two rows of teeth, sparkling white, which gave sufficient proof that the savage, more cleanly than his American neighbour, did not spend his day chewing tobacco leaves.*

'I have said that at the moment we turned about, putting our hands to our arms, the Indian had stopped. He underwent the rapid examination we made of his person with absolute impassiveness, with a glance direct and motionless. As he saw that we on our side had no hostile feelings, he began to smile: probably he saw that he had alarmed us.

'That is the first time I was able to observe how completely the expression of gaiety changes the faces of these savage men. I have had a hundred occasions since to make the same remark. A serious Indian and a smiling Indian are absolutely two different men. There reigns in the immobility of the first a savage majesty which gives you an involuntary feeling of terror. Does this same man smile, his face takes on an expression of *naïveté* and benevolence that gives it real charm.

'When we saw our man's face relax, we addressed him in English; he let us speak at our ease, then signed that he did not understand. We offered him a little brandy which he accepted without hesitation as without thanks. Speaking always by signs, we asked for the birds he was carrying, and he gave them to us in exchange for a small piece of money. Having thus introduced ourselves, we saluted him and went off at full trot.

'At the end of a quarter of an hour's rapid march, having again glanced behind, I was confounded again to see the Indian behind the crupper of my horse. He was running with the agility of a wild animal, without pronouncing a single word or seeming to lengthen his stride. We stopped, he stopped; we went on, he followed. We went on at full speed; our horses, raised in the wilderness, cleared all the obstacles with ease: the Indian doubled his pace; I saw him now on the right now on the left of my horse, jumping over the bushes and falling noiselessly to earth. One would have said one of these wolves of northern Europe which follow riders in the hope that they will fall from their horses and be the more easily devoured.

'The sight of this set face which, now losing itself in the forest obscurity, now reappearing in the daylight, seemed to float at our side,

---

* So far as the present writer is aware, this is almost the only reference in all of Tocqueville's and Beaumont's papers to the habit which so provoked and disgusted Mrs. Trollope and Dickens.

ended by making us uncomfortable. Not being able to conceive what induced this man to follow us at so precipitate a pace, and perhaps he had long been doing so when we discovered him the first time, it occurred to us that he was leading us into an ambush.

'We were occupied with these thoughts when we perceived before us in the woods the end of another carbine; soon we were alongside the bearer. We took him at first for an Indian. He wore a kind of short coat which, folded closely about the waist, revealed an erect and well-proportioned figure. His neck was bare, and his feet covered with moccasins. When we came near him and he raised his head, we at once recognized a European * and we stopped. He came to us, shook hands with cordiality, and we began to converse.

'—Do you live in this wilderness? said we to him.—Yes, answered he, there's my house.

'And he showed us, among the leaves, a hut much more miserable than the usual *log house*.

'—Alone?—Alone.—What do you do here?—I go through these woods and kill to right and left the game to be found on my path; but there are few good shots to be had now.—And this kind of life pleases you?—More than any other.—But are you not afraid of the Indians?—Afraid of the Indians! I would rather live in their midst than among the whites. No, no, I am not afraid of the Indians; they are worth more than we, if we have not brutalized them by our liquors, poor creatures!

'We then showed our new acquaintance the man who was so obstinately following us and who had stopped a few feet away and was standing as motionless as a mark (*terme*).

'—That's a Chippewa, said he, or as the French call them, a *sauteur*. I bet he is returning from Canada where he has received the annual presents of the English. His family cannot be far from here.

'Having spoken thus, the American signed to the Indian to approach and began to speak to him in his tongue with extreme facility. It was remarkable to see the pleasure which these two men of birth and customs so different found in exchanging their ideas. The conversation evidently turned on the comparative merits of their arms. The white, after having examined the gun of the savage very attentively:

---

* 'To be suppressed, I think, has too much the air of a reminiscence from Cooper.' Toc. marginal note.

'—There's a fine carbine, said he; the English have doubtless given it to him to use against us, and he will not fail to do so in the first war. It's thus that the Indians draw on their heads all the misfortunes which overwhelm them, but they don't know any better, poor people! —Do the Indians, said I, use these long and heavy guns with skill?— There are no shots like the Indians, retorted our new friend with the accent of most profound admiration. Examine these small birds which he has sold you, sir: they are pierced with one ball, and I am very sure that he shot only twice to get them. Oh! said he, there is nothing happier than an Indian in the regions whence we have not yet made the game flee; but the large animals scent us at more than three hundred miles and in withdrawing they make before us a sort of desert where the poor Indians can no longer live, if they do not cultivate the earth.

'As we resumed our journey:—when you come by again, our new friend called, knock on my door. It is a pleasure to meet white faces in these parts.

'I have related this conversation, which in itself contains nothing remarkable, to make known a type of man we have since often met on the edges of settlement. They are Europeans who, in spite of the habits of their youth, have ended by finding in the freedom of the wilderness an inexpressible charm. Clinging to the American solitudes by taste and passion, to Europe through their religion, their principles and their ideas, they mingle love of the savage life with the pride of civilization and prefer the Indians to their compatriots, without however acknowledging them as equals.

'We resumed our way, then, and, advancing always with the same rapidity, at the end of a half hour we reached the house of a pioneer.

'Before the door of this cabin an Indian family had taken up its temporary residence. An old woman, two young girls, several children were grouped about a fire to the heat of which were exposed the still palpitating parts of an entire deer. A few feet away an Indian, altogether naked, was warming himself in the rays of the sun, while a small child rolled in the dust near him.* It was there that our silent

* 'Arrival at the small clearing of Little Spring. Flying camp of Indians. Men, women, children about the fire, eating potatoes and partly roasted corn. . . . Profile handsome enough, full face ugly. Cheekbones too protuberant. In spite of what we have been told, they are only to be feared when drunk; otherwise honest and gentle. The proof is that the master of Little Spring had left his wife and his six small children in the midst of this Indian horde, and had gone hunting that very morning. Aspect of the region from Little Spring to Grand Bank [?], very broken country.' Toc. diary note, 24 July.

companion stopped; he left us without taking leave and went to sit gravely among his compatriots.

'What had induced this man to follow our horses thus for two leagues? That's something we were never able to divine.

'After having lunched at this place we remounted and pursued our way through a tall but rather thin grove. The woods had once been burned, as could be seen from the ashy remains of some trees fallen in the earth. The soil to-day is covered by ferns, which stretch as far as one can see under the forest foliage.

'Some leagues further on my horse lost its shoe, which caused us a lively uneasiness. Near there, fortunately, we met a planter who succeeded in replacing it. But for this happy encounter, I doubt whether we would have been able to go any further, for we were approaching the extreme limit of the clearings. This same man, who thus put us in a position to pursue our way, invited us to hasten, the day beginning to fall and two long leagues still separating us from *Flint-River* where we wished to sleep.

'Soon, in fact, a deep obscurity began to envelop us. It was necessary to walk. The night was serene, but glacial. There reigned in the depth of these forests a silence so profound and a calm so complete that one would have said that all the forces of nature were as if paralysed. One heard only the uncomfortable buzzing of mosquitoes and the footfall of our horses. From time to time one sighted in the distance an Indian fire before which an austere and still profile sketched itself in the smoke.

'At the end of an hour we arrived at a place where the road forked, two paths opened off the spot. Which of the two to take? It was a delicate choice. One of the two ended at a stream whose depth we did not know, the other at a clearing. The moon, which was then rising, showed ahead of us a valley filled with a thousand debris; further on we saw houses.

'It was so important not to lose ourselves in such a place at such an hour that we resolved to inform ourselves before going further. My companion stayed behind to hold the horses, and I, throwing my gun on my shoulder, descended into the valley.

'Soon I perceived that I was entering a very recent clearing. Immense trees, with their branches not yet lopped off, covered the ground. By jumping from one to the other I came near the houses fairly rapidly. But the same stream we had already encountered separated me from them. Happily its course in this place was obstructed by some great oaks which the pioneer's axe had doubtless felled there. I succeeded in working my way along these trees and finally arrived on the other bank.*

'I approached the two houses with caution, fearing that they might be Indian wigwams. They were not yet finished. I found the doors open and no voice replied to mine. I returned to the bank of the stream where for some minutes I couldn't keep from admiring the supreme horror of the place.

'This valley where I found myself seemed to form an immense amphi-theatre, surrounded by the foliage of the woods on all sides, as by black drapery, and in whose centre the rays of the moon, breaking, came to create a thousand fantastic beings which played with each other silently in the forest debris. Beyond that, no sound whatever, no noise of life rose from this solitude.

'At length I thought of my companion, and I shouted to him to tell him the result of my search and to get him to cross the stream and come and find me. My voice echoed a long time in the surrounding solitudes, but I got no response. I shouted again and still listened. The same deathly silence reigned in the forest. Uneasiness seized me, and I ran along the stream to find the trail which I knew crossed it lower down.

"Arrived there, I heard in the distance the footfall of horses and soon after I saw Beaumont himself appear. Astonished by my long absence, he had decided to advance toward the stream. He had already begun to descend the slope when I had called. My voice had not then been able to reach him. He told me that on his side he had made every effort to make himself heard and, like me, had been frightened at not receiving a response. But for the ford, which served us as a meeting place, we would perhaps have hunted each other a large part of the night.

'We set forth again promising each other faithfully not to separate any more, and three quarters of an hour from there we finally caught sight of a clearing, two or three cabins and, what pleased us even more, a light. The river, which stretched like a violet thread at the end of the valley, convinced us that we had arrived at Flint River.†

* 'I then see by the light of the moon that they have built a rude dam and have begun to construct a building which is probably to be a saw-mill.' Toc. diary note, 24 July.
† 'I get down from my horse; I march straight toward the light which struck my eyes. After walking about five minutes I am near enough to distinguish a wooden

'Soon, in fact, the baying of dogs made the woods ring and we found ourselves before a *log house*, separated from it by a single barrier. As we were preparing to cross it, the moon showed us on the other side a great black bear which, upright on its hind feet and drawing its chain in, showed as clearly as it could its intention to give us a fraternal accolade.

'—What a devilish country is this, said I, where they have bears for watchdogs.—We'll have to call, answered my companion; if we tried to cross the fence we should have difficulty making the porter understand.

'We shouted, then, at the top of our lungs and so well that a man finally put his head out the window. After having examined us in the moonlight,—Enter, gentlemen, said he. Trink, go lie down! To your kennel, I say, these are not thieves.

'The bear retreated waddling, and we entered. We were half dead with fatigue. We ask our host if we can have hay for our horses.— Surely, he answered; and he set to work to scythe the nearest field with all the calm of Americans and as he might have done at midday. Meanwhile, we unsaddled our mounts and tied them, for want of a stable, to the fence we had just crossed.

'Having thus cared for our travel companions, we began to think of our own lodgings. There was only one bed in the house; the toss having given it to Beaumont, I pulled my mantle about me and, stretching out on the floor, slept as profoundly as becomes a man who has just done fifteen leagues on horseback.'

---

house, without a door and half roofed over. Somebody was moving inside without showing themselves, and it seemed to me that they were trying to hide the light which illuminated the interior. Finally, assuming the softest and most humble voice in order to reassure the people of this dwelling who might take me for a thief, I ask if they can tell me where is the house of Mr. Todds (the name of the man with whom we wished to stay at Flint River). At that there appears a half-clothed woman, carrying a torch in her hand, who tells me in the most obliging tone that Mr. Todds' house is in the neighbourhood at no great distance.—This unhappy woman was alone in this house, abandoned and open to all the winds.—I didn't have time further to commiserate her lot, and I returned to Tocqueville, not without difficulty, as I got caught in a swamp where for the moment I thought I should remain. Finally we found shelter at Mr. Todds. . . .' Bt. to Chabrol, 2 August, on board the *Superior* on Lake Huron (BBlb).

'Mr. Todds,' here referred to, was Major John (Joseph) Todd, Pontiac pioneer and first settler of Flint, who, with his wife 'Aunt Polly' Todd, kept a little inn later noted as the half-way house to Saginaw.

## XXI

## FORTNIGHT IN THE WILDERNESS (*Cont.*)

'THE next day, 25 July, our first care was to inquire for a guide.

'A wilderness of fifteen leagues separates Flint River from Saginaw, and the road there is only a narrow path, scarce recognizable to the eye. Our host approved of our plan, and soon after he brought us two Indians in whom he assured us we could place every confidence. One was a child of thirteen to fourteen years, the other a young man of eighteen. The body of the latter, without yet having acquired the vigorous shape of maturity, gave already, however, the idea of agility united to strength. He was of medium height, his figure straight and slim, his limbs flexible and well proportioned. Long tresses fell from his bare head. Moreover, he had carefully painted on his face lines of black and red in the most symmetrical way; a ring passed through the membrane of his nose, a necklace and earrings completed his apparel. His accoutrements of war were no less remarkable. On one side the battle-axe, the celebrated tomahawk; on the other a long sharp knife, with whose aid the savages lift the scalps of the vanquished. From his neck was suspended a bull's horn which served him as a powder-box, and in his right hand he held a rifle. As with most of the Indians, his glance was fierce and his smile kindly. Beside him, as if to complete the tableau, walked a dog with straight ears, narrow muzzle, much more like a fox than any other animal, and whose fierce air was in perfect harmony with the countenance of his conductor.

'After having examined our new companion with an attention of which he did not seem an instant aware, we asked him what he wanted as the price of the service he was going to render us. The Indian answered a few words in his tongue and the American, hastening to speak, told us that what the savage asked would be valued at two dollars.

'—As these poor Indians, added our host charitably, do not know the value of money, you will give me the dollars and I shall willingly undertake to furnish him the equivalent.

'I was curious to see what the worthy man called the equivalent of two dollars, and I followed him very softly to the place where the bargain was consummated. I saw him deliver our guide a pair of moccasins and a pocket handkerchief, objects whose total value certainly did not reach half the sum. The Indian withdrew very much pleased . . . and I slipped away silently, saying like La Fontaine: Ah! if the lions knew how to paint!

'Furthermore, it's not only the Indians whom the American pioneers take for dupes. We were ourselves daily victims of their extreme avidity for gain. It's very true that they do not steal, they are too enlightened to commit such an imprudence, but I have never seen an inn-keeper of a large city overcharge with more impudence than these inhabitants of the wilderness among whom I thought to find primitive honesty and the simplicity of patriarchal customs.

'All was ready: we mounted and, fording the stream (Flint River) which forms the extreme boundary between civilization and the wilderness, we entered once and for all into the solitude.

'Our two guides walked or rather jumped before us like wildcats across the obstacles in the path. Did a fallen tree, a stream, a marsh present itself, they pointed out the best way, crossed themselves, and did not even look back to see us get out of our difficulties. Used to counting only on himself, the Indian has difficulty conceiving that another may have need of help. He knows how to render you a service at need, but no one has yet taught him the art of making it appreciated through courtesies and attentions. This manner of conduct would have elicited some observations on our part, but it was impossible to make our companions understand a single word. And then we felt ourselves completely in their power. There, in fact, the ladder was upside down. Plunged into a deep obscurity, reduced to his own resources, the civilized man was marching like a blind man, incapable not only of guiding himself in the labyrinth he was traversing but even of finding there the means to sustain life. It's in the same difficulties that the savage triumphed. For him the forest had no veil; he was as if at home; he marched there with his head in the air, guided by an instinct more certain than the mariner's compass. At the summit of the tallest trees, under the thickest foliage, his eyes discovered the prey near which the European passes and repasses a hundred times in vain.

'From time to time our Indians stopped. They put their hands on their lips to invite us to silence and signed to us to dismount. Guided by them, we managed to reach a place whence the game could be seen. It was a singular spectacle to see the scornful smile with which they guided us by the hand like children and finally conducted us near the object which they themselves had seen long ago.

'As we advanced, however, the last traces of man disappeared. Soon everything ceased even to proclaim the presence of the savage, and we had before us the spectacle we had so long run after: the interior of a virgin forest.

'In a thin grove through which objects can be seen at quite a distance, rose in a single bound a high clump composed almost entirely of pines and oaks. Obliged to grow on very circumscribed soil and almost entirely deprived of the sun's rays, each of these trees rises by the shortest way to seek the air and the light. As straight as the mast of a vessel, it shoots up beyond all the surrounding forest, and it is only in the upper regions that it tranquilly spreads its branches and envelops itself in their shade. Others soon follow it into that elevated sphere and all, interlacing their branches, form as it were an immense dais, above the earth which bears them.* Beneath this still humid vault the aspect changes and the scene takes on a new character.

'A majestic order reigns above your head. Near the earth, on the contrary, everything offers the image of confusion and chaos: trunks incapable of longer supporting their branches have broken at half their height and present to the eye only a torn and pointed top. Others, long shaken by the wind, have been precipitated to earth in one piece. Torn from the soil, their roots form so many natural ramparts behind which hundreds of men could easily find cover. Immense trees, retained by the surrounding branches, hang suspended in the air, and fall into dust without touching the earth.

'With us there is no region so little peopled, where a forest is so abandoned to itself that the trees, after having calmly lived out their life, finally fall of decrepitude. It's man who fells them in the prime of their age and who clears the forest of their debris. In the American

---

* 'I measured a pine which is 20 feet in circumference, and an oak which is 18.' Bt. to Chabrol, 2 August, on board the *Superior* on Lake Huron (BBlb).

solitude, on the contrary, all-powerful nature is the only agent of ruin as it is the only power of reproduction. As in the forests within the domain of man, death strikes here without ceasing, but no one takes away the debris it has made; each day adds to their number. They fall, they accumulate, one on the other; there is not the time to reduce them quick enough to dust and prepare new places. There are to be found, lying side by side, several generations of dead. Some, in the last stages of dissolution, present to the eye only a long streak of red dust on the ground; others, already half consumed by time, still preserve their shape. Finally there are some, fallen yesterday, which stretch their long branches on the ground and at each instant arrest the steps of the traveller by unforeseen obstacles. . . .

'It has often happened to us to admire on the ocean one of those calm, serene evenings when the sails fluttering peacefully along the masts leave the sailor ignorant of the direction whence the breeze will come. This repose of all nature is not less imposing in the solitudes of the new world than on the immensity of the sea.

'When at midday the sun darts his rays at the forest, one often hears in its depths as it were a long sigh, a plaintive cry prolonged into the distance. It's the last effort of the expiring wind; everything about you then enters into a silence so profound, a stillness so complete, that the soul feels penetrated by a sort of religious terror; the traveller stops, then he gazes about:

'Pressed against each other, their branches intertwined, the forest trees seem to form only a single whole, an immense and indestructible edifice, under whose vaults reigns an eternal obscurity. In whatever direction one looks, one sees only a field of violence and destruction, trees broken, trunks torn; everything proclaims that the elements here make perpetual war, but the struggle is suspended, the movement is suddenly arrested. At the order of a great power the half broken branches have remained hung from trunks which seem no longer able to support them; trees already uprooted have not had the time to reach the ground and have remained suspended in the air.

'He listens, he holds his breath fearfully the better to catch the slightest sound of existence which may strike his ear. No sound, no murmur reaches him. It has more than once happened to us in Europe to find ourselves lost in the woods: but always some sounds of life come there to strike the ear. It was the distant ringing of the nearest village bell, the footfalls of a traveller, the axe of the woodchopper, the sound of a shot, the barking of a dog, or only that confused rumour which rises from a civilized country.

'Here not only man is missing, but even the voices of animals are not heard. The smallest of them have left these regions to go nearer human habitation, the larger to go farther away; those who remain keep hidden under shelter from the rays of the sun. Thus everything is still, everything in the woods is silent under the foliage; one would say that the Creator has for a moment turned his face away and that the forces of nature are paralysed.

'It is not in this single case, furthermore, that we have remarked the singular analogy existing between the aspect of the ocean and of a wild forest. In one spectacle as in the other the idea of immensity besieges you. The continuity of the same scenes, their monotony even, astonishes and weighs down the imagination. The feeling of isolation and abandonment, which had seemed so heavy to us in mid-Atlantic, I have found more strong and poignant perhaps in the solitudes of the New World.

'On the sea, at least, the voyager contemplates a vast horizon toward which he always directs his glance with hope; he sees before him as far as his eye can carry, and he perceives the sky. But in this ocean of foliage who can indicate the road? In vain do you climb on the summit of the highest trees, others higher still surround you. Uselessly do you climb the hills, everywhere the forest seems to go along with you, and this same forest stretches before you even to the arctic pole and the Pacific ocean.

'You can travel thousands of leagues in its shade and you advance always without seeming to change your place. . . .

'. . . But it is time to return to the route to Saginaw. We had already proceeded for five hours in complete ignorance of the place where we were when our Indians stopped and the older, whose name was Sagan-Cuisco, made a line in the sand. He pointed to one end of it crying:—*Michi-Couté-ouinque* (the Indian name for Flint River) and to the other extremity pronouncing the name of *Saginaw*, and, making a point in the middle of the line, he indicated that we had reached the half-way point and that we should rest a few minutes.

'The sun was already high on the horizon, and we would have accepted with pleasure the invitation made us, if we had seen some water at hand; but not seeing any in the neighbourhood we signed to the Indian that we wished to eat and drink at the same time. He understood us at once and set off with the same speed as before. An hour later he stopped again and showed us thirty yards off in the woods a place where he made a sign that there was water.

'Without awaiting our reply, and without helping us to unsaddle our horses, he went there himself; we hastened to follow him. The wind had recently blown down a tall tree at this place; in the hole formerly occupied by its roots, a little rain water was to be found. This was the fountain to which our guide conducted us, without seeming to think that one might hesitate to use such a drink.

'We opened our sack. Another misfortune! The heat had absolutely spoiled our provisions, and we saw ourselves reduced for all dinner to a very small piece of bread, all we had been able to find at Flint River.

'Add to that a cloud of mosquitoes drawn by the nearness of water, whom one had to fight with one hand while carrying the morsel to the mouth with the other, and you will have the idea of a picnic dinner in a virgin forest.

'While we ate our Indians sat, arms crossed, on the fallen tree of which I have spoken. When they saw that we had finished, they made sign that they too were hungry. We showed them our empty sack; they shook their heads without saying anything. The Indian does not know what regular meal hours are; he gorges himself with food when he can, and then fasts until he again finds something to satisfy his appetite: the wolves do the same in like circumstance.

'Soon we thought of remounting, but we perceived with great fright that our mounts had disappeared. Bitten by the mosquitoes and pricked by hunger, they had gone from the path where we had left them, and it was only with difficulty that we were able to put ourselves on their trail. If we had remained inattentive a quarter of an hour, we would have awakened like Sancho with the saddle between our legs. We blessed the mosquitoes who had so quickly made us think of leaving, and we put ourselves on the road again.

'The path we were following immediately became more and more difficult to recognize. At each instant our horses had to force a passage through thick clumps or jump over the trunks of the immense trees barring the path.

'At the end of two hours of extremely hard travelling we finally arrived on the bank of a shallow but very inaccessible stream. We forded it and, arrived on the top of the opposite bank, we saw a field of corn and two cabins quite like log houses. On approaching we discovered that we were in a small Indian settlement: the pretended log houses were wigwams. Further, the most profound solitude reigned there as in the surrounding forest.

'Before the first of these abandoned dwellings Sagan-Cuisco stopped. He carefully examined all the objects round about, then, putting down his gun and approaching us, he first traced a line on the sand indicating in the same way as before that we had yet only covered two thirds of the journey; then getting up he showed us the sun and signed to us that it was fast sinking toward its setting. He then looked at the Wigwam and closed his eyes. This language was most intelligible: he wished to have us spend the night at this place. I admit that this news greatly surprised and hardly pleased us. We hadn't eaten since morning and we were only moderately anxious to sleep without supping. The sombre and savage majesty of the scenes which we had witnessed since morning, the complete isolation in which we found ourselves, the fierce countenances of our guides with whom it was impossible to enter into understanding, none of these besides was of a nature to beget trust in us.

'There was in the conduct of the Indians something singular which did not reassure us at all. The route which we had just followed for two hours seemed still less frequented than the one we had been on before. No one had ever told us that we were to pass an Indian village; and every one had assured us, on the other hand, that we could go in a single day from Flint River to Saginaw. We were therefore unable to understand why our guides wished to retain us overnight in the wilderness.

'We insisted on going ahead. The Indian indicated that we should be surprised by the darkness in the woods. To force our guides to continue their route would have been a dangerous attempt. We decided to tempt their cupidity. But the Indian is the most philosophic of men. He has few needs, and correspondingly few desires. Civilization has no hold on him. He is ignorant of and despises its comforts (*douceurs*).

'I had however noticed that Sagan-Cuisco had paid particular attention to a small osier bottle hanging at my side. A bottle that doesn't break! That was a thing whose utility had appealed to his senses and which had excited his real admiration. My gun and my bottle were the only parts of my European accoutrements which had seemed to excite his envy. I made a sign to him that I should give him my bottle if he conducted us at once to Saginaw. The Indian thereupon appeared violently torn. He looked again at the sun, then the earth. Finally, deciding, he seized his carbine, twice putting his hand on his mouth, he uttered the cry: ouh! ouh! and threw himself before us into the brush.

'We followed him at full trot and, forcing our way through, we had soon lost the Indian dwellings to view. Our guides ran thus for two hours with greater speed than they had before made.*

'However the night gained on us and the last rays of the sun had just disappeared in the trees of the forest when Sagan-Cuisco was seized with a violent nosebleed. Habituated though this young man appeared to be, with his brother, to bodily exercise, it was evident that fatigue and want of food were beginning to exhaust his strength. We ourselves began to fear that they would renounce the attempt and want to make us sleep at the foot of a tree. We therefore decided to have them alternately ride our horses.

'The Indians accepted our offer without astonishment or humility.

'It was a strange sight to see these half naked men gravely established on English saddles and carrying our gamebags and our guns slung on bandoleers, while we walked painfully afoot before them.

'Night finally came. A glacial humidity began to spread under the foliage. The obscurity then gave to the forest an aspect new and terrible. One saw about one only confused piled-up masses, without order or symmetry, forms bizarre and disproportioned, incoherent scenes, fantastic images which seemed borrowed from the sick imagination of a man in fever. The gigantic and the ridiculous were as close together there as in the literature of our age. Never had our steps awakened more echoes, never had the silence of the forest appeared to us so formidable. One would have said that the buzzing of mosquitoes was the only breathing of this sleeping world.

'As we advanced the shadows became deeper; only from time to time

* 'From time to time a shed of oak bark and the remains of a fire. We only encounter a single human being, a woman asleep with a child near a fire. . . . Now and then the stream across our path. We kill several pieces of game and wish to stop. The Indian signs that we must now carry out our enterprise.' Toc. diary note, 25 July.

  'From time to time, as we were very tired, we slowed the steps of our horses, but the Indian would turn and cry Saginaw!! Saginaw!! pointing to the sun which was already beginning to sink, and he would set off at full speed.

  'The distractions of hunting had made us lose a little time; occasionally also I would stop when I saw in the woods a wild flower which seemed pretty, and I would get off my horse to pluck it.' Bt. to Chabrol, 2 August, on board the *Superior* on Lake Huron (BBlb).

a firefly traversing the woods traced as it were a luminous thread in its depths. We realized too late the justness of the Indian's advice, but it was no longer a question of going back.

'We therefore continued as rapidly as our strength and the night allowed. At the end of an hour we came out of the woods and we found ourselves in a vast prairie. Our guides then stopped, and three times uttered a savage cry which echoed like the discordant notes of a *tam-tam*. An answer came from the distance. Five minutes after we were on the bank of a river whose far bank the darkness made it impossible to see. . . .

'The Indians halted at this place. They wound their blankets about them to avoid the bites of the mosquitoes and, hiding in the grass, they soon formed but a scarcely perceptible ball of wool in which it would have been impossible to recognize the form of man.

'We ourselves dismounted and waited patiently for what was to follow. At the end of a few minutes a gentle sound was heard and something approached the bank.

'It was an Indian canoe, about ten feet long and, as usual, formed of a single tree. The man who crouched in the bottom of this frail embarcation wore the costume and had all the appearance of an Indian. He spoke to our guides who, at his orders, hastened to take the saddles off our horses and to place them in the pirogue. As I myself was preparing to get in, the seeming Indian came towards me, put two fingers on my shoulder and said to me in a Norman accent that made me tremble: Don't go too fast, people sometimes drown themselves here (*y en a des fois ici qui s'y noient*). Had my horse spoken to me I don't think I should have been more surprised.

'I stared at the speaker whose face, struck by the first rays of the moon, was gleaming like a ball of copper: Who are you? French seems to be your tongue, said I, and you have the appearance of an Indian? He replied that he was a *bois-brûlé*, that is to say the son of a Canadian and an Indian woman. I shall frequently have occasion to speak of this singular race of half-breeds which covers all the frontiers of Canada and a part of those of the United States. For the moment I thought only of the pleasure of speaking my mother tongue.

'Following the counsels of our compatriot the savage, I seated myself in the bottom of the canoe and held myself as steady as possible; my horse, which I held only by the bridle, entered the river and began to swim, while the Canadian propelled the craft with his paddle, all the while singing softly, to an old French air, the following couplet, the first lines of which alone I caught:

> Entre Paris et Saint Denis
> Il était une fille, etc.

'We arrived thus without accident at the other bank; the canoe returned at once to get my companion. I shall remember all my life the moment when he for the second time approached the bank. The moon, which was full, was then rising precisely over the prairie which we had just crossed; half of its disk only appeared on the horizon; one would have said a mysterious gate through which the light of another sphere was escaping to us. The rays coming from it were reflected in the water and shimmered to where I was. On the very path where trembled this pale light advanced the Indian pirogue. One saw no oars, heard no noise of paddles. It glided swiftly and without effort, long, narrow and black, like a Mississippi alligator making toward the bank to seize its prey. Crouched in the point of the canoe, Sagan-Cuisco, head on his knees, showed only the gleaming tresses of his hair; at the other extremity the Canadian paddled in silence, while behind him Beaumont's horse made the water of the Saginaw break away under the impulse of his powerful breast.*

'There was in the ensemble of this tableau a savage grandeur which then made and has since left a profound impression on our minds.[1]

'Disembarked, we hastened to betake ourselves to a house which the moon had just discovered a hundred paces from the stream and where the Canadian assured us we could find lodging. We did in fact succeed in establishing ourselves comfortably and we should probably have repaired our strength if we had been able to get rid of the myriads of mosquitoes with which the house was filled; but that's what we never were able to accomplish.

'The animal they call *mosticos* [*sic*] in English and *maringouin* in French Canadian is a small insect in every respect like the *cousin* of France, from which it differs only in size. It is generally larger; and its sting is so strong and sharp that only linen goods can guarantee against it. These small flies are the scourge of the American solitudes. Their presence would suffice to render a long sojourn there insupport-

---

* 'This system of navigation did not seem at all reassuring to me, and I confess that it appeared to me almost certain that it would be necessary to swim to get across.' Bt. to Chabrol, 2 August, on board the *Superior* on Lake Huron (BBlb).

able. For my part, I declare that I have never experienced a torment like to what they made me suffer during the whole course of this voyage and particularly during our stay at Saginaw. During the day they prevented us from sketching, from writing, from keeping still a single instant; at night they circled about us by thousands, each part of the body that we left uncovered instantly served as a rendez-vous. Awakened by the pain caused by their bite, we covered our heads with our sheets; their sting went right through. Hunted, pursued by them thus, we arose and went to breathe the air outside until the excess of fatigue finally procured us a painful and interrupted sleep.

\*

\*     \*

'We went out very early, and the first spectacle which struck us, on leaving the house, was the sight of our Indians who, rolled in their blankets near the door, slept beside their dogs.

'We then saw for the first time in broad daylight the village of Saginaw which we had come so far to seek. A small cultivated plain, bordered on the south by a fine tranquil river, on the east, west, and north by the forest, composes at present the whole territory of the city that is coming into being.

'Near us rose a house whose structure proclaimed the well-to-do character of the proprietor. It was the one where we had just spent the night. A dwelling of the same kind was to be seen at the other end of the clearing. In the interval, and along the edge of the woods, two or three log houses were half lost in the foliage.

'On the opposite bank stretched the prairie like the boundless ocean on a calm day. A column of smoke then escaped from it and rose peacefully toward the sky. By following it to earth one finally discovered two or three wigwams whose conic form and pointed peak melted into the prairie vegetation. An overturned cart, some oxen going back of themselves to the plowing, some half-tamed horses completed the tableau.

'Wherever one looked the eye sought in vain the steeple of a gothic tower, the wooden cross marking the way or the moss-covered doorstep of the presbytery. These venerable remains of the antique Christian civilization have not been carried into the wilderness. Nothing there as yet recalls the idea of the past and of the future. One doesn't even encounter any asylums sacred to those who are no more. Death has not had time to reclaim its domain nor to mark out its fields.

'Here man still seems to enter life furtively. Several generations do not gather round his cradle to express hopes often fallacious, and give themselves over to premature rejoicings which the future will belie. His name is not inscribed in the registers of the city; religion does not come to mingle its touching solemnities to the solicitudes of the family. The prayers of a wife, some drops of water sprinkled on the child's head by the father's hand, noiselessly open to him the gates of heaven.

'The village of Saginaw is the last point inhabited by the Europeans, toward the northwest of the vast peninsula of Michigan. It can be considered an advance post, a sort of refuge that the whites have come to place among the Indian nations.

'The revolutions of Europe, the tumultuous clamours rising ceaselessly from the regulated universe, reach here only at long intervals, like the echo of a sound whose nature and origin the ear can no longer distinguish.

'Now it will be an Indian who, passing through, will relate with the poetry of the wilderness some of the sad realities of life in society; a newspaper forgotten in the haversack of a hunter, or simply that vague rumour that spreads by unknown ways and rarely fails to warn men that something extraordinary is happening under the sun.

'Once a year a vessel, mounting the Saginaw, comes to tie this detached link in to the great European chain which already envelops the world with its coils. It brings to the new establishment the divers products of industry, and in return takes away the fruits of the soil.

'Thirty persons, men, women, old men, and children, at the time of our passage composed the whole of this little society, scarce formed, germ confided to the wilderness that the wilderness is to make fruitful.

'Chance, interest, or passions had gathered these thirty persons in this narrow space. Between them were no ties; they differed profoundly from each other. One noted among them Canadians, Americans, Indians, and half-breeds.

'Philosophers have believed that human nature, everywhere the same, varied only following the institutions and laws of the different societies. That's one of those opinions that seems to be disproved at every page of the history of the world. Nations like individuals all show themselves there with a face that is their own. The characteristic features of their visage are reproduced through all the transformations they undergo.

Laws, customs, religions change, empire and wealth come and go, external appearance varies, clothes differ, prejudices replace each other. Under all these changes you recognize always the same people. It's always the same people, which is growing up. Something inflexible appears in human flexibility.

'The men who inhabit this little cultivated plain belong to two races which for more than a century have existed on the American soil and obeyed the same laws. Yet they have nothing in common between them. They are still Englishmen and Frenchmen, such as they show themselves on the banks of the Seine and the Thames.

'Enter this cabin of boughs, you will meet a man whose cordial welcome, joyful face and half-opened mouth will at once proclaim a taste for social pleasures and a carefree attitude toward life. At first you will perhaps take him for an Indian. Subjected to the savage life, he has voluntarily adopted its clothes, usages, and almost its morals; he wears moccasins, a mink cap and wool cape. He is a tireless hunter, lies in his blind, lives on wild honey and bison meat.

'Yet this man has none the less remained a Frenchman, gay, enterprising, glorious, proud of his origins, passionately fond of military glory, more vain than calculating, man of instinct, obeying his first impulse rather than his reason, preferring fame to money.

'To come to the wilderness, he seems to have broken all the ties which attach him to life. One sees no wife and children with him. This state is contrary to his customs, but he submits himself easily to it as to everything. There is in the nature of the French something malleable and yet inflexible. Delivered to his natural bent he would normally feel home-loving. None more than he prefers to rejoice himself by the sight of his paternal tower. But he has been torn, in spite of himself, from his tranquil rounds; his imagination has been struck by new pictures; he has been transported under another sky: this same man has suddenly felt possessed by an insatiable need for violent emotions, for vicissitudes and dangers. The most civilized European has become the adorer of the savage life. He will prefer his savannahs to the city streets, hunting to agriculture. He will play with existence, and live without care for the future.

'The whites of France, said the Indians of Canada, are as good hunters as we. Like us, they despise the comforts of life and brave the terrors of death; God had created them to dwell in the cabin of the savage and to live in the wilderness.

'A few yards from this man lives another European who, subjected to the same difficulties, has stiffened himself against them.

'This one is cold, tenacious, pitiless arguer. He binds himself to the soil and wrests from the savage life all that he can take from it. He struggles ceaselessly against it, despoils it daily of some of its attributes. Piece by piece he transports into the wilderness his laws, his habits, his customs and, if he can, even the niceties of advanced civilization. The emigrant of the United States esteems only the results of victory; he holds that glory is a vain noise, and that man is come into the world only to acquire ease and the comforts of life. Brave, but brave by calculation; brave because he has discovered that there are several things harder to bear than death; adventurer surrounded by his family, who yet cares little for intellectual pleasures and the charms of social life.

'Placed on the other side of the stream, amid the reeds of the Saginaw, the Indian throws from time to time a stoic glance at the dwellings of his European brothers. Don't go and believe that he admires their works or envies their lot. In the nearly three hundred years that the American savage has struggled against the civilization which thrusts and envelops him, he has not yet learned to know and to esteem his enemy. The generations succeed each other in vain with the two races. Like two parallel rivers they have for three hundred years been flowing toward a common abyss. A narrow space separates them, but they do not mingle their floods.

'It is not, however, that the native of the new world lacks natural aptitude; his nature seems obstinately to reject our ideas and our arts. Lying on his blanket, in the smoke of his hut, the Indian regards with scorn the comfortable dwelling of the European. As for him, he takes a proud pleasure in his misery, and his heart swells and lifts at the evidences of his barbarian independence. He smiles bitterly on seeing us torment our lives to acquire useless riches. What we call industry he calls shameful servitude. He compares the labourer to the ox painfully plowing his furrow. What we call the comforts of life he calls children's toys and women's playthings. He envies us only our arms. When man can shelter his head at night under a tent of foliage, when he can light a fire to drive off the mosquitoes in summer and protect himself from cold in winter, when his dogs are good and the country full of game, what more could he ask of the eternal being?

'On the other bank of the Saginaw, near the clearing of the Europeans and, so to speak, on the confines of the old and new worlds, rises a rustic cabin, more comfortable than the wigwam of the savage, more rude than the house of the civilized man (*homme policé*): it's the dwelling of the half-breed.

'When we for the first time presented ourselves at the door of this half-civilized hut, we were surprised to hear in the interior a soft voice singing to an Indian air the canticles of penitence. We stopped a moment to listen. The modulation of the air was slow and profoundly sad; one easily recognized the plaintive melody which characterizes all the songs of man in the wilderness.

'We entered: the master was absent. Seated in the centre of the apartment, her legs crossed on a mat, a young woman was making some moccasins. With her foot she was rocking a child whose copper skin and features proclaimed its double origin. This woman was dressed like one of our peasants, except that her feet were bare and her hair fell freely on her shoulders. Seeing us, she fell silent with a sort of respectful fear. We asked her if she was French.—No, she answered, smiling.—English?—No, said she. She lowered her eyes and added: I am only a savage.

'Child of the two races, brought up in the use of two languages, nourished in diverse beliefs and cradled in contrary prejudices, the half-breeds forms a composite as inexplicable to others as to himself. The images of the world, when they come to reflect themselves in his rude brain, appear to him only a tangled chaos from which his spirit could not extricate itself. Proud of his European origin, he despises the wilderness, and yet he loves the savage freedom which reigns there; he admires civilization and is unable to submit himself completely to its empire. His tastes are in contradiction with his ideas, his opinions with his ways. Not knowing how to guide himself by the doubtful light which illumines him, his soul struggles painfully in the web of universal doubt: he adopts contrary usages, he prays at two altars, he believes in the Redeemer of the world and the amulettes of the charlatan, and he reaches the end of his career without having been able to untangle the obscure problem of his existence.

'Thus, in this unknown corner of the world, the hand of God had already thrown the seeds of diverse nations. Already several different races, several distinct faces found themselves here face to face.

'A few exiled members of the great human family have met in the immensity of the woods. Their needs are common; they are scarce thirty in a wilderness, where everything defies their efforts; they have to struggle together against the beasts of the forest, hunger, the inclemency of the seasons; and they throw at each other only looks of hatred and suspicion. The colour of their skin, poverty or wealth, ignorance or knowledge, have already established indestructible classifications among them: national prejudices, the prejudices of education and birth divide and isolate them.

'Where find in a narrower compass a more complete tableau of the miseries of our nature? One trait however is still lacking.

'The profound lines which birth and opinion have traced between the destinies of these men do not end with life but stretch beyond the tomb. Six religions or sects share the faith of this embryo society.

'Catholicism, with its formidable immobility, its absolute dogmas, its terrible anathemas and its immense recompenses; the religious anarchy of the Reform; the antique paganism, are represented here. Here they already adore, in six different manners, the Being unique and eternal who has created all men in his image. They dispute here with ardour the heaven that each claims as his exclusive heritage. Moreover, in the miseries of the solitude and the evils of the present, human imagination exhausts itself creating inexpressible pains for the future. The Lutheran condemns the Calvinist to eternal fire, the Calvinist the Unitarian, and the Catholic envelops them all in a common reprobation.

'More tolerant in his rude faith, the Indian limits himself to excluding his European brother from the happy hunting grounds he reserves for himself. Faithful to the confused traditions handed down by his fathers, he consoles himself easily for the evils of life, and dies tranquil, dreaming of the always green forests that the axe of the pioneer will never disturb, where the deer and beaver will come to be shot at during the numberless days of eternity.

*
*   *

'After dinner we went to see one of the richest proprietors of the village, Mr. Williams.* We found him in his shop, busy selling Indians a number of objects of small value, such as knives, glass necklaces, earrings, etc. It was pitiful to see how these unhappy people were being treated by their civilized European brothers.

'Furthermore, all whom we saw rendered striking justice to the

* Either G.D. or Ephraim S. Williams, both agents of the American Fur Company.

savages. They were good, inoffensive, a thousand times less inclined to theft than the white. It was a pity only that they were beginning to learn the price of things. And why that, if you please? Because the profits of the trade with them daily became less great. Do you perceive here the superiority of civilized man? The Indian would have said, in his rude simplicity, that he daily found it more difficult to deceive his neighbour; but the white discovers in the perfection of language a happy *nuance*, which expresses the thing but saves the shame.

'On returning from Mr. Williams, it occurred to us to ascend the Saginaw a certain distance to shoot the wild duck which people its banks.* As we were busy with this hunt, a pirogue detached itself from the river reeds and some Indians came to meet us to examine my gun, which they had seen from far off. I have always noticed that this arm, which yet is not extraordinary in any way, procured me among the savages an altogether special attention. A gun which can kill two men in a second and fires in the rain was, according to them, a marvel above all value, a masterpiece without price. Those who approached us exhibited, according to custom, a great admiration. They asked whence came my gun. Our young guide replied that it had been made on the other side of the great water, among the fathers of the Canadians, which, you may believe, did not render it less precious in their sight. They observed that, as the sight was not placed in the middle of each barrel, one could not be as certain of one's shot: a remark to which I admit I did not well know what to reply.

'Evening having fallen, we re-embarked in the canoe and, trusting to the experience we had acquired in the morning, we set out alone to ascend an arm of the Saginaw that we had only glimpsed.

'The sky was without a cloud, the atmosphere pure and still. The river rolled its waters through an immense forest, but so slowly that

---

* Apparently game was still plentiful in Michigan, and the two friends were willing to take a shot at anything:

'During this last expedition my gun was a great resource. I had a horse so quiet that I shot the game I encountered from his back. I killed several very beautiful birds of prey, some wood pigeons . . . all prettier than the last. I saw many quail, pheasants, wild turkeys, deer; and I didn't kill a single one. Hunting was not only a matter of pleasure, it also served a real purpose. Nothing is so rare as to find fresh meat in the small wilderness inns; we therefore ate our own birds nearly all the time. The pigeons especially were very good. At Saginaw I saw some humming birds. I shot at them but missed; nothing is harder to hit.

'In general it is difficult to conceive that one can in places so lost as Saginaw live as well as we have done; not a tavern where we have not found tea.' Bt. to his father, Detroit, 1 August 1831 (Michigan) (BBlb).

it would have been almost impossible to say in what direction the current was flowing.

'We have always thought that, to get a just conception of the forests of the new world, one should follow some of the rivers which flow in their shade. The rivers are, as it were, the great roads by which Providence has been careful, since the beginning of the world, to pierce the wilderness to render it accessible to man. When you clear a passage through the woods the view is most often very restricted, even the path where you walk is a human work. The streams, on the contrary, are roads which retain no trail, and their banks freely reveal all that a vegetation vigorous and abandoned to itself can offer in the way of great or curious spectacles.

'The wilderness there was the same as it appeared six thousand years ago to our first fathers:

'A solitude flowery, delightful, balmy, a magnificent dwelling, a living palace, built for man but into which the master had not yet entered. The canoe slid without effort or noise. There reigned about us a universal quietness and serenity. We ourselves soon felt as it were softened by such a spectacle. Our words began to come more and more rarely. Soon we expressed our thoughts only in a whisper, finally we fell silent; and, lifting our paddles in unison, the two of us sank into a tranquil reverie full of inexpressible charm.

'Whence comes it that the human languages, which find words for all griefs, meet an invincible obstacle in trying to communicate the sweetest and most natural emotions of the heart?

'Who will ever faithfully paint these rare moments in life when physical well-being prepares you for moral tranquillity and when, before your eyes, as it were, a perfect equilibrium is established in the universe; when the soul, half asleep, balances between the present and the future, between the real and the possible; when, surrounded by beautiful nature, breathing a calm and balmy air, at peace with himself in a universal peace, man lends his ear to the even beating in his arteries whose every throb marks the passage of time which, for him, seems thus to flow drop by drop in eternity.

'Many men perhaps have seen the years of a long existence accumulate without once experiencing anything like what we have just described. Those could not understand us. But there are several, we are sure, who will find in their memory and at the bottom of their hearts the colours for our images, and will feel awaken, on reading this, the recollection of some fugitive hours which neither time nor the cares of life have been able to efface.

'A shot which suddenly rang out in the woods drew us from our reverie. The noise seemed at first to roll with fracas on the two banks of the river; then it retreated growling until it was entirely lost in the surrounding forest. One would have said a long and formidable war cry uttered by civilization in its march.

'One evening, in Sicily, we happened to lose our way in a vast swamp which now occupies the site where formerly was built the city of Himera. The impression with which we were inspired by the sight of this famous city now become a savage wilderness was profound. Never had we encountered on our way a more magnificent witness to the instability of human things and the miseries of our nature.

'Here again it was a solitude; but the imagination, instead of turning back and trying to mount toward the past, plunged ahead and lost itself in an immense future. We asked ourselves by what singular permission of fate we, who had been able to contemplate the ruins of empires which no longer exist and walk in wildernesses made by man, we, children of an ancient people, were led to witness one of the scenes of the primitive world and see the still empty cradle of a great nation.

'These are not the more or less hazardous foreseeings of human wisdom. They are facts as certain as if they were already accomplished. In a few years these impenetrable forests will have fallen, the noise of civilization and of industry will break the silence of the Saginaw. Docks will imprison its banks: its waters which to-day flow unknown and tranquil through a nameless wilderness will be thrust back in their flow by the prows of vessels. Fifty leagues still separate this solitude from the great European establishments, and we are perhaps the last travellers to whom it has been given to contemplate it in its primitive splendour. So great is the impulse which draws the white race toward the utter conquest of the new world.

'It's this idea of destruction, this conception of near and inevitable change which gives in our opinion so original a character and so touching a beauty to the solitudes of America. One sees them with melancholy pleasure. One hastens in a way to admire them. The idea of this natural and wild grandeur which is to end mingles with the superb images to which the march of civilization gives rise. One feels proud to be a man, and at the same time one experiences I know not what bitter regret at the power God has given us over nature. The soul is agitated by these ideas, these contrary sentiments. But all the impressions it receives are great and leave a deep mark.

*

*    *

'We wished to leave Saginaw the next day, 27 July, but, one of our horses having a saddle sore, we decided to stay one day longer. For want of other pastime we went hunting in the prairies which border the Saginaw below the clearings.

'These prairies are not marshy as one might believe. They are plains more or less large where the wood doesn't come, though the soil is excellent; the vegetation is thick and three or four feet high. We found but little game, and returned early. The heat was stifling, as at the approach of a storm, and the mosquitoes even more bothersome than usual. We walked only surrounded by a cloud of these insects, against whom one had to make perpetual war. Disaster for him who was obliged to stop! He delivered himself then defenceless to a pitiless enemy. I recall having been forced to load my gun on the run, it was so difficult to stay still a moment.

'As we were crossing the prairie on our return, we noticed that the Canadian who was acting as our guide was following a small path and was looking at the ground with the greatest care before making a step.—Why are you being so careful, I asked him, are you afraid of getting wet?—No, he answered, but I have made it a habit when crossing the prairies always to look where I step so as not to step on a rattlesnake.—What the devil, said I, jumping into the path, are there rattlesnakes here?—Oh! certainly, replied my Normandy American with his imperturbable sang-froid, *y en a tout plein*.

'I reproached him then for not having warned us sooner; he maintained that, as we had on good shoes and rattlesnakes never bit above the ankle, he had not thought that we ran great danger.

'I asked him if the bite of the rattlesnake was mortal; he replied that one always died of it in less than twenty-four hours if one did not have recourse to the Indians. These know a remedy which, given in time, saves the victim, he said.

'However that may be, the rest of the way we imitated our guide and, like him, watched where we were stepping.

'The night which followed this burning day was one of the most painful of my life. The mosquitoes had become so bothersome that, even though overwhelmed with fatigue, it was impossible to shut my eyes.

'Toward midnight the storm which had long been threatening finally broke. Unable longer to hope for sleep, I got up and opened the door of our cabin to at least breathe the freshness of the night. It was not yet raining, the air appeared calm, but the forest was already tossing, and there came from it deep moans and long clamours. From time to time a flash of lightning illuminated the sky. The quiet course of the Saginaw, the small clearing on its banks, the roofs of the five or six cabins, and the belt of enveloping foliage appeared then for an instant like a sublime evocation of the future. Then everything was lost in the most profound obscurity, and the formidable voice of the wilderness made itself heard again.

'I was watching this great spectacle, moved, when I heard a sigh at my side and, by the lightning, I saw an Indian leaning like me against the wall of our dwelling. The storm had doubtless just interrupted his sleep, for he cast a fixed and troubled glance on his surroundings.

'Was this man afraid of the thunder? or did he see in the shock of the elements anything but a passing convulsion of nature? Did these fugitive images of civilization, which surged up of themselves in the tumult of the wilderness, have for him a prophetic meaning? Did these groans of the forest, which seemed to be fighting an uneven battle, reach his ear like the secret warning of God, a solemn revelation of the final fate reserved to the savage races? I could not say. But his agitated lips seemed to be murmuring some prayers, and all his lineaments seemed graven with superstitious terror.

'At five in the morning we thought to leave. All the Indians of the neighbourhood of Saginaw were absent. They had gone to receive the presents annually made them by the English, and the Europeans were busy with the labours of the harvest. We therefore had to make up our minds to go back through the forest without a guide.

'The enterprise was not so difficult as one might suppose. In general there is but one path in these vast solitudes; and it's only a matter of not losing the trail to reach the end of the journey.

'At five in the morning, then, we recrossed the Saginaw. We received the farewells and the last counsels of our hosts and, having turned our horses' heads, found ourselves alone in the forest.

'It was not, I confess, without seriousness that we began to penetrate these humid depths. This same forest about us then stretched behind us all the way to the pole and the Pacific ocean. A single inhabited point separated us from the limitless wilderness, and we had just left it. But these thoughts only led us to hasten our horses along; and at the end of three hours we came near an abandoned wigwam on the solitary banks of the river Cass. A grassy point jutting into the river in the shade of some tall trees served as our table, and we sat down to lunch, having in perspective the river whose waters, limpid as crystal, coiled through the woods.

'On leaving the wigwam of Cass river, we encountered several paths. We had been told which one to take. But it is easy to forget some details, or to be misunderstood in such explanations. . . . We did not fail to find it so that day. They had spoken of two roads; there were three. It is true that two of these three joined further on in one, as we later learned; but we did not know that then, and our embarrassment was great.

'After having well examined, well disputed, we did as do almost all great men, and took a chance.* We forded the stream as best we could and pushed ahead rapidly toward the southwest. More than once the trail seemed about to disappear among the clumps. In other places the road seemed so little frequented that we found it hard to believe that it led elsewhere than to some abandoned wigwam. Our compass, it is true, showed us that we were always going in the right direction; however, we were not completely reassured until the discovery of the place where we had dined three days before.

'A gigantic pine, whose wind-torn trunk we had admired, made us recognize it. We continued our way with no less rapidity, for the sun was beginning to fall. Soon we reached the thinned space that usually precedes the clearings. As night was about to surprise us, we caught sight of Flint river; a half hour afterwards we found ourselves at our host's door. This time the bear received us like old friends and only sat up on his hind legs to celebrate his joy at our happy return.

'During the entire day, we did not meet a single human being; on their side the animals had disappeared. They had doubtless withdrawn under the foliage to flee the heat of the day. Only from time to time we discovered, at the bare summit of some dead tree, a hawk which,

* We saw nothing wiser than to abandon to our horses, dropping the bridle on their necks, the solution of the difficulty.

motionless on one leg and calmly sleeping in the sun's rays, seemed sculptured in the very wood he had made his perch.

'It was in the midst of this profound solitude that we suddenly thought of the revolution of 1830, whose first anniversary (29 July 1831) we had just reached. I cannot say with what impetuosity the memories of the twenty-ninth of July took possession of my spirit. The cries and smoke of combat, the sound of cannon, the rolling of musketry, the still more horrible tolling of the tocsin, this entire day with its enflamed atmosphere seemed suddenly to rise out of the past and place itself a living tableau before me. This was only a sudden illumination. When, raising my head, I glanced around, the apparition had already disappeared. But never had the silence of the forest seemed colder, its shades more deep, or its solitude so complete.'

*

\*  \*

The day was Tocqueville's birthday. He was just twenty-six years old.

*

\*  \*

On the thirty-first of July the two friends found themselves back in Detroit. Their expedition in the wilderness was over. Before closing the story, however, two interesting experiences, for which Tocqueville did not find room in his narrative, should be recorded. Both took place in Detroit, on their earlier passage through from Buffalo.

The first was an interview with the famous old priest, Gabriel Richard.[2] Father Richard, after a birth and education in France, had come to America forty years before; and since 1798 he had been associated with Detroit and with the development of the whole region of the Upper Lakes. Missionary, teacher, writer, empire-builder, he had founded the first schools, both for the Indians and the whites, established the first Michigan newspaper, assisted in the beginnings of the University of Michigan, laboured for the spread of Catholicism among the frontiersmen, and on occasion not disdained to minister to the spiritual needs of his fellow settlers of whatever denomination. In a sense the traders, trappers, and pioneers of the whole Northwest had been his parishioners for a generation. Friend and associate of the leading men of Detroit, he had even been elected by a community predominantly Protestant to serve a term as Territorial Delegate to Congress, eight years before. But now, care-worn and devoted, he was at last growing old.

The rumour of his name and deeds had, as a matter of course, fallen on the sharp ears of Tocqueville and Beaumont, even while they were still in New York. On landing in Detroit, they therefore went straight to seek him out, and an interview ensued. They were, they felt, rewarded for their pains. In due course, as a result, the substance of the conversation found its way into their notes, to be preserved for future use. To-day these documents take on an additional interest, for they afford one of the few intimate glimpses, saved for posterity, of the revered patriarch in his last year of service.

On disembarking in Detroit, wrote Beaumont, 'we paid a visit to an old Catholic curé, Mr. Richard, who had been described to us as a fine old man capable of giving us many precious documents on Michigan. We found him in his Presbytery teaching school to a dozen children. He speaks French very well. He was born in Saint-Ange and left France at the moment when the French revolution began to persecute the Catholic clergy. It was then that he decided to come to Detroit. Since that time he has not left this place and has not ceased to labour at the *conversion of the infidels.* Here as with us it's the character of the Catholic clergy to make as many proselytes as possible. The good man, who attaches more importance to this end than to any other, discoursed to us at length of his successes in this line, which occasionally annoyed us a little, because we asked him questions to which he did not reply. We were however much pleased with his conversation. The remarkable thing about his position is that he has been sent to Congress by the Protestants, in spite of his quality of Catholic priest. This at first seemed to us very surprising, but here they do not think as we do in religious matters; the same hostility does not exist between the sects, and they never ask to what religion a man belongs to form an opinion about him. What astonishes me is that the Protestants should thus have chosen him, in spite of the extreme freedom with which he himself attacks them. He makes bitter war on them. "Their sects," said he, "are without number. There are now 450 of them, they don't believe in anything at all, they are neither Episcopalians nor Methodists nor Presbyterians: they are *rienists!*"

'Furthermore, he thinks as I do that this multiplicity of different cults will one day end, either in natural religion, that is to say in the absence of all outward cult, or in Catholicism.'[3]

Tocqueville, in an abbreviated diary note, had this to say of their interview with the old priest: 'Conversation wandering but interesting. The Protestants begin to preponderate in Michigan because of the immigration. However, Catholicism gains some converts among the most enlightened. Opinion of Mr. Richard on the extreme coldness of the upper classes in America on religious matters, one of the causes of the extreme tolerance. Indeed, complete toleration; you are not asked to what religion you belong but whether you are capable of employ. The greatest service that one can render religion is to separate it from the temporal power. . . . System of the United States for the new states. One accustoms them by degrees to governing themselves. . . .'[4]

The following autumn, while labouring among those suffering from the great cholera epidemic, Father Richard was himself to be stricken. In four days the venerable man would be dead.

Before setting out for Saginaw, Tocqueville and Beaumont had one other experience that struck them as illuminating. 'I forgot to tell you,' Beaumont wrote a friend,[5] 'that on information given us that Saginaw and its neighbourhood was infested with *cousins* or mosquitoes, we went to a Mme de Moderl [?] of Detroit to buy some mosquito netting. While she was giving us what we asked, my eyes happened to encounter a little print posted in her store. This print represents a very well dressed lady and at the bottom is written: *Mode de Longchamps 1831*. How do you find the inhabitants of Michigan who give themselves the styles of Paris? It's a fact that in the last village of America the French mode is followed, and all the fashions are supposed to come from Paris.

'From this anecdote you will believe that Detroit is very civilized. It is, however, not very far from the wild forest and the latter's inhabitants. At half a league you see woods which begin and do not end. Besides, here is something that happened only last year and that proves more than all one could say. A bear, bayed by the hounds near the forest, came into the main street of Detroit and ran down its whole length, to the entertainment of the Americans, whose gravity probably did not betray them even on this occasion.'[6]

\*

\*    \*

It will be remarked that this is a somewhat inadequate—if spectacular—description of Detroit in 1831. The fact was that though Tocqueville and Beaumont were to see Detroit on three separate occasions in all, they apparently never bothered to take advantage of its social and intellectual resources. The story of the bear hunt was therefore the first and last description of this flourishing and by no means uninteresting western community that we have from their pens.

In a sense, the two young travellers were missing an opportunity. Yet it should be remembered that they had seen American towns before, and had come to Detroit to explore two altogether different features of Michigan civilization. They were interested in the pioneer and the Indian; and for these they went straight—as their manuscripts attest—to be instructed on the spot. If Tocqueville and Beaumont can be criticized, therefore, it is only for what they said, or failed to say, of the Michigan frontier.

On examining Tocqueville's *Fortnight in the Wilderness*, with the appended notes, the reader is perhaps surprised to find Saginaw described as if it were the last western outpost of American civilization. This was, as Tocqueville himself discovered a week later, an exaggeration. It is also amusing to find the two energetic young men undergoing such hardships to reach Saginaw by the overland route, when this trading post might have been attained with ease and in about half the time by water, had only a steamboat been available. The student is forced to recognize, however, that this adventurous journey netted the keen investigators the information and experiences that they had come for, and could have got in no other way.

Tocqueville and Beaumont were determined, in the first place, to see and study the American pioneer settlers. They were also, wrote Beaumont, 'persuaded that there are thousands in France who would find it to their advantage to come to America and buy excellent land cheaply. But the majority are ignorant of the state of affairs. Perhaps it would be rendering a service to our country to make conditions known. Ordinarily the difficulty for those emigrating to a new country lies in the difference of language; but this obstacle would not exist in Michigan where a quarter of the population speaks French.'[7] In other words, the two young explorers sought exact information, statistics, on the conditions of settlement in Michigan; and, in addition, a broad understanding of the significance and future of the whole American frontier. In both endeavours they were notably successful.

It is really extraordinary to total up the information they collected on their brief trip, and see what a clear grasp of that strange institution, the American frontier, they were able to get. Hardly a phase of pioneering, hardly a significant aspect of the westward movement escaped their attention. They soon discovered, for instance, that trail-making and roads preceded settlement, rather than the reverse. They recorded the part played by the government in stimulating and regulating expansion through public land-office sale, in small sections, of the territories acquired for the nation from the Indians. Thanks to Gabriel Richard, Tocqueville was even able to see how the territorial governments were really training schools for statehood. And on the procedure of settlement, their inquiries were extensive. They got data on the number and character of the new settlers who, at the moment, were pouring westward and crowding the facilities of Detroit. They watched the new arrivals at work. And, lastly, with meticulous care they investigated the prices of land, the costs of settlement, and all the details of clearing, cultivation and household economy among the pioneers.

At the same time, Toqueville gained a lively impression of the frontier environment, and the frontier types. One would have to go far to find a more striking picture of the vast forests of the northwest in their primitive state, unkempt and dangerous, magnificent but doomed. Yet, for all the poetry of Tocqueville's imagination, one is not allowed to forget that there were swamps, and fevers, and (above all) mosquitoes, these last alone making the newly-opened lands a purgatory scarce bearable for ordinary man. Amid these imposing surroundings Tocqueville also placed at least one representative of all the types that he found inhabiting or roaming through these frontier communities. Inn-keepers, farmers, fur-traders, half-breed hunters, and full-blooded Indians: all were encountered by the two friends, and their appearance in this habitat vividly described. Only the circuit-riding Methodist is missing.

Perhaps the most striking feature of the essay, however, is the insight it gives into the fundamental character of Michigan pioneering. With their usual perspicacity, Tocqueville and Beaumont soon realized that the westward movement in that region, diverse and tumultuous though it seemed, was being carried forward, directed and dominated by New Englanders.[8] Essentially, the settlement of the peninsula was the expansion of New York and New England, through the emigration of a lean, argumentative, and persevering race of townsmen. As a consequence, the two young Frenchmen utterly failed to find the backward, primitive communities they had anticipated, or even the uneducated, unprogressive rural peasantry they might have expected, from their own experience in the provinces of France. About the practical, religious-minded, solitary pioneer there was nothing rustic, save his log cabin and his temporary surroundings. Unlike the French Canadian, he proved to have the character, the education, the interests, and the ambitions of a civilized city-dweller. Instead, therefore, of finding all the stages in the past history of man recapitulated on a small scale within the territory of Michigan, Tocqueville and Beaumont were forced to proclaim that they had encountered a modern society.* Men so recently arrived, of such moral fibre, yielding so little to the exigencies of the frontier, naturally had developed no peasantry, no true villages. Small as a settlement like Pontiac was, it was yet not a village. Rather it represented, as a German critic bluntly put it, *ein Fragment von municipaler Civilisation.*[9] Its first cabin, as Tocqueville himself more gracefully said, was 'the ark of civilization lost in the midst of an ocean of leaves.'

Even the wilderness, limitless and unconquerable though it had at first seemed, was evidently about to disappear. Looking about him with a seeing eye, Tocqueville realized that the frontier was sweeping westward with incredible speed; nothing could stop the Americans, he was certain, short of the Pacific. On the morrow of his visit, he sadly predicted, the mighty forests would be gone.

*

*    *

But what of the Indian? Here Tocqueville and Beaumont were obviously less happy in their experiences and observations.

They saw the native American, it was true, in a large variety of situations. They studied him in his degradation in a civilized community; they watched him in the frontier forests, they were with him on the trail and in the fur-trader's post. They even enquired of him from those who, through long association, should have known him well. Being men of intelligence, Tocqueville and Beaumont could not help but recognize that the Indian was indolent, improvident, and unadaptable. They therefore detected some of the fatal flaws of character, unfitting him for civilization. Lastly, they realized that contact

---

* The force of Tocqueville's discovery, as a critique of Turner's 'frontier' thesis, must be apparent to present-day readers. In a later letter, Tocqueville said that they had found civilization advancing like a forest fire (*incendie*) through the wilderness.

with the whites drove away his food supply, while their alcohol brutalized and destroyed him.

Yet the fact remains that this fortnight in the wilderness gave Tocqueville and Beaumont a more favourable opinion of the savage than the experience of the white race would seem to justify. Against the received judgment of generations of Americans, the two young Frenchmen were coming to look on the Indian as in many ways a noble and an admirable being. He did not steal, it seemed; and, when not excited by conflict or strong drink, he was the most harmless creature in the world—kindly, peaceful and trustworthy. In striking contrast to his oppressors, he was an honourable person. In short, his character had been traduced by calumniators, and, all things well considered, he had been much wronged by the whites. Tocqueville and Beaumont were moved to sympathy with him.

This was an extraordinary conclusion for two such intelligent and level-headed young men to have reached. In fact, the opinion seems so strange, and was later to exercise such an influence, particularly on Beaumont's work, that some explanation is needed.

The explanation is, it happens, relatively simple. Tocqueville and Beaumont had come to America full of impressions from Cooper and Chateaubriand, and full of the liberal and romantic notion, so firmly fixed in the French heart, that the red-skin was that paragon long sought of the philosophers: a noble savage. Their first view of the degenerate Iroquois of Oneida Castle and Buffalo had therefore, in a reaction that was unavoidable, appalled and horrified them. All their convictions seemed destined to be taken away from them. But they could not believe that those were fair specimens of the Indian race. So in Buffalo they had jumped at the opportunity to come to the frontier, and verify the facts by contact with savages still uncontaminated by civilization.

In other words, the two friends had proposed to base their opinion on a first-hand study of the Indians of Michigan Territory; and in the end this is exactly what they did. But these Indians of the peninsula were, unfortunately, scarcely more representative of the race than the drunken remnants of the Five Nations. Instead of being of the fierce Iroquois, of the war-like Sioux or predatory Apache, 'Sagan-Cuisco,' and the other savages whom Tocqueville and Beaumont saw, belonged to the relatively peaceful and harmless tribe of the Chippewa, known to the French Canadians as *Sauteurs*. The result was that the two investigators were deceived. Just as on landing they had taken New York for typical Americans, so in Michigan they at once assumed that all the different nations of red-men were like the scattered, harmless hunters whom they had before them. Relieved, furthermore, at the restoration of their convictions, and instinctively sympathetic to the viewpoint of the Canadians, the idealistic young men gave play to their imagination. Stories of Indian treachery and barbarity were forgotten; the squalor of the savage was overlooked. Helplessness became injustice; improvidence, lack of white man's avarice; and stoic stupidity once more noble pride.

\*

\*    \*

The expedition to the wilderness, to resume, left the friends with a rich store of memories, and with some illusions. Big, easy-going, generous-hearted Beaumont was to be particularly influenced by the latter, when he came to write his book. Not having a Yankee's cold, calculating egotism, he was already gathering materials for a story of the wrongs of the American Indian. Soon the wrongs of the American negro were to eclipse even these thoughts, and steal the main theme of his novel. Nevertheless, the great scenes of the tragedy would in the end take place on the shores of the Saginaw, 'mid those vast and mournful forests of Michigan, indelible in his memory.

As for Tocqueville, who out of loyalty was never to publish his *Quinze Jours*, he, also, would not forget the trip to Saginaw. In later, more troubled years, it was to give him calm and peace of mind to recall the fortnight in the wilderness that he and Beaumont had had together. He was often to refer to its incidents in conversation with his friends—especially to the 'delighted wonder' with which he had heard the Canadian Indian at Saginaw begin to sing:

> Entre Paris et Saint Denis
> Il était une fille. . . .

# XXII

## ON THE UPPER LAKES

'STILL another unforeseen voyage!' was Beaumont's next greeting to his family. It was 11 August; he was sitting on the deck of a steamboat crossing the upper end of Lake Michigan.[1] 'Instead of returning to Buffalo 1 August, we left for Green Bay. Here we have been more than ten days en route, and when we return to Buffalo, we shall have made 1810 miles, that is to say, 603 leagues in two weeks. . . .

'The day we proposed to leave Detroit to return toward the State of New York, we learned that a superb steamboat, *the Superior*, was passing at that very moment, going to the Great Lakes to make a run through their entire extent. For a long time the papers had been advertising this excursion, which was represented as of a nature deeply to excite the curiosity of amateurs. We went to visit the vessel. It was already almost filled with travellers, with English and Americans who for the most part had no other interest in this trip than that of passing their time agreeably for several days. The captain assured me we would not be more than eight or ten days en route. The opportunity was tempting. For the first time a great vessel was venturing into these distant regions; and for him who wishes to see things close up, this was not simply a pleasure trip. In short, we decide to engage places; they give us two fairly uncomfortable beds in the *Gentlemen's* cabin and, in less than an hour, we make the decision, we install ourselves, and we are sailing on the river Ste. Clair [*sic*] leading to the lake of the same name, which itself leads to Lake Huron.'

The steamboat was, they were told, to make the only visit of the summer to Sault Ste. Marie, Mackinac and, finally, Green Bay on the far shore of Lake Michigan.* Before they well knew what had hap-

---

* For a long time, as Beaumont had observed, daily notices in the papers had been calling the attention of the 'travelling public' to the excursion, 'as affording an opportunity of viewing the splendid scenery of the Upper Lakes; the intention of the trip being to accommodate *Parties of Pleasure* at a season of the year when the voyage through the lakes is both agreeable and healthful.'[2] The *Superior*, released from the Buffalo-Detroit run for the purpose, was of 350 tons; her accommodations were

pened, therefore, the prison commissioners were off with a boatload of sightseers. Just as Beaumont might have foretold, once out of the New York penitentiaries, they could not rest from travel. Nor were they simply on pleasure bound. As before, for him who wished 'to see,' such an expedition was bound to be instructive. They could view the old French frontier post of Ste. Marie, investigate the fur-trading station in the straits of Mackinac, study the Indian colony at Green Bay. The voyage was also destined to be otherwise important to the two inquisitive students of American civilization. For, if the vast majority of their new companions seemed of no consequence whatever, they soon made the acquaintance of one man—a Catholic priest—whose experiences and opinions they could turn to use.

'Of these two hundred individuals with whom I find myself,' Beaumont reported,* 'there are three quarters and a half of whom I have nothing to say. I haven't much more to tell you of the second half of the last quarter. However, you shall know that among our travelling companions is an Englishman, Mr. Vine [Vigne],† a fine fellow, an intrepid traveller, who was in Russia last year and who told me yesterday that he hopes to be in Egypt next spring; Mr. Mulon [Mullon],‡

---

'spacious and elegant.' She carried, Beaumont discovered, about 200 passengers. 'Each has his bed on board. You see by that the size of our ship. It's an enormous ambulating house.'

* There are available, in all, four accounts of this excursion on the *Superior*. Besides Beaumont's long letter to his brother, already cited, and the information scattered through Tocqueville's manuscripts,[3] there is an account by one of their fellow-passengers, the Englishman G.T.Vigne, included in his *Six Months in America*, London, 1832; and also a series of four letters by an American on board, published in the *Detroit Courier*, 18 August, 25 August, 1 September, and 8 (?) September 1831. Each of these has its merits. As neither of them can compare with Beaumont's story, however, they will be quoted only when they supply pertinent information not otherwise given.

† Godfrey Thomas Vigne, 1801–1863, had already begun the career of indefatigable travel that was to make him and his books of interest to geographers and empire-builders alike. The following season this sharp-eyed student of the world, who was 'neither a professional author nor a commissioned tourist,' was to be in Persia, not in Egypt; thence he would proceed to India, for a seven-year exploration of Kashmir and Afghanistan, emerging at length to describe the northern and western sections of India for his fellow-countrymen at a time when British supremacy had not yet been established in those regions.

‡ James Ignatius Mullon, son of William Mullon of Emmitsburg, Md., had been educated in his father's school and at Mount St. Mary's, and assigned to the Cincinnati cathedral. While there he had become the first editor of the *Catholic Telegraph*, the only Catholic paper of that period still publishing to-day. He had also made a missionary journey with Bishop Fenwick in 1829 to Mackinac, Green Bay, and Arbre Croché. In 1832 he became President of the Athenaeum of the diocese, and in 1834 transferred to the diocese of New Orleans, where he continued.

Catholic priest from Cincinnati (Ohio). He is coming to Michilli-machinac [*sic*] for the express purpose of issuing a public challenge to a Presbyterian minister on a point of religious dispute. Mr. Mul[l]on is a large dry man whose Catholic zeal borders on intolerance. The religious spirit in this region in nothing resembles what it is in the state of New-York and especially in the large cities. In New-York, in Albany, the different sects live in peace, one beside the other, and seem to be friends. The same union does not exist here between the different communions. "These Presbyterians," Mr. Mul[l]on said to me, "are wicked as vipers; you crush their heads and they rise on their tails." . . .

'Beside Mr. Mul[l]on, we have two other ecclesiastics, a Presbyterian minister and an Episcopalian.* The majority on the steamboat is Presbyterian. Consequently, it was the Presbyterian who the other day (Sunday) officiated. The ceremony took place in the gentlemen's cabin. The Episcopalians, who are not so particular, accommodate themselves very well to the service of their brothers in Protestantism, and in general the disciples of one sect hear with equal satisfaction the ministers of a different sect. This may be tolerance, but may I die if it is faith.—As for Mr. Mul[l]on, he is not so indifferent in this matter. He but appeared in the place of the ceremony, and when he saw what was going on there, he fled as from hell. As for me, I was sitting near my bed when the service began, and I did not leave my place, listening and sleeping turn by turn, according as the preacher raised or lowered his voice. . . .' †

'We arrived the second of August at Fort Gratiot, which is situated at the opening of Lake Huron at the beginning of the river St. Clair. Our arrival in this place was picturesque enough. It was evening: the sun had just gone down, stormy clouds covered the sky, lightning flashed on all sides. We were dancing on the deck, to the sound of the violin and hautboy (*Cor anglais*). Lake Huron and its immense waters spread before us like those of the ocean. It was in this situation that,

---

* Probably Rev. Lucius Smith, of Christ Church, Batavia.

† Among the remaining passengers, Beaumont spoke of three or four young men, *fort bons garçons, mais plus ou moins nuls* (which included, doubtless, the correspondent of the *Detroit Courier*). The 'company of women' was 'not much richer.' They impressed him as a frivolous and giddy lot. Among others he noticed a romantic Englishwoman who 'would be charming if she were ten years younger.' The Miss Clemens in question was soon to make him regret her existence (see next chapter). 'The first day we know nobody; now we are on friendly terms with all the world.'

the ball being over, the orchestra played the Marseillaise for us. I forgot the beautiful in this music to see only the memories which it recalled to me. It was just a year since I had heard it for the first time, sung in Paris on the Place Vendôme and in the court of the Palais Royal. This air thus played was like an echo of the cannon of July, still thundering in the world. But who would have been able to predict to me that a year later I should come to hear it on Lake Huron?'

'We were to remain but an instant at Fort Gratiot, but the weather was so bad and the wind so contrary that we anchored. Two days passed without conditions becoming more favourable, and we had to spend them in a place where there was nothing at all to see. . . .'

There were, however, wet prairies and forests within stone's throw; consequently, game and adventure enough for two enthusiastic nimrods. 'I go to hunt in the meadows on the other side of the river St. Clair,' Tocqueville jotted hastily in his diary. 'We first go to the fort. In the forest on the way, the sound of an Indian drum. Some cries. We see approaching eight savages entirely naked except for a small clout. Surprise of the men, smeared with colour from head to foot, their bristling hair full of mud, with a pigtail behind. Wooden clubs in hand, jumping like devils. Fine men. Dance to amuse themselves and to gain money. We give them a shilling. Cries, the war-dance, horrible to see. What degradation. Another dance —— * heads to the ground. We do not know how to get across the water. Huts in the swamps on the other side. A [canoe?] detaches itself and comes. Terrifying navigation. Good hunt in the swamp.'

*

* *

The *Superior* left Fort Gratiot on 4 August, and made the crossing of Lake Huron in fine weather. The passengers were astonished at the 'unimagineable' clearness of the water. When members of the crew

---

* Word illegible. Tocqueville's diary note of 3 August is supplemented by Vigne's account: 'I saw an Indian dance: the performers, an old man and his sons, advanced towards us, on a forest path, looking like wood demons, jumping and racing with each other, and uttering a small shrill cry at intervals; they were nearly naked, bedaubed all over with clay, and began the dance with light clubs in their hands: sometimes they writhed on the ground like snakes, at others they shook their clubs at each other, and used the wildest and most extravagant gestures. The old Indian beat time on a small skin stretched across a piece of hollow tree. When stooping to the ground and looking upwards, his features and figure reminded me of the celebrated statue of the "Remouleur" in Florence.' *Six Months in America*, II,95–96.

peeled potatoes and threw them over the bow, it was possible to distinguish them clearly to a depth of forty feet. Some of the Americans soon tired of this, and in their boredom professed to see in Lake Huron —as Beaumont reported—only a great *piece* of water. Not so the observant French travellers.

'The immense stretch of coast that we had just passed,' Tocqueville admitted,[4] 'does not present a single noteworthy view. It is a plain covered with forests. The ensemble, however, produces a profound and durable impression. This lake without sails, this shore which does not yet show any trace of the passage of man, this eternal forest which borders it; all that, I assure you, is not grand in poetry only; it's the most extraordinary spectacle that I have seen in my life. These regions, which yet form only an immense wilderness, will become one of the richest and most powerful countries in the world. One can affirm it without being a prophet. Nature has done everything here. A fertile soil, and outlets like to which there are no others in the world. Nothing is missing except civilized man, and he is at the door.'

'On nearing Ste. Marie, as the lake narrows,' Beaumont continued his story, 'you encounter a multitude of islands of all sizes, midst which you have to pass. . . .' So crooked was the channel that once they only missed 'by an inch or two running hard aground.' They were told that as one went north in this region, the soil became more barren; hence there were fewer whites, and more Indians. In fact Beaumont began to notice 'canoes filled with Indians, altogether savage. At the noise of our boat and of our music they left their forests and came to cast a curious eye on our *steamboat*. I can understand their stupefaction. For even to a European these great vessels propelled by steam are without gainsaying one of the marvels of modern industry. While some of them were admiring our manner of navigating, we threw them two or three bottles of brandy, which they received with the liveliest manifestation of joy and gratitude. In the same way they received some pieces of bread that we let fall in their canoe. . . .*

---

* Of this scene Vigne wrote: 'It was a remarkably fine evening: as the steamer passed rapidly on, her paddles seemed to take infinite pleasure in defacing the astonished surface of the water, and splashed away through the liquid crystal with as little ceremony as if they had been propelling a mere ferryboat. Every thing besides was hushed and tranquil: the very passengers, who had all assembled near the forward part of the deck, were intensely gazing upon the scene around them; and watched in almost breathless silence, as the vessel rounded each bend in the deep, but comparatively narrow river, that developed in quick succession some new and more beautiful object at every turn. Suddenly we heard the screams of Indians, who had descried us from

'When we arrived near Sault Ste. Marie, it was late; we therefore remained in our vessel till the next morning. The place where we brought to was charming, and all evening long we had concert and ball. The echo from the forest was such that it entirely repeated what the hautboy (*Cor anglais*) played. Out of curiosity of this fact, I also wanted to make harmony in the virgin forests of America; and at midnight I played on deck the variations of *Di Tanti Palpite*.* Nothing equals the beauty of such a night. The sky was sparkling with stars which were all reflected in the depths of the water; and from place to place on the bank were to be seen the fires of the Indians, whose ear an unaccustomed sound had struck and who doubtless for the first time listened to the airs of Rossini and Auber.

'The sixth of August early in the morning we entered the village which bears the name of Sault Ste. Marie. . . .† Everybody at Ste. Marie speaks French. There are as many Indians as Canadians there. Each day the two populations mingle further. This half-European, half-Indian population is not disagreeable. There is in Indian faces something fierce that is softened by this mixture. The eyes of the savage have a natural vivacity that I have seen with no white man, their defect is to be hard and severe at the same time. But this fire burning in their glances is of great beauty when, without ceasing to be as lively, it loses something of its primitive rudeness, which is what happens through the union of the Indian and the European. The

their wigwams on one of the islands, and were paddling after us in a canoe with all their might. One of them was a chief, who displayed the flag of the United States. In the course of the afternoon, we had been amusing ourselves by shooting with rifles at a bottle attached to a line about forty yards in length; this had been left hanging from the stern, and the endeavors of the Indians to catch hold of the string afforded us no little amusement. Their faces were deeply stained with the red extract from the blood root (Sanguinaria Canadensis); they were in the best possible humor, and their wild discordant laugh, and the still wilder expression of their features, as they encouraged each other to exertion with quickly repeated and guttural exclamations enabled us to form some idea of their animated appearance, when excited to deeds of a more savage description. By dint of the greatest exertion, they contrived to seize the string; they held on for a moment by it; it snapped, and the canoe was instantly running astern at the rate of seven or eight knots. They again had recourse to their paddles, and used them with redoubled energy; we then slackened our pace for a moment or two, and threw them a rope, by which they soon pulled themselves under the stern. We conversed with them through the medium of an interpreter, and made them presents of bread and spirits. They seemed very thankful, and threw us some pigeons which they had killed, and fired a *feu-de-joie* with their fowling-pieces at parting.' *Six Months in America*, II,101–103.

* *Di tanti palpiti*, an *aria* from Rossini's 'Tancredi.'
† 'On our arrival, the whole population on the bank or on the roofs of the houses. Only once a year do they see a vessel like ours.' Toc. diary note.

Canadians call *métiches* (*métis*) those who come of this double origin. I have seen some young *métiches* girls who seemed to me of noteworthy beauty.

'No sooner arrived at Ste. Marie than we took a canoe to go see Lake Superior. Miss Clemens, Miss Thomson,* Mathilda † and some other ladies came with us. We mounted the river two leagues and went as far as a place called *Pointe aux Pins*, where is the beginning of Lake Superior. This lake much resembles all the others; I believe however that its waters are the purest of all. In addition to its immense size, it has also in common with the sea an ebb and flow. I was enchanted by this promenade. The boatmen who guided us were Canadians, of charming gaiety. While paddling they did not stop singing to us a number of old French songs, some of whose couplets are altogether droll. The little time that I have spent with the Canadians has proved to me with what difficulty national character, and especially French character, is lost. ‡ The French gaiety which they have preserved contrasts singularly with the glacial self-possession of the Americans. It is also to be remarked that the French of Canada are more gay than are we now in France. . . .

'We spent an hour or two at the *Pointe aux Pins*. There I was presented to an Indian chief, who fell into admiration before my *fusil à piston*. I fired a shot before him. He was so satisfied that to show me his gratitude he gave me a small tortoise shell.'

Tocqueville had been standing by, watching the savage dogs nosing about the Indian encampment. The chief asked to see his gun. 'Costume of the chief,' he noted,[5] 'red pantaloons, a blanket, his hair drawn to the top of his head. Two feathers therein. I fire my gun before him. He admires and says that he has always heard that the French were a nation of great warriors. I ask him what his feathers mean. He replies with a smile of joy that it is a sign that he has killed two *scouts* [Sioux] (he is of the *sauteur* nation and always at war with the other). I ask him for one of his feathers saying that I shall wear it in the land

* 'Miss Thomson is a small woman, svelte as a wasp, light as a butterfly, lovely as a cupid, and stupid as a goose, etc., etc.'

† Anna Mathilda Macomb, 1812–1834, was the sixth child of Major General Macomb, at the moment head of the American army. Beaumont thought her 'likeable and fairly pretty.'

‡ 'The whole population of Ste. Marie is French. They are the ancient French, gay and jolly (*en train*) as we no longer are. We have rediscovered here the French language of a century ago, preserved like a mummy for the instruction of the present generation.' Toc. to his father, 14 August 1831 (YT; *O.C.*,VII,47–51).

of the great warriors, and that they will admire it. He takes it out of his hair at once and gives it me, then stretches out his hand and shakes mine.' The grave little Frenchman was much tickled by this solemnity.*

'I took a view of Lake Superior,' continued Beaumont, 'after which we returned on the river Ste. Marie. We bravely *descended the rapids in a canoe*. There is no danger because you are guided by skilful boatmen who know the river and its rocks marvellously well. But the boat goes down so fast, and you see yourself surrounded by so many rocks, contact with any one of which would break your canoe into a thousand pieces, that it is hard to repel a feeling of fear. Besides, we ought not to have feared for ourselves, since we had ladies with us. They gave us the example of courage themselves, and not one let the least cry escape. We stayed a very brief time at Ste. Marie, and the same day, the sixth of August at three o'clock, we left, heading for Michilimackinac. . . .'†

'The land which bears this great name is an island, which is located between Lake Huron and Lake Michigan.'

---

* Two months later, when trying to explain, a little mockingly, to a cousin of his back in France, the grotesque pride of the American Indians and their scornful pity for all the comforts and precautions of the European, Tocqueville remembered this interview, and embroidered it, tongue in cheek: 'Of all my European accoutrements,' he wrote, 'they envied only my *fusil à deux coups*. This arm, however, had on their attitude the same effect as the penitentiary system produced on the Americans. I recall, among others, an old chief whom we encountered on the banks of Lake Superior, seated by his fire as motionless as befitted a man of his rank. I established myself by his side, and we engaged in a friendly conversation, with the aid of a French Canadian who served as interpreter. He examined my gun, and remarked that it was not made like his. I told him then that my gun was not afraid of the rain and could be fired when wet (*dans l'eau*). He refused to believe me; but I fired it off in front of him after having dipped it in a nearby stream. At this spectacle the Indian gave signs of the most profound admiration; he examined the weapon afresh, and gave it back to me, saying with emphasis: "The fathers of the Canadians are great warriors!" As we were taking leave, I noticed that he was carrying on his head two long hawk feathers. I asked him what this ornament signified. At this question he began to smile very agreeably, the while showing two rows of teeth that would have done honour to a wolf, and replied that he had killed two Sioux (the name of a tribe hostile to his) and that he wore these plumes in sign of his double victory. "If you would be willing to yield me one," said I, "I would wear it in my own country, and I would say that I had it of a great chief." It seems that I had touched a soft spot, for at that my man arose and, detaching one of the feathers with a majesty that had its comic side, gave it me. Then from under his blanket he thrust out his naked arm and gave me a great bony hand, from which I had much pain withdrawing mine after he had shaken it.' Toc. to Mme de Grancey, New-York, 10 October 1831 (*O.C.*,VII,74–75).

† Henry R. Schoolcraft was absent at this time, which accounts for Tocqueville and Beaumont's failure to mention him.

As nothing remarkable struck Beaumont's attention on this second leg of their voyage,* he got out his paints. Immediately he was besieged by the ladies. They wanted their portraits.

He used Vigne's colours to paint a blue bird instead.

*
* *

The long hours of this passage also supplied the two friends with an opportunity to chat with the Catholic priest whom they had found on board, and to whom they had instinctively gravitated. He seemed, Tocqueville noted, 'very ardent in his zeal.'

'*Q*. Do you think that the support of the civil power is useful to religion?

'*A*. I am profoundly convinced that it is harmful. I know that the majority of Catholic priests in Europe have a contrary belief; I understand their point of view. They distrust the spirit of liberty whose first efforts have been directed against them. Having, besides, always lived under the sway of monarchical institutions which protected them, they are naturally led to regret that protection. They are therefore victims of an inevitable error. If they could live in this country, they would not be long in changing their opinions. All religious beliefs are on the same footing here. The government neither sustains nor persecutes any one; and doubtless there is not a country in the world where the Catholic religion counts adherents more fervent and proselytes more numerous. I repeat, the less religion and its ministers are mixed with civil government, the less part will they take in political dissensions, and the more power religious ideas will gain.

'*Q*. In the United States, which sects are the most inimical to Catholicism?

'*A*. All sects join in the hatred of Catholicism; but only the Presbyterians are violent. They are also those who are the most zealous.

'*Q*. Do you sometimes encounter traces of the work of the Jesuits among the Indians?

'*A*. Yes. There are tribes which retain confused notions of the religion taught them by the Jesuits, and which return very quickly to Christianity. At Arbre Crochu [*sic*] there are families which received the first principles of Christianity 150 years ago; and they still con-

* 'Fleet of 22 Indian canoes, going in the opposite direction and returning home after having received presents from the English.' Toc. diary, 7 August 1831.

serve a few traces of it. When one can reach them, the Indian tribes generally recall with veneration the memory of the *Black Robes*. From time to time one still encounters in the wilderness crosses once raised by the Jesuits.

'*Q.* Is it true that the Indians have a natural eloquence?

'*A.* Nothing is more true. I have often admired the profound sense and conciseness of their speeches. Their style has something Lacedemonian about it.

'*Q.* Do they still make war with the same ferocity?

'*A.* The same. They burn, and torment their prisoners in a thousand ways. They scalp the dead and the wounded. They are, however, mild and honest men when their passions are not irritated by war. . . .

'*Q.* Are the Indians of Arbre Croché fervent?

'*A.* (Here the face of Mr. Mul[l]on lit up in an extraordinary way.) I do not know their equals as Christians. Their faith is entire, their obedience to the laws of religion is entire. A converted Indian would rather let himself be killed than to fail in the rules of abstinence. Their life becomes very moral. You could see with what eagerness the Indian population of Ste. Marie came to find me as soon as it was known there was a priest on board. I have baptized many children.

'*Q.* How does the American clergy recruit itself?

'*A.* Up to the present most of the priests have come from Europe. We are only beginning to have American-born (which is much better). We now have twelve or thirteen seminaries in the Union. In the last forty years Catholicism has made unbelievable progress among us.

'*Q.* How are the expenses of the cult paid?

'*A.* Voluntary gifts. The pews which each family has in the church form the principal revenue.

'*Q.* How are the bishops named?

'*A.* The Pope names them directly, but usually he consults the body of existing bishops. He has sometimes happened not to do it, and then his choices have rarely been happy.'

Thoughtfully, Tocqueville recorded this conversation in his notes. Then he made a *remark*. '*Mr. Mul[l]on*,' he wrote, 'like all the Catholic priests I have met up to now, differed essentially from the Protestant ministers: 1. In that he appeared profoundly convinced, and entirely devoted to his ministry. 2. In that he showed a strong leaning toward intolerance, and little belief in the good faith of his adversaries. 3. In that he appeared, not an enemy of civil liberty, but little fond of democratic government by the masses of the people. This, however, is an imperceptible distinction which I need to render more positive by further inquiries.'

It would be difficult to find a better illustration of Tocqueville and Beaumont's method.* Perceiving that Father Mullon was a bitter opponent of Protestantism, they had foreborne to pursue the subject of the Presbyterians. Instead, they had asked him about things of which a vigorous missionary might have a less biased opinion and a more intimate knowledge. They had questioned him about the Jesuits, and about the organization of his church. In particular, having heard in New York, and again from Gabriel Richard, that the separation of church and state in America was an inestimable benefit to all religious communions, even to the Catholic, they had decided to see what this downright priest would say in the matter.

On answers to questions thus directed, the investigators felt they could place some reliance. Father Mullon's absolute approval of the separation of church and state, especially, had gone far to convince them that the principle was a sound one. Notwithstanding the opinion of most Frenchmen, therefore, Tocqueville and Beaumont were coming to believe that it could even be applied, with advantage, in France. Beaumont, in his letter home, admitted his almost complete conversion to Mr. Mullon's views. And for Tocqueville, his future book was to make a similar announcement.†

\*

\*    \*

On the morning of 7 August, the *Superior* rounded the point of Mackinac Island and entered the harbour. 'Nothing but the pencil can give an adequate idea of the picture spread, from this point of view, before the sight,' reported an American in his letter to the *Detroit Courier*.⁶ 'One of the French gentlemen on board had his sketch book out at once, his eye in fine phrenzy rolling from beach to precipice, apparently taking every beauty into his mind, whatever may have been his success in transferring them to his paper.'

---

* Even their failure to consult the Presbyterian and Episcopalian ministers on board was characteristic. Though they were not regular Catholics, they were conscious of having much in common with a Catholic priest, and apparently found no difficulty in approaching him; whereas a certain lack of sympathy with the Protestant ideals and temperament deprived them even of the desire to consult its clergy.
† *Dém. en Am.*, II,ch.9.

'This small island,' Beaumont admitted, 'is the most picturesque thing I have yet seen in this region. Generally the soil is very flat, and the accidents of nature are very rare. (I am speaking of the country bordering the Great Lakes.) Michilimackinac on the contrary is almost entirely bordered by cliffs. It is defended by a fort, which is little fortified by the hand of man but draws a great advantage from its natural position. It is occupied by a hundred men of the American army. The population of the island, composed of the same elements as that of Ste. Marie, is more numerous than in the latter place; it is reckoned at about 400 souls. Furthermore, the population is altogether industrial and commercial. Everybody speaks French, and there are some wealthy and distinguished inhabitants, among others Mr. and Mme Abbet [Abbott] * who received us with the greatest kindness, though Tocqueville and I presented ourselves at their door entirely unaccompanied. The only things which appear to agitate this island are the thirst for riches and religion. Like all Americans, they are unbelievably keen to make money. But they have also, which all Americans do not, a religious warmth which makes veritable enemies of the votaries of the different sects. The Catholic religion and the Presbyterian communion divide the believers. The Catholics are the more numerous. It was to Michilimackinac that our priest of the steamboat, Mr. Mul[l]on, was coming.†

'We passed the whole of the seventh in this island. I saw few Indians there; several days before there had been a great number, but they were already far away. They cover immense distances in tiny canoes which, in their smallness, almost resemble the small boat which you made twenty years ago and on which, a new Columbus, you crossed the ocean of Beaumont-la-Chartre, that is to say, the spring in the lower garden. We spent the day visiting two natural curiosities of the island. The first is an arch cut by nature in a very high rock. Some call it the *Rocher Percé*, others the *Arche du Géant*. The fact is that this rock is of extraordinary shape. I observed it from every direction. I climbed to its top with Tocqueville and two companions. Nothing is easier; the only thing to fear is dizziness. We had a guide who was so unfortunate

* Samuel Abbott, of prominent Detroit family, was agent of the American Fur Co. and an authority on Mackinac Island. Apparently his conversation dwelt on the state of the fur trade.
† 'Mackinac is the rendezvous of the Northwest American Missionary Establishment. It contained six missionaries; of whom four were Presbyterian, one a Catholic, and one of the Church of England, and a large establishment for the instruction of one hundred children, of whatever persuasion.' Vigne, *Six Months in America*, II,112-113.

as to have the vertigo; at once the poor devil began to tremble in all his limbs; he only recovered by letting himself slide gently to the bottom. In order to judge the point of view, I and the Englishman took a small barque, and a short distance out we both of us sketched the Giant's Arch.

'The other no less curious phenomenon is in the middle of the island. It's a pyramid which seems to lift itself regularly to a height of fifty feet, and which is composed of one rock, never touched by the hand of man. In the rock are crevasses and faults where the Indians sometimes deposed the bones of the dead. I found a small fragment of these relics, and it's *one of the riches* that I shall bring back to my country.'

While Beaumont was sketching, Tocqueville was off, 'as usual,' on an inquisitive tour of inspection. He went to call on the curé, who wasn't in. Instead he met Madame La Framboise, a respectable woman partly of Indian extraction, whose family was well known at Mackinac and in the adjoining regions. Nothing loath, this half-breed lady gave her French visitor some interesting details on her life and family history. She then showed him a letter written by an Indian girl, and some Indian books of prayer.

Tocqueville wandered on, and came to a bivouac of Canadians along the shore. The chief of the band of traders was a *bois-brûlé*, with the air and manners of the French, gay, open, energetic. 'I sat down at their fire, and I had with their chief the following conversation: I have only taken in this conversation,' Tocqueville noted in his diary, 'what accorded with all the notions I had already received.' *

'*Q.* What has become of the Hurons and the Iroquois who played so great a role in the history of the colonies?

'*A.* The Hurons have almost disappeared. The Iroquois, half destroyed also, have almost all mingled with the Chippewas. Many are established at Green Bay and in the neighbourhood. The Iroquois form an astute nation always ready to join our side or the English, as fortune seems to incline.

'*Q.* Have you something to fear from the Indians in trading with them?

'*A.* Almost nothing. The Indians are not thieves, and besides we are useful to them.

---

* This procedure was characteristic with Tocqueville, whenever he had begun to make up his mind about a question.

'*Q*. Do you think the Indians are better or worse, in proportion as they are nearer or further away from the Europeans?

'*A*. I think they are much better when they have no contact with us, and certainly happier. There is more order, more government among them as one advances further into the wilderness. I make an exception, however, for the Christian Indians and especially for those who are Catholic. Those are the best of all.

'*Q*. Have the distant Indians, of whom you speak, chiefs?

'*A*. Yes, sir, they have chiefs whose power is very respected in peace. They are hereditary, and their origin is lost in the night of time. They name a special chief (the bravest) to lead them to war. They don't exactly have a system of justice. However, when a murder is committed, the murderer is delivered to the family of the dead. Often he succeeds in buying himself off. More often still, he is killed and buried with his victim.

'*Q*. How do the Indians you speak of live?

'*A*. In an ease absolutely unknown near European establishments. They do not cultivate the land. They are much less well clothed, and use only bows. But game is in extreme abundance in their wilderness. I imagine it was thus all the way to the Atlantic before the arrival of the Europeans. But the game flees toward the west with unbelievable rapidity. It precedes the whites by more than a hundred leagues. The Indian peoples which surround us die of hunger if they do not cultivate the ground a little.

'*Q*. Is it that the Indians do not realize that sooner or later their race will be annihilated by ours?

'*A*. They are unbelievably careless of the future. Those who are half educated already, or on whose heels we tread, see with despair the Europeans advancing toward the west, but there is no longer time to resist them. All the distant western tribes (I have heard it said that there were a good three million of them) do not seem to suspect the danger that is menacing them.

'*Q*. Is it true that the Indians love the French?

'*A*. Yes, sir, extremely. They do not consent to speak anything except French. In the furthest wildernesses, the quality of being a Frenchman is the best recommendation with them. They always remember our good treatment of them when we were masters of Canada. Besides, many of us are allied to them, and live almost as they do.'

It was late when Tocqueville returned. He must have been smiling to himself at the recollection of how the chief of the *voyageurs* had 'sirred' him. As he passed a savage hut, an Indian family was chanting a canticle of the church in its native tongue.

\*

\*  \*

'In the night of the seventh to eighth we left Michilimackinac,' Beaumont continued his account. 'The morning of the ninth we arrived at Green Bay. You will find this place indicated in one of the corners of Lake Michigan. We left there again the next day, the tenth.

'I passed my time there in quite an original way. Many of the Indian huts \* were on the river bank. I went steadily from one to the other. I was alone. I talked as much as possible with the savages I found. A few knew a little French, not one but knows how to say: *bonjour*. That's already a way of beginning a conversation. Besides, they are very fond of the French. When I found some who did not understand a word of French, I spoke to them by signs. . . . If I wanted to give them extreme pleasure, I had but to show them my album. There is one fairly good-looking young Indian girl who gave me a collar of pearls and shells for an American *Pic-vert* [green woodpecker] that I had painted. There's trading for you, about which I know nothing. You perceive that through seeing Americans I take on their industrial spirit. Happily I have for me the anecdote of the ladies asking for their portraits. . . .

'In the hut of one of my savages I amused myself painting the face of a small Indian. I made a bird on one cheek, a galloping horse on the other, and a cat on his chin. His comrades were in admiration of my masterpieces. You know that it is the custom of the Indians to paint their faces. They do it very crudely, without taste or art. Therefore they were charmed by colours arranged with some method. I have learned the ways of the Indians better in half a day thus passed in their midst than I should have done in reading thousands of volumes. I shall not undertake a description of the subject; taken by and large they seem excellent people. But it's the rough diamond, crude, unpolished, which consequently seems and really is inferior to other stones, far less precious but embellished by art. While I was on my expedition among the savages, Tocqueville was hunting, and nearly drowned himself. He is

---

\* Green Bay was the centre of an Indian colony of Menominees and Iroquois, the latter having been given land and transported there by the U.S. Government, upon decision to remove them from western New York.

very shortsighted; he encounters a stream and thinks it very narrow; he therefore does not hesitate to swim across. But he had been mistaken, and this river was actually so wide that he was utterly worn out when he reached the other bank. These are dangers never run by those who do not know how to swim very well.*

'All the lands surrounding Green Bay are so flat that there is no sort of view, unless it be that of Fort Howard, which is occupied by some American companies. All the military posts in this lost country have no other object than to hold the Indians in respect and to expel them always further and further. In this respect the American army has little to do; the Indians are in general resigned to their lot. . . .' And Beaumont sent his family a short description of the United States army, its pay, and its duties. He and Tocqueville had obtained their information from the Major in charge of Fort Howard,† whom they had gone to interview. This curiosity satisfied, Tocqueville had once again returned to the subject which was preoccupying them.

Would the Indians ever 'bend themselves' to civilization? The Major thought not. They feared work, despised the comforts of the white man, and were too proud to change. Would they ever unite to attack the whites? Again the Major said no. Too few realized the danger; and they were too busy with their private wars. Their character, he insisted, was *unconquerable*. And he regaled them with the anecdote of the young Indian who, after being educated in a white school, went back to the taking of scalps.‡

The rest confirmed what the Canadian fur-trader had said. They returned to the *Superior*, and Beaumont sketched the fort, amusing himself by inserting the vessel at her pier, with a few bored Americans on deck, and an Indian establishment in the foreground.

'Speaking of Indians,' Tocqueville was later to tease his sister-in-law, 'do you know what Atala, or some one of her sort, is like? I must describe her, so that you may judge of her resemblance to Chateaubriand's Atala. Atala is an Indian woman, the colour of very dark brown *café-au-lait*, whose straight and gleaming hair falls like two drum sticks well down her back. Ordinarily, she has a large, almost aquiline

---

* In Tocqueville's diary there is only: 'I go hunting alone. River crossed by swimming. Canoe, plants in the depths of the water. I lose myself a moment, return to the same spot without suspecting it.'
† 'Major Lamard' [?], 12 August 1831. 'A well educated and intelligent man. For a year and a half he was stationed at Prairie du Chien.' [7]
‡ Cf. *Dém. en Am.*, II,275–276 note.

nose, a large mouth armed with sparkling teeth, and two great black eyes which, in full day, much resemble a cat's eyes at night.

'Don't think that with this natural beauty she neglects adornment. Not at all. First she makes about the eyes a black stripe; then underneath a beautiful red line; then a blue; then a green; until her face resembles a rainbow. Then she hangs from her ear a kind of Chinese carillon, which weighs half a pound.

'The most *worldly,* moreover, pass through their nostrils a great ring of tin, which hangs on their mouth and produces the most gracious effect. They add, also, a necklace composed of large plaques on which are engraved various wild animals.

'Their clothing consists of a kind of linen tunic which falls a little below the knee. They drape themselves ordinarily in a blanket which, at night, serves as their bed.

'You are not at the end of the portrait. The fashion in the forests is to turn the feet in. I don't know if it is more unnatural than to turn them out; but our European eyes have difficulty getting used to this kind of beauty.

'Imagine, to obtain it, the Indian girl binds her feet from childhood, so that at the end of twenty years *les deux pointes du pied se trouvent vis à vis l'une de l'autre en marchant.* Then she carries off all homages, and is reputed among the most *fashionable.*

'All I know is that I wouldn't, for all the gold in the world, fulfil by her the role of Chactas. The Indians, it should be said, are more attractive than their women. They are great, carefree huskies (*grands gaillards*), set on their legs like stags, and with like agility. They have, when they smile, a charming expression; and are devils incarnate when angry. We have seen less of them than we should have liked, but the forests are being depopulated with such unbelievable rapidity. . . .'

'We left Green Bay 10 August,' wrote Beaumont, 'and came back to Michilimackinac by which our way passed to return to Detroit. Chance had it that at the moment of our arrival at Michilimackinac Mr. Mul[l]on was pronouncing his controversial discourse against the Presbyterians. Tocqueville and I went to hear him in the Catholic church. We found many people there. The religious quarrel in question excited a lively sensation among the people. Mr. Mul[l]on spoke with extreme warmth and with much talent. But it seemed to me that he treated his adversaries with a violence and severity that had nothing evangelical about them.'

Apparently the Presbyterians had declined to meet Father Mullon in debate, as he had expected. Mr. Vigne, the Englishman, considered the performance anything but edifying:[8] 'Having been, or fancying himself to have been very much wronged, he entered into a long explanation of the affair. He read letters and papers, and commented upon them in his robes from the altar; he made a long tirade, in which sarcasm and ridicule were successively prominent, and wound up his speech more suited to the bar than the pulpit, by accusing his adversary of telling a "thumper." Whether he was in the right or the wrong was little to the purpose: in common, I believe, with every one that heard him, I thought the whole proceeding was exceedingly disgraceful.'

'If his moderation is not perfect,' concluded Beaumont a little more charitably, 'one must at least admire his zeal; for it is a fact that he came 200 leagues to sustain his thesis, and he will have 200 leagues more to cover to return.*

'We left Michilimackinac the twelfth, and we are now on Lake Huron, where I continue the letter that I began day before yesterday. To-morrow, the fourteenth, we shall be at Detroit . . . and we shall at once return to Buffalo. . . .'

Thus ended their first western tour. On 17 August Tocqueville and Beaumont were back at the point from which they had started, thirty days before: the poorer for a month lost from their mission, but well compensated by the experiences they had enjoyed and by all the information they had acquired on the pioneer, the Indian, and the missionary of the northwestern frontier.

In many ways theirs was an unique achievement. Only two unusually determined students, as persevering and relentless as a New Englander himself, could have continued a serious investigation in the face of such hardships, and such distractions. And only two extraordinarily attractive and tactful young men could have made such an appeal to men of all types and characters. Dour Yankees, canny inn-keepers, voluble traders, stern Indian fighters, zealous missionaries: all had felt the charm of the young Frenchmen, and had yielded their confidence. One after the other had been pleased to talk about himself, and had let himself be persuaded to discourse at length about the region and its diverse peoples.

Tocqueville and Beaumont even brought back with them the esteem

---

* On 19 November 1831, Mullon baptized 'five adult converts from the wanderings of indefinite Protestantism.' Information furnished by T.A.Thoma.

of the uninteresting tourists. Shortly after the return of the *Superior*, there appeared in the Detroit press [9] a notice that two French Prison Commissioners had been among the passengers on this excursion. 'We have seldom,' wrote the correspondent, 'met with gentlemen better qualified, by their natural temperaments, acquisitions and habits, for Tourists in a foreign land. It was refreshing to hear their expressions of admiration, poured forth with the most winning enthusiasm, as some new scene of beauty opened before them. They sketched the most picturesque views, that they might, as they said, give pleasure to their friends on their return. And they looked with curious but kindly eye, on the beginnings of improvement in this newly explored region.

'They intended, when they left this city, to visit Niagara, and be in Cambridge, at the annual commencement. Wherever they may go, we trust they will receive all the attention, due to foreigners, of cultivated minds and gentlemanly feeling.'

# XXIII

## THUNDER OF WATERS

Tocqueville and Beaumont had an unhappy time at Niagara: a woeful and uneasy visit.

Not that the Falls disappointed the two young men. On the contrary, they were thrilled, spellbound—even (and this was wonderful) practically speechless. From the moment when in their carriage, still a league and a half away on the river road from Buffalo, they first heard the grumble of the cataract—heavy mutterings as of distant thunder in the darkness—they were overawed. And next morning when, after a night in the little village of Niagara Falls, they caught their first glimpse of the Falls itself, they were dumb with astonishment. No description they had ever read had prepared the French commissioners for what lay before them. Even the magnificent word picture of Chateaubriand seemed insignificant as they stood on the brink of the river and looked down into the gorge. Only the romanticist's remark that the cataract resembled 'a column of water of the deluge' measured up to the spectacle. That, and the Indian name Niagara, 'Thunder of Waters.' To try to convey an idea of the scene to their families was hopeless. They did not even make the attempt.

Instead, they were content to explore and to see. The weather was glorious. By day, the smoke of waters rising from the canyon was covered by a rainbow; at night, a white bow, pale in the brilliant moonlight, seemed to bridge the gulf. Tocqueville and Beaumont examined the Falls from every angle. They crossed the bridge from the American side to the island; they crossed the island toward the horseshoe falls on the Canadian side; they clambered out to a rock surrounded by water and overhanging the very precipice. Then their insatiable curiosity got the better of them. They changed to canvas suits, and hired a guide to take them under the Falls.

For so frail a person as Tocqueville, this was no easy venture. An impetuous wind almost swept him off his feet, and threw in his face a torrent of blinding spray. It was, he said, as if ten fire hoses had been turned on him at once. The further they went, the harder it became to breathe. When, finally, at the end of a hundred yards, they reached the jutting rock which terminated the passage, the Frenchman was almost sick from suffocation. Only after pressing his mouth a long time against the rock of the arching wall behind him, was he able to lift his head. 'There reigns in this place,' he later wrote his mother,[1] 'a profound and terrifying obscurity, now and again relieved by a flicker of light. Then you see the whole river, seemingly descending on your head. It is difficult to describe the impression produced by this ray of light, when, having let you a moment glimpse the vast chaos which surrounds you, it abandons you again amidst the darkness and fracas of the cataract.'

Retreating, Tocqueville and Beaumont emerged again safely, and went on with their explorations. They crossed to the Canadian side. After pausing to drink the King's health (out of courtesy to their English friend Vigne), they next proceeded to visit all the sights to be seen on that bank of the river. Beaumont made more sketches, Tocqueville did more dangerous climbing. In all, they spent two busy days examining the celebrated Falls and gorge of Niagara. Characteristically, their explorations were thorough, from top to bottom.

The eager prison commissioners were, without any question, both surprised and pleased by what they found. The thundering Falls went beyond their wildest imaginings; and the still river above, the green tree-grown plateau in which it lay, held for them an unexpected, quiet charm. Satisfied with what he saw, Tocqueville's restless mind yet misgave him. Inevitably, he conjured up a vision of the future. In spite of the tourists, the whole region was still wild and almost untouched, much as nature had made it. 'But,' he warned a friend,[2] 'if you wish to see this place in its grandeur, hasten. If you delay, your Niagara will have been spoiled for you. Already the forest round about is being cleared. The Romans are putting steeples on the Pantheon. I don't give the Americans ten years to establish a saw or flour mill at the base of the cataract.'

Absorbed by such activities and speculations, Tocqueville and Beaumont should have been in the best of spirits. Yet the two adventurous young friends were really miserable, inwardly so miserable that they could hardly enjoy Niagara at all. For this there were two reasons.

The first was worry. On arriving in Buffalo from the West, they had received bad news from home. According to the papers, the men of the July Revolution in France were planning an attack on the hereditary peerage, particularly on the members of the upper chamber who had been appointed by the recently deposed Charles X. Tocqueville was torn by anxiety. The Comte, his father, was a peer, had, in fact, been elevated to that body, as a reward for faithful service, in the last years of the Bourbon regime. 'Never,' wrote the young traveller,[3] 'have I felt myself a prey to more profound melancholy. . . . I was convinced that a crisis was imminent at home, and that civil war was about to start, bringing in its train so many perils for the very ones who are dearest to me. . . . These visions slide in between me and my surroundings; and I can't, without deep sadness and a sort of shame, see myself busy admiring cascades in America, while the destiny of so many loved ones is, perhaps at this very instant, compromised.'

Ever of an anxious and foreboding mind, Tocqueville feared the worst. The result was that the great natural phenomenon, which he and Beaumont had come so far to see, meant at bottom very little to him. There was not a moment, he wrote again, that he would not give America and all its curiosities to find himself back in France. If he explored Niagara none the less, and with his usual thoroughness, it was simply because the news was still uncertain, and there was, for the moment, nothing better to do.

The other trial that contributed to spoil their visit to the Falls was infinitely less tragic, though nevertheless annoying. This time, misfortune took the shape of a woman. In a sense, though they never could have foreseen it, the two amiable and courteous young men had only themselves to blame. As Beaumont, the chief victim, was the first to admit, their adventure even had its comic side.

'Hardly arrived at Buffalo,' he began,[4] 'we left again for Niagara. We had for travelling companions MR. Vi[g]ne an Englishman, and an Englishwoman Miss Clemens. I think I spoke to Achille of these two persons, who figured among the passengers of Green Bay. The first is an altogether likeable man; he travels for instruction and pleasure both. The second is the best person on earth; but it is impossible to be more boring. She has an altogether romantic imagination; she lives only on fictions, emotions, and moonlight. When she sees something which pleases her, she expresses herself only by exclamations, and with her there is no admiration without ecstasy. At twenty she would be charming; she is at least forty, which makes her only ridiculous. She has taken a passionate liking for us. I had the misfortune to be polite; she believed I wanted to be gallant. When we were on the steamboat, I was driven to many manœuvres to escape the charms of her conversation. Now it was verses that I had to hear her declaim; sometimes a charming point of view that she wanted to admire with me. Usually I got rid of her on pretexts good or bad. But there was no way to escape her on leaving Buffalo. 'I shall go,' said she, 'show you my favourite location (*séjour*), and do you the honours of the place.' It is certain that she spends half her life near the cataract; one might call her *la folle de Niagara*. Why doesn't she place herself under the Falls? Perhaps the *douche* would cure her.

'However that may be, we thus embarked with our elderly travelling companion, and in three hours we arrived at the place nearest to the Falls. . . . We explored the two banks successively, in order to judge all the views. I made a sketch which I hope will give you an idea of them. Miss Clemens bothered us a great deal during our sojourn in her domain. She was always proposing walks, boat rides, etc., etc., etc., . . . One day she was so impatient to go with us, that at the moment when Mr. Vi[g]ne, Tocqueville, and I were leaving, gun on shoulder, to go see a very picturesque site called the *Whirpull* [*sic*], she attached herself to our steps in spite of all our efforts to make her remain behind. Seeing that reason could do nothing with her spirit, we thought that it was necessary to convince her by the aid of arguments of another nature. Consequently we began to walk with extreme speed. It was perhaps the hottest day of the year. It was noon. We were dying of the heat. The need of avoiding a sentimental old woman gave us spur [?]. I, especially, kept at the head of the company, because I had suffered more than the others from strokes of boredom. We really had the appearance of a band of deer pursued by a fierce hound. We were all breathless. We leapt barriers like stags. I believe that in like case I should have jumped the reservoir of Beaumont-la-Chartre twenty times in succession. But more tireless than we, like unto a pack of hounds who have been promised their part (*la curée*), our beautiful Englishwoman cleared all obstacles with unbelievable legerity and, in spite of all our efforts, after a good hour's run, we hadn't gained fifty yards on her. In despair, we halted. At length, having seen what we wished to see, we returned with our intrepid *Dulcinée*. We began a flight of the same kind. This time we were more happy, and we manœuvred so well that she lost sight of us and we fled like convicts who have broken the prison gate. On our return we were nearly all ashamed of our rudeness. But while, to console ourselves, we were eating a good dinner, we received a small note in which she begged our pardon for having separated from us. We were much tempted not to pardon her. However we thought that she would profit by the lesson. If I had known how much she would annoy us the next day, I should certainly not have forgiven her.*

'This poor woman has overwhelmed me with benefits, and I blush to think how ungrateful I am. She has given me a very good work on the art of perspective, a charming book containing a poem of Thomas Moore, various biographical sketches of the great men of England, and finally a few verses of her own composition, some of which are remarkably well made. I should reproach myself for having received all that, if it had been in my power to refuse. But I declare that no power on earth could resist the will of Miss Clemens, and I suffered veritable violence. . . .

'We passed the eighteenth and nineteenth of August at Niagara,' concluded the long-suffering squire, 'the twentieth we embarked on Lake Ontario on the steamboat *Great Britain.* . . .'

---

* The reader who cares to examine *Six Months in America* (II,133) will admire the admirable British restraint with which Mr. Vigne later described the flight from Miss Clemens: 'At about two miles below the fall, the river again becomes a torrent,' his account of their adventure begins. 'I proceeded along the edge of the chasm through which it rages, in order to visit "the Whirlpool," whose deep and gloomy appearance well repaid me for a very hot walk.'

## XXIV

## LOWER CANADA: A LOST EMPIRE?

BUT it was French, this *Montréal.* . . ! The Rev. John Power, in New York, had warned them; yet it was as pleasant a surprise as they could remember.

Two weeks later, when investigation had somewhat accustomed the young continentals to the nature of Lower Canada, Tocqueville wrote to Abbé Lesueur:[1] 'I am astonished that this country is so unknown in France. Not six months ago I believed, with every one else, that Canada had become completely English. In my mind had always stuck the returns of 1763, which gave the French population as only 60,000. But since that time the rate of increase has been as great there as in the United States; and to-day there are in the single province of Lower Canada 600,000 persons of French descent. I tell you that you can't dispute them their origin. They are as French as you and I. They even resemble us more closely than the Americans of the United States resemble the English. I can't express to you what pleasure we felt on finding ourselves in the midst of this population. We felt as if we were home, and everywhere we were received like compatriots, children of *old France*, as they say here. To my mind the epithet is badly chosen. Old France is in Canada; the new is with us. . . .'

Such was the thought that only first really penetrated the French commissioners as they rounded the mountain and came within sight of Montreal. In a matter of hours the idea was to ripen into a firm conviction.

Tocqueville and Beaumont did not have the time to stay long in this island city. But they had a letter of introduction (probably from John Power) for the Superior of the Catholic Seminary, a Frenchman who had come over from St. Sulpice not many years before, and who turned out to be a most likeable and distinguished clergyman.*

'I don't believe there is a happier people in the world than the

* Joseph-Vincent Quiblier.

Canadian,' he told them.[2] 'It has *des mœurs très douces,* no civil or religious dissensions, and pays no tax.

'But is there not some vestige of the feudal system remaining?' The antique character of the city and the surrounding country-side had evidently made a strong impression on the two Frenchmen.

'Yes, but it's rather a name than an actuality. The greater part of Canada is still divided into *seigneuries.* Those who inhabit or who buy a piece of land therein are required to pay a rent to the *seigneur,* and the rights of transfer. But the rent is only a bagatelle. The *seigneur* has no honorary rights, no superiority whatsoever over his tax payer. I think he is less far above him than the European farmer is over his tenant.

'*Q.* How are the expenses of the cult covered?

'*A.* By the tithe. The clergy in general has no landed property. What one calls the tithe is the twenty-sixth part of the harvest. It is paid without repugnance as without difficulty.

'*Q.* Have you any convents of men?

'*A.* No. In Canada there are only convents of women. And these religious women lead a very active life, bringing up children or caring for the sick.

'*Q.* Have you freedom of the press?

'*A.* A liberty complete and unlimited.

'*Q.* Have they sometimes tried to turn it against religion?

'*A.* Never. Religion is too respected for a journalist to let himself make the least attack on it.

'*Q.* Are the upper classes of society religious?

'*A.* Yes, very.

'*Q.* Is there any animosity between the two races?

'*A.* Yes; but it is not very lively, it does not extend to the habitual intercourse of life. The Canadians * pretend that the English government gives places only to Englishmen, the English on the contrary complain that it favours the Canadians. I think that there are exaggerations on both sides in these complaints. In general there is little religious animosity between the two peoples, legal toleration being complete.'

Tocqueville and Beaumont wondered. In their patriotic French hearts a hope was being born.

---

* 'The English and the French mingle so little that the latter keep exclusive possession of the name *Canadians,* the others continuing to be called *English.*' Toc. diary note, 28 August 1831.

'Do you believe that this colony will soon escape from England?' they next asked.

'*A*. I do not. The Canadians are happy under the present regime. They have a political liberty almost as great as that enjoyed in the United States. If they became independent, there are a multitude of public expenses which would fall to their charge. If they joined the United States, they would be afraid that their population would soon be absorbed in the deluge of emigration, and that their ports, closed during four months of the year, would fall to nothing if they were deprived of the English market.'

This was not very encouraging. The two political scientists changed the subject.

'*Q*. Is it true that education is spreading?

'*A*. Within a few years, a complete change has come about in this matter. The impulsion is now given and the Canadian race which is growing up will not resemble that which now exists.

'*Q*. Are you not afraid that enlightenment will injure the religious principle?

'*A*. It is not yet possible to know the effect that will be produced. I believe however that religion has nothing to fear.

'*Q*. Is the Canadian race spreading?

'*A*. Yes, but slowly and little by little. It lacks that adventurous spirit and that scorn of the ties of birth and family that characterize the Americans. The Canadian removes only to the farthest extremity of his parish and [of the commune] of his parents, and he goes to establish himself as near as possible. However, the movement is great, as I said, and it will multiply a hundredfold, I think, with the increase of enlightenment.'

So there was some hope for the French-Canadians after all. Tocqueville and Beaumont were much intrigued; and promptly resolved to find out just as much as they could about the little-known survivors of the once-great Empire of France in North America. They introduced themselves to Dominique and Charles J. E. Mondelet, two enterprising young French-Canadians, not much older than Beaumont, who were practising law in Montreal.* The brothers Mondelet seemed to be 'men of intelligence and good sense.'

---

* It was probably John C. Spencer of Canandaigua who had given them a letter of introduction to these two brothers (see above, p.216). The questions and later activities of Tocqueville and Beaumont make it interesting to realize that Dominique

'In what proportion is the French population to the English in Canada?' was Tocqueville and Beaumont's opening question.[3]

'*A*. 9 to 10 [9 out of 10?]. But almost all the wealth and trade is in the hands of the English. They have their families and relations in England, and find facilities that we do not have.

'*Q*. Have you many newspapers in French?

'*A*. Two.

'*Q*. In what proportion are their subscribers to the subscribers of the English papers?

'*A*. 800 out of 1300.

'*Q*. Have these newspapers influence?

'*A*. Yes, a very marked influence, though less than the newspapers in France are said to obtain.

'*Q*. What is the position of the clergy? Have you remarked in it the political tendency it is accused of having in Europe?

'*A*. It is perhaps possible to discern in the clergy a secret tendency to govern or direct, but that's a very small matter. In general, our clergy is eminently national. This is partly the result of the circumstances in which it finds itself placed. In the first days of the conquest and up to our times, the government in an underhanded manner worked to change the religious opinions of the Canadians in order to make them a body more homogeneous with the English. The Church therefore found its interests opposed to those of the government and allied to those of the people. Every time that it was a question of struggling against the English, the clergy has therefore been at our head or in

Mondelet (1799–1863) was in that very year, 1831, elected to represent Montreal in the Assembly of Lower Canada. There he joined the group of moderate constitutional reformers who were seeking to increase the power of the native French-Canadian population in the legislative and executive administration of the Province, without, however, attacking the supremacy of the Empire or severing the tie with England. The following year, in a move to conciliate the *habitants* by giving them representation in the executive branch, the Governor appointed him to the Executive Council. But at this the extreme Canadian nationalist party in the Assembly, in a characteristic fit of inconsistency and animosity, declared his seat vacant and proclaimed him a traitor to his race. In 1834, therefore, he and John Neilson (*q.v.* below), both beaten by Louis Joseph Papineau and the extremists, withdrew from politics and accepted an appointment to go and investigate the American penitentiary reforms —thus following in Tocqueville and Beaumont's footsteps. The two Canadians used *Du. Syst. Pén.* as a guide, and returned with a verdict in favour of the Pennsylvania System. In 1842, after the abortive revolution of 1837–1838, the famous Durham Report, and the Union of the two Provinces, Dominique Mondelet and his brother, Charles Joseph Elzéar Mondelet (1801–1876), were appointed to judgeships, a career in which each attained advancement and distinction. See especially: *Canada and Its Provinces*, III,315; and the John Neilson Papers, Public Archives of Canada.

our ranks. *Far* from opposing the ideas of liberty, it preached them it-self. All the measures in favour of public education that we have taken, almost by force and in spite of England, have found a support in the clergy. In Canada it's the Protestants who sustain aristocratic ideas. The Catholics are accused of being demagogues. What makes me think that the character of our priests is peculiar to Canada is that the priests who from time to time come to us from France show the government on the contrary a condescension and a docility impossible to conceive.

'*Q*. Are morals pure in Canada?

'*A*. Yes, very pure.'

That same afternoon, 24th August, Tocqueville and Beaumont went on board the fine steamboat *John Molson*, for the twenty-hour trip to Quebec.[4] The capital of Lower Canada was their real destination; and without seeing the old citadel and the heart of the Province they knew that they could not really hope to understand the character and prospects of the French race in Canada. On their way down to the wharf, however, they had taken the opportunity to observe the townsmen narrowly, had examined their houses and looked into their shops. And what they had seen, together with what had been told them in their brief conversations, had suggested some interesting reflections. Next morning, therefore, as the steamboat sped down the St. Lawrence, Tocqueville got out his pocket note-book. The title he gave his entry was: *Canada. Outward Appearance*.[5]

'Canada is without comparison the portion of America so far visited by us which bears the greatest analogy to Europe and above all to France. The banks of the St. Lawrence are perfectly cultivated and covered by houses and villages in every way similar to ours. All traces of the wilderness have disappeared; cultivated fields, church steeples, a population as numerous as in our provinces have replaced it.

'The towns, and in particular Montreal (we have not yet seen Quebec), bear a striking resemblance to our provincial towns. The basis of the population and the immense majority are everywhere French. But it is easy to see that the French are the conquered people. The well-to-do belong for the most part to the English race. Even though French is the language almost universally spoken, the majority of the newspapers, the posters, and even the signs of French shopkeepers, are in English. Commercial enterprises are almost all in their hands; they are truly the governing class in Canada.

'I doubt whether it will long be thus. The clergy and a great part

of the classes not rich but enlightened are French, and they are beginning to feel their secondary position keenly. The French journals
that I have read carry on a constant and animated opposition to the
English. Up to now the people, having few needs and intellectual passions and leading a very comfortable material life, has but imperfectly
discerned its position as a conquered nation and furnished but feeble
support to the enlightened classes. But within the last few years the
House of Commons, almost entirely Canadian, has taken measures
to spread education in profusion. Everything announces that the new
generation will be different from the present one, and if within the
next few years the English race does not prodigiously increase its
immigration and succeed in confining the French in the area which
they to-day occupy, the two peoples will find themselves face to face.'

Altogether, Tocqueville was inclined to be optimistic. 'I do not believe
that there can be an indissoluble union between them,' he concluded.
'I therefore still hope that the French, in spite of the conquest, will
succeed some day in forming a fine empire in the New World, more
enlightened, more moral, more happy than that of their fathers. For
the present, this division between the two races is singularly favourable to the domination of the English.'

*

*    *

*Québec* proved even more fascinating than the keenly inquisitive
French magistrates had anticipated. On the first two days they investigated everything, visited all the points of interest to tourists
within or in the near vicinity of the old, steeply-built capital. Naturally, as Frenchmen and as gentlemen of imagination and sympathy,
they felt the appeal of what they saw. The vast, onward-moving St.
Lawrence, the high-road of the old Empire, seemed to them more
beautiful and more majestic than they had thought possible. They
looked up at the ancient citadel of the governors, and thought it very
strong. They visited the Convent, and humbly acknowledged the
character and distinction of the *religieuses*. All such, wrote Beaumont,[6]
'have disappeared in France.' They rode to the Plains of Abraham,
and Beaumont was moved to sketch the simple obelisk which recalled to the descendants of both nations the romantic struggle of
Montcalm and Wolfe. Already they had visited the picturesque spot
where the Montmorency streamed over the precipice and dropped,

two hundred and forty feet, to the St. Lawrence. Beaumont had made a drawing of the falls, and embellished it with water-colours. And twice from the ramparts of *Québec*, looking out over the crowded lower town, he sought to transfer to his album the magnificent and smiling scene. From the steep, gabled roofs in the foreground, the glance lighted down on the wide, moving river, with the boats at anchor and the great isle of *Orléans* below. Thence, magnetically, the vast current drew the eye far into the distance, where on its banks the peaceful white houses of Beaufort and Lorette clustered and sparkled in the sun, 'mid their yellow fields, and underneath the long, green, horizontal mountain range. Beaumont had never before seen a region at the same time so fertile and so picturesque. The beauty of the country defied the best efforts of his art. And Tocqueville himself admitted: 'I have never in Europe seen a tableau more animated than that presented by the environs of Quebec.' [7]

'But what has interested us most keenly in Canada,' Tocqueville hastened to assure Abbé Lesueur, 'are its inhabitants.' 'All the labouring population of Quebec is French,' he jotted in his diary on 27 August. 'One scarce hears anything but French in the streets. However, all the signs are in English; there are only two theatres, which are English. The interior of the town is ugly but has no analogy with American cities. It resembles in striking fashion the interior of the majority of our provincial towns.

'The villages that we have seen in the neighbourhood bear an extraordinary resemblance to our fine villages. Only French is spoken there; the population appears happy and well off. The stock (*sang*) is markedly handsomer than in the United States. The race is stronger, the women haven't that delicate and sickly air which characterizes the majority of American women.'

Thirty years later, when publishing some of Tocqueville's Canadian notes in the *Œuvres Complètes*, Gustave de Beaumont was silently to drop out the passage just quoted.* His motives, obviously, were charitable. After the lapse of years, the youthful Tocqueville's remarks about American women seemed needlessly sharp, and—whatever the truth of the matter—it was wiser not to risk giving offence. Perhaps the gentle editor was right. Certainly, Tocqueville had found himself in a disparaging mood while in Quebec. For so many months he had had to be courteous, to swallow his dislikes, to 'express nothing

---

* Cf.*O.C.*,VIII,253.

but pleasure':—now, suddenly, it was almost as if he were at home, in France, again. The contrast was too great; in his relief and relaxation the long-bottled-up emotions came pouring out. In fact, so home-like and attractive seemed the country of Lower Canada that he was beginning to romanticize its people. All the sympathy and generous admiration that their coldness, their materialism and conceit, had prevented the eager young idealist from bestowing on his American hosts, was now flowing out toward these robust and smiling descendants of the early French colonists. Of course religious matters were better ordered here than in the United States. Nor was that all.

'Religion is not accompanied by any of the accessories which it has in the countries of southern Europe, where its power is strongest,' Tocqueville continued. 'There are no convents of men, and the convents of women have useful aims and give examples of charity regarded with lively admiration by the English themselves. You see no madonnas along the roads; no bizarre and ridiculous ornaments, no *ex-voto* in the churches. The enlightened religion and the Catholicism here excite neither the hatred nor the sarcasm of the Protestants. I confess that for my part it satisfies my spirit more than the Protestantism of the United States. The *curé* is of a truth here the pastor of his flock. He is not a religious business man like the majority of American ministers.* Either one has to deny the utility of a clergy, or have one like the Canadian.

'I went to-day to a reading room.[8] Almost all the journals printed in Canada are English. They have about the dimensions of those of London. I have not yet read them. There appears at Quebec a paper called the *Gazette*, half English, half French, and a paper altogether French called *Le Canadien*. These journals have about the dimension of our French newspapers. I read several numbers with care: they carry on a violent opposition to the government and even to all that is English. The *Canadien* has for superscription: *Our Religion, Our Language, Our Laws*. It is hard to be more frank. The contents correspond to the title. Everything that can enflame the great or small passions of the people against the English is brought up with care in this journal. I saw an article in which they said that Canada would never be happy before she had an administration Canadian by birth, by principle, in ideas, in prejudices even; and that if Canada escaped from England it would not be to become English [American?]. In this

* Cf. above, p.156 note.

same paper were to be found quite pretty pieces of French verse.* Therein were also described some prize-givings at which the students had played *Athalie, Zaïre,* the *Mort de César.* In general the style of this journal is common, compounded of anglicisms and strange figures of speech. It much resembles the journals published in the canton of Vaux in Switzerland. I have not yet seen in Canada any man of talent nor a production which gave evidence of it. He who is to stir up the French population and raise it against the English is not yet born.'

A man who 'was to' stir up (*qui 'doit' remuer*) the French population and raise it against the English! This was pretty strong and definite language for a young man, supposedly disinterested, and but newly arrived in the Province.

Of course, for some days, Tocqueville and Beaumont had been reading the *Gazette* and *Le Canadien.* In other words, they had at once come to understand that there actually was a struggle going on in Lower Canada between a certain group of French-Canadians and the government. The elective Assembly, largely dominated by the French-Canadians, and fervently supported by *Le Canadien,*† seemed to be trying to change the constitutional organization of the Province, and to be attacking the Governor and his English subordinates in the positions of executive responsibility. In *Le Canadien,* there was talk of the abuse of office by the judges: the judges sat as well in the Upper House or Legislative Council, it appeared, and used their position to block every bill calculated to benefit the *habitants* and uphold their religion. Furthermore, the Governor filled the rest of the Legislative Council with English appointees and members of the 'château clique,' to protect and perpetuate British misrule. This was an injustice to the Canadian people. The Upper House should be elective, like the Lower, and under its control. Then, of course, the crown revenues should also come under the exclusive control of the Assembly. All these matters— and many others relating to the privileges and tyranny of the British minority—were aired with animus and vituperation by *Le Canadien.* After perusing its pages, therefore, Tocqueville and Beaumont had

---

* 'The Canadian gazettes all contain small fragments of literature in prose or verse, a thing that is never found in the vast columns of the English journals. This versification has the character of antique French poetry. It has a simple, a naïf turn far removed from our great words and the affected simplicity of our present literature, but it deals with small or antiquated ideas.' Toc. diary note, 29 August 1831.
† For the position of the *Gazette,* see below, pp.328,341.

good cause to reason that all was not just as it should be in Lower Canada.

On the other hand, this newspaper, as Tocqueville himself confessed, gave little evidence of talent or real ability. And quite clearly neither he nor Beaumont had been introduced, either in Montreal or Quebec, to the small and able group of radical nationalists who were chiefly responsible for this agitation. Had they, for example, had the opportunity to converse with their leader, the fiery and popular speaker of the Assembly, Louis Joseph Papineau, they might have gathered from him a more exact notion of the aims and prospects of the French-Canadians—and possibly even the idea that an eventual rising against the English was inevitable. But if Papineau was to lead a minority of the *habitants* to actual revolt in 1837, this was still the year 1831, and much would have to happen before even the extremists would abandon the method of political agitation and the goal of constitutional change for the program of complete independence by armed force.

Who, then, had said anything about a Rebellion to Tocqueville and Beaumont? about an uprising of the French-Canadians against their conquerors?

Nobody. That is, nobody but Tocqueville and Beaumont themselves. As a matter of fact, every one whom they had interviewed had discountenanced the idea, as neither necessary nor possible. The Mondelet brothers had talked a little about religious differences, but without suggesting anything serious. And to their question as to whether the colony 'would soon escape from England,' the distinguished Superior of the Montreal Seminary had returned a categoric 'No,' with the flat statement that the Canadians were 'happy under the present regime.' The columns of *Le Canadien*, it was true, gave the lie to this last assertion, and the editors appeared definitely to be trying to drive the English out of Lower Canada. But Tocqueville and Beaumont had apparently begun to *look around* for signs of racial 'animosity' and unrest some time before that bitter and homely little sheet fell into their hands. An observer might even have accused them of *looking forward* to trouble, and to a rebellion.

The fact was, Tocqueville and Beaumont's French hearts were beginning to get the better of them. The unexpected presence of half a million Frenchmen in North America, the sudden encounter with a vast and growing people, French in all but government, and free, powerful, and great but for the shameful peace of 1763, had aroused the commissioners' most patriotic instincts. At once indignation at the lot of their fellow countrymen—hatred of the British conquerors—hope for a different future—had arisen in their breasts. They had inquired for French newspapers, at once procured themselves copies. Then with characteristic directness and impatience, the very first day after their arrival in Quebec, Tocqueville had gone to interview an English merchant on the subject. Whether he confessed it to himself or not, it was as if he were reconnoitring the camp of an enemy.

'Do you think you have anything to fear from the *Canadians?*' was his bold, if mild-voiced approach.[9]

'*A.* No. The lawyers and the wealthy of French blood detest the English. They make a violent opposition to us in their papers and in their House of Commons [Assembly]; but it's only talk, that's all. The mass of the Canadian population has no political passions, and besides almost all the wealth is in our hands.

'*Q.* But are you not afraid that this numerous and compact population, to-day without passion, may have some to-morrow?

'*A.* Our numbers are increasing every day; soon we shall have nothing to fear on this side. The Canadians hate the Americans even more than they do us.'

To which Tocqueville added a *Note.* 'In speaking of the Canadians, there painted itself on the phlegmatic physiognomy of Mr. ***** a sentiment of hate and scorn most visible. It is rare that one speaks with so much passion of those from whom one has nothing to fear.' Perhaps so. The inquisitor was perhaps right. But it was rare also for the impartial Tocqueville to ask questions of such passionate intensity. Had he himself no hopes, no fears, no ill-suppressed desires? Complete objectivity seemed to fail both of the parties to this conversation, and about equally. Certainly the scholarly detachment, habitual with the Frenchmen, was conspicuous by its absence.

*

*     *

The next day, the same that saw Tocqueville devouring the propaganda of *Le Canadien* in some reading room in the city, he and Beaumont encountered their English tourist friend, Mr. Vigne, once more; and together they went to inspect the Inferior Court of King's Bench.

'We entered a spacious chamber filled with benches, occupied by a crowd whose appearance in every detail was French,' Tocqueville began his account of the visit.[10] 'At the end of the chamber were painted in large scale the British arms. Below this painting was placed the judge, in robe and bands. Before him were ranged the lawyers.

'At the moment that we came into the chamber, they were pleading a case of defamation. It was a question of fining a man who had called another a *pendard* and a *crasseux* [a dirty rogue?]. The lawyer was pleading in English:

'*Pendard*, said he, pronouncing the word with an altogether British accent, signifies a man who has been hung. No, gravely amended the judge, [*pendard* signifies] one who merits to be hung. At this word the attorney for the defence rose with indignation and pled his cause in French; his adversary replied in English. The two sides . . . [harangued?] each other in both languages, without probably understanding each other perfectly. From time to time the Englishman made an effort to express his ideas in French, in order to follow his adversary more closely. Occasionally the latter did likewise. The judge kept trying, now in French, now in English, to restore order; and the officer of the court called for silence! giving this word the English and the French pronunciation alternately. With calm restored, witnesses were produced. Some kissed the silver Christ on the cover of the Bible and swore in French to speak the truth; the others swore the same oath in English and, as Protestants, kissed the other side of the Bible, which was plain. Thereupon they cited the *coutume de Normandie*; they based their arguments on Denisart,[11] the decrees of the *Parlement* of Paris, and the Statutes of the reign of George III. After which the judge, because the word *crasseux* conveys the idea of a man devoid of morality, of discretion, and of honour, condemns the defendant to a fine of six louis or ten pounds sterling.

'The lawyers I saw there, and who are said to be the best in Quebec, gave evidence of talent neither in matter nor expression. They singularly lack distinction. They speak French with the accent of middle-class Normans. Their style is vulgar and full of oddities and English locutions. They say that a man is chargé [charged] ten louis when they mean that *on demande* of him ten louis, and they add . . .

'Enter the *boîte* [box], they cry to a witness, to tell him to place himself on the bench where he is to testify. . . .

'On the whole the tableau has about it something bizarre, incoherent, burlesque even. Fundamentally, the impression produced was sad, however. I have never been more convinced than on leaving that place that the greatest and most irretrievable misfortune for a people was to be conquered.'

Which brought the two French observers back to the fundamental question: Were the French-Canadians doing anything to remedy their plight, anything to free themselves from the alien yoke? To their satisfaction, Tocqueville and Beaumont now found themselves in a fair way to gather some first-hand information on this important subject.

It happened that they had brought with them from Charles Mondelet at Montreal a most flattering letter of introduction to a certain citizen of Quebec, one John Neilson.[12] This gentleman was a Scotchman who had come to Canada as a boy, and succeeded his uncle in the editorship of the *Quebec Gazette*—that half-English, half-French journal that Tocqueville had come across in the reading room. For the past thirteen years he had been a member of the elective Assembly of Lower Canada, a loyal representative of the French-Canadians and a fervent leader in their cause. Twice within the last decade he had been sent to England to argue their grievances; and only a few months before he had been thanked publicly for his services, and presented with a silver vase by the speaker of the Assembly. Throughout Canada John Neilson was known as a man of ability and distinction.*

On the 27th, then, Tocqueville and Beaumont called and presented their letter of introduction. They found Mr. Neilson open and hospitable, and courteous and attentive to a degree. He spoke French, they were pleased to note, 'with as much facility as his own language'; and his every word manifested a 'lively and original disposition.' Soon they were pouring out their questions, and he was answering as best he could. That same day he took them on an expedition along the river. And for days thereafter he devoted himself to showing them the country-side and introducing them to the life and civilization of Lower Canada.

The conversations that they came to have with him were naturally too numerous and long to be recorded in detail. But the first touched on such vital thoughts, and threw such a flood of light on certain aspects of the main question, that Tocqueville contrived a fairly extensive résumé of it in one of his diaries. Apparently this colloquy took

---

* Born in Scotland in 1776, Neilson had come to Quebec at 14, and since 1818 he had represented Quebec in the Assembly. At this time he was just beginning to separate from the more violent nationalists of the French-Canadian party (see below).

place that very day as the three of them were on their way to the ancient Jesuit settlement at Lorette.

'*Q*. What does Canada cost the English government every year?'[13] Evidently Tocqueville and Beaumont had resolved to begin at the bottom, with Great Britain's reasons for keeping her dominion in Canada.

'*A*. From two hundred to two hundred and fifty thousand pounds sterling.

'*Q*. Does it bring in anything?

'*A*. Nothing. The taxes exacted by the tariff are employed in the colony. We would fight rather than surrender to England a cent of our money.

'*Q*. But what interest has England in keeping Canada?

'*A*. The same that large landholders have in conserving great possessions which figure among their properties but which cost them heavy expenditures and often involve them in troublesome suits. However, it cannot be denied that England has an indirect interest in keeping us; in case of war with the United States the St. Lawrence is a canal by which she can make her merchandise and her armies penetrate into the heart of America. In case of war with the peoples of northern Europe, Canada furnishes all the [ship-]building materials she needs. Besides, the burden is not as heavy as supposed. England is obliged to have the empire of the sea, not for her glory but for her existence; the expenses which she is obliged to make to attain that supremacy render the occupation of colonies much less costly for her than it would be for a nation which had no other object than the conservation of her colonies.'

These things being so, Tocqueville and Beaumont told themselves, England would never voluntarily withdraw from Canada, never even be willing to grant the French-Canadians in Lower Canada their independence. That left only the alternative of force.

'*Q*. Do you think the Canadians will soon shake the yoke of England?

'*A*. No, unless England forces us to. Otherwise it is absolutely contrary to our interest to become independent. We still form only 600[000] souls in Lower Canada; if we became independent, it would not be long before we were enveloped by the United States. Our population would, as it were, be annihilated by an irresistible mass of emigration. We must wait until we are numerous enough to defend our nationality, then we will become the Canadian people. Left alone the population here augments as fast as that of the United States. At the time of the conquest in 1763 we were only 60,000.'

Tocqueville and Beaumont must have had to struggle to control their expressions. Mr. Neilson's answer had certainly been disillusioning. Not only did this leader of the French-Canadian cause foresee no early stroke for freedom; he actually thought independence contrary to the French interest! They ventured their next question, therefore, with a kind of quiet desperation.

'*Q*. Do you think that the French race will ever succeed in freeing itself from the English? (This question was put with the tact required by the race of the respondent.)

'*A*. No. I believe that the two races will live and will mingle on the same soil, and that English will remain the official and business language. North America will be English, fate has decided. But the French race of Canada will not disappear; the amalgam is not as difficult to make as you think. That which above all maintains your language here is the *clergy*. The clergy forms the only *enlightened and intellectual* class here which *needs* to speak French and speaks it with purity.'

That settled it. Mr. Neilson evidently entertained no hopes for the revival of New France. Though a leader in the Assembly, he was as positive as any American that the continent belonged to English-speaking peoples. For him, too, destiny had decided. Later Tocqueville began his record of this conversation with the remark (evidently suggested by the statement above) that Mr. Neilson's 'birth and social position, in discord one with the other, sometimes produce singular contrasts in his ideas and conversation.' *

---

* Clearly, Tocqueville and Beaumont did not fully comprehend their guide's position. Mr. Neilson had been a champion of the French-Canadian cause since first entering politics. As this very conversation was to show, he entertained a deep affection for the *habitants*, their simple ways and quaint, antique customs. Furthermore, he wished to see these descendants of the early French colonists develop into a happy, educated, and largely self-governing people; he had always, for example, opposed the Union of Lower Canada with Upper Canada under one Assembly, fearing that this would lead to the destruction of the French-Canadian individuality and to the absorption of the *habitants* in the English population. On the other hand, Neilson was loyal to England and believed strongly in the Empire tie: according to him the French-Canadians were not yet fit for complete self-government. It followed, therefore, that responsible government was out of the question, and that the Upper House or Legislative Council should remain appointive, rather than be elected by the *habitants*. One other factor influenced his opinion. Neilson had always believed in reform by constitutional means; and now that he was approaching sixty he was growing distinctly more conservative in his ideas. As a consequence, he was beginning to feel that the nationalist leaders were becoming unreasonable in their demands. Three years later,

But if they now had to guard themselves from confiding in Mr. Neilson their own indignation and their still unextinguished hopes, there were still many things that he could tell them.

'What is the character of the Canadian peasant?' they asked.

Mr. Neilson was enthusiastic: 'In my opinion they are an admirable race.' And he went on to describe their virtues and social customs, apparently with such volubility that all Tocqueville could do that evening was to record a sort of condensed summary of what Mr. Neilson had said.

'The Canadian peasant is simple in his tastes, very tender in his family affections, very pure in his morals, remarkably *sociable*, polite in his manners; with all that very ready to resist oppression, independent and war-like, brought up in the spirit of equality,' Tocqueville quoted their guide. 'Public opinion here has an unbelievable force. There is no public authority in the villages, yet public order is there better maintained than in any other country in the world. Does a man commit a fault, he is shunned, he has to leave the village. Is a theft committed, the guilty one is not denounced, but he is dishonoured and obliged to flee. A capital execution has not been seen in Canada for ten years. Natural children are almost unknown in our country-sides. I recall the conversation of (I have forgotten the name): for two hundred years not one had been seen. Ten years ago an Englishman, having come and established himself, seduced a girl; the scandal was frightful.*

'The Canadian is tenderly attached to the soil which saw him born, to his church, to his family. That is why it is so hard to get him to go seek his fortune elsewhere. Besides, as I said, he is eminently *sociable*. The friendly reunions, the divine office in common, the assembly at the door of the church, these are his only pleasures.

'The Canadian is profoundly religious, and pays the tithe without repugnance. Each could free himself of it by declaring himself a

---

in 1834, this was to lead to a definite split with Papineau and his followers, and to his own defeat for re-election to the Assembly. After investigating American prisons with Dominique Mondelet, therefore, he was to join the Constitutional Association, go to London in 1835 as its representative, and in 1836 make a last effort to prevent the rebellion. On the outbreak of hostilities and the suspension of the government, he was to be appointed a member of the Special Council for the two Provinces. And in 1841, after the Union which he had opposed was finally consummated, he was to be elected as a conservative to the United Legislature.

* 'There reigns in all the villages a purity of morals that one would believe *fabuleuse*, if it were spoken of in our European cities.' Bt. to his father, Albany, 5 September 1831 (BBlb).

Protestant, there are no examples yet of such a deed. The clergy here forms only a corps knit to the people. It shares the ideas of the people, enters into their political interests, co-operates in the struggle against the government. Risen from the people, the clergy exists for the people only. They accuse the clergy here of being demagogues. I have not heard it said that the same reproach is made against the Catholic clergy in Europe. The fact is that it is liberal, enlightened, and yet profoundly believing; its morals are exemplary. I am a proof of its tolerance. A Protestant, I have twice been named to our House of Commons, and never have I heard it said that the smallest religious prejudice was advanced against me by no matter whom.* The French priests who come from Europe, little like ours in their *mœurs*, are absolutely different in their political tendencies. I was saying to you that a great spirit of sociability existed among the Canadian peasants. This spirit leads them to help each other in all critical circumstances. Does a misfortune happen to one of them? The whole commune does its best, usually, to repair the damage. Lately the barn of ***** came to be struck by lightning. Five days afterwards it had been rebuilt by the neighbours, without charge.

'*Q*. There are some remains of feudalism here.

'*A*. Yes, but so light that they are scarcely perceived. 1. The *seigneur* receives for the lands which he originally conceded an almost insignificant rent. It's from 6 to 8 francs, for example, for 90 *arpents*. 2. One is obliged to grind at his mill, but he may not ask more than a price fixed by law, which is below what one pays in the United States with free competition. 3. There are rights of *lods et vents*; that is to say that when the proprietor of an infeudated piece of land sells it, he is obliged to give a twelfth part of the price to the *seigneur*. This charge would be quite heavy were not the dominating trait of the population that of remaining invincibly attached to the soil. Such are the vestiges of the feudal system in Canada. Otherwise, the *seigneur* has no honorary rights, no privileges.† There is no nobility, and there could be none. Here, as in the United States, one has to work to live. You find no *fermiers* [tenants]. The *seigneur* is therefore ordinarily

---

* 'Mr. Richard, Catholic *curé*, is sent to Congress by a Protestant population. Mr. Neilson, Protestant, is sent to the Canadian House of Commons by a Catholic population. Do these facts prove that religion is better understood, or that its force is diminishing? They prove, I think, both.' Toc. diary note, 29 August 1831.

† 'The *seigneur* has a privileged stall in church.' Bt. to his father, Albany, 5 September 1831 (BBlb).

himself a cultivator, and yet however much on a footing of equality the *seigneurs* are now placed, the population does not regard them without some fear and jealousy. It's only by embracing the popular side that some of them have succeeded in having themselves elected to the House of Commons. The peasants remember the state of subjection in which they were held under the French government; there is especially one word which has remained in their memory like a political scarecrow, that's the *taille*. They no longer know the sense of the word precisely, but it always represents for them something insupportable. I am convinced that they would take up arms if the attempt were made to establish some sort of tax to which this name were given.'

At this point Tocqueville and Beaumont brought the conversation back to the political situation of the peasants. They had some definite questions to ask about the governmental institutions of Lower Canada.

'*Q*. What are the conditions of eligibility for being elected to the Chamber of Commons?

'*A*. There are none.

'*Q*. Who are the electors in the country-side?

'*A*. Those who have forty pounds of income from land.

'*Q*. Do you not fear so great a mass of electors?

'*A*. No. Every man is a proprietor, he is religious, loves order, his choices are good, and though he takes a great interest in elections, they are hardly ever accompanied by disturbances. The English wanted to import among us their system of corruption, but they failed completely against the morality and honour of our peasants.'

So the Canadians believed in self-government, in the beneficent effects of equality and manhood suffrage, just as did their confident neighbours to the south! But in the United States men of intelligence attached one condition to the successful operation of a democracy. Peoples had to educate themselves before they were fit to govern themselves, the New Yorkers had admitted. Now how did the Canadians feel about that?

'At what point is primary education?' Tocqueville and Beaumont wanted to know.

Mr. Neilson replied that that was 'a long story. In the time of the French there was no primary instruction. The Canadian had his arms always in his hand; he could not spend his time at school. After the conquest, the English occupied themselves only with their own. Twenty years ago the government wanted to establish education, but went about it tactlessly, and shocked religious prejudices. The government made us believe that it wished to take over the instruction and direct it in favour of Protestantism. That's what *we* said anyhow, and the project failed. The English said that the Catholic clergy wanted to retain the people in ignorance. Neither side was speaking the truth, but that's the language of parties. Four years ago the House of Commons saw clearly that if the Canadian population did not educate itself, it would end by being entirely absorbed by a foreign population rising at its side and in its midst. Exhortations were made, encouragements given, funds were created, finally school inspectors were named. I am one, and I am just back from making my tour. Nothing is more satisfying than the report that I have to make. The impulsion is given. The population is seizing with remarkable activity the opportunity to instruct itself. The clergy has aided us in our efforts. Already we have in our schools half the children, about 60,000. In two or three years I have no doubt but that we shall have them *all*.

'I hope that then the Canadian race will begin to leave the banks of the river and advance toward the interior,' Mr. Neilson continued. 'Up to now we stretch out about 120 leagues on both banks of the St. Lawrence, but this line is rarely two leagues wide. Beyond, however, there is to be found some excellent land, that is almost always given away for nothing (this is literally true) and that can easily be put into cultivation. The price of labour is three francs in the towns, less in the country; food is very cheap. The Canadian peasant himself makes all the necessities; he manufactures his shoes, his clothes, all the linens which cover him.'

'I have seen it,' noted Tocqueville. As a matter of fact, on the road to Lorette, he and Beaumont had stopped to question a number of the fine peasants who so strikingly resembled the peasants of Tocqueville's own Normandy. It appeared that the *habitant* of Lower Canada frequented Quebec as little as the true Norman went to Paris. And on being asked the reason why, when he was so near, he said that he never needed to, because 'it was the *créatures* who did the weaving and made his clothes.' *Créatures*! The word came straight from the *patois* of lower Normandy. Suppose he and Beaumont ever came to be exiled from France. . . .

'Do you think the French can come to live here?' Tocqueville turned to Mr. Neilson.

'*A*. Yes. Our House of Assembly passed a law a year ago to abolish the law of *escheats*. At the end of seven years of residence, the foreigner is a Canadian and enjoys the rights of a citizen.'

Then this refuge was open to them. A few days later Tocqueville was instructing his sister-in-law: [14] 'If ever you go to America, dear sister, it's there [Canada] that you must settle.'

\*

\* \*

Still conversing, the three sightseers reached the Indian colony of Lorette. Mr. Neilson showed them the ancient church founded by the Jesuits and said: 'The memory of the Jesuits is adored here.' \*

Tocqueville and Beaumont found the houses of the Indian 'very clean.' Curiously enough, the Indians themselves 'spoke French and had an almost European appearance, even though their clothes were different.' Almost all were of mixed blood.

'I was astonished not to see them cultivating the earth. Bah! said Mr. Neilson to me, they are gentlemen, these Hurons; they would consider it dishonouring themselves to work. Scratch the earth like oxen, say they, that's only good for the French or the English. They still live by hunting and by the small pieces of work (*par des petits ouvrages*) done by their wives. . . .'

Beaumont and Tocqueville referred to more heroic times. Yes, Mr. Neilson was convinced that the Indians had always had a predilection for the French. 'It's in becoming savages yourselves that you have obtained from the savages an attachment that still endures,' he told them. It was particularly the unbelievably daring *voyageurs*, the fur-traders, who had subjugated the Indians in their forest. To-day? Only this handful of Hurons was left.

Later in the week Mr. Neilson was to recur to the subject. 'These poor people will disappear completely,' he told them. 'But they are succumbing victims of the *hauteur* of their soul. The least among them believes himself at least the equal of the Governor of Quebec.'

\*

\* \*

'28 August 1831. Mr. Neilson came for us to-day to take us to see the country. . . . The result of this promenade could not have been

---

\* This episode is abbreviated from the last pages of the diary note which contains the above-quoted conversation.

more favourable to the Canadian population. We found lands well cultivated, houses breathing prosperity. We entered several of them. The *grande salle* is garnished with excellent beds, the walls are painted white, the furniture very clean, a small mirror, a cross or some engravings representing subjects from Holy Scripture complete the ensemble. The peasant is strong, well constituted, well clothed; his address has the frank cordiality which the Americans lack; he is polite without servility, and receives you on the footing of equality but with kindness. As a matter of fact, those with whom we were had in their manners something distinguished which struck us (it is true that we were taken to the first families of the village); otherwise this race of men seemed to us inferior to the Americans in education, but superior in the qualities of the heart. One is not in any way aware here of the *mercantile* spirit which appears in all the actions as in all the conversations of the Americans. The reason of the Canadians is little cultivated, but it is simple and straightforward; undeniably they have fewer ideas than their neighbours, but their sensibility appears more developed. They live a life of the heart, the others of the head.' *

Which of the two races Tocqueville and Beaumont preferred, and for what reasons, it is not very difficult to guess. It was almost as if in Lower Canada they had found an idyllic people, not as civilized or developed as the peoples of modern Europe, it was true, but Frenchmen without the vices and sophistication of their nineteenth-century cousins in France, a race without immorality or crime or hatreds, a people simple, innocent, religious, and content.

'We discovered there, especially in the villages at some distance from the cities,' Tocqueville began his ideal portrait of the *habitants* some days later, 'the ancient habits, the ancient customs of France. Clustered about a church, surmounted by a cock and a cross marked with the *fleur-de-lis*, are to be found the houses of the village; for the Canadian proprietor does not like to isolate himself on his land like the Englishman or the American of the United States. Their houses are well-built, solid without, clean and neat within. The peasant is rich and pays not a cent of taxes. There is gathered four times a day about a round table a family composed of vigorous parents and buxom, merry children. After supper one sings some old French *chanson,* or perhaps one relates [the tale of] some ancient prowess of the first Frenchmen

---

* Here again Beaumont altered and somewhat toned down the phrasing of the original (*O.C.*,VIII,261).

of Canada, or of some great strokes of the sword given in the times of Montcalm and the wars with the English. Sundays, one plays, one dances after the service. The *curé* himself takes part in the common merriment so long as it does not degenerate into licence. He is the oracle of the place, the friend, the counsellor of the population. . . .

'. . . Would one not be tempted to believe that the national character of a people depends more on the blood from which it is sprung than on the political institutions or the character of the country? There you have Frenchmen mingling for the last 80 years with an English population, subordinated to the laws of England, more separated from the mother country than if they dwelt at the Antipodes. *Eh bien!* They are still Frenchmen, trait for trait; not only the old ones, but all, even to the *bambin* twisting his forelock. Like us, they are animated, alert, intelligent, apt to scoff and easily carried away, great talkers and very hard to control when their passions are fired.* They are fighters *par excellence*, and love fame more than they do money. . . .'

One day Tocqueville and Beaumont were introduced to Jean Thomas Tascherau,† one of the founders of *Le Canadien* and now a judge on the Court of King's Bench—the only French-Canadian office-holder in the government's employ at Quebec, they were told. 'What's more, it's a "good thing" for him,' Beaumont recorded, 'for he has a salary of 25,000 francs. I dined with him at a relative's. In this last-named Canadian I rediscovered the French gayety and the antique customs of our fathers. Since I have been in America, it's only in Canada that I have seen people laugh. At dessert, each one has to sing a song. Good nature, cordiality, you are sure to find these sentiments among the Canadians.'

There was no resisting such people. Time and again Tocqueville and Beaumont were taken by surprise by some unexpected, piquant jest; and often they found themselves smiling and laughing almost in spite of themselves. In Lower Canada—as nowhere else to a comparable degree—the wine of life flowed salty and full-flavoured.

Especially among the villagers. One day Tocqueville asked a peasant 'why the Canadians let themselves be hemmed in their narrow fields

* 'A Canadian said to me to-day that in the House of Assembly the discussions were lively, hot-headed, and that often they adopted hasty resolutions of which they repented when the head had cooled. Would one not suppose that one was hearing of a French chamber?' Toc. diary note, 2 September 1831.

† J.T.Tascherau (1778–1832), who was also a member of the Legislative Council of Lower Canada, told Beaumont that his family came from Touraine, and that the Tascheraus of Beaumont-la-Chartre were his relatives.

when at twenty leagues they could find fertile and uncultivated land. Why, he replied, do you prefer your wife even though your neighbour's has prettier eyes.'[15] The inquisitive young prison commissioner detected 'a real and profound feeling in this response.'

'*To sum up,*' he wrote a few days later as he was leaving the land of his enchantment,[16] 'this people resembles the French prodigiously, or rather they are still Frenchmen, trait for trait, and consequently absolutely different from the English who surround them: gay, lively, mocking, loving glory and fame, intelligent, eminently sociable. The people in general is more moral, more hospitable, more religious than in France. It's only in Canada that one can find what in France is called a *bon enfant.* The Englishman and the American is either coarse or frigid.'

And again: 'A peasant said to me: when you come right down to it, the English are not white.'

*

\* \*

Obviously, neither Tocqueville nor Beaumont had made a real study of the English in Canada—or even once tried to understand the difficuties under which the representatives of that race were labouring.

As a matter of fact, of the ruling half of the population, and of more than half of the area of Canada, the two friends remained in complete and almost deliberate ignorance. Huron, Erie, and Ontario bounded the vast triangular wedge of Upper Canada on two sides. In the course of their steamboat travels from Sault Ste. Marie to Montreal, therefore, the young Frenchmen had never been far from British territory, and had actually almost circled the Upper Canadian peninsula. Yet never a glance had they thrown in the direction of York or Ottawa. Apparently it had never even occurred to them that it might be interesting to investigate what a British colony was like.

It followed that they knew nothing of the English, Irish, and American settlers of that province; nothing of the wealthy British oligarchy (known as the 'Family Compact') which monopolized the offices and emoluments under the colonial government; nothing, even, of the land question or the Anglican settlement. Of the aspirations of the popular Assembly, under such agitators as William Lyon Mackenzie, they were utterly unaware. In fact, of the disputes which were beginning to generate unrest and dissatisfaction, and which would shortly bring on a rebellion in that Province, even as in Lower Canada, they had not heard the first word.

Nor did they really know so very much more about the situation facing the government at Quebec. For, as their own manuscripts showed with tell-tale clarity, the keen-eyed commissioners had been confining their inquiries almost exclusively to the French-Canadian population. Tocqueville had, indeed, ventured one brief verbal duel with an English merchant; and a visit to one of the Inferior Courts of Quebec had occupied an hour or two. But that was all. The two friends had deliberately passed up a chance to study the English newspapers in the reading room that they had found. More important still, they were making no effort to meet the British official class or to be presented to Governor Aylmer.

As a consequence, neither Tocqueville nor Beaumont was aware of the fact that the French-Canadian problem, with which they were so much concerned, was really only part of a larger and even more fundamental clash of interests between the mother country and the majority of the inhabitants of Canada in both Provinces. Had the two Frenchmen but investigated, they would have made the discovery that the Colonial Office in London—and the British officials in both Upper and Lower Canada—were facing more than a racial issue. Once again Englishmen were clumsily wrestling with the problem that had disturbed the relations between England and her thirteen colonies in the previous century—and finally led to the revolt and independence of the Americans. In a word, it had once again become a question of how to keep and govern a distant and fast-growing dependency.

Specifically, the British task was to reconcile the supremacy of the Empire with the increasing demands of the colonists of Upper and Lower Canada for representative and responsible government. And as yet no solution had suggested itself. To conciliate the popular leaders and the democratically elected Assemblies in the two Provinces by changing the Upper Houses from Appointed to Elective bodies, at the same time yielding to the Assemblies complete control over the revenues, would only be to transform the inter-cameral feuds into concerted attacks on the executive, with the purse strings in the hands of the populace. Immediately Canada would lose much of its discipline; to the mother country it might even become a liability rather than an asset. And of course the vested interests in Upper Canada would be exposed to the democrats, while in Lower Canada the British minority would have to be abandoned to the mercies of the French-Canadian nationalists. On the other hand, all other proposals only seemed to augment the exasperation of the political agitators, and to expose the fabric of government to attacks now steadily increasing in intensity.

It was a fact, then, that racial animosity was only partly responsible for the troubles of the British governor and his appointees in Quebec. That the masses in Lower Canada happened to be French in blood, traditions and prejudices, only embittered a struggle that would have been going on anyhow, had the inhabitants been English to a man.

But Tocqueville and Beaumont missed this truth. As their own papers demonstrate, they had not given themselves the opportunity to appreciate the wider significance of the struggle upon which they had happened. Obviously, they were not interested in Englishmen (they thought they knew the British character from their contacts with the Americans); and curiously enough they were not even interested in British colonial difficulties as in a problem in comparative government. What did intrigue them, what was commanding their attention even to the exclusion of everything else, was the fate of the French race in Canada. And on this narrower and more personal problem they had been conducting some very curious investigations.

'29 August. To-day we rode out on horseback to see the country-side without a guide,' Tocqueville noted in his diary.[17]

'In the commune of Beaufort, at two leagues from Quebec, we saw the people coming out of church. Their clothes proclaimed the greatest affluence. Those who belonged to a distant hamlet were returning by carriage. We went aside into the lanes, and we chatted with all the inhabitants we met, trying to lead the conversations to serious subjects.'

What Tocqueville and Beaumont meant by 'serious subjects,' or why he and Beaumont had chosen that morning to ride out alone without a guide, he did not say. But . . . 'Here is what seemed to result from these conversations: 1. There reigns at present among them a great prosperity; land in the neighbourhood of Quebec is extremely dear, as dear as in France, but also it brings in greatly. 2. The ideas of this population seem still little developed. However, they already feel very clearly that the English race is encircling them in an alarming manner, that they are wrong to enclose themselves in a line instead of extending into land still free. Their jealousy is keenly aroused by the daily arrival of newcomers from Europe. They feel that they will end by being absorbed. One sees that all one says on this subject stirs their passions, but they do not clearly perceive the remedies.'

Lest the student be tempted to believe that the honest peasants of Beaufort had simply burst out with these confessions of impotence and fear, let him examine the last sentence again. 'One sees that all one says on this subject stirs their passions' . . . ! So it had not been until after Tocqueville and Beaumont had accused them of betraying their race that the light-hearted *habitants* had discovered in themselves the uneasiness and the forbodings that the young Frenchmen sought. And Tocqueville and Beaumont had, definitely, been seeking. Clearly, no other explanation will account for the extraordinary character of the record here presented. The prison commissioners had come out from Quebec without Mr. Neilson precisely so that unimpeded they could discuss the future of Lower Canada with the Norman peasants, perhaps even suggest to them a racial policy, at least discover whether it was not within the range of possibility to arouse them to a struggle for independence and greatness.

In short, for the moment the two investigators had cast discretion to the winds, and were acting the role of instigators of revolution. There was no other name for what they were doing. If the Superior of the Seminary at Montreal and their religious advisers, if the Mondelet brothers and their lawyers, if John Neilson and their politicians: in other words, if their best-educated leaders were content that these descendants of the French colonists should remain subject to Englishmen and to the British crown, Tocqueville and Beaumont were not. Their French blood boiled at the thought, a fine fire of patriotism was raging within them. It was shameful, they felt, that these poor peasants had been allowed to remain so long in ignorance of their true destiny.

Happily, it was perhaps not yet too late. 'One sees that all one says on this subject stirs their passions,' Tocqueville was pleased to record, 'but they do not clearly perceive the remedies. The Canadians are too fearful of leaving the sight of their church; they are not shrewd enough. Oh! You are right enough, but what do you propose? Such are their responses. They evidently feel their position as a conquered people, they do not count on the goodwill, not precisely of the Government, but of the English. All their hopes are bound up in their representatives; they appear to have for them, and particularly for Mr. Neilson, that exalted attachment that in general oppressed peoples have for their protectors. Yet he is English, said they, as if in astonishment or regret. Several seemed perfectly to understand the need of education and to rejoice keenly over what had just been done in its favour.

'On the whole,'—Tocqueville was summing up the impressions of the morning—'this population seemed to us capable of being directed, though still incapable of directing itself. We arrive at the moment of the crisis. If the Canadians do not come out of their apathy within twenty years, it will be too late. Everything indicates that the awakening of this people is near. But if in this effort the middle and upper classes of the Canadian population abandon the lower classes and allow themselves to be drawn into the English movement, the French race in America is lost. And it will be a real pity, for there are here all the elements of a great people. The French of America are to the French of France what the Americans are to the English; they have preserved the greater part of the original traits of the national character, and have mingled with it more morality and simplicity. They are disembarrassed, like the Americans, of a mass of prejudices and false points of departure which produce and perhaps will always produce the miseries of Europe. In a word, they have in themselves all that is necessary to create a great memento of France in the New World. But will they ever succeed in completely reconquering their nationality? That is what is probable, without unhappily being certain. A man of genius, who would understand, who would feel and be capable of developing the national passions of the people, would have here an admirable role to play. He would soon become the most powerful man in the colony. But I don't yet see him anywhere.'

It has already been remarked that Tocqueville and Beaumont had failed to meet Louis Joseph Papineau, who by 1831 had himself already done more than any other French-Canadian nationalist to arouse the *habitants* to a sense of their wrongs and an interest in political action. So whether the prison commissioners would have recognized in him any of the signs of future greatness it is impossible to say. In making their sweeping statement, however, Tocqueville and Beaumont had not forgotten their guide, John Neilson, or his (more conservative) friends.

'There is already in existence at Quebec a class of men forming a transition between the French and the English,' Tocqueville's note continued. 'These are Englishmen allied to Canadians, Englishmen . . . [dissatisfied with?] the administration, Frenchmen holding office. This class is represented in the periodical press by the *Gazette de Quebec*,* mixture of French and English, in the political assemblies by Mr. Neilson and probably several others whom we don't know. This is the class that I fear the most for the future fate of the Canadian population. It excites neither their jealousy nor their passions; on the contrary, it is more Canadian than English in interest because it makes opposition to the government. At bottom, however, it is English in customs, ideas, language. If it ever took the place of the upper and enlightened classes among the Canadians, the nationality of the latter would be lost without redress; they would vegetate like the *bas-Bretons* in France.'

'Happily,'—just as Mr. Neilson himself had said—'religion puts an obstacle to marriage between the races, and creates in the clergy an enlightened class which has an interest in speaking French and in cultivating French literature and ideas.' On the other hand, Tocqueville realized, there was no aristocracy to assist the church.

'We have been able to perceive in our conversations with the people of this country a fund of hatred and jealousy against the *seigneurs*,' he was forced to admit. 'Yet the *seigneurs* have, so to speak, no rights, they are of the people as far as it is possible to be so, and are almost all reduced to cultivating the earth. But the spirit of equality in *Démocratie* is alive there as in the United States, even though it is not so *raisonneur*. I have discovered at the bottom of these peasants' hearts the political passions which brought on our Revolution and still cause all our miseries. Here they are inoffensive, or nearly so, because nothing resists them. We believe we have remarked also that the peasant did not see without pain the right the clergy have to exact the tithe, and did not consider without envy the riches that this tax puts in the hands of some ecclesiastics. If religion ever loses its empire in Canada, it's by this breach that the enemy will enter. . . .'

'31 August 1831. To-day we went with Mr. Neilson and a Canadian named Mr. Viger† along the right bank of the St. Lawrence as far as the village of St. Thomas, situated ten leagues from Quebec. That's the point where the St. Lawrence assumes a width of seven leagues, which

* That very day, 29 August, the *Gazette* announced: 'Among the strangers now visiting this Province, and at present at Quebec, are MM. de Beaumont and de Tocqueville lately sent by the French Government to collect information on the state of the penitentiaries in the United States. . . .' Quoted, *Columbian Centinel*, 10 September 1831.
† Probably Denis Benjamin Viger (1774–1861), member of the Legislative Council, one-time delegate to England, and mutual friend of Papineau and Neilson.

it keeps for fifty leagues. All the country-sides we traversed are admirable in their fertility. Joined to the St. Lawrence and to the mountains in the North they form the most complete and magnificent tableau. The houses are *universally* well built. They all breathe an air of plenty and cleanliness. The churches are rich, but in very good taste. Their interior decoration would not be out of place in our cities. In this portion of Canada one hears no English. The population is only French; and yet when one encounters an inn or a trader, the sign is in English.'

During this scenic excursion, also, Tocqueville and Beaumont had pursued their inquiries on the future of Canada. 'Five or six years ago,' they were informed,[18] 'the English government wanted to unite all Canada in a single assembly. That was the measure best adapted to dissolve the Canadian nation entirely. Thus the whole people awoke at once, and it's since then that they know their strength. . . .'

'The nomination of the officers of the militia belongs to the government,' Tocqueville noted, 'but the House of Assembly having decided that to be an officer of militia it was necessary to reside in the locality of one's command, the result has been to put the direction of the armed force almost exclusively in the hands of the Canadians. . . .'

'Several *curés* told me that in their commune there was not a single individual speaking English. They themselves didn't understand it, and took us for interpreters. . . .'

'It was curious,' Beaumont wrote his father, 'to see good country *curés*, like those of Marçon and Beaumont-la-Chartre, preaching liberalism and talking like demagogues. . . .'

'The fact is,' Tocqueville explained this phenomenon to Abbé Lesueur, 'The fact is, that it (the clergy) is the first to resist oppression and the people see in it their most constant support. Thus the Canadians are religious by principle and by political passion. . . .'

'The power of religion over society is very great,' Beaumont agreed. 'The Catholic clergy is universally respected; there is not a philosopher who is not at the same time a religious man, or at least who dares appear the contrary. I went for a promenade one day with one of the *démocrats* of Quebec; he never passed in front of a church without making the sign of the cross. . . .'

Altogether, the clergy seemed to Tocqueville the most distinguished class in Lower Canada. 'All those whom we have seen are educated, polite, well brought up,' he wrote.[19] 'They speak French with purity. In general they are more distinguished than most of our *curés* in France. One sees in their conversation that they are *all Canadian*. They are united in heart and in interest to the population, and argue its needs very well. In general, however, they seemed to us to harbour sentiments of loyalty to the king of England and sustain the principle of legitimacy. Yet one of them said to me: We have everything to hope now; the administration [ministry?] is *democratic*. They are in the opposition to-day, and would certainly foment rebellion if the government became tyrannical. . . .'

What, then, were Tocqueville and Beaumont's final conclusions? The two friends themselves were not entirely certain. By the end of their stay in Quebec, however, it was becoming obvious that their first rosy hopes—their bright vision of the early emergence of a great French Empire in North America—had been too optimistic by far. Lower Canada might remain French in blood and customs: in fact Tocqueville and Beaumont were willing to prophesy as much. There might even be an uprising or rebellion of the French-Canadians. But all the probabilities seemed to favour the victory and continued domination of the British conquerors. It was a regretful young prophet, therefore, who, on the deck of the *Richelieu* steaming up the St. Lawrence to Montreal, on the first day of September 1831, got out his pocket notebook to sum up their investigations in some 'General Remarks':

'We have noticed through the conversations that we have had with several Canadians that their hatred was directed more against the government than against the English in general,' Tocqueville wrote.* 'The instincts of the people are against the English, but many Canadians belonging to the upper classes did not seem to us animated to the degree that we believe [they should be?] by the desire to preserve intact the trace of their origin and to become a people entirely apart.

---

* Beaumont summed up his opinions in certain sentences which are to be found scattered through his letter to his father from Albany (cited above). 'There are in Canada some germs of discontent, of uneasiness, of hostility against England,' he wrote. 'The people, properly speaking, isn't fully conscious of what it feels; but the enlightened class, which is not yet very numerous, is taking care to lead it, and to furnish arguments to its passions. . . .' On the other hand, the government was trying to swamp the *habitants* with immigrants. 'What augments the danger is that the wealthy class in Canada is entirely English; the English there hold all the *haut commerce* and industry in their hands; they fill the two large cities of this country, Quebec and Montreal. They do their utmost to annihilate the Canadian population, whose poverty they despise and whose happiness they do not understand. . . . It is probable that all that will end in a violent conflict. But it would be difficult to foresee which of the two populations will get the better of the other. . . .'

Several did not seem far from amalgamating with the English, if the latter would adopt the interests of the country. It is therefore to be feared that with time, and above all with the immigration of the Irish Catholics, the fusion will take place, and it cannot do so except to the detriment of the race, the language, and the customs of the French.

'However, it is certain:

'1. Lower Canada (happily for the French race) forms a separate state. Now in Lower Canada the French population is to the English population in the proportion of ten to one. It is compact. It has its own government, its own parliament. It really forms a distinct national body. In the Parliament composed of 84 members, there are 64 French and 20 English.

'2. The English up to now have always kept apart. They sustain the government against the mass of the people. All the French journals are in the opposition, all the English are ministerial, with the exception of one alone, *The Vindicator* at Montreal. And that was founded by Canadians.

'3. In the towns the English and the Canadians form two societies. The English affect a great luxury. There are only very limited fortunes among the Canadians. Thence small-town jealousies and vexations.

'4. The English have all the foreign trade in their hands and direct all the domestic trade. Thence again, jealousy. The English each day take possession of the lands which the Canadians thought reserved for their race.

'5. Finally, the English show themselves in Canada with all the traits of their national character, and the Canadians have retained all the traits of French character. The odds are therefore that Lower Canada will end by becoming a people entirely French. But it will never be a numerous people. Everything around them will become English. They will be a drop of water in the ocean. I am much afraid that, as Mr. Neilson said with his brusque frankness, fate has in fact decided that North America will be English.'

\*

\*　　\*

So much for prophecy. For commentary and confirmation, the student has but to go to the pages of history. There he will find that in 1837, or about six years after the documents just quoted were penned, the rebellion foreseen of the two young prison commissioners did in fact take place. Or, rather, there were two rebellions, the French-Canadians being led by Louis Joseph Papineau, and the democrats of Upper Canada by William Lyon Mackenzie. Leaders of a sort did, then, arise. On the other hand, the priests of Lower Canada proved far less revolutionary than Tocqueville and Beaumont had prophesied the emergency would show them. And, just as they feared, John Neilson repudiated the cause and joined the conservatives. Under such circumstances, of course, there could be but one answer. The *habitants'* uprising petered out ignominiously. Fate had indeed decided. It was not long before Lower Canada was joined to Upper Canada in a common government—the hope of a new France-in-America totally extinguished.*

*

*     *

'We left Quebec on the 31st of August,' Beaumont concluded his Canadian letter home. 'We mounted the St. Lawrence as far as Montreal in the steamboat *Richelieu*; we arrived at Montreal the 2nd of September and left that city immediately to go to Albany. A steamboat (the *Voyageur*) took us to St. John, where we embarked on Lake Champlain in a steamer (the *Phoenix*). The 4th of September we arrived at Whitehall, and there we took a carriage in which we reached Albany to-day. During this crossing the only remarkable thing I saw was the country midst which Lake Champlain is situated; the mountains of Vermont, visible in the distance, are very high.

'I have seen several persons at Albany to-day. We are still treated with the same kindness. We are leaving this evening for Boston, where we are going to recommence the Penitentiary System, somewhat forgotten for the last month. We shall stay there a fortnight or three weeks, after which we shall betake ourselves to Philadelphia. Adieu.'

* The writer omits at this point an unfinished essay, by Tocqueville, on penal colonies and on 'Why the French are unsuccessful colonizers' (version published by Bt., O.C.,VIII,267–272).

7

# PART V: NEW ENGLAND: THE HEART OF THE EXPERIENCE

## XXV

## TO STOCKBRIDGE, BOSTON, AND BAD NEWS

On the seventh of September, Tocqueville and Beaumont turned east from Albany and took the road to Massachusetts. At last, after long postponement, they were off to visit New England and the famous city of Boston.

At the very start of this journey they did allow themselves one last diversion, in the shape of a detour to Stockbridge. For they were keen to get a glimpse of a certain celebrated authoress, whose name was Catherine Maria Sedgwick.* A lady novelist of distinction in the United States? Here was indeed a phenomenon! They had heard about her in New York, and had prevailed upon her enterprising and eccentric brother, their friend Henry Dwight Sedgwick,† to give them a letter of introduction.

Alas, when they reached Stockbridge, their bird had flown! Miss Sedgwick had invited them to stop, but through an unfortunate accident she had herself gone off that very morning for a visit, and was not to get back until the following day.

As a matter of course, the rest of the Sedgwick clan invited the two French commissioners to stay and abide her appearance. Nor were these Sedgwicks an uninteresting company. The elder brother, Theodore (2nd), had married Susan Ridley, an authoress in her own right;‡ and he himself was the most distinguished farmer in the neighbourhood, having represented that part of Massachusetts for three succes-

---

* Catherine Maria Sedgwick, 1789–1867, had had an excellent education, and was managing a private school for young ladies, in addition to turning out a work of fiction every two years. Her *Redwood* had already been translated into a number of foreign languages.

† H.D.Sedgwick, the second son of the Massachusetts Federalist, Theodore Sedgwick, had been born in 1785, and was to die at Stockbridge in December of that very year, 1831. A writer of influence on the Common Law, he was also an opponent of slavery, and an ardent advocate of free trade.

‡ She had already published *Morals of Pleasure*, and *Young Emigrants*.

sive sessions in the legislature.* His son, Theodore (3rd), was a young man of promise, who had recently graduated from Columbia, and who would one day, as attaché of the legation in Paris, be of immense assistance to Tocqueville in the composition of his book (remaining thereafter a life-long friend).†

But the acquaintance of the Sedgwicks in general, however intelligent and lively the others might be, was not what Tocqueville and Beaumont were after. And apparently they did not even realize that in Susan Ridley Sedgwick they had another American authoress right under their noses. It was Catherine Maria whom they had come to view. 'Her brothers and sisters received us *à merveille*,' Beaumont admitted;[1] 'but this did not satisfy our purpose, which was to see a lady whose works have rendered her famous. Of course we could have seen her by staying a day longer at Stockbridge; but we were too impatient to arrive in Boston, where we knew that letters were awaiting us.' So, after Beaumont had made a hasty sketch of the singular red church at Stockbridge, they took up their journey again, and set out on the trail across the Berkshires toward Boston.

'The country through which we passed is remarkably picturesque,' Beaumont recorded. 'The great number of mountains there encountered, and the picturesque aspect by them produced, form a striking contrast with all that part of western New York through which we journeyed on our way from Albany to Buffalo. You know that this latter region is always flat, and that nothing is so rare there as to see a hill or a valley. We were struck by the appearance of riches and prosperity reigning in Massachusetts; everything there proclaims a happy population; it is no longer that wild nature that one meets with everywhere in the states of the west; the virgin forest has long since disappeared and you no longer find a single trace of it. Massachusetts, which as you know once bore the name of New England, is evidently a *vieux pays*: I call *old* a country counting 200 years of existence. Two centuries are a veritable antiquity in this country, where the majority of the towns boast hardly 10 or 20 years of existence. One sees in Massachusetts neither tree trunks in the fields, nor houses of logs serving as habitations; the fields are carefully enclosed, the culture is varied, and everything indicates that the inhabitants draw from the earth all the benefit possible, because the ranks are already crowded there. . . .'

---

* A Democrat, Theodore Sedgwick 2nd helped put through the Boston & Albany R.R.
† See below, ch.LV,pp.731–32.

Fresh from the humble, whitewashed villages of the French-Canadians, Tocqueville was particularly impressed with the aspect of the towns along their route. 'The houses,' he wrote,[2] 'are almost all charming (especially in the villages); a luxurious cleanliness, which is astonishing, reigns there.'

A contrast of another sort struck Beaumont. 'I don't know why this people, which appears so content, is generally of such feeble and delicate health,' he pondered. 'The women in particular are extremely thin and appear all of them affected in the chest. I don't know whether this state of things must be attributed to the climate, which is variable and passes without stay from one extreme to the other, or to the manner of life of the women. Here it is an unknown thing to see a woman working on the soil, or busying herself in any way with the labours in the field; whence it results that her labours are all within, and are limited to the cares of the household. Perhaps this shut-in life is unhealthy. I have not seen, since being in America (except in Canada) a single woman bearing the slightest analogy to our peasant women.

Their trip was fast, and a day and a half after their departure from Stockbridge, the young commissioners reached Boston. The celebrated metropolis of the New Englanders did not seem so very large. But, without and within, it breathed a quiet charm that they had not encountered in New York.

'Boston is a city of sixty thousand souls,' Beaumont wrote. 'Its harbour is magnificent; it is situated on the middle of an island, and you reach it from every side by means of causeways which have been constructed across the water. Much less commercial bustle is to be seen there than in New-York, but the general aspect of the town is much more agreeable. The latter lies on a flat terrain and offers to the eye, no matter from which side it is observed, but a single row of houses. Boston, on the contrary, is built on uneven and mountainous ground, in such a way that to the observer at a certain distance, it presents some charming views. It contains many private houses constructed with taste and elegance; [yet] in the matter of public edifices, I see but the government house [State House] in the least remarkable. . . .'

It was Saturday evening, the ninth of September. The new arrivals went to the Marlboro Hotel[3] on Washington Street;—then ran to collect their mail.

\*

\*   \*

No! No! No! It *could* not be that he was dead, the good abbé Lesueur!

'It was yesterday evening, my friend,' the distracted young Tocqueville lamented to his brother Édouard next morning,* 'It was yesterday evening that I found the fatal bundle announcing the death of Bébé. I was already uneasy, the last mail had brought me no letter from him. Knowing his exactitude and his tenderness, I suspected that his illness was more grave than you said; and a number of times on the road I repeated to Beaumont that I trembled to learn some great misfortune on reaching Boston.

'Yesterday, even though it was very late, I had them give me my letters at the post. On opening the bundle and not seeing his writing, I knew the cruel truth. In that moment I experienced, my dear Édouard, the keenest and most poignant grief that I have ever felt in my life. It was a regret that words cannot render. I loved our good, old friend as if he were our father; he had always partaken of the cares, the worries, the tenderness of one; and yet he only clung to us by his will alone. And he has left us for always, and I wasn't able to receive his last benediction.

'It's useless to say, my friend, that one should accustom oneself in advance to the idea of separation from an old man of 80 years. No, one doesn't get used to the idea of seeing disappear, on a sudden, the support of one's childhood, the friend, and what a friend, of one's whole life. I hope at length to be able to stiffen myself against this frightful unhappiness, but there will remain at the bottom of my soul, none the less, an idea poignant because it is true, that we have lost what neither time nor friendship, nor the future whatever it may be, can restore to us, something which it is given to but few people to find in this world, a being whose every thought, whose every affection concerned us alone. I have never seen nor heard speak of a like devotion. . . .'

And Tocqueville remembered with anguish how joyfully he had been looking forward to his own home-coming. Now he would never receive another welcoming embrace, or see the tears of happiness standing in the old priest's eyes. Perhaps it was as well. 'Who knows the fate reserved for his adopted family?' And surely it was to an eternal happi-

---

* Toc. to his brother Édouard, Boston, 10 September 1831 (YT; published in *O.C.*,VII,58–64). This letter of lament is famous, and has often been quoted for its glowing tribute to abbé Lesueur.

ness that this brave and devoted counsellor had gone. Never had Tocqueville been so convinced of the immortality of the soul. 'Yesterday evening I prayed to him as to a saint. . . .'

'12 Sept. Here are already two days that I have been here,' the stricken Tocqueville finally resumed. 'I begin to take up the thread of my occupations, to be able from time to time to get outside myself. But one has to withdraw into oneself occasionally, and then I can't tell you what heartrending emotions I experience. Each man has his manner of feeling. I, I would I could flee the entire world.

'I have not yet said a word to Beaumont of the thing that preoccupies me unceasingly; and I should consider myself happy to be alone. . . .'

Still trembling from the shock, and exiled amid a strange people in an alien land, it was no easy thing for the young man to swallow his misery. His thoughts were for ever recalling to him how the good Bébé 'had watched since we were in the world over our first childhood with that daily vigilance of all the moments and that tender solicitude rarely found in others than a mother. It was on his knees that we acquired our first notions of good,' Tocqueville proudly remembered.[4] 'It was he who began for us that first education whose effects one feels the rest of one's life, and which has made us, if not distinguished, at least honourable men.

'I confess to you that this sorrow has singularly diminished for me the interest of the voyage that I have undertaken. The objects which claim me are still the same, but it seems as if I saw them in a different light. There are moments when I desire to be back in Europe, and yet, I will allow, the idea of returning is not without bitterness. . . .'

For the news from France was worse, even, than before. The summer elections had, it seemed, gone very badly for the conservatives. The regime of Casimir Périer was apparently doomed. And God alone knew what excesses the new Chamber might commit. After reading their mail, and the foreign news in the papers, Tocqueville and Beaumont could not but fear that civil and international war were imminent. 'The state of Europe seems to me to be that of a volcano ready to explode,' was Beaumont's expression.[5] And the prospect that France would soon be tranquillized, under a firm and stable government based on the consent of all the great parties, seemed slight indeed. The day for their own return, therefore, was still far off in the future. Certainly this was true if they were to carry out their scheme of returning only at the propitious moment for entering politics.

But the package of letters, collected the night of their arrival in Boston, had announced still another sinister fact. The administration of Justice in France was moving for a curtailment of their eighteen-months' leave of absence, and for their recall within the year. The news was that their friends at home were doing their utmost to arrest this measure, but the issue was still uncertain.

Under the circumstances, Tocqueville and Beaumont were less appalled than thrown into inextricable doubt and a mood of brooding despondency. The irreparable loss of abbé Lesueur, Tocqueville wrote his friend Chabrol after a week in Boston,[6] 'joined to all the news which reaches me from Europe, has cast my spirit into such a profound sadness and discouragement that I am become almost a stranger to all I see, and consider objects without intelligence as without interest.

'I believe it absolutely necessary in order to be happy, or at least tranquil, to be able to set your mind to work on theoretical subjects. And to-day the positive present draws me and absorbs me entirely. I can't make myself study with care the institutions, the morals, the laws of a foreign people, when my country is in such a critical position; nor amuse myself divining what will become of America in four centuries, when I don't know whether, this very day, France is not prey to civil and foreign war. In a word, my regrets, my hopes like my fears, all are with you. Only my body is in America. . . .

'In this state of mind, I confess that I have not been so sensitive as you think to the brutal measure (your adjective is just) which takes away six months of our leave. This shortening of time will make us miss an essential part of our travels, the visit to Louisiana; but, at least, I will find myself among my family and friends to struggle with them, if it is necessary, against civil war, the Cossacks, and the cholera morbus.*

'I still regard it as possible, however, that the measure depriving us of our leave will be revoked. It is all the more unjust in that it forces us to return in the month of January, a time of year in which one drowns right handsomely on the ocean, instead of the month of April. What renders the position of those who will act for us more difficult is that, at bottom, one year is sufficient to visit the penitentiaries. But what is to be done is already done at the present hour, the extension is granted or refused; so it is useless to discuss it further, and I await, with what patience I can muster, the result.'

* See below, p.524.

1. The Young Tocqueville

2. Prefect and Secretary

Comte de Tocqueville dictating to his son Alexis. The artist has thrown
the young Tocqueville considerably into the background, but his expression
of expectant interest is very clear in the original. The Prefect, on the other
hand, is brilliantly painted: surprised, as it were, at the happy instant of
capturing an elusive thought, to put it into words. Note his decoration, and
the sword of a Peer of France.

3. Gustave de Beaumont at 35

4. VIEW OF THE HUDSON AT 'YOUNKER'

Notice Tocqueville returning from his hunt, their sloop tied up at the
landing, and the artist himself sketching the scene from the slope above.
In a subsequent, embellished version, a bush was to be substituted for
Beaumont's profile.

5. View of Lake Oneida from Frenchman's Island
From the Romanet Album. The original contained one figure and no boats.

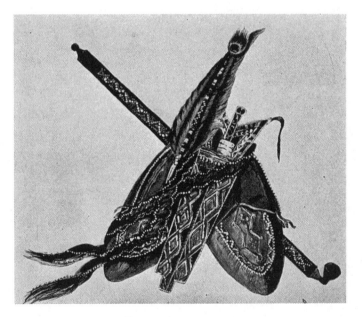

6. Indian Accoutrements
From a sketch in color

7. Ready for the Wilderness

'Straw hat, jacket gray, gamebag white, wicker bottle hung around neck, Indian pipe in hand, portmanteau black, trousers gray, horse bay.'

8. The Guide and the Osier Bottle

Tocqueville is reclining against the fallen tree. An embellished version contains two horses (carefully tied!) and the Indian's small dog.

9. VIEW OF THE ST. LAWRENCE FROM QUEBEC

From the Romanet Album

10. STOCKBRIDGE: THE RED CHURCH

11. THE EASTERN STATE PENITENTIARY 'OUTSIDE PHILADELPHIA'
From the Romanet Album

12. FORT HOWARD AT GREEN BAY
From the Romanet Album

# XXVI

# THE CHILLINESS OF BOSTON—AND THE POLES

MEANWHILE, Boston—Massachusetts—all New England—awaited their investigation.

But Alexis de Tocqueville was suddenly guilty of an extraordinary lapse. For seven days he took no notes, apparently made no observations, wrote his family nothing about the Americans.

Obviously, he was too stunned, too overwhelmed by sorrow, to take much *interest* in his surroundings. But a week was a long time, in fact too long a time, for his exacting conscience to allow him to remain in idleness, even under the most extenuating circumstances. There had to be, therefore, some other, more adequate explanation.

It was contained in Beaumont's first letter from Boston.

'From the moment of our arrival here, we tried to put ourselves in relation with the best in the town,' the unsuspecting young Frenchman reported to his family.[1] It had not occurred either to him or to Tocqueville that there was anything presumptuous in such an attempt.

Hitherto, at the mere mention of their official errand, distinguished Americans had simply fallen all over each other out of eagerness to welcome them. But, Beaumont had to confess, 'the first day we were not happy in our attempts; we were unable to *accost* anyone. We found ourselves in an embarrassing position, because we had no letters of introduction for Boston. When, after these unfruitful efforts, Tocqueville and I found ourselves face to face, we began to make some pretty melancholy reflections: "Is it, by chance," said we, "that up to now we have owed the kind reception given us everywhere entirely to some scraps of paper whose bearers we were? Is it that, reduced to our intrinsic value, we do not merit the least consideration? There's something to diminish our self-esteem; we were beginning to think ourselves distinguished men; but when we have for us only our personal merit, they don't even look at us!! etc., etc." and other plaints of the same nature. . . .'

Tocqueville and Beaumont were a pair of young innocents. Clearly, they had come to Boston assuming that the inhabitants were even as other mortals in America:—free, open, democratic, and easily impressed. Nor had they realized their mistake until they had actually bumped their boyish heads against shut doors. Then, in the midst of their consternation, they had for the first time noticed a certain coolness—not to say frostiness—in the social air. Evidently the residents of this New England metropolis were in possession of a considerable supply of reserve, of most un-American reserve. Almost one had the impression of being on the continent, and among aristocrats.

But Beaumont was not inclined to be critical. 'The fact is, arriving without recommendation, we were received with less eagerness,' he explained. To which, on second thought, he added: 'It has seemed to us that here people throw themselves less at the head of strangers than in New-York.' The unconscious understatement was delicious.

Not even the dignified leaders of Boston's most exclusive society, however, could long keep their doors shut against the two visitors from France. By the beginning of the third day, it was already beginning to be realized who Tocqueville and Beaumont were, and what was their 'social position': and signs were not lacking that soon they would be treated 'exceedingly well.' Perhaps it was the magic word *Penitentiary* that was once again proving the *open-sesame*.

'. . . We profit from a very natural error into which the Americans fall,' Tocqueville was to write a month afterwards.[2] 'In the United States, they have neither war, nor pestilence, nor literature, nor eloquence, nor fine arts, nor revolutions; no great excesses, nothing which awakes attention in Europe. They enjoy there the most insipid happiness which can be imagined. In politics they are occupied discussing whether a road must be repaired, or a bridge built, or a stone placed edgewise or flat; one might even get interested over such questions, but to become hot discussing them!

'In the United States, then, the execution of a fine prison seems as important as the pyramid of Cheops, neither more nor less. And consequently, we, who pass in some sort as the penitentiary system made man, when they place us alongside, we appear like giants. You well understand that, for the French government to have charged us to visit the prisons, it is necessary that we be men of the first flight, for what is there greater than a prison? If we were to say to these poor people that there are not a hundred persons in France who know just what the penitentiary system is, and that the French government is so far innocent of the large views imputed to it that at the present hour it probably doesn't even know that it has commissioners in America, they would be utterly astonished, no question.

'But you appreciate that the truth consists in not saying what is false, and not in saying all that is true. . . .'

It happened, therefore, that on 12 September, or the third morning after their arrival in Boston, Tocqueville and Beaumont once again found themselves in an American parade. The occasion was a public rally on behalf of the far-away Polish people, at that very moment engaged in a desperate struggle for independence.

'I was present the twelfth of this month at a rather curious ceremony,' Beaumont began his description of the day. 'The Bostonians celebrated the consecration of two flags that they were sending to the Poles. On this occasion the militia and the regular troops gathered; the authorities, the learned bodies, etc., etc., assembled; and the procession paraded to a place called *Faneuil house*, where habitually are held the political meetings of deliberative assemblies. We took part in the procession, it goes without saying, in our role of distinguished foreigners. On entering the Hall we saw an immense gallery entirely filled with very well-dressed ladies, without admixture of any man. In almost all public meetings in the United States, this separation of men and women takes place. The *séance* was opened by an invocation on behalf of the Poles pronounced by a Congregational minister. The holy man blasted despotism and oppression with all his power and uttered a pompous eulogy of insurrection and liberty. Thereupon were unfurled to the regards of the audience the two flags, on which different inscriptions were to be seen, among others the last words of Poniatowski: "It is better to die with glory than to surrender." Great applause broke out in the assembly, especially when they pronounced the name of Lafayette, to whom the flags will be addressed so that he may see that they reach their destination. Finally, they sang hymns, odes, etc.'

Of this celebration, as was to have been expected, the newspapers of Boston and the vicinity soon published full and vivid descriptions. And the phrasing of their accounts was such that no reader could fail to realize the importance of the occasion. 'The ceremony of the consecration of the standards about to be forwarded to the Poles by the Young Men of Boston, was a brilliant and imposing affair,' one newspaper proclaimed.[3] 'The military escort was composed of the most beautiful body of troops we have seen for many years. It consisted of six companies of light infantry, all in splendid uniforms, and a battalion of the *United States Infantry*, under Capt. Frazier, fine looking troops, in a state of the most perfect discipline, and admirably equipped. A corps of Cavalry covered the flanks of the procession. The two superb Bands of Boston were employed on the occasion. In the procession were noticed, Maj. Gen. Macomb, of the U.S. Army, President Quincy of Harvard University, two distinguished French gentlemen, who are on a tour through the United States, to inspect our Prisons, by order of the French Government, and other eminent individuals. . . .

'The Rev. Dr. Beecher then fervently and eloquently invoked the Divine Blessing on the cause of the Poles, and of civil and religious freedom generally—praying that the rod of the oppressor might be broken, and the oppressed of all nations be emancipated, etc. The auditory were with difficulty repressed from a hearty and *noisy* expression of their approbation after the Rev. Doctor's patriotic and truly Republican sentiments. . . .'

So it had been Lyman Beecher [the father of Henry Ward Beecher] who had so castigated tyranny! And in his ministerial garments, as well! Whatever the approbation of the good republicans of Boston, Tocqueville at least was so shocked that the extraordinary words of the prayer, to Beaumont a pompous eulogy, engraved themselves indelibly on his memory. And years afterward he was to recall this scene in detail, as an illustration of how in the United States there was 'not a single religious doctrine which shows itself hostile to equalitarian and republican institutions.'

'I was, for the moment,' he would write for his own countrymen of France,* 'I was, for the moment, dwelling in one of the largest cities of the Union, when I was invited to attend a political reunion whose object was to come to the aid of the Poles. . . .

'I found two to three thousand persons together in a vast hall prepared to receive them. Soon afterwards a priest, clothed in his ecclesiastical garments, stepped to the edge of the platform meant for the

---

* *Dém. en Am.*, II,ch.9 ('*De la religion considérée comme institution politique . . .*'), pp.218–220.

orators. The audience, after uncovering, stood silent, and he spoke as follows:

'God, all-powerful! God of War! Thou who didst sustain the courage and guide the arm of our fathers when they were upholding the sacred rights of their national independence; thou who madest them triumph over an odious oppression, and hast granted our people the benefits of peace and of liberty, oh Lord! turn a favourable eye toward the other hemisphere; look with pity on the heroic people which struggles to-day as we did formerly, and in defence of the same rights! Lord, creator of all men on the same model, do not allow despotism to deform thy work and maintain inequality on the earth. God all-powerful! watch over the destinies of the Poles, make them worthy to be free; let thy wisdom reign in their councils, thy strength be in their arms; scatter terror over their enemies, divide the powers plotting their ruin, and permit it not that the injustice, of which the world was witness fifty years ago, be accomplished to-day. Lord, who holdest in thy mighty hand the heart of peoples as of men, raise up allies in the holy cause of right; make the French nation rise at last and, quitting the repose in which its leaders hold it, come to fight once more for the freedom of the world.

'Oh Lord! do not ever turn thy face from us; let us always be the most religious people, as the most free.

'God all-powerful! Hearken to-day to our prayer; save the Poles. We ask it in the name of thy well-beloved Son, Our Savior Jesus Christ, who died on the cross for the salvation of all men. *Amen*.

'[And] the whole audience, deeply moved (*avec recueillement*), repeated *amen*.'

It was now time for the lay orators to step forward on the stage.

'The address to the audience, by Josiah Quincy, Jr., was peculiarly felicitous, and called forth tumultuous plaudits,' the *Boston Evening Transcript* commented next day.[4] 'It was succeeded by the Address to the Polish Nation, (composed and read by David Lee Child), breathing an ardent and devoted attachment to the cause of Liberty. The letter to general LaFayette, committing the standards to his charge and custody after their arrival in France, was neat and pertinent . . . and the appointed exercises were conducted with perfect decorum and propriety.'

According to the *Columbian Centinel*, which enlarged on the proceedings with particulars (and a certain amount of unconscious humour),[5] 'One of the most affecting objects visible in the hall, was the name of the gallant SKRZYNECKI just over the bust of John Adams and the portrait of John Hancock. It would cheer his noble spirit in the midst of his perils and privations to know how he is appreciated in a remote land of strangers. On the opposite side of the hall, between the names of WASHINGTON and LAFAYETTE appeared the name of the immortal KOSCIUSCO. The whole ceremonies were performed in the most effective manner. May the standards reach their destination, and find the gallant Poles in a situation to rally about them. . . .

'. . . On no former occasion, excepting perhaps when Mr. Webster pronounced his memorable Eulogy on the two Presidents, have we seen old Faneuil so much thronged.'

In short, as the writer in the *Transcript* so complacently remarked, the day had 'passed off happily, and we believe satisfactorily to the Young Men who charged themselves with the active duties of the occasion.' Now there was only one small fly still noticeable in the ointment of their satisfaction: 'We understand that a small amount is still requisite to defray all the expenses which have occurred—but we doubt not that the deficiency will soon be supplied by the open handed liberality of our fellow citizens.'

As a matter of fact, the deficit was but a paltry $150. The meeting cost $800, and $650 had already been subscribed. The cause was noble. It could not fail.

What the Poles themselves thought of this state of affairs, and of the gifts thus purchased for them, they naturally had no way of saying. Possibly their opinion in the matter was of no consequence, anyhow. For, only a short time after, their gallant rebellion was to be defeated, and overwhelmed. The fine efforts of their Boston friends were therefore doomed to be wasted, in any case. Whether wise or foolish, whether well or poorly chosen, no Massachusetts aid could possibly be forwarded to them, or avail them, then.

Meanwhile, however, not knowing what the future held, Beaumont and some of the other marchers in the parade were unable to view the proceedings so philosophically.

'A great number of the participants found this patriotic folderol ridiculous,' the young Frenchman noted. 'What use will these Boston flags be to the Poles? This manifestation of enthusiasm for the cause of the brave Poles would mean something only if, with their phrases, some money were sent at the same time. Now, they scarcely had enough to cover the expense of the ceremony. I have seen a crowd of sensible people who regretted this foolishness; but it was organized by some young men, who got everything started without there being any way to stop them. Happily for the United States, such things take place with impunity; but I think that in France we act *chez nous* exactly as if we were in the United States.'

## XXVII

## THE ARISTOCRATS UNBEND

BETWEEN Charlestown Prison and the Poles, Tocqueville and Beaumont were pleased to discover, the reserve of Boston society was melting rapidly.

Near them in the parade, for instance, had been Josiah Quincy, Jr.* This distinguished gentleman, after a career as a lawyer, Congressman, farmer, and Mayor of Boston, was now, it appeared, President of a college for young men, a short way up the river. Immediately, President Quincy expressed great interest in their studies, and soon he was supplying them with documents and information of considerable value. Also in the procession had been the retiring Mayor of Boston, the last of the federalist aristocrats, Mr. Harrison Gray Otis,† who now invited them to his house. There Tocqueville and Beaumont met his wife, and at once gained entrance to the circle around his daughter-in-law, Mrs.H.G.Otis,Jr., (or 'the widow Otis' as the young men of Boston called her). The last-named lady was a rollicking, romping, good-humoured woman, full of fun, and speaking French with great fluency and volubility. Beaumont, in particular, was much taken by her.

More quiet in manner, and representative of Boston's conservative families, was the travelled and cultivated George Ticknor,‡ Professor

* 1772–1864. Of brilliant mind and manifold attainments, his life was an admirable illustration of the variety achieved by many Americans in the course of their careers.
† 'Harry' Otis, 1765–1848, was noted for his witty oratory, his determined championship of New England interests, and for the exuberant hospitality he dispensed at the mansion built for him by Charles Bulfinch at 45 Beacon Street. In him Tocqueville encountered a Federalist who would live to be eighty-three without acquiring any faith in democracy. For Otis 'the country was always going to the dogs.'
‡ George Ticknor, 1791–1871, had studied in Germany, and brought back a large library from the continent. A founder of the Boston Public Library, and future author of a *History of Spanish Literature*, his greatest contribution was to be his discovery for American students of the superiority of continental scholarship. For his many contacts with Tocqueville in later years, see his *Life, Letters, & Journals*.

of Languages at Harvard, who was to become, and throughout his life remain, a friend and admirer of Tocqueville's. Then, of course, their visits to the new penitentiary at Charlestown brought the French commissioners the acquaintance of the philanthropists and social workers of the city as well. They were introduced to Samuel Atkins Eliot, who, as an official of the Boston Prison Discipline Society, became much interested in the progress of their researches.* At the prison, four days after the parade for the Poles, they met and made a deep impression upon Mr. Francis Calley Gray,† an official prison inspector, and a State Senator as well. The Tappan brothers, philanthropists and reformers of note, inspired Beaumont with great respect.‡ And, inevitably, they were soon being shepherded about, instructed, guided, and assisted, by the indefatigable secretary of the Boston Prison Discipline Society, the Rev. Louis Dwight.§

Apparently at the suggestion of their new friends, the first thing Tocqueville and Beaumont did was to move to a new hotel. 'We are lodged here in the best inn in the city (Trement Hotel),' Beaumont wrote at the end of their first week.² 'Everything in it is on a grand scale; about 150 strangers are to be found there at the moment, you are magnificently served, and it is scarcely more dear than elsewhere. . . .'

'. . . It has seemed to us that here people throw themselves less at the head of strangers than in New-York; but there is more true courtesy. There are in society others besides business men. They are interested here in the fine arts and in literature; there is a class of persons engaged in neither trade nor industry and whose pastime is to live with all the *agréments* provided by an advanced civilization. This class, composed of those who have received from their parents a large enough fortune to live without engaging in business, is not very numerous; but it is agreeable.' And it was beginning to show a lively interest in the two newly-arrived visitors from France. In fact, by the end of the first four days,

* The father of a future president of Harvard, Mr. Eliot (1798–1862) was particularly interested in music and politics, becoming President of the Academy of Music, Mayor of Boston, and Congressman, before he died.

† F.C.Gray, 1790–1856, the son of a very successful shipping merchant, was a Fellow of Harvard, and interested in a number of philanthropic and literary enterprises, such as the Athenaeum, the Historical Society, the State Lunatic Asylum, etc.

‡ It was John Tappan (and either Benjamin or Lewis?) whom Beaumont encountered. 'I declare that I have never met anyone whose character and virtues inspired in me a more profound respect.' *Marie*, II,319, footnote 2.

§ Louis Dwight, 1793–1854, a graduate of Yale, was a nephew of Theodore Sedgwick, and related to Timothy Dwight. For his prison activities, see below, pp.431–32.

Tocqueville and Beaumont suddenly realized that they had now been accepted as completely as they had at first been snubbed by the exclusive society of Boston.

'We dined the other day at Mr. Sear's,' Beaumont was soon boasting.* 'He has a fortune of five or six millions, his house is a kind of palace, he reigns there in great luxury, he treated us with splendour, I have never anywhere seen *dinners more sumptuous*. Among the ornaments of the table was a very pretty lady who is, I believe, his niece. I chatted at length with her, but I don't even know if I shall see her again, so the attention is a pure loss. It's absolutely the same with all the beauties I meet. We see a good number of them in society. We take fire *3 or 4 times a week*, one driving out the other. But the faces are always new, and I think, God pardon me, that we always tell them the same things, at the risk of complimenting a brunette on the whiteness of her skin, and a blond on the ebony of her hair. But all that is a bagatelle and occupies but a very small place in the lives of two men of politics, utterly devoted to speculations of the most elevated order.

'We have already been present at two Balls, and we shall see a third this evening. The *toilette* of the women is exactly the same as in France; the French mode dominates in the United States, and people are perfectly in touch with the least revolutions that it undergoes. Many ladies have questioned me on this subject, and I replied to them (with the same assurance as if they had consulted me on the penitentiary system) of *coques* (bows?) as learnedly as *Michalon* or *Alcibiade* could have done.

'Music is cultivated here with a little more success than in New-York; but the mass haven't the inner feeling for music. There is a museum where paintings are shown, but as I have not yet seen them, I will ask your permission to speak no further of it. . . .'

Altogether, Tocqueville was surprised to discover how much at home he was coming to feel in the strange city of Boston. 'What we have seen of the inhabitants up to this moment differs completely from what we saw at New-York,' he wrote at the end of eleven days.[3] 'Society, at least the society in which we have been introduced, and I think that it is the first, resembles almost completely the upper classes in Europe. Luxury and refinements reign. Almost all the women speak French well, and all the men whom we have seen up to now have been in Europe; their manners are distinguished, their conversation turns

* Probably David Sears.

on intellectual matters, one feels oneself delivered from those commercial habits and that financial spirit that render the society of New-York so vulgar. There are already in existence at Boston a certain number of persons who, having no occupation, seek out the pleasures of the spirit. There are a few who write. We have already seen three or four very pretty libraries of an altogether literary character. (It must be noted, though, that we hardly see any but distinguished men, yet they are otherwise distinguished than those of New York.) It appears, however, that the prejudice against those who do nothing (a very useful prejudice on the whole) has still great strength in Boston, as in all the states that we have traversed up to now. In Boston the labours of the spirit are directed especially toward religious matters. Out of 25 semi-periodical works or pamphlets to be found at the Athen[a]eum, 12 have more or less to do with religion.'

In other words, the men of Boston were serious, moral, religious-minded gentlemen, with whom an earnest young political philosopher could converse with profit and satisfaction.

'Boston, 16 September,' noted Tocqueville. '—I said to Mr. Dewight [Louis Dwight], Protestant minister of great zeal, who was telling me of the good effects of education: There are people in France who have a blind love for instruction. They believe that simply by having taught a man to read, write, and count, one has made of him a good citizen, and almost a virtuous man. Does the same error exist in America?

'He answered: Doubtless not. No one would be found here to sustain the thesis, so often maintained in Europe, that education can have ill effects; but each takes it for granted that the instruction given will be moral and religious. There would be a general outcry, a kind of popular uprising against the man who would introduce the contrary system, and each would say that no education at all would be better than instruction given in that manner. It's in the Bible that all the children learn to read.

'Mr. Dewight added that he thought that the religious principle was making progress in the United States. He said that published reports showed that the number of those who had taken the (Protestant) communion had greatly augmented this year. He admitted, however, that Unitarianism had 13 churches (if I remember correctly) in Boston. There are 60 churches in all there, to 60,000 souls.

'I have, however, already heard a man of *esprit* maintain that if religious instruction was preferable to all other kinds, he thought education in general, however given, more useful to the people than igrance.'

Obviously, Tocqueville still clung to the opinion of a conservative Frenchman. For the moment, however, he was diverted from a further pursuit of this subject by the discovery of two most interesting individuals.

Sometime in the course of their first week in Boston, he and Beaumont were presented to a prominent and wealthy citizen named Joseph Coolidge Jr. Mr. Coolidge was, it seemed, a shipping merchant engaged in the China trade; in other words, he was as much a business man as any New Yorker. But Tocqueville and Beaumont soon realized that he was a man of wide information. Furthermore, he showed himself not insensible to their rank and station,* and what they told him of their researches into American political institutions seemed to interest him intensely, and to kindle in him a most active desire to help them.

The consequence was that at ten o'clock in the morning, on Saturday the seventeenth of April, the young Frenchmen found themselves being shepherded by Mr. Coolidge, past the door of a house on Somerset Court, into the study of the Reverend Jared Sparks.†

The famous editor and historian, who had made a number of friendly contacts in France in the course of his search for documents and materials in Parisian archives, was delighted to see them. He inquired of their families and connections; he listened with interest to what they and Mr. Coolidge had to tell him of their American studies. Then he rose and showed them his manuscripts.

It was, they at once realized, an extraordinary collection. Mr. Sparks even had the papers of the great Washington. And what papers! Toc-

---

* Joseph Coolidge Jr., 1798–1881, had married Eleanor W. Randolph, one of the granddaughters of Thomas Jefferson, and was therefore a friend and correspondent of N.P.Trist, in Washington. In the letter of introduction which he gave Tocqueville and Beaumont to Trist, he wrote: 'They are extremely intelligent and interesting men, greatly curious to inform themselves of the true state of things here, and very sensible to any attentions which they receive. M. de Tocqueville is "parent" to the chevallier de la Luzerne, (who was in this country during our revolution-war.) and also known to M. de Chateaubriand. . . .' Trist Letters, Library of Congress.
† J.Coolidge Jr. to J.Sparks, Friday evening (Sparks Letters, Widener Library, Harvard). Sparks, 1789–1866, had raised himself from a poor Connecticut farmer boy to a position of influence in the Unitarian movement, and to the ownership of the *North American Review*. As an editor of historical documents, of course, he was already widely known.

queville's astonishment was audible. 'Mr. Sparks,' he wrote in one of his diaries that evening, 'Mr. Sparks, erudite inhabitant of Boston who has already published the correspondence of all the ambassadors and men of mark of the time of the American Revolution, and who is at this moment working on a life of Washington, showed me to-day (17 Sept. 1831) several volumes full of accounts or of copies of letters coming from the hand of Washington. These are business letters and some books of accounts bearing on his administration of the army or his personal property. The whole is kept with a care, a clearness, a precision and detail that would do honour to a clerk. The writing is fine, tranquil, perfectly identical on all the pages. He signs everything, even copies of letters, and one would say that one saw in each signature a facsimile. It is hard to conceive how a man whose ideas were so broad could bend himself to such details.'

Tocqueville's own ideas were broad enough to be those of a leader, he hoped, but he had to confess himself awed by such mastery of passion and such patience. His own hand was a miserable and impatient scratching, without power or self-confidence, and betraying but too clearly the unhappy twistings of a nerve-ridden, doubt-tortured soul.

Meanwhile, Beaumont was examining the 'mass of letters from all the political figures who in the last thirty years have played or still play a role. Among others,' the commissioner was interested to note,[4] 'he has all the correspondence of Washington, many letters of Mde. de Stael, of Louis Philippe, during the emigration of Lafayette, etc.—' Naturally, the hand of his demagogical cousin caught the young Frenchman's eye. 'There is,' he reported, 'one truly curious letter written by this last, while in prison at Ollmütz; he speaks of *the new infamies* of M. d'Orléans, and speaks of the *horrible assassination* that the Convention has just committed in condemning Louis XVI (in '93).—Poor Lafayette. . . .'

But Tocqueville was impatient to engage their unexpectedly erudite host in conversation, and ventured a question about the man who now held the great Washington's place at the head of the American government. 'The majority of enlightened men now recognize,' Mr. Sparks soberly replied,[5] 'that General Jackson is not made to fill the office of President; his lack of experience in matters relating to civil government, and his great age, render him incapable of it. Yet he will be re-elected.

'And why that? said I.

'Our people, replied Mr. Sparks, does not resemble yours. Public opinion, with us, is created slowly; it is never taken by surprise, although very subject to error. They worked long and industriously to get it into people's heads that General Jackson was a great man, and that he did honour to America. They finally succeeded in getting this believed. One has not yet had time to lead the people back to other sentiments, and the majority is still assured to the general.'

Mr. Sparks believed, then, that in the United States the tides of public opinion moved slowly but (once started) with an irresistible and overwhelming force.

*

*     *

'18 Sept. 1831. To-day,' noted Tocqueville, 'Mr. Clay (Mr. Clay is a planter from Georgia; I have rarely seen a man more likeable or better informed)* pointed out to me several of the fine *chalets* of Boston, and said that the majority of those who had built these sumptuous dwellings had made their fortunes themselves, and had risen from very low. He added: Fortunes change hands here with unbelievable rapidity. It has been remarked that to a rich father succeeded almost always a poor son, and that a family shone only during one generation. Whence comes that? said I. I understand that your inheritance law is favourable to the destruction of fortunes. But an even more "democratic" law exists in France. Fortunes diminish little by little, without doubt, but they do not melt away like yours.

'The reason for this difference, replied Mr. Clay, is that in France the great fortunes are territorial, and that they are all commercial in New England. You know that here and in general in America it is impossible to procure tenants; the contrary is an exception; land costs too little and its produce sells too cheaply for any one to want to cultivate it unless he is the proprietor. Without tenants, no great territorial fortunes. Now the great commercial fortunes are gained and conserved by industry and skill, qualities that are not transmitted like dollars, and rarely pass from father to son. In the South, on the contrary, where our slaves replace our tenants, fortunes do not disappear any more quickly than with you.

'This led us to speak of slaves. Mr. Clay said to me: There are in our southern provinces a great number of districts where the whites are un-

* It has not been possible to identify Mr. Clay.

able to acclimate themselves, and where the blacks live and prosper. I imagine that in time the black population of the south, in measure as it becomes free, will concentrate in this part of the American territory, and that on the contrary the white population will little by little move away. In this manner, a population entirely descended from the Africans will be formed there, which will have its own nationality and enjoy its own laws. I cannot see any other solution of the great slavery question. I do not believe that the blacks will ever intermingle sufficiently with the whites to form with them but a single people. The introduction of this foreign race is, furthermore, the great and the only evil sore (*plaie*) in America.

'Note—The impossibility of which Mr. Clay spoke of founding territorial fortunes in the north of the United States (impossibility which cannot be brought into question), is it not the chief contributor to the commercial, industrial, speculating spirit which so extraordinarily distinguishes the men in this part of the Union? The passion to get rich has only commerce and industry by which to satisfy itself in New England.'

Obviously, Tocqueville was now, after long pursuit down the path of his original error, at last headed back in the right direction. At least, he was finally beginning to realize, even if only dimly as yet, that he had perhaps exaggerated the influence of the American inheritance laws.* Might not the abundance of free land, and the character of the labour supply, have something to do with the absence of the family estates? Certainly the commercial occupations of the New Englanders accounted at least in part for the rapid dispersal of fortunes and the general equality of conditions which were such striking features of American civilization.

Beaumont, too, was almost ready to concede the point. 'By nature, it [the Boston aristocracy] is somewhat changeable, because the equal partition of the inheritance does not allow a fortune to remain long in the same family,' he wrote.[6]—So much for his rooted conviction.—'On the other hand, the inheritance laws here are far from being as *démocratique* (equalitarian) as they are with us. In France the equal division between all is compulsory; here, when the father of the family dies, the law divides the patrimony equally; but he has the right to give all his property, personal and real, to a single one of his children, and when he does so his wish is carried out. This right, which renders paternal

* Cf. Livingston conversation, etc., above pp.117,126–28,164.

authority much more efficacious than it is with us, has a very great moral influence on all society, outside of the advantage that it has in preventing the extreme division of properties.'

Yet if this were so, how was it that there was visible in ancient Massachusetts no unpropertied and discontented class of men, disinherited by their fathers, and disposed to trouble the peace of the State? If all did not share equally, what happened to the losers?

Here again, an explanation was immediately forthcoming. Opportunities a-plenty, it seemed, awaited the younger sons. On reviewing their journey from Stockbridge to Boston, Beaumont elucidated the matter to his family in the following words:

'This increase in the population in Massachusetts has nothing alarming for American society; each year a great number of persons leave the country and go into the west of the State of New York to seek cheap land and form new settlements. For that they have only 50 leagues to cover, and they find as many acres as they desire at 10 shillings (about 6 or 7 francs) an acre. In this way a superabundance is never to be feared; there is never any real misery, and the people being always content, or at least being free to become so, does not feel the slightest disposition to be discontented with the government. Each one, on the contrary, remains indifferent to the administration of the country, to occupy himself only with his own affairs. Thus all the skill of the government, here, consists in not making itself felt, and the less the administration administers, the more content people are. It's a society going ahead on its own; the only thing which could interfere with its progress would be to take a hand in it. Almost all the Americans in the least distinguished with whom I speak of this state of affairs understand perfectly this peculiar situation of their country, and they regard with pity our European theorists who would apply the institutions of the United States to peoples whose position bears not the slightest resemblance to that of America.'

Tocqueville, too, was startled by this discovery. 'I have been astonished up to now to see to what point the enlightened men of America reason justly on the affairs of France,' he wrote that Sunday in some *General Remarks.* 'I have not yet encountered a single one who thought us in a state to support the Republic, or democratic institutions. Perhaps it is because, seeing at close range the path taken by popular passions acting in their own country in perfect freedom, they are better situated than we to judge how difficult it is to obtain a good government, and above all a stable government, from such elements; since all believe that a people, to be republican, must be poised, religious, and very enlightened. Many admit that, beside these conditions, it is necessary that there be found a condition of material happiness such that there be hardly ever any interior unrest resulting from unsatisfied needs. These last imply, or boldly state, that America must arrive at a monarchy in a given time. But this time is assuredly very far off. The enlightened classes judge M. de Lafayette without any kind of infatuation.* Almost all think that the regime of the Restoration was the happiest combination for France and that the present revolution is a crisis, dangerous and perhaps fatal for the liberty of Europe. The middle classes, the masses, and the newspapers representing popular passions, have on the contrary a blind instinct which drives them to adopt the principles of liberty professed in Europe, and the men who foster them. It's thus that the most religious nation in the world favours with all its wishes the success of the political party which with us professes the most unconcealed hatred against all religions.'

In other words, there were two schools of opinion in the United States. And the good people of Boston belonged, almost to a man, among the 'enlightened' and the sensible. Aristocrats at heart, they agreed with him and with Beaumont, with their families and with all the reasonable liberals of France.

'Father, who has just written me and whose letter I received at the same time as yours, says some very just things on the exceptional position of the United States,' Beaumont assured his brother, Jules. 'It seems as if he had seen with his own eyes what goes on here; and I am entirely of his opinion, that American society, its progress and its prosperity, prove nothing at all, and offer nothing for the imitation of the old nations of Europe. But I am none the less satisfied thoroughly to understand this republic, of which they speak so much and from which they claim to draw so many arguments in favour of "democratic" innovations. There are many people who, in good faith, consider the United States a powerful argument in favour of republics; I am very glad to be in a position to reply to them. The study of contemporary peoples is like that of history; you must study them less to seek examples to follow, than to learn to beware of the imitations people desire to make.'

* 'He is judged a *niais* here: the English word applied to him is *Visionary*.' Bt. to his brother Achille, 25 September 1831 (cited, note 4).

Beaumont's letter was a confession, then, that he and Tocqueville had, for the moment, veered sharply back to their original opinion. Forcibly reminded of the difference between the French peasant and the American citizen by their sojourn in Lower Canada, and now confirmed in their impression by the superior minds of Boston, the two young investigators were once again convinced that the United States could serve only as a warning, never as an example, to France. On the other hand, they did not now fall into the error under which their families were still labouring—the error of supposing that the American experiment would soon fail. The time for a monarchy in the United States, Tocqueville had written, was 'assuredly very far off.' And Beaumont thoroughly agreed.

'I think that you don't grant the United States a long enough future,' he wrote his brother Achille. 'I readily believe that the state of affairs in which they find themselves could not perpetuate itself durably; but it seems to me that the extraordinary circumstances in which they are placed will not change before one, perhaps two centuries, and American society will sustain itself as it is as long as it will have the same conditions of existence. . . .'

## XXVIII

## BOSTON (*Cont.*)

## SOCIAL OBSERVATIONS AND LESSONS ON
## THE JURY

'Tocq. and I are still at Boston,' Beaumont wrote home at the end of
the second week;[1] 'we pass our time there in perpetual motion and
in the midst of a rolling fire of occupations of all kinds. It is without
contradiction the most interesting city that we have seen up to the
present. We are exerting every effort to penetrate to the bottom of
things, and I think that we shall succeed. We see people of all kinds,
of all nationalities, and of diametrically-opposed opinions. We hear
them embitter the grievances of one against the other, and by deducting
from each opinion the exaggeration given it by a thousand passions we
have the truth. There is not a minute of our time unoccupied; we are
pursued by invitations; we hardly ever dine at our hotel, and almost
every evening we have a ball, or a political meeting.'

Obviously, such pursuits gave the two friends an admirable opportunity to study the ways of American society.

'There reigns an unbelievable outward equality in America,' Tocqueville had recorded on the seventeenth.[2] 'All classes are constantly meeting, and there does not appear the least arrogance resulting from different social positions. Everybody shakes hands. At Canandaigua I
saw a district attorney [John C. Spencer?] give his hand to a prisoner.

'The inequality produced by riches and education are to be found,
it is true, in private life. In general the wealthiest and most enlightened
live among themselves. But for a stranger these inequalities are not perceptible, and the fact is that they are, I believe, less felt [here] than
everywhere else. I don't believe that there is an *occupation* which by itself lowers the individual therein employed. You constantly read in the
papers these words in praise of a man: *he keeps a respectable . . .*
[*house?*] *in such place.* It is evident that the white servants regard them-

selves the equals of their masters. They talk familiarly. In the steamboats we at first wanted to give a tip to the steward. They prevented us, claiming that this would be to humiliate him. In the inns I have seen them sit down beside us at table when everybody else had been seated and served. It is, furthermore, almost impossible to find servants in America. They say that they give *the help* (the word is characteristic) and wish to be treated like neighbours who might come momentarily to help their neighbours. They have to eat with the masters.'

In Boston society, of course, such vulgar practices were not allowed. But Tocqueville soon had an 'anecdote' to show that even in America's most aristocratic circle, there was no means of gaining money, lawfully, which was considered dishonourable. One evening, he wrote, 'I found myself in a Boston salon behind two respectable *gentlemen,* who appeared to be discussing with interest an important subject. How much will that bring you said one? It's a good piece of business, replied the other, about a hundred dollars each. Of a truth, returned the first, that's, as you say, a good piece of business. Now it was a question of nothing less than of two pirates who were to be hanged the next day. One of the interlocutors, who was the city-marshal, was obligated by his position to be present at the execution and to see that everything was done in due order. The law allowed him, for the performance of this duty, a hundred dollars per hanged man, and he was speaking of these two patients as of a yoke of oxen that he was to sell the following day at market.' *

Next, Tocqueville turned his attention to *Morals.*

'American morals are, I believe,' he wrote on the 21st,[3] 'the purest existing in any nation,† which may be attributed, it seems to me, to five principal causes:

'1. Their physical constitution. They belong to a northern race, even though almost all living in a climate warmer than that of England.

'2. Religion still possesses there a great power over the souls. They have even in part retained the traditions of the most severe religious sects.

'3. They are entirely absorbed in the business of making money. There are no idle among them. They have the *steady* habits of those who are always working.

---

* These Boston experiences were to give Beaumont materials for an extensive note on 'L'égalité universelle' in the United States. *Marie*, I,383–385.

† Was Tocqueville forgetting his opinion of French Canada?

'4. There is no trace of the prejudices of birth which reign in Europe, and it is so easy to make money that poverty is never an obstacle to marriage. Thence it results that the individuals of the two sexes unite . . . ,* only do so from mutual attraction, and find themselves tied at a time in life when the man is almost always more alive to the pleasures of the heart than to those of the senses. It is rare that a man is not married at 2- † years.

'5. In general the women receive an education that is rational (perhaps even a bit *raisonneuse*). The factors above enumerated make it possible without great inconvenience to allow them an extreme liberty; the passage from the state of young girl to that of a married woman has no dangers for her.

'Mr. Clay, who appears to have occupied himself with statistical researches on this point, told Beaumont that at Boston the prostitutes numbered about 2000 (I have great difficulty believing this). They are recruited among country girls who, after having been seduced, are obliged to flee their district and family, and find themselves without resource. It seems that the young blood of the city frequents them, but the fact is concealed with extreme care, and the evil stops there, without ever crossing the domestic threshold or troubling the families. A man who should be not convicted but suspected of having an intrigue would immediately be excluded from society. All doors would be shut to him.

'Mr. Dewight was saying to me that a venereal disease was a mark of infamy which was very hard to wash away. On the other hand, the police do not concern themselves in any way with the prostitutes. The Americans say that it would be to legitimate the evil to oppose to it such a remedy. Mr. Dewight said to us (what we had already had occasion to remark in the prison reports) that of all the prisoners those who most rarely reformed were the women of bad morals.'

*

*    *

'We have found here some men truly distinguished by their knowledge,' wrote Beaumont,[4] 'among others a German, Mr. Lieber.'

So they had met the young man who was to give their future Prison Report its American translation, and who, more than any other publicist

* Illegible.
† The second digit is illegible.

in the United States, would parallel Tocqueville's political philosophy in his own writings.

Franz Lieber, or Francis Lieber as he was now coming to be known, boasted only 31 years. But in his brief life he had already known the joys of patriotism, the fires of idealism, the thirst for knowledge, and the bitterness of failure and exile. Born but two years before Beaumont, he had volunteered to fight for Germany's independence when still a boy, and faced Napoleon at the battles of Ligny and of Waterloo, where he was severely wounded. With the Emperor gone, the future had seemed bright. An enthusiastic disciple of Jahn, and a leader in the physical culture movement, the idealistic student had talked with his youthful companions of the liberation of the Germans, and of better days for the fatherland. But the reaction, and the Austrian repression, had set in, and Lieber had been imprisoned for several months for his 'liberalism,' prohibited as well from studying in any German university. At length escaping from the surveillance of the authorities, he had gone to join the Greeks in their struggle for independence. Quickly disillusioned, however, by the most un-Homeric character of the race that he had come to help save, he had retreated to Italy, and joined the family of the philosopher Niebuhr, as tutor. Finally, despairing of a future in Germany, he had sojourned for a while in London, and in 1827 come to America.

In Boston, he had established a swimming school. That, and the intelligence and industry of the young man, had won for him a number of friends and the respect of the educated citizens. Before long he was known in a number of eastern cities for his lectures on history and politics. And his *Encyclopedia Americana* was now giving him a national reputation. This last was an extraordinary achievement. After the briefest of residences in Boston, he had announced his intention of getting out an encyclopedia in English; and, undaunted by the difficulties, he had set to work. Now, thanks to his great learning, his indefatigable curiosity, and an industry little short of Herculean, half the volumes were already out. With characteristic enthusiasm and energy, however, he was already contemplating another publication, which was to be nothing less than a history of representative institutions up to the present time.[5]

A scholar with a leaning toward political philosophy, a philanthropist with an intense interest in prisons, a warm-blooded humanitarian with a tender concern for the human race, such was the man whom Tocqueville and Beaumont now discovered.

They were taken to his home on the evening of Sunday, the eighteenth of September. Already Lieber knew them for *zwei sehr wohl unterrichtete Leute.*' * The three young men were delighted with each other. The enthusiastic German, whose proudest boast in later years was to be that he was the American 'de Tocqueville,'† found himself particularly attracted by Beaumont's generous and easy-going disposition; and in the ensuing days the sympathetic idealists saw a good deal of each other.[6]

Mr. Lieber 'got himself expelled from Germany for the exaggeration of his political principles. He had to come to the United States to cease to be a Republican,' Beaumont delightedly reported to his family.[7] In using the word *Republican*, of course, Beaumont had the French variety in mind. 'Since seeing with his own eyes the differences existing between America and Europe he regards as *idéalogues* those who would give us the government of the United States. He spends the time of his exile composing a work called the *Encyclopedia Americana*; he has already issued seven volumes of it. This work is very highly thought of; and he has sold it to his publisher for the bagatelle of 100,000 francs. He gave us an example.'

'22 Sept. 1831. Mr. Lieber . . . said to me this evening,' Tocqueville noted in his diary: 'We Europeans, we think to create republics by organizing a great political assembly. The Republic, on the contrary, is of all the governments the one that depends most on every part of society. Look at this country! The Republic is everywhere, in the streets as in Congress. If an obstacle embarrasses the public way, the neighbours will at once constitute themselves a deliberative body; they

* Lieber had met them at 'old Mrs. Otis's' that same day (Perry, *Life and Letters of Francis Lieber*, p.91), and there made the appointment. *'Heute Abend werde ich die Herrn Tocqueville and Beaumont bei mir sehen, die von französischen Gouvernment hierher gesannt sind um die Gefangnisse zu studieren, die bekanntlich so vorzüglich in Reinlichkeit, Disciplin u[nd] Menschlichkeit in diesem Lande sind. Es sind zwei sehr wohl unterrichtete Leute, u[nd] obgleich jung, schon procureurs du Roi.'* Franz [Lieber] to *'Meine geliebten Eltern und Geschwister,'* Boston, 18 September 1831 (Lieber Papers, Huntington Library, courtesy of the Library and of Ch.B.Robson).
† 'There is a peculiar class of political philosophers or publicists, which might be called historico-philosophical publicists, the three most prominent of which, so far as I know, are Montesquieu, De Tocqueville, and Lieber. I really write this with perfect calmness. "So much the worse," you say, perhaps. I don't know. . . .' Lieber to S.B.Ruggles, Columbia, S.C., 23 October 1856 (Lieber Papers, Library of Congress).

will name a commission and will remedy the evil by their collective force, wisely directed. Does a public ceremony, a banquet, take place, you will likewise see a gathering, a deliberation, and an executive authority arising therefrom. The concept of an authority preceding that of the parties interested does not exist in any one's head. The people has the Republic to the marrow of the bones.

'Another time he said to us: How can a man who has seen America believe that it is possible to transplant its political laws to Europe, and especially at one fell swoop? Since seeing this country I can't believe M. de Lafayette in good faith in his theories; one can't deceive oneself so grossly. For my part, I feel myself inclined to believe every day more strongly that constitutions and political laws are nothing in themselves. They are dead creations to which the morals and the social position of the people alone can give life.

'We asked him: Is it true that morals are as pure here as they pretend?

'He replied: Morals are less good in the lower classes than among the enlightened; however I think them superior to those of the same classes in Europe. As for the educated, their morals are as perfect as it it possible to imagine them. I don't believe that there is a single intrigue in Boston society. A woman suspected would be lost. The women there are, however, very coquettish; they even display their coquetry with greater boldness than with us because they know that they cannot go beyond a certain point, and that no one believes that they overstep that bound. After all, I like still better our women of Europe with their weaknesses, than the glacial and egotistical virtue of the Americans.

'*Q*. To what do you attribute the unbelievable mastery that one obtains here over the passions?

'*A*. To a thousand causes: to their physical constitution, to Puritanism, to their habits of industry, to the absence of an unemployed and corrupted class, such as a garrison for example, to the early marriages, to the very construction of the houses, which renders the secret of an illicit liaison almost impossible to keep.

'*Q*. They say that the young men are not *sages* before marriage.

'*A*. No. they are even, like the English, gross in their tastes, but like them they make a complete separation between the society in which they habitually live, and that which serves their pleasure. These are like two worlds which have nothing in common together. The young men never seek to seduce honest women.

'As we were walking with Mr. Lieber, he pointed out a gentleman passing near us and said: This man is the sheriff, he was a colonel in the army; we were out in society at the mayor's yesterday with him.'

Tocqueville and Beaumont recognized the 'city-marshal' who had discussed his hanging fees before them with such *sang-froid* the evening before.

'Well,' said Francis Lieber, 'two months ago I saw him hang two men.'

'How is that possible?' Tocqueville remembered asking.

'*A.* In America, sheriffs fulfil the functions of executioners.

'*Q.* And no shame attaches to such functions?

'*A.* Not the slightest. The sheriff in executing the criminal is only obeying the law, like the magistrate who condemns him to death, and there attaches to his profession neither hatred nor scorn. It's this respect for the agents of the law, deriving from the extreme respect that one has for the law itself (because one makes it) which is the cause that the people feels no animosity against the officers of police, the collectors of taxes, the customs men. All these places are honoured.'

This conversation, and the incident which occasioned it, were to stick in Lieber's mind. For four years later, in the rather autobiographical impressions of his adopted country, which he published under the title, *The Stranger in America*,* he was to make use of the anecdote to illustrate the difference between the American and the continental point of view. As a convert to the American attitude, Lieber had been entertained by Tocqueville's astonishment. His own version of the conversation, consequently, was not without a certain spice.

'If you go from England to the United States, you find that there the law is held in still higher respect,' Franz Lieber would write.[8] 'But to see the whole truth, to feel the full weight of what I say, it is necessary to see the law administered on minor occasions, to see riots quelled by citizens themselves sworn in for the occasion, to see banks and mints without sentinels, to travel thousands of miles and never meet with a uniform; and farther, to observe that what the law requires is held honourable. No man looks upon a district attorney as upon a tool of government because he prosecutes in the name of the United States.

'I was once with Messrs. —— sent by their government to this country to inquire into our ——, in a Boston party. A gentleman of fine appearance attracted their attention; "Who is he?" they asked. "The

* This was actually a reissue of Lieber's *Letters to a Gentleman in Germany . . .* , 1834.

sheriff," I replied. "The sheriff?" said one of them: "is not the sheriff the officer who directs the infliction of capital punishment?" "He is," I answered. "And did he superintend the execution this morning?" "He did," was my answer. "And he here! *ma fois* that is rather too much!" exclaimed my friend, in whom, though a gentleman of clear mind, all the European prejudices against every person who has any thing to do with the administering of capital punishments were excited; but reflection soon came to his aid, and he was struck with the rationality of this state of things.

'The more civilized a nation the fewer are the prejudices against professions and classes,' was Lieber's conclusion.

Returning to the walk and discussion, as reported by Tocqueville: 'He [Lieber] said to us again, speaking of Germany: Our misfortune is that of not forming a single people. There is a literary Germany, but no political Germany. I regard political union as much more important and much harder for a people to achieve than liberty. I should regard it as a great happiness that all the Germans should be subject to the same yoke, were the yoke of iron. They would then become a single people, and with time they would be *free*.

'Reflection. What disturbs us the most in Europe are the men who, born in an inferior rank, have received an education which gives them the desire to leave it, without furnishing them the means. In America, this inconvenience of education is hardly felt; instruction always furnishes the natural means to enrich oneself, and creates no social unrest.'

*

\*    \*

Two days before, perhaps at the instigation of Lieber himself, Tocqueville had begun to make a very sober investigation of a subject that had not hitherto engaged his attention. Thus far he and Beaumont had analysed the social life of two great cities; at Albany they had searched for the administrative machinery of an American State; and in Michigan Territory they had gained a first-hand impression of the westward-moving frontier. But the theory and practice of local self-government within each State they had quite neglected. Yet how explain the success of these now independent British colonies—as contrasted with the failure of the French in Canada—without a thorough understanding of what 'American decentralization' meant?

'20 September 1831. Mr. Quincy, president of the University of Cambridge, said to me to-day:[9] The State of Massachusetts is a union of small republics, which name their own magistrates and carry on their own affairs.

'But [questioned Tocqueville] what is the tie which unites them (*le lien central*)?'

'The legislature, replied Mr. Quincy. These small republics have a sphere of action fixed by law, beyond which they fall in complete dependence upon the great political body which represents the people. When the particular communities violate the law they are sued before the courts by the State Attorney General. They can even be sued by all those whom they injure. Such and such a town has the responsibility of repairing a road, but neglects to do so. I smash my carriage on it; I at once bring action against the town for damages.

'Mr. Quincy also said to me: I believe we are still more beholden for our present happiness to circumstances strangers to our will than to our Constitution. Here all the material needs of man are satisfied. Besides, we live in freedom, and know nothing else! Massachusetts was nearly as free before the revolution as to-day. We have put the name of the people where was the name of the king; otherwise nothing has been changed with us.'

So President Quincy, like many of his fellow-Bostonians, acknowledged the importance of the rich, unsettled continent to the young American republics. But Tocqueville was not content with this, now familiar, thought. For, more than ever before, it was becoming plain to him what excellent results these ex-colonials were drawing from the accidents of their situation.

'Note,' he wrote. 'One of the happiest consequences of the absence of government (when a people is so fortunate as to be able to get on without it, a rare thing) is the development of individual power which never fails to result. Each man learns to think, to act for himself, without counting on the aid of an outside power which, however vigilant one suppose it, is never able to respond to all social needs. The man, thus accustomed to seeking for his well-being only from his own efforts, rises in his own opinion, as in the estimation of others, his spirit expands and grows strong at the same time. Mr. Quincy gave an example of this state of things when he spoke of that individual attacking a city which has allowed the public way to fall into disrepair. It is thus with everything here. Does a man conceive the idea of some social improvement, a college, a hospital, a road, it doesn't occur to him to go to the authorities. He publishes a plan, offers to execute it himself, calls the strength of other individuals to aid his own efforts, struggles hand to hand against each obstacle. I confess that in the last analysis he often succeeds less well than if the public authorities had been in his place, but in sum the general result of all these admirable enterprises far surpasses what any administration could undertake, and furthermore the influence exercised by such a state of affairs on the public and moral character of the people would more than compensate for all the differences, did any exist.* But we must repeat, there are few peoples who are thus able to get on without government. Such a state of affairs has never been possible except at the two extremities of civilization. Savage man, having only physical needs to satisfy, also counts only on himself; for a civilized man to do as much, he must have reached that social state where his intelligence permits him to perceive clearly what is useful, and where his passions do not prevent his executing it.'

This was almost to admit that the American political civilization was the highest that had yet been evolved. And certainly Tocqueville was not far from giving the American *ideal*, at least, his complete approval. 'The greatest care of a good government should be to habituate people, little by little, to doing without it,' he concluded.

Next day, he and Beaumont encountered their talented friend, Senator Gray, once more.

'Have you,' said Tocqueville,[10] 'a collection of laws regulating municipal government?'

'No,' replied Mr. Gray. 'We have some general principles. All the rest is shaped by custom.' And he proceeded to elucidate. Apparently the State had no right to interfere with the interior government of a municipality, with its police, its revenues, or its own particular affairs. 'The admitted rule is that so long as the town acts only for itself and does not injure the rights of any one, it is all-powerful in its sphere.' What happened when a town disobeyed a law? The Attorney General cited it before the grand jury of the county in which it was situated. If circumstances warranted, it was fined. If it refused to pay, then in theory the party injured could sue the individual inhabitants. Actually, of course, the towns always avoided such an ordeal by paying promptly.

---

* Convinced of the importance of the liberty of individual initiative in a democracy, Tocqueville was later to emphasize the idea throughout his work. The influence of Lieber and Quincy, in this connection, may best be discovered in *Dém. en Am.*, II,ch.6 (end); and III,Pt.2,ch.5.

There were, then, certain general laws to which even the towns had to conform—and judges before whom they might be hailed.

'Have the judges great political power?' was Tocqueville and Beaumont's next question.

'*A*. Our courts form the first power in the state. It is admitted by everybody that they can refuse to apply a law that they hold to be unconstitutional; and it happens every day that they do so. I regard this power accorded to the judges as one of the greatest guarantees of liberty that a people can have. The judges, furthermore, do not misuse it. They do not excite complaints. The people knows them, it participates in their judgments by the jury. I see one of the great advantages of the jury in civil matters in the relation I have just mentioned; and the union and mutual confidence that it creates between the people and the magistracy greatly augment the moral power of the latter.

'*Q*. Since you are speaking of the jury, explain to me why in America, or at least in the State of New-York, you do not try by jury the cases where it is a question of lack of good faith, and other affairs of the same kind touching the conscience. It's especially for deciding such cases, it seems to me, that the jury is useful. What does your court of chancery signify?

'*A*. You must first know that the court of chancery is not organized in the same fashion in Massachusetts. Here the cases you speak of are, like all the rest, within the competence of the jury, unless the parties desire the contrary. If the court of chancery has been established completely in the State of New-York and in many other States of the Union, it's that they have followed the English laws blindly. Now this is why the oddity, that you remark and that I admit, exists in the English laws. England is a country where, in the beginning, the use of Roman law had absolutely ceased. All legislation was based on custom, and all trials judged by the jury. But, as the nation became more civilized, the defects of customary law began to make themselves felt; those defects were such that I don't think that a people could ever have become enlightened while remaining subject to customs. Little by little, they took bits from the *written law*. It was the ecclesiastics, the most educated and enlightened class, who began to operate this change. By knowledge and ambition, the priests drew a great number of causes to their tribunal, under one pretext or another. In general, these were the cases which, founded on bad faith, touched the conscience. Now before the ecclesiastical courts, and with the written law, there was no jury. The cases therefore ceased to be submitted to juries. Later on, the court of chancery succeeded to the ecclesiastical courts, and even though the same reasons for dispensing with the jury no longer existed, they continued from habit in the same way. It's thus that an institution born of the power of the Roman Church has perpetuated itself even to us, republican Protestants.'

\*

\* \*

'22 September 1831. The jury is a political institution, even when applied to civil matters,' noted Tocqueville. 'That's the general idea which must never be lost sight of, that's the starting point from which to judge it.

'I went to-day to attend a hearing in the Circuit Court. The case was this: A ship had been insured, it perished. The underwriter claimed that the vessel was not seaworthy. The suit was carried before a jury which declared by its *verdict* that the ship was in a state to navigate at the time of the contract. Appeal from the sentence of the jury to the Circuit Court. This court, presided by a judge of the United States Supreme Court, could not decide the case itself but sent it back before another jury.

'The lawyer of the insured (Mr. Fletcher, a very good lawyer of Boston)\* began by answering several charges made against the jury which had rendered the verdict in his favour. The jurors were capable men; they had given the affair sustained attention. Entering then upon the point of law, he maintained that if juries were conceded discretionary power to annul the verdicts of other juries, the institution of the jury was become a representation without power. He admitted, however, that in cases where the jury might have acted with passion, or had fallen into palpable and evident error, there was ground for cassation. But he claimed that outside of these extraordinary cases, and every time that the jury had but followed, in a doubtful question, an opinion not shared by the judge, the latter had no right to alter the *verdict*. He went on from this to plead the facts.

'We were unable to be present at the Reply, but in the interval we chatted with one of the judges, who said to us: I see that what you have just heard astonishes you; you aren't able to get a clear idea of

---

\* Probably Richard Fletcher, 1788–1869, a graduate of Dartmouth who had studied law with Daniel Webster and was a recognized expert in commercial law and marine insurance.

the limits within which the rights of the juror and those of the judge are exercised. These limits are, as a matter of fact, determined more by practice than by theory. In fact, we have the right to quash the verdicts of the jury for any motives whatsoever and to send the case back before other men. But it's a right we use only in the last extremity, and when the error or passion can escape nobody. The people sets great store by the judgment of jurors, even in civil matters; it watches with extreme jealousy lest any blow be struck at the moral power of the jury. When a judge sets aside a verdict, he assumes an immense responsibility. For my part, I don't believe I have done so more than ten times in my life; and when I see that the jury has been moved by reasons which, without convincing me, have nevertheless some weight, I leave the matter to its judgment, and respect its opinion. 99 appeals out of a hundred fail. Consequently, out of 50 plaintiffs, perhaps not one comes to us. It's thus that the institution of the jury, that one could render almost illusory by following theory, regains all its power in practice.'

Tocqueville was deeply impressed. And he had learned a valuable lesson. For he was beginning to see that the jury was a great deal more than a judicial device. Clearly, it was one of the means whereby a self-governing people might hope to keep a constant control over its own affairs. At the same time, just as Senator Gray had said, to sit on a jury in a civil trial was to become acquainted with one's rights and duties as a citizen, and to learn to trust the judge. In other words, the jury was also a wonderful school of self-government—a political institution indispensable to the successful operation of a republic.

The young Frenchman felt as if he were at last laying bare the vital organs of American democracy. He began to study the jury as a political institution with an intense concentration.

Five days later he seized a favourable opportunity to pump the legal solicitor for the city of Boston, Mr. Charles Pelham Curtis.* With methodical thoroughness they explored almost the entire subject of litigation. How a man could bring a suit—before what court or courts he would have to go—what the names and jurisdictions of the four Massachusetts courts of first instance were—when they sat and how trials were conducted and in what cases a judge might overrule a jury: all these and many other questions were elucidated by the agreeable solicitor. Mr.

---

* A graduate of Harvard in 1813, Curtis had studied law with William Sullivan (*q.v.* below, p.406), become first legal solicitor for the city of Boston, and served for four years as member of the City Council. He is also remembered as one of the originators of the Boston Farm School for indigent boys.[11]

Curtis even went into particular detail on the Court of Chancery, which he said Massachusetts had imported from England only thirty years before, 'though to be at home in that field, one needs the feeling for it that practice gives.'

A little bewildered, Tocqueville realized that there were two more questions that he wanted to ask.

'*Q*. Don't you think that much of your procedure could be simplified? And can you give me a satisfactory reason for all the rules which govern you?

'*A*. No. Our legislation has been a gradual growth, left to us by our fathers. Habit has familiarized us with its spirit and practices. But it would be impossible to apply it, as we now know it, to another people. There is no logical principle governing it.

'*Q*. Do you think that the jury is, after all, useful in civil suits?

'*A*. For my part, and many think as I do, I believe that in almost all the suits, and even when it's a question of fact, the judges offer greater guarantees of capacity than the jurors.

'The people, however, is extraordinarily attached to judgment by jury, even in civil suits, and it would be absolutely impossible to deprive us of it.'

The conversation ended there. But Tocqueville was further than ever from abandoning the subject. There was more in American legal institutions than met the eye, apparently; and the deeper one probed into the Anglo-American use of the jury, the more obvious it became that the jury had an importance quite other than juridical. What Mr. Curtis said recalled, in particular, certain ideas that had fallen from the lips of Mr. Fletcher and the judge in the insurance case a few days before. Tocqueville was moved to record some *reflections*.

'Here is what seems the clearest result of the preceding conversation,' he noted:

'It is evident that all the legislation of England, and of America consequently, is an ancient fabric, constructed out of pieces brought together at different times, and in which one must not seek new ideas, or a logical principle, or methodical order.

'*At present*, it seems to me certain that in the beginning the judgment by jury was applied to everything. This was, in fact, the only judicial principle of our fathers the Germans. But this judicial form can subsist only in a society which is in its infancy and where all the cases are founded on an appreciation of fact.

'In measure as the societies of Europe became civilized, the difficulty of restricting themselves to the jury became more and more plain. On the continent, and especially in France where the advantages of something new have always more struck the spirit than those of the old, they did away with the jury to establish permanent courts.

'In England, on the contrary, where the human spirit proceeds more slowly, where the necessity of logic does not preoccupy man as much as with us, and where they are far more guided by every-day facts and arrested by the fear of a complete change, in England, instead of destroying the jury they have made inexpressible efforts to conserve it its place in the law.

'Each century, while making the social state undergo a new progress, showed the impossibility of judging such and such a class of cases by the jury. As these difficulties presented themselves, some new expedients were invented to combat them.

'It's thus that the multiplication of the suits (and they multiply in proportion as society grows more enlightened and wealthy) made obvious the impossibility of applying the jury to the decision of everything. A minimum was therefore fixed above which the jury would not be consulted.

'As the law became more perfect, the necessity was felt of establishing a permanent court to interpose between the litigants and prevent their doing things, while awaiting judgment, that would prejudice their rights; and this tribunal had to be created.

'When one began to discern more clearly the *interest* of suits, it was perceived that only half justice was rendered in reducing cases to damages. And on the other hand, it was felt that the moment a tribunal ordered a *performance*, there could be a discussion on the motives for its decision, and the difficulties over its execution could only be remedied by return to the judge who rendered it. Now the jury is a judge chosen for the specific case, which disappears after having pronounced. The institution of the jury was not abandoned, however; instead there was created beside it a tribunal to handle this kind of suit.

'Finally, even in cases where it was only a question of money, it was felt, as the law became more complicated, that the fact became constantly entangled with the law, and could scarcely be separated from it. Even yet they didn't despair of keeping the jury, but rendered its *verdict* divisible. The judge remained master of questions of law, of the interpretation of acts; the jury found itself confined, not in appearance but in reality, to questions of fact.'

'From all that,' Tocqueville concluded, 'it results that the jury in civil matters is by nature an institution adapted to the needs of an infant society and not to the exigencies of an enlightened and perfected legislation. The laws of England attest the near impossibility of adapting it completely to an advanced social state, and leave it gravely in doubt, whether the jury is useful to justice, in the sphere reserved for it.'

On the other hand, Tocqueville now added, 'its political usefulness is immense, and it is from this point of view that one must envisage it.'

The reasons were becoming increasingly obvious. 'The judges forming a body entirely apart would either constitute a danger for liberty or soon lose their power.

'It gives the habit of discussing public affairs to a multitude or persons.

'It teaches the people to take a hand in its own affairs, and to regard as its business all the interests of society.

'It gives a great outside power to [the administration of] justice, it prevents the magistracy from becoming a body apart from the people, and gives it a force that is immense and almost always useful in political questions.

'Established in civil as well as criminal affairs, it so controls the habits, and so enters into the ideas and customs that it becomes impossible to take it away in criminal matters. Now, it is impossible to conceive of a people among whom the jury is solidly established who are not a free people.

'Furthermore, I cannot believe that one could safely give a permanent judicial body the right to interpret the *constitutionality* of the laws, did the jury not exist.

'Now, this power of the judges is one of the greatest remedies of the defects of *Démocratie* [popular government?].'

*

* *

Clearly, Tocqueville was at last beginning to feel that he had a sufficient command of the history of the English jury to understand its presence in America. And of its importance, especially and chiefly from the political point of view, he no longer entertained any doubts. As a matter of fact, a number of the ideas * that he was later to put forward in his Commentary had already assumed a striking and definite form in his mind. In a really notable chapter on 'The Jury in the United States considered as a Political Institution' he would one day bear eloquent testimony to these early Boston observations.[12] Indeed, he would rehearse them, use, quote them—thought for thought and even almost word for word.

* If the ideas were originally suggested by Mr. Curtis, they were to be affirmed and strengthened—and the very wording of the last few paragraphs foreshadowed— by a conversation that Tocqueville was soon to have in Philadelphia with a young lawyer named Gilpin. See below, pp.529–30.

XXIX

## WITH THE LEADERS OF CHURCH AND STATE . . .

TOCQUEVILLE and Beaumont stayed on in Boston three and a half weeks; they could not get away. The last ten days of their visit, in particular, were so crowded with engagements and useful occupations that they had never an instant of quiet to themselves. 'We live in a sort of whirlwind which scarce gives us time to know what we are about,' wrote Tocqueville. 'Ideas, impressions, faces succeed each other with inexpressible rapidity. We are swept along by a current midst which it is impossible to stand still a single instant.'

In spite of its obvious disadvantages, this life of headlong activity was an excellent tonic for Tocqueville in his bereavement. It served, as nothing else could have done, to distract him from thoughts of France and home. 'For a man as absent of mind as I,' he confessed,[1] 'this manner of observing is often worth nothing. Ordinarily, I remember what I had to say to a man after I have left him never to see him again, or at least not until the other world, where I shall no longer be interested in questioning him. And yet, I will admit, this kind of feverishness has its charms. The monotony of Versailles was killing me. Besides, you know that the great object in this life is to forget, so far as it is possible, that one exists. Now I defy any one to imagine an existence (except that of a minister, however) which draws a man more completely out of himself. . . .'

In justice, Tocqueville should also have added that in his life he had met with few experiences that, on the whole, were more stimulating or worthwhile. Beaumont, at least, appreciated this. 'I think that we have never so well employed our time,' his account of their last week in Boston began.[2] 'We were unceasingly in touch with the most distinguished persons of Boston, and that city possesses a great number. In no city of the United States (Philadelphia excepted) is there so much intellectual life; we found there what up to the present we had not been

390

able to encounter in America, that is to say, a superior class possessing the tone and the manners of the societies of Europe. This class is not very numerous at Boston, as you well believe, but still it exists, and it is all the more curious to examine because it finds itself thrown, as if by hazard, in the midst of a republican society, whose principle is an absolute equality and with which it forms a strange anomaly. I took on all the facts I observed a mass of notes, which will serve me later on, if on my return I accomplish my projects of literary composition.*

'Right up to the end we were treated at Boston with extreme distinction; each day we had new invitations. Here is how, generally, we spent our day. When we could get up a little early, we made notes on the *objects to be observed*. Ordinarily this labour was not long, in view of the fact that we breakfasted at half past seven (such is the rule of the hotel where we were). After breakfast we ran to the post to see if some letters hadn't come for us from France by the New York bag. We rarely had the joy of finding any; but then how happy we were when a packet had arrived!

'We could scarce pass once or twice in a street without being approached by someone; it was moreover a series of perpetual engagements from one day to the other. When we could escape the visits and the necessity of making them, we went to spend a few instants at the library of the Athenaeum; but even this place was not a certain asylum from the ingenious searches of our good friends; and when we were encountered they always demonstrated to us that we were under the obligation to go see such and such remarkable public establishment, such and such distinguished man who wished to see us, etc., etc., etc. In this way we made more than one boring expedition. For example, when it was necessary to spend an hour in a hospital examining, in full representation, all the miseries of human life, I confess that I would willingly have yielded my place to another. . . .

'To return to the history of our life at Boston, you shall know that almost every day we were invited to dinner in the city. We made some excellent meals, they live very well in Boston. They have but a single fault, which is that of drinking too much.† One has all the difficulty in

* On Beaumont's notes, see below p.393, footnote.
† In résumé, what most struck Beaumont about Boston society were its intellectual distinction, its aristocratic snobbishness, and its heavy drinking! [Such is the tenacity of family character and local tradition that it would be a bold man who to-day, more than a hundred years afterward, would proclaim any one of these three qualities to have been lost.]

the world avoiding the toasts which are offered. The dinner usually takes place at 2 or 3 o'clock; it is prolonged quite late because they have, here as in England, the habit of staying at table, when the dinner is finished, in order to drink and make conversation at the same time. However, at 6 o'clock one can withdraw without offending any one, and that is what we always did, because we were usually engaged to take tea somewhere. Now tea is taken at half past 6 or 7 o'clock; it was not without its use for us in helping us digest. After having spent one or two hours, in the house where we took tea, we had to return to our hotel in order to dress so as to put ourselves in *costume de bal*. We had balls or *soirées dansantes* every day, and sometimes 2 or 3 the same day. . . .'

It was a mad round, but Beaumont, at least, enjoyed it thoroughly. He and Tocqueville were now known all over Boston as 'men of intelligence, information, and highly pleasing manners';[3] and their debut into society could only be described as a great success. At the balls, the gay Gustave continued to encounter the arch Mrs. Otis; so he danced and danced with her—and carefully avoided saying anything about it to his family. Francis Lieber might tease him and pretend;[4] but of course there was nothing serious in it. So why make his family anxious? It would be better to give them something more reassuring to read—a general estimate of Boston women, for instance.

'. . . There is here a considerable number of pretty women, but not a single beauty,' he had accordingly written.[5] 'Here, as in New-York and, I believe, all the United States, they are, in the matter of music, of an *unbelievable barbarity*. The women do what they can to play and sing *passably*; but their physical organization does not allow them to succeed. As for the men, they are too *occupied* to make music, and have too little natural taste to hear with pleasure that made by the others. It's probably for that reason that they have made up their minds not to listen to the women, when they sing or play the piano. I have for some time so neglected the *instrumental* line that I pardon the Americans their indifference in the matter of harmony. I haven't five minutes to play the flute, and I am on the eve of losing my fine talent.—It is, in truth, a pure bagatelle . . .' For, as the young magistrate had already been careful to state, he and Tocqueville were 'men of politics' —and— 'utterly devoted to speculations of the most elevated order.'

Posterity might smile at the high-flown phrase; yet it carried to his family a very faithful picture of the young Frenchmen's daily preoccupation. They might dance, and chatter, and flirt with the young ladies of Boston; but it was the stiff and somewhat craggy fathers who really interested the 'distinguished' commissioners. With all their social graces, Tocqueville and Beaumont preferred the company of Boston's leading men: intelligent, well-informed, tough-minded gentlemen, with whom they could reason and argue and discuss, and forget the frivolities around them.

'Among the persons whom we most enjoyed seeing and whose society presented to us the greatest interest,' Beaumont informed his family,[6] 'are Mr. Webster, the most remarkable orator of the United States; Mr. Adams, ex-president of the United States, a sort of dethroned king who is full of *esprit* and whose conversation is most interesting. Mr. Channing, writer of the greatest merit, also keenly interested us.' And they met the distinguished Congressman and editor, Edward Everett, with his older brother, Alexander, the diplomat.

Perhaps it was Senator Webster who surprised them most. Every one had spoken to them of this unusual statesman. Joseph Coolidge, it was true, thought him a little too proud and overbearing. But people in general seemed to consider him one of the strong men of the nation— and spoke of his defence of his country's unity, in Congress the year before, as one of the great achievements of their generation. Particularly among the manufacturing element were his praises to be heard. 'At Boston,' noted Beaumont, 'there is a numerous party naturally favourable to the tariff; it's that of the manufacturers and their adherents; [whose] great establishments [are] at Lowell. Mr. Webster was by principle opposed to the tariff, and several years ago he pronounced a discourse in Congress to combat it. But he emits a contrary opinion since a great number of forces are engaged in enterprises which would be overturned without the succour of the tarriff (analogy with our iron manufactures).'

That was on the eighteenth of September.* Undaunted by his reputation, the two young prison commissioners resolved to beard the 'God-like Daniel.' The introduction was effected; and Tocqueville took the plunge. They were interested in the reform of criminals, one gathers that he said; to that end they had come to investigate the American penitentiary systems.

---

* MS. at Beaumont-la-Chartre. Except for this single sheet, containing also a remark of Mr. Sears and the Sparks conversation cited below (p.400), all of Beaumont's American diaries or notes have apparently been lost. [See below, p.546.]

Disaster. The great man was not interested. 'I have never forgotten what De Tocqueville said to me when I met him coming from his first interview with Webster,' Francis Lieber wrote twenty-one years afterwards.[7] 'The Frenchman had heard a great deal of Webster, and of course was most anxious to converse with him on prison discipline; but Webster paid no attention to the subject, said it was useless to try to reform criminals. He took, as De Tocqueville thought, a very common lawyer view of the whole; and, added he, "Webster, like thousands of statesmen, cares only for power." '

On the whole, Lieber agreed with his French friend. In the German's eyes, the Senator's great weakness was an indifference to humanitarianism. 'I do not say that Webster was exactly as he had appeared in that one conversation, in which he had fairly displeased De Tocqueville; but he had not, as it seems to me, that greatest and rarest of qualities of a statesman or a ruler,—a union of the sense of power with the naturalist's perception of the pulsations of life,—typified, possibly in Charlemagne in the highest degree—he who conceived the idea of normal schools and normal farms while beating back the hordes of Hungary. . . .'

From Webster, then, the two friends derived but small satisfaction. And if they conversed again, Tocqueville made no notes of what passed.

But there were other gentlemen, more sympathetic to the objects of their mission, and infinitely more philanthropic by nature. So Tocqueville and Beaumont did not allow themselves a moment of discouragement.

In particular they were attracted to an unassuming, frail little minister named Joseph Tuckerman. The Rev. Mr. Tuckerman belonged, it appeared, to the Unitarian faith; in fact, he was one of the most zealous in what seemed to the Frenchmen a mistaken cause, being 'Minister at Large' under the auspices of the Benevolent Fraternity of Churches, which he had helped to organize. But his real mission was among the poor. Inspired by an intense compassion for the downtrodden and the suffering, he was making a scientific study of pauperism and the administration of charity. He gave them a letter that he had published on the societies of temperance, and the seven reports that he had written on charity and the education of the poor.* Natur-

* Joseph Tuckerman, 1778–1840, was a classmate and friend of Dr. Channing, and had roomed with Joseph Story at Harvard. With Channing he was recognized as one

ally, he was interested in prison reforms, as well. And it soon became apparent to the French commissioners that the penitentiary system inspired in him the most sanguine hopes.

'Among the estimable philanthropists, who seemed to us to entertain some illusions on this point, we shall cite Mr. Tukerman [*sic*] of Boston,' Tocqueville and Beaumont were later to note in their Prison Report.[8] 'He (*qui*) hopes that the day will come when, all the wicked being regenerated, prisons will no longer be needed. It is certain that if there were many men as passionately devoted as he to the cause of humanity, his hope would not be chimerical. Mr. Tukerman's name ought to be pronounced only with respect; he is the living image of beneficence and virtue. A disciple of Howard, he spends his life in good works, and aspires to relieve all human miseries; feeble of body, pale and almost extinguished, he has only a breath of life; but in the presence of a good deed to be done, one sees this sort of human phantom quicken and become filled with energy. Mr. Tukerman, who on certain questions may perhaps deceive himself, does not the less render immense services to society. His charity toward the poor of Boston has given him the right to be their supervisor; and if his kindness toward them is extreme, it must also be said that nothing equals his severity toward them. They love him because he is their benefactor; but they respect him and fear him, because they know the austerity of his virtue. They know that his interest in them depends on their good conduct. . . .'

After the lapse of a year, Tocqueville and Beaumont's admiration still kindled at the thought of what they had seen. 'Mr. Tukerman does more for the good order and the police of Boston than all the aldermen and justices of the peace together.'

Furthermore, he had given them some opinions on public education that seemed to the two friends, by reason of his experience in the field, of great value. On the twenty-seventh of September, Tocqueville had ventured to recur to the topic that Louis Dwight had first broached.

Mr. Tuckerman said to them: 'For God's sake, do not create in France a fund for the support of a school. Or, at least, make it so insufficient that it serves only as an encouragement. We have observed

---

of the leaders of the new Unitarian movement; but his great work was as the first modern poor relief advocate. In this field his principles gained for him an international reputation; and his influence was to revolutionize the methods of dealing with the poor. In England the Tuckerman Institute at Liverpool, in France Baron Degérando were to carry forward his ideas.

that when the towns knew that the government paid all the funds for education, they became quite indifferent about their schools. Whereas, when they put their own money into it, they took a great interest in seeing that it should be well employed. It's to this cause that we attribute the superiority of Massachusetts schools over those of Connecticut.

'The same thing had already been said by Mr. Spencer at Canandaigua,' Tocqueville recalled. 'He claimed that the same remark applied to every kind of town or district interest.'[9]

In other words, paternalism and centralization had the same deadening influence in the field of education as in politics. On the other hand, some system of inspection by the state was admitted to be desirable.

'Mr. Tukerman said to me to-day (27 Sept. 1831) that that which was lacking in the State of Massachusetts was that there was no central authority having the right to visit the schools, inspect them, and publish each year, as is done in New-York, reports showing their present state, the number of children therein received. . . .'

In the absence of such reports, Tocqueville thought it well to take some general notes.

'*Public Instruction,*' he wrote. 'In New England the law obliges all towns containing 80 families or proprietors to have a school where are taught reading, writing, English grammar, geography, and arithmetic at least six months a year.

'It obliges all the towns having 500 families to have a school where is taught the history of the United States, the art of surveying, geometry, algebra.

'Finally, in each town containing 4000 inhabitants, the master shall be equipped to teach Latin, Greek, and the history of other countries.

'One perceives what place is occupied by primary instruction and elementary subjects. It is immense. Everywhere the history of the country and geography are necessary parts of the instruction. . . .'

'*Blacks.* In Massachusetts the blacks have the rights of citizenship, they may vote in elections. But prejudice is so strong that it is impossible to receive their children in the schools.'

## XXX

## SPARKS—AND LOCAL SELF-GOVERNMENT

On the twenty-eighth of September, Tocqueville and Beaumont called on Mr. Edward Everett, formerly the editor of New England's leading periodical, the *North American Review*, and now a representative of Massachusetts in the Congress of the United States. Unfortunately, the noted New Englander was away for the day.[1]

Their friend Senator Gray, however, had some further thoughts on the subjects which they discussed together a few days before. At that time, he had given them specific information on the legal status of the New England town, and the practical operation of the American jury system. Now the learned prison inspector wanted to emphasize the importance of such institutions for any self-governing people. He said to Tocqueville:[2]

'I regard it harder still to establish municipal institutions among a people than great political assemblies. When I say municipal institutions, I mean to speak not of the form but of the spirit which makes them work (*qui les vivifie*). The habit of treating all affairs by discussion, and of proceeding in all, even the smallest, by means of majorities, that habit is harder to acquire than all the others. Yet it's the only one which makes governments really free. It's that habit which distinguishes New England, not only from all the countries of Europe, but even from all the other parts of America. Even our children never go to their master [to settle their differences], they regulate everything among themselves, and there is not a man of fifteen years among us who has not a hundred times already fulfilled the functions of a juror. I have no doubt but that the last man of the people of Boston has a more truly parliamentary spirit and is more accustomed to public discussions than the majority of your deputies. But on the other hand, we have been working for 200 years to form this spirit, and we had as a starting point the English spirit and an altogether republican religion.

397

'*Q*. Do you think that the *political character* of the inhabitants of New England is owing largely to their natural character?

'*A*. Natural inclination is of some effect, but it's above all the result of the laws, and even more of custom.' *

The next day another Bostonian referred to New England's British heritage.

'29 Sept. 1831,' Tocqueville noted. 'Mr. Everett (Alexander), former United States minister to Spain and a distinguished writer,† said to me this evening: The starting point of a people has an immense bearing, the consequences for good or ill have an influence by which one is unceasingly surprised.

'The English, our fathers, permit imprisonment for proven debt,' Mr. Everett illustrated; 'they even allow, what is much less justifiable, imprisonment before the proof. That legislation was passed on to us. But they are attacking it, and several states have begun to modify it. In the State of New-York, by virtue of a law which will go into effect next year, imprisonment for debt has been absolutely abolished. In Kentucky they have abolished imprisonment for debt where the debt was proven, and yet have continued to allow the plaintiff to have his adversary imprisoned before the judgment, so difficult to conquer are the habits that its origin gives a nation.'

In short, Mr. Alexander Everett was implying that no one could fully understand American institutions without some knowledge of the ancient island antecedents from which they had sprung. It was the Rev. Jared Sparks, however, who really brought home to Tocqueville and Beaumont the full significance of this suggestion. Encountering the learned New England historian that same day, the two curious young investigators soon found themselves listening to one of the most comprehensive and luminous expositions of the origins of American political institutions that it had been their privilege to hear.

'I believe that our origin is the fact which best explains our government and our ways,' Mr. Sparks began.[3] 'We came here republicans and religious enthusiasts. We found ourselves abandoned to our own devices, forgotten in this corner of the world. Almost all societies, even

* A comparable verdict was to be rendered by Tocqueville, *Dém. en Am.*, II, end ch.9.
† Alexander Everett, 1792–1847, after a brilliant career at Harvard, had taught at Exeter, studied law with J.Q.Adams, and represented the United States in various diplomatic capacities in Russia, the Netherlands, and Spain. At the moment he was a member of the Massachusetts Legislature.

in America, have begun at the point where the governing authority was concentrated, and then have spread from this central point. Our fathers, on the contrary, founded the *town* before the *state*. Plymouth, Salem, Charlestown existed before one could say that there was a government of Massachusetts; they only united together later on, and by a voluntary act. You perceive what power such a starting point must have given to the *esprit communal* which so eminently distinguished us even among Americans and in the midst of republican principles. Those who would imitate us should well reflect that our history has no precedents.'

'New England is the cradle of American Democracy,' Mr. Sparks pursued. 'It's there that landed a group of men who immediately organized the principle of universal representation of the people: each time that a question of any sort arose, the entire population was called together; thence the origin of the town meetings. It was the inhabitants of Massachusetts who carried their customs into Connecticut; and as they enjoyed the advantage of having put their free principles into practice, they founded in Connecticut a pure "democracy" better ordered and more rational than anywhere else. This starting point of Massachusetts is constantly cropping up; and the town meetings are nothing else than the application of this "democratic" principle. . . .'

But did not the practice of pure democracy have its drawbacks, did not the political parties take advantage of the opportunities, thus provided, to arouse the ignorant voters to disturb the state? Tocqueville and Beaumont wanted to know.

Apparently not. In America the practice of almost pure democracy entailed no 'inconveniences.' For in the first place, Mr. Sparks pointed out, there were 'no *Political Parties* properly so called: only local interests, and personal rivalries.' There was, he admitted, 'a general politics for the whole nation,' which was to be found, discussed in all the local newspapers. As a rule, people 'all took sides for or against the administration.' But their differences were those of personal preference, rather than of principle. At the moment, for example, the great struggle was 'between the friends of General Jackson and the friends of Mr. Clay.' Which might be, doubtless, a national question. But such disputes did not, generally speaking, seriously disturb the individual States.

In the second place, the freedom of the press, in America unlimited, tended to give the newspapers 'a purely local influence.' 'There are,' said Mr. Sparks, 'about 1000 Journals in the States; a great city paper has little influence on the other cities of the State; each city has its paper which it prefers to all the others; this paper is dedicated to the defence of the interests of the locality. Here there is nothing resembling your Paris Journals, or their influence. [Of course] the liberty of the press is not free from excesses with us; the papers are sometimes guilty of defamation. If it is against private individuals, these complain, and the papers are sued in the courts; but if it is against public officers, the latter never complain; they would have the right but never make use of it.'

At bottom, the key to American self-government was to be found, said Mr. Sparks, in one great principle. 'The political dogma of the country is that the majority is always right. Altogether, we find it very good to have adopted it.' Sometimes, he admitted, the theory did not always work out in practice. And he 'cited some examples.' 'Occasionally the majority wanted to oppress the minority.* Happily, we have in the *veto* of the Governor and above all in the power that the judges have to refuse to execute an unconstitutional law, a guarantee against the passions and the errors of *Démocratie* [the masses in an unlimited democracy?].'

But such precautions were really, Mr. Sparks hastened to add, a comparatively small matter. 'In the midst of this great freedom and this limitless *Démocratie*, the power, the government of society is scarce to be perceived,' Beaumont noted. 'The first functionary of the State is the Governor. It's he who names to a great number of public appointments; he is in continual relations with the Legislature and the Senate; he has the right to pardon, and to veto the laws passed by the Legislature. This veto arrests the going into operation of the laws, and he prolongs it as long as he chooses. The Governor is named only for one year, like the members of the Senate and the Legislature. The advantage of this is to render the offices temporary and passing; they are thereby less important, less coveted, and less apt to excite ambitions and . . . intrigues. The Governor is often re-elected; he whom we have now, Mr. Lincoln, has been Governor for seven years. If the members of the Senate and the Legislature were entirely renewed, it would have one inconvenience, that of having legislatures unskilful in affairs, and ignorant of the traditions. But although all cease each year to be members, it is recognized by experience that three quarters of

* The reader will encounter this phrase again.

them are always returned to the chambers by re-election. . . . The Governor and the two chambers form the legislative power, and give laws to the whole State; otherwise the action of the central government is difficult to feel and harder still to define. . . .'

Unfortunately, said Mr. Sparks, there was no book which would explain the general principles governing the action of the State, or show how all the localities were 'united by a common bond, without any one of them losing the least portion of its independence.' In all 'local matters,' however, it was understood that 'the smallest aggregation of men is sovereign, and regulates its affairs without the central government mixing in, the least in the world. . . . I was just speaking of the "democratic" spirit of New England,' Mr. Sparks harked back. 'It is, to tell the truth, the starting point of the republican institutions in the United States. New-York borrowed our principles from us. In the beginning New-York was not at all what the city and state are to-day. It was a royal colony; the aristocratic ways of England had been imported there; later on the State of New-York took our institutions, or rather our institutions penetrated into the State of New-York. . . .'

Tocqueville had one last question: 'Is it necessary for the President of the United States to have a majority in Congress to govern?' he asked.

If Mr. Sparks was surprised at such complete ignorance of the Federal Constitution, his reply was still patient and courteous. 'No, the contrary often occurs. General Jackson,' he explained, 'did not have a majority in Congress.'

\*

\*    \*

Suddenly Tocqueville and Beaumont were face to face with a dilemma. Going along as they had done hitherto, they could not possibly hope to get to the bottom of the vast questions they were now investigating in the few short days that remained.

Almost from the very start in New York, they had realized the tremendous difficulty of the task ahead of them. So they had at once set to work to sharpen their tools and to perfect a methodology of inquiry. In the most natural way, both Beaumont and Tocqueville had early learned to use their letters home as store-houses of information and theory, while Tocqueville had gradually fallen into the habit of keeping a number of narrative and topical diaries. But this had not been sufficient. So Tocqueville had developed the knack of memorizing and recording the daily conversations that were slowly coming to assume an ever more important place in their investigations. And both young men had early begun to practise the gentle art of flattery. For enthusiasm, they found, opened the hearts of all their hosts, secured them a friendly hearing and unlimited assistance, and above all led the pleased Americans to shower them with valuable books and printed documents otherwise hard to obtain. By the end of their visit to Albany, as a consequence, Tocqueville and Beaumont had already collected, of such materials, a whole trunk full.

Now, however, all these devices were proving insufficient. Never before, it was true, had they conversed with such interesting and well-informed men. And never had their calculated flattery worked so efficiently. It was really almost scandalous, so to victimize the great men of Boston. 'We have a complete collection of books, pamphlets, memoirs, which they gave us,' Beaumont boasted.[4] 'We couldn't help laughing that we never returned home our pockets empty. When we were presented to an author, we were sure, with a few compliments, to hook onto his work, and we never missed.'

On the twenty-first, for example, Francis Lieber had sent them the seven volumes of his *Encyclopedia Americana*, with a note saying that he would be glad to forward the other five to any address as they appeared. Then the venerable Joseph Tuckerman had insisted that they accept his reports on pauperism, and his *Letter to the Mechanics of Boston* on the Temperance reforms. From the zealous and indefatigable Louis Dwight, the two friends had collected a complete set of indispensable annual *Reports* of the Boston Prison Discipline Society. Senator Gray had listed for them the Massachusetts official documents that might be of use to them in their inquiry, and was sending them a letter that he had published on Harvard University. And from President Josiah Quincy, in addition to the catalogue and annual report of the college, they had obtained a copy of his address to the citizens of Boston on the bicentennial of the city, the year before, and a very valuable little book on New England local government called the *Town Officer*.[5]

The trouble was, the most serious conversations, and all the random documents in the world, seemed only to scratch the surface of each subject. And, now that they had begun to delve into the inner workings of civil government in New England, Tocqueville and Beaumont were discovering such depths of ignorance in themselves that they were almost desperate. Some more effective method of gathering detailed factual knowledge and precise information on the particular topics under investigation—some device as well for acquiring the general principles and political theories involved—would quickly have to be invented.

Tocqueville and Beaumont had an inspiration. They would set their friends to work collecting the information required. A man so interested in their studies, and so well informed that he could discourse to them all evening about the origins and character of American government, would certainly be willing to take a few hours to collect his thoughts and write them a considered essay on some particular point. And his essay, if they could obtain such a thing, would be more authentic and valuable than any of Tocqueville's memorized conversations. At the very least, it would do no harm to try.

But here was a curious difficulty. The first necessity, they discovered, was to refresh their own memories as to how things were ordered in France. 'Our sojourn in Boston was most useful to us, we found there a crowd of distinguished men and a mass of precious documents,' Tocqueville was soon writing to his magistrate friend Chabrol;[6] 'but we are constantly made aware that the greatest obstacle in the way of learning is knowing nothing. On a multitude of points we don't know what to ask because we are ignorant of what exists in France and because, without comparisons to make, the mind doesn't know how to proceed. It is therefore absolutely necessary that our friends of France furnish us in part with what we need, if we wish to acquire some useful notions here.'

Specifically, what Tocqueville wanted out of Chabrol was an analysis of French administration, with particular attention to the domestic organization known as the Ministry of the Interior. 'What strikes every traveller in this country the most, whether he tries to reflect or not, is the spectacle of a society proceeding all alone, without guide or support, by the single fact of the concourse of individual wills. It's useless to torment the spirit seeking for the government; it is nowhere to be perceived, and the truth is that it does not, so to speak, exist.'

How, then, account for 'the 1200 employees of the Ministry of the Interior'? He had never, Tocqueville confessed, given the matter a moment's thought hitherto. Now he was genuinely puzzled, and begged for something positive in the way of information. 'Don't be afraid of details.' *

Next Tocqueville approached his friend Blosseville† about the administrative courts in France, requesting an outline of their organization and particularly some notion as to their political importance. What he needed, he suggested, was 'some of that information which is not to be found in books and whose greatest merit is that it comes from a person on whose judgment and elevation of mind one has learned to count.'[7]

As a matter of course, then, Tocqueville appealed to the Comte his father. 'You could, dear Father,' he wrote from Hartford,[8] 'render me a great service, which, with the leisure that you now enjoy, would not cost you much, I think. Here is what I wish to say. One of the things which most particularly attracts my attention in the United States is the internal administration of each State, and after that of the entire Union. I try so far as it is possible to understand with clarity what part of the government is given to the towns, to the provincial [State] bodies, and finally to the central government in matters having to do with the administration of the country. In this examination, one great obstacle arrests me. Each fact is without particular physiognomy for me, and without great significance because I can make no comparisons. Nothing would be more useful for judging America well than to know France. But it's this last point that doesn't exist. I know in general that with us the government concerns itself with almost everything; a hundred times the name *centralization* has been dinned into my ears, without its being explained. I have never had the time or the opportunity to examine the play of the different administrative circuits which cover France.

* By way of aside, Tocqueville went on to explain what it was that made their researches in America so difficult. 'The unfortunate thing about our position here is that we are obliged to concern ourselves with too many things at a time. When an idea comes to us, if we do not instantly fix it on paper, we are almost certain never to see it again.

'If, when we are talking with a particular man, we are not able to ask him the most useful questions on the spot, it is a lost opportunity. We never have time to bring a man around to an idea by an indirect route. One must seize on the wing a multitude of things which would demand a detailed examination, and pass from one subject to another with a rapidity of which I had no conception. Consequently I am not absolutely certain that I shall not go mad before returning to France. One's brain is here in a continual fermentation. . . .'

† Ernest de Blosseville, a Versailles acquaintance, and author in that very year of a history of penal colonies in Australia. Though Blosseville was in favour of penal colonies, Tocqueville and Beaumont were becoming more and more dubious of that solution. See below, and *Du Syst. Pén.*, p.3.

'You have acquired cognizance of these different things, my dear papa, through reflection and necessity. You have seen the administration acting in great matters and in small, and I think that the subject is familiar enough to you for you to be able, without putting yourself to any inconvenience, to furnish me with the documents which I need.

'I should like to know what exists with us in the way of internal administration, what are first of all the general principles accepted in this field; secondly, what are the applications, that is to say, what portions of independence remain to the *commune*, what it may and may not do, what are the powers of the councils of the *arrondissement* and of the department, finally, just what the prefect and the central government take a hand in. If you could, my dear papa, decompose for me this word *centralization*, you would render me an immense service, not only at the present moment, but for the future.

'There, as you see, is an altogether positive labour. If you could join to it in a second part a few political observations, the utility of the whole would be very much greater. Thus, I would know at what point, in your opinion, the action of the central government should stop, what kind of independence one may give to the *communes*, what is the usefulness of the administrative courts, what power may without danger be accorded to the departmental assemblies.

'The evil is that if you undertake this little labour, you mustn't, my dear papa, delay sending it to me, for the time passes and our sojourn here is limited. . . '

*
*    *

Meanwhile, of course, certain eminent Bostonians had already been approached. And they had responded gallantly. Beaumont, for example, had drafted a long list of questions which he and Tocqueville proposed to send to the Attorneys-General of the several States; and Senator Gray had immediately corrected it for mistakes in English. A certain Mr. Nathan Hale, editor of one of the greatest Massachusetts newspapers, the *Boston Daily Advertiser*, had promised to write them an essay [or send them some documents?] on the press in the United States. And the distinguished lawyer and author, William Sullivan, had said that he would be only too glad to put his knowledge and experience at their disposal.[9] So Tocqueville and Beaumont now drafted a series of twenty-seven precise and searching questions, covering all branches of the administration of justice from the powers of the Attorneys-General to the use of the Jury, for Mr. Sullivan to answer in writing at his earliest convenience.*

The man for whom they reserved their chief appeal, however, was Jared Sparks. No Bostonian of their acquaintance seemed to have made such a profound study of the political institutions of New England; and certainly no one possessed a greater grasp of the entire subject of township government, or could so lucidly explain its character and practical operation. Now, as Tocqueville pointed out to his French friends, it was precisely the local institutions of the New Englanders that were coming to absorb his attention. For in the decentralization first developed in Massachusetts must lie the whole secret of the success of American 'democracy.' Certainly, there was visible in New York and Massachusetts no faintest trace of an all-powerful, all-providing centralized administration such as had proved the undoing of the French colony in Canada. Yet sovereignty and administration had to exist somewhere. The answer was obvious. 'The State of Massachusetts is a union of small republics,' Josiah Quincy had said.

So Tocqueville and Beaumont now drew up a long list of queries which they wished Mr. Sparks to consider and to answer. 'Are there any general principles regulating the relations of the towns with their members, of the towns with each other, and of the towns with the state?' they first wanted to know. What, in the second place, were the powers exercised by each township, and what limitations were placed on its competence? This subject was treated in ten specific questions. Next, five questions were so phrased as to bring out whatever defects such a system of local self-government might possess. 'Have you sometimes in town affairs,' they asked, 'felt the need or the usefulness of a central administration, of what we call centralization? Haven't you remarked that this independence of the [constituent] parts injured the harmony of the whole, prevented uniformity in the state, and interfered with national enterprises? In a word, what is the bad side of your system, for the best systems have one?' Finally, there were sections dealing with the functions—such as those of education and road main-

---

* Convinced that the permanence of American political institutions depended upon the spread of popular education, William Sullivan (1774–1839) had just written the first two of his notable 'class books' (*The Political Class Book*, 1831; *The Moral Class Book*, 1831). He was conceded by all to be cheerful, sensible and of great intelligence, though his writing was perhaps too simple and lucid for the fashion of the day. Before they left, he sent Tocqueville and Beaumont a copy of the address that he had made before the Suffolk Bar on Boston as the cradle of statesmen.

tenance—that by their very nature seemed to require a centralized, uniform administration. In all, Tocqueville and Beaumont had thirty-three questions to ask of Mr. Sparks; and later on they thought of some more to send him through the mail.

The two hopeful young Frenchmen handed their list to Mr. Sparks on the first of October, and gave him an address in Washington to which he could forward his reply.

The result was more gratifying than they had any right to expect. The erudite and obliging historian wrote them an elaborate paper, which he entitled: *On the Government of Towns in Massachusetts.*

*

\* \*

Tocqueville and Beaumont did not receive the essays, written by Chabrol, Blosseville, and Hervé de Tocqueville in answer to their questions about the government of France, until well on in the following December or January. And Mr. Sparks' paper did not reach them until they were about to sail for home in February 1832. Moreover, all four of these documents were of such weighty and solid workmanship as to demand the most thoughtful and extended study for their proper digestion and assimilation. Necessarily also their length precludes their reproduction here.[10]

Before passing on to the story of Tocqueville's and Beaumont's last days in Boston, however, a word or two on the individual character of these essays, and on the results thus obtained by the overburdened young investigators, will not be out of place.

It is to be noticed, first of all, that the materials contributed by their friends included both detailed statements and some general remarks. In other words, Tocqueville and Beaumont acquired knowledge of both fact and theory. For both France and New England they were given the specific information that would make clear the daily operation of the political institutions described, and the philosophy that justified and explained the type of government employed. If Tocqueville, as a political philosopher, was more interested in the basic ideas, the practice was none the less important to know. Only through the factual could he safely approach the general principles involved.

Now it seemed that in both fields the institutions of France and of New England were in the most violent contrast. This was the second point that could not escape remark. The able Hervé de Tocqueville had begun his really notable survey, or *Glance at the Administration of France*, for example, by the following striking generalization:

'It is fundamental (*de principe*) in France that the King is the chief of the administration, and its director.

'This administration is divided into two portions, that which deliberates and that which executes. The latter is at the choice of the King; the acts of the former are not valid until after having received his approbation or that of his delegates.

'The Royalty exercises a general tutelage over all the branches of the administration. It names, it directs, it approves, it prevents. . . .'

Again, the loyal prefect of Charles X insisted: 'Without the tutelage exercised by the King over the administration there would be no more monarchy. . . . This high power is necessary to maintain unity and to prevent each administrative fraction from abusing its independence. Without it the intimate union of all the parts of the State would soon be replaced . . . [by a mass?] of small republics.'

And later on he summed up the case in the phrase: 'In a Monarchy surrounded by powerful and jealous States, a centre of unity is necessary.'

So much for the faith in which Tocqueville had been born. But when he turned to Sparks' *Observations on the Government of Towns in Massachusetts*, the young political scientist read:

'In considering this subject, it is necessary to keep in mind the mode in which the country was originally settled. The first establishment was at Plymouth, and consisted of only one hundred and one persons, surrounded by a vast wilderness, uninhabited except by a few savages. As far as the rights and forms of government were concerned, the new settlers, when they landed, were in a state of nature.* For mutual convenience and security they agreed on a system of social and political regulations, which had the effect of laws. This was the simplest form of a republic. Each person had a voice in the several councils, and all rules and decisions were established by a majority of voices. As circumstances required it they adopted new regulations, or laws, but always upon the same principles, that is, the equal rights of each individual, and the power of a majority to control the whole. The people chose a governor, and other suitable officers for administering the government, to whom limited powers were granted and whose duties were prescribed by the people themselves.

* See footnote below.

'Within a few years other settlements were established by new emigrants from England, and being remote from the original settlement at Plymouth, and from each other, they adopted similar modes of government, acting, for all essential purposes, as independent republics, after the model and under the general guidance of the earliest establishment. In this way they soon acquired the knowledge and habits of local government, and from these habits, thus early rooted, and never abandoned, has been derived the present municipal system of New England.

'As the settlements increased in numbers it was convenient for them to unite under some form of government, in order to protect themselves from the Indians, and for other advantages common to all parties. There commenced the system of representation in proportion to the numbers of the people, and by a free suffrage in elections, which is in fact the basis and the continuing support of all the political institutions. When the settlements, or towns as we may now call them, first agreed to this union, they had individually, in their own hands, the power which pertains to a social or political compact. Thence it is obvious that they would give up no more than was essential to the general interests without divesting themselves of their primitive rights or deranging their local forms of government already established. There again is another principle of the American institutions, which is, that a superior government exercises such powers only as are delegated to it by an inferior, or, in other words, by the people. . . .'

Again Sparks wrote: 'The laws of the state on municipal subjects have grown out of the early habits and previous usages of the towns, and by producing uniformity they now consolidate them into one political body, at the same time that they allow all the liberty requisite for local self-government. The laws are made by representatives sent from the towns. The representatives are accustomed to act constantly as political agents in managing town affairs, and from the habit of acting upon the same principles, though living in different parts of the state, they come together with similar views and are qualified to judge of the nature, utility and consequences of any laws designed to affect the whole. Hence the groundwork of the state government is in the towns, and each town is in some sort an epitome of the state. To abridge their liberties, or restrain their power of political action, would be to undermine and destroy the whole fabric. . . .'

In short, France and America stood at opposite poles. There was no other interpretation. In the one (as with the Romans) the state was supreme; in the other, the people. In France, the Monarchy was the rightful and necessary source and organ of sovereignty; in New England, the theories of Rousseau were law, and government was only a compact between sovereign individuals.*

In each country, moreover, these so contrasting theories were put into daily and successful practice. The merest glance at the detailed analyses provided in the four essays sent him by his friends showed Tocqueville that much. For example: In New England, according to Sparks, the towns, being corporate bodies, could 'buy and sell, contract loans, and maintain actions in a court of justice.' In France, such actions were considered the privilege of the government, and generally were allowed only after careful examination and specific permission given by the authorities higher up. In New England again, the counties and the towns took care of the roads, and private companies were even allowed by the legislature to establish turnpikes and levy tolls. In France, on the other hand, nothing could be done except with the approval and often through the agency of the governmental engineers. In the one country, in short, the interests of the people were considered to be known only to the King; in the other, the welfare of each locality was its own, daily concern.

One further contrast now clamoured for recognition. It concerned the attitude of the governed, under each system. Loyal as they were to their own fatherland, Tocqueville's French correspondents all had criticisms to make of the way their highly centralized administration worked in practice. It tried to do too much, interfered too much in the petty domestic concerns of the *commune*. Above all, the necessity of securing authorization from the Ministry of the Interior for each small act, for each needed improvement, resulted in long, 'desolating'

---

* Professor Charles McLean Andrews has shrewdly pointed out that Sparks' memoir was in reality a skilful combination of two old but persistent theories, neither of which is altogether acceptable to historians to-day: (1) The theory of natural liberty and the social compact; and (2) the theory of the town as the source of sovereignty and residuary legatee of political power. (The American Academy of Political and Social Science, *Annals*, May 1899, pp.111–112.)

It must be recognized that Tocqueville's exaggerated opinion of the importance of the New England town rested on a wider foundation than the views of one counsellor (see above, p.397; below, p.411). Yet Professor Andrews makes a telling comment when he reveals Sparks entertaining a philosophy of government in complete sympathy with the States' Rights or compact theory of the Constitution, though the scene was Boston, stronghold of Federalist thought, and the time the epoch of Webster's great speech, and of his ascendancy.

delays. 'Thence,' wrote Hervé de Tocqueville, 'the constantly repeated recriminations against *une fatiguante centralisation.*'

Mr. Sparks, on the other hand, like almost all the Americans whom Tocqueville and Beaumont had ever met, was content with his country's institutions, proud even with the pride of one who is conscious of some superiority. Every word of his persuasive essay breathed out a calm and confident satisfaction. The contrast was complete.

What, then, were to be Tocqueville's conclusions? Here perhaps the travelling inquisitor would himself have found it hard to specify. It would be said later that 'some of the most authentic information which Tocqueville obtained upon the subject of town government in New England came from that pioneer of American institutional history, Jared Sparks.' [11] And this was, in large measure, what happened. To be exact, for his description of the towns, the town meetings, and selectmen, for his analysis of the activities and spheres of action of this smallest governmental unit in New England, the future commentator was in the end to draw directly from three principal sources: the first a collection of the Laws of Massachusetts (given him in all probability by Senator Gray); the second a volume called the *Town Officer* (which Josiah Quincy had put into his hands and which enumerated the officers of the towns and their legal duties); and the third, Sparks' essay *On the Government of Towns in Massachusetts.*

But the influence of Sparks' thought on the young Frenchmen went beyond a mere supplying of information. It will not escape the reader of *De la Démocratie en Amérique* that for his description of representative local institutions Tocqueville selected the New England State of Massachusetts. And the township organization in this State he portrayed with an approval strongly reminiscent of his Boston mentor. It would, perhaps, be too much to say that Tocqueville idealized the local institutions that Sparks told him of during his visit (for it must be remarked that Tocqueville had had no personal experience of such institutions, had never, for example, attended a town meeting). But throughout his chapter on American local self-government he kept calling his countrymen's attention to the good effects that from these institutions flowed.*

Finally, his book was designed to suggest to the French reader how France might benefit by the American example. Of course, it was too much to hope that a France surrounded by hostile nations would ever

---

* See below, chs. LV, LVI, LVIII; and *Dém. en Am.*, I, ch.5.

be able to dispense with a strong central government. In that he agreed thoroughly with Chabrol, Blosseville, his father, and the great majority of his fellow-countrymen. But centralization, Tocqueville pointed out, was of two kinds: legal (*gouvernemental*), and administrative. Now the first was an excellent and necessary thing. A uniform code of laws, made, revised, and developed by a central legislature, and bearing equally on all parts of the nation, was infinitely to be desired. So, too, was the control of national institutions by the national government. In other words, all the common interests belonged of right within the sphere of action of the State.

On the other hand, each *commune* should be encouraged to look after its own interests, choose its own officers, make its own regulations. And, whenever possible, the State should act only through such agents, rather than through its own. In America, Tocqueville pointed out, the town loaned its agents to the government; the town tax collector, for example, gathered the State taxes as well. But in France, the central government loaned its agents to the *commune*, and the State collector took in the communal dues. That was what he called *administrative* centralization. It was unnecessary, it fostered a bureaucracy, it stifled the slightest spirit of local self-reliance, it deprived the people of a chance to share in a little power and responsibility, it left them hardly even an interest in their own development. At all costs, then, the kind of decentralization represented by flourishing, active, locally controlled communal governments must be fostered in France. They might seem crude; undoubtedly the tiny governments would betray incoherence, would be guilty of mistakes. But 'the *political* advantages which the Americans draw from decentralization would nevertheless make me prefer it to the contrary system.

'Of what importance is it to me, after all, that there is an authority which is always afoot, which sees that all my pleasures may be quietly enjoyed, which flies before my feet to ward off all dangers, without my even bothering to think about them; [of what importance is all that to me] if that authority, at the same time that it removes the smallest thorns from my path, is absolute mistress of my liberty and my life; if it monopolizes action and existence to such a degree that all about it must languish when it languishes, that all sleep when it sleeps, that all perish if it dies? . . .'[12]

'I have visited the two nations which in the highest degree have developed the system of provincial liberties,' Tocqueville the commentator was to proclaim in his magnificent conclusion,[13] 'and I have listened to the voices of the parties dividing those nations.

'In America, I found some men who aspired, secretly, to destroy the "democratic" institutions of their country. In England, I found others noisily attacking the aristocracy. Among them I have not encountered a single person who does not regard provincial liberty as a great good.

'I have seen, in these two countries, the ills of state imputed to an infinity of diverse causes, but never to communal liberty.

'I have heard the citizens attribute the greatness or prosperity of their country to a multitude of reasons, but I heard them *all* place in the front line and rank at the head of all the other advantages local liberty.

'Shall I believe that men, naturally so divided that they agree neither on religious doctrines nor political theories, fall into accord on a single fact—the very one they can judge best, since it passes each day under their eyes—and [believe also] that this conviction is erroneous?

'It's only the peoples possessing few or no local liberties who deny their usefulness: which is to say that those only who do not know the institution speak ill of it.'

\*

\*    \*

All this, however, was still far in the future as Tocqueville and Beaumont made out their list of questions for Jared Sparks, and reflected on what he had told them already.

'The two great social principles which appear to me to regulate American society, and to which one must always return to discover the reason for all the laws and habits which govern it,' wrote Tocqueville on the thirteenth of September,[14] 'are these:

'1. The majority may err in some particulars, but on the whole it is always right, and there is no moral force superior to it.

'2. Each particular individual, every society, town, or nation, is the only legal judge of its own interest, and so long as it does not injure the interest of another, no one has the right to intervene.

'I think,' added Tocqueville in a postscript for his own more mature reflections, 'I think that this note must never be lost sight of.'

A second reflection came to him. 'A government entirely *démocratique* is a machine so dangerous,' he noted, 'that *even in America* they have been obliged to take a number of precautions against the errors

and the passions of *démocratie*. The institution of two Chambers, the
veto of the governors, and above all the institution of judges' were the
safeguards that Mr. Sparks had mentioned.

'Another principle of American society that one must never lose
sight of:

'Each individual being the most competent judge of his own interest, society must not push too far its solicitude for him, for fear that
he will end by counting on society and will load it thus with a task
which it is incapable of performing.

'It's by virtue of this principle that the Americans claim that without judicial police they succeed in discovering more criminals than we,
because when a crime is committed, all the population takes a part in
uncovering and pointing out the authors, a task that an administration
could never accomplish in the same way.

'But the happy mean in these theories is difficult to seize.

'In America, free habits have created free political institutions, in
France it's for free political institutions to create the habits. There
is the goal at which we must aim, but without forgetting the starting
point.'

*
*  *

The thought of 'free political institutions' still running in their
heads, Tocqueville and Beaumont encountered their merchant friend,
Joseph Coolidge Jr. The opportunity was too good a one to be missed,
so the two friends promptly sounded him out on the subject of one
of those institutions: the American jury system.

In Massachusetts, he told them, all those who voted at elections could
sit on juries. Now, the electoral qualification being very low, this meant
that practically the entire male population was called to do jury duty.

'Do you remark that there are inconveniences in thus taking jurors
from all classes?' Tocqueville and Beaumont asked.[15]

'*A*. No. But our people is the most enlightened existing in the world.

'*Q*. Is the burden of jury duty heavy?

'*A*. No. Your name is very rarely drawn.

'*Q*. You submit to it easily?

'*A*. Yes. It is regarded, however, as very disagreeable to be on a jury.

'*Q*. Do the jurors receive indemnity?

'*A*. Yes, they receive a light indemnity.

'*Q*. Do you think that the rule of unanimity is a good one?

'*A*. I am not prepared to answer that question. However, I am tempted to believe it bad, and what makes me think so is that it often happens that the jurors are unable to agree, and then recourse has to be had to others.' *

Tocqueville and Beaumont next switched the conversation to a subject that was once more beginning to interest them deeply.

'No,' said Mr. Coolidge. 'We are not afraid of Catholicism in the United States because we are persuaded that here it will modify itself so that it will have no influence on our political *mœurs*. Here we have remarked that the Catholics always voted with the most democratic party. It is true that they are the poorest. Baltimore, where they dominate, is the most democratic in the Union. Charles Carroll is Catholic.

'*Q*. Do you sometimes feel the absence of government?

'*A*. No. Far from that, we are only occupied by the fear of seeing it taking a hand in things where its action is not indispensable.'

From several points of view this seemed an unsatisfactory conversation. Like so many others, it opened whole fields of exploration, only to abandon them immediately. And Tocqueville and Beaumont thought they knew a better way. At least there could be no harm in asking Mr. Coolidge whether he would consider a series of carefully prepared questions and send them the answers later on.

The suggestion was well received. Mr. Coolidge seemed willing, even anxious, to lend them whatever aid was within the power of a practical man of affairs; and Tocqueville and Beaumont at once set to work. They made out a set of forty-two questions, beginning with a number on the administration of justice and the jury system, and passing on to the character of the press, the place of religion, the influence of education on society, the powers of the Federal Government, and the character and effects of elections. Later they added five more on the keeping of vital statistics and the laws of divorce.

This was an odd assortment of questions to throw at an unassuming China merchant. But if Mr. Coolidge was a little nonplussed by the number and variety of the problems presented for his decision, he set doggedly to work. And a few months later Tocqueville and Beaumont had his answers.

---

* Tocqueville was later to add a Note: 'From this conversation result two facts of great consequence. *The first* that the number of jurors is immense. *The second* that their functions are not gratuitous.'

The two French Commissioners found them modest yet comprehensive: simple, reasonable, and straightforward. Altogether, they provided the investigation with a good deal of valuable information; and they certainly presented Mr. Coolidge in an attractive light. For the student of Tocqueville's later opinions, one or two are particularly curious and interesting:

'22. The characters of persons who are candidates for public office are often violently and slanderously assailed in the newspapers,' Mr. Coolidge wrote. Tocqueville and Beaumont had evidently been puzzled to account for the virulence of some of the American press. 'Editors of newspapers also are very much in the habit of abusing one another for the amusement of the public. An Editor generally seems to mind no more being called hard names (an office-hunter, scoundrel, slanderer, or liar) than an actor on the stage regards similar abuse from one of the characters in the play—Private persons are very rarely attacked in the papers.'

'28. I believe that the foundation of our political institutions rests upon the virtue of the people. This virtue cannot be maintained without religion.'

'30. In general the better classes of Protestants are glad to have Catholic Priests here to take care of the lower class of Irish, thinking the Catholic far better than no religion. . . .'

'31. . . . I certainly do not consider the Catholic religion as particularly favorable to republican institutions, and yet I believe a very large part of the people of this country might become Catholics without endangering our present forms of government. . . .'

'34. I believe that the influence of general education is always beneficial to society. The tendency of cultivating the mind is usually to improve the morals. And this tendency I think is most strong in regard to the moderate instruction which alone can be given to the lower classes. If I had leisure I could demonstrate this opinion by an appeal to facts. That popular instruction is less beneficial without religion, I admit. But that any class of the people are the better for being left destitute of education, I cannot believe.'

'35. To say that the Government is not seen at all in the United States is a pardonable hyperbole. It interferes perhaps less frequently and less offensively with individuals than most other governments. It is not supported by an armed force. It is supported by the good will of the people. . . .'

# XXXI

## MR. ADAMS AND DR. CHANNING

On the evening of the first of October, there was given by one of the notables of Boston, Alexander Everett the diplomat, a small but distinguished dinner. His brother Edward Everett made a note of the fact in his skeleton diary;[1] so the names of some of the guests were preserved for posterity. 'I dined to-day with Alexander,' he jotted in his characteristically colourless fashion. '—Mr. Adams, Sir James Colleton, & Messrs. Tocqueville & Beaumont, the French Commissioners for visiting prisons, were present. . . .'

At last, then, the two friends were face to face with a President— or, rather, an ex-President—of the United States. What their feelings had been on receiving the invitation they did not specify. But it must almost have seemed to the visitors as if they had been asked to meet Royalty; for Mr. Adams occupied a position among Americans superficially not so different from that of Charles X in France. Yet apparently the honour was not all theirs. At least Alexander Everett acted as if he thought John Quincy Adams would be interested in them, just as they were in him. And when they came to go in to dinner, Tocqueville found himself placed, not merely within sight and hearing, but actually in the seat of honour immediately at the side of this illustrious personage.

Apparently Tocqueville and Beaumont had taken pains to arrive promptly at Alexander Everett's. At all events, they were on hand when the former President made his entry. 'He was received with much politeness, like a distinguished guest, but that was all,' recorded the astonished Tocqueville. 'The majority of the company called him *Sir*. A few gave him, by courtesy, the name of *President*.'

The French Commissioners studied the important guest with curiosity. 'Mr. Adams is a man of 62 years, who appears still in possession

of all his mental and bodily vigour,' Tocqueville later noted in his diary.*
'He speaks French with facility and elegance. I was placed beside him
at table, and . . .'

Naturally, with such an arrangement, but one thing could happen.
And in a moment or two the cool-minded New Englander found himself listening intently to what the dark young man at his side was saying. In a rush of French, a volley of remarks—all of the most serious
and arresting character—were being addressed to him. Apparently
the commissioner of the Government of France was intent on sounding
to the very bottom of American politics and civilization.

'I expressed to him the astonishment I felt on seeing how far the
American people get on without government,' Tocqueville afterwards
began his résumé of the conversation. 'Among other things I touched
on the right that all opinions had to send their representatives to a place
designated in advance, and to unite them in a Convention.'

Tocqueville was evidently thinking of the two impending Conventions, which everybody was discussing. It seemed that the enemies of
the protective tariff were shortly to meet in Philadelphia, in a proposed
Free Trade Convention; while the Friends of Domestic Industry
held their own Convention simultaneously in New York. The famous
ex-secretary Albert Gallatin was to preside over the first; and Edward Everett himself was to speak at the second.

'Mr. Adams,' according to Tocqueville, 'replied: The use of these
conventions dates only from five or six years. To-day we have them
for every kind of thing. But to express my opinion frankly to you, I
think that these assemblies are dangerous, they usurp the place of
political bodies and may end by absolutely thwarting their action.

'We discussed the character of Americans in general, and he said:
There are two facts which have a great influence on our character: in
the north, the religious and political doctrines of the first founders of
New England; in the south, slavery.

'Do you regard slavery, I said to him, as a great evil (*plaie*) for the
United States?

'Yes, unquestionably, he answered, it's in slavery that are to be found
almost all the embarrassments of the present and the fears of the future.

'*Q*. Are the inhabitants of the south aware of this state of things?

* 'Mr. Adams has just been named to Congress. Many people are astonished that he
has accepted. He is the first President to have re-entered public affairs.' Toc.
diary note (Non-Alph.II).

'*A.* Yes, at the bottom of their hearts. But it's a truth, concern over which they are not aware that they show. Slavery has modified the whole state of society in the south, added Mr. Adams. There the whites form a class which has all the ideas, all the passions, all the prejudices of an aristocracy, but don't deceive yourself. Nowhere is equality among the whites greater than in the south. Here we have a great equality before the law, but it ceases absolutely in the habits of life. There are upper classes and working classes. Every white man in the south is a being equally privileged, whose destiny is to make the negroes work without working himself. We can't conceive how far the idea that work is dishonourable has entered the spirit of the Americans of the south. No enterprise in which negroes cannot serve as the inferior agents can succeed in that part of the Union. All those who do a large trade at Charleston and in the cities have come from New England. I remember that a representative from the south being at my table in Washington could not keep from expressing his astonishment at seeing white domestics occupied in serving us. He said to Mr[s.] Adams, I find it a degradation of the human race to use whites for domestics. When one of them comes to change my plate, I am always tempted to offer him my place at table. From this laziness in which the southern whites live great differences in character result. They devote themselves to bodily exercise, to hunting, to racing; they are vigorously constituted, brave, full of honour; what is called the point of honour is more delicate there than anywhere else; duels are frequent.

'Do you think that it is really impossible to get on without the blacks in the south? said I.

'I am convinced of the contrary, returned Mr. Adams. The Europeans work in Greece and in Sicily, why should they not in Virginia and the Carolinas? It's no hotter there.

'*Q.* Is the number of slaves increasing?

'*A.* It is diminishing in all the states to the east of Delaware, because there they cultivate wheat and tobacco, cultures for which the negroes are rather a charge than useful. Therefore one exports them thence to the provinces where cotton and sugar are cultivated. In those of the western States where they have been introduced, they remain in very small numbers. I know nothing more insolent than a black, added Mr. Adams, when he is not speaking to his master and is not afraid of being beaten. It is not even very rare to see negroes treat their masters very ill when they have to do with a weak man. The negresses especially make frequent abuse of the kindnesses of their mistresses. They know that it isn't customary to inflict bodily punishments on them.'

Here was Tocqueville's opportunity to bring up Nullification, and the future of the Union. But another question was in the front of his mind.

'We spoke of religion, which Mr. Adams appeared to regard as one of the most . . . guarantees of American society. I asked him if he thought that the religious principle was decaying in the United States.

'If one compares the present state with that of a century ago, yes, answered he. But if you compare what exists to-day with what existed forty years ago, I believe that religion has gained among us instead of losing. Forty years ago the philosophy of Voltaire in France, the school of Hume in England, had unsettled all the beliefs of Europe. The repercussions made themselves strongly felt in America. Since then the crimes of the French Revolution have made a strong impression on us; there has been a reaction of feeling, and this impulse still makes itself felt.

'Remark however, said I, the road that beliefs have travelled since leaving Catholicism. Do you not think that their march continues, and do you not see in the Unitarianism of this country the last link that separates Christianity from natural religion?

'Mr. Adams assured me that such was his opinion. He added: On the other hand, all the Unitarians of Boston loudly disclaim this consequence of their doctrine, and maintain themselves with firmness in the outpost that they occupy.

'Mr. Adams seemed to think that one of the [greatest] guarantees of order and interior tranquillity in the United States was the movement of the population westward. Still many generations will pass, added he, before we find ourselves too crowded.'

So, at long last, the ageing statesman and the inexperienced philosopher had reached the essential question: the destiny of North America. The safety that lay in an unsettled frontier: that was by now a familiar idea. But Tocqueville had been hearing rumours of a sectional dispute that might bring an immediate menace:

'I then spoke to him of nearer dangers to the Union,' he wrote, 'and of the causes which might bring about its dissolution.' Could Tocqueville but have known, it was only about a fortnight before that the anxious ex-President had written at length on the very subject of

Nullification to both John C. Calhoun and their host Alexander Everett.[2] But this evening he apparently felt too depressed to want to say anything about it to a stranger. 'Mr. Adams,' concluded Tocqueville, 'did not answer, but it was easy to see that on this point he had no more confidence than I in the future.'

*

* *

'2 October 1831. To-day I went to see Mr. Channing, the most celebrated preacher and most remarkable author of the present time in America (in the serious style),' Tocqueville recorded in one of his diaries. It was their last evening in Boston; but they could not forego the opportunity of meeting the famous Unitarian divine. Their friend Joseph Tuckerman had secured the appointment for them.[3]

'Mr. Channing,' Tocqueville noted, 'is a small man, who has the air of being exhausted by work. His eyes, however, are full of fire, his manners warm-hearted. He has one of the most penetrating voices that I know. He received us with great kindness, and we enjoyed a long conversation, of which here are some parts:

'We spoke to him of how little religion existed in France, and he replied: I take the liveliest and most constant interest in France; I believe that to her destiny is joined the destiny of all Europe. You exercise an immense moral influence round about you, and all the nations of the continent will follow you in the path you take. You have in your hands the power for good and for ill in a higher degree than any people that has ever existed. I am unable to believe that we must despair of seeing France religious; everything in your history gives witness that you are a religious people. And besides! I think that religion is a need so pressing for the heart of man that it is against the nature of things for a great people to remain irreligious. I hope on the contrary that you will make the human species take a new step toward perfectibility, and that you will not, like the English, stop half way. They have stayed in the Protestantism of the 17th century; I am confident that France is called to the highest destinies, and will find a religious form still more pure.'

Here was Dr. Channing in a characteristic mood.* Clearly, he would

---

* William Ellery Channing, 1780–1842, had the character of an ascetic and a mystic, eating little and subjecting himself to great hardships and fatigue. He had been acknowledged leader of the Unitarians since his famous discourse (Baltimore, 1819) at the ordination of Jared Sparks; and was interested in Europe as well as in philanthropy.

have continued in the same vein for hours, had not Tocqueville and Beaumont finally taken the bit in their teeth. 'I give myself full rein in the examination of religious questions,' Beaumont later confessed to his family.[4] 'I live only with Presbyterians, Methodists, Unitarians, etc. I break lances with them, in a way to persuade them that I am a warm Catholic; the truth is that I have never felt myself so attached to my religion as since the time that I have seen the aberrations of the other cults. . . .'

At this point Beaumont and Tocqueville elected to discuss some of the most obvious objections to Dr. Channing's own faith. 'We spoke to Mr. Channing of Unitarianism,' Tocqueville's account pursued, 'and we told him that many people belonging to other Protestant sects had spoken to us of it with disfavour.

'The question between us, said Mr. Channing, is whether the 17th century can return, or whether it is past without return. They opened the road, and have the pretension to stop precisely at the point where the first innovator himself stopped. We, we claim to go ahead, we maintain that if human reason is steadily perfecting itself, what it believed in a century still gross and corrupted cannot altogether suit the enlightened century in which we live.

'But are you not afraid, I said to him frankly, that by virtue of purifying Christianism you will end by making the substance disappear? I am frightened, I confess, at the distance that the human spirit has travelled since Catholicism; I am afraid that it will finally arrive at natural religion.

'I think that such a result, returned Mr. Channing, is little to be feared. The human spirit has need of a positive religion, and why should it ever abandon the Christian religion? Its proofs fear nothing from the most serious examination of reason.

'Permit me an objection, said I. It applies not only to Unitarianism but to all the Protestant sects, and even has a great bearing on the political world: Do you not think that human nature is so constituted that, whatever the improvements in education and the state of society, there will always be found a great mass of men who are incapable from the nature of their position of setting their reason to work on theoretical and abstract questions, and who, if they do not have a dogmatic faith, will not exactly believe in anything?

'Mr. Channing replied: The objection that you have just made is in fact the most serious of all those that can be raised against the principle of Protestantism. I do not believe, however, that it is without answer. 1. In the first place, I think that for every man who has an upright heart, religious questions are not as difficult as you seem to believe, and that God has put their solution within the reach of every man. 2. Secondly, it seems to me that Catholicism does not remove the difficulty; I admit that once one has admitted the dogma of the infallibility of the Church, the rest becomes easy, but to admit this first point, you have to make an appeal to reason. (This argument appears to me more specious than solid; but as we had but a limited time, I envisaged the question from another angle and resumed:)

'It seems to me that Catholicism had established the government of the skilful or aristocracy in Religion, and that you have introduced Democracy. Now, I confess to you, the possibility of governing religious society, like political society, by the means of *Démocratie* does not seem to me yet proven by experience.

'Mr. Channing replied: I think that you mustn't push the comparison between the two societies too far. For my part, I believe every man in a position to understand religious truths, and I don't believe every man able to understand political questions. When I see submitted to the judgment of the people the question of the tariff, for example, dividing as it does the greatest economists, it seems to me that they would do as well to take for judge my son over there (pointing to a child of ten). No. I cannot believe that civil society is made to be guided directly by the always comparatively ignorant masses; I think that we go too far.'

\*

\*     \*

This last was strong language for an American—and not at all the common belief. That very day, to illustrate the point, the French commissioners had discussed the subject with their southern friend, Mr. Clay. 'Mr. Clay,' noted Tocqueville in the same diary, 'is a most ardent Presbyterian. He pled with special warmth the cause of *Démocratie* and religion. We are in a special and very favourable position, I admit, said he, and yet I do not despair of all the enlightened nations following our example.

'What, said I, you believe that a time will come when the great nations of Europe will be able to adopt your limitless *démocratie*?

'I hope so, he replied, especially those which have already arrived, or will arrive at Protestantism. I believe Protestantism indispensable to a republican people.'

That Protestantism and Republicanism almost naturally went together, Tocqueville was beginning to concede. By a happy accident, only the previous day he had been trying to define for himself the exact connection.

'There is in each religious doctrine a political doctrine which, by affinity, is joined to it,' he had ventured to affirm.[5] 'This point is incontrovertible in the sense that where nothing interferes with this tendency, it surely shows itself. But it doesn't follow that it is impossible to separate religious doctrines from their political effects. On the contrary, in all the countries of the world, material interests have been seen to operate this separation. The Catholics in Canada and the United States are the invariable supporters of the "democratic" party. Does it follow that Catholicism leads to the "democratic" spirit? No, but that the Catholics are poor, and come almost all from a country where the aristocracy is Protestant.'

*In general*, then, Tocqueville could not agree with Mr. Clay. But in the case of the United States, the Protestantism of the founders really seemed to have been a support.

'(The Protestant) Religion,' pursued Mr. Clay, 'is with us the surest guarantee of liberty. It proceeds in accord with liberty and consecrates her principles. If we should ever cease to be religious, I should regard our state as very dangerous. This opinion is shared by all the enlightened among us. We know that the emigrants to the west are somewhat leaving behind the religious habits of their fathers. This spectacle fills us with lively fear, and we are so convinced of the political danger of letting an irreligious society establish itself near us, that we spend enormous sums to aid the westerners in establishing schools and churches. Many New England families are going to settle in the valleys of the Mississippi solely to form a nucleus of religious men.

'I said to Mr. Clay: What still singularly favours the Republic with you is the fact that you form a number of small and almost entirely separated nations.

'That is even more true than you think, he replied. Not only does each State form a nation, but each town of the State is a small nation, each ward of a town is a small nation, has its particular interests, its government, its representation, its political life in a word. So long as France is in Paris, you will have the government of the populace.'

Religion—the Township organization: here were two of the fundamental reasons for the success of the American experiment. And as
they were saying good-bye to him, Jared Sparks harked back to a
third:

'The landed estates are no longer subdivided in Massachusetts,' he
reminded them. 'The oldest alone almost always has the whole property.

'And what happens to the other children? said I.

'They emigrate to the West.'

To Tocqueville this fact had 'an immense significance.'

# XXXII

## TWO MASSACHUSETTS PRISONS

There was (in the opinion of the young Frenchmen) just one serious drawback to being a prison commissioner in America: whether one would or not, one had to keep on inspecting the prisons.

And this was true even in Boston, centre of light and refinement. For almost in the shadow of the Tremont Hotel and the prosperous palaces of Beacon Hill, where under the State House dwelt in ease and luxury the most civilized society that Tocqueville and Beaumont had yet discovered in America, two grim, forbidding institutions waited. And one was a prison, and one was a reformatory.

No further away than neighbouring South Boston, behind the doors of an unobtrusive 'House of Reformation' for the young, twenty-five juvenile delinquents had recently been gathered, in seclusion to be broken and in discipline to be trained, against eventual release. Nor had the welfare of their elders, the adult criminals of the State, been in any wise overlooked. For they now had a penitentiary on the approved Auburn model. In Charlestown across the waters of Back Bay, dominating the shore and rising against the sky, the great walls of the new state prison obtruded on the view.

For two whole months, of course, Tocqueville and Beaumont had given the subject of prisons but scant attention. Ever since leaving Auburn they had been running away, fugitives—as it were—from the grim business which had brought them to the United States. In association with the gentle Chippewas of Michigan, and in the company of the cheerful, backward *habitants* of the St. Lawrence valley, they had blithely gone about more congenial explorations, in their excitement forgetting for the moment the more civilized savagery of the great New York penitentiaries, whose inmates were the true outcasts of American society. Unfortunately, that had been a vacation, and vacations could not be prolonged for ever. So, with a sigh, the two friends had at last faced the necessity of beginning their long-postponed investigation of New England prisons. They had set out for Massachusetts.

For some days after their arrival in Boston, nevertheless, neither Tocqueville nor Beaumont went near the prison at Charlestown, or the reformatory in South Boston. Probably Beaumont was too upset by the astonishing coolness of the Bostonians, too busily concerned making the first contacts so as to gain an *entrée* and a welcome into Boston society. Certainly Tocqueville was too overwhelmed by grief to care. If it had depended on him, he would gladly have put off their investigation of Massachusetts' prisons until the end of their stay.

Unfortunately, the good citizens of Boston would not hear of such a thing. Once it had penetrated their heads that two distinguished commissioners had come all the way from France to study the American penitentiary reforms, nothing would satisfy them until they knew that the intelligent young foreigners approved the fine new institutions of their State. Nor were the eminent philanthropists and men of letters alone in their curiosity. Even the ladies of Boston, Tocqueville found, were interested in the philosophy of the subject, and importunate in their questions. 'The penitentiary system being our industry, we have to exploit it, whether we will or not, every single day,' he wryly confessed.[1] 'Each man finds the means to slip us a pleasant little phrase on the prisons. At all the receptions and dinners we attend, the mistress of the house or her daughter would think herself lacking in breeding if she did not begin by speaking to us of hanged men and of whipping (*fessade*). It's only after exhausting a subject known to be agreeable to us, and on which it is supposed that we will have something to say, that any attempt is made to steer the conversation to more vulgar topics.'

No sooner had Tocqueville and Beaumont begun to go about in Boston society, therefore, than a visit to Charlestown prison became imperative. On the fourteenth of September (just two days after the parade and celebration on behalf of the Poles), the unfortunate young investigators might consequently have been observed, with great show of eagerness, bending reluctant steps toward their third great American penitentiary.

\*

\*    \*

Charlestown prison, as it had been called, was ancient; and its
new name,* new wing, new discipline and regulations, were just
two years old. But already the Auburn system had made its indelible
mark on the institution. The same fortress-like walls frowned down
upon the approaching Frenchmen. For convenience and added security,
the penitentiary even jutted out a little into Back Bay, so that on three
sides it was surrounded by water, by means of which supplies and
building materials could be landed from barges directly at the gate.

Tocqueville and Beaumont entered, and were received by the warden
and his staff. The prison, it appeared, now harboured about 250 inmates, who at night slept in the solitary cells of the Auburn cell-block,
and by day were employed in the usual variety of occupations. The
rule of silence, of course, was rigidly enforced. And contraventions
of the discipline were punished by the whip, or—as the expression
went—by stripes, the number of stripes being determined by the
seriousness of the offence.†

Naturally, the arrival of the French commissioners created something of a sensation in the Massachusetts institution. But not even so
momentous an occurrence was allowed to disturb the sombre regularity of the routine. To get an inkling of the oppressive monotony
of this prison, one had but to glance at the deputy-warden's record.
On 14 September, the day of Tocqueville and Beaumont's first visit,
Charles Lincoln Jr., the dull and somewhat illiterate official in question, wrote:

| Commissioners | Wednesday 14 Mesrs Beaumont & Topville ['cque' |
| from | written above in pencil]—commissioners from the |
| France | Govt of France, for the purpose of Inspecting the |
| | Prisons, Discipline etc etc in this Country—called |
| | at this Institution, this day. |

They were rec'd and conducted through the different Departments of the Prison by the Warden
and such information and Advice as was calculated to facilitate and aid them in the great object

---

* Massachusetts State Penitentiary.

† The reader who cares to investigate this aspect of an 1831 penitentiary has but to
go where Tocqueville and Beaumont went that September day, and look into the
prison journal, which the deputy-warden then kept, and which is still preserved
in the warden's safe. There he will find that offences were fairly frequent, but the
punishments (apparently) not extreme in cruelty. Four stripes constituted an average
whipping; and such entries as 'Charles Gardiner, punished two stripes for dis-
obedience and talking' were characteristic of the deputy-warden's journal.

of their mission was communicated to them.
A Freight of Anthracite Cole from Philladelphia
and two Freights of Stone from the Railway quarry
—came up to the wharf to discharge this day.

Arms and Equipments Inspected and found in
good Order.

Revd L. Dwight officiated in the evening services. . . .

Again, two days later, the deputy-warden wrote:

| | |
|---|---|
| Inspector | Friday Sept 16 Hon F.C.Gray and the French |
| F. Commissions | Commissioners—with two German Noblemen |
| Gent. from Germany | from Transylvania visited & Inspected the Prison |
| | in the morning & Hon. Sherman Leland in the |
| Inspector | afternoon. . . . |

And on the eighteenth the entry was:

| | |
|---|---|
| Doct Fay | Sunday, 18 Sept 1831—Revd Doct. Fay offeciated |
| F Commissioners | in the Chapel accompanied by the Chaplain— |
| | Warden, Deputy & other officers and the French |
| | Commissioners. . . . |

So Tocqueville and Beaumont had visited the prison on a Sunday,
and attended its Sabbath school. Just as before at Sing Sing, the two
Frenchmen were anxious to study the religious and moral aspect of
these American houses of penitence and reform. Hence the repetition
of this painstaking performance. What they saw here, however, impressed them much more favourably than had the neglected and sparsely
attended school at Mount Pleasant. At all events, Jared Curtis, the
prison chaplain, was deeply flattered by their remarks to him; and a
month later, in his report to the Governor of the State, he was pleased
to write: 'The Commissioners sent out by the government of France,
to examine the best constructed and best regulated Prisons in the
United States, were present one Sabbath, during the whole of the
exercises of this [Sunday] school, were very attentive to the manner
in which it was conducted, and the instructions communicated by the
teachers, and expressed themselves highly pleased with an exhibition
so novel, and at the same time so interesting, in an Institution like
this. . . .'

Meanwhile, one other feature of Charlestown penitentiary had commended itself to Tocqueville and Beaumont's particular attention:

the prison was very well run. For this the warden, William Austin, was obviously responsible. The deputy-warden might be ill educated, and some of the regulations might not be ideal, but Mr. Austin was admirably fitted for his post . . . which was, after all, the thing that really mattered. In other words, it was noticeable that the French commissioners were becoming more and more convinced of the importance of the office of warden. Whatever the powers of Prison Inspectors like Senator Gray, and however perfect the rules or diligent the other officers in the institution, an American-style penitentiary required an able man at its head. Happily, the Americans, themselves, seemed well aware of this necessity. 'It's thus that Auburn prison has had in turn as directors Mr. Elam Lynds, formerly a captin in the army, and Mr. Gershom Powers, New York State judge,' Tocqueville and Beaumont were later to point out to their government.[2] 'At Wethersfield Mr. Pillsbury, at Singsing Mr. Robert Wiltse, at Boston Mr. Austin, a former naval captain, are all men distinguished by their knowledge and their capacity. To a high rectitude and a deep sentiment of duty they associate wide experience and that perfect understanding of men so essential in their role. . . . The inferior officers, the deputy-wardens are not as distinguished, either in social position or in talent. They are generally, however, intelligent and honest. Charged with supervising the work done in the shops, they have almost always a special, skilled knowledge of the professions practised by the inmates.'

Even the deputy-warden and the keepers, then, could sometimes provide statistics and useful information. But those of Auburn, Tocqueville and Beaumont now found, had done the job so well under persistent questioning, that astonishingly little was left to be learned from an intensive study of the practices at Charlestown. On examination, everything in the Massachusetts State Penitentiary seemed familiar. And all the statistics which Tocqueville and Beaumont wanted were contained in the series of annual reports of the Inspectors. A day or two of personal investigation proved more than ample for their purposes, therefore; and if the two young Frenchmen continued to put in an occasional appearance at the penitentiary, it was more to satisfy the proprieties and to avoid offending the delicate sensibilities of their Boston friends, than in the hope of making any startling, new discoveries about the operation of an Auburn-style prison.

This was no indication, however, that their dutiful visits to Charlestown had been without their reward. For, in addition to making the acquaintance of Inspector Gray, they were by this means enabled to meet and enlist the aid of Massachusetts' most learned penologist, the Reverend Louis Dwight.

A graduate of Andover Theological Seminary, Mr. Dwight had originally intended to enter the ministry, but an accident had so weakened his lungs as to make him give up hope of preaching, so he had become an agent for the Tract and American Education Societies, and in 1825 had made a long journey through the southern and middle-Atlantic States, distributing Bibles. Curiously enough, this expedition had led the young agent directly to his grand vocation. For, having occasion to visit the prisons along his route, he had at once become conscious of the abuses prevailing in those institutions; and further investigation had inspired him with the resolve to dedicate himself to their eradication, to give his life to penitentiary reform. Immediately upon his return, therefore, he had helped found the Boston Prison Discipline Society, and ever since he had acted as its secretary, directing its activities, gathering its information, and publishing its annual *Reports*, a set of which he now presented to the French commissioners.

Tocqueville and Beaumont were delighted, for these *Reports* were really invaluable. In them was presented the history and present state, not only of the Massachusetts prisons, but of all the prisons and penitentiaries worth knowing about in the Union. Having a 'peculiar aptitude for statistical experience,' Secretary Dwight had, it seemed, spared no pains to collect all the most striking and pertinent documents on the subject of the old abuses and the new reforms. Moreover, he knew how to present his information in the most telling fashion. The Prison Discipline Society itself, Tocqueville and Beaumont were later to report, did a vast amount of good, spending thousands of dollars in the cause and paying for the services of chaplains in at least five of the penitentiaries that they knew about. But 'one of its greatest riches lies in the zeal of Mr.L.Dwight, its secretary, who is to be seen searching out with indefatigable ardour all the documents calculated to enlighten public opinion, neglecting no journey, however unpleasant, when he pursues the truth; visiting the good prisons with the bad; pointing out the vices of some, the advantages of others; indicating the gains made and those still to be made. He labours unceasingly at the work of reform.'[3]

Altogether, Tocqueville and Beaumont were well content to have made Mr. Louis Dwight's acquaintance.

*

* *

'Abuses' and 'errors' in the management of prisons were certainly less common in the United States than in France. Yet even the great penitentiaries of Sing Sing, Auburn and Charlestown were not, Tocqueville and Beaumont now knew, each without some fairly obvious defects. In addition, the Auburn penitentiary principle was itself still open to question.

The same could not be said about the reformatories for juvenile delinquents. 'No one,' the French commissioners were to write in their government report,[4] 'no one disputes the necessity of houses of refuge for young convicts.' In all times and in all countries, people have recognized the inconvenience of putting in the same place and submitting to the same regime both youthful delinquents and criminals whom the years have hardened in crime. Only in the United States, however, had a real solution for the problem been discovered. Beginning a few years before with the recognized principle of separation, the progressive American philanthropists had recently gone on to develop an institution which seemed to meet all the most crying needs of the situation. In the new reformatories—or Houses of Refuge, as they were generally called—many even of the most advanced penitentiary devices were being employed, and with marked success. As a matter of fact, the results promised and already obtained were so astonishing, that many people regarded these Houses of Refuge as the real hope of the future, the only prisons which were both preventive of crime and truly reformatory of the criminal.

Tocqueville and Beaumont had been introduced to this type of penal institution on Bloomingdale Road, just outside New York City, the preceding June; and they had studied the New York House of Refuge with the most meticulous and approving care. No sooner did they now make their first visit to the House of Reformation in South Boston, however, than they realized that here was the paragon of all reformatories.

To begin with, the House of Reformation was in charge of an extraordinarily devoted and capable man, an Episcopal minister, E.M.P.Wells by name. Francis Lieber, himself, was moved to admiration by this gentleman's wisdom and character. 'We know of no in-structer,' the young German was to write in his translation of Tocque-ville and Beaumont's Report,[5] 'We know of no instructer who has seen deeper into the human heart, and knows more thoroughly to what principles in the human soul he safely may apply, than Mr. Wells.'

In the second place, there was the man's system. Guided by his intuitive understanding of youth, and relying on his hold over their affection and esteem, Mr. Wells had devised a code of regulations and discipline for the inmates of the House of Reformation that was probably unique in the annals of penal endeavour. On arrival the visit-ing French commissioners were presented with a copy of these ex-traordinary rules, which they were to reproduce in the appendix of their Report. So interesting and of such unusual importance were these rules, that they might easily have been advanced as a sufficient study for penologists for generations to come.* As Francis Lieber remarked, however, 'the system of education and correction which Mr. Wells has established . . . is one of those subjects which cannot but be misunder-stood, if it be exhibited in a rapid sketch, because it is formed on so original a basis.' The same applied with even greater force to an inanimate body of regulations. Instead of being content with a mere summary of Mr. Wells' rules, therefore, Tocqueville and Beaumont devoted long days of study and reflection to an analysis of Houses of Refuge in general, and to a particular description of the Boston House of Reformation now under their eyes; and the results they would later include in their Report to the government of France.

In general, Tocqueville and Beaumont were to point out,[6] the Amer-ican Houses of Refuge all took two kinds of children: those that had actually been convicted of breaking the law, and those that were sent in as a precautionary measure. Inevitably, then, such an institution had to be half prison and half college. Equally, the length of each sentence had to be left indeterminate, to be decided later by the warden or directors of the establishment, according to the conduct and progress of the individual delinquent. 'In any case, even when a child leaves the house of refuge as a result of good conduct, he never ceases to remain under the eye (*sous le patronage*) of the directors until he at-tains his twentieth year.'

So much for the inhabitants and the general aims common to all

* See *Du Syst. Pén.*, pp.359–366.

the Houses of Refuge. The French commissioners had next to investigate the daily regulations and discipline.

In the establishments at New York and Philadelphia, they were to report, the children were separated in solitary cells at night, but allowed to associate and converse during the day. They were educated in a sort of primary school, and in addition worked for eight hours in the shops where each of them was being taught a trade. Furthermore, a noticeable endeavour was made to form and strengthen their characters. On admission, each child was given two very simple admonitions: '1. never lie; 2. do the best you can.' A register was kept on his conduct. And he was then put in the class indicated by his age and known morality. Apparently Mr. Hart, of the New York House of Refuge, had defined his top class at that 'in which the children do not swear, never lie, never use any obscene or unseemly expression in their conversation, and who are as zealous at school as in the shop. According to Mr. Wells of Boston, this same class is composed of those who make positive, regular, and constant efforts toward the good.'

Was there a difference in approach, indicated by this slight shift in emphasis? From the first moment Tocqueville and Beaumont were almost certain that there was. For they had at once noticed that in a number of interesting details this Boston House of Reformation was striking out for itself.

The manner in which Mr. Wells divided the time of the children seemed to indicate, for example, that he was particularly interested in the moral education of his charges. 'In this last house of refuge, only five and one half hours are devoted to work in the shops; besides four hours spent in school, more than an hour is given to religious instruction, and all the children have each day two hours and a quarter of recreation. Those hours of leisure are not those that profit the young inmates the least. Mr. Wells, the superintendent, takes part in all their games, and while their physical strength is developing by means of bodily exercise, their moral character is being formed under the influence of a superior man who, though visible to their eyes, really conceals himself in their midst, and whose authority is never greater than at the moment when he is not making it felt.'

Mr. Wells appeared also to have another means of influencing the character of his stray and delinquent children: his system of rewards and punishments. In the establishments at New York and Philadelphia—that was to say, in an ordinary House of Refuge, 'the punishments inflicted on children who break the rules are:

1. Deprivation of recreation;
2. Solitary confinement in a cell;
3. Reduction of food to bread and water;
4. And in serious cases, bodily punishments, that is to say, whipping.'

'At Boston, bodily punishments are excluded from the house of refuge; the discipline of this establishment is entirely moral, and reposes on principles which partake of the highest philosophy. . . .'

\*

\* \*

Here Tocqueville and Beaumont came to a particular analysis of the House of Reformation as it revealed itself to their fascinated eyes during their industrious visits of the latter half of September. By a curious accident, the description that they would write would one day constitute one of the few sources available to future penologists on this noble and interesting experiment.\*

'At Boston the admission of a child to the refuge is accompanied by circumstances which have appeared to us worthy of being reported: the establishment forms a miniature society, in the image of the world. To be received in its midst, it is not only necessary to know the laws and submit to them voluntarily, but also to be accepted as a member of the society by all those who already form a part of it. The reception, consequently, is preceded by a time of trial, after which the candidate is admitted or refused by majority vote. . . .

'Everything there tends to lift up the souls of the young inmates, and render them jealous of their own self-respect and of the respect of their equals: to accomplish that one pretends to treat them like men, and like members of a free society.

'We envisage this theory from the point of view of discipline, because it has seemed to us that the high opinion they give the child of his morality and social condition is not only calculated to operate his reform, but is also the cleverest way of obtaining from him an entire submission.

'It is, first of all, a principle well established in the house, that none can be punished for a fault unforeseen either by the laws of God, by

---

\* It seems to be literally true that, but for Tocqueville and Beaumont, very little would to-day be known of this idealistic adventure in humanitarianism.

the laws of the country, or by those of the establishment. That's the first of the principles in criminal matters proclaimed in the house of refuge. The regulation also contains the following:

' "As it is outside of the power of man to punish lack of respect toward the Divinity, whoever will have made himself guilty in this respect will merely be forbidden all participation in religious services, the criminal being thus abandoned to the justice of God which awaits him in the future."

'In the Boston house of refuge, the child excluded from religious service suffers, in the eyes of his comrades and in his own opinion, the most terrible of all punishments.

'Elsewhere it is written that children will not be allowed to denounce the faults, one of the other; and in the next article, it is added that none shall be punished for a fault sincerely confessed. In France we are acquainted with public establishments where betrayal is encouraged, and where it is practised by the good subjects of the house.

'There exists also at Boston a register of moral conduct, in which each one figures with his good notes and his bad; but what distinguishes this register from those to be found in the other houses of refuge is that at Boston each child himself gives the notes concerning himself. Every evening the young inmates are successively interrogated; each one is called on to judge his conduct during the day; and it's on his own declaration that the note about him is written. Experience demonstrates that he always judges himself more severely than he would be judged by others. Thus one is often forced to moderate the severity, even the injustice of the sentence.

'When difficulties arise over the moral classifications, or when young inmates have broken the discipline, then a judgment takes place. Twelve jurors taken from among the children are got together and they pronounce, either the condemnation or the absolution of the accused.

'Each time it's a question of electing among them a magistrate or a monitor, the community assembles, proceeds to the elections, and the candidate obtaining the majority of the votes is proclaimed by the presiding officer. Nothing so serious as the manner in which these electors and these jurors of ten years exercise their functions.'

Even as they looked back on what they had seen, Tocqueville and Beaumont were incredulous. Nor could one wonder. A more extraordinary sight for two French aristocrats than a prison democracy of ten-year-old children it would have been difficult to imagine.

'We will be pardoned for having entered into the workings of this system, and pointed out its smallest details,' Tocqueville and Beaumont pursued. 'Needless to say, we don't take these infant citizens seriously. But we have thought it our duty to analyse a system so remarkably original. Besides, there is in these political games, which harmonize so well with the institutions of the country, greater depth than one supposes. It may be that these childhood impressions and this precocious practice of liberty will help render the young delinquents more obedient to the laws later on. And, without bothering ourselves with this political consequence, such a system is at least powerful as a means of moral education.

'In fact, one perceives what efforts these young souls are capable of, in whom all the feelings calculated to lift them above themselves are made to vibrate.

'The discipline, however, has other weapons that it uses when the moral means we have just pointed out have been insufficient.

'The children whose conduct has been good enjoy great privileges.

'They alone participate in the elections, and alone are eligible; the vote of those belonging to the first class even counts twice: a kind of double vote of which the others can't be jealous because it depends only on themselves to obtain the same favour. The good children are in charge of the most important keys of the house. They go out from the establishment freely, and leave their places in the assemblies, without needing permission; their word is believed on all occasions, and their birthdays are celebrated. Not all the good children have all these privileges; but whoever belongs to a good class has the right to one or the other of them.

'The punishments laid on the class of bad children are:

'Depriving them of the electoral right, of eligibility; furthermore, they may not enter the superintendent's house, nor speak to him without his permission; and they are forbidden to talk to the other young inmates. Finally, if it be necessary, they lay on the delinquent a punishment that affects him materially. Perhaps he is made to wear handcuffs; perhaps his eyes are bandaged; or, finally, he is shut in a solitary cell.

'Such is the system of the house of refuge of Boston.'

The account was finished. It simply remained, then, to sum up the conclusions which personal experience and observations suggested.

'The system (*celui*) of the New-York and Philadelphia establishments, though infinitely less noteworthy, is perhaps better,' their account would read: 'not that the Boston house of refuge does not seem to us admirably directed and superior to the two others; but its success appears to us much less the work of the system itself than of the distinguished man who puts it into practice.

'We have already said that the putting together of the children at night is the serious vice of this house of refuge. The system established there reposes, furthermore, upon a high theory that might not always be understood perfectly; and its application would lead to grave embarrassments did not the superintendent find within himself immense resources to conquer them.

'At New-York and Philadelphia, on the contrary, the theory is simple. Isolation at night, classification during the day, work, schooling: everything in such an organization of affairs is easily understood and executed. It requires neither a profound genius to invent this system nor a continuous *tour de force* to maintain it.

'In summary on this point, the Boston discipline belongs to a much more elevated realm of ideas than those of New-York and Philadelphia; but its practice is difficult.

'The system of these latter establishments, founded on a simpler theory, has the merit of being within the competence of the whole world. It is possible to find superintendents suitable for the Philadelphia system; but one must not hope to encounter men like Mr. Wells.

'In spite of the very marked differences distinguishing the two systems, one of which can be put into practice only by superior individuals while the other is at the level of ordinary intelligences, let us recognize, in conclusion, that in the one case as in the other, the success of the houses of refuge depends, essentially, on the superintendent. . . .'

\*

\* \*

Yet it was undeniable, after all, that the American penitentiary principle had its virtues, no matter who applied it. Especially when it was compared to the prison practices prevailing in France. 'Everywhere they recognize the incontestable advantages of this system, which is now generally adopted in all the states of the Union,' Beaumont wrote his brother.[7] 'I haven't the slightest doubt of its superiority. The only question in France will be that of the expenses to be made to introduce it. Such establishments are easily built by a nation which has nothing else to do but concern itself with its internal administration and no great expense weighting its budget; but we are in a quite opposite position. I think that with us, we ought only to aim at successive and partial ameliorations; and when a prison is built, it will not cost more to build it in one way than another.'

After all that they had seen, this was not a very radical program. No doubt, then, that the philanthropists of Boston were somewhat disappointed at the dubious tone of the commissioners. 'They felt,' Louis Dwight was to state in the next *Report* of the Boston Prison Discipline Society, 'they felt, while here, that it was a matter of great uncertainty what would be the result of their labors.' However, the young foreigners were unquestionably an able and well-meaning pair. So before they got away, Messrs. Tocqueville and Beaumont found themselves being invited to become corresponding members of the great Society, which meant that they were to keep their friend the Secretary, Louis Dwight, informed of all their activities and successes on their return to France. The amiable commissioners promised faithfully.

Meanwhile the two friends had, in their turn, secured a promise from Francis Lieber that he would translate their Report for publication in America as soon as it came out. Their two-week prison study in Boston was over; and they began to gather up their papers and belongings preparatory to departure.

'Anyhow, we shall return rich in documents and observations,' was Beaumont's conclusion; 'we shall be incontestably *les premiers pénitenciers* of the universe: may we only on our return find some sort of a government to which to render account of our mission. . . .'

## XXXIII

## SEEN (AND NOT SEEN) IN CONNECTICUT

On the twenty-first of September Beaumont had written his family: 'We are leaving here [Boston] the twenty-ninth of this month, and going to Wethersfield near Hartford, in Connecticut.—There is there a famous prison, which we absolutely must examine; and though we should prefer to busy ourselves with something other than the Penitentiary System, we yet do not want to neglect our duty.'

Eventually, of course, the two Frenchmen found it impossible to get away from Messrs. Sparks, Coolidge, Gray, Channing, and John Quincy Adams as soon as they had expected. It was not until the third of October, therefore, that they finally turned their backs on the most civilized society that they had yet seen in America and set out to pay their first visit to the State of Connecticut.

What impression the opulent and blooming little capital of Hartford made on them, the commissioners did not say. It was not at all unlikely that they were taken about, shown the sights, told the story of the early days of the colony, introduced to the famous 'Charter Oak,' and presented to some of the first families of the town. But, if so, not a word of comment or description found its way into their manuscripts. 'It's a very small town,' was all Tocqueville would say; '. . . its greatest merit in our eyes is its location at one league from one of the most celebrated prisons of America.' And during their stay in Hartford only three people made a sufficiently strong impression on Tocqueville to receive mention in his notes.

The first was a judge, who on the fifth of October unwittingly gave confirmation to something Jared Sparks had said only a day or two before on the subject of America's westward movement. 'Last year I was in Congress,' he informed them. 'I found there 36 members originally from Connecticut, so great is our emigration. Connecticut itself has only six representatives.' *

* Toc. diary note (Non-Alph.II). The name of the judge is illegible.

The same day, a mere stripling from Massachusetts, one Robert Charles Winthrop, made an even more startling remark.* Only twenty-two years old, and with his career all ahead of him, this bearer of a distinguished Boston name already entertained quite definite opinions. 'It is sad to state but true that with us the most enlightened provinces are those which produce the most criminals,' he said to Tocqueville. 'This assertion astounded me,' the Frenchman recorded; 'it was the first time I had heard anything like that in America. Have you obtained the proof of this fact? said I.' 'It suffices to compare the state of the population with the number of crimes,' was the answer. '*Note*,' wrote Tocqueville. 'This observation merits confirmation.'†

Again, on their second day in Hartford, Tocqueville and Beaumont were taken to the hospital of the deaf-mutes to see the famous Julia Brace. This visit was inevitable. For Julia Brace was a girl singularly afflicted by fortune: She was not only deaf and dumb, but blind as well. Yet she remained cheerful, she did many of the things the other inmates did, and at times she showed extraordinary flashes of intelligence. As a result she had become the greatest curiosity or—as people then said—the most *interesting object* within many miles. '5 Oct. 1831. To-day at the hospital of the deaf-mutes at Hartford I saw a girl deaf, mute, and blind,' Tocqueville noted in his diary.[1] 'She was able to sew, however, and was threading a needle. From time to time she smiled at her thoughts. It was a singular spectacle. How can the ridiculous or the amusing appear to a spirit thus immured, what form does it take? The Director said to me that she was gentle and very easy to

* Toc. diary note (Non-Alph.II). Winthrop, who had just received an A.M. from Harvard, and his admission to the Suffolk Bar after three years of study with Daniel Webster, was to achieve prominence as Congressman, Speaker, and successor to Webster in the Senate. He would be one of the early readers of Tocqueville's book, long President of the Massachusetts Historical Society, and a member of many learned and benevolent associations, both in the United States and abroad.

† Before completing their Report, Tocqueville and Beaumont did verify this observation. At least, they satisfied themselves that crime actually had been on the increase, and most of all in Connecticut 'which, in point of education and enlightenment, occupies the first rank in the whole Union.' (*Du Syst. Pén.*, pp.390–392.) On the contrary, the State where the increase was the least noticeable was Pennsylvania, 'where the population is comparatively ignorant.' Neither Francis Lieber nor Judge Martin Welles (q.v. below) were to agree with this reading of the situation. Each would persist in his belief that ignorance was probably the greatest cause of crime, and Welles was of the opinion that the increase noted could be attributed rather to the new prison and the stricter enforcement of the law. On the whole this error would not interfere with his very high opinion of Tocqueville and Beaumont and their work: it was not surprising that some facts should have escaped them in so wide a field. *Hazard's Register*, April 1835, pp.252–255. See also *Du Syst. Pén.*, pp.114,410.

control. He added that her sense of smell was so perfected that in a pile of dirty linen she recognized her own clothes by the smell. In the same way she knew who was the man or woman who approached her.' *

Obviously, Tocqueville and Beaumont were astonished and touched. And apparently their curiosity about Hartford was now satisfied. For without further inquiry or exploration, the preoccupied prison commissioners set out for Wethersfield.†

And once again it was a new prison, on the Auburn model, that they found. By the bend in the wide Connecticut River stood the characteristic cell-block, the workshops, the chapel and warden's office, all, of course, enclosed within a high wall. As usual, the warden seemed to be an able man; and the prison inspectors drawn from among the most distinguished citizens of the State.

The French commissioners had already met, and corresponded with, the Reverend G. Barrett, the chaplain of the penitentiary; and soon they were on excellent terms with two of the prison inspectors, Samuel Howard Huntington‡ and Martin Welles,§ both graduates of Yale College in New Haven, and men of intelligence and standing in the State. Mr. Huntington, a lawyer of Hartford, at once found himself trying to explain Connecticut criminal procedure—as well as prison practice—to the distinguished visitors. And Judge Welles, who had himself been largely responsible for the location of the New Connecticut State Prison at Wethersfield, was no less delighted to be able to explain the fine points of the institution whose construction he had so carefully supervised. As a matter of fact, after a morning's inspection, he even took them home with him, to dine in the famous old Webb house where he lived, and to discuss prison matters and the care with which juries were selected in Connecticut.

* 'They have already had three or four negroes in the establishment; I was assured that no difference was discerned between their intelligence and that of the whites.'
† Their notes indicate that, while in Hartford, they must have met Gregorio Perdicaris, Professor of Greek at Washington College, and also, of course, the head of the Deaf and Dumb Asylum, Laurent Clerc. Very probably they made the acquaintance of William C. Woodbridge, the educator, as well.
    Tocqueville's method of reaching Wethersfield recalls his foresight in bringing so many shoes to America. 'As the weather is superb, we go there and return, every day, on foot, which is altogether healthy and economical.' Toc. to his father, harfort, 7 Oct. 1831, YT.
‡ Huntington, 1793–1880, came of an old Hartford family.
§ Welles, 1787–1863, had a lawyer's training, and some local experience in Whig politics. He later developed a large interest in Ohio lands, and died in a town bearing his own name.

The penitentiary itself, so far as Tocqueville and Beaumont could judge from its construction and its regulations, was much like the other Auburn-style institutions that they had visited. But in the fields of discipline and economy it presented some innovations that were worth examining.

'At Singsing, the only chastisement in use for punishing the contraventions of the established order is that of the whip,' the commissioners were to write in their Report.[2] 'The application of this disciplinary punishment is extremely frequent there, and the least fault draws it down on the delinquent. This penalty is preferred to every other for several reasons. It produces the immediate submission of the delinquent; his work is not interrupted a single instant; the chastisement is painful but does not injure the health; finally, it is believed that no other penalty would produce the same results. The same principle is admitted at Auburn, but it is singularly tempered in its execution. The penitentiaries of Boston and Baltimore, a little more severe than Auburn, are yet much less so than Singsing. Wethersfield differs from all the others by its extreme mildness.

'In this last prison they do not reject the use of corporal punishment, only its application is avoided as far as possible. Mr. Pillsbury, superintendent of the establishment, has assured us that in the last three years he has only once found himself under the necessity of inflicting stripes. It's a hardship to which resort is only had when it has been well demonstrated that all other softer ways have been tried in vain. Before using it, they try the influence of absolute solitude on the recalcitrant inmate; they shut him up in his cell day and night, without allowing him the resource of work; if we are to believe the employees in the prison, nothing is rarer than to see a prisoner resist this first trial. Scarcely has he begun to undergo the rigour of absolute isolation than he begs the favour of resuming his place in the common shop, and submits with good grace to all the exigencies of discipline. However, in the event that he is not cowed from the first instant, some additional hardships are added to his isolation, such as the entire privation of light, the diminution of his food; sometimes his bed is even taken away, etc., etc. If the inmate persists in his resistance, then, and then only, is sought in the whip a more effective instrument of submission. The directors of this establishment appear to feel a marked aversion for corporal punishments; yet they would deeply regret not being invested by law with the right to inflict them. They dislike and avoid the application of a cruel punishment; but they find, in the right they have to set one, a powerful leverage on the inmates.'

Then there really was some hope of running an Auburn-style penitentiary without the use of the whip! At least, here was a practical demonstration. 'The temperate discipline of Wethersfield appears sufficient for the success of the establishment,' the commissioners concluded.

Even more extraordinary, however, was the marked economy with which the prison was administered. Not only were the running expenses at Wethersfield less than elsewhere, but the labour of the convicts actually returned an annual profit to the State. At Auburn it was only in the last two years that the penitentiary had ceased to weigh in the budget of New York; and, in spite of strenuous efforts, the great prison at Sing Sing was still running at a loss. But here in the small prison of the State of Connecticut, 174 inmates were apparently in the process of earning more than twice what it cost to keep them. According to the statistics available, in three and a half years a mere handful of convicts had returned, in clear profit to the Connecticut treasury, more than seventeen thousand dollars. And Judge Martin Welles was certain that the same results could be obtained elsewhere. As a matter of fact, he even went so far as to draw up for the two Frenchmen a careful note, analysing the probable cost and returns of a prison of 500, if properly built and run.

'The characteristic of the modern system,' he stated,[8] 'is the substitution of vigilance for material force.' In other words, the keepers, and not the walls, really stood between the inmates and their freedom in a new-style penitentiary. That being so, the prisons did not need to be so heavily or durably constructed. In the second place, the convicts, constrained to silence, could safely be allowed to work together, by which means alone could profit be assured to the State. And a real profit could be made, even in France where labour was cheap. In a prison for 500, rightly constructed and administered, Judge Welles was confident that the annual return to the State should better fourteen thousand dollars.

To this the Rev.G.Barrett had but one thought to add: the modern American penitentiary actually did reform some of the criminals confined within its walls. In Wethersfield, he pointed out in a brief note that he submitted to the French commissioners on 7 October, the convicts read the Bible, placed in their cells by the State, with great care; and on Sundays they listened to the sermons with marked attention.

'Afterwards,' he wrote,[4] 'they often ask eagerly about the meaning of the words that they have just heard.

'When the principles of Holy Scripture are engraved in the heart of a convict, one may certainly believe that his reform is complete. We have reasons to think that this result has sometimes been obtained. I should be tempted to believe that among the total number of actual convicts, 15 or 20 can be found in this state. . . .

'. . . If the keepers are what they should be; if the condemned, separated at night, work in silence during the day; if a continuous surveillance is united with frequent moral and religious instruction; [then] a prison can become a place of reform for the convicts and a source of revenue for the State.'

Of the positive reform of criminals, Tocqueville and Beaumont remained, as before, more than a little sceptical. Elam Lynds' downright disbelief had made too strong a mark on them for optimism to seem reasonable. From the material point of view, however, Wethersfield was immensely impressive. And the two friends were entirely ready to say so. For, two days after their departure, the *Hartford Mirror* had the following report to make of the French commissioners:

'. . . They have been through many prisons in the Union, but express an opinion that for regularity of discipline, for the good order that prevails throughout the institution, for the neatness and precision with which its concerns are managed, as well as for the profits made to accrue from the labor of the convicts, that the Wethersfield prison is not inferior to any which has come under their inspection.' *

Privately, to his family, Beaumont characterized the Connecticut State Penitentiary as a 'very fine prison.'

\*

\*    \*

* The quotation concludes: 'This speaks well for the directors and the more immediate presiding officers of the Institution in question.'
    It is amusing to note that the *Boston Evening Transcript*, having, like most American newspapers, no really good staff of news-gathering reporters, had completely failed to notice Tocqueville's and Beaumont's presence in that city during September. Being, however, well versed in the art of news clipping or borrowing, the paper now reprinted the announcement of the *Hartford Mirror* verbatim. Alas! A certain neighbourly jealousy could not be suppressed. So the last sentence (above) was carefully omitted, and the following added instead:
    'We wish the above gentlemen would visit the Massachusetts State Prison, at Charlestown, as we feel confident that they cannot go away without bearing ample testimony to the neatness and precision of every department. The moral discipline is also fast gaining ground on the inmates. We have not room to say more at this time.'

*Erreur!*

Tocqueville and Beaumont were mistaken, terribly mistaken.

At the very moment when they were making their visit, and unhesitatingly setting the stamp of their approval on the institution, trouble was brewing at Wethersfield. As a matter of fact, for some time past things had been going far from satisfactorily in the management of the penitentiary; and that month of October 1831, a secret but bitter controversy was raging between certain of the inspectors over the way the warden, Amos Pillsbury, was running the prison. Strange to relate, the two principals in the argument were none other than Tocqueville and Beaumont's two friend, Mr. Martin Welles and Mr. Samuel Huntington.

Judge Welles, in grim privacy, was certain that warden Pillsbury was tyrannizing over the inmates, and peculating on the side. Sick prisoners were constantly being abused, and forced to work when their health should have forbidden it. Later Mr. Welles and the prison physician, Dr. Samuel B. Woodward, were to testify that Pillsbury always accused sick prisoners of 'playing the old soldier,' and would not let them see the doctor soon enough. Again, there was the matter of food. Welles was convinced that the convicts were stinted while the warden took some of their food for use in his own house.

There was a book kept in the prison to receive the written suggestions of the State inspectors. On the fifth of September 1831, therefore, the judge had made an entry asking for an 'entire revision' of the diet. But on the seventeenth, Mr. Huntington had countered with an entry in the same book opposing any change. On the twenty-ninth, Mr. Welles had returned to the attack with the charge that the peas stipulated for in the penitentiary regulations had not been used. To which Mr. Huntington on the sixth of October—that is, the day after Tocqueville and Beaumont's arrival—replied that peas had been used, and the rice was satisfactory. This was too much for Mr. Welles, who on the nineteenth, apparently after considerable investigation, put it down in black and white in the director's book that no purchase of rice had been made in two years, which was a violation of the by-laws.

Finally, there were some other abuses almost too disgusting to record about this model prison. The well, it seemed, had run foul, and had been allowed to remain thus—the prisoners having no other water to drink—for five or six weeks. Again, the ventilation of the cell-block was bad, and the heating worse. Mr. Huntington had a theory that the stove—defective enough as it was—would work better without a draft of air from the outside! During the winter of 1831–1832, consequently, the temperature indoors was often to be below the 50° mark. And when Mr. Welles protested, Mr. Huntington was to put himself on record in the director's book as opposing *overheating*. Again, the warden was quite obviously employing certain of the inmates for personal service, in direct contravention of the prison rules.

All this was to come out three years later, when the scandal reached its head and the legislature appointed a committee to investigate the abuses and take testimony.* Meanwhile, of course, Tocqueville and Beaumont's prison Report had appeared, and had been translated by Francis Lieber—with the ironic consequence that each side in the controversy would try to justify its conduct and opinion by citation to the distinguished French commissioners' book:

> George Stillman, called by A.P. [Amos Pillsbury].—'In October, 1831, Dr. Woodward was visiting at my home, and spoke of the French Commissioners, who were then here. He said he understood they considered this the best organized Prison they had found, either in this country or in Europe. While he was speaking, they passed, and he said, "they are going down to Judge Welles' to dine." '

Obviously, here was an attempt to use Tocqueville and Beaumont to vindicate Pillsbury and discredit Judge Welles' charges and Dr. Woodward's testimony. To which the judge was to counter by trying to show that it was the regulations rather than the practice, the principles of the penitentiary rather than its management, that the distinguished Frenchmen had commended in their 'valuable report.'

Unfortunately, the plain fact of the matter was that Tocqueville and Beaumont had approved almost everything in the whole concern. During the three days of their intensive inspection, the abuses later to be aired before the world had passed unnoticed, though right under their noses. It would probably be too strong to suggest that naturally a whip was not needed to control inmates weakened by long and systematic starvation. But when Tocqueville made the remark—as he now did in a preliminary report to the Ministry of Justice in Paris—that Wethers-

* *Minutes of the Testimony Taken before J.Q.Wilson . . . Committee for the General Assembly to inquire into the condition of Connecticut State Prison . . . with their Report and Remarks upon the Same*, Hartford, 1834 (Yale College Pamphlets, v. 1895), pp.30–31,89–93.

field presented *toutes les garantées de sûreté et de salubrité qu'on peut désirer*, he clearly was guilty of a misunderstanding of the fact.

\*

\*    \*

There was such a thing as going too fast, perhaps. In their haste, at least, the two travellers were immediately guilty of a second, and very singular omission.

They had fully intended to visit New Haven, with its small but distinguished college of Yale, from whose classrooms had issued several of the Americans whom Tocqueville and Beaumont found most distinguished.\* They had planned to go that far by stage, and then take a boat on to New York. Their plans had been intelligent enough.

But there were boats every day which went the whole way, it appeared. In other words, not only did a man go on board at Hartford one noon, to step off in New York the next, but there was the beautiful trip down the Connecticut included. The temptation was too strong to be resisted . . . especially as they had a good deal of writing to do.

For Tocqueville had just received a letter from his cousin, the influential Le Peletier d'Aunay, strongly urging him and Beaumont, if they

---

\* It is a matter of no little interest to note how many of Tocqueville and Beaumont's acquaintances and informants were college graduates. Their manuscripts contain the names of more than 250 individuals, of both sexes, whom they met in America. Of these about 32 were foreigners, or Canadians, and a like number are not sufficiently identified to make any judgment possible. Of the remaining 177, however, a really surprising number had been college-trained. Harvard contributed 18 (possibly 21) to the list, Yale 9 (counting two non-graduates), Columbia 8, Princeton (College of New Jersey) 11, and Pennsylvania 5. Two each had been educated at Dartmouth, Williams, and Union; and at least ten more at West Point, Bowdoin, Georgetown, etc., a total of approximately 70 in all. In this group, Tocqueville and Beaumont met two college presidents and two presidents-to-be, 8 professors, 6 trustees, and a number of individuals holding honorary degrees, to say nothing of about 12 Americans who had been educated abroad.

On closer analysis an even more striking result is obtained. Of the 72 persons who may be said to have contributed the most to Tocqueville and Beaumont's understanding of American institutions, 15 had been trained at Harvard, 5 at Princeton, 3 at Yale, and 1 at Columbia; while 9 had been educated abroad. One reason for the preponderance of Harvard men, perhaps, was the commissioners' long stay at Boston, their failure to stop longer in Connecticut or New Jersey. At this period the colleges seem to have been catering largely to a local clientele.

However that may be, the conduct of Tocqueville and Beaumont in the matter of higher education appears extraordinary. They met the Presidents of Harvard and Columbia, but, so far as can be ascertained, they neither visited, nor studied, a single college in the United States!

Apparently it never occurred to them that such institutions could have any bearing on the character of American civilization.

did not wish their eighteen-months' leave to be curtailed, to use a little tact and report home on their investigations to their superiors in the Ministry of Justice. This seemed a reasonable thing to do. So now the two friends had the *Garde des Sceaux* as well as the Minister of the Interior on their correspondence list. And if they did not wish to be too late, they would have to interest him at once.

On Saturday the eighth of October, therefore, Tocqueville and Beaumont went on board a steamboat for New York. And Tocqueville sat down to organize a long report on the prisons of New York, Massachusetts, and Connecticut. 'The prisons have pretty well bored us,' Beaumont confided to his family; [5] 'we see always the same thing. We have now no, or very few, new observations to make, and if we always inspect the prisons of the cities where we go, it's solely to fulfil a necessary formality. It really is necessary that our mission last some time longer, since the opportune moment for returning to France has not yet arrived. Thus from time to time we address to the Minister of Interior very circumstantial reports proving to him more and more the necessity of continuing the inquiry that we've begun. It results from our reports that it is impossible, at present, to know what to think; but that very probably new researches will bring happier results.'

## XXXIV

## CONNECTICUT AFTERTHOUGHT

In after years Connecticut became a symbol to Tocqueville.

Quite recently, for example, there was rediscovered and published the vivid anecdote related by a Congregationalist historian in 1876. According to William C. Fowler's best recollection, not long after Tocqueville's *Democracy in America* was published, some Americans were celebrating the Fourth of July in Paris, and invited Monsieur de Tocqueville to be present.[1] It happened that a native of the State mentioned the name of Connecticut.

> . . . Upon this Monsieur de Tocqueville arose and exclaimed:
>
> 'Connect-de-coot, Vy, messieurs, I vill tell you, vid the permission of de presidante of this festi*val*, von very *lee*tal story, and then I vill give you von grand sentiment, to dat little State you call Connect-de-coot. Von day ven I was in de gallery of the House of Representatif, I held one map of the Confederation in my hand. Dere was von leetle yellow spot dey called Connect-de-coot. I found by the Constitution he was entitled to six of his boys to represent him on dat floor. But ven∙I make de acquaintance person*elle* with de member, I find dat more than tirty of the Representatif on dat floor was born in Connect-de-coot.* And then ven I was in the gallery of the House of the Sen*at*, I find de Constitution permits Connect-de-coot to send two of his boys to represent him in dat Legislature. But once more ven I make de acquaintance person*elle* of the Senator, I find nine of de Senator was born in Connect-de-coot. So, den, gentlemen, I have made my leetle speech; now I will give you my grand sentiment:
>
> 'Connect-de-coot, the leetle yellow spot dat make de clock-peddler, de school master, and de senator. De first, give you time; the second, tell you what you do with him; and de sird make your law and your civilization;'
> —and then, as he was resuming his seat amidst roars of laughter, he rose

---

* See above, p.440.

again, and with that peculiar gesticulation which characterizes all Frenchmen in moments of excitement, he shook his finger tremulously over the
assembled *confrères*, and exclaimed to the top of his voice, 'Ah! gentleman, dat leetle yellow State you call Connect-de-coot, is one very great
miracle to me.'

Whether this echo of the later Tocqueville is altogether authentic
may perhaps be questioned. Certainly the accent seems theatrical: a
rather vulgar version of English to attribute to a traveller who had
been so practised in the tongue. In the matter of sound, it is possible that
the Connecticut historian exaggerated.

However that may be, both the facts and the sentiment expressed are
unmistakable. Quite aside from the reader's recognition of the origin
of Tocqueville's information, it was characteristic of him to take Connecticut as a miracle or a symbol. He was always generalizing, and
therefore always singling out the individual as a representative of an
idea or a type, to sharpen his focus and to emphasize his meaning. At
the very moment of his departure from the State, he was thinking
of Connecticut as a symbol of New England, and of New England as
a reproduction—or exposition in miniature—of all America. During
his last two days in Wethersfield, for instance, Tocqueville had been
trying to fix clearly in his mind certain characteristics of New England
decentralization.

From a conversation that he had had with Inspector Huntington, he
had gathered that there was no true hierarchy of control or inspection
in the administration of justice, whether in Connecticut or elsewhere.[2]
Secondly, in this New England State (again, as in all America, apparently) the function of the department of justice was to prosecute,
not to gather the evidence. Once more, he had learned that 'in the State
of Connecticut, which contains 290,000 souls, there are 8 counties, an
average of 36,000 souls per county. In each county there are 10 or 12
towns (the town is the lowest unit in the American system), there are
therefore about 3000 in each town. Wethersfield has 3000.'

In other words, from observations in Connecticut, Tocqueville was
now prepared to generalize about the size and name and administration of America's smallest and most important unit of self-government.
From a month's contact with the Yankee Jacks-of-all-trades, furthermore, he now believed he could explain the reason for what he called
the

*INTELLIGENCE OF THE PEOPLE IN AMERICA*

'It has been remarked in Europe that the division of labour rendered men infinitely more capable in the details to which they applied themselves, but diminished their *general capacity*. The worker thus classified becomes past master in his specialty, a brute in all the rest. Example of England. Terrifying state of the working classes in that country.'

'What makes an ordinary American such an intelligent man is the fact that division of labour does not, so to speak, exist in America. Each does a bit of everything. He does each thing less well than the European who does nothing else, but his general capacity is a hundred times greater. Chief cause of superiority in the usual affairs of life and in the government of society.'[3]

There was also another cause that helped account for the practical intelligence of New Englanders and Americans. 'The general principle in the matter of public education is that any one is free to found a public school and to direct it as he pleases. It's an industry like other industries, the *consumers* being the judges and the state taking no hand whatever. . . . You ask me if this unlimited liberty produces bad results. I believe that it produces only good,' Tocqueville was soon writing to a professor friend in Paris.[4]

'. . . The effort made in this country to spread instruction is truly prodigious. The universal and sincere faith that they profess here in the efficaciousness of education seems to me one of the most remarkable features of America, the more so as I confess that for me the question is not yet entirely decided. But it is absolutely clear in the minds of the Americans, whatever their opinions political or religious. The Catholic himself in this matter gives his hand to the Unitarian and the Deist. Thence results one of those powerful efforts, quiet but irresistible, that nations sometimes make when they march toward a goal with a common and universal impulse.

'There has never been under the sun a people as enlightened as the population of the north of the United States. Because of their education they are more strong, more skilful, more capable of governing themselves and standing their liberty: that much is undeniable.'

Finally, there has been found among Tocqueville's American manuscripts a brief, but most significant note. It is undated, but its content identifies it with this period in Tocqueville's investigations. Certainly it sums up, in a precise catalogue, a number of the truths that he had but recently verified about the history and nature of American society. He had now found, Tocqueville thought, the 'causes of the social condition and the present political organization in America.'[5]

1. *Their origin*, fine starting point, intimate mixture of religion and spirit of liberty. Cold and reasoning race.
2. *Their geographical position*. No neighbours.
3. *Their Activity*, commercial and industrial. Even their vices are now helpful to them.
4. *The Material Happiness* which they enjoy.
5. *The religious spirit which reigns*. A Republican and equalitarian religion.
6. The diffusion of *useful* education.
7. Very pure morals.
8. Their division into small states. They are incapable of a great state.
9. The lack of a large capital where everything is centred. Care in avoiding such a large place.
10. Communal and provincial activity, which enables every one to find employment at home.

This list was more than an empty enumeration. It teemed with ideas for Tocqueville's future book. Whole chapters were one day to be fashioned from the items thus catalogued. Point 2, the geographical position, was to help suggest his opening chapter on the 'Configuration of North America,' and also to supply some telling reasons for the success of the Federal principle in the United States, its failure elsewhere. The second chapter of *De la Démocratie en Amérique* (cf. Point 1) was to be entitled: 'Du point de départ et de son importance pour l'avenir des Anglo-Américains.' Thanks to Jared Sparks, Alexander Everett and many another, Tocqueville was often, after his Massachusetts investigations, both to think and speak of the inhabitants of the United States as Anglo-Americans. Again the assumptions (Points 3 and 4) about American materialism and industrial activity—thoughts first suggested to Tocqueville and Beaumont by their experiences in New York—were to underlie much of Tocqueville's future argument. New York and New England had prompted the emphasis on the republican nature of Protestantism and the *usefulness* of American education (Points 5 and 6). And it was from Albany, Massachusetts, and Connecticut that Tocqueville was later to draw most of his observations on the necessity and real advantages of decentralization in a democracy (Points 8, 9, and 10).[6]

Whether he knew it or not, as Tocqueville bade farewell to New England and turned southward, certain portions of his future commentary were already emerging into articulate expression.

PART VI: PHILADELPHIA AND BALTIMORE

XXXV

# THE HEAVENLY PRISON OF THE
PHILANTHROPISTS

'I ARRIVED in New-York from Hartford the eighth or ninth of this month,' Beaumont wrote to his father on the sixteenth of October. 'We stayed in this last city but two days. This sojourn was indispensable for finishing certain negotiations begun relative to our penitentiary investigation: it was also necessary to put ourselves into shape for the journey which we are going to make in the South. We can't carry all our belongings with us, especially since in travelling we are constantly accumulating piles of gift-books: it would be something of a nuisance to drag a library with us. We therefore made up our minds to leave half our possessions at New-York: we selected with as much *discernment* as possible what to leave and what to carry with us; and after these preparations we embarked for Philadelphia, the capital city of Pennsylvania. A steamboat took us half way, and we negotiated the rest of the route by carriage. We arrived in Philadelphia the twelfth.'

The city filled them with astonishment. Indeed, Paris was not thus curiously constructed. Nor had the cities of New York and New England—Broadway with its windings or the confusion of streets on Beacon Hill—led them to expect so revolutionary a spectacle, even in pragmatic America.

'This city of 200,000 souls resembles none of those that I have seen up to now,' Beaumont was forced to confess. 'It is of a regularity that one is tempted to find too perfect. Not a street but traverses the entire city in one direction or another; and all of them are laid out with geometric precision. All the edifices are neat, kept up with extreme care, and have all the freshness of new buildings. It's a charming city, very favourable to those who have no carriage, since all the streets are bordered with wide side-walks; and its sole defect, I repeat, is to be monotonous in its beauty.'

'Philadelphia is an immense city,' Tocqueville began his description

457

of what they had found.[1] 'You can convince yourself of it for it occupies the entire space between the Delaware and the Schuikil [*sic*]. All the houses are of brick, and without *portes cochères* following the English custom, and the streets straight as a string. The regularity is tiresome but very convenient. Philadelphia is, I believe, the only city in the world where it has occurred to people to distinguish the streets by numbers and not by names. The system of streets is so regular that, starting from the Delaware where is Street No. 1, one goes up number by number all the way to the Schuikil.

'I am living in Street No. 3. Don't you find that only a people whose imagination is frozen could invent such a system? Europeans never fail to join an idea to each external object, be it a saint, a famous man, an event. But these people here know only arithmetic.'

Philadelphians were clearly a little wanting in humour and imagination. 'But we must not speak ill of them,' Tocqueville amended, 'for they continue to treat us admirably. Philadelphia, beyond all others, is infatuated to the last degree with the penitentiary system, and as the penitentiary system is our *industry,* they vie with each other in pampering us.'

The two commissioners had brought with them a great many letters of introduction and had, Beaumont reported at the end of their first week,[2] 'carried a larger number to their address, but up to now we haven't enjoyed much society, because from the instant of our arrival we have been absorbed by the men of the penitentiary system. The city doesn't exist where prisons, the care of administering them, the theories concerning them, in a word all that is connected with this system, play a greater role or occupy a larger place than at Philadelphia.'

'There are here above all two kinds of men who take a prodigious interest in prisons, although they envisage the subject differently,' Tocqueville explained. 'These are the theorists and the practical men: those who write and those who act. Between these two classes a struggle is going on to see which will monopolize us most completely. A week before our arrival the head keeper of the establishment had come to leave his card with the Consul of France and ask that he be notified the very instant of our arrival in this city: while the Society established to examine into the penitentiary theories assembled at the same time and named a committee to aid us in our research.'

It was a fact. The two friends had not been forced to seek out either the prisons of the State, or the prison administrators, or indeed the philanthropists who might be expected to take an interest in their mission. For the prison, the so-called Eastern State Penitentiary outside of Philadelphia, was one of the famous monuments of the region; and wardens and theorists alike were, to put it mildly, penitentiary enthusiasts. The French commissioners had come to study the second great American penitentiary principle, the Pennsylvania system of absolute solitude, and the one thing these Philadelphians made absolutely impossible for Tocqueville and Beaumont was solitude—or even, as Beaumont noted, a reasonable enjoyment of Pennsylvania society.

It began with the celebrated and venerable Quaker association of prison reformers. For better than a generation, these true friends of humanity had been carrying forward their kindly, idealistic ameliorations of the Pennsylvania penal system. They still called themselves with humility and pride the Philadelphia Society for Alleviating the Miseries of the Public Prisons. It was but two years before that they had seen their ambitions crowned in the new penitentiary; and now the French Government was come to investigate their handiwork.

On the tenth of October therefore—a good two days before the arrival of the interesting visitors—the Society had made careful preparations to receive them. A resolution had been passed in meeting 'to furnish the said commissioners with such assistance and information as they may require in relation to the examination of the prisons and prison discipline of Pennsylvania.' [3] And, as Tocqueville reported, a committee of three had been appointed to carry this resolution into effect. To this committee the chairman of the Society had named Messrs. Roberts Vaux, George Washington Smith, and James J. Barclay.

All three were men of character and standing in the community, and intensely and actively concerned with the new prison reforms. Barclay * was a college graduate, lawyer, and philanthropist. More important, he had been one of the founders of, and was destined long to preside over, the Philadelphia House of Refuge, which Tocqueville and Beaumont were soon to visit. Smith, after graduating from Princeton, had travelled widely in Europe and Asia. The son of a Federalist judge, and himself a man of means, he had returned to become one of the founders of the Pennsylvania Historical Society, and an advocate of the new railroads against the canals, and one of the State's leading

* James J. Barclay, then in his late thirties, was a graduate of the University of Pennsylvania, and was about to enter on a presidency of the Philadelphia House of Refuge that would span the next fifty years. Living beyond his ninetieth year, he is still remembered in Philadelphia today.

humanitarians. The Pennsylvania theory of prison discipline was one of his great hobbies, and two years before he had published a defence of the solitary system of confinement.* With him Tocqueville was to enjoy several conversations of no little interest.

Yet the man who really counted was the senior member of the committee, the devout Quaker, Roberts Vaux. Interested in all branches of idealism and philanthropy, Vaux was unquestionably one of the leading men of the State. He had helped found innumerable institutions, not least among them the Deaf and Dumb Asylum, the Historical Society, and the Pennsylvania public school system. He was an active opponent of slavery and an influential friend of the Cherokee Indian. Finally, and herein lay the reason for his appointment, Vaux himself had been responsible for the building of the experimental Eastern State Penitentiary. In fact, it was due almost entirely to his unflagging and persistent efforts that the Quaker theories of self-reform under solitary confinement were now at last being given practical demonstration and world-wide publicity. If the French Commissioners were to be persuaded of the value of their system, the Society for Alleviating the Miseries of the Public Prisons could not have entrusted the task to more expert or enthusiastic hands.†

In addition, as Tocqueville immediately realized, there were also the practical reformers, the men who actually administered the system, the guardians and State Inspectors who were anxious to impress the new visitors with the lessons drawn from practical experience. Chief among these was the warden of the great prison, Samuel R. Wood, who had been so forehanded as to inquire for them of the French counsel. Wood, it seemed, had been moved by a feeling of religious duty to abandon a career of promise in order to devote himself entirely to the success of the new establishment.‡ He was a direct man, of impressive administrative capacity.

* G.W. Smith (1800–1876), *Defense of the Pennsylvania system in favor of the solitary confinement of prisoners*, 1829.

† A man of some *esprit* and humour—naïve, literary, and philosophic—Roberts Vaux was easily one of the most public-spirited men of his day, and an outstanding penologist. In addition to his *Notices of the original and successive efforts to improve the discipline of the prison at Philadelphia, and to reform the criminal code of Pennsylvania* (1826), and other penitentiary pamphlets, Vaux presented Tocqueville and Beaumont with up-to-date reports on Pennsylvania temperance and school reforms, and later secured the election of his two French friends to the Pennsylvania Historical Society. See *Du Syst. Pén.*, pp.vi,7,41,110,etc.

‡ Wood was warden from 1829 to August 1835. Two of his published letters on prison matters were to be cited in Tocqueville and Beaumont's report; Tocqueville was to keep a record of his remarks on illegitimate children, and the ability

The two commissioners, as Beaumont reported, had reached Philadelphia on the twelfth. On the thirteenth they were already caught.
On that first day, Tocqueville wrote, 'we received an invitation to dine
with the warden [Wood] and a letter from [Roberts Vaux] a Quaker
(theorist *par excellence*) who, without saying *Monsieur*, but thee-thou-
ing us, begged us to come sup with him and some of his friends. Our
own interest being to listen to all the world without taking anybody's
word for the truth, we act most agreeably toward both sides, and accept with open hands the books and dinners they give us.' Beaumont
felt some consternation at the feast prepared by Roberts Vaux. 'We
had to digest a great dinner, where we figured in the midst of all the
philanthropists of the *pays*.' And already they had been forced to visit
the prison by the practical men. Judge Coxe, one of the State Inspectors,* had that day accompanied them there for their first sight of
it. He had also taken advantage of the opportunity to discourse to them
on the subject of the criminal code of Pennsylvania, in an endeavour to
impress them with the advantages of lighter punishments and shorter
sentences. That evening, also, at Mr. Vaux's dinner, the talk of course
had hardly deviated from the penitentiary.

As Tocqueville noted in his diary:[4] 'Mr. Vaughan,† the pupil of
Franklin, an old man much esteemed in Philadelphia, said to me this
evening while speaking of the penitentiary system: Our Walnut Street
prison is in a frightful state. It was different when the Quakers directed it, but the political party opposed to the Quakers having triumphed some [years] ago in the elections, the Quakers were all kicked
out of office.

'—But, said I, what have politics and prisons in common?

'—Nothing, unquestionably, replied Mr. Vaughan, but posts of all
kinds excite the envy of men, and when a party triumphs, it takes pains
to get hold of them for its partisans.

---

of negroes (diary Alph.B); and his name and character were to be referred to
again and again in *Du Syst. Pén.* See pp.54,274,etc.

* Charles Sydney Coxe, 1790–1879, Associate Judge of the District Court for the City
and County of Philadelphia. Others who helped Tocqueville and Beaumont with
their investigations were Inspector Thomas Bradford (much interested in prison
schooling); Dr. Franklin Bache (1792–1864), the descendent of Benjamin Franklin,
who was the penitentiary physician; and John Bacon and William Hood.

† John Vaughan, 1755–1841, was a prominent merchant and much given to hospitality. Of English birth, great vivacity and wide interests, he had become the accredited liaison officer for Philadelphia society, and was particularly fond of introducing Englishmen and other foreigners to the 'Wistar Parties' and the social circles
of the city.

'—This effect of the popular system is so well known, added Mr. Coxe, judge in Philadelphia and present at the conversation, that to try to remedy the evil the legislature has given the nomination of the warden to a commission composed for the most part of judges. It was thought that, being magistrates for life, they would be less inclined to carry politics into their selection.'

'At bottom,' Tocqueville later informed his family, 'these are all excellent people, but political rivalries, and above all small-town rivalries, preoccupy them almost as much as if they were Frenchmen. Someone said to me the other day: the result of the last elections has been to take the direction of the prisons away from very capable men. But what, said I, have elections and prisons in common? Not much, was the answer, but there as elsewhere the posts are given to the victorious party. You will admit that it's not necessary to travel two thousand leagues to see such things as that.'

\*

\*     \*

Next day, the fourteenth, *Poulson's Daily American Advertiser* informed Philadelphia of the arrival of the French prison commissioners; and their penitentiary investigations began in earnest.

They were showered with verbal information and with printed documents. Roberts Vaux and his committee supplied them with all available reports and notices on their beloved Eastern State Penitentiary at Cherry Hill, together with Vaux's published correspondence on the subject of the Pennsylvania discipline, and a copy of the constitution of their society. Warden Wood wrote them a letter on penitentiary practices. They accumulated Job R. Tyson's *Essay on the Penal Laws of Pennsylvania*, Mathew Carey's *Reflections on the Penitentiary System*, and a report on the medical statistics of Philadelphia. They visited the old Walnut Street jail where the eighteenth-century Quakers had first experimented and built their earliest solitary cells, but which was now an overcrowded and old-fashioned prison of the congregate type. They took a look at the House of Refuge of the city, conversed with the warden, and collected its annual report.[5]

They visited the Eastern State Penitentiary.

The prison was new, just two years old. Its still uncompleted cell-blocks radiated outward like the spokes of a wheel from a central hub or observation chamber. Each cell, a one-story and rather commodious affair, faced inward on a common corridor, and opened behind into its own walled garden. Meanwhile, about this articulated organism had been raised a high, rectangular enclosing wall. From the outside, then, the wheel was invisible.

Instead (Tocqueville and Beaumont were to report to their government),[6] 'Gigantic walls, crenellated towers, a vast gate of iron give to this prison the aspect of a vast *châteaufort* of medieval times.' Standing on a hill, it was unquestionably a massive and impressive construction. The ambitious Society for Alleviating the Miseries of the Public Prisons had secured the plans from the leading prison architect of America, and were very proud of their handiwork. 'This penitentiary,' they boasted, 'is the only edifice in this country which is calculated to convey to our citizens the external appearance of those magnificent and picturesque castles of the middle ages.'

Very true. But why did a penitentiary on the Pennsylvania plan need a surrounding wall? With the inmates never leaving their own individual double-cells, it seemed a needless ornament and expense. The wall of the Eastern State alone cost $200,000, Tocqueville and Beaumont were to point out, and the rest of the prison was being finished on the same lavish scale. Before completion it would cost Pennsylvania in the neighbourhood of $432,000, which would raise the price of its two hundred-odd cells to more than $1600 apiece. The expense seemed absolutely fantastic.

'I believe that Philadelphia represents the abuse of the philanthropic theories which in other states we have seen wisely applied,' Beaumont therefore observed. 'The prison is truly a palace; each prisoner enjoys all the comforts of life; the building of such a prison costs *un prix fou*; there is not a cell for a single inmate but costs from two to three thousand francs. I wonder to myself how one would manage in France if it were necessary to build such prisons for thirty-two thousand convicts (that's the number of inmates in the various prisons in France).

'Although we are at once struck by the vicious side in such a system, we are obliged to continue our examination with the same interest and the same attention as if we hoped to draw thence a real profit. We have to do with well-intentioned people, who attach an immense importance to their experiments and who would be hurt by a superficial investigation quite as much as by a severe *critique*. So we pass whole days at the penitentiary. This labour is not altogether without its use, for it is interesting to learn how one may go wrong on the right road.'

But Beaumont was more bored than Tocqueville. For his colleague was absorbed in an unique investigation.

They had begun by examining the prison registers for a record of the health, conduct, and moral state of the prisoners. Dr. Bache and the inspectors insisted that the health of the inmates was good; and in the matter of discipline the warden's books recorded little but exemplary conduct. Suddenly it occurred to Tocqueville to wonder what kind of an infraction of discipline a convict confined alone and without contacts, night or day, could commit. And as for their mental state under such a regime, how could books or warden say?

So Tocqueville made an extraordinary request. He wanted to visit each of the prisoners alone in his cell, without the presence of any keeper, so as to find out if possible what the prisoners themselves thought of the institution. The idea must have come as a shock to the Warden and Inspectors, for neither then nor earlier had it been the practice of even the most conscientious penologists to consult the prisoners for information. There was something a little preposterous in the idea. But Tocqueville was in earnest: he felt it his duty. And the Philadelphians were certain of their penitentiary.* So the consent was given . . . and Tocqueville embarked on his 'delicate' task alone. Beaumont would no doubt have been willing to join in these solitary conversations, but both friends agreed that to go together would probably destroy the atmosphere of confidence and trust so necessary to create in the minds of the prisoners if frank answers were to be elicited.

Armed with a pencil and a few small sheets of paper, Tocqueville got a cell unlocked and entered the semi-obscurity within. After a few moments: 'No. 28—' he scratched down.† 'The inmate knows how to read and write, he was condemned for murder. He says that his health, without being bad, is poorer than it was outside the prison. He strongly denies having committed the crime which was the cause of his condemnation; otherwise he confesses readily that he was a drunkard, turbulent, and irreligious. But to-day, he adds, his soul is

---

* Samuel Wood gave the order. 'We have no other interest than that of the truth,' he said. 'If there is something vicious in the prison that I direct, it is important that we know it.' *Du Syst. Pén.*, p.274 (Note O).

† The prisoners had been assigned numbers in the order of their arrival (and seniority) at the institution. Tocqueville could only take pencil notes of an abbreviated character at the instant, but later he wrote them out into the tragic and very moving series of conversations from which quotation is here made. See *Du Syst. Pén.*, pp.318ff.

changed: he finds a sort of pleasure in the solitude, and is tormented only by the desire to see his family again and give his children a moral and Christian education, something he had never considered.

'Do you think you could live here without work?' the Frenchman asked.

'*A.* Work seems to me absolutely necessary to existence; I think I should die without it.

'*Q.* Do you see the keepers often?—*A.* About six times a day.—*Q.* Is it a consolation to you to see them?—Yes, Sir: it's a sort of joy to glimpse their faces. This summer a cricket came into my yard. *It looked like company for me.* When a butterfly or any other animal enters my cell, I never do it any harm.'

The solid door clanged to behind the strange visitor—and Tocqueville proceeded to a second cell.

'No. 36.—The inmate has already undergone a prior punishment in the Walnut-Street prison; he declares that he prefers life in the penitentiary to what it was in the old prison. His health is very good, and the solitude doesn't seem unbearable.

'On being asked whether he is forced to work, he answers, no. But labour, he adds, should be regarded as a great favour. Sunday is the one day in the week that is most interminable, because on that day work is forbidden.

'*Q.* What is, in your opinion, the principal advantage of the new system of imprisonment to which you are subjected?—

'*A.* Here the inmate knows none of his companions and is unknown to them. It was a prison friend who, on leaving Walnut-Street, got me again to commit a theft.

'*Q.* Is the nourishment they give you sufficient?—*A.* Yes, Sir.

'*Q.* Do you think the yard annexed to your cell necessary for your health?—*A.* I am convinced one couldn't do without it.'

The third acquaintance that Tocqueville made among the inmates of the great experimental institution was very communicative.

'No. 41.—This inmate is a young man; he admits that he is a criminal; he weeps during the whole course of our conversation, especially when spoken to about his family. Happily, he says, here no one can see me. He hopes, therefore, to be able to return to the world without stigma, and without being rejected by society.

'*Q.* Do you find the solitude hard to bear?—*A.* Ah! Sir, it's the most frightful torture one can imagine.—*Q.* But your health doesn't suffer from it?—*A.* No, it is very good, but my soul is very sick.—*Q.* What do you think about most often?—*A.* About religion; religious ideas are my greatest consolation.—*Q.* Do you occasionally see a minister?— Yes, every Sunday.—*Q.* Do you enjoy talking with him?—*A.* It's a great happiness to be able to converse with him. Last Sunday we were to-gether an hour; he promised to bring me news of my father and my mother to-morrow. I hope they are alive; for the year that I have been here I haven't heard from them.—*Q.* Do you consider labour an alleviation of the solitude?—*A.* One couldn't live here without work. Sunday is a day that takes a long while to pass, I assure you.—*Q.* Do you believe that without injuring the health of the inmates it would be pos-sible to suppress the yard adjoining the cell?—*A.* Yes, on setting up a continuous current of air in the cell.—*Q.* What notions have you as to the usefulness of the system of imprisonment to which you are sub-jected?—*A.* If there is any that can make men re-examine and correct themselves, it's this one.'

The fourth inmate Tocqueville introduced himself to was a hardened criminal in feeble health, who said that he had been transferred to Cherry Hill at his own request. The first few days in the penitentiary he had been sick, for want of exercise and a sufficient current of air in the cell, he thought. Tocqueville himself found the cells wonderfully clean and odourless, despite the presence of a latrine in the corner of each.* He proceeded with his curious inquest.

No. 61 had been condemned for 'hors-stealing,' it seemed. 'No one, he says, can conceive what horror there is in continued solitude. On being asked how he manages to pass the time, answers that he has but two pleasures: working, and reading his Bible. The Bible, he says, is the greatest consolation. This inmate appears strongly agitated by ideas and even passions of a religious nature: his conversation is animated; he can't speak for very long without being moved and having tears in his eyes. (We have made the same observation with all those seen up to the present.) He is of German origin, lost his father early, was badly brought up. He has been in prison a year. Good health. According to him the yard adjoining the cell is absolutely neces-sary to the health of the inmates.'

---

* 'Each cell is aired by a ventilator, and contains a *fosse d'aisance* whose construction makes it perfectly odourless. One must have seen all the cells of the Philadelphia prison, and have passed entire days in them, to form an exact idea of their clean-ness and the purity of the air one breathes in them.' *Du Syst. Pén.*, p.58,note.

No. 22 turned out to be a negro of thirty-four, already condemned once for theft. 'Do you find the regime of the prison where you are at this moment as rigorous as they say?' he was asked.

'*A*. No; but that depends on the mental disposition of the man shut up in it. If the prisoner doesn't take to the solitary confinement, he falls into irritation and despair; if on the other hand he at once perceives all the gain that can be drawn from his situation, it isn't unbearable to him.

'*Q*. You have already been detained in the Walnut-Street prison?

'*A*. Yes Sir, and I can't imagine a greater lair of vice and crime. There a minor offender needs but a few days to become a complete scoundrel.

'*Q*. So you think the penitentiary is superior to the old prison?

'*A*. It's as if you asked me if the sun were more beautiful than the moon.*

Altogether, the readiness of the prisoners to talk, and their fertility of expression, were amazing. Only two of the forty-four prisoners whom Tocqueville saw were suspicious or taciturn, though several went right on working during their interview. Generally, too, the inmates agreed in their answers. Walnut prison had injured the morals of all those who had been sentenced there. The first days of solitude in the Eastern State were a severe trial. One convict who was still in his third week was convinced that he would never come out alive. 'Here,' he said, 'the soul is very sick'—and sobbed at the thought of his wife and children. On entering, Tocqueville had found him weeping at his work. Again, on the other hand, almost all regarded the Bible as a great consolation. Tocqueville found an octogenarian occupied in its tranquil perusal. And a negro, the first prisoner ever sent to the penitentiary, insisted on reading to his unexpected visitor the parable of the good pastor, so much comfort it gave him.

Tocqueville was not bored. Originally he had undertaken these interviews more as a necessary task—out of a feeling of duty—than for any other good reason. But soon, as Beaumont was later to write,[7] he was 'carrying them on with extreme interest, now struck by the singular consequences of isolation for the human soul, now moved by the moral miseries whose secrets were unveiled before his eyes, often [again] held by the fascination of these solitary interviews beyond the

* 'We have thought it our duty to reproduce the inmates' replies textually.'

hours fixed by the discipline of the place, [and] always detained by the poor prisoners, ingenious to prolong the rare accident of conversation with a man, little they suspected with what man.'

In twelve days Tocqueville had made eight visits to Cherry Hill.* But the conversation that interested him perhaps more than all the others was reserved almost for the end. He had gone in to interview a man of forty years, who had been convicted of highway robbery.

'I was fourteen or fifteen years old when I came to Philadelphia,' the prisoner began his story. It was a life history that seemed to Tocqueville to illuminate the whole penitentiary problem. 'I was the son of a poor farmer in the West, and I came to seek my livelihood by working in a large city. Not being recommended to any one, I found no work; and, the very first day, for want of shelter, I was reduced to sleeping on the deck of one of the vessels in the harbour. It was there that they found me in the morning; the constable arrested me, and the mayor condemned me to a month in prison, as a vagabond. Associated during this month of detention with a crowd of evildoers of all ages, I lost the honest principles that my father had given me; and, on leaving the prison, my first act was to join several young delinquents of my own age, and help them to commit several thefts. I was arrested, judged, and acquitted. I believed myself thenceforth beyond the reach of justice and, full of confidence in my cleverness, I committed several other violations of the law which brought me once again before the assizes. This time I was condemned to imprisonment for nine years in the Walnut-Street jail.

'Q. Didn't this punishment make you realize the necessity of reforming yourself?

'A. —Yes, sir; yet it wasn't the Walnut-Street prison that made me regret my criminal acts. I confess that I was never able to repent of them, nor even thought of doing so during all my stay in that place. But I wasn't long in noticing that the same individuals reappeared there over and over again, and that, whatever the skill, the strength, or the courage of the thieves, they always ended by being taken. That led me to reflect seriously, and I adopted the firm resolution to abandon for ever, on getting out of prison, so dangerous a mode of life. That decision made, my conduct improved, and after seven years of im-

* The journal of Warden Wood is still preserved, and gives both the dates of their visits and the names of the Pennsylvania Inspectors who accompanied them. (Courtesy of Henry L. Woolman, through whose kindness the journal was brought to the prison for consultation.)

prisonment I obtained my pardon. I had learned the tailor's trade in the prison, and I soon was able to get a favourable position. I married; and I began to earn my living easily enough; but Philadelphia was full of people I had known in prison; I was in constant terror of being betrayed by them. One day, indeed, two of my old room companions presented themselves to my employer, and asked to speak to me. At first I pretended not to recognize them; but they forced me soon to admit who I was. They then demanded that I lend them a considerable sum; and, on my refusal, they threatened to betray to my master the history of my life. I promised then to satisfy them, and suggested that they come back the next day. As soon as they were gone, I left myself; and, going on a boat at once with my wife, I left Philadelphia and betook myself to Baltimore. Again I was easily able to get a job in that city, and for a long time I led a very comfortable existence, when one day my master received a letter from one of the constables of Philadelphia warning him that he had an ex-convict from Walnut among his workmen. I don't know who could have brought this man to such an act. It's to him that I owe my being here. As soon as he had received the letter I speak of, my master dismissed me with ignominy. I ran to all the other tailors of Baltimore, but they had been warned, and refused to receive me. My misery then constrained me to go work on the railroad then being built between Baltimore and the Ohio. My chagrin and the fatigues of such a manner of life weren't long in giving me a violent fever. I was sick a long time, and used up my resources. Scarcely recovered, I had myself taken to Philadelphia, where the fever attacked me again. When I began to convalesce, and saw myself at the end of my means, without bread for myself or family, when I thought of all the obstacles I encountered in earning an honest livelihood, and of all the unjust persecutions that I had been made to undergo, I fell into a state of inexpressible exasperation. I said to myself: Very well! Since they force me to it, I shall become a thief again; and if there exists a single dollar in the United States, were it in the pocket of the President, I will have it. I called my wife; I ordered her to sell all the clothes that we didn't need; and with the money I had her buy a pistol. Supplied with that weapon, and during the time when I was still too feeble to walk without crutches, I got myself to the outskirts of the city; I stopped the first passerby and forced him to give me his pocketbook. But I was discovered that very evening. I had been followed from afar by the man I had robbed; and, my weakness having forced me to stop in the neighbourhood, they had no trouble in capturing me. I readily admitted my crime, and they sent me here.

'What are your resolutions for the future?' the sympathetic Frenchman asked.

'*A*. I don't feel disposed, I tell you frankly, to reproach myself for what I have done, or inclined to become what is called a good Christian, but I am determined to steal no more, and I see a possibility of succeeding in that. When in nine years I leave here, no one will know me any longer in the world; no one will know that I have been in prison; and I will have made no dangerous acquaintances there. I shall be free to earn my living in peace. That is the great superiority I find in this penitentiary and what makes me feel, in spite of the severity of discipline in vigour here, that I prefer a hundred times to be here to having to live once more in the prison of Walnut-Street.'

To take down *verbatim* such detailed stories as this last was of course impossible. So Tocqueville contented himself at the moment with some rapid notes, then wrote out the whole conversation afterwards. As documents for their penitentiary book, these prison interviews would be absolutely priceless.

Some weeks later, wishing to show them to his colleague, Tocqueville couldn't find them. He searched again, but in vain. Finally, convinced that he had lost them, he sat down to write out what his memory could recall, and 'so profound had been the impression made on his soul by these lonely interviews,' Beaumont was one day to proclaim,[9] 'that in a few hours he retraced them all on paper, without any confusion, and without omitting a single one. The next day, no longer looking for his notes, he found them. One could see, in comparing them with his recollections, how exact the latter had been, and with what prodigious fidelity his memory had reproduced the whole. A few details only had been forgotten, but nowhere was the *pensée-mère* absent. . . . Alexis de Tocqueville did not have a memory for words or numbers,' Beaumont testified, 'but to the highest degree he possessed a memory for ideas; once entered into his mind, an idea never escaped.'

'If it is true,' their prison report was to phrase one of those ideas acquired at Cherry Hill,[10] 'if it is true that in establishments of such nature all the evil comes from the relations of the inmates with each other, one is forced to acknowledge that nowhere is this vice more surely avoided than at Philadelphia, where the prisoners find it materially impossible to communicate. And it is incontestable that this perfect isolation shelters the prisoner from all harmful contagion.'

Experience and logic had also impressed a second idea on Tocqueville. 'As in no other prison is the solitude more complete than at Philadelphia, so nowhere is the necessity of labour more absolute. It would thus be inexact to say that in the Philadelphia penitentiary they impose labour; it can more reasonably be said that the privilege of working is accorded. When we visited this penitentiary we conversed successively with . . . .'

Again, a third idea was to persist in Tocqueville's mind till it found expression in their report.[11] 'The only critical instant (at Philadelphia) is that of entering the prison. The solitary cell of the criminal is for several days full of terrible phantoms . . . but when he has triumphed over the terrors that were driving him to insanity or despair . . . and has sought in labour distraction from his miseries, then, from that moment on, you have him cowed, and submissive for ever afterwards to the rules of the prison.'

These and other convictions the grim Eastern State had driven home.

\*

\* \*

There was one important idea, however, that had not been able to find entrance into Tocqueville's or Beaumont's mind—and this despite the best efforts (and apparent success) of the Philadelphia reformers, who were certain that they had convinced the young commissioners of the absolute perfection of the Pennsylvania system.

'It gives me pleasure to assure thee,' the good Quaker Roberts Vaux wrote to the Governor of the State on the eighth of November.\* 'It gives me pleasure to assure thee, that Monsr De Beaumont, & Tocqueville the Commissioners appointed by the French Government to examine the Prisons, Jail discipline, & criminal codes of our Country,

---

\* On 24 October, H.D.Gilpin wrote to Edward Livingston in Washington: '. . . It has been very pleasant for some weeks. Among other strangers we have had the two French gentlemen DeBeaumont & DeTocqueville who are examining the state of our criminal code. They brought me a letter from the Duke of Montbello, but I have not seen much of them, for their time has been passed almost entirely at the Penitentiary. With that institution they appear to be strongly and favorably impressed. They spoke much of you, and were well informed in regard to your code. By the by, I sh<sup>d</sup> mention that Mr. Vaux expressed to me much regret that you were in Philadelphia without his having met you. He is very anxious that you sh<sup>d</sup> use your influence to have the Penitentiary building at Washington, on the plan of ours; . . .' Gilpin Papers, Historical Society of Pennsylvania.

after having sought information at Auburn, Sing-Sing, Weatherfield [*sic*], Boston, & New York City, have passed a week at the new Penitentiary near the Town, & have pronounced unhesitatingly in favour of the Penna system, this is a Proud result for some of us, who have given much attention & time in the promotion of the actual plan; & as these Gentlemen have solely sought the *truth* I regard their verdict of vast importance for humanity, & the triumph of mild laws, & adequate reformatory penal jurisprudence.—They will report under these impressions & thus our honest Commonwealth will be presented *to the World*, in this respect on the highest point of improvement. The State may be congratulated in this matter.'

Apparently Governor Wolf, on receipt of this information, thought so too. For in his meassage to the State legislature on the sixth of December he was to boast that 'Foreigners, whose especial business it has been to visit the penitentiaries in this country . . . have with one voice awarded the meed of merit to that established in the Eastern Penitentiary of Pennsylvania.'

Even the *National Gazette* was to report that the French Commissioners 'were fully convinced of the superiority of the system of the *separate confinement of offenders.* . . . This decision,' Philadelphians were informed, 'should be regarded as entitled to great consideration and weight, proceeding from minds eminently gifted, and otherwise qualified by professional and general studies, for the important duties assigned them. They were brought to the judgment we have mentioned after a calm and philosophical investigation of principles, and a thorough inspection into the practical operation of the Pennsylvanian punishment, inflicted upon prisoners whom they saw and conversed with in the most confidential manner.'[12]

Of the thoroughness of the investigation there could be no question. Only the *United States Gazette* detected a reservation behind the tactful enthusiasm of the commissioners. 'They doubt the possibility of introducing the same arrangement in France, on account of the *first* cost. The prison is here built; the cost is already met. There it would be necessary to incur anew the whole expense of the erection of buildings.'[13] Even so, after philosophical consideration, the gifted investigators 'express their approbation of the new penitentiary . . . and consider it superior to any other they have seen.'

Yet actually Tocqueville and Beaumont were full of doubts. After completing their survey of the second of America's great penitentiary systems, they were sure of neither the absolute nor the comparative merits of the two schools of practice. Eleven days after Vaux had announced his triumph to the governor, Tocqueville informed his friend Chabrol:[14]

'As for the penitentiary system, which is our industry as Lucas would say, we can say without vanity that the subject has been exhausted by us. We have the materials to prove that the penitentiary system reforms and that it does not reform; that it is costly and cheap; easy to administer and impracticable: in a word, that it suits or does not suit France, according to the taste of the interviewer; and we guarantee to support each of these assertions with very pertinent examples.

'This is in fun. The truth is that our trip has demonstrated to us two or three great Penitentiary truths which may be of use. But, from the point of view of its applicability to France, there remain in our mind doubts that we shall frankly set forth on our return. . . .'

XXXVI

## SOUNDING THE PENNSYLVANIA MIND

'I was raging to have to occupy myself with prison matters when around me I saw a host of distinguished men, whose conversation would have been a source of light for me had I had the leisure to talk with them,' Beaumont later confessed.[1] 'However, I saw enough of Philadelphia society to judge that it is most agreeable and contains in its midst some individuals of very great merit.'

The very first day, 12 October, they had met the distinguished lawyer and linguist, Peter S. Duponceau. The old gentleman, it appeared, had been a countryman of theirs but was now become a thorough American.* To his fellow Philadelphians he was known as a notorious punster, a lover of music, and a friend to all visiting Frenchmen, shepherding them often, as did John Vaughan with English travellers, to the famous 'Wistar Parties.' To Tocqueville and Beaumont his first words were a warning against the over-emphasis placed in English-speaking countries on prisons as instruments of punishment.[2] In Philadelphia of the philanthropists Duponceau retained his balance.

On their third day, 14 October, they enjoyed some conversation with the scion of a distinguished New England family, Charles Jared Ingersoll, lawyer, writer, friend of the Bonapartes.† And that evening

* His had been an extraordinary career. Born on the Ile de Ré, he had learned English from the soldiers. In 1777 he had come to the American colonies with Steuben, helped drill Washington's army, and become assistant to Robert Livingston, the Secretary for Foreign Affairs of the Confederation. Settling in Pennsylvania, his skill in handling the cases of aliens and the business of the French consular agents had soon brought him to the top. An enterprising and curious soul, he had also published some works on the language of the Indians (which Tocqueville was to cite in his *Démocratie*); and now he was engaged in some experiments with the culture of silk.
  Trained as an ecclesiastic, and at first an anti-Federalist, he lived to think that he had been in error in both of these matters.
† Son of Jared Ingersoll, Connecticut representative at the Federal Convention of 1787, and himself of some diplomatic experience abroad, Charles Jared Ingersoll (1782–1862) had been Federalist candidate for Vice-President in 1812, and District Attorney for Pennsylvania by appointment of President Madison. Recently removed

they went, seemingly in Ingersoll's company, to a play. It was to the
evenings almost exclusively that their social explorations had to be
confined. In his first letter from Philadelphia Beaumont proceeded to
describe these diversions.[3]

The play, a French piece on Napoleon presented by a New Orleans
troupe, was terrible. And the audience seemed to Beaumont even more
extraordinary. Apparently only strangers, prostitutes, or lower class
people attended. And they paid not the slightest attention to the stage,
but walked about, drank together, and argued as if nothing else were
going on.*

'The day following we were invited to a musical *Soirée* at the home
of Mr. Walsh, a very distinguished Philadelphian. They sang well
enough: that is to say that neither American men nor women figured
in the concert, all the entertainment was provided by an Italian and
some French women. The Americans, who are by nature as cold as
ice, were throughout tempted to regard the Italian *amateur* as a lunatic,
because he, while singing, gesticulated a great deal and assumed dramatic attitudes. The concert ended in some waltzes and quadrilles.'

On the whole, Beaumont had been much impressed. 'The most lov-
able and sprightly man [of Philadelphia] is without contradiction Mr.
Walsh,' he was later to report. The man's conversation 'sparkled with
sallies and witticisms.'[4] A stylist of great facility and the editor of a
newspaper and a quarterly, both widely read, Mr. Walsh was the
literary leader of Philadelphia. 'He has two charming daughters,
who do not spoil the attractiveness of his house,' Beaumont noticed.
'At frequent intervals he gives small *soirées*, where we did some fine
waltzing, I promise you. They play at his house some very good music,
which would I am sure compare very well with the music of Galle-
rande. At the last concert I heard an Englishwoman, Miss Sterling, who
is *d'une très grande force* on the piano. Anne Walsh, the younger [of
the daughters], sings marvellously; she was a real success in the *duo*,
*Amour sacré de la Patrie*, which she sang with Mr. Dirigi [?], a
little Italian who is not wanting in talent but who, because of his af-
fectation and his grimaces, makes one die laughing. . . .†

---

from that office by Andrew Jackson, he was now devoting himself to local politics,
internal improvements, and poetry.
* For a short essay on the three theatres of Philadelphia, see *Marie*, I,393,395.
† Educated at a Jesuit College, deafness had forced Robert Walsh (1784–1859) to give
up the practice of the law for a career in journalism and letters. A contributor to
Dennie's celebrated *Portfolio*, and founder of the *National Gazette*, he became a

'Many of my evenings have been spent in small gatherings, simple, not very brilliant, but very agreeable. Don't expect of me a description of *mœurs*, that would be to enter upon a path without end; all that I can say is that this society is very happy. The women practise an unrestrained coquetry. But all the world agrees in acknowledging that they stop there.* Among the husbands, there are some who are amiable enough to deserve their good fortune; but in general they are much more happy, and much better treated by their wives, than their qualities give them the right to be. The fact is that, with the exception of a small circle of literary men whose civilized ways and European manners quite recall our most agreeable *salons*, it can be said that at Philadelphia, as in all the other cities of the United States, the American men are occupied with but one single thing, their business. . . .'

Such occupation, of course, did not prevent their treating Tocqueville and Beaumont '*according to our merits*.' The evening of their fourth day, 'we passed . . . with the Philosophical Society of Philadelphia, to which we were presented by Mr. Duponceau, a very well informed ex-Frenchman, who is president of the Society.' But Beaumont was not impressed by America's most distinguished academy. 'I was bored,' he confessed, 'and saw no one there who inspired me with the desire to see him again.'†

Toward the end of their second week in Philadelphia, Tocqueville sat down to write his mother. ' . . . Prisons, learned societies, and *salon* gatherings in the evening: there's our life,' he summed up.[5] 'I continue in very good health, that's a point that you will be glad to find settled. The autumn here is admirable, the sky pure and sparkling as on the most beautiful summer days. The woods have a very much more varied foliage than in Europe at the same time of year. All the shades of red and green are mingled together; this is really the moment when America appears in all her glory.'

---

pioneer and authority in the field of literary periodicals. Long residence in Europe had made him a bitter critic of Napoleon; and his *Letter on the Genius and Disposition of the French Government* was to reach four editions in England.

To Tocqueville and Beaumont, this entertaining *raconteur* presented no less than seventeen different pamphlets (and, very possibly, others as well). One bundle was addressed to Tocqueville and Beaumont at the 'Mansion House, South 3rd Street,' where they were probably staying. See below p.537

* Dannery, the French Consul, in a later letter to Beaumont, mentioned several of their lady acquaintances, among others a Miss Lewis and Malvina Willbert, who had married Capt. Pelet. Beaumont probably had not forgotten her big black eyes, which finally had found what they were looking for, he said. 8 Oct. 1832 (BB).

† This was an exaggeration.

It also appeared to be the moment when Philadelphia society resumed its full activity. That very day, the twenty-fourth, Job R. Tyson had delivered the annual discourse before the Historical Society; * and Tocqueville and Beaumont had been present at a formal dinner attended by a number of the leading citizens and celebrities of the city. Thus they had encountered the former ambassador to France and Senator from Louisiana, James Brown.† Mayor Benjamin W. Richards, a handsome and imposing man,‡ they had already conversed with at the Philosophical Society. Now they also talked to his friend, the Quaker editor and librarian, John Jay Smith,§ and to the Recorder of the City, the indefatigable Joseph McIlvaine.¶ Most of these men were politicians, perhaps, but each had his merits. At least Tocqueville wanted to correct the distorted picture of American society that his family had just received. It seemed that one of their companions and friends of the Atlantic crossing was now back in France and had reported very unfavourably on his experiences in the United States.

'*De grâce*, don't believe half the unfavourable things that S. . . . has told you about this country,' Tocqueville begged. 'He has no personal experience of it, and what he knows he has learned from a certain class of Frenchmen whom alone he saw and who, in America as elsewhere, seem the representatives of all the defects common to the spirit of our compatriots. With England, this country here is the most curious and instructive that one could visit, and, beyond England, it has the unique privilege of being at the same time in its virility and infancy, which gives it the most extraordinary aspect in the world.

* Job R. Tyson, 1803–1858, was a member of the Prison Society and a school director, and solicitor for the Pennsylvania Railroad. He apparently gave Tocqueville and Beaumont copies of his address and his *Essay on the Penal Laws of Pennsylvania* (1827).

† Born in Virginia, James Brown (1766–1835) had known a career as Indian fighter, and administrator and judge in Louisiana Territory, as well.

‡ One of nineteen children in a family of Welsh origins, Benjamin W. Richards (1797–1851) had graduated from Princeton with honours in 1815, and married a daughter of Joshua Lippincott, by whom he was to have eleven children of his own. He was a man of generosity, courtesy and conviction, interested in politics, an advocate of public schools, and a director in many commercial and philanthropic enterprises. See below, p.535.

§ John Jay Smith, 1798–1881, was librarian of the Philadelphia Library, and interested in negro emancipation.

¶ Joseph McIlvaine was shortly to die at the unripe age of 38; but some idea of his judgment and native capacity may be obtained from a study of the long essays on the judiciary and penal system of Pennsylvania that he was in the course of the next few months to compose for Tocqueville and Beaumont's benefit. See below, pp.530–35.

'. . . I admit that the inhabitants of the country are not all the most agreeable company.* A great number smoke, chew, spit in your beard. But they do not the less form a race of very remarkable men. Besides, if they don't stand upon ceremony, they bear the same conduct in others admirably. There is nothing so difficult as to annoy an American. Unless you plant your fist in his face, he doesn't suspect that you wish to offend him: he attributes everything to chance and not to your design. Yet those are the things that profoundly irritate S. . . . He would be quite willing to see the Americans liars, dissolute, irreligious, thieves even; but that they should step on your feet without asking your pardon, and spit a great distance without taking . . . . (illegible), those are so many abominations that one cannot suffer, and that dishonour a people. The fact is, I recognize, that generally speaking they lack refinement, grace, and elegance; at each instant in America you are aware of the absence of a superior class which, if it existed, would give the example to all the rest. But, after all, that's a superficial thing at which it is not reasonable to halt.'

What *should* one think of Americans, then? Tocqueville was not yet prepared to say. He had, he told his father, some notebooks 'of inestimable value.' But whether he would ever publish anything on the United States, he truly did not know.

'It seems to me that I have some good ideas, but I don't yet know in what framework I will place them, and the [idea of] publicity frightens me. . . .'

*

*    *

In Philadelphia, it so happened, it was democracy—the people's control of their own government—that was beginning to attract Tocqueville's most earnest attention.† The fact was, he was now trying to block in a hitherto neglected section of the map or chart that he had

---

* This paragraph has been scratched out in the original (possibly by Beaumont?).

† 'We spend our time as profitably as we can,' was Beaumont's phrasing. And on 26 October he proceeded to describe to his sister-in-law the demographic investigations that had lately begun to occupy *him*.[6] Three races of men, the original Quakers, the later German immigrants, and the people who had been brought from Africa, the blacks, seemed to Beaumont of particular fascination in Pennsylvania. Whether Tocqueville's companion was now at last beginning to envisage the possibility of writing his own separate book on America, he did not say. But the letter in which he discussed his new-found racial enthusiasms made it perfectly clear that he had not lost his perennial interest in phenomena of a less solemn sort:

'The young ladies are raised here in great freedom. . . . I hope that they will not make me lose mine. I can even say that I am certain they won't, for I would rather

been constructing of American society. On first landing in the country, he had immediately been impressed with environment and background. He had learned about the English origins and the religious foundations of America's democratic society. In New York, and later in New England, he had then begun to study the actual structure of American Republicanism: the shape of the government; where it was organized and how operated. From landlords, lawyers, and historians he had learned about State governments and town meetings: about the administration of justice, and the jury system: about the separation of state from church and press: in a word, about the absence of strong government and the presence of free opinion.

Now he was seeking the people's part. What role, in a society of such origins and under a government of such a character, did the private citizen play? If American democracy rested on the average man, what were his political privileges, what were his political activities?

The *suffrage* and the *right of assembly* drew Tocqueville's eye—especially at first the right of assembly, or what he called 'Association.'

While still in New York on his way from Connecticut, Tocqueville had been speculating on the extraordinary use that American citizens seemed to make of this right of Assembly. 'The power of association has reached its uttermost development in America,' he noted in one of his alphabetical diaries.[7] 'They associate in the interests of commerce, for objects political, literary, religious. It's never by an appeal to a superior authority that success is sought, but by an appeal to individual resources, oganized to act in harmony.

'The most extreme effort of association seems to me to be in the temperance societies, that is to say in an association of men who engage mutually to abstain from a vice, and who find in the collective force an aid in resisting something that is most intimate and most personal to each man, his own inclinations. The effect of the temperance societies is one of the most remarkable things in this country.' *

From the reports of the Societies of New York and Pennsylvania, and from their friend Mr. Tuckerman's *Letter to the Mechanics of Boston*, Tocqueville was to estimate that there were at the moment

---

be hanged than marry a foreigner. . . . They claim that to-night we will hear an Englishman who sings marvellously well. I have difficulty believing this, for the English, like the Americans, compose an anti-musical race. . . .'

* 'At Baltimore, it's an association that provides the racing prizes, establishes the track, and presides at the races.' 30 Oct. 1831.

140 temperance societies in existence in Maine, 209 in Massachusetts, 202 in Connecticut, 727 in New York, 124 in Pennsylvania, and more than two thousand in the whole nation. Already it was claimed that liquor consumption had been cut in two in New York, and in Pennsylvania had dropped 500,000 gallons. All this Tocqueville was to consider sufficiently curious to be worth mention in their future Prison Report.[8]

On the whole, however, Tocqueville was tempted to doubt the usefulness of such institutions in France. In America, of course, the abuse of alcohol was worse than anywhere else, temperance societies therefore more useful. But that was not his thought. Instead, he was afraid that in France the people would abuse the privilege of 'association,' especially should the right of assembly be allowed to political minorities. There had just been held two conventions of a political nature in the United States: one—a free trade convention—had been occupying the centre of the stage in Philadelphia just a few days before Tocqueville's arrival; the other—a meeting of the friends of industry, or a pro-tariff convention—had been holding its sessions simultaneously in New York. Tocqueville was appalled when he thought what the consequences of such democratic activities might be in France.

'The right to assemble in convention is the most extreme consequence of the dogma of the sovereignty of the people,' he began some reflections on the subject, 14 October.[9] And again, after recording the debates and the resolutions of the Philadelphia Convention, he returned to his fear: 'Of all that I have seen in America, it is this convention which has most struck me as being, [for] us, a dangerous and impracticable consequence of the sovereignty of the people.'

Not every American, however, was prepared to agree.

'Id. To-day I was at the home of Mr. Ingersall, lawyer and ex-member of the legislature, and I expressed to him what I have just written. He replied:

'The dangers of which you are afraid are in my opinion less to be feared. When men can speak in liberty, you can bet they won't act. Besides, notice this, the object of the convention is not to act but to persuade. It represents an opinion, an interest, and doesn't aim to represent the nation, which, itself, is all together in Congress. The convention, on the contrary, starts from the fact that it does not represent the majority, but wishes to act on public opinion and change the majority by persuasion.

'But, said I, the opinion and interest you speak of is able to put its arguments forward daily by means of the press.

'You appreciate, replied Mr. Ingersall, the immense preponderance that an assembly has over an obscure journalist or the individual effort of a man of talent. As for me, I regard the right of assembling in convention as the logical consequence of the dogma of the sovereignty of the majority. There are some opinions which, by the very fact they are shared by the minority, would be for ever repressed by the majority, if by the side of the public assemblies which express the all-powerful wishes of the majority there were not to be found gatherings (likewise supplied with the moral power that numbers give) which may plead the interests of the minority and make, not laws, but speeches calculated to win over the majority itself.

'Very well, I answered, nothing is certainly more logical, but I shan't ask for any other instances to prove how inapplicable are the immovable laws of logic to the affairs of this world. Suppose a people imperfectly habituated to the government of laws and the reign of persuasion, give it passions and great political interests, allow beside the law-making majority a minority to arise which charges itself solely with preambles and stops at plans, and you will see what becomes of public order. Don't you perceive that in the character of almost all men there is only a step, the easiest step in the world to take, between proving that a thing is good and executing it? Besides, are there not certain political questions where the majority is so uncertain that each party may pretend itself the majority? Thus you let be created, at the side of the directing power, a power whose moral authority is as great, which yet, though feeling itself strong enough to struggle against the established order, will respect it because of the metaphysical consideration that the convention is made to enlighten opinions and not constrain, to persuade and not act.

'Mr. Ingersall confessed that he had spoken only for the United States, and for the present time. Being capable of following out the logical consequences of our principles without danger, said he, we do well to do so. Generally speaking (*du reste*) my conviction has always been that one should make laws for peoples, and not peoples according to laws. I can imagine that an assembly like the Philadelphia convention would have great dangers for France. Yet it seems to me that the association against foreigners [?] has some analogy with our use of conventions. The thing that would make conventions so dangerous for you is the concentration of all France in Paris. I fancy an assembly of factious people, held in Paris, might have a destructive power over the whole state. There is nothing like that in America. In general I am firmly persuaded that as long as you do not give your provinces *une forte individualité* you will never be certain of remaining free.'

Tocqueville was silent, impressed, dubious.*

In his *Démocratie*, four years later, he would devote a whole chapter to 'Political Associations' (when discussing the faith of the people in their own government, in America). To illustrate, he would retell the entire story of the Philadelphia Free Trade Convention, almost word for word as given here. Mr. Ingersoll's explanation and his own misgivings would be repeated. As for France, Tocqueville would still be afraid: 'I suppose a people imperfectly habituated to the use of liberty, or seething with profound political passions,' he would write.† 'Beside the law-making majority, I place a minority which undertakes merely to *consider* and which stops short at *proposals*; and I cannot help believing the public order exposed to great hazards.' As for America, on the other hand, the case was different. More dangerous and less necessary than a free press, the freedom of Assembly was yet justified because the people was habituated to its use, and could employ it particularly in preventing the tyranny of the majority. In a country of frequent and universal voting, the majority was at the same time precisely determined, all powerful, yet susceptibile of losing control through desertion from the ranks. In such surroundings, a minority convention could indeed play a peaceful *and* successful role. 'Of all the causes which contribute to moderate the violence of political Associations in the United States, the most powerful is perhaps the universal vote.'‡

*

*    *

---

* As to Ingersoll's last suggestion, Tocqueville jotted down the following memo: 'The Americans are so afraid of centralization and the influence of capitals that they almost always take care to place the seat of legislative and executive powers far from the chief cities. Thus the seat of the legislature and government of the State of New-York is at Albany. The seat of the government of Pennsylvania is at Harrisburg, a small town in the interior, and not [at] Philadelphia; that of Maryland at Annapolis and not at Baltimore.

'In criminal justice, roads, prisons, in general in all enterprises requiring rapidity of execution or continuity of plan, the want of centralization makes itself felt in America.' 23 Oct. 1831 (Alph.B).

† *Dém. en Am.*, II,33.

‡ *Dém. en Am.*, II,40.

In Philadelphia Tocqueville turned to examine the question of the suffrage.

The exact qualifications for voting he could get later from the printed source. At the moment he was anxious to get an expression of opinion. Were the masses, who had recently won an almost universal manhood suffrage, wise in their selection of representatives at the elections? In other words, was unlimited voting—a complete self-government—thus far a practical success?

Benjamin W. Richards, about to be reappointed Mayor of Philadelphia for another term by the Select and Common councils of the city, seemed to think so. He 'said to me to-day that in general the people showed great good sense in their choices,' Tocqueville noted on 16 October.*

'It has not always been thus in France, I replied. With us there is an ancient enmity in the people against the upper classes which has brought it about that when the people have been master they have often been seen to elect men [who were] without education and who presented no social guarantee.

'Mr. Richards returned: we have never seen the like here. It is true that in America what may be called the upper classes have never had privileges and have never separated themselves openly from the people in politics. Our situation, however, has to be appreciated. One may say that our republic is the triumph and the government of the middle classes. In the Middle States and those of New England, for example, there exists no true tie between the people and the classes that are altogether superior. The latter betray but little faith in the wisdom of the people, a certain scorn for the passions of the multitude, a certain distaste for its manners; in fact, they isolate themselves. The people on their side, without animosity exactly, but by a sort of instinctive repugnance, seldom name them to office. They choose their candidates ordinarily from the middle classes. It's really they who govern.

'Do you believe that that is a good thing?' Tocqueville asked.

'*A.* The middle classes are the most useful to society, and we find them as apt in public affairs as the rest. What I tell you, however, is not to be found in the South. In the West, also, the march of society is so rapid, there is such a confusion among all the social elements to be encountered there, that it is impossible to make such a remark.'

It was even difficult to get unanimity of opinion on the results of

* Richards 'appears much esteemed in this region,' Tocqueville observed.

the suffrage in New England and Pennsylvania, Tocqueville discovered. Their venerable friend, Peter Duponceau, for example, disagreed sharply with Mayor Richards' opinion. 'I have heard it said,' Tocqueville angled,[10] 'I have heard it said that you have put your affairs in the hands of those incapable of directing them.' 'That is very true, replied Mr. Duponceau, it is rare that the choice falls on a man of talent. All the offices are distributed according to political considerations. It is party spirit and intrigue that are the impelling motives, here as under monarchies. The master, alone, is different.'

Again, Tocqueville heard words of dispraise from James Brown. The wealthy ex-senator from Louisiana was certain that the voters were often mistaken in their choices. And Tocqueville, himself, was inclined to this opinion. Surely the system of manhood suffrage did not always produce perfection. 'Since landing in America,' he wrote, 'I have practically acquired proof that all the enlightened classes are opposed to General Jackson, and the populace sticks to him, and he has the mass in his favour.' Again Tocqueville noted: 'The dogma of the Republic is that the people is always right, just as The King Can Do No Wrong is the religion of monarchical states. It's a great question whether one is more false than the other. But what is certain is that neither one nor the other is true.'[11] The whole problem of leadership in a democracy would therefore have to go over for further investigation.

Meanwhile, it was interesting to hear that universal voting power—that is, equal participation in controlling the government—was not producing complete social equality in the city of brotherly love. Instead, another influence was making itself felt: that of wealth.

Mr. Ingersoll, the lawyer, had first mentioned the subject. 'I think there is more *social* equality with you at home than with us,' he had ventured.[12] 'With you, according to my understanding (*je crois*), talent and wealth are on the same footing. Here talent opens all doors, but wealth gives a decided pre-eminence.'

Duponceau was particularly eloquent and scornful on this subject.[13] 'Equality exists only on the street,' he said. 'Money creates extreme inequalities in society. A man of talent, whatever his fortune, is no doubt everywhere received; but he is made to feel that he is not rich, and his wife and children are not received. We can't have anything to do with (*fréquenter*) those people, say the women, they have only two thousand *piastres* income, and we have ten. It's this immoderate desire to shine that throws so many families into luxury and spoils the simplicity of life. The same desire to shine is to be noticed from State to State. How much money vanity has made us throw out of the window!'

But this was getting away from the subject under investigation, namely, the further political effects of universal suffrage. If the representatives of the people were not always of the first order of talent, what influence did frequent elections have on the character of the government itself?

While still on his way to Philadelphia, Tocqueville had already made a note on this topic.[14] The frequency of elections made it possible, he thought, for those in office to exercise a power more tyrannical than that of the most despotic governments; because the people, being able to switch the majority and throw out the ruling party at the next election, was not afraid of a permanent oppression. 'It's thus that the select men of New England have the right to have posted the names of the drunkards in the taverns and to prevent the tavern-keepers and even third parties, under penalty of fine, from furnishing them wine. A censorial power of that kind would revolt people in the most absolute monarchy. Here they submit to it easily. Once things are begun in this style, the magistrate has the more power the lower the franchise and the shorter the terms of office. Nowhere is there more of the arbitrary than in a Republic, because there it is not to be feared. . . .'

Tyranny by the majority? despotism in a democracy? Tocqueville's American friends would have been astonished and shocked at the line that his thought was taking. Only Jared Sparks had mentioned the word 'tyranny' in connection with majority rule. Yet Tocqueville had been born an aristocrat; by instinct he hated uniformity, the slightest loss of personal independence, even the dictation of public opinion. Already he had some of the materials in hand for his famous and oft-controverted chapter on the 'Despotic Character of Office-holders under the Empire of American Democracy.' *

Yet there were two points where democratic tyranny was nothing but pure weakness. In the first place, the participation of all, and the frequency of changes in control, robbed government in America of all the regularity, perseverance, and order that a single despot could impart.† In the second place, and this was far more serious, even the office-holders were apparently unable to resist the majority. In Penn-

---

* *Dém. en Am.*, II,30. For comment on this celebrated *dictum*, see below, pp.766–67.
† Toc. diary note, Philadelphia, 25 Oct. 1831 (Port. III). See also *Dém. en Am.*, II,98.

sylvania, George Washington Smith pointed out,[15] the majority were anti-temperance. Instead of posting the names of drunkards, therefore, the legislators were even afraid to place a tax on *eau-de-vie*. Curiously enough, their devoted friend Roberts Vaux was just emphasizing the danger of such weakness. On the twenty-seventh of October, in prophetic mood, the philanthropist gravely said to Tocqueville:[16]

'I regard manufacturers as a social necessity, yet as a harmful necessity. They deprave the population and often expose it to frightful want. The introduction of the industrial system in a country as completely democratic as ours is especially to be feared. In France and in England, when the industrial population experiences needs and wishes to trouble public order, there exists an exterior force ready to maintain the peace. But where with us is our authority independent of the people?

'I replied: But take care, what you say has wide implications (*une grande portée*). If you admit that the majority can sometimes desire disorder and injustice, what becomes of the principle of your government?

'Mr. Robert[s] Vaux answered: I'll confess to you that I have never approved the system of universal voting rights; in very truth it hands over the governing power to the most passionate and least enlightened classes of society. Here we really have no guarantees whatever against the people; our legislative powers have not the slightest independence. I would wish that the Senate were chosen by the large property-holders, but, being chosen by the same electors as the legislature, it offers no more resistance than the latter to popular passions.'

\*

\* \*

One other conversation, because of its variety and interest, is worth quoting here.

It was the twenty-eighth of October, the day of Tocqueville and Beaumont's departure from Philadelphia. The elegant and experienced James Brown was bemoaning the decline of Quaker influence.

'Since we are now on the Chapter of Religion,' said Tocqueville,[17] 'tell me what I must think of the religious principles in this country. Do they exist only on the surface, or are they deeply rooted in the heart? Are they a belief, or a *political* doctrine?

'I believe, said Mr. Brown, that for the majority religion is a respectable and useful thing rather than a demonstrated truth. I believe that a pretty fair indifference toward dogma exists at the bottom of their souls. They never speak of it in the churches, [instead] it's morality that is discussed. But I am not acquainted with any materialists in America; I am convinced that a firm belief in the immortality of the soul and the theory of rewards and punishments is, one can assert, universal; there's the common ground on which all the sects meet. I have been a lawyer for twenty years, and I have always observed a great respect for the sworn oath.

'We spoke of New Orleans, where he lived for twenty years. He said to me: There is in New Orleans a class of women dedicated to concubinage, the women of colour. Immorality is for them, as it were, a profession carried on with fidelity. A coloured girl is destined from her birth to become the mistress of a white. When she becomes marriageable, her mother takes care to provide for her. It's a sort of temporary marriage. It lasts ordinarily for several years, during which it is very rare that the girl so joined can be reproached with infidelity. In this fashion they pass from hand to hand until, having acquired a certain competence, they marry for good with a man of their own condition and introduce their daughters into the same life.

'There's an order of things truly contrary to nature, said I; it must be the cause of considerable disturbance in society.

'Not so much as you might believe, replied Mr. Brown. The rich young men are very dissolute, but their immorality is restricted to the field of coloured women. White women of French or American blood have very pure morals. They are virtuous, first, I imagine, because virtue pleases them, and next because the women of colour are not; to have a lover is to join their class.*

'Is it true, said I, that there is a great difference in character between the Americans of the North and those of the South?' Tocqueville and Beaumont were looking ahead. That very evening they would reach Baltimore, and before long they were planning to explore the whole South. They had heard that the Americans inhabiting the Slave

---

* Beaumont was later to make use of these extraordinary customs to heighten the colour and underline the tragedy in his own book. See below, pp.517ff.; and *Marie*, I,139–141. The same day, 28 October, Tocqueville made a memorandum of a quite different kind. One of the great reasons accounting for the maintenance of morality in America, he thought, was the equalitarian spirit. Only where there were sharp class divisions, and young girls of lower station to be seduced, could the young men live a profligate life without damage to their social reputation. This conclusion was to be adopted in both of Tocqueville and Beaumont's books. See Toc. diary note (Port. III); *Dém. en Am.*, II,83; *Marie*, I,348.

States were a quite different order of being from the middle class and commercial population of the North.

'An immense difference, answered Mr. Brown. The Americans of the North are all intelligence and activity; the pleasures of the heart hardly hold any place in their lives; they are cold, calculating, reserved. The Americans of the South, on the contrary, are open and lively; the habit of command gives their character a certain *hauteur* and an altogether aristocratic susceptibility on the point of honour. They are much inclined to laziness and regard work as a degradation.'

# XXXVII

## BALTIMORE

TOCQUEVILLE and Beaumont did not anticipate that their flying excursion into Maryland would be one of the chief turning points—perhaps for Beaumont even the critical experience—of their American tour.

Philadelphia had been so vastly intriguing. Prisons and Quakers, lawyers, writers, and philanthropists had disputed the hours of their stay. A city of brilliant lights and shadows, the two Frenchmen had found it, so full it was of wonderfully ill-assorted things. Here fertile minds and prison institutions, love of the arts and mathematical regularity, flourished together. By turns, Tocqueville and Beaumont had been exasperated and amused, harassed, bored, and stimulated. Particularly had they been instructed. Behind a Quaker *façade* they had found a strange conglomeration of races. Within the rectangular pattern of Penn's new-world metropolis they had discovered a really cultivated society. By its leaders they had been informed in the workings of popular self-government. And from its lowly outcasts they had received flashes of insight into the prison problem and the criminal's shadowy mind. Certainly, their two weeks in Philadelphia had been interesting and valuable enough.

Yet as Tocqueville and Beaumont journeyed out from the Quaker city, on the twenty-eighth of October, they were approaching an even stranger experience: their first contact with the South and with a city of the South. The experiment would give them a threefold sensation. To both young men, Baltimore was to be a social experience of no small curiosity. For Tocqueville, again, the conversation of the Marylanders was to arouse an intense intellectual excitement. And for Beaumont, finally, the sight of his first slave State was to be an emotional stimulant of far-reaching personal consequences.

\*

\* \*

489

'We have made to Baltimore, capital of Maryland, a little excursion that I shall have to tell you about,' Beaumont wrote to his brother on the eighth of November, when he and Tocqueville were once more settled in Philadelphia.[1] '. . . The very day of our arrival they gave a great subscription ball at twenty-five francs a ticket. If it had been necessary to pay this price, you may well believe that we should not have gone. But in our quality of foreigners of distinction we were admitted gratis. Thus on our very first day we had a chance to see gathered together all the finest society of Baltimore. The women of this city have a great reputation, and truly they deserve it. I saw a quantity of very pretty ones. They dress well, are very attractive, and excessively coquettish, though I am persuaded that this coquetry is not very dangerous for them and that it's a path in which they well know how to stop. I did however see a little Miss Randolp[h], roguish as a demon, and more giddy than a May-bug, who, I believe, will be guilty of some follies, were it only from malice, when she shall have cast her choice on some one as ready as she to commit them.*

'The following day we enjoyed a spectacle of another kind: we had a very fine horse race. Every year at Baltimore there are races of this sort which last three or four days. On this occasion all the finest horses of Virginia and New-York State are brought together, to compete. The meet takes place in an enclosure situated at two leagues from the city; in other respects things pass exactly as in our races of the Champ de Mars. The day I speak of, I saw five horses race against each other. They had to cover a distance of four miles, that is to say, a league and a third. The two horses which distinguished themselves among the five are *Black Maria*, a New-York mare, and *Trifle*, a small Virginia mare. The latter bears a name which portrays her very well: truly she has the air of a *bagatelle*. She is so slender, so slight, and appears so weak, that one would believe she would fall at the first gallop; she is as it were transparent, her muscles are visible through her skin; it always seemed to me she was going to break like glass. None the less she twice in succession took the prize, which was 4,000 francs. *Black Maria*, whose name recalled to me the one of Beaumont la Chartre, lost, but with honour. The first time *Trifle* covered the four miles in seven minutes, and the second time in eight minutes, minus a few seconds. Between the first and second run there was but a half-hour interval. The horses in this country are not of a breed

* Mary Randolph?

peculiar to America. There were no horses in this region before the Europeans came; so this was one of the things that caused the Indians the most astonishment. The horses I saw run are of Arab stock. Here at the meets there is one thing that we never see at home, and that's a trotting race, which always follows the main race. In this country they have a breed of trotters who are really extraordinary and against whom the English horses find it impossible to compete to advantage.' *

Tocqueville, of course, had not missed the opportunity to make some observations. The dance, he admitted, was a 'brilliant assembly,' and the women 'were remarkably pretty' though 'dressed in bizarre fashion.' But the cost of the tickets reminded him of what Charles Jared Ingersoll had said about the influence of wealth. 'This ball can give an idea of the state of society in America,' he noted.[2] 'Money is the only social distinction, but look with what *hauteur* it ranks people. In France one would scarce have dared set the price of entry to a public affair so high; it would have been considered an insolent pretension on the part of the wealthy to set themselves off from the rest.'

As for the horse races, 'the horses were fine but the jockeys ridiculously clothed. There was a great crowd in carriages and on horseback. Altogether, though, it wasn't quite the style of Europe.

'A negro having taken the liberty of entering the arena with some whites, one of them gave him a volley of blows with his cane without this deed appearing to surprise either the crowd or the negro himself.'

'But that's enough of horses,' Beaumont's letter pursued; 'let us come to the men. We were charmed by those of Baltimore. The week that we spent in that city was a *real carnival*; we went from feast to banquet steadily. Not a single day did we dine at our inn; it was a series of new *galas* [?].'

In a word, the French commissioners had experienced none of the usual difficulties in gaining an *entrée* into the best society. In Boston a certain haughty reserve had been their greeting. In Philadelphia the penitentiary enthusiasts had at first monopolized them. But in Baltimore they were taken at once into the heart of the best families. Four days after their *début* at the race ball they found themselves at a din-

---

* Tocqueville and Beaumont evidently saw the fourth and last day of the race-meet at Central Course. Spectators to an estimated number of 10,000 were present; and the celebrated horse *Eclipse* was shown before the race started. According to the *Baltimore Republican and Commercial Advertiser* (31 Oct.), *Trifle*, by *Charles*, beat *Black Maria*, by *Eclipse*, in 8 minutes, and in 7 minutes 55 seconds, with *Collier* and *May Day* trailing. The purse was for $700.

ner with many of the leading citizens of Maryland. The Governor, George Howard, a son of 'Peggy' Chew, was there.* So was the Chief Justice of the Criminal Court.† Among the other guests were the influential Ebenezer L. Finley, and a distinguished architect and engineer, Mr. J.H.B.Latrobe. The rest had been scions of the reigning families of the city.

Three days after that the Governor himself gave a feast in their honour. And meanwhile they had visited the famous Charles Carroll of Carrollton; and made the acquaintance of the leading lawyers, doctors, journalists, and educators of the region. One evening Beaumont even attended a 'children's ball.'‡

'An incredible luxury is paraded at their great dinners,' he wrote. 'If these people give such dinners often, they must ruin themselves. There are, though, some very rich men among them. Mr. Charles Carroll, for example, has easily four hundred thousand *livres de Rente*. . . .§

'The day of our departure from Baltimore, we were beginning to succumb under the weight of the entertainment. The last was given us by the Governor of Maryland, Mr. Howard, who assembled a great many people in our honour. It was necessary to gulp down a great many toasts, which, however kindly intended, had for us the great drawback of making us drink too much, a thing to which we are not yet accustomed.

'On our return to Philadelphia, we saw in a Baltimore paper a very flattering article about us, in which was rendered a striking tribute *to our merit and our virtues*.¶ It is perfectly true that each day we

---

\* His mother had been a Tory, and daughter of Chief Justice Benjamin Chew. Howard himself was perhaps the foremost Federalist in Maryland, and had just been re-elected to the Governorship after being appointed to serve out the term of Daniel Martin, deceased. He was a slave-holder, and owned the great estate 'Waverly' near Woodstock, Anne Arundel County.

† Probably Nicholas Brice, Chief Judge of the City Court.

‡ The 'very pretty' children, he reported with great solemnity to his little French niece Clémence, were girls between the ages of ten and sixteen, all very well educated. He had a very interesting conversation with one, who was but twelve. She was 'so nice and well brought-up that I twice had her out to dance.'

§ 'I also saw at Baltimore a Frenchman whom I was glad to encounter: Mr. De Menou (Count Jules) who is allied to the Tocqueville family and who knows my uncles André, Charles and Armand. He told me also that he had seen my father in Touraine. His great merit is that he spoke to us of France and of our friends. He is, moreover, a character of the first abilities, who remains in America one knows not quite why.'

¶ 'Messrs. de Bourmont and Toqueville, the commissioners appointed by the French Government to visit and inspect the prisons and penitentiaries of this country, are at present in Baltimore, having visited a number of the establishments of that nature

gain in self-possession and that now, when we are on exhibition, we utter, with great tact, the most agreeable remarks in the world.

'I should never finish if I told you everything we did at Baltimore. There was, notably, one very interesting thing to be examined, to wit, the *slavery* which still exists there legally. On this point I made many observations which, to my mind, are not very favourable to the people to whom they apply; but all that will probably be published in the great work which is to immortalize me, and it's to that publication that I refer you to learn the rest. . . .'

\*

\*   \*

While Beaumont had been initiating his 'observations,' and drawing some first conclusions on the great institution of slavery—an activity that was indeed to have literary consequences—Tocqueville had been engaged in investigations of no small interest but of a quite different kind.

Of course the local penal institutions were first examined: and penitentiary and almshouse did not want for visits. But here, fortunately, there was little new to see. The commissioners could note that the penitentiary brought in dividends to both State and convict, since the inmates, contrary to the rule elsewhere, were paid for all the work done after a certain required minimum had been completed. Otherwise, there was nothing worthy of remark.[3] It happened, then, that Tocqueville was free to pursue his political investigations after his heart's desire. He began with a long and most instructive interview, his subject being the suffrage question that had so tantalized him in Philadelphia.

'30 Oct. 1831,' he noted in one of his diaries.[4] 'Conversation with Mr. Latrobe, a very distinguished Baltimore lawyer.* He said to us:

in the north. We believe the general opinion of these gentlemen is satisfactory in regard to their arrangement and discipline. They have examined attentively our jail and penitentiary, with similar conclusions. We hope every facility will be afforded to these gentlemen, in extending their curiosity to others of our institutions, and who, by their intelligence and general information, are very competent to appreciate them with justness.' Leading editorial in the *Baltimore American*, 5 November 1831. This notice was later made use of by *Poulson's American Daily Advertiser*, *Saturday Courier*, and New York *Atlas*.

* John Hazlehurst Bonval Latrobe, 1803–1891, was the son of the architect and engineer Benjamin Henry Latrobe, and a man of wide interests and accomplishments. Educated at St. Mary's College (Baltimore) and at West Point, he was an author, an artist, a champion of the Baltimore and Ohio R.R., an inventor on a small scale, and a devoted leader in the cause of negro repatriation in Liberia. In 1832 he was to publish *Pictures of Baltimore*.

I believe that the constitution of Maryland is the most democratic in America. No property qualification is required of the electors; every man who is a citizen of the United States and has resided a year in the Republic is an elector.

'Do you not find, said I, that this universal suffrage has its inconveniences?

'It has some, said Mr. Latrobe. The elections are not always wise. It has been noticed that we have fewer men of talent in our legislature than the Virginians have in theirs.

'So, I returned, because your legislation is so "democratic" it is therefore a mistake to say that Maryland is the region in the United States where the aristocratic spirit most shows itself?

'Mr. Latrobe replied: Our outward customs have in effect retained an aristocratic turn that exists neither in the laws nor even in our political habits. Thus, there is more luxury here than anywhere else. In the streets you will see carriages with four horses, jockeys, liveries after a fashion; the members of the different families distinguish themselves by the names of their estates.

'Formerly your laws, in common with your customs, were aristocratic?

'Yes, Maryland was founded by English noblemen, and in addition the first emigrants professed the Catholic religion, which is itself favourable to aristocracy. They therefore divided the territory into large holdings. But America is not favourable to the existence of great territorial fortunes, as the proprietors are never able to draw a great revenue from their lands. Up until the revolution, however, Maryland presented the appearance of an English province; birth was as highly prized there as on the other side of the Atlantic; all the power was in the hands of the great families.

'What changed this state of things?' Tocqueville asked.

'The inheritance law.* With equal division, the fortunes were rapidly divided up. A few families, like that of Charles Carroll for example, because they had but one representative during several generations, saved their fortune; but in general the great holdings have been fractioned into a thousand pieces. With the small proprietors and with commerce was born our "democracy." You see what progress it has made.

* Again one wonders whether it was not the custom, rather than the law, that was fundamental. See *Dém. en Am.*, I,63–64; also index, under *Inheritance*, below.

'But how have the great families borne this change; what is their position in relation to the people, and what is the opinion of the populace respecting them?'

'The masses are not hostile toward the members of the old families, as you seem to believe. They elect them to all the offices without distinction drawn. On their side, the members of the old families don't *manifest* any hostility to the situation as it exists. This state of affairs is due to two circumstances: when the war with Great Britain broke out, the great families of Maryland embraced the cause of independence with ardour; they shared the passions of the people and led them on the field of battle. After the war of independence the political question that divided sentiments was the question of the constitution. The nation split into Federalists, who wanted to give a very strong central authority to the Union, and Democrats or Republicans, who wanted to preserve for the States an almost complete independence. The latter party, which won in the end, was the more popular. Now it happened that the nobles of Maryland, through love of power and the desire to preserve their local importance, almost all of them embraced this cause. There you have, then, two great occasions on which they went along with the people and won rights on its behalf. Just a moment ago I spoke of Federalists and Republicans, and I said that the Republicans won the victory in the end. That is to say, they finally got into power. Otherwise, once masters of the government, they directed it very nearly as their adversaries would have done. They accepted a central authority, a standing army, a navy. . . . Never can oppositions govern with the principles which brought them into power. Now, realistically speaking, there are no parties in the United States; everything is reduced to a question of men; there are those who have the power and those who want to have it, the people *in* and [the people] *out.*'

That was exactly what innumerable Americans had told Tocqueville before.* He made haste to return to the question of popular elections.

'From what class does the people most often select [its representatives],' he queried.

'From the lawyers. The United States are governed by lawyers; it's they who have almost all the posts. The president is a soldier, but look at his cabinet. Not a single secretary but is a lawyer. The lawyers have an even greater preponderance here than in the rest of the Union

* See *Dém. en Am.*, II,ch.2, esp.pp.7–8.

because it is accepted that before the election the candidates speak to the people. We often see the eloquence of one of them upset an election that the real merits of his adversary ought to have settled.

'Does slavery still exist in Maryland?' Tocqueville was now ready to change the subject.

'Yes, but we are making great efforts to get rid of it. The law allows the export of slaves but not their importation. Cultivating grain, we can very easily do without the blacks. It's perhaps even an economy.

'Is it permitted to free one's slaves?

'Yes, but we often notice that freeing them produces great troubles, and that the freed negro finds himself more unhappy, and more stripped of resources than when a slave. An odd thing is the fact that to the west of the Chesapeake the black population is growing faster than the white, and that the exact opposite is happening to the east of the same bay. That comes, I think, from the fact that the west has remained divided in great estates, which do not attract the free and industrious population. Baltimore, which to-day counts more than 80,000 souls, didn't have thirty houses at the time of the Revolution. . . .'

And Latrobe explained how the wars of Europe and the ruin of Santo Domingo had contributed to the city's extraordinary growth. To Tocqueville's mind, however, the mention of the blacks had suggested questions about the whole civilization to which this slavery had given rise.

'Is it true that great differences exist between the Americans of the North and those of the South?' he now asked.

'Yes, in Baltimore we think we can recognize a Yankee, or even an inhabitant of New-York or Philadelphia in the street.

'But what are the chief traits that distinguished the North and the South?

'I should express the difference in this way. What distinguishes the North is its enterprising spirit, what distinguishes the South is *l'esprit aristocratique* [spirit of chivalry?]. The manners of the inhabitant of the South are frank, open; he is excitable, irritable even, exceedingly touchy of his honour. The New Englander is cold and calculating, patient. While you are with the Southerner you are welcome, he shares with you all the pleasures of his house. The Northerner, after having received you, begins to wonder whether he couldn't do some business with you. (After drawing this lively portrait Mr. Latrobe appeared to fear that he had spoken to us too frankly; and he added several details to diminish the effect.) *

'But your present legislation, your inheritance law among others, must be changing the aspect of your society?' Tocqueville was back on the subject of democracy. The South might once have been aristocratic, might still be based on slavery, but its manhood suffrage and equalitarian legislation must now be moulding it nearer and nearer to the character of the middle-class, self-governing North.

'Yes,' answered Mr. Latrobe, 'there existed with us formerly a race of proprietors dwelling on their estates. They were, on the whole, the most distinguished men of the region; they had received an excellent education, had the manners and ideas of the English upper classes. We still have a certain number of these *gentlemen farmers*, but the inheritance law and "democracy" is killing them, in two or three generations they will have disappeared.

'Do you not regret that it should be thus?

'Yes, from certain points of view. This class was, in general, a nursery for distinguished men for the legislature and the army. They formed our best statesmen, our finest characters. All the great men of the Revolution, in the South, came from this class. And yet I am brought to believe that, taken altogether, the new order of things is better. The upper classes with us are less remarkable now, but the people is more enlightened; there are fewer distinguished men, but a more general happiness. In a word, every day we are growing more like New England. Now New England, in spite of what I have just told you about it, is far superior to us in all that constitutes the economy of society. I believe that the whole American continent is destined one day to model itself on New England, and what is hastening the movement is the continual importation of Northern men which is taking place in the South. Their desire for wealth and their enterprising spirit thrust them constantly among us. Little by little all commerce and all the control in society are falling into their hands.'

Yet the North had repudiated slavery. 'Do you believe that it would be possible to do without slaves in Maryland?' Tocqueville wanted to know.

'Yes, I am convinced of it. Slavery is, in general, a very costly method of farming . . .' and Mr. Latrobe went on to explain why. Only in

* Beaumont, however, was to treasure the expression. See *Marie*, I,380.

the far South, and only on such staple crops as tobacco and sugar, could negro slaves be put to profitable use. In Maryland, as slavery disappeared, the culture of tobacco would follow, he thought. 'It is better to lose this branch of revenue than keep it. All this that I tell you is not just personal opinion, it's the expression of a public conviction. In the past fifteen years a complete revolution has taken place in the popular mind in this matter. Fifteen years ago one wasn't permitted to say that slavery could be abolished in Maryland, to-day no one contests it. . . .' *

In addition to economic reasons, the inheritance law was in part responsible, Mr. Latrobe agreed.† By parcelling up the estates, it brought in the small proprietor and the competition of a rapidly increasing free white labour class. Tocqueville took up another point of comparison between the South and the North.

'Is it true that in Maryland public education is infinitely less advanced than in New England?' he asked.

'Yes. We are but entering on the path trod for 200 years by the Northerners. The greatest obstacle that we are experiencing lies in the opinion of the people itself. A singular thing has often happened with us, and still sometimes happens: the enlightened classes of society, feeling the need for popular education, are unceasingly labouring to spread it; but the [lower?] classes, which do not yet see the necessity of giving their money to attain this result, do not nominate to office those who would thus work for their happiness in spite of them.

'Do you realize that what you are telling me there is a very strong argument against the sovereignty of the people?

'No, not at least to my mind. The people is often blind, it falls into unbelievable errors. But I have always noticed that it ended by learning its own interests; and then it does more than the strongest power could. Thus, for public education, it was long impossible for us to do anything, but now public opinion is beginning to turn to our side. The shove has been given, and nothing could stop it now.'

Tocqueville in his questioning was apt to resemble a nun telling over her rosary, his thoughts seemed chained together, one topic always suggested the next. Now the association of Maryland and education drew onto his tongue the name of the religious group that in Europe would have been the most hostile to free public education.

* Compare *Marie*, I,310–313; *Dém. en Am.*, II,331.
† Echoed in *Dém. en Am.*, II,330–331.

'What is becoming of the Catholics in America?' he asked.

'They are taking on an extraordinary increase, and following a very clever policy. . . . In the last twenty years they have, with great skill, turned all their efforts toward education. They have established seminaries and schools (*collèges*). The best institutions of education in Maryland are Catholic; they even have schools in other States. These are full of Protestants. There is perhaps not a single young man of Maryland who, having received a good education, has not been brought up by Catholics. Although they take good care not to speak to the students about their beliefs, you appreciate that they always exercise a certain influence. Furthermore, they have very adroitly turned most of their efforts to the education of women. They think that there where the mother is Catholic, the children must almost always be the same. . . .' *

*

*   *

What a strange civilization Maryland represented! Here was a society that somehow combined medieval traits like aristocratic traditions, a Catholic training, and the institution of slavery, with the most modern democratic political practices. The obvious confusion of ideas and standards intrigued Tocqueville into further inquiries.

He easily verified what he had heard about the former resistance of the common people to free, tax-supported education. From a Catholic priest, the vice-president of the College of St. Mary, he also obtained confirmation of what Latrobe had said about the organization and educational activities of the Catholic church.† Yet even in Maryland, it seemed, the priests were content with the separation of church and state. Could it be, then, that religion and its ministers in America never exercised more than an indirect influence over politics and government? If so, how profound was this much-advertised faith, anyhow? Tocqueville decided to ask the distinguished physician, Dr. Richard Spring Stewart.‡

* It is instructive to notice how many of the topics broached by Tocqueville in this long conversation were questions of which Latrobe could speak from long study or personal experience. Considering their ages of 26 and 28, the conversation did them great credit.

† Conversations 2 and 4 Nov. (diaries Non-Alph.II and Alph.B). See also *Marie*, II,190–191. The priest referred to may have been Father John Mary Joseph Cranche, consecrated bishop of Natchez and an ardent missionary.

‡ Dr. Stewart, 1797–1876, was a graduate of St. Mary's College, and of the University of Maryland where he had studied medicine. In 1828 he had become president of

'He said to me: In America the doctors exercise a certain amount of political influence. In the small localities they have the confidence of the people, and are often sent to the legislatures and to Congress. Ministers are also sometimes sent there, but the case is very rare. Generally the tendency is to keep the clergy in church and separate it from the state.

'What is your opinion on the religious feeling in the United States? I confess that I am tempted to see a great indifference at the bottom of all religious beliefs. I estimate that the mass of the enlightened classes have numerous doubts on the subject of dogma, but are careful not to betray them because they feel that a positive religion is a moral and political institution very important to preserve.

'There is some exaggeration in that portrait. In the United States the great majority, even among the enlightened classes, but especially among the people, is truly believing, and firmly sustains the opinion that a man who is not a Christian offers no social guarantee. That opinion is still so deeply rooted that it is the source of an intolerance of which you can have no idea. It gives the clergy a great indirect influence. Thus, if a minister, known for his piety, should declare that in his opinion a certain man was an unbeliever, the man's career would almost certainly be broken. Another example: A doctor is skilful, but has no faith in the Christian religion. However, thanks to his abilities, he obtains a fine practice. No sooner is he introduced into the house than a zealous Christian, a minister or someone else, comes to see the father of the house and says: look out for this man. He will perhaps cure your children, but he will seduce your daughters, or your wife, he is an unbeliever. There, on the other hand, is Mr. So-and-So. As good a doctor as this man, he is at the same time religious. Believe me, trust the health of your family to him. Such counsel is almost always followed. It cannot therefore be said that the clergy is precisely a civil influence with us, but it is certain at least that *Religion* exercises an immense power outside of the church and still has a prodigious influence in the affairs of the world.

---

the Maryland Hospital for the Insane and was one of the leaders in the movement (made famous by Dorothea L. Dix) to improve the treatment of these unfortunate members of society. The tenor of his remarks to Tocqueville makes it interesting to note that he was not, himself, regarded as a professing Christian, though 'possessed of most of the Christian virtues in a high degree.' For this conversation, see Toc. diary note, 1 Nov. 1831 (Non-Alph.II, quoted with omissions and alterations, *O.C.*,VIII,288).

'That state of affairs must create a good many hypocrites?

'Yes. But above all it prevents people's speaking of it. Public opinion accomplishes with us what the Inquisition was never able to do. I have seen, I have known a multitude of young men who, after receiving a scientific education, thought they had discovered that the Christian religion was not true. Carried away by the fire of youth, they began to maintain this opinion openly; they became indignant at the intolerance of the zealous Christians, and placed themselves in a position of open hostility. Well! Some were obliged to leave the country, or to vegetate there miserably. The others, feeling that the struggle was unequal, were constrained to return, outwardly, into the ways of religion, or at least keep their mouths shut. The number of those thus beaten by public opinion is very considerable. Anti-religious books are not published with us, or at least the thing is very rare. Irreligion is, however, beginning to gain entrance into several newspapers. There is a journal of this character in Boston, one in New-York, one in New Jersey, another in Cincinnati; but the gains of this school of thought are very slow. Yet several of our great men have shared it. Washington's opinion in the matter of Christianity is unknown, he never explained himself. But Jefferson, Franklin, John Adams were decidedly deists. On the other hand, it must be acknowledged that with us a great many men of talent have been and are still firm believers. I imagine, however, that their number is diminishing.'

Agnosticism might be gaining, reasoned Tocqueville, but one fact was obvious. Even in the matter of opinion—of religious faith—the majority exercised a tyrannical control. The really great might stand above dictation; but for the average man there was no escape. He had to conform, or see himself suspected and despised. So Tocqueville once more found himself wrestling with the problems of majority rule, or popular self-government—a topic which the Marylanders, fortunately, were delighted to discuss.

'3 Nov. 1831,' noted Tocqueville at the beginning of a new diary.[5] 'Yesterday I went to a dinner at the house of Mr. James Carrol[?].* The Governor of Maryland—Mr. Howard, son of Colonel Howard—, the chief justice of the criminal court, Mr. Finley and several others were there. Most of these gentlemen belonged to the old families of Maryland. They talked a good deal about the political constitution of this state, and everybody fell into agreement that they had lowered the

* It has not been possible to identify this man.

suffrage qualification much too far. As a result, said these gentlemen, it's really the least enlightened portion of the nation that governs the rest. Subsequently I took Mr. Finley* aside, and had with him the following conversation:

'I am sorry, said he, that you didn't come to Baltimore at the beginning of last month. The members of the legislature were being chosen then, and the spectacle of our elections would have interested you deeply.

'Can't you tell me what it was like? I replied.

'All the more easily, said Mr. Finley, because I played a role in it. The Republicans, or anti-Jackson party, had chosen me as their candidate. My adversary was, at the same time, one of my best friends. Two days before the election we went together to Washington Square, where platforms had been erected for the orators of the town-meeting. I got up the first, and began to expose to the crowd of spectators, there were at least ten thousand, the mistakes that General Jackson and the present administration had made since coming to power. My adversary, on the other hand, defended the government. When I say that we did, we tried to do, for at each instant those opposed to the orator drowned his voice with hooting. Several men even came to blows. There were several limbs broken; and every one finally went to bed. The next day my adversary and I left to tour the different parts of the county. We travelled in the same carriage, ate at the same table, lodged at the same inns, and then appeared as opponents on the same platforms.

'But do you fear nothing from such disorderly and tumultuous assemblies?

'Personally, I believe this system of hustings detestable. But it doesn't offer the dangers you imagine. Our people is habituated to these election forms. It knows exactly how far it can go and how long it can consecrate to these political saturnalias. The night of an election, in which blows with clubs have been exchanged, Baltimore is as peaceful as Rome on Ash-Wednesday. Besides, the excesses of "democracy" save us in part from the dangers of "democracy." All public offices are for one year. The party that fails this year hopes to succeed the year after; why should it wish to resort to illegal means?

* Toc. diary note (Non-Alph.III). Ebenezer L. Finley had served on the committee that welcomed Lafayette to Baltimore in 1824. In 1832 he was to act as one of the secretaries of the meeting of Baltimore citizens to protest the nullification proceedings of South Carolina.

'You reason like a man who has never seen a people agitated by political passions that are *real* and *profound*,' Tocqueville protested. 'With you everything up to now is on the surface. No great material interests are at stake.

'That may be true. Notice that I am speaking only about us, and for the present time,' Mr. Finley replied.

Again Tocqueville was led to compare the institutions of Maryland with what he had already seen in America. 'No doubt the municipal government, with you as in New England, convokes the town meeting?

'It should be so; but with us the custom is different. In Maryland any individual, by announcing its place and purpose in a journal, can bring on a meeting. At the time of the elections I saw some innkeepers announce gatherings of this kind near their taverns, so as to attract a crowd thither; and the announcement was followed by complete success.

'Is it true that you demand no suffrage qualification?

'Not the slightest. I have seen elections carried through the almshouse poor, whom one of the candidates had brought.

'Is it that you approve such an order of things?

'No. In pushing *démocratie* (equality?) to its last limits, we have really confided the direction of society to those who have no interest in stability, since they possess nothing and have little education. What's more, we have built our social structure on ground that is always moving. With us each year, not only the public officials are changed, but also principles, manners of government, and parties succeed each other in power with unbelievable rapidity. Social positions, fortunes, are drawn into this universal confusion. There is no continuity in [public] undertakings.

'But it's you yourselves, members of the upper classes, who made the present laws. Fifty years ago you were masters of society.' Tocqueville was now quoting his authority, Mr. Latrobe.

'Yes, certainly,' Mr. Finley conceded. 'But each party, in order to get into power, wished to flatter the people, and win its support by giving it new privileges. It was thus that, by degrees, the most aristocratic state in the Union has become the most democratic.'

Tocqueville treasured this explanation of the Maryland paradox and was one day to venture to repeat parts of it in his book.* Mean-

* See *Dém. en Am.*, I,64.

while he got together some further observations on the character and consequences of universal suffrage. His first remark [6] was that 'birth has preserved an influence in America. The men who bear the names celebrated in the history of the colonies or made famous in the war of the Revolution are *assez volontiers* called to high places, particularly to offices of honour. Thus, in Massachusetts the governor is Mr. Lionel [Levi] Lincoln and the lieutenant governor Mr. Winthrop, both descended from early governors of the colony. In the State of New-York the lieutenant-governor is Mr. Livingstone [*sic*], scion of the greatest family of the region. In Maryland the governor is Mr. Howard, the son of the famous Colonel Howard and the representative of one of the oldest families. All these gentlemen are very ordinary individuals and evidently owe their elevation simply to their names. The populace is attracted by these intellectual distinctions, from which it feels there is nothing to fear. Birth appeals to its imagination without exciting its envy. The same is not true of wealth. The rich are not persecuted, but are left aside.'

Wealth was more influential than talent, Mr. Ingersoll had said: birth more influential than wealth, Tocqueville's observations seemed to indicate. But perhaps the people did not always pause at such amiable distinctions.

'How doubt the pernicious influence of military glory in republics?' Tocqueville had written on the first of November.[7] 'What was it that directed the choice of the people to General Jackson, apparently a very mediocre man; what is it that assures him the suffrage of the people despite the opposition of the enlightened classes? The battle of New Orleans. Yet that battle was a very ordinary feat of arms; and the people thus beguiled is the most anti-military, prosaic, and cold-blooded people in the world.'

The portrait was severe, almost acid. But the more he thought about the matter, the more convinced Tocqueville became that manhood suffrage did not result in the election of the best leaders, not even in America. Instead, the rule of the people meant the choice of mediocre officials, the tyranny of the majority over private opinion, and, finally, the failure of popular self-control. By self-control Tocqueville meant the restraining of the turbulent masses within a lawful and orderly sphere of action. Governments were designed to preserve the peace between the governed. Yet an administration founded on its popularity with the majority would often be unable to defy the majority, especially when the people were excited, or more particularly in cases of mob lawlessness. Tocqueville had an anecdote that seemed to demonstrate this theory. The story came from a Baltimore journalist.

'4 Nov. 1831,' his memorandum was dated. 'Mr. Cruse,* a man of much *esprit* [and] the editor of one of the principal journals of Baltimore, said to me to-day: we have no authority outside of and superior to the people; whatever it desires one has to submit to. The militia, itself, is the populace, and is of no use when it partakes or condones the passions of the majority. Twenty years ago we witnessed a terrible example of this. It was the time of the war against England, a war that was very popular in the South. A journalist allowed himself to attack the war sentiment violently. The masses gathered, broke his presses, attacked the house where he and his friends (belonging to the first families of the town) had taken refuge. An attempt was made to call the militia; it refused to march against the rioters and did not respond to the call. The municipal authorities could rescue the editor and his friends only by sending them to prison. The mob wasn't satisfied. At night it came together and marched against the prison. Again they tried to get out the militia and were unable to do it. The prison was taken by assault, one of the inmates killed on the spot, the others left for dead. An effort was made to prosecute in the courts, but the juries acquitted the guilty parties.'

So much for the executive authorities, the majority, the militia, and the jury system. But the most glaring weakness of a popular administration would show itself, Tocqueville surmised, in still another place. On the third of November he was conversing once more with Mr. Latrobe. As he noted in his papers:

'I said to-day to Mr. Latrobe: I can only just in the last extremity admit that *la Démocratie* (the masses) can regulate the internal affairs of society. But I can't believe that it is fit to conduct its foreign policy. All the peoples that have influenced the world, all those that have executed grand designs without, have been directed by strong aristocracies. I should cite the Romans in times past, the English in ours.

'Mr. Latrobe replied. I agree with you on that point. That is indeed the reef for "democracy." But we haven't yet encountered it; we have no neighbours. In general, he added, I think that America proves

---

* Toc. diary note (Port.III). Peter Hoffman Cruse, 1795–1832, was a graduate of Princeton, editor of the *Baltimore American*, and a noted conversationalist.

absolutely nothing in favour of republican institutions (*la République*).' *

\*

\* \*

On the evening of the fifth of November, Tocqueville and Beaumont went to see the patriarch of Maryland, Charles Carroll of Carrollton.

'Charles Carroll is the last survivor from the signers of the Declaration of Independence,' Tocqueville began his account of their visit.[8] 'He is descended from a very old English family. He possesses the most vast domain existing to-day in America. The estate on which he lives contains 13,000 acres of land and 300 negro slaves. He has married his granddaughter to the Duke of Welesley. He is a Catholic.

'Charles Carrol[l] is 95 years old, he is very erect, has no infirmity, [only] his memory is uncertain. Still, he converses very well, like a well-informed and agreeable gentleman. He was educated in France.†

'He received us with much kindness and affability. The conversation turned on the great epoch of his life, the Revolution. He recalled to us with very natural pride that he had signed the Declaration of Independence, and that by that proceeding he risked both his existence and in addition the largest fortune there was in America.

'I ventured to ask him if from the beginning of the quarrel the colonies had had the thought of separating from Great Britain.

'No, replied Charles Carrol[l]. We were strongly attached, at heart, to the mother country. But by degrees she forced us to separate from her. With great good nature he added: No, unquestionably we did not think things would go so far. Even while signing the Declaration of Independence we thought that Great Britain, frightened by that step, would seek to make up with us, and that we could still become once more good friends. But the English pushed their point, and we ours.

'We spoke of the government of the United States,' Tocqueville recalled. 'Charles Carrol[l] seems to show regret for the old aristocratic institutions of Maryland. In general, everything in his conversation breathed the tone and ideas of the English aristocracy, combined

---

* Note (Non-Alph.III). Tocqueville would later enlarge on this 'reef' for democracy. See *Dém. en Am.*, II,105–108.

† 'He told me that he had been brought up in France by the Jesuits, who, says he, are people of great merit. . . . He spoke to me about his excellent friend Lafayette, who, says he, is an ignoramus in politics.' Bt. to his brother Achille, Philadelphia, 8 Nov. 1831 (BBlb).

sometimes in original fashion with the ways of the democratic government under which he lives, and the glorious memories of the American
Revolution. He ended by saying to us: *a mere Democracy is but a mob.*
The government of England is the only one that suits us, said he;
if we get along with ours, it's because each year we can push our in-
novators into the west.'

Tocqueville was much struck by the appearance and conversation
of the patriarch. 'All the ways and habits of mind of Charles Carrol[1]
make him completely resemble a European gentleman,' he reflected.
'Probably the great proprietors of the South, at the time of the Revolution, were much on this model. This race of men is disappearing to-
day, after having furnished America her greatest men. With them
is being lost the tradition of the better born; the people is growing
more enlightened, knowledge is spreading, a middling capacity is
becoming common. The outstanding talents, the great characters, are
more rare. Society is less brilliant and more prosperous. These diverse
effects of the march of civilization and *lumières*, merely suspected in
Europe, appear in full light in America. To what primary cause are
they due? I don't yet see this clearly.' *

James Carrol [?], who had been standing by (or who heard Tocqueville repeat the opinions of the old gentleman), ventured to modify
the impression that the two young commissioners had received.

'You mustn't exaggerate the inconveniences that "democracy" has
for us,' he said. 'No doubt in a mass of details, in a great number of
particular cases, the people doesn't show common sense. Yet on the
whole the machine goes and the State prospers. Certainly universal suffrage has its dangers, but it has this advantage that with it there does
not exist a single class hostile to the others. There is a general satisfaction spread through the nation. I believe that, whatever may be the inconveniences of "democracy," *when it can subsist*, it still produces more
good than misery. It spreads throughout the whole social body an activity and a life that another government would not know how to create. On the other hand, I am very far from thinking that it can subsist

---

* Beaumont, in his own book (*Marie*, I,312–313), was to quote the celebrated patriarch
on the subject of slavery:
  'It's erroneous, he said to me, to believe that the negroes are necessary for the
  exploitation of certain crops, such as sugar, rice, or tobacco. I am convinced that
  the whites would get used to it easily if they were to undertake it. Perhaps, at first,
  they would suffer from the change introduced into their habits; but soon they
  would get over that difficulty, and, once used to the climate and work of the blacks,
  they would accomplish twice as much as the slaves.'

everywhere. I think that we are placed in unique circumstances, and that we don't prove anything.

'What is the opinion of the rich classes in society on the actual state of affairs?' Tocqueville asked him.

'The upper classes perceive the blunders and passions of the mass (*peuple*) very clearly; they believe that in a number of respects they would be more successful in leading society. Yet they recognize that, all considered, the State prospers. They submit to the actual order, whose goodness in the final result they acknowledge, while still pointing out the defects in the details.'

On the whole, Tocqueville thought their instructor was probably right. 'Mr. James Carrol is a cool and just mind, on whom I believe one may rely,' he noted. Besides, there was also that other remark by J.H.B. Latrobe to be considered. After admitting that America might prove nothing for other peoples, in their conversation two days before, Mr. Latrobe had made an emphatic statement: [9]

'Not enough account is taken of habits in the history of peoples, as with individuals,' he had insisted. 'One must seek far back the reasons which enable us to support a republic. The greatest, in my opinion, is that we are used to it. What is to be explained is how that habit became established. What was it that, during the first ten years after the Revolution, made us experience such great social unrest? The fact that we were not yet accustomed to governing ourselves as an independent State, even though we had long been used to administering ourselves in each particular State.'

\*

\*    \*

Tocqueville's visit to Baltimore—with his first exploration of Southern society—was over. And still he did not know exactly what to think of all the contradictory things that he had seen and heard.\*

Out of the confusion of his thoughts, however, there gradually

---

\* In addition to the interviews quoted above, Tocqueville and Beaumont had met the Governor's brother, Dr. William Howard, who was a civil engineer and who talked to them about an Illinois canal; a man named Williamson, who gave them some information about legal procedure; George Henry Calvert, brother-in-law of Dr. Stewart; Z.H.Miller and Archibald [?] Stirling. Either in Baltimore or in Washington they also encountered Roger Brooke Taney who, in December 1831, succeeded Berrien as Attorney-General of the United States. To Calvert, Stirling, and Taney they were later to send copies of their Report on the prisons. Meanwhile John McEvoy, clerk of the prison, and Richard W. Gill, a lawyer, would forward to them statements on crime and punishment in Maryland. See *Du Syst. Pén.*, pp.vi,180.

emerged three conclusions. It was as if he were selecting three ideas, three solid verities about which he could hope to arrange and harmonize all the pieces of information that he had been gathering, all the jumbled lumber of his conversations.

The first of his pegs was a conclusion as to the practice of democracy in the southern half of the United States: a basic comparison between the two sections.

On the sixth of November, he put his comparison in black and white. 'So far as I can judge,' he wrote in his diary,[10] 'the Republic does not seem to me a social state as natural and appropriate to the South as it is in the North of the United States. Does this result from differences in enlightenment between North and South, or in physical constitution and the resulting differences in character in the two sections? Or, rather, [is it that] the enlightened classes are not made for leadership in a democracy; do they in the South more easily betray the secrets that the same classes in the North conceal? This is what I still do not know. What's certain is that my impression is not the same in the two parts of America. The North presents to me, internally at least, the image of a government strong, regular, durable, and perfectly appropriate to the moral and physical state of men. In the South there is in the march of affairs something feverish, disorderly, revolutionary, passionate, which does not leave the same impression of strength and durability.'

So much for a preliminary statement about the South.

Tocqueville's second thought had to do with the reasons for the strange success of self-government in America. Clearly democracy was working better in practice than one would, from theoretical considerations, have supposed possible. For this there had to be some explanation—and Sparks and Alexander Everett in Boston, Ingersoll in Philadelphia, and Finley and James Carrol [?] in Baltimore had all been hinting at the secret. Perhaps J.H.B.Latrobe, in his emphatic way, had stated the matter as clearly as had any one. At all events, Tocqueville was obviously echoing American opinion as well as his own thoughts when he wrote his important paragraph on *The Superiority of Custom over Law*.[11]

'After one has well reflected on the principles or causes that make governments act, on those that sustain and animate them,' he began his memorandum; 'when one has spent much time calculating with care what is the influence of the laws, their relative goodness and their tendency, one arrives always at this conclusion: that above all these considerations, outside all these laws, one encounters a superior might, which is the *spirit* and *customs* of the *people*, their *character*. The best laws are incapable of making a constitution work in despite of the *mœurs*, the *mœurs* draw profit from the worst laws. This is a truism, but one to which my studies bring me back unceasingly. It is placed in my mind like a central point; I see it at the end of all my ideas. Yet the laws help to produce the spirit, habits and character of the people. But in what proportion? That is the great problem, about which one cannot reflect too much. I believe that the customs (*ces choses*) have an existence permanent and independent of the laws.' *

Finally, Tocqueville's investigation had given him a third conclusion to set down.

If American democracy in some respects worked better than the laws would lead one to expect, in other respects it worked considerably worse. To the student it showed itself full of flaws; on the idealist it heaped the most unexpected disappointments. In short, popular governments posed a problem: the problem of their own mediocrity. Here, then, was another riddle requiring reflection.

'Why, when civilization spreads, do the outstanding men grow fewer?' Tocqueville asked himself.[12] 'Why, when there are no longer any lower classes, are there no superior classes? Why, when the knowledge of government reaches the masses, are great geniuses missing from the direction of society?

'America poses these questions clearly, but who can resolve them?'

---

* Returning to this thought in his commentary, Tocqueville was to hammer the idea home with the following statement: 'I have but one word more to say on this subject. If I have not succeeded in the course of this work in making the reader feel the importance that I attach to the practical experience of the Americans, to their habits, to their opinions, in a word to their *mœurs*, in the maintenance of their laws, I have missed the principal object that I proposed for myself in writing.' *Dém. en Am.*, II,225.

# XXXVIII

## BEAUMONT'S *MARIE*

IN Maryland Tocqueville studied democracy.

But Beaumont saw the blacks. And the spectacle of the negro determined his literary career.

A simple comparison will suggest how much Baltimore meant to the older of the visiting Frenchmen. Six months before, during the Atlantic crossing, he had written his father about their plan for a joint book on American political institutions. That had been in April 1831, at the beginning; but the co-operative labour had been faithfully undertaken, with the result that in January 1835, three years and some months later, he and Tocqueville were to fulfil the promise, and to publish. Only by that time there would be two books; and each of the two friends would have composed his own individual work. The projected joint-masterpiece on democracy would be Tocqueville's.

And Beaumont's book would bear the title: *Marie, ou l'Esclavage aux États-Unis.* . . .

*
* *

The origins of Beaumont's interest in the negro—and the exact moment of his decision to consecrate his labours to American slavery—will probably never be determined. For his voluminous notes on the subject, and his diary, have apparently been lost.*

---

\* On the first of December, Beaumont wrote to his sister Eugénie: 'For some time past I have been an observer so *intrepid*, and so indefatigable, that my notes are assuming immense proportions and my diary is of inordinate length. . . .' Again, many years later, he was actually to produce what purported to be a quotation from that diary. See below, p.546, and *O.C.,*V,28–33.

Yet neither that diary, nor those notes, have ever come to light. Perhaps they were destroyed, perhaps they have simply been lost and will again appear some day. In the latter event an immense amount of interesting material, some of it duplicating Tocqueville's notes, some of it contributing new adventures and new sidelights to fill out the story of their American experiences, will become available.

511

From Tocqueville's own records, however, and from the writings of Beaumont that remain, a fair outline of the story can be given.

The curiosity of the two students of American society was apparently first attracted to the great colour problem by the blacks of Philadelphia. Neither Tocqueville nor Beaumont had ever been in a city of such a large negro population before. The 'darkies' were everywhere—and were everywhere treated with extraordinary contempt. Yet they were supposed to be free. The cluster of notes in Tocqueville's hand, dated from their October sojourn in Pennsylvania, reveals a sudden sharp awareness on the part of the prison commissioners. All at once they had become conscious of a negro problem in America. They began to take notice, to ask questions.[1]

At first they were interested chiefly in comparing the blacks to the whites—or rather in letting their American friends make the comparison. Tocqueville and Beaumont wanted to get an understanding of American race prejudice.

'Many persons in America, and of the most intelligent, have maintained to me that the negroes belong to an inferior race,' Tocqueville began the twenty-second of October. 'Many others have maintained the contrary thesis. The latter in support of their opinion generally cite the aptitude of negro children in their schools, [and] the example of certain negroes who, in spite of all obstacles, have acquired an independent fortune. Mr. Wood of Philadelphia related to me, among others, the instance of a negro of this city who has acquired an enormous fortune and owns several vessels whose crew and captains are black.'

About the native abilities of the negroes there was, then, some difference of opinion. But in the white man's feeling and conduct toward his darker brothers there seemed to be a strange, grim unanimity. Without any question, the whole black race was being maltreated.

In Massachusetts, Tocqueville had noticed, the negroes were allowed to vote, but were not permitted in the white schools.* In Philadelphia the discrimination was universal. In the Walnut Street prison they were separated from the white convicts, even at meals. Perhaps that was natural. But when the commissioners visited the House of Refuge, an institution more philanthropic than penal, not a single black child was to be seen. 'It would be degrading to the white children,' the Director had explained, 'to associate them with beings given up to public scorn.'

* See above, p.396.

Life was hard enough for this despised race; their very mortality rate was double that of the whites.* And even into the grave the hatred of society pursued them; they were not allowed interment in the same cemetery.

What made perhaps the strongest impression on Beaumont, however, was his experience at the play. 'The first time I entered a theatre in the United States,' he was later to recall,† 'I was surprised at the care with which the spectators of white skin were distinguished from the black faces. In the first gallery were the whites; in the second, the mulattoes; in the third, the negroes. An American, near whom I was placed, pointed out to me that the dignity of the whites required this classification. However, my eyes wandering to the gallery of the mulattoes, I noticed there a young woman of striking beauty, whose complexion, of a perfect whiteness, betrayed the purest European blood. Entering into all the prejudices of my neighbour, I asked him how a woman of English origin could be so shameless as to mingle with the African women.

'That woman is *coloured*,' he answered.

'What? *Coloured*? She is whiter than a lily!'

'She is *coloured*, he repeated coldly. The tradition of the country establishes her origin, and every one knows that she numbers a mulatto among her ancestors.

'He pronounced these words without further explanation, as one would utter a truth which, to be understood, needs but to be stated.

'At the same instant I made out in the gallery of the whites a face that was half black. I demanded the explanation of this new phenomenon. The American replied: The woman who now attracts your attention is white.

'—What? White! Her complexion is that of the mulattoes.

'—She is white, he insisted. The tradition of the country says that the blood flowing in her veins is Spanish.'

All this was hard for the two Frenchmen to comprehend. They began to bring up the subject with their Philadelphia acquaintances. On the twenty-fourth of October they had a conversation with John Jay Smith, which Tocqueville thought worth adding to his latest collection of documents. Mr. Smith, incidentally, had taught in a coloured Sunday School, and was familiar with anti-slavery thought. Tocqueville

* Compare *Marie*, I,169; and *Dém. en Am.*, II,334.
† *Marie*, I,iv–v.

wrote: 'Mr. Smith, a very able and well-informed Quaker, said to us to-day that he was perfectly convinced that the negroes were of the same race as we, just as a black cow is of the same race as a white cow. . . .

'We asked him if the blacks had the rights of citizenship. He re-plied: Yes, in law. But they can't present themselves at the polls.

'Why so?

'They would be maltreated.

'And what becomes of the reign of law in this case?' Tocqueville and Beaumont wanted to know.

'The law with us is nothing if it is not supported by public opinion. Slavery is abolished in Pensylvania,' Mr. Smith explained, but '. . . the people are imbued with the greatest prejudice against the negroes, and the magistrates don't feel strong enough to enforce the laws favourable to them.' * And the Quaker went on to talk about the problems of slavery in the South.

Tocqueville and Beaumont asked him 'what in his opinion was the only means of saving the South from the ills he foresaw.'

'He answered that it was to attach the negroes to the soil like the serfs of the Middle Ages. Serfdom (*la glèbe*) is an evil institution, he said, but it is infinitely better than slavery, properly so called. It would serve as a transition to a state of complete freedom. But I am perfectly certain that the Americans of the South, like all other despots, would never consent to give up the least portion of their power; they would wait till it was torn from them.'

Three days later, Tocqueville and Beaumont decided to consult their friend Duponceau on this perplexing question. The old man was very pessimistic. He said:

'The great rankling sore (*la grande plaie*) of the United States is slavery. The evil only grows. The spirit of the century tends toward giving the slaves their liberty. I don't doubt that the blacks will even-tually all become free. But I believe that one day their race will disap-pear from our soil.'

'How so?' Tocqueville wanted to know.

'With us white and black blood will never mingle. The two races abhor each other, and yet are obliged to live on the same soil. This situation is contrary to nature. It must end in the destruction of the weaker of the two hostile peoples. Now the white race, supported as it

* Toc. diary note (Port.III). See the echo in his book, *Dém. en Am.*, II,319.

is in the West and the North, does not perish in the South. The blacks will arm against it, and will be exterminated. We shall not escape from the position our fathers put us in when they introduced slavery, except by massacre.'

The next day the two commissioners left Philadelphia for their excursion into Maryland. But already Beaumont had written to his family about his interest in the coloured population of Pennsylvania. 'They [the blacks] are no longer slaves,' he had summed up his first impressions and conclusions, 'according to the Constitution they are the equals of the whites and have the same political rights. But laws don't change customs. One is accustomed here to see in a negro *a slave*, and as such one continues to treat him. It is curious to see what aristocratic pride is to be found among *these free men*, whose government reposes on the principle of absolute equality. The colour white is here a nobility, and the colour black a mark of slavery. The fact is not difficult to seize, but it's the consequences that one has to foresee. Each day the ignorance of the blacks diminishes, and when they shall all be enlightened it is much to be feared that they will avenge by violence the scorn in which they are held.'

*

\* \*

It was at the end of October in the year 1831 that Beaumont reached Baltimore. From the point of view of his new interest the time could hardly have been better chosen. For it so happened that the whole preceding year had for his new hosts seemed ominous with signs of a coming disaster. The previous New Year's Day, out of a clear sky, the abolitionist William Lloyd Garrison had suddenly begun the publication in Boston of a rabid anti-slavery sheet called the *Liberator*. In August, or just two months past, Nat Turner's rebellion had then broken out in Virginia. The planters of the Old Dominion had cursed the incendiary propaganda of the New England fanatic, and suppressed the rebellion ruthlessly. To many it seemed as if the whole of Southern society was reposing on a sleeping volcano. In Maryland itself, the autumn of Beaumont's arrival, there were whispered fears of a slave insurrection in Kent and Queen Anne counties. To put it quite simply: at the end of October 1831, talk of race violence was not confined to Philadelphia.

Beaumont and Tocqueville went to the horse races, and saw a negro caned for presuming to enter the enclosure with the whites.

A day or so later they were told that a master could have his slave imprisoned as long as he chose, provided only that he paid the expenses.

The following day, 4 November, they discovered that free negroes in Maryland paid the school tax with the whites but couldn't send their children to the schools.

At the same moment Mr. Latrobe made a gloomy prophecy. The thoughtful supporter of the Colonization movement had been explaining to Tocqueville how Maryland was gradually learning to substitute cereals for tobacco, small freeholds for large estates, free white labour for slaves. Now he said:

'I am very much afraid that the next legislature will make unjust and oppressive laws against the blacks. People want to make living in Maryland unbearable for them. We mustn't deceive ourselves; the white and black population are in a state of war. Never will they mingle. One of them will have to yield place to the other.'

Again in democratic America, Beaumont had been faced with the unmistakable evidence of injustice and race oppression. But the full horror of slavery and slave trading was only brought home to him that very day.*

He and Tocqueville had been visiting the Almshouse outside the city. During the course of their inspection their ears had suddenly been assaulted by a frightful howling, which issued apparently from one of the locked cells. The jailor explained that the cell contained a negro who was violently insane. There was in Baltimore, it seemed, a well-known slave-trader, feared and hated by the entire black population. This notorious dealer in human flesh had carried a slave from Virginia into Maryland, and abused him so frightfully on the way that the black had lost his reason. The negro's madness now took a peculiar form. He imagined that he saw the trader night and day, constantly following him, looking for the opportunity to tear off portions of his flesh. He was a great strapping fellow, foaming mad. And in his fury, he howled.

Beaumont and Tocqueville were introduced into the cell. The madman was 'one of the finest negroes' they had ever seen, and apparently 'in the prime of his life.' 'When we entered his cell,' Tocqueville afterwards recorded, 'he was lying on the floor rolled in a blanket which was his only covering. His eyes rolled in their sockets and his face expressed at the same time terror and fury. From time to time he threw

* Toc. diary not (Port.III). Compare *Marie*, I,88–90.

off his covering and raised himself on his hands, crying: Get away, get away, don't come near me. It was a horrible sight. . . .'

On Beaumont in particular the spectacle of the negro's madness made an indelible impression. He could not get the scene out of his mind. And four days later he was writing to his family about 'the great work which is to immortalize me. . . .'[2]

*
*   *

A word about that 'great work' is now in order.

When it finally appeared, in 1835, it bore the title *Marie*. It had also a subtitle: *Ou l'Esclavage aux États-Unis, Tableau de Mœurs américaines*; it was cast, very curiously, in the form of a two-volume novel; it contained long notes and appendices.

The novelesque character of his book Beaumont felt called upon to explain in a foreword to the reader. 'Everything in it is grave, except the form,' he warned. 'My principal object has not been to create a romance. The fable which serves as frame for the work is one of extreme simplicity. I have no doubt that under a more skilled and practised pen it would have been susceptible of the most interesting and even dramatic developments. But I do not know the art of the romancer. . . . During my sojourn in the United States I saw a society which offers with ours both harmonies and contrasts; and it seemed to me that if I succeeded in reproducing the impression that I received in America, my recital would not be entirely lacking in usefulness. It is these altogether real impressions that I have attached to an imaginary story.

'I am quite conscious that in offering the truth under the veil of a fiction I run the risk of pleasing nobody,' the apology continued. 'Will not the serious public spurn my book at the mere sight of its title? And the frivolous reader, attracted by a light appearance, will he not halt before the seriousness of the matter? I do not know. All that I can say is that my first object has been to present a series of solemn observations; that, in this work, the facts at bottom are true and only the persons imaginary; finally, that I have tried to clothe my work with a less serious surface in order to attract that portion of the public which seeks in a book, all at the same time, ideas for the mind and emotions for the heart.'

Having thus explained the form of *Marie*, Beaumont summarized its matter, its freight of solemn observations, in the following weighty paragraph:

'The existence of two million slaves in the midst of a people with whom social and political equality has attained its highest development; the influence of slavery on the ways (*mœurs*) of free men; the oppression with which it weighs down the heads of the unfortunates subjected to servitude; its dangers for the very beings in whose favour it is established; the colour of the race which furnishes the slaves; the phenomenon of two populations living together, touching each other, without ever fusing or mingling; the grave collisions that this contact has already produced; the more serious crises that it can give birth to in the future: all these causes unite in making it clear how important it is to know the lot of the slaves and the free blacks in the United States. I have tried, in the course of this work, to offer a tableau of the moral consequences of slavery on the coloured people who have become free. . . .'

To put the matter in a nutshell, *Marie* was intended to be neither more nor less than a study of the great conflict that the author had discovered in Philadelphia and Baltimore.

So much for Beaumont's expressed purposes. His actual methods, or the real contents of his work, now merit consideration.

The skeleton or framework of *Marie*, as Beaumont stated, was a simple, romantic tale. In a word, it revolved about the sorrowful experiences of an American family who had had the misfortune—like the woman in the second gallery at the theatre—to have a mulatto among their ancestors. To be exact, the whole tragic romance was presented in the form of a story told by a French exile, named Ludovic, who had been discovered by a fellow-countryman living alone in the wilds of Saginaw. Exiled Ludovic's mournful narrative went as follows:

After a troubled youth in a land whose ancient social order was going to pieces, he had crossed the Atlantic in the hope of finding a happier people and some chance for a successful political career. Landing at Baltimore, whose harbour reminded him of the enchanting Bay of Naples, he had been taken into the home of a New Englander named Nelson. This man was a successful and respected merchant, of strong Presbyterian convictions and humanitarian views, who had long resided in New Orleans, and was now, with his son Georges and his daughter Marie, come to establish himself in Baltimore. The Frenchman was at first repelled by the Puritanism and the intense interest in money of the father. But with Georges, a youth of fire and idealism, Ludovic had at once struck up an intimate friendship. Together they had explored the city, and taken part in the dinners and balls given by its best society . . . only to come to the bitter conclusion that in Maryland no great political careers were possible.

At this juncture Ludovic had discovered Marie. Hitherto she had always avoided him, he could not guess why. But one day he followed her on one of her mysterious errands—and found himself at the Almshouse. There he had watched her on her mission of sympathy and succour to the poor and the demented. She had even been able to still for an instant the ravings of the crazed negro who mistook every one for the hated slave-trader come for his morsel of flesh. Ludovic had spoken to Marie. They had fallen in love. He already knew that she could draw soft, harmonious music from harp or piano; instruments with which American women in general made only noise. In Marie, then, the exile had thought to find happiness.

A terrible revelation awaited him. It came from the mouth of the anguished Nelson. In New Orleans the stern New England father had married a beautiful orphan, who had given him two children, Georges and Marie. Then a would-be seducer of his wife had discovered proof that one of her ancestors had been a mulatto. The taint of negro blood had alienated their friends, thrown them into disgrace. His wife had died of grief, and he and his children had fled. Here, in Baltimore, no one knew their secret; but it might be discovered at any time. Ludovic could not wed Marie; their happiness would be too fragile; the misery of their life, should Marie's origins again be discovered, would be too awful to contemplate—for even in the North there was no toleration of black blood.

Transported by generous emotions, and untouched in any case by the race prejudices of the Americans, Ludovic wanted to go through with the marriage. But, at Nelson's express command, he consented first to make a six-months tour of the North, to see for himself how the free blacks and mulattoes were treated. He left for New York, Philadelphia, and Boston.

He had been north only long enough to discover that a literary career was as hopeless as a political, when Nelson and Marie arrived suddenly from Baltimore. At a local election for Congressman some one had betrayed the secret of Georges' origin—and the Nelson family had been forced once more to flee. Undaunted, Ludovic again proposed to marry Marie, and this time her friendless father consented. He knew a Catholic priest, John Mullon, who would perform the ceremony, and a Presbyterian minister who would ratify it.

The labouring classes of New York, however, were irritated by negro competition, and inflamed at the news of a marriage of a white with a black. In the very midst of the wedding ceremony, therefore, the doors of the church were stormed, the solemnization prevented. While the militia stood calmly by, Ludovic, Marie, Nelson, and Mullon only just escaped with their lives.

This time the unfortunates resolved to leave civilization behind altogether. Like Tocqueville's Oneida Frenchman, they fled westward to live among the Indians. Encountering a band of Cherokees, whom Nelson had befriended in Georgia but who were now being transported by a cruel government,* the poor wanderers settled in the Michigan peninsula, at Saginaw. There the last strokes of fate descended. Marie died of a fever. And the news came that Georges had been killed in Georgia leading a conspiracy of Cherokee Indians and enslaved blacks against their white oppressors. Life seemed to hold nothing more. Nelson devoted himself to a ministry among the Indians; and Ludovic, in his solitary cabin, lived on with his bitter memories.

That was Beaumont's story. But it would do the author an injustice to suggest that this tragic romance constituted his whole attack on American race relations, or that a pure fiction alone supported his indictment.

Instead, the entire narrative was interspersed, filled out, clothed, with the most earnest and factual discourses on the state of Northern feeling, and the nature of the public ordinances in regard to the blacks. These discourses Beaumont disguised as arguments and conversations between the various protagonists in his tragedy. Through the mouths of Nelson and Georges, therefore, he hoped to pour into his readers' ears all the information and all the conclusions that he himself had gathered in America on the lot and destiny of the negro race.

Then he took one further step. It has been suggested that *Marie* was one-half text and one-half notes or appendices. For his first appendix, Beaumont wrote a 76-page essay—without any fictional skeleton—'*on the social and political condition of the negro slaves and the free coloured people.*' Laws were cited, the most interesting statistics given, an

* Compare Tocqueville and Beaumont's encounter with the tribe of Choctaw Indians, at Memphis, below, pp.595–98!

attempt even made to weigh the possible remedies or solutions for the negro problem. The plot of *Marie* was designed to arouse the readers' sympathy and indignation, the text and notes to supply all the information needed for a careful appraisal of America's great scourge. In Beaumont's mind, *Marie, ou l'Esclavage aux États-Unis* . . . was nothing if not a serious and weighty contribution to the world's knowledge of American negro servitude.

Yet the author was not willing to rest there. During his own travels through western New York he had been touched by his encounters with the degraded remnants of the Iroquois, and roused to anger by their unfortunate history. Into *Marie*, therefore, he succeeded in weaving a sub-plot exposing the second of America's race problems, the Indian problem, with all that it contained of white man's greed and redskin suffering. And again there was a solemn and well-informed appendix—this time of 85 pages—'*on the ancient state and present condition of the Indian tribes of North America.*' Tocqueville had filled his *Démocratie* with political science, with a profound commentary on American political institutions. Beaumont intended his own work to cover the field of American social relationships.

As a consequence, he firmly inserted into the text and notes of *Marie* a number of short essays on other topics that might be considered to throw light on social conditions in the United States. Remarks on the morality, the home life, the business interests and the musical disabilities of the Americans studded the pages. Disquisitions on bankruptcy, the duel, the sociability of the Americans and their hatred of the English were imbedded in the notes. A long appendix 'on the religious movement in the United States' summed up Beaumont's carefully gathered thoughts on this subject and lent added interest to the second volume. From the mouth of Ludovic, again, came extended and rather unfavourable notices of the unliterary character of American society; and —like his creator, the author—the French exile had much to say about the virtues and defects of American women. In a word, *Marie* was the vehicle for an encyclopædia of information—and a whole system of thought.

Nor did Beaumont draw only from stores of knowledge and opinion. His very experiences in America, the accidents and incidents of his own travels, went into the composition of his work. Just as with Tocqueville and himself, for example, Ludovic had been driven from France by the impossibility of beginning a political career in a land whose social order was crumbling, whose institutions were in revolution. Like their new friend Francis Lieber, again, Ludovic had first thought to find employment fighting for the Greeks. He came to Baltimore and saw the same society, the same almshouse, the same mad negro, that Tocqueville and Beaumont had encountered there. Mr. Finley had described a typical Maryland election: Georges Nelson participated in one and was betrayed. Mr. Cruse had told them the story of the riots of 1812 and the helplessness of the militia: at Ludovic's wedding in New York the militia were called out but could not be induced to march against the mob. Most striking of all, perhaps, was the resemblance between the incidents of Ludovic's western flight and the story of Tocqueville and Beaumont's 'Fortnight in the Wilderness.' The same Indians went off to receive presents from the English. Ludovic and Marie attempted the same hazardous journey overland, on horseback, from Detroit to Saginaw. Again appeared the majestic forest, the fearful trail, the swarms of mosquitoes, and the pioneer who calmly gathered hay for their horses in the dark. Again it was necessary to procure an Indian guide, who naturally indicated the progress of the journey by a line drawn in the sand. For the purposes of the tragedy, Marie caught the very same seasonal fever that Beaumont's Pontiac host had talked about.* At Saginaw there even came the oppressive heat and the great awe-inspiring storm of Beaumont's experience, and in the midst of the storm Beaumont let his heroine die. Then, when the storm was over and the tragedy played out, there arrived from Detroit a comforter, a priest —and the name of the priest was Richard.

*

\* \*

*Marie, ou l'Esclavage aux États-Unis* . . . was not destined to be a great book. In spite of several re-editions it never seriously rivalled Tocqueville's *Démocratie*. Perhaps this was because, as Beaumont himself admitted, he had tried to interest a great many people. As a commentary on the American scene, and an interpretation of New World doctrines, *Marie* was apparently too romantic, too sentimental and too interrupted, too much concerned with social issues, too little with political. It could not satisfy the students, the serious readers. As a novel, on the other hand, the intended masterpiece left even more to be de-

---

\* Possibly this idea was also drawn from Beaumont's experience when Tocqueville fell ill of a fever in Tennessee. See below, pp.579–80.

sired. Beaumont had all the generosity, the sympathy, the indignation thought necessary in a romantic writer of his day, but—alas—he did not have the art. Neither in ability nor intention was he a genuine novelist.

From *Marie*, therefore, the reader must not expect a great story or a systematic treatise. Instead he will find some of the scattered elements of each. Particularly will he discover large chunks of information and fragments of critical thought, which, had they but been gathered together and carefully integrated, would have formed the body of a stimulating social commentary: a book not without value as a serious companion-piece to Tocqueville's institutional study.

Even as it was written, however, Beaumont's *chef-d'œuvre* was, and has remained, illuminating. For, whether his own countrymen realized the fact or not, every page reflected the author's American experiences, every chapter was based on earnest and prolonged investigation. In essence, therefore, *Marie, ou l'Esclavage aux États-Unis* . . . was both a mirror of Beaumont's American adventures, and a serious study—by a conscientious observer—of a very important subject.

It follows that to the readers of the present work the book of 1835 will seem strangely and wonderfully familiar. The sentiment expressed in the romantic tragedy will seem a reminiscence of Beaumont's letters home to his family. The essays on slavery will recall his Baltimore experiences. Despite some rearrangement, *Marie* will be a book of echoes.

In October and early November 1831, all this lay hidden in the future. But, as Beaumont reviewed his Baltimore visit, a passionate indignation was already burning in his heart, a fateful idea already marching to the conquest of his mind.

# XXXIX

## PHILADELPHIA AGAIN

SEVERAL considerations of weight made Tocqueville and Beaumont glad to return from their Baltimore excursion for another fortnight in Philadelphia.

The first of these reasons was a matter of discretion. They probably said very little about it to any one. But the fact was that in Maryland the feasting was so steady and so bibulous that they had become afraid for their digestions. 'In Baltimore they positively crammed us with dinners,' Beaumont wrote.[1] Especially, so much drinking had its inconvenience. So the two friends escaped with relief to the lighter, yet hardly less fashionable, suppers of Philadelphia.

Again, to the young commissioners the jump back northward had this important advantage, also: it made them feel nearer to their friends and families in France, who were at this moment very much in the front of their minds.

Just before their departure from Philadelphia, Tocqueville and Beaumont had received word that the Asiatic cholera was stalking Europe. The dread disease was still far off: *Dieu merci*, it had not yet reached France. But that was only a respite, apparently; nothing could stop its progress, they were told; in a matter of a few months their loved ones would certainly be exposed. Against that danger there was said to be one medicament, only one remedy that might work: 'catjeput oil' from China.* Tocqueville and Beaumont had never before heard of the specific, and did not quite know whether to believe in it or not; but on information that the supply of genuine oil in France was already exhausted, they hastened to do what they could. 'We put ourselves in motion, running to all the Pharmacists and Druggists in Philadelphia,' Beaumont had written on 26 October.[2] 'The first place we went

---

* Cajeput or Cajuput oil is an essential or volatile oil made from the leaves of a small tree of the myrtle family, found in the Moluccas.

had only one ounce. We seized it with extreme avidity, and would have paid 100 *Louis*, had it been asked. At length, at other stores we found as much as we wanted. We have just made up a package containing two bottles full of this oil; we are addressing it to Chabrol, our mutual friend at Versailles; he will undertake to divide the package between the Tocqueville and Beaumont families. . . . They told us that cajeput oil is taken only in very small doses, not exceeding five drops, save for beginning again after some hours.

'I shall tell you that at the bottom of our hearts we think we've done something absolutely useless; it seems to us as clear as day that there is at Paris and in all the cities of France as much cajeput as could be desired. If that is true, you will have a good laugh over our remittance from America, and over our simpleness; but we are assured that none exists in France [and] that it is a question of life and death. That being the case, hesitation is not possible, and we should rather take the chance of doing something absurd and even ridiculous than risk omitting an act so useful. . . .'

Even so, there had been further difficulties. Tocqueville had not been able to find out whether the oil in question would be allowed through the French customs. So, by advice of a druggist, he had carefully labelled the bottles *Oil of Cubebs*. For a moment he had felt relieved. Then, just as he was about to send them off, he had remembered that Oil of Cubebs was celebrated as a remedy for the pox (*vérole*). Somehow he could not openly address his friend a drug of such shameful character. In desperation he had substituted the name of a mutual acquaintance at Versailles—who would not mind, perhaps.[3]

Again, during their first visit to Philadelphia, there had been other news. Chabrol was defending the usefulness of the prison mission in the *Moniteur*, which told the commissioners that their interests were being watched over at home. But the activity of the Chamber was disquieting, and particularly the attitude of the *Royalistes*. Tocqueville had once again begun to fear that the latter would touch off a Civil War in France. The thought was profoundly saddening. 'Bound to the Royalists by agreement on a few principles and by a thousand family ties,' he had written Chabrol,* 'I see myself in some sort chained to

---

* Toc. to Chabrol, Philadelphia, this 18 Oct. 1831 (YT). Tocqueville's father, the Comte, was even afraid that his letters to America were being opened, but Tocqueville found the seals unbroken.

a party whose conduct appears to me often lacking in honour and almost always extravagant. I cannot fail myself to suffer deeply from their mistakes, even while condemning them with all my power. The more I examine myself, my dear friend, the more I think that I was not made to live in a time of revolution. Had it but been necessary to labour for society, I should perhaps have been able to render a few services; but I could never attach myself to the banner of a [mere] party, no matter what party. . . .'

In another characteristic letter of about the same date, Tocqueville explained some of the additional difficulties that had so often plagued him in the past and that were still at times returning. Writing to a discouraged young friend in France, the commissioner soberly admitted that in his own boyhood he had been profoundly troubled by the elusiveness of happiness. Finally he had come to the conclusion that the search was futile. 'There is hardly a man who has been continually unhappy; there are hardly any who are continually happy. Life is therefore neither an excellent nor a very poor thing but, permit me the expression, a mediocre thing partaking of both. You must not expect or fear too much of it,' Tocqueville counselled his friend. Again he gave expression to his own philosophy: 'Life is neither a pleasure nor a sorrow, it's a grave matter with which we are charged, and in which it is our duty to acquit ourselves as well as possible.'[4]

This goal remained, even though perfection in conduct was likewise out of the question. In that same troubled boyhood Tocqueville had made a second terrible discovery: it wasn't possible to find what was true. Instead of the great demonstrable verities that (he had fondly imagined) awaited every sincere seeker, there had faced him only inextricable doubts. Rarely had any one struggled so desperately against doubt—and that struggle was still going on. 'I finally convinced myself that the search for absolute, *demonstrable* truth, like the search for perfect happiness, was an effort after the impossible.' The only practical thing was to determine what was most probable and then go ahead as if no doubt existed. And Tocqueville advised his correspondent to do likewise. Yet Tocqueville's boyhood victory over himself was still imperfect. In America, reading the dispatches from France, he still felt a prey to uncertainty. 'I consider doubt one of the greatest miseries of our nature; I place it immediately after sickness and death,' he wrote. And in one of his diaries he set it down:

'If I were charged with the classification of human ills, I should do it in this order:[5]

1. Sickness
2. Death
3. Doubt'

All this had been in October, prior to their departure for Baltimore. Now Tocqueville and Beaumont were once again examining the newspapers of Philadelphia for foreign news, following with anxiety the inexorable march of the cholera toward western Europe, studying their letters from home as if somewhere between the lines there could be read the outcome of the party struggles and the secret of their country's future. Their superiors in the Ministries of Justice and Interior were still urging an early return. Everything seemed to be conspiring to draw them back to France. The commissioners began to fear they would have to curtail their trip into the Mississippi valley and the Southwest.*

In a moment of particular anxiety, Beaumont wrote to his family: 'I promise faithfully that I shall never [again] undertake such travels, so long as France is in such a situation.'†

*

* *

Meanwhile, the same letters from France reminded the two commissioners that there was a third reason for their presence in Philadelphia. They had left some of their Pennsylvania investigations unfinished.

This time it was not the prisons or the penitentiaries that required attention. 'On this matter we are now highly skilled,' Beaumont was

---

* Beaumont now thought that they would have to be back in France in April.

† That still another problem—of a very personal sort—was weighing on Tocqueville's mind at the moment of his return to Philadelphia is evidenced by the rough draft among his papers of a letter to his friend Louis de Kergolay. It concerns an offer of marriage. Apparently a certain Mr.L., a man of some wealth, had inquired of Kergolay whether Alexis de Tocqueville might not like to marry his daughter. Being already deeply in love with the English girl, Mary ['Marie'] Mottley, whom he was later to marry, Tocqueville had to make his excuses. Only, for some reason, he preferred to keep quiet about this particular impediment. So he pointed out that he couldn't give up his mission in America, with any honour to himself. Then, somewhat ingenuously, he argued that he had not even had the pleasure of meeting Miss M., as yet; and without the assurance that they would some day love each other—a knowledge that he could only acquire through making her acquaintance—the thought of marriage was out of the question. Finally, and in this he was perfectly sincere, money did not mean very much to him, he said. Toc. to Louis de Kergolay, Philadelphia, 8 Nov. 1831 (TT).

jubilant to report.[6] To their great relief he and Tocqueville realized that the penal phase of their American tour was almost over.

Certain of their inquiries into the political institutions of Pennsylvania, however, had barely been begun. Édouard de Tocqueville, for example, wanted to know all about the banking system. For another correspondent Tocqueville felt it necessary to sketch a tableau of all American society. And for some time past their long-suffering friend Chabrol had been awaiting an essay on the organization of Civil and Criminal Justice in the United States.[7]

The administration of justice, it so happened, had begun to interest Tocqueville deeply. Here was a topic, a branch of political knowledge, that he would certainly have to master before he could write about American democracy. Yet thus far he had rather neglected the subject. The role and activity of the people he had just examined with care: the manhood suffrage, the liberty of assembly, the right of jury trial, the freedom of the press; all these had fallen under his scrutiny. Before that he had also given some attention to the machinery of self-government, both in the local communities and in the State. Eventually, when he reached Washington, he would of course investigate the Federal machinery as well, particularly the legislative and executive powers. All these special inquiries would leave the third organ, the judiciary branch (both State and Federal), alone of the important agencies practically untouched. He had thought to make a start on such a study in Boston, but other matters had intervened. Tocqueville made up his mind to remedy the omission at once.

Already, before his return to Philadelphia, he had collected a few scattered and miscellaneous observations. On the sixteenth of October, for example, James J. Barclay, Secretary of the Prison Society, had spoken to him of the Pennsylvania courts and the provisions for summoning witnesses; while judge Coxe had emphasized the powers of the Public Prosecutors. In Baltimore a Mr. Williamson had outlined the procedure for the impeachment of judges, and discussed the function of the grand jury. Again, a few days after establishing himself once more in Philadelphia, Tocqueville visited a United States court, where a counterfeiter was being tried. George M. Dallas, the Federal Attorney for the Eastern District of Pennsylvania, was kind enough to let him look over all the documents in the case.* Afterwards Mayor

---

* All these 'documents' were entered in a special diary for criminal and civil justice, 'Cahier F.' George M. Dallas, 1792–1864, was to be one of the leaders of the Demo-

Richards praised the impartiality of the judges. And that evening he had been able to note down a reflection or two of his own on the influence of the bench.

All this, however, was unsatisfactory. What Tocqueville wanted was not a few ill-assorted fragments of information, but a reasoned and systematic description of the whole judiciary system of Pennsylvania. He sought for a lawyer who would be able and willing to supply his need.

On the fifteenth of November—or two days after the court trial— Tocqueville found his man in the person of Henry D. Gilpin, a rising young practitioner of the city, who was soon to succeed George M. Dallas as United States District Attorney, and who would one day be District Attorney of the United States.* The Duc de Montébello had given him a letter of introduction to this son of the celebrated Joshua Gilpin, and Tocqueville had delivered it dutifully in the early days of his first visit to Philadelphia. Then the prison investigation and their Baltimore excursion had prevented his taking advantage of the opening. But now he was free. And the result was a conversation, or rather a discourse by Mr. Gilpin, that covered four mortal hours.

Henry D. Gilpin had studied under J.R.Ingersoll, and was a very well-informed young man. He began, therefore, with a short history of English law: from the earliest common law, to the statute law, and the gradual erection of exceptional courts, such as the Court of Chancery, with its Equity Law and its special jurisdictions. Shifting then to Pennsylvania, Gilpin outlined the judicial organization of his State. He described the circuits, the differences between the Inferior and Superior Courts, and the lack of a real 'appeal' from one to the other. Under questioning from Tocqueville he made clear which parts of the English practice had been retained, which parts abandoned. Under further questioning he drew a careful distinction between the judge

---

cratic party in Pennsylvania, Vice-President of the United States under Polk, and U.S. Minister to England in Buchanan's administration. Since graduating from Princeton with honours, he had already served for a time as Gallatin's secretary in Europe, and in 1828 had been Mayor of Philadelphia.

* Valedictorian of his class at the University of Pennsylvania, Henry D. Gilpin, 1801– 1860, was shortly to be appointed Government Director of the United States Bank, and later, as Attorney General of the United States, would edit the Papers of James Madison. Of Quaker descent, Gilpin represented another instance of sound Pennsylvania ability turning to the support of Andrew Jackson. Democratic enthusiasm was apparently perfectly compatible with an interest in literature and the arts, as well; for Gilpin had for six years been editing the *Atlantic Souvenir*, a literary annual, and was later to become President of the Pennsylvania Academy of Fine Arts.

and the jury, naming the functions and powers of each. He spoke of written evidence and oral testimony. He showed how the law protected the individual against false judgments of the jury by writs of error and retrials; against bad judges by the remedy of impeachment. He answered all the questions Tocqueville could think to ask. And then, as a final contribution, he gave his own opinion of the value of the American jury system. The whole interview made for his listener a priceless document, to be saved, studied, used. And when Tocqueville himself came to publish his personal opinion of the jury system, he would conclude with Gilpin's remarks, paragraph by paragraph and almost word for word.*

One might suppose that a four-hour interview of such authority and encyclopædic content would have sufficed Tocqueville, at least for a considerable time. But the commissioner was now in full cry, and almost immediately he was off in pursuit of fresh documents.

His first victim was the Recorder of the City, the young and energetic Joseph McIlvaine. Though only 31, a year older than Gilpin, McIlvaine himself presided over a local city court, and seemed to the commissioners 'extremely intelligent and capable.' So Tocqueville asked him about the composition and payment of the jury, and about its possible adoption in foreign countries. When Tocqueville explained to the Recorder 'how things *se passaient* in France, the *exposé* seemed to cause him [the Philadelphian] great astonishment.' But the young man was none the less convinced that—with certain modifications— the jury system would prove its value even there.

Suddenly, as their days in Philadelphia were growing short, it occurred to the two commissioners that they might make use of the willing and intelligent Recorder, even after their departure. That is, they would make out a list of questions, which he would consider at his ease, and answer at some length in writing while they were in the South. Like Mr. Coolidge of Boston, Mr. McIlvaine proved as accommodating and agreeable as one could desire. In fact, he seemed so anxious to contribute to what he called 'the laudable and interesting object of your visit to this country,' that Beaumont was even to venture to send him some further questions, six weeks later, from New Orleans.

* See also Tocqueville's 'Lesson on the Jury,' above, pp.384–89. A glance at his commentary (*Dém. en Am.*, II,190) will indicate that Tocqueville's final judgment would be a skilful synthesis of his Boston and Philadelphia impressions. For a full account of the Gilpin conversation, see Cahier F.

The result was that Mr. McIlvaine very nearly wrote a book for the French Commissioners before he got through. At least, his labours on their behalf were enormous. On the seventh of February following, he was to send them the first of three long essays of his own composition.* It would be a treatise on the history of the penal code of the state, enumerating the capital offences under the harsh English code, describing the modifications advocated by the Quakers, quoting from the humanizing laws passed after the Revolution, mentioning the recent establishment of solitary confinement with labour, and winding up with an analysis of offences and punishments as of the year 1831. For prison commissioners, destined before long to write a report to their government, this document would obviously be of no inconsiderable value.

Their great harvest, however, was to be reaped from the two even longer letters or essays that McIlvaine would have composed, copied, and sent them by the eighth of February, just before their sailing. The first would be the much-desired written account of the judicial organization in Pennsylvania, a document that would correct and supplement Tocqueville's recollection of his Gilpin conversation. The letter would be a monumental piece of work. It would begin with a concise but illuminating analysis of the judicial machinery of the State, from the Justices of the Peace at the bottom, through the Court of Common Pleas, upward to the Supreme Court, mentioning in each instance the composition of the court and the jurisdiction covered. Next, McIlvaine would describe the usual procedure in Criminal and in Civil cases, following the story step by step: from arrest to indictment, to arraignment, to plea, to the selection of the jury, to argument and testimony, to the charge of the court, the decision of the jury and the motion for retrial. After mentioning the exceptional city courts, McIlvaine would then go on to point out what, after mature consideration, he thought to be the defects of the Pennsylvania system and the necessary precautions to take in employing the institution of trial by jury. Under this last head he would put at Tocqueville and Beaumont's disposal, in reasonable and compact language, the vast knowledge and the great stock of wisdom that he and his fellow-lawyers in America had slowly been accumulating out of long experience and observation of the use of juries. As for the adoption of the jury system in France,

---

* For these three essays, see the Tocqueville papers, under the heading BIc; also McIlvaine's accompanying letter (BB).

McIlvaine would have a specific recommendation to make. The jury, if employed at all, should be given control in certain cases, and this not only because it educated the citizens in self-government but because it protected the bench from popular passions.

The jury system, he would suggest, 'should apply to all cases where fraud is alleged, where the genuineness of any paper is disputed, where a contract is alleged to have been made upon a void consideration—or for the sake of a benefit which has not been obtained—and in other cases which will readily occur to you.

'A judge, in order to maintain his standing of just influence, should be protected from the necessity of deciding all questions not referable to fixed and settled principles. Matters resting in mere opinion or depending on the degree of credit to be attached to witnesses, to which no positive legal standard can be applied, are decided by a jury with more satisfaction to the parties concerned and with an equal chance of a just result.

'It is to the adoption of this principle by our laws more than to any barrier which the constitution has provided that the independence of the American Judiciary must be attributed.

'In proportion as the government of France approaches a democratic form, or as the popular voice increases in its influence, will the necessity of such protection be felt by the judges. The sooner, therefore, that the people at large are made acquainted with the trial by jury and prepared by experience for its proper exercise, the better.

'I take it for granted'—McIlvaine would wind up his effort with a friendly flourish—'I take it for granted the march of France will be onward to free and liberal institutions.

'That her march may be *calm, reflecting, peaceful* and victorious—and that the result may be increase of light and knowledge and happiness is the sincere wish/of your obedient serv./Jos. McIlvaine.'

Even yet, however, the Recorder's labours would not be done. Beaumont would have sent him a whole list of questions from New Orleans and a third letter would have to be written. Some of these questions would again concern judicial matters—the impeachment of judges, the duties of district attorneys, the attendance of witnesses—and McIlvaine would return clear and reasonable explanations. Others would be of more general character: the registry of births and marriages, the law in regard to divorce. Finally, there would be the [for Tocqueville and

Beaumont] inevitable question on the inheritance law, on *'Successions.'*
To this query McIlvaine would reply as follows:

'The political effect of the law of successions by which the property
of a person dying intestate is divided equally among all his children
male and female is altogether advantageous.

'It effectually prevents rich families from continuing rich through
more than two generations unless the family wealth be kept up by
constant industry.

'The consequence is that *mere idlers* are not sufficiently numerous in
any community to form a distinct class—and that respectability and
influence attach themselves exclusively to the industrious and useful
portion of society.

'Among the moderately wealthy classes, the operation of the principle of equal division is necessarily favourable in a country opening so
wide a field to industry and enterprise.

'Each child receives enough to start him on the road to wealth but
not sufficient to encourage him in idleness.

'Where a moderate property in land only is left, a minute subdivision of estates is not the consequence, as I have understood it to
be in France.

'One of the children generally takes his father's farm, becoming
responsible to the others for the payment of their shares in money at
a reasonable period. The rest move off to the west where a small sum
will purchase a large tract of land, or they enter into the trades and
occupations which the nearest city affords.

'Our principle of Partition among joint heirs of land is a good
one. . . .' And McIlvaine would explain how the court proceeded in
order to prevent the continual subdivision of small estates.

'An article which I remember to have read in the Edinburg quarterly Review upon the effect produced in France by the abolition of the
law of Primogeniture, insisted greatly upon this subdivision of landed
property, as an evil of much importance.

'It will be felt probably in proportion as the people want knowledge
and enterprise and a desire to better their condition, and as they are
disposed to drag through life in the same dull track which their fathers
before them pursued.

'Such is not the genius of our population. They are perhaps on the
opposite extreme, exhibiting too great eagerness for change, and too
little stability in the pursuit of any single object.'

Whatever his views of French character, apparently McIlvaine would agree perfectly with the commissioners, with Mr. Livingston of New York, and with all the others whom Tocqueville had consulted on the influence of the American inheritance laws. Apparently he, too, would contribute to Tocqueville's self-deception, confirming the Frenchman in his erroneous and disastrous belief that it was the inheritance law more than any other one cause that had created American democracy.

Yet one had to be careful not to read the Recorder of Philadelphia too hastily. For actually the acute and energetic young man did not mean what, superficially, his words seemed to indicate. Instead, he would at once go on to explain two facts that Tocqueville and Beaumont did not seem to realize and that badly needed pointing out. The first was that the law of equal partition applied only to the estates of those dying intestate. The second was that it was the *custom*, even of those making wills, to divide their property fairly equally. In other words, the equal partition of property that was everywhere to be remarked was the result, fundamentally and originally, of *custom*, not of *law*. In short, Tocqueville was wrong. Democracy was not the result of the subdivision of property, itself the unavoidable result of the inheritance law. Instead, the equal partition of estates had existed in custom before it had entered the law. The custom might be democratic in nature, but it had not caused the rule of the people. Originally it had been coeval with other equalitarian customs, latterly it had shown itself in harmony with a multitude of popular practices. The most that could therefore be said was that custom and law were now in perfect agreement.

In McIlvaine's letter, this thought would be phrased as follows:

'The parent has an absolute right to dispose of all his property by will, and may entirely cut off any or all of his children. . . .'

On the other hand, 'the provision made by law for the equal distribution of property among the heirs in equal degree is so generally acquiesced in that few men would make their wills, but for the sake of designating their Executors, of providing for the comfort of their widows, or of so limiting the shares of their daughters as to secure them against the debts or extravagances of the future husbands.

'Inequalities of distribution among children occur so seldom, as not to be worth notice, and not to be referable to any distinct motives or causes. . . .'

'I must apologize for the bad handwriting & perhaps the loosely expressed sentiments of this document,' the Recorder was to conclude this third essay. 'It has been written in about six hours of constant sitting without an opportunity to read over or correct any part of it.'

*

* *

With Gilpin's remarks in their notebooks, and written answers promised by Joseph McIlvaine, Tocqueville and Beaumont could now abandon the judiciary system and turn their attention to the collection of documents of a more miscellaneous nature.*

From Samuel L. Southard,† a very prominent citizen of New Jersey, they obtained assurances of a written digest of the Penal Code and practice of his State. From R.W.Gill, the Baltimore attorney, they could already count on some remarks on capital punishment and crime in Maryland. They wrote to Richard Riker, the New York Recorder, asking for statistics on indictments and punishments in New York. They even ventured to send their friend Coolidge in Boston some further queries of a general nature.[8] And in Philadelphia their acquaintances sprang nobly to their aid.

Benjamin W. Richards, busy though he was, promised them some personal statements on the organization and expenses of the counties and cities of Pennsylvania.‡ And the distinguished Nicholas Biddle, President of the Bank of the United States, volunteered some verbal information on a subject that still puzzled Tocqueville considerably: the strange absence of party government in America.[9]

'What I find hardest to understand in America is the existence and means of action of the political parties,' Tocqueville explained. 'In France, and elsewhere in Europe, society is divided by two or three

* On the twenty-sixth of November, Tocqueville sent his friend Chabrol two essays: one, on American justices of the peace, was for a mutual acquaintance; the other was the long promised analysis of the American judiciary system for Chabrol himself. It made an able and illuminating document, as may be judged from its trenchant opening:
  '. . . There are in the United States two entirely distinct Civil Justices: the Federal justice and the justice of each State. Each State forms an independent sovereignty: there's the principle. The States have ceded certain portions of their rights to the *Union*: there's the exception. . . .'

† Southard, 1787–1842, was a graduate of Princeton who had many acquaintances in Virginia through having tutored in the Taliaferro family. In a varied career, which perhaps illustrated one of McIlvaine's remarks, he had already been a prosecuting attorney, State legislator, Secretary of the Navy, and State Attorney General. In 1832 he was to become Governor of New Jersey, and immediately thereafter to go to the United States Senate, where he continued until his death. The information requested by Tocqueville and Beaumont he forwarded on 27 December.

‡ These were eventually delayed, and were only sent the following April, after Tocqueville and Beaumont had left the country.

great ideas around which positive interests and passions rally. In America I see nothing similar; one would say that there existed here only coteries and no parties, properly speaking. Personalities are everything, principles insignificant.

'Mr. Biddle answered: I can understand your having trouble grasping the existence and activity of parties in America, for we ourselves no longer know where we are. All the old parties have intermingled, and to-day it would be impossible to say what is the political faith of those who favour the administration and of those who attack it.

'But it was not always thus, said I?' Tocqueville was waiting to see if Mr. Biddle would offer the same explanation that Latrobe had given them in Baltimore.

'Certainly not, replied Mr. Biddle; this is entirely new with us. For a very long time we were divided into federalists and republicans. Those two parties were much like those you have in Europe; they possessed political doctrines; to which interests and passions attached themselves. They fought each other unmercifully, until finally the Federal party, always weak in numbers, was absolutely annihilated by its adversary. Weary of their position of vanquished, the federalists in the end abandoned their own party; they identified themselves with the victorious party, or under different names took up special causes. But their party standard has indeed been struck down for good. This revolution was just being completed when General Jackson arrived in power; and he has pretended to recognize no ancient distinctions of party in his appointments. Since then there are people who support the administration and others who attack it, people who put forward a measure, others who disparage it. But there are no parties properly speaking, opposed the one to the other and adopting contrary political faiths. The fact is, there aren't two practicable ways of governing this people now, and political passions can only be exercised over small administrative details, not over principles.'

Tocqueville approached another puzzling feature of American administration. 'With you the chief of state can have the majority in Congress against him without the public business suffering?' he asked.

'Yes, unquestionably our political machine is set up so it can go ahead on its own. The case you speak of has already presented itself several times; even now the President has lost the confidence of Congress and the enlightened classes. His proposals are not adopted, his appointments rejected by the Senate; yet public affairs go as well as before and no one has any fears for the future. I regard it as the greatest proof of the goodness of our institutions that we find it so easy to get on without government, or to go ahead in spite of the administration.' Mr. Biddle would not always be able to treat the power of President Jackson so lightly. But not yet had the war been declared between them. For the present, the great banker was full of confidence.

Finally, for Tocqueville and Beaumont, there was the really amusing case of their friend Robert Walsh, the enthusisatic *littérateur*. As an editor of wide reputation, Mr. Walsh was in possession of a variegated collection of pamphlets and publications which his friends and associates in the literary profession had sent him. Suddenly it seems to have occurred to him that he could do some house cleaning to the profit of the young French commissioners. The latter, at least, were presently in receipt of a perfect avalanche of printed documents, many of them, it seemed, the presentation copies of the authors to Mr. Walsh.

Among others, for example, the benevolent editor sent: *The First Annual Report of the New York Young Men's Society* (1830); Mr. Gray's letter on Harvard University (1831); *The Annual Oration of the Zelosophic Society of the University of Pennsylvania*; a Lecture on the *Infant School System of Education* (1830); an *Address on the Formation of Teachers* (1830); an *Address delivered at the request of the Sunday School Union of Maryland* (given by E.L.Finley, the orator, to Mr. Walsh); a *Report of the Select Committee of the House of Representatives of Massachusetts relating to legalizing the study of Anatomy* (marked by Tocqueville *Curieux*); an article *On the Penetrativeness of Fluids* (1830); an *Introductory lecture to a Course of Anatomy in the University of Pennsylvania* (1831); another on Chemistry; a third on 'demonstrative anatomy'; the *Report of the Danville and Pottsville Railroad Co.* (1831); *The Liberal Preacher* (a monthly publication of sermons, Boston); a copy of the *Christian Examiner*; and the *New England Magazine* (for October 1, 1831).

Just what Tocqueville and Beaumont thought of this shower of documents, they did not say. We know only that Tocqueville tied them up in bundles, brought them all back to France, took them to his Normandy Château. A hundred years later Mr. Walsh's pamphlets would still be there, their condition indicating that perhaps after all they had served as edification only . . . for worms.

*

\*    \*

Learning that the commissioners of the French Government were almost at the end of their visit, the Philadelphians multiplied their parties and their attentions.

Roberts Vaux and Warden Wood made haste to supply them with some letters of introduction to Harrisburg and the West.* And, in the thought perhaps that he would be able to give them some interesting information on the country they were going to see, they were presented to the interesting soldier, diplomat and traveller Joel R. Poinsett.†

'Philadelphia, 20 Nov. 1831,' Tocqueville wrote in his diary: [10] 'Mr. Poinsett, who was long ambassador of the United States to Mexico and who passes for a very remarkable man, said to me this evening:

'It's in Kentucky and Tennessee that the character of the Americans of the South can be judged. The Kentuckians are descended from the Virginians; they have never been mingled with foreigners; they have preserved their own character and customs better than the men of any other province. Ohio, Illinois, and all the West, on the contrary, are being peopled by means of an emigration from all parts of the Union, but particularly from New England. There is in these emigrants a restlessness of spirit that is extraordinary. It never happens that the land remains in the hands of the man who clears it. When it begins to produce, the pioneer sells it and plunges anew into the woods. It seems as if the habit of moving, of upsetting, of cutting, of destroying, had become a necessity of his existence. Very often the second proprietor cannot free himself to settle down, either. When the land is in full production, he sells it in his turn and goes farther on to improve a new lot. But the third or fourth settlers; it's they who form the population. The others are like advance guards of civilization in the wilderness of America.'

---

* Addressing them 'at Boyers, Chestnut St.,' to which they had apparently gone in preference to the Mansion House, on their return to Philadelphia, Vaux took the occasion to recommend his friend J. Francis Fisher, a Harvard graduate, who would be in Paris the next winter. 'Anticipating the pleasure of seeing you at coffee this evening at any hour you please after 5 O'Clock, I salute you with gt. respect.' 20 Nov. 1831 (BB).

† A Charlestonian by birth, Joel Roberts Poinsett, 1779–1852, was one of the most striking and cosmopolitan figures of his generation. He had tutored under Dr. Timothy Dwight at Greenfield Hill in his 'teens, studied medicine at Edinburgh University and military science at Woolwich Academy, travelled for nine years in Europe and Asia, been sent on a special mission to South America by President Madison, served in Congress, and represented the United States for four years in Mexico, where he made himself unpopular by introducing an alien brand of Masonry into the country—and immortal by bringing back the Poinsettia to the United States. At the moment he was just arrived from Liverpool, and about to act as President Jackson's agent against the Nullifiers in South Carolina. For Tocqueville and Beaumont's later meeting with him in the South, see below, pp.643ff.

In this manner the last week passed. 'Not a minute of each day but is employed to definite purpose,' Beaumont wrote his family.[11] 'We spend much of our time boring ourselves, or, if you will, amusing ourselves in society. Yet in that we act not for our pleasure but through duty. It is impossible to decline the *soirées dansantes* when one is young and handsome. It is even necessary to appear to enjoy ourselves hugely. We see our time consumed, then, in the accomplishment of small social obligations, while we can't find an instant to give to the labours which alone in our eyes have a true importance. . . .

'. . . In Philadelphia it's above all the suppers which are fashionable. The last that we attended was at the home of the Mayor, who in our honour had gathered together all the social and intellectual notabilities of the city. They made us earnest entreaties to induce us to stay longer. We were only able to escape by promising to return; but as we make the same promise everywhere it is probable that we shall nowhere keep it.

'One of the richest men of the city, Mr. Burd,* came the eve of our departure to ask us to dinner at his house one of the following days. We were unable to accept, since we had made all our arrangements for leaving. This dear, good man was much cast down by our refusal; he had sent out a multitude of invitations and everywhere announced a great *fête*, always in our honour. Supplications and entreaties were in vain. All that proves to you what important personages we are in this land. I believe we'll never make as much noise in France.'

On the twenty-second, Tocqueville and Beaumont finally set forth for the Ohio valley and the Southwest. Their friends bade them adieu. Roberts Vaux prepared to have them elected members of the Historical Society of Pennsylvania. And the newspapers resounded with their praises.

'We are glad,' *Poulson's American Daily Advertiser* republished one article on the twenty-fifth,[12] 'We are glad to witness the testimonials of respect and approbation which have attended the travels and researches of Messrs de Beaumont and De Tocqueville, Commissioners deputed by the Government of Louis Philippe, to inspect the prisons of this country. These tributes have been induced by the bland demeanor and intelligent liberality of the commissioners. They have passed over many interesting sections of the United States; especially

* Edward Shippen Burd, who had just been elected one of the Trustees of the University of Pennsylvania.

over some regions in the north west, peculiarly calculated to give them just ideas of the unhewn and original America. The recital of their tour thus far, and the favourable impressions awakened in its prosecution, is unusually interesting. After inspecting sundry institutions of criminal punishment in the South and South-west, they will return hither and embark for France in February next.'

PART VII: OHIO AND MISSISSIPPI

## XL

## JOURNEY TO THE OHIO: THE HAZARDS OF
## STAGE AND STEAM

'MY journey from Philadelphia to Pittsburg[h] is one of the most arduous that I have taken,' Beaumont wrote his sister a week later:[1] 'the roads are detestable, the carriages even worse. We travelled night and day during three times twenty-four hours. At 30 leagues from Philadelphia we encountered the Allegheny Mountains, where we were pounced on by a horrible cold. During almost all the remainder of the journey we proceeded in the midst of a perpetual tornado of snow such as had not been seen for a long time, especially at this season of the year.*

'The Alleghenies are not very high but they don't terminate,' he continued. 'They are less mountains than an interminable succession of hills cut by a thousand valleys, all extremely picturesque. I admit, though, that I admired the beauty of the country very little, it was too cold. There are no pretty countrysides without verdure; and one is necessarily a cold admirer when freezing.

After covering 100 leagues by carriage, we had arrived at Pittsburg[h], the most industrial town of Pennsylvania, the Birmingham of America, where the air is constantly obscured by the multitude of steam engines that run the shops. We stayed there but an instant, which I employed in writing a word or two to my father.' With Tocqueville he also visited the Western Penitentiary of Pennsylvania in the city.†

---

* Beaumont did not realize that this blizzard, the like of which he had probably never seen before, was only a foretaste of the weather that was to accompany them almost to New Orleans. At the request of the Minister of Justice they were now hurrying so as to get back to France within the year.

† They found sixty-four prisoners, in a neglected prison, using the cells indiscriminately and communicating with each other all the time. They were perfectly unoccupied, as the prison contained no shop where they could work. John Patterson, the warden, was of ordinary capacity; and on the whole this penitentiary represented all the abuses of the original Pennsylvania theory, without any of the later improvements.

'After that we embarked for Cincinnati, not in a carriage, but in a steamboat. On the Ohio there are always a great number of steamboats going from Louisville to Pittsburg[h] and from Pittsburg[h] to Louisville (Louisville is beyond Cincinnati on the road toward the Mississip[p]i).'

It was a welcome change, particularly for Tocqueville, who could once more resume the writing of letters and the recording of observations on the country they had been seeing. Travelling with them on their steamboat, the *Fourth of July*, was, for instance, a great landholder from the State of Illinois. 'He drew me,' Tocqueville noted,[2] 'an admirable picture of the fertility of the country, and added that it was being populated with extreme rapidity.'

'Many Europeans come there, said I?'

'No, he answered, the majority of emigrants come from Ohio. Isn't this fact characteristic of the nature of the country and the character of its inhabitants? It was only 40 years ago that Ohio began to be settled. Its chief city has been in existence only 30 years. And already the new generation finds too little opportunity there to get rich and takes up the march again toward even newer countries.'

Yet, if here was an American trait so obvious as to have struck Tocqueville even before he had been two months in New York City, he now knew that there were other groups of men, there were even whole races within the bounds of North America, who somehow strangely failed to partake of this western restlessness.

'It was fifty years ago at least that the German colonies came to establish themselves in Pennsylvania. They have preserved intact the spirit and customs of their fatherland. All about them is stirring a nomad population, with whom the desire to grow rich has no bounds, which clings to no spot, is arrested by no ties, but shifts wherever the prospect of fortune presents itself. Immobile in the midst of this general movement, the German limits his desires to the gradual amelioration of his position and that of his family. He is always working, but abandons nothing to chance; he enriches himself surely, but slowly; he

---

What could be the explanation of such laxity? Tocqueville and Beaumont thought that local indifference on the part of the public was responsible. 'In a government where strength and continuity are nowhere to be found, those things only are well done that excite the interest of the public and that yield glory and profit on that account to the individuals who take a hand in them.' (*Du Syst. Pén.*, note d, pp.266–267.) On 27 January 1832, Patterson sent them a page statement, that they had requested, on the Western Penitentiary (BB).

clings to the domestic hearth, confines his happiness within his own horizon, and feels no curiosity to know what there may be the other side of his last furrow.' *

*

* *

'The banks of the Ohio must be delightful in the fine season,' Beaumont continued his account of their downward passage. 'This river flows for quite a while between enclosing mountains. These mountains, a chain of the Alleghenies, offer a prodigious variety of sites, each more picturesque than the last. After a day on the water we arrived within a league of a small town named Wheeling. There, one of the drollest and most singular adventures happened to us; but there's no way of relating it in a letter. Just remember, though, this *passage* in my letter, and when I get back I'll tell you a story that will make you laugh.'

Eugénie must have wondered what this droll adventure was, but no enlightening word was to come from America. And Tocqueville's family were never to hear of it at all. That is, not until his arrival home.

For the plain fact was that during the night of 26–27 November the two young Frenchmen had been shipwrecked and very nearly drowned. And both were afraid to tell their already apprehensive families.

Tocqueville did relate the story in a letter to Marie Mottley, but the letter has long since been destroyed or lost.‡ He also had sufficient faith in the discretion of his friend Chabrol to confide in him at the end of the long-promised essay on Civil Justice in Pennsylvania.[3]

---

* 'To-day (26 Nov. 1831), descending the Ohio below Pittsburg[h], we passed before the colony of Economy. The town of Economy is situated on the bank of the Ohio in a fertile plain. There are there now 1000 inhabitants, who are living in great prosperity and increasing rapidly each year the common stock (*fonds social*). This society is one of the most remarkable in existence. Mr. . . . ., the founder, is the uncontrolled head of the enterprise. He directs the common labours and renders no accounts. All the other members of the society are only employees having an eventual right to the common property when the ties shall be broken; but up to then they receive only enough to live comfortably. If some of them want to withdraw, they may; but they leave behind what they put in. Should the entire society wish to dissolve, it could; but there has been no desire to do so, and its affairs are prospering unbelievably. The society already owns an immense area of land.' Toc. diary note, Alph. B.

† Marie Mottley, probably after her husband's death many years later, made fair copies of those parts of Tocqueville's letters that she wished to save, then apparently destroyed the entire correspondence between them. In any case, the invaluable letters that Tocqueville wrote her from America have never been recovered.

'Marie will tell you, my dear friend, that these lines only just missed being the last ever addressed to you by me,' he wrote on the twenty-eighth of November. 'Day before yesterday, in the evening, our vessel, driven by the current and all the force of steam, smashed itself like a nutshell on a rock in the middle of the Ohio. The noise, as we learned afterwards, was heard at a quarter of a league all around. The cry of: *we sink* resounded immediately; the vessel, the gear, and the passengers started in company for eternity.

'I have never heard a more villainous sound than the water made rushing into the ship. . . .'

What had happened was that their vessel had struck a rock on a well-known obstruction to navigation called Burlington Bar. And the Bar had, in the last analysis, saved them.

Thirty years later, in his *Notice* of the life of his friend, Beaumont undertook to recreate the scene from some pencil notes which he claimed to have made at the time. Internal evidence casts considerable doubt on the contemporaneous character of the sketch. There are too many obvious errors, there is too much breathlessness in the punctuation.* Yet this dubious and abbreviated narrative remains to-day the only substantial account of the accident that almost cut off Tocqueville and Beaumont in the inception of their careers, and that came so close to robbing the world of Tocqueville's *Démocratie*.

'. . . 1st December (1831), departure from Wheeling, at ten miles from Pittsburg, on the steamboat ——,' Beaumont's narrative began:

The Ohio charged with blocks of ice. Its banks covered with snow. Navigation said to be dangerous at night, especially when cloudy. Nevertheless we keep on steadily . . . towards midnight, cry of alarm! *all*

---

* This passage in his biographical sketch, Beaumont introduced with the following explanation. '. . . here, to render more rapid a recital that is only intended for a sketch, it is fitting, for lack of notes by Alexis de Tocqueville which are wanting for this incident, to reproduce textually those of his travelling companion, just as he traced them in pencil from day to day.' *O.C.*,V,28.

Unfortunately for the reputation of the supposed extract that follows, the date given for the accident is out by five days, the wreck took place above Wheeling (not below, as Beaumont's account suggests), the subsequent stay at Cincinnati is shortened from four days to one, and the whole account of their adventures, to the moment of their arrival in New Orleans, has the air of a clumsy amateur fake. Without much risk of injustice, one may conclude that Beaumont's narrative represented less the pencilled jottings of an observer on the spot than the emotions of a romantic traveller, recollected in tranquillity. The so-called daily diary was constructed, either several weeks, or many years, after the events that it described. (Whether Beaumont lost the diary, that he really had been keeping, in this wreck, or mislaid it somewhere later, there seems to be no way of ascertaining.)

*lost!* It's the voice of the captain, we have struck against a reef (Burling-ton Bar); our boat has stove itself in; it is going down before one's eyes. Solemn moment: two hundred passengers aboard, and only two skiffs (*chaloupes*) each able to hold ten to a dozen persons. The water rises, rises; it already fills the cabins. Admirable *sang-froid* of American women; there are fifty there; not a cry at the sight of approaching death. Tocque-ville and I throw a glance at the Ohio, which at this place is more than a mile wide and whose current is drawing down enormous cakes of ice; we grasp each other's hand in farewell. . . . Suddenly the boat stops sinking; its hull is hanging on the very reef that broke it; what saves it is the very depth of its injury and the speed with which the inrushing water makes it settle on the rock. . . .

No more danger. . . . But what's going to become of us, planted thus in the middle of the river like prisoners on a hulk?

Another steamboat, the *William Parsons*, passes and takes us aboard. . . . We continue our journey. . . .*

The reader may smile a little at the touching spectacle of the two young stoics solemnly shaking hands after throwing a scornful glance at this ice-filled Ohio. Perhaps, children of a more romantic day, they did just that. But in any case the gesture was one of a moment only. For their minds were filled too utterly with the sensations of the disaster: the cry of the captain, the villainous sound of inrushing water, the heroic silence of the women on board. Even after the *Fourth of July* ceased sinking, one could not but admire the calmness of the Americans.

'I had, during my sojourn in America, a thousand occasions to see (*juger*) the *sang-froid* of the American,' Beaumont was by and by to testify in his *Marie.*[4] 'I shall cite but one example. As I was coming down the Ohio on a steamboat with a number of merchants and their merchandise, our vessel, called the *Fourth of July*, struck a reef known as Burlington-Bar and stove itself in. This is not the place to retail the circumstances of this accident, or its dangers—which one would think exaggerated by the imagination or memory of the traveller. I shall limit myself to the statement that, the ship having submerged, all the

* On 8 December, the *Nashville Republican and State Gazette* quoted a Louisville news-paper:

ANOTHER STEAMBOAT SUNK!

'The Steamboat 4th July, Powell commander, on her passage from Pittsburgh to this place, struck a rock at Burlington Bar, between Pittsburgh and Wheeling, and sunk. She was loaded with goods, principally for Cincinnati. We understand that she is insured for eight thousand dollars, by the Louisville Marine and Fire In-surance Company.'

commercial goods it contained were either destroyed or damaged; and yet, faced by a fact that for some meant a considerable loss, for others complete ruin, the American merchants uttered not a single cry of desolation or despair.'

Of course, sons of the aristocracy were capable of reticence, and could also play the man. 'When I get back I'll tell you a story that will make you laugh,' Beaumont had soon been writing. They had been set ashore and had spent the night at a hut on the snow-covered bank of the river. Soon another steamboat came by and carried them down to Wheeling.

*

*    *

They kept on down the river. Perhaps there was no other adequate transportation available. Quite as likely the two commissioners had begun unconsciously to absorb some of the even-tempered equanimity of fatalistic Americans. For as the long vibrating hours of steamboat routine began again their endless procession,* Tocqueville's thoughts reverted once more to the larger and less accidental America. It was a rare day, anyhow, that did not give birth to some fresh observation, or find a conclusion maturing in his mind.† And now he had two decisions ready, two vital judgments to record.

'There is one thing that America demonstrates invincibly of which I was hitherto doubtful,' he wrote in one of his diaries.[5] 'This is that the middle classes are capable of governing a state. I don't know if they would come off honourably from really difficult political situations, but they are adequate for the ordinary conduct of society, despite their petty passions, their incomplete education, their vulgar manners. Clearly they can supply practical intelligence, and that is sufficient.'

The implications of Tocqueville's statement were of great significance. It wasn't just that he was now echoing what so many of his acquaintances in Philadelphia and Baltimore had suggested. It went much farther than mere repetition. For here, at long last, the liberal

---

* The 'most attractive towns' that Beaumont saw from their vessel, he said, were Marietta and Gallipolis.

† In this instance, keyed up by their adventure to a pitch of emotional exuberance, Tocqueville first unburdened himself of a delicious, satirical little essay on American women, before and after marriage. The United States was the 'eldorado of husbands,' he asserted; and in proof he proceeded to tell over the virtues of their 'reasonable' and devoted wives, with the greatest seriousness and solemnity. Toc. to his sister-in-law, Mme Édouard (?), On the Ohio, 28 Nov. 1831 (TT), rough draft.

aristocrat was admitting his doubts conquered. It *was* possible for a middle class to govern itself by democratic means, and adequately, too.

'In France,' the diary note continued, 'In France the middle classes have very narrow prejudices against the upper classes; but perhaps the upper classes themselves are too much swayed by the unfavourable impression which is aroused in them by the vulgarity noticeable in the manners and habits of mind of the middle classes. From this incontestable fact are drawn arguments of a political incapacity which does not exist, at least in the degree supposed.

'Another point demonstrated by America is that virtue is not, as it has long been pretended, the only thing which can preserve Republics, but that enlightenment more than anything else facilitates that social state. The Americans are hardly more virtuous than others, but they are infinitely better educated (I speak of the mass) than any other people of my acquaintance. I don't wish to say just that it contains more men knowing how to read and write (to which perhaps an unreasonable value is attached), but the mass of those possessing an understanding of public affairs, a knowledge of laws and precedents, a feeling for the best interests of the nation, and the faculty of understanding them, is greater in America than any place else in the world.'

There was Tocqueville's first decision, noted down. His second was entitled 'Concerning Equality in America.' That was to say, he had now finally made up his mind also about the oft-disputed question of how much equality there really was in American social (as distinguished from political) life.

'The relation between the different social positions in America is hard enough to understand, and foreigners ordinarily fall into one of two errors,' he prefaced his remarks. 'Either they imagine that in the United States there exists no distinction between man and man except that of personal merit, or else, struck by the high position occupied here by riches, they come thereby to believe that in a number of our European monarchies, in France for instance, one enjoys an equality more real and more complete than in the American Republics. I think, as I said above, that there is exaggeration in these two ways of interpreting things.

'And first of all, let us carefully establish the terrain. It's not a question at this moment of equality before the law: that kind is complete in America. It is not only a right but a fact. One can even say that if inequality exists somewhere elsewhere there operates in the political world an ample compensation in favour of the middle and lower classes, who, with historic names, fill almost all the elective places.

'I speak of equality in the relations of social life; that equality which brings it about that certain individuals gather in the same places, share each other's ideas and pleasures, link their families. It's here that one must distinguish France from America: the differences become essential.

'In France, whatever people say, the prejudice of birth still exercises a very great power. Birth still forms an almost insurmountable barrier between individuals. In France the professions still to a certain degree classify those that follow them. These prejudices are of all the most inimical to equality, because they create distinctions that are permanent and almost ineffaceable, even with the aid of fortune and time. Those prejudices don't exist in America. Birth is a distinction, but it doesn't classify those who have it, it creates neither right nor incapacity, no obligations toward the world or toward oneself. Classification by professions is likewise almost unknown. It does indeed establish some practical difference between the position of individuals, and in this a difference of fortune is even more effective, but it creates no fundamental inequality, for it does not in any way prevent the intermarriage of families (that's the great touchstone).

'Yet one must not think that in America all the classes of society mingle in the same *salons*. Nothing of the kind is true. The people of the same professions, the same ideas, the same education, choose each other by a sort of instinct and gather together, exclusive from the rest. The difference is that no arbitrary and inflexible rule presides at this arrangement. Thus it shocks no one; it is final for nobody, and no one can be wounded. In this way, less in America than anywhere else do you see the ardent desire of one class to partake not only of the political rights but of the pleasures of others. There's what distinguishes American society favourably from ours. And unfavourably.'

At this point Tocqueville turned to examine the other extreme in interpretation. 'The first of all distinctions in America is money,' he agreed. But this pre-eminence was not permanent or fundamental, he was convinced. Pride of wealth showed itself much more impudently and offensively in the United States than in France, where 'Talent' and 'Merit' were held in high esteem. But what else could have been expected?

'In America, in the absence of all material and exterior distinctions, riches presented themselves as the natural scale by which to measure the merit of men. Furthermore, the Americans are a people very little sensitive to the pleasures of the spirit. Exclusively occupied in making money, they must naturally have a sort of veneration for wealth. It excites their envy, but tacitly they recognize it as the prime advantage.

'In sum then, men in America, as with us, are arranged according to certain categories in the course of social life; common habits, education, and above all wealth establish these classifications. But these rules are neither absolute, nor inflexible, nor permanent. They establish temporary distinctions, and do not form classes properly so called. They give no superiority, even in opinion, to one man above another, so that even though two individuals never meet in the same *salons*, if they meet on the public square, one looks at the other without pride, and in return is regarded without envy. At bottom they feel themselves equal, and are.'

Again Tocqueville wrote: 'When one wishes to estimate the equality between different classes, one must always come to the question of how marriages are made. That's the bottom of the matter. An equality resulting from necessity, courtesy or politics may exist on the surface and deceive the eye. But when one wishes to practise this equality in the intermarriage of families, then one puts one's finger on the sore.'

The journey to Cincinnati was nearly over. It was the thirtieth of November and the next day would see them at their destination. Already Tocqueville had forgotten the steamboat accident and was looking forward to what the new western cities had to show.

'We are arriving in Cincinnati after a journey that the snow and the cold have made pretty uncomfortable,' he finished a letter to his father. Of steamboat accidents, not a word.

And in his diary he wrote:

'What's extremely curious in America is to examine the leanings and instincts of a democracy free to act as it chooses, and to see to what social state it forcibly conducts the society it dominates. This study is particularly interesting for us Frenchmen who are marching perhaps toward Despotism, perhaps toward the Republic, but certainly toward a "Democracy" (Equality) without limit.' *

---

* This last paragraph, with only the slightest rephrasing, Tocqueville was to employ verbatim in his introduction to a chapter on the reign of *démocratie* in America. *Dém. en Am.*, II,ch.5,p.43.

## XLI

## CINCINNATI

Of course Tocqueville and Beaumont had been west before: their tour of the Great Lakes had offered spectacles. There had been the old French port of Detroit; there had been the primeval naked wilderness, making its last silent stand against the pioneer. They remembered Buffalo, a lake village that was growing into a town. And even before that, Tocqueville had written home from Utica that for an American city twenty years was already a considerable antiquity. Along the valley of the Mohawk, in other words, and into the Territory of Michigan, they had been able to watch the process of settlement, see the American people expand.

But now, in the Ohio valley, they were in the main channel of the westward rush: in the stream-bed where had flowed and was still flowing the greatest tide of settlement and expansion that the modern world had perhaps known.

Tocqueville and Beaumont stepped ashore from their steamboat the first of December. Cincinnati was 'the most curious' town Beaumont had ever seen. 'I don't believe there exists anywhere on earth,' he wrote his family,[1] 'a town which has had a growth so prodigious. Thirty years ago the banks of the Ohio were a wilderness. Now there are 30,000 inhabitants in Cincinnati. During the last five years the population has doubled.'

Tocqueville was equally impressed by the 'singular spectacle' of Cincinnati, 'a city which seems to want to rise too quickly for people to have any system or plan about it. Great buildings, thatched cottages, streets encumbered with debris, houses under construction, no names on the streets, no numbers on the houses, no outward luxury, but the image of industry and labour obvious at every step.'[2]

It was always hard, Tocqueville thought, to know for certain what gives birth and growth to towns. Chance, he guessed, had a good deal to do with it, especially the accident of geographic location. In the case

of Cincinnati, for instance, the settlement had been made in an extraordinarily fertile valley, which had brought farmers, then manufactures,
then, naturally, a thriving trade that reached all the way from New
York to New Orleans. And Cincinnati, of course, was only the symbol
of the whole region.

'The entire State of Ohio presents a spectacle no less extraordinary,'
Beaumont decided.[3] 'It possesses a million inhabitants, the whole lot
arrived in this area within 30 years. Everywhere there reigns an appearance of well-being and of universal prosperity. The soil is extremely
fertile and there is no region more happily situated for commercial
enterprises.' *

Yet such an interpretation of Ohio was obviously superficial. 'These
facts are easy to see,' he went on, 'but when you want to examine this society closely, its character and physiognomy become quite difficult to
judge.

'The population of Ohio is made up of very dissimilar elements. The
first settlements in this region were made by inhabitants of New England, which still sends a great number of emigrants. On the other hand,
some came and still are coming every day from Virginia and the other
Southern states, whose customs are very different from those of the
North. Finally there are in Ohio some Germans and Irish come from
Europe with still different ideas and customs. All these diverse peoples
find themselves amalgamated together, and their combination creates
a moral being whose portrait it would be very hard to draw.'

Perhaps, thought Beaumont, 'the character of this society is that of
having none. . . .'

But before agreeing to any such sweeping generalizations, both he
and Tocqueville felt that a really intimate inquiry into Ohio civilization
was in order.†

*

*   *

* 'Without being more thickly populated than many of the provinces of Europe, Ohio
could have ten million inhabitants,' Tocqueville noted with a sort of wonder. 'The
fertility of the country is apparently inexhaustible; it is admirably watered by three
or four small rivers, affluents of the Ohio, which mount toward the Great Lakes.'

† Tocqueville and Beaumont did not pause long over the prisons of Ohio. The State,
which 'certainly does not have the enlightenment of New England, possesses a penal
code much more humane than those of Massachusetts and Connecticut,' they were
to report. But as for the application, that was barbarous. 'We sighed profoundly when
at Cincinnati, visiting the *maison d'arrêt*, we found half the prisoners there loaded
down with irons, and the rest plunged in an unhealthy dungeon. What Ohio had
was a bad prison regime, not a penitentiary system.' *Du Syst. Pén.*, 26–28,32.

'My pockets are full of letters of recommendation for the inhabitants of Cincinnati,' Beaumont wrote home the first of December. Apparently he might with justice have boasted that these inhabitants were also the most distinguished of the place. At all events, before the end of the second day he and Tocqueville had met (*and interviewed*) no less than six of the most notable or promising characters of this raw but bustling community.

On 2 December, for instance, Tocqueville's diary noted a 'conversation with Mr. [Bellamy] Storer, the leading lawyer of Cincinnati.' Four years later Storer would also be a Congressman.* That same day, Tocqueville conversed with Timothy Walker, a newly arrived young Harvard graduate, whose distinguished career was to embrace the teaching and the judging of Ohio law.† After meeting the even more youthful Salmon Portland Chase,‡ Tocqueville next asked questions of Dr. Daniel Drake, perhaps the leading practitioner of the region and founder of a medical college in Ohio.§ Finally, he interviewed the prosecuting attorney of the county,¶ and had the good fortune of conversing with the notable John McLean, once Postmaster General under

* Born in Portland, Maine, Bellamy Storer (1798–1875) had been educated at Bowdoin, studied law under Chief Justice Parker, and come to Cincinnati in 1817. He had been a J.Q.Adams man, the editor of a party newspaper, and a leading spirit in a religious band of young men, called the 'Flying Artillery,' who went from town to town to promote revivals.
† Timothy Walker, 1806–1856, was the brother of a mathematician and had himself for three years taught mathematics at the famous Round Hill School of Cogswell and George Bancroft, before coming to Cincinnati and being admitted to the bar. In 1833 he was to help found the Cincinnati Law School, where he was to teach and administer for more than a decade. Apparently the profession of the law was one of the first special skills or refinements to make the transit into the Ohio valley successfully. How crude Ohio standards were, however, was to be revealed very shortly.
‡ Not quite twenty-four years old, the future statesman and jurist was the son of a farmer and tavern-keeper, and nephew of Bishop Philander Chase. After studying at Cincinnati and Dartmouth, and teaching while reading law with William Wirt at Washington, he had settled down in Cincinnati to a career as a reformer in the fields of the law and the anti-slavery movement. He had had some trouble in passing his legal examination in the East, and it was said that 'the only reason he was not rejected utterly was because he intended to practice at Cincinnati, O., where any sort of lawyer was supposed . . . to be good enough.' On one occasion counsel in defence of James B. Birney, he soon came to be known as 'Attorney General for runaway negroes.'
§ Of pioneer Kentucky background, Dr. Daniel Drake (1785–1852) had laboured for many years at the task of introducing sound medical learning into the western valley. Professor successively at Transylvania (Lexington, Ky.), Jefferson Medical College (Philadelphia), and Cincinnati Medical College, he had also edited a medical journal and was widely known for his advanced scientific ideas. In 1850, he would publish his great work: *A Systematic Treatise, Historical, Etiological and Practical, on the Principal Diseases of the Interior Valley of North America*.
¶ Daniel Van Matre, a graduate of Yale.

Presidents Monroe and Adams and now, by President Jackson's appointment, an Associate Justice of the Supreme Court of the United States.* From all these new acquaintances the two French commissioners gathered materials on Ohio and the rising American West.

Bellamy Storer, for instance, was of the opinion that the people of Ohio had made a bad mistake in not keeping to the doctrine of the separation of powers. Specifically, he accused them of trying to give the legislature control over the judiciary.

'Do your judiciary institutions differ from those of the other States?' Tocqueville asked him.[4]

'Notably in one particular,' he answered: 'our judges are named by the legislature, and are appointed only for seven years. In all the Union I believe that only Vermont has done as we.

'Do you think this innovation a good one?' Tocqueville wanted to know.

'*A.* I think it very pernicious. Judges ought to be independent of political passions; that's the greatest safeguard of our liberties. Here they are under the yoke of party spirit.

'*Q.* Is the evil realized by the masses?

'*A.* I think so. We are hoping soon to change that portion of our constitution. But for that it will be necessary to assemble a convention and we are afraid that with the political passions now aroused it will not be well composed. The convention that in 1802 made our present constitution was very poorly composed. At that time Ohio was peopled by individuals for whom very little could be said and the elections suffered from the morality of the electors. We have yielded too much to "Democracy" here.'†

Tocqueville was impressed, and recalled Mr. Storer's opinion at the next opportunity.

'2 December 1831—Mr. Walker, very distinguished young Ohio lawyer,' he noted in his diary.

---

* The son of an Irish weaver, John McLean (1785–1861) had, like Dr. Drake, come to Ohio by way of Kentucky, with only the education that a farmer boy could procure. President Jackson had tried to get him to continue as Postmaster General, and had also offered him the posts of War and Navy in his cabinet, before appointing him a Supreme Court Justice. In the latter capacity, he was later to deliver a dissenting opinion (against slavery) in the famous Dred Scott case.

† It is interesting, in this connection, to note that Justice McLean had at one time been elected by the people of Ohio to serve on the State Supreme Court, 1816–1822; and Storer himself was later to sit as a judge in the Superior Court of Cincinnati for nineteen years.

'*Q.* Do you believe that your system for nominating judges is a good one?

'*A.* I think it very dangerous; and trial has already made evident its vices. In general our constitution tends toward a too boundless "democracy." It has some other defects as well: our legislature, for example, is too small a body. This robs it of a part of its moral force; one is never certain it really represents the wishes of the people.'

Here was interesting confirmation. Tocqueville progressed to another aspect of the West: its restless prosperity.

'*Q.* I have heard of the extreme fertility of this part of your territory. Is what people say true?

'*A.* Yes. I was born and passed a part of my life in Massachusetts. There an acre returns from 25 to 30 bushels per year; here the return is between 70 and 80.

'*Q.* Is it true that a portion of the population of Ohio is already starting to move to the right bank of the Mississip[p]i?'

Mr. Walker had himself arrived in Cincinnati from the East only that very year.

'Yes,' he answered, 'here's what's happening. Those who possess lands generally keep them and remain here. But their sons go to seek their fortune further west, in the States where the lands are as yet uninhabited. Furthermore, our towns here receive each year a host of workers and artisans from the other States, or from Europe. These men stop here for two or three years. The price of labour is so high (a third more than in New England) and living costs are so cheap that in two or three years they get together a [tidy] capital. Then they leave us and go west to buy lands and become proprietors.

'*Q.* Is it true that there are no idlers in your towns?

'*A.* I know no one without a profession, and who does not follow it.'

Timothy Walker may have told Tocqueville that for three years he had taught in an eastern school.

'What is the state of public education in Ohio?' Tocqueville wanted to know.

'*A.* The State of Ohio, which contains about 25,000,000 acres, is divided regularly into *townships*, each one of which contains the same number of acres. When Congress governed Ohio, as a territory, it ordered that the thirty-sixth part of all the lands in each township should not be sold but should serve to support public education. The same rule was established on behalf of religion. We are already finding in this reserve our greatest resources for the establishment of schools. What slows up the progress of education with us is the want of good teachers.

'*Q*. Does the government concern itself with education?

'*A*. There is a distinction to be made. Any one is free to establish a school or a college; here the State takes no hand in education. But you perceive that on its own part the State undertakes to supply free education, and in that case retains the directing control, though indirectly it is true. Thus, the schools are placed under inspectors, not of the central government, but named in each locality, who examine the masters, their methods, and the progress of the pupils.

'*Q*. With what other State has your communal organization the most in common?

'*A*. With the system of Pennsylvania, which is the State nearest to us.'

That same day Tocqueville had the chance to question another lawyer and a pedagogue, newly arrived for a career in the West. Salmon Portland Chase, future Secretary of the Treasury and Chief Justice of the Supreme Court, was waiting for his first clients, an empty interval that he was filling by editing the Statutes of Ohio, with notes and an historical introduction. If his choice of language was any indication, apparently the tall young man was already of that humourless and opinionated disposition that was to make him such a trial to Lincoln and the future Republican party. To Tocqueville he said:[5]

'We have carried "Democracy" to its last limits. The right of voting is universal. Thence result, especially in our towns, some very bad elections. For instance, the last four members elected for the county of Cincinnati are absolutely unworthy to occupy the position to which they have been elevated.

'*Q*. But how did they get themselves chosen?

'*A*. By flattery, something distinguished men will never do, by mingling with the populace, by base flattery of its passions, by drinking with it. And it's not just to the State Assemblies that the people frequently send such men. Many are to be found in Congress. In spite of everything, however, it's still the influence of men of talent that rules us.

'*Q*. But don't you think that when the right of suffrage is so broad, the people must necessarily often make poor choices?

'*A*. I think so, and I am convinced that no distinguished men in the Union but believe a very wide suffrage harmful. However, they can't struggle against the flood of public opinion which is steadily heading in that direction. We have had before us the example of Virginia. Virginia was the one State of the Union where the proprietors had succeeded in maintaining, up to the present, a tax qualification for voting. Last year, they were finally overcome. They have begun to lower the amount of the tax. Now it's no longer in their power to stop. It's only in New England, and particularly in Massachusetts of which I can speak because my family came from there, that the people is sufficiently enlightened and master of its own passions to elect invariably the most noteworthy. But I believe that's an exception.'

Tocqueville was ready to change the subject. 'What are the ordinary revenues of the State of Ohio?' he asked.

'*A.* About half a million francs. But it often makes extraordinary expenditures. The canals have already cost it 6,000,000. It covered this by a loan. What proves how scarce capital still is in America is the fact that to find this sum it was necessary to go to Europe.

'*Q.* Have you in Ohio the communal organization of New England?

'*A.* No; our system resembles more that of Pennsylvania. We have town-ships, but they do not, as in New England, form one single same individuality, having but one will and one government. In Ohio the town-ship often contains *a town*, having its own separate government independent of the town-ship. I find the New England system more supple and perfect.

'*Q.* Don't you think that they did a dangerous thing in Ohio to have the judges named by the legislature and to limit their terms to seven years?

'*A.* Yes, I believe the measure dangerous. In America the judges are created to hold the balance between all the parties, and their duty is particularly to oppose the impetuosities and errors of "Democracy" (popular passions?). But springing from them, depending on them for the future, they can't possess that independence. Yet Vermont has gone much further still than we; for they have their judges elected every year.'

On the whole, Salmon P. Chase did not seem to think highly of American democracy, or of his adopted State.

\* 

\*   \*

John McLean, on the other hand, appeared to think well of the Federal principle. At least, Tocqueville noted, the United States Justice was insistent on the duality of the Union and on the value of such an arrangement for large and far-flung Republics.[6]

'He said to us: What seems to me most favourable with us for the institution and maintenance of Republican institutions is our division by states. I don't believe that, with our "Democracy," we could long govern the entire Union, were it composed of but a single people. All the more so, for the great nations of Europe. I add that the federal device is singularly favourable to the happiness of peoples. The legislature of a vast population can never enter into the detail of local interests like the legislature of a small nation. With our federal organization we have the happiness of small peoples and the strength of a great nation.'

Tocqueville had encountered this Federal idea before and would recur to it more than once. Now he wanted the affable Justice to answer some questions on contemporary politics.

'Do you know how many electors there are in Ohio?

'*A.* About 150,000. At the election of General Jackson 130,000 voted. An election is much less tumultuous than you suppose because of the extreme care they have taken to avoid large assemblages of people. Each town-ship has its electoral college. In six hours the election is done, in the whole State, without tumult, journeying, or expense.

'*Q.* Do you know why there are so few banks in Ohio?

'*A.* There were forty or more some ten years ago, but they all failed, and the people entirely lost confidence in them. Besides, the great quantity of paper that they had issued had given a false value to the different articles of consumption. Now only the bills of the Bank of the United States are received.

'*Q.* Aren't there some who wish to destroy the privilege of the Bank of the United States?

'*A.* Yes, certain party men are exploiting to their own profit the instinctive hatred that the idea of privilege or monopoly always arouses. I don't think the adversaries of the Bank in good faith. Its effects are obviously excellent, especially in the West where it furnishes a currency that is safe and portable. Aside from its other advantages it has that of preventing the establishment of bad banks. It refuses to take their notes and in this way discredits them on the spot.'

The questions continued and Mr. McLean described the Civil and Criminal Jurisprudence of Ohio. Apparently many of the refinements, many of the special courts and jurisdictions of English practice had been

lost on their journey into the wilderness.[7] Even New England practice
had been modified. There existed, for example, no Attorney General in
Ohio, but only District Attorneys, whose salary was set by the judges,
usually at a fairly low figure. There was no law school, either, in the
West.* 'To be a lawyer,' Tocqueville noted, 'one must have spent two
years in the study of a lawyer and pass an examination before a committee named by the judges.'

The judges themselves, of course, were selected by the people, through
their proxy the legislature. Even the necessary and valuable institution
of the jury seemed filled with the humblest citizens.

'I went to-day to view the Court of Common Pleas in Cincinnati.
The jury appeared to us composed of individuals belonging to the lowest class among the people.'

\*

\*	\*

On 3 December, Tocqueville had a second conversation with Timothy
Walker. This son of Massachusetts and Harvard was Tocqueville's own
age, but he seemed remarkably well informed and his observations radiated good sense. 'Important,' Tocqueville wrote at the top of his
record, and underlined the word.

Apparently the conversation began with a question about manhood
suffrage and political equality in Ohio.

'Our Constitution,' Walker explained,[8] 'was made at a time when
the democratic party, represented by Jefferson, triumphed throughout
the Union. It's impossible not to recognize under the power of what political feelings it was drafted. It is "democratic" beyond all bounds. In
it the government is much weaker even than in any other. The governor amounts to absolutely nothing, and receives but 1200 dollars.†
The people name the justices of the peace and [word illegible] the ordinary judges. The legislature [House of Representatives?] and the Senate
change every year. In general, what distinguishes our legislation from
that of all the new States of the West are the boldness in innovation,

---

\* As mentioned above, Timothy Walker was to remedy this defect in 1833. Later on,
Storer would be one of the professors in the school thus founded.

† Tocqueville was later able to use this example of parsimoniousness to illustrate what
he thought was one of the natural jealousies of democratic government: *Dém. en
Am.*, II,74–76. In similar fashion, what Justice McLean had said about the Bank,
and what Mr. Walker was about to say concerning the movement of the centre of
population and influence into the Mississippi valley, were to provide materials and
thoughts for Tocqueville's final chapter on 'the present and future of the three
races,' *Dém. en Am.*, II,373,389,404–405.

the scorn of the past and of precedents, the urge to do something new and to get rid of legislative technicality, in order to get swiftly to the bottom of things. You run into this same freedom of spirit everywhere. Nothing is fixed, nothing is regulated with us, in civil society or even in religious life. Everything goes forward from an individual impulsion that denotes a total absence of established opinion.'

'Does the populace often make wise choices?' Tocqueville wanted to know. It was a question that had plagued him much in the last month.

'No,' said Timothy Walker; 'its choices are almost always mediocre or bad. Here you see a permanent and active jealousy in "Democracy" (the masses?), not only against the upper classes—they don't exist— but against all those who emerge from the ranks by their wealth, their talents or their services. We had a striking example of this at the last election. General Harrison, a former member of Congress and a well-known general, [once] governor of a territory and twice minister abroad, put himself up for our legislature. He failed. His chief adversary was a young man whom we saw three years ago selling cakes at the street corner. Since then, it is true, he had entered into the study of the law. He won.

'In Massachusetts, which I regard as the most perfect model of a republican government, one doesn't openly solicit votes. The people themselves almost always choose the most noteworthy men. In the West the candidate has to go harangue his partisans at the cross-roads and drink with them in the taverns.'

Crossroads and taverns! The words must have wakened an echo in the French commissioners' minds. For had they not encountered the same conditions in the South as well as the West? The hustings of Baltimore! One thought immediately of their friend Finley and his disagreeable experiences.

'Doesn't,' asked Tocqueville, 'Doesn't this excessive development of the "democratic" principle frighten you at all?'

'Yes,' confessed the young lawyer. 'I wouldn't say so in public, but between ourselves I admit it. I am frightened by the current that is carrying us on. The United States, it seems to me, are in a crisis; we are at this moment trying out a "democracy" without limits; everything is going that way. But shall we be able to endure it? As yet no one can say so positively.'

This was exactly what Tocqueville would have been inclined to say himself. He could hardly have stated his own dubious attitude more concisely. From the problem of political equality, therefore, he now passed on to that of the Federal principle.

'I perceive the distinctive traits which characterize the social politics of the western States. Do not these bring into Union affairs interests which really belong to them alone and are of a nature to upset the present equilibrium?' he wanted to know.

'The answer to that,' said Timothy Walker, 'requires some development. The West has no interests contrary to the rest, at least at present, and there is no indication that it must have any later on. The North of the United States is almost exclusively industrial, the South entirely agricultural. The West is both at the same time. Nothing promises a future collision between its interests and those of the other parts of the United States. Yet its growth must necessarily give another face to the Union. There are already 5,000,000 inhabitants in the Mississip[p]i valley. I haven't any doubt but that twenty years from now the major portion of the population of the United States will be west of the Ohio: the greatest wealth, the greatest strength will be found in the Mississip[p]i and Missouri basin. At that point it will be necessary to change the location of the capital which [otherwise] would be placed at one edge of the empire. This removal of strength and wealth will necessarily bring on new combinations impossible to foresee.

'*Q*. But aren't you afraid that it will be impossible to keep this immense body together?' In spite of Justice John McLean, Tocqueville was beginning to wonder how so vast an Empire could possibly remain united under republicanism. With immediate local interests pulling against a weak Federal bond, diffraction began to loom on the distant horizon: a sort of inevitable catastrophe toward which the American experiment was fated to march.

The Cincinnati lawyer was not sure. 'Up to now,' he answered, 'everything prospers; at the bottom of men's hearts there is even a strong instinct that attaches all to the Union. Yet I am not without uneasiness as to its duration. There are several causes weakening the Federal tie. In all the States, in the first place, there is a store of jealousy against the central government; that's easy to perceive. The excessive development of the "democratic" (equalitarian) principle in the West makes the new States even more impatient of the yoke of the Union and the restrictions that it places on their sovereignty. The tariff trouble leaves me also disquieted. South Carolina has truly adopted a menacing attitude; and it is supported by almost all the States of the South. The party chiefs in that portion of the Union seem resolved to seize the power, whatever it may cost; they are kindling what seem to me unreasonable passions. The growth of the North, the growing feebleness of the South, have in part destroyed the equilibrium of the Union. Another question, which presents itself for the future in menacing guise, is the problem of all the uncultivated lands. It [the Union] thus possesses immense areas engulfed within the new States. The latter are beginning loudly to demand the possession of these lands. The States of Indiana and Illinois have already made energetic representations. There's a point of collision between the States and the Union.* There are several others also.'

Tocqueville passed on to questions of a different kind.

'Is it true that the present administration is distributing all the offices to its dependents without bothering to examine their capacity?'

Some enemy of President Jackson's had been talking to the French commissioners! Bellamy Storer was an Adams man, Salmon Portland Chase leaned obviously toward anti-democratic principles, and Justice McLean was reputedly opposed to the 'spoils' system. What would Walker say?

'Yes,' it was true, he answered. 'When General Jackson came to power he displaced 1200 officeholders, for no other reason than to replace them with his own partisans. Since then he has gone ahead along the same lines. The offices have been used to pay for services rendered to himself. That's the thing for which I most reproach him: he has introduced corruption into the central government, and his example will be followed. All the journalists who followed him have been given places. Appointees all the way to the Supreme Court have been chosen from among his friends.'

Such a state of affairs, Tocqueville reasoned, was hardly a guarantee of ability in the running of the Federal government, that unifying influence in which so much faith was placed. He thought naturally of other influences which might temper the ill effects to be expected from a decentralized 'mobocracy.' Education he had already discussed with Mr. Walker. There remained one other fundamental safeguard.

'*Q.* To come back to Ohio, is it true that religious ideas are here less powerful than in the other parts of the Union?

---

* Applying the thought to Ohio lands, Tocqueville was to make use of this illustration in his book: *Dém. en Am.,* I,261–262 note.

'*A*. There are many unbelievers in Ohio; especially do they show themselves more openly than elsewhere, because, as I said before, here less than anywhere else is there a system of ideas ready made to which submission must be given. Each person is more himself, but the rank and file (*classe*) of the people is at least as much and perhaps more penetrated by religious feelings than in any of the other States of the Union, without forgetting New England.

'*True*, it is a less enlightened religion. Living in the woods, having to struggle against the hardships of life, the inhabitants of the new States cannot receive the same instruction as those of the old. The sect of Methodists prevails in all the Mississip[p]i and Ohio valley. But the want of established rules, of steady practice (*méthode suivie*), makes itself felt in this matter as in all others. Many of the settlements have neither church nor regular worship. Travelling ministers come to preach the gospel. The first-comer often carries out that office. You don't see in the countrysides here, as in those of New England, pastors of recognized capacity and fixed salary.'

So much for religion, and the political and physical state of the American Northwest. Tocqueville now felt himself in possession of the essential information. About another part of the West, however, about that vast area lying just south of the river and stretching all the way to New Orleans, he was still ignorant. People insisted that the Southwest was different. Kentucky, for instance, was utterly unlike its neighbour just to the North.

'Is it true that a great difference exists between the aspect of Ohio and that of Kentucky?' Tocqueville asked.

'*A*. Prodigious. And yet Kentucky was settled twenty years before Ohio, its lands are as good, the climate more temperate, the country admirable. Nevertheless, Ohio has three times as many inhabitants as Kentucky; its business is ten times as great. The population of Kentucky is growing, but its prosperity is stationary. The only explanation that can be given for this difference is that slavery reigns in Kentucky and not in Ohio. There work is dishonourable, here held in esteem. There there is laziness, here activity without limit. Kentucky receives no emigrants; Ohio attracts the industrious inhabitants from all parts of the Union. The South, which receives none, sends its inhabitants. The poor classes of the South arrive in Ohio because they can work there without shame. I see no reason why slavery should cease in Kentucky. The present population, while recognizing the evils it causes, can't learn to get on without it; and there is no emigration.

'*Q*. You have made in Ohio some very severe laws against the blacks.

'*A*. Yes, we are trying to discourage them in every possible way. Not only have we made laws allowing their expulsion at will, but we annoy them in a thousand ways. A negro has no political rights; he cannot be sworn, he cannot bear witness against a white. This last law leads sometimes to the most revolting injustices. Lately I was consulted by a negro who had furnished a very great number of foodstuffs to the master of a steamboat. The white denied the debt. As the creditor was black, and his workmen, who were black also and might have been able to depose in his favour, could not appear in court, there wasn't even any way to bring suit.

'*Q*. Do the laws often change?

'*A*. Unceasingly. That's one of the great inconveniences of our "Democracy"; yet a large portion of our legislation is good.'

The interview was finished; and it had ended on a hopeful note.

Despite all the 'inconvenience' of manhood suffrage and the rule of the many, 'a large portion' of Ohio legislation was 'good'! Perhaps such cheerfulness was characteristic of the West. At all events, Dr. Daniel Drake, with whom they talked the same day, was essentially optimistic.

'Our "Democracy" is without limits, and I confess that the populace is not happy in its choices,' he said.[9] 'I've noticed that in general the outstanding men do not obtain the votes.

'Yet the State enjoys an immense prosperity. The enterprises are great and favourable to the general well-being. I have never heard of the slightest resistance to law. The people are happy and tranquil.'

How to account for this seeming contradiction? Dr. Drake had an interesting hypothesis.

'If there were but one demagogue in charge of our affairs, things would doubtless go very badly. But they control each other, injure one another,' he said. It followed, therefore, that 'the ill effects resulting from the elections by the people are not as great as one might believe.'

## XLII

## OHIO—OR REFLECTIONS ON THE MANUFACTURE
## OF AN AMERICAN STATE

TocQUEVILLE and Beaumont paused in Cincinnati a little less than four full days. But so earnestly had they employed their time that the brief interval had been more than enough to fill their heads with new ideas. It followed that, before they came to leave, they were already drawing up the *dossier* of Ohio.

'We are very pleased with the visit that we have just made to Cincinnati,' Tocqueville wrote his mother; [1] 'it was most interesting. We didn't have any idea what the States of the West were like. One can estimate their character very swiftly once one has seen the others; but without [first] seeing them it is impossible even to imagine them. All that there is of good or of bad in American society is to be found there in such strong relief, that one would be tempted to call it one of those books printed in large letters for teaching children to read; everything there is in violent contrast, exaggerated; nothing has fallen into its final place: society is growing more rapidly than man.'

Actually, when they looked back on what they had seen, and began to analyse their conversations with the ambitious young men of Cincinnati, Tocqueville and Beaumont discovered that they had already reached five definite conclusions about this first western State of their experience. The print was so plain on the face of the region that even strangers could read.

To begin with, Ohio was an example of American expansion, of a characteristic growth so prodigious as to defy the imagination. In the second place it was the community where better than anywhere else the principle of a complete democratic self-government was actually realized and put into practice. In the third, this State was so new and so mongrel in its composition that it had as yet no standards and no character of its own. Again, it illustrated, thought Tocqueville, what must be a law of American civilization: the progressive abandonment of English institutions by the American people as they moved westward. Finally, the comparison of Ohio with its neighbour to the South demonstrated beyond the shadow of a doubt the essential vice of the institution of slavery. Each of these five ideas, in Tocqueville's opinion, merited a little elaboration. And together they would give him a commentary on American expansion, a picture of how American communities were manufactured, an insight into the essential nature of the new American West.

Growth, equalitarian, confusion: there is perhaps no need to trace out Tocqueville's insistent reiterations on this theme.[2] Whether the West was prospering 'because of, or in spite of' its democratic forms of government, the two commissioners still found it impossible to determine, but of these three distinguishing characteristics they were in no doubt whatever.

Now Tocqueville came to their fourth discovery about Ohio and the new regions that it represented.

In investigating the criminal procedure and the civil jurisprudence of the State, he and Beaumont had found several innovations and a number of simplifications from the current practices in New England and Pennsylvania. 'In civil law it has simplified English legislation to an astonishing extent and, so far as I have been able to judge up to now, has fairly completely shaken off the rule of tradition. I imagine that it is the same in the political world,' Tocqueville had noted. Now he began to develop this thought.

'The new States of the West, and in particular the State of Ohio, stand in the same relation to the older States of the Union as these last stand to Europe. I elucidate.

'The Americans in coming over brought with them what was most "democratic" in Europe. They arrived in America having left behind on the other side of the Atlantic the greater part of the national prejudices in which they had been raised. They became a new nation, adopted new habits and customs, something of a national character. To-day a new emigration is commencing, producing the same effects. The new emigrants carry into their adopted country the "democratic" principles even further disengaged from all alliance, even less characteristic customs, minds even freer from precedents. It's a curious thing to observe in the laws the trace of this intellectual and physical movement. A de-

fective English law (and there are many) is imported into America by
the first emigrants. They modify it, adapt it after a fashion to their
social condition; but they still retain for it a superstitious respect, and
are unable to rid themselves of it entirely. The second emigration
takes place; these same men plunge once again into the wilderness. This
time the law is modified in such a way that it has almost lost the stamp
of its origin. But it requires still a third emigration before it ceases to
exist. And when one reflects that this law was probably given to the
English by the Saxons, one can't restrain one's astonishment at the influence exercised by the point of departure on the good or evil destinies of peoples.'

Was it the influence of the frontier, or the loss of ancestral baggage
while on the march, that caused an emigrating society to alter?
Tocqueville did not try to choose; rather his diary note hinted at a
double process. There was adaptation, and also accidental loss, apparently. Culture and institutions never travelled intact.

Here was an astonishingly clear perception of what was happening
and had been happening for more than two hundred years in the slow
manufacture of North American society. Grasping the great tableau for
the first time in its entirety, Tocqueville was almost swept off his feet
as he tried to sketch the panorama that he had glimpsed, for his family
back in France.

'The Europeans, on coming to America,' he wrote, 'left behind them,
in large part, the traditions of the past, the institutions and customs of
their fatherland, they built a society which has analogies with those of
Europe, but which at bottom is radically different. In the last forty
years, from the midst of that new society has gone out another swarm
of emigrants marching west, as once their fathers came to the coasts
of New England and Maryland. Like them abandoning the ideas of
their fatherland together with the soil that bore them, they are founding in the valleys of the Mississip[p]i a new society which has no
analogy with the past and is connected to Europe only in language. It's
here one must come to judge the most singular state of affairs that has
doubtless existed under the sun. A people absolutely without precedents, without traditions, without habits, without dominating ideas
even, opening for itself without hesitation a new path in civil, political,
and criminal legislation; never casting its eyes about to consult the
wisdom of other peoples or the memory of the past; but cutting out its
institutions, like its roads, in the midst of the forests which it has come

to inhabit and where it is sure to encounter neither limits nor obstacles. . . .'

In his eloquence, Tocqueville had almost forgotten what he called 'the point of departure,' and seemed actually to be discounting its influence. Yet he did not mean to contradict himself. What he was really describing was a tendency: a continuous, persisting, irresistible flight; not an accomplished fact. For always, as he well knew, there would remain in the background near or remote, that other moulding and definitive influence, the strong current of the English inheritance and tradition.

\*

\* \*

'One other very remarkable thing,' and Tocqueville was now drawing the deadly parallel against slavery, 'One other very remarkable thing in Ohio is this: Ohio is perhaps the State in the Union where it is easiest to see in striking and parallel fashion the effects of slavery and freedom on the social state of a people. The State of Ohio is separated from that of Kentucky by one single river. On the two sides the soil is equally fertile, the position as favourable, yet everything is different. . . .' And Tocqueville proceeded to run through the catalogue of contrasts: of energy against sloth, of enterprise and rapid growth against stagnation and brutality.* Like Timothy Walker he found it 'impossible to attribute those differences to any other cause than slavery. It brutalizes the black population and debilitates the white.'

'. . . Man is not made for servitude,' Tocqueville concluded his survey of Ohio. 'That verity is *perhaps even better established by the master than by the slave.*'

---

* The comparison between Ohio and Kentucky was to serve as an argument for Tocqueville's book: *Dém. en Am.*, II,323–327. He was never to forget the impression that the two banks of the Ohio made on him; and later, in political life, he was to lead the fight in the Chamber of Deputies for the abolition of slavery in the French colonies. *O.C.*,I,xxxviii.

# XLIII

## THE WINTER ROAD TO MEMPHIS

'I HAVE just left Cincinnati, my dear Jules,' Beaumont began a letter to his oldest brother the evening of the fourth of December. 'Embarked on a steamboat, here I am descending the Ohio and voyaging toward the West, where I am going to meet the waters of the Mississip[p]i. We decided to pass by New Orleans in order to go to Charleston; this is certainly not the shortest road on the map, but it is incontestable that we will get there this way much more promptly than by any other route.'

As a matter of fact, the two commissioners were proposing to add an extra 1800 miles or so to their itinerary. Originally they had seriously projected an overland journey from Cincinnati southeastwards: through Kentucky, the tip of Virginia, the northeast corner of Tennessee, then North and South Carolina, on a straight line through to Charleston. Their time was limited; and once they had seen Ohio they would want to strike as fast as they could for the old South. The plan disregarded the mountains, however, and also the time of year, as they soon found out. Every one hastened to tell them that travelling through the Cumberland region was 'horribly difficult,' especially in winter. The roads were 'detestable' and it would take them two weeks to make a journey that would be 'without interest or pleasure.' The circuit by the Mississippi and New Orleans, on the other hand, had great advantages.

'We are sorely tempted to take this last route,' Beaumont had confessed to his sister a few days before.[1] 'We are curious to see *The Great River*, as Mr. de Chateaubriand calls the Mississip[p]i, not that we expect to find blue herons, rosy flamingoes, monkeys and parrots, all gathered together on the bank to watch us pass—as indeed we might anticipate from the fine description of Meschacebé * to be found in the

---

* Chateaubriand's name for the Mississippi. It is, of course, suspected that the famous romanticist never saw a number of the wilderness regions in America that he described.

first pages of Attala [*sic*]. But, without trusting the dreams of the imagination, it's certain that it [the Mississippi] is one of the most magnificent rivers on earth, and from this point of view well worth the trouble of a few hundred leagues to see it. In any case New Orleans, [in] the ancient French Colony to which our ancestors gave the *charming name of Louisiana*, excites our interest even more. Finally, our last reason for lengthening our circuit thus would be that, to go from New Orleans to Charleston, we would have to cross the States of Alabama and Georgia, where are to be found some Indian tribes, the Creeks, Cherokees, and Chactas, whose customs and ways of life are curious and well worth examining.'

The alternative had seemed more and more alluring. And now he and Tocqueville had made up their minds. New Orleans it would be. After the briefest possible pause in Cincinnati, they were already on their way.

'To-morrow,' Beaumont continued his steamboat letter, 'to-morrow morning we arrive at Louisville (town situated on the banks of the Ohio in Kentucky), and if we can at once find a steamboat leaving for New Orleans, we shall not stop a moment at Louisville. Once set sail from this town we shall make about 100 leagues a day; and according to this calculation we shall arrive in New Orleans in less than seven or eight days.'

'The steamboats on which one descends the Ohio and Mississip[p]i are in general very fine and very comfortable,' Beaumont explained. 'Each passenger has a bed on board; three good meals are served. There is, of course, the men's side and the women's side, as in the public baths. The two sexes come together only to eat. As the Americans are not chatterers it's seldom that a man speaks a word to a woman, even when they both know each other. Otherwise the time is spent in reading, writing, looking at the country, and asking questions. Sometimes the steamboat is so shaken by the operation of the engine that it is impossible to write legibly. It happens to-day by chance that the boat on which I am has an extraordinarily gentle motion, so I have decided to write you a note which will be short or long depending on the time we take to reach Louisville. . . .'

So as the boat continued down the Mississippi, Beaumont began to describe for his brother all the things that he had thus far seen in Ohio and the West.

He wrote and wrote. It should have been an overnight journey, but next morning he was still writing; still they had not reached their destination. Suddenly, he was interrupted and had to break off——

*

* *

It was ten days later, the fifteenth of December, before Beaumont could write again. And he was not, as he had anticipated, in New Orleans. Instead, he found himself stuck at a small log house somewhere in the wild forests of western Tennessee. The spot was called Sandy Bridge. And both the circumstances and the manner of his getting there required, thought Beaumont, some explanation.

'Before giving you any details on my trip, I think, dear Mother, that I ought to tell you what place it is that I find myself in at this moment,' he began.[2] 'Sandy Bridge is nothing but a small inn, built of logs placed one on top of the other, and situated on the road which leads from Nashville (capital of Ten[n]essee) to Memphis, a small town on the banks of the Mississip[p]i between the 34th and 35th degrees of latitude, just about on the boundary separating Ten[n]essee from the State of Mississip[p]i. In the room where I write there are three beds, on which stopping travellers throw themselves, whatever their numbers or sex. An immense fire burns in a chimney like those of the ancient *châteaux*. It's big enough to contain ten logs, each three feet around. Despite this fire, which would roast an ox, one freezes in the room. Just a little while ago I wanted to take a glass of water that had been brought me, but having been so imprudent as to leave it five minutes without drinking it, I found it entirely frozen. This is accounted for by two things: the first is that outside it is at 8 or 10 degrees; and the second is that between the different logs that make up the walls of the house there are cracks wide enough to allow the air to circulate freely. This rigorous cold is quite extraordinary, when you consider our latitude, which is that of Egypt; but such is the climate of America that in the southern States, where during the summer the heat is excessive, you die of cold in the winter.

'To come back to my small lodging, you know that it is situated on the road from Nashville to Memphis, but I haven't told you its real geographic position. I can't give you an altogether clear indication, because there is on the said road not a single town, not a single place marked on the map. But imagine a straight line starting from Nashville and ending at the spot where my preceding explanations have enabled you to place Memphis. That line represents a stretch of about 100 leagues. Well, I am 35 leagues from Nashville and 60 leagues from Memphis. You see now quite clearly where I am.

'My hosts are good people, very proud though inn-keepers, and very lazy though poor. They are proud because they are in a region of slaves. Not a small landowner, however wretched, but possesses two or three slaves. The latter are, in the house of the whites, an obligatory furnishing, as is a chair or a table. It results from this that all those who are not black, and who are consequently free men, consider themselves privileged beings; and likewise that colour is a veritable nobility in this country. The convenience of being served by slaves makes the whites indolent and lazy; and the fertility of the country, which produces much without labour, reinforces this disposition. Finally, the climate, which during the fine season is excessively hot, adds its encouragement. However, I have less faith in the influence of the climate than in that of slavery; for if men were indolent or hard-working according to the degrees of cold and heat registered on the thermometer, the inhabitants of this region, so lazy in summer, would have to be very active in winter. Now that's what doesn't exist. My small landowner regards work as an infamous thing, belonging of right to his slaves. His customs are feudal; he spends his time hunting, riding, or doing nothing. He has a superb rifle, which he uses with great success against the roe, the deer, and other game. Without the least difficulty he kills birds with a ball. This rifle is so heavy that I have all the trouble in the world carrying it. This morning I wanted to hunt a little; I walked through the woods for an hour or two; I saw a number of charming birds, notably some red and yellow parrots unequalled in their beauty. But, armed as I was, I couldn't kill a single one. While walking with me, my little republican *seigneur* asked me to whom the woods in France belonged. He doesn't understand the advantage it is for an individual to own forests, because he is surrounded by woods belonging to nobody and which nobody troubles to take. When we need a fire, they go cut a thick oak in the woods and the slaves of our Lord *seigneur* have soon made logs of it.

'No doubt you are asking yourself what I am doing in this Sandy Bridge Inn where I appear installed without knowing when I'll get away. To relieve you from embarrassment I will tell you that in coming from Nashville here I was in a small public carriage which was open and resembled in every respect a *charabanc*. Tocqueville and I found ourselves with several other travellers, going night and day, and rivalling each other freezing when, to warm us up, fortune sent us three small accidents which almost caused us to get stuck on the road. First the traces, then a wheel, then the axle-tree of our carriage broke. By means of some oaks cut in the forest, which follows the whole road, we managed to repair our poor cart, which was in pieces, *limping with all four feet*, on our arrival at this place. This will sufficiently explain why we can't continue our journey. So long as they have not repaired the limbs of our carriage we must resign ourselves to staying here.

'But, you say, why the devil did you come to Nashville? and why are you going to Memphis? I answer this question at once. You will recall perhaps that in my last letter to Jules I announced my arrival at Louisville in a steamboat going down the Ohio. And it is a fact that at the moment of closing the letter every one around me was saying "We are only 7 or 8 leagues from Louisville now." Well, no more than two hours were required to get there, according to the ordinary progress of steamboats. But all of a sudden we are arrested in our navigation by an invincible obstacle, which we were far from anticipating. For two or three days past the weather had been very cold; the cold had set in so hard that the Ohio was covered with cakes of ice; nevertheless the boats kept on. But what was our stupefaction when, at the moment of our arrival at Louisville, we find the Ohio entirely frozen, and our steamboat is forced to stop. The distance of 7 or 8 leagues, which was nothing for our boat, became a very great one for us. They throw us on shore, with our packages, at a small village called Westport. There we find it impossible to get transportation to town. After much looking, however, we succeed in getting a wagon, in which we put our trunks and our night bags. This vehicle advances toward Louisville escorted by a driver, and us two. In this fashion we covered our 8 leagues in the snow, along a small path which winds very agreeably through the woods, amid a perpetual succession of mountains and valleys. Nothing is more picturesque for an amateur, but when one is tired the fine undulations of the terrain lose much of their merit.

'On arriving in Louisville we escaped from one difficulty to fall into another. No doubt it was a great deal to find shelter and rest after real fatigue; but short of taking up winter quarters in Louisville, what to do, what was to become of us, where to go? . . . The Ohio being obstructed by ice, all our plans were upset. To retrace our steps, re-passing exactly all the places by which we had come, was an *odious* thing and the very idea revolted us. To await the thawing of the Ohio was to take a big risk, though every one assured us that the freeze would certainly not last two days. We took a middle course which seemed to us, and which we still think, the wisest. As there is a constant procession of steamboats on the Mississip[p]i, we thought that if we could reach this river, which never freezes, we would be sure to find transportation by water, the only kind that does not take a mortal time. . . .'

\*

\* \*

So that was the explanation? Ice on the Ohio, the overland decision, and a carriage break-down in Tennessee? It certainly seemed so, Beaumont's accounts were so circumstantial. Certainly it was all that he allowed his family to know; and Tocqueville made his letters home even less informing.

But one wonders a little about those families. Did Beaumont's mother scent nothing wrong? Wasn't it a little curious how very circumstantial, how extremely methodical he made his tale? It was almost as if he explained too much, as if he had a guilty conscience.

He did. And with good reason. He was hiding something. His story was true, or almost true. But it did not go far enough. He had left something important out.

What that omission was will appear as Beaumont's narrative is retold, and given its full development so far as the documents surviving from that critical fortnight will permit.[3]

\*

\* \*

The story of the ice, to begin with, was substantially true. Tocqueville and Beaumont left Cincinnati for the 100-mile journey to Louisville late on the fourth of December. That night the already bitter weather turned even colder and the freeze set in. The passengers might have been prepared had they known that twenty-four hours before the Hudson River at Albany had been closed by ice. But there was no way of getting such news. What was the astonishment of the French commissioners, therefore, when next morning at 8 o'clock the Ohio was found frozen solid before them! The cold had set in 'with such fury' that they were caught. 'Decidedly, water journeys do not go well with us,' Tocqueville thought.

'At the present moment we find ourselves obliged to open a path painfully through the ice. Thanks to the current and steam we still manage to force a passage; but we are afraid of splitting our vessel apart with the effort demanded of it. Add to that the fact that your ears freeze if you but stick your head outside. It's the cold of Russia (a Siberian cold). They don't remember ever having seen the like in this region. . . .

'. . . Just now the vessel is cracking from poop to prow.'

This was too much for the captain and pilot, who decided to retire till the unseasonable weather moderated. 'Twenty-four hours spent in a little creek, to which we fell back to await the thaw,' noted Beaumont.* 'The thaw doesn't come. The cold increases.

'The captain makes up his mind to set us on the shore, which we approach by breaking the ice little by little, thus opening a passage for our boat.

'Disembarked at West-Port, small village in Kentucky, situated at about twenty-five miles from Louisville.

'Impossible to find either carriage or horses to carry us to Louisville; necessary to make the journey on foot; our luggage thrown into a cart with which we keep pace. We march all day through the woods in a half-foot of snow. America is still nothing but a forest. . . .'

'A great jovial pioneer of the neighbourhood,' according to Tocqueville, had 'offered to carry our trunks to Louisville in his cart. Our travelling companions, to the number of ten, came to the same decision, and there we were all marching, on foot, in the midst of the woods and mountains of Kentucky, where a loaded wagon had never been since the beginning of the world. It got through, however, thanks to the good shoulder shoves and the daring spirit of our driver; but we were marching in the snow, and it was up to our knees. This manner of travelling finally became so fatiguing that our companions began to abandon us one after the other.'

It was small wonder. Even hardened westerners might balk at having to walk 25 miles, through six inches of snow, and all in one day. For the slender Tocqueville it must have been a real hardship. One

---

* These notes are again the 'pencilled' jottings in the diary that has never since been found. They can only be trusted for the main facts, and are unreliable as to date.

cannot help noticing that for him Beaumont's 'half-foot' of snow seemed 'up to the knees.' Yet when travelling, or when he had set out to do something, it was not his custom to stop. 'Repose was antipathetic to his nature,' there was no use arguing with him, Beaumont well knew.[4] So now it did not seem to occur to Tocqueville to imitate their American companions. 'As for us,' he concluded his account of the incident, 'we stuck to our point, and finally arrived in Louisville, toward nine o'clock in the evening.

'Next morning we learned that the Ohio had frozen below as well as above the point where we were, and that we would have to set up winter quarters in Louisville if we did not prefer to turn around and retrace our steps. There was a third alternative to be taken, however. On the banks of the Mississip[p]i, in the State of Tennessee, we were told that there was a small town, called Memphis, where all the steamboats going up or coming down the river stop to take on wood. If we could reach this place we would be sure to resume our navigation, as the Mississip[p]i never freezes.

'This information having been given us by those most worthy of confidence, we did not hesitate, and we left Louisville for Memphis. One hundred and fifty leagues, about, separate the two towns; the journey had to be made by the most abominable roads, in the most infernal carriages, and above all in the most unbelievable cold you can possibly imagine: the order of nature seemed to have been turned upside down just for us. Tennessee is almost beneath the lattitude of the Sahara desert in Africa. Cotton and all the exotic plants are grown there. And when we were crossing it, it was freezing at 15°; nothing like it had ever been seen. . . .'

It had been a horrible journey of two days and two nights. But worse was to come. On reaching Nashville Beaumont learned 'with anguish' that the Cumberland was frozen over.

'The eleventh of December, departure from Nashville. The further we advance toward the South the more bitter the cold becomes. Never in the memory of man has anything like it been seen, they say. That's what people always tell travellers who come only once. . . .'

But Beaumont was mistaken. They were indeed in the grip of extraordinary weather. It was beginning to be colder all over the United States than Americans had known it for a long generation. That very month was to prove the coldest December since 1776. On the fifteenth of the month, or four days after Tocqueville and Beaumont's passage through the Tennessee capital, a Nashville newspaper was to announce that the Cumberland had been so thickly frozen over only twice before in the memory of the oldest inhabitants, the winters being those of 1787–88 and 1795–96. Not since the winter of '96 had passengers been able to cross on the ice. On the sixteenth the thermometer was to stand at '*14 degrees below zero*!!!'.[5] And at the end of the month a Nashville correspondent would write to President Andrew Jackson that 'we have a Continuation of the most cold and sevear weather ever. Known in this Country—Our river is frozen Over and has been so. for more than twenty days past—sufficiently so to bear any weight.'[6]

Nor was this all. In far-away New York, on the twenty-sixth of December, Beaumont's friend Philip Hone was to notice an extraordinary thing: 'The East River was closed by Ice this morning and two or three hundred persons walked across from Fulton Street to Brooklyn. On the turn of the tide the Ice went out, and the Steam Boats were again plying.'[7]

And in Cincinnati, on the fifteenth of January, Tocqueville's intelligent young lawyer, Timothy Walker, would be writing to George Bancroft: 'So stern a winter has never been known here—The river closed when there was but little coal in the city, and what there was soon rose to 50 cts per bushel. . . .'[*]

But much of this was still in the future as Tocqueville and Beaumont set out from Nashville toward Memphis on the far western frontier of the State. It was the eleventh of December and the two friends were beginning the second leg of their journey, the stretch on which they were to become stranded because (so Beaumont would inform his family) their carriage broke down. Tocqueville was never to describe what happened at all, but Beaumont was one day to publish some notes that would show how much he failed to tell his family at the time. These stenographic jottings, from which quotations have already been made, went as follows:

'. . . Cold of ten degrees below freezing. The cold increases steadily. Our *stage* changes to an open charabanc.' [It was a demonstration of

---

[*] George Bancroft Papers, 1830–1832, Massachusetts Historical Society. In January it was to be so cold that a newspaper like the *Richmond Enquirer* (*q.v.*, 17 Jan.) had to reduce the size of its sheet for want of the usual supply of paper. And early in February, torrential rains, with the thawing of the winter's heavy snows, were to bring on a terrible Ohio river flood. Fed by all the streams of the State, this river was to swamp Marietta and reach a flood stage of 64 feet at Cincinnati. Business would be suspended in all the river towns but Gallipolis, from Steubenville to Cincinnati.

how little prepared they were in Tennessee for zero weather.] 'Fright-ful roads. Perpendicular descents. Way not banked; the route is but a passage made through the forest. The trunks of badly cut trees form as it were so many guard-stones against which one is always bumping. Only ten leagues a day.—You have some very bad roads in France, haven't you? an American says to me.—Yes, Sir, and you have some really fine ones in America, haven't you? He doesn't understand me. American conceit.

'After Nashville, not a town on the way. Nothing but a few villages, scattered here and there, all the way to Memphis.

'The eleventh of December, the braces and a wheel, then the axle-tree broken. Half the journey covered on foot. We blame our bad luck. Go ahead and complain, we are told; day before yesterday two travellers on the road broke, one an arm, the other a leg.'

Here were the three accidents of Beaumont's letter home. But did the charabanc stop for any time? It did not.

'The twelfth, the cold still more rigorous; we cross the Tennessee, carrying down great cakes of ice, in a ferry. Tocqueville benumbed by the cold; he experiences a chill. He has lost his appetite; his head af-fected; impossible to go any further, we must stop. . . . Where? How? No inn on the road. Extreme anguish. The stage keeps on. . . . Here finally is a house: Sandy-Bridge (name of the place), Log-House! No matter, they set us down. . . .

'Thirteenth of December; what a day! what a night! The bed where Tocqueville is lying is in a chamber whose walls are made of oak logs not even squared, placed one on top of the other. It is so cold it would crack a stone. I light a monster fire; the flame crackles on the hearth fed by the wind which rushes in on us from all sides. The moon sends us its rays through the interstices between the chunks of wood. Tocqueville gets warm only by stifling himself under his blanket and the pile of coverings I load on him. No succour to be gotten from our hosts. Depth of our isolation and abandonment. What to do? What is going to happen to us if the illness gets worse? What is this illness? Where to find a doctor? The nearest more than thirty miles away; more than two days required to go get him and return; on my return what will I find? *

'Mr. and Mrs. Harris (the name of our hosts), small Tennessee

---

\* Again the diary quotations give evidence of having been manufactured some time after the event.

proprietors. They possess slaves; in their position as slave-holders, they do nothing. The husband hunts, walks, rides; certain gentlemanly airs; small aristocrats with feudal customs, giving asylum to travellers for one hundred *sous* a day.

'The fourteenth, Tocqueville better. It will not be an illness; too weak however to proceed. Difficulty of finding food that will be good for him. Prodigies of diplomacy to get from Mrs. Harris a rabbit that Mr. Harris has shot, and that I make my patient eat in place of the eternal *beacon* (pig's flesh).'

The next day Tocqueville was better still and Beaumont sat down to write his mother an expurgated account of their Kentucky and Tennessee adventure. 'No doubt you are asking yourself what I am doing in this Sandy Bridge Inn where I appear installed without knowing when I will get away,' he laboriously explained. 'To relieve you from embarrassment [it was Beaumont who was embarrassed] I will tell you that in coming from Nashville here I was in a small public carriage which was open. . . . three small accidents . . . cart, which was in pieces . . . can't continue.'

Once again the two friends had been driven to practise a deceit in order not to worry their foreboding families.* But it had been a close call this time.

'The fifteenth of December, great progress'; Beaumont's notes continued, 'the sixteenth, Tocqueville entirely well; his appetite returns. Great desire to flee as soon as possible this inhospitable place. The stage from Nashville to Memphis passes. What a stage! Tocqueville climbs in, not without pain. The cold is still intense. Journey of two days and two nights. New accidents, not serious but not without discomfort.

'The seventeenth, arrival at Memphis. Alas! The Mississip[p]i also is covered with ice and navigation suspended.

'Memphis!! large as Beaumont-la-Chartre, what a fall! Nothing to see, neither men nor things. . . .'

---

* After Tocqueville's death, Beaumont saw in this illness, if not the first sign of the malady that had finally cost his life, at least the symptom of the frail and delicate constitution that so plagued and hindered him in his career. *O.C.*,V,33–34.

# XLIV

## TENNESSEE REFLECTIONS

'ON finally arriving in Memphis,' Tocqueville took up the thread of his letter to his father, deliberately interrupted at Nashville, 'on finally arriving in Memphis we found that, several miles above, the Mississip[p]i itself was frozen over; several steamboats were caught in the ice; you could see them but they were as motionless as rocks.'

'Within the memory of man,' Beaumont assured his family,[1] 'nothing like it has ever been seen: for the inhabitants of the South it's a subject of stupefaction. However, the weather has moderated to-day and we are hoping for the thaw, which would soon start navigation again. We are resolved to await it a week. If it doesn't come in that interval, we shall leave for Washington by retracing our steps. . . .'

It would, as Beaumont remarked, be an *odious* and *revolting* necessity. But even with luck as bad as that, after all his hardships and sufferings, Tocqueville was not sure he would regret their adventure.

'If it were not for the vexation we feel in seeing our plans just about foiled (without its yet being in the least our fault),' Tocqueville wrote, 'we should not regret the expedition just made through the forests of Kentucky and Tennessee.' The reason, to one who knew Tocqueville as well as did his father, must have leaped to the understanding. Obviously the young man must have had his curiosity aroused; must have seen and heard things on his journey that would repay, in intellectual coin, any amount of physical discomfort and disappointment. Yes, Tocqueville acknowledged it; he had a new enthusiasm.

'We made the acquaintance there of a kind of man and a way of life that we had no conception of,' he announced. 'This part of the United States is peopled by a single type of man only, the Virginians. They have retained the physical and moral character that belongs to them; they form a people apart, with national prejudices and a distinctive character.'

There had also been a second discovery: 'For the first time we have had the chance to examine there the effect that slavery produces on society. On the right bank of the Ohio everything is activity, industry; labour is honoured; there are no slaves. Pass to the left bank and the scene changes so suddenly that you think yourself on the other side of the world; the enterprising spirit is gone. There, work is not only painful: it's shameful, and you degrade yourself in submitting yourself to it. To ride, to hunt, to smoke like a Turk in the sunshine: there is the destiny of the white. To do any other kind of manual labour is to act like a slave. The whites, to the South of the Ohio, form a veritable aristocracy which, like the others, combines many prejudices with high sentiments and instincts. They say, and I am very much inclined to believe, that in the matter of honour these men practise delicacies and refinements unknown in the North. They are frank, hospitable, and put many things before money. They will end, nevertheless, by being dominated by the North. Every day the latter grows more wealthy and densely populated while the South is stationary or growing poor.'

Some of these ideas, of course, had first come to Tocqueville in Ohio. But now he had the proof, the ocular demonstration. And a whole fresh set of notions had been suggested by their stage-coach experiences, or brought to his attention by some of the acquaintances that they had made en route.

In Louisville, for instance, while recuperating from their forced march through the snow, and waiting to see if the ice in the lower Ohio would not break, Tocqueville had managed to interrogate a 'Mr. McIlvain, one of the greatest merchants of Louisville.' *

'I am told that the prosperity of Louisville has shown great progress in the last few years?' Tocqueville had ventured.[2]

'Immense,' answered the business man. 'When I came to settle here seven years ago, Louisville had only 3,000 souls; there are 13,000 to-day. By myself at the moment I am doing more business than the whole commerce of Louisville seven years ago.

'*Q.* Whence comes this rapid growth?

'*A.* Principally from the unbelievable stream of emigration toward the West. Louisville is become the emporium of almost all the merchandise coming up the Mississip[p]i to provision the emigrants. I believe Louisville is called to become a very large city.

* B.R.McIlvaine?

'*Q*. Is it true that there is a great difference between the prosperity of Kentucky and that of Ohio?

'*A*. Yes, the difference is striking.

'*Q*. What is the cause?

'*A*. Slavery. I regard slavery as more prejudicial still to the masters than to the slaves. The slaves of Kentucky are treated very gently, well fed, well clothed, nothing is so rare as to see them flee their master's house. But slavery prevents the emigrants coming to us. They deprive us of the energy and enterprising spirit which characterize the states where there are no slaves.'

This was exactly what Timothy Walker had said. But Tocqueville wanted to develop the economic argument a little further. 'Is it true that slavery prevents a State from becoming manufacturing?

'*A*. Many people think that negroes cannot become good workers in factories. I believe the contrary. When the blacks are placed young in a factory, they are as apt as the whites to become good workmen. We have examples of this in Kentucky; several plants run by slaves are prospering. If the South is not as industrial as the North it's not because the slaves are not able to serve in the factories, it's because slavery deprives the masters of the industry necessary to establish and direct them.

'*Q*. Is it true that public opinion is beginning to be against slavery in Kentucky?

'*A*. Yes, in the last few years an unbelievable revolution has occurred in people's minds. I am convinced that if one made a count of opinion by the head in Kentucky the majority would be found to be for the abolition of slavery. But one doesn't know what to do with the slaves. Our fathers did us a horrible injury in bringing them among us,' McIlvain admitted.

'*Q*. But since opinion against slavery is so pronounced, why has Missouri so obstinately refused to abolish it when it would be so easy?

'*A*. At that time the revolution I spoke of a moment ago had not yet occurred. Besides, it is so convenient for new settlers to have slaves to help them cut the trees and clear the lands in a region where it is hardly possible to find free workmen, that it is understandable that the less immediate benefit of the abolition of slavery has not yet been appreciated at its true value in Missouri. I believe, however, that now they realize the mistake they have made.

'*Q*. Is the black population increasing rapidly in Kentucky?

'*A*. Yes, but it can never become dangerous for the white population. Kentucky is divided into small holdings; on each one of these small properties is a white family owning several slaves. The division of land and the type of cultivation, which requires a small number of slaves, prevents our seeing here, as in the States further south, hundreds of negroes tilling the fields of one white man. With us, slavery is a great evil, not a danger.

'What do they raise in Kentucky?' Tocqueville eventually wanted to know.

'*A*. Corn, wheat, hemp; tobacco.

'*Q*. Do you think that for these various kinds of crops it would be more economical to use slaves than white workmen?

'*A*. I believe the contrary. Slaves work less well than free white men, and furthermore they have to be taken care of at all times; you have to raise them and support them in old age.'

If there was a contradiction in a point of view which regarded negroes as competent for manufacturing but uneconomic for agriculture, Tocqueville had seemed not to notice it. Their stage started for Nashville, and he had begun his observations of the countryside and its people.

He found the Kentucky-Tennessee plateau, he later noted,[3] 'filled with hills and rather shallow valleys through which flow a multitude of small streams. It's an attractive but uniform region.

'The soil in the two States seemed still almost entirely covered by forests. Once every so often a line of rails, some burnt trees, a field of corn, a few cattle, a cabin of tree trunks placed one on the other and roughly squared, announced the isolated dwelling of a settler. You see hardly any villages. The habitations of the farmers are scattered in the woods.

'Nothing is more rare than to encounter a house of brick in Kentucky; we didn't see ten in Tennesse[e], Nashville excepted.

'The cabin of the Kentucky and Tennessee country is generally divided into two parts, as seen in the margin.* All about are a number of huts serving as stables.

'The interior of these dwellings attests the indolence of the master even more than his poverty. You find a clean enough bed, some chairs, a good gun, often books, and almost always a newspaper, but the

* Here was inserted a rough diagram.

walls are so full of chinks that the outside air enters from all sides with . . .

'You are hardly better sheltered than in a cabin of leaves. Nothing would be easier than to protect oneself from bad weather and stop the chinks, but the master of the place is incapable of taking such care. In the North you see reigning an air of cleanliness and intelligence in the humblest dwellings. Here everything seems sketchy, everything a matter of chance; one would say that the inhabitant lives from day to day in the most perfect carelessness of the future. . . .'

What was the reason for this singular state of affairs in the prosperous West? 'Almost all the farmers that we have seen, even the poorest, have slaves. These are covered with rags, but generally seem strong and healthy. . . .'*

And Tocqueville took a moment to paint for his father an ideal picture of a Tennessee cabin.

It was in one of the many forested valleys of the region, he wrote, 'that we discovered one evening a cabin, made of wood, whose poorly-joined walls allowed one to see a great fire flaming in the interior. We knock: two great roguish dogs, big as donkeys, come first to the door. Their master follows close, grips us hard by the hand, and invites us to enter.† A fireplace as wide as half the room, and with an entire tree burning in it, a bed, a few chairs, a carbine six feet long, against the walls of the apartment, a few hunter's accoutrements which the wind was blowing about as it chose, and the picture is complete. Near the fire was seated the mistress of the lodge, with the tranquil and modest air that distinguishes American women, while four or five husky children rolled on the floor, as lightly clad as in the month of July. Under the mantel of the chimney two or three squatting negroes still seemed to find that it was less warm there than in Africa. In the midst of this collection of misery, my gentleman did not do the honours of his house with the less ease and courtesy. It's not that he forced himself to move in any way; but the poor blacks, soon perceiving that a stranger had entered the house, one of them by orders of the master presented us with a glass of whisky, another, a corn cake or plate of venison; a third was sent to get wood. The first time I saw this order

---

* Page torn.
† 'You push open a door hung on leather hinges and without a lock. . . . Here you find a family of poor people leading the lazy life of the rich. . . . Not even the most miserable planter of Kentucky or Tennesse[e] but represents marvellously the country gentleman of old Europe.' Cahier E.

given I supposed that it was a question of going to the cellar or wood-house; but the axe strokes that I heard ringing in the wood told me soon that they were cutting down the tree that we needed. It's thus they do everything. While the slaves were thus occupied, the master, seated tranquilly before a fire that would have roasted an ox to the marrow of his bones, enveloped himself majestically in a cloud of smoke, and between each puff related to his guests, to make their time seem less long, all the great exploits that his hunter's memory could furnish him.'

Apparently Tocqueville had chosen for his model of the typical Tennessee homestead the very wayside cabin where Beaumont had lodged him during his chill and illness. Even a fever was not enough to drug the observer's instinct in him. Not for long, at any rate. For on the fourteenth Beaumont had cooked him a rabbit, and on the fifteenth and sixteenth the same watchful companion had discovered signs of rapid recovery in a returning appetite and a great impatience to be off. One other sign there had been, also. Still lying on his bed, Tocqueville had now begun to interrogate their host, the story-telling Mr. Harris.

'I came from South Carolina to settle in this country several years ago,' Mr. Harris told him.[4]

'*Q.* Tell me why all the habitations that we encounter in the midst of the woods offer so poor a shelter against bad weather. The walls show such chinks that rain and wind can come in without trouble. Such a dwelling must be disagreeable and unhealthy for the proprietor as for the stranger. Would it be so very difficult to make them tight?' It was a difficult topic, and in the bitter chill of the room Tocqueville was trying hard to be tactful.

'Nothing would be easier,' the American answered, 'but the in-habitant of this region is generally indolent; he looks on work as dis-agreeable. Provided he has enough food, and a house capable of giving him a half shelter, he is content and thinks only of smoking and hunting.

'*Q.* What, in your opinion, is the main reason for this indolence?

'*A.* Slavery. We are habituated to doing nothing for ourselves. There are no farmers in Tennessee so poor that they do not have one or two blacks. When he has no more than that he is often obliged to work with them in the fields. But the moment he has a dozen, which is very frequently, he has a white to oversee them and himself does absolutely nothing but ride and hunt. Not a farmer but passes a part of his time hunting and has in his possession a good rifle.

'*Q*. Do you think that farming by slaves is economical?

'*A*. No. I believe it more costly than the employment of free whites.'

That settled it, at least in Tocqueville's mind. 'It is proved, then, that one could get on without slavery,' he wrote in his diary. 'Public opinion in these two States seems altogether favourable to this doctrine. But slavery is an evil whose roots are so deep that it is almost as impossible to shake it off after perceiving its harm as before.'

Meanwhile, the position of the slave remained—what it had been. And Tocqueville illustrated for his father by an experience that he and Beaumont had had the day that he was taken with a chill.

'I must tell you one other small anecdote, that will enable you to judge what value is attached here to the life of a man, when he has the misfortune to have a black skin. About a week ago we had to cross the Tennessee river. To reach the other side we had only a paddle-wheel boat operated by a horse and two slaves. We ourselves got across all right, but as the river was full of drift ice the master of the boat was afraid to try to take the carriage across. "Don't worry," one of our travelling companions said to him, "we'll make up if necessary the value of the horse and the slaves." This argument removed all objection: the carriage was taken on and got across.'

\*

\* \*

It was in Memphis, looking at their odyssey in retrospect, that Tocqueville penned most of these notes on slavery and the dwellings of the forest pioneers. Naturally, the strange, feudal aristocracy of the region did not escape a similar analysis.

They had not seen many individuals, and these perhaps not of the best. But everywhere the Southerners had seemed to conform to a distinct type.

'In the sections of Kentucky and Tennesse[e] that we traversed the men are tall and strong,' Tocqueville wrote in his diary.[5] 'They have a national physiognomy and a rough and energetic appearance. They are not, like the inhabitants of Ohio, a confused mixture of all the American races; on the contrary, they are all sprung from the same stem and belong to the great Virginia family. They possess, then, to a much greater degree than all the Americans we have seen up to now, that intuitive love of country, a love mingled with exaggeration and prejudices, entirely different from the reasoned sentiment and refined egoism that bear the name patriotism in almost all the States of the Union.'

'. . . Nothing in Kentucky or Tennesse[e],' however, seemed to Tocqueville to convey 'the idea of so developed a society. On this point these two States differ essentially from those newly settled by the Americans from the North, where is to be found in germ the high civilization of New England. In Kentucky or Tennesse[e] you see few churches, no schools; society, like the individual, seems to provide for nothing.

'And yet, it's not quite a rustic society. There is none of that simplicity full of ignorance, prejudices and . . .* that distinguish agricultural peoples in inaccessible countries. These men still belong to one of the most civilized and reasoning races in the world. Their customs have none of the *naïveté* of the fields; the philosophical and argumentative spirit of the English crops up there as in all parts of America; and there is an astonishing circulation of letters and newspapers in the midst of these wild forests. We were travelling with the mail. From time to time we stopped before what they called the post. It was almost always an isolated house in the depth of the woods. There we dropped a large packet, from which doubtless each inhabitant of the neighbourhood came to take his share. I don't believe that in the most enlightened rural district in France there is carried on an intellectual exchange as rapid or as large as in these wildernesses. . . .'

Of course, 'it would be ridiculous to try to judge an entire people after having lived with it eight or ten days,' Tocqueville admitted. But already he was beginning to believe that the 'whole history' of Kentucky and Tennessee peculiarities could be summed up in a single phrase: 'They are southerners, masters of slaves, made half wild by the solitude, and hardened by the hardships of life.'

\*

\*      \*

One other *suite* of observations, and Tocqueville's catalogue of his recent thoughts would be complete.

His approach was often philosophic. He dealt, with himself, with Beaumont, and with others, customarily in such sweeping generalities

* Page torn.

that his diary notes fatigue the reader and sometimes dull one's appreciation of what he had to say.

But this time he was venturing into a new field. He was making a departure so radical that it took him almost completely beyond his usual field of thought. Not of political customs, not of social habits, not even of personal adventures was he now thinking.

For he had turned to economics.

Travelling with the mail, he and Beaumont had had their eyes opened. In the wildest of American forests there was, they could not help noticing, 'an astonishing circulation of letters and newspapers.'

To another, less thoughtful observer, this fact might not have meant very much. But to Tocqueville it suggested a whole theory of economics and civilization. Briefly, he felt he had now discovered for himself at least one infallible '*Means of increasing the public prosperity.*' This, if it could be proved, was a theory of no small importance. So, as soon as he felt strong enough, Tocqueville sat down to develop his idea in a short essay.

'Almost all political precepts,' he began,* 'contain in their statement something so general, so theoretical, and so vague that it is difficult to draw from them the least profit in practice. Almost always they are remedies whose utility depends still more on the temperament of the patient than on the nature of his illness.

'I know but one single means of increasing the prosperity of a people that is infallible in practice and that I believe one can count on in all countries as in all spots.

'This means is naught else but to increase the ease of communication between men.

'On this point the spectacle presented by America is as curious as it is informing.

'The roads, the canals and the mails play a prodigious part in the prosperity of the Union. It is well to examine their effects, the value set on them, and the manner of obtaining them.

'America, which is the country enjoying the greatest sum of prosperity ever yet accorded a nation, is also the country which, proportional to its age and means, has made the greatest efforts to procure the easy communication I was speaking of.

'In France there are large and very concentrated populations through which winds no road, with the result that they are more separated

---

* Cahier E. For an echo, see *Dém. en Am.*, II,245 and note, 397–399.

from the rest of the nation than half the world formerly was. I don't doubt it would take longer and cost more to have ten sacks of wheat brought from certain *communes* in lower Brittany to Paris than to transport to the same spot all the sugar of the colonies.

'In America one of the first things done in a new State is to have the mail come. In the Michigan forests there is not a cabin so isolated, not a valley so wild, that it does not receive letters and newspapers at least once a week; we saw it ourselves.

'It was especially in such circumstances that I felt the difference between our social state and that of the Americans. There are few rural districts in France where, proportionately, as many letters and newspapers are received as in these still wild regions of America where man still struggles against all the hardships of life and gets a glimpse of society only once in a while.

'America has undertaken and is finishing some immense canals. It already has more railroads than France. There isn't any one who does not recognize that the discovery of steam has added unbelievably to the strength and prosperity of the Union, and has done so by facilitating rapid communications between the diverse parts of this vast body.* The States of the South, where communication is less easy, are those that languish by comparison with the rest.

'Of all the countries of the world America is the one where the movement of thought and human industry is the most continuous and swift. Not an American but knows the resources of all the parts of the vast country he inhabits; all the men of intelligence know each other by reputation, many by sight. I have often been struck with astonishment on seeing to what an extent this is true. I believe that I have never happened to speak to an American about one of his fellow-countrymen without finding him aware of the latter's present position and life history.

'I realize that this extreme industrial and intellectual movement is singularly favoured by education, by the kind of government enjoyed in America, and by the special position in which the Americans find themselves. The populations of America are not sedentary, even among the old nations. They are almost entirely made up of entrepreneurs, who feel the need of means of communication with a vivacity, and employ them with an ardour, that one could not expect of the routine

---

* Had Tocqueville pursued this thought, the whole emphasis of his book would have been different. Cf. above, ch.XIV.

and lazy minds of our peasants. The effect of a road or a canal is therefore more felt, and above all more immediate, in America than it would be in France.

'Thus we would have to carry on among ourselves as the Americans do for the new districts of the West: open the road before the travellers, assured that the latter will present themselves sooner or later to use them.

'As for the means used to open communications in America, here's what I have remarked on this point.

'It is generally believed in Europe that the great maxim of the American government is *laisser-faire*, to remain a pure spectator of the advance of society, in which individual interest is the great agent. This is a mistake.

'The American government doesn't concern itself with everything as does ours, it is true. It doesn't pretend to provide for and execute everything, it distributes no premium, does not encourage commerce, does not patronize belles-lettres and the arts. But as for the great works of public utility, it rarely abandons the responsibility for them to private people; it's the government itself which executes. The great canal joining the Hudson to Lake Erie was built at the expense of the State of New-York; the one joining Lake Erie to the Mississip[p]i is the work of the State of Ohio. The canal uniting the Delaware to Chesapeak[e] Bay is a State enterprise. The great roads leading to distant points are ordinarily undertaken and carried out by the State and not by companies.

'Note well, however, there are no rules in this matter. The activities of companies, of communities, of individuals contribute in a thousand ways to those of the State. All the enterprises of moderate scope or limited interest are the work of communities or companies. The turnpike or toll roads often parallel the State roads. The railroads set up by companies carry on in certain sections of the country the work of the canals over the main arteries. The county roads are kept up by the districts through which they pass. No exclusive system, then, is known here. Nowhere does America exhibit that systematic uniformity so dear to the superficial and metaphysical minds of our day.

'In institutions, in laws, in the government of society, and in daily life, all on the contrary is different and varied.

'Everything adjusts itself to the nature of man and of the region, without having the pretension to bend them to the rigour of an inflexible rule. From this variety rises a prosperity pervading the whole nation and each of its parts.

'To come back to the roads and all the other means of carrying rapidly from place to place the produce of industry and of thought, I do not pretend to have made the discovery that they served the prosperity of a people. That's a truth universally felt and recognized. I say only that America makes you put your finger on this truth, that it throws the fact more in relief than any other country in the world, and that it is impossible to travel through the union without becoming convinced, not through argument but by the witness of all the senses, that the most powerful, infallible way of increasing the prosperity of a country is to favour by all possible means a free intercourse among its inhabitants.'

## XLV

## ENCOUNTER WITH CHOCTAW INDIANS—AND
## AN ACCIDENT

'AT last, at last, dear Mother, the signal has been given, and here we are sailing down the Mississip[p]i with all the speed that steam and the current united can give a vessel.' It was the twenty-fifth of December, Christmas, seven long days since they had first caught sight of the isolated, disappointing little river town of Memphis. Tocqueville was beside himself with relief.

'We were beginning to despair of ever getting out of the wilderness in which we found ourselves imprisoned,' he wrote his mother.[1] 'If you wish to trouble to look at the map you will see that our position was not gay. Before us, the Mississip[p]i half-frozen, and no ship to take us down; over our heads a Siberian sky pure and icy.—One could turn back, you will say.—That last resource eluded us. During our sojourn at Memphis the Tennessee had frozen, in such a way that carriages were no longer getting across. Thus we found ourselves in the middle of a triangle formed by the Mississip[p]i, the Tennessee, and impenetrable wildernesses to the South, as isolated as on a rock in the ocean, living in a small world made expressly for us, without papers, without news of the rest of mankind, with the prospect of a long winter. It was in this fashion that we spent a week.

'But for the worry, however, these days passed pleasantly enough. We were staying with some nice people who did their best to be agreeable to us. Twenty paces from our house began the most admirable forest, the most sublime and picturesque place in the world, even in the snow. We had guns, powder, and lead as much as we wanted. A few miles from the village lived an Indian nation (the Chickasaws); once on their lands we always found a few who asked nothing better than to hunt with us. Hunting and war are the only occupations, as the only pleasures, of the Indians. We would have had to go too far to find true game in any quantity. But in revenge we killed a number of pretty birds unknown in France: a performance which hardly raised us in the estimation of our allies but which had the virtue of amusing us perfectly. In this fashion I killed birds that were red, blue, yellow, without forgetting the most brilliant parrots that I have ever seen.'

'I think,' Beaumont was writing to his brother on that same day,[2] 'I think we should have died of boredom and despair if we had not had to sustain us our accustomed philosophy and each a *fusil de chasse*. We awaited *better times* wandering through the surrounding forests and exploring the shores of the Mississip[p]i. Tocqueville and I killed a multitude of charming birds, among others some parrots of charming plumage; they were green, yellow and red. We killed four on the same hunt. The only difficulty is to kill just one, the death of the first makes all the others come; they perch on the head of the hunter and have themselves shot like ninnies.*

'These hunts gave us the opportunity to see some very picturesque sites on the left bank of the Mississip[p]i,' Beaumont continued. 'I should draw up for you a description of them if M. de Chateaubriand had not written his in a way to discourage amateurs. Besides, I did not have the chance to see *the Great River* and its neighbourhood in all their beauty. Winter gives to all nature a sombre and lugubrious tint, and the snow with its whiteness animates the tableau not at all, it's the whiteness of death. Thus it was only by comparison that I found beautiful the scenes offering themselves to my eyes; when I experienced some admiration it was my imagination that was responsible.

'Hunting was difficult on a slippery and mountainous terrain; but the fatigue that we acquired on our walks was a veritable blessing. It made us feel the need of repose, and at least the hours passed in sleep disembarrassed us momentarily of our cares and alarms.'

'Thus passed our time,' Tocqueville agreed, 'lightly as to the pres-

---

* Beaumont later recalled Tocqueville's joy on killing two parrots of the most beautiful plumage. And twenty-five years later, in a letter to this same companion, Tocqueville was to say how glad he was that he had kept *jusqu'à ce jour le même ami avec lequel je chassais les perroquets à Memphis*. Wandering in the snow-covered forest of *Compiègne*, there had suddenly flashed on his mind *les bois du Tennessee que nous parcourions il y a vingt-cinq ans*. O.C.,V,33;VI,288–289.

Beaumont's sketchbook makes it almost certain that what he and Tocqueville had mainly been shooting were Carolina Paroquets.

ent; but the future would not leave us tranquil. Finally, one fine day, we saw a wisp of smoke on the Mississip[p]i, on the edge of the horizon. The cloud drew nearer little by little and out of it came, not a giant or a dwarf as in fairy tales, but a great steamboat, coming from New Orleans and which, after parading in front of us for a quarter of an hour, as if to leave us in uncertainty whether it would stop or continue its journey, after blowing like a whale, finally steered toward us, broke the ice with its heavy timbers and tied up to the bank. The entire population of our universe turned out on the shore of the river which, as you know, formed at that time one of the extreme frontiers of our empire. The whole city of Memphis was in a ferment; they didn't ring the bells because there are no bells, but they cried hurrah! And the new arrivals stepped down on the beach like Christopher Columbuses.

'We were not saved yet, however; the destination of the boat was up the Mississip[p]i all the way to Louisville, and we, our business was to go to New Orleans. We had luckily about fifteen companions in misfortune who were no more anxious than we to take up winter quarters in Memphis. There was therefore a general *rush* for the captain. What would he do in the upper Mississip[p]i? He would infallibly be stopped by the ice. The Tennessee, the Missouri, the Ohio were frozen over. Not one of us but insisted that he had seen it with his own eyes. He would be arrested without fail, damaged, perhaps even smashed by the ice. As for us, we were speaking only in his own interest. That went without saying: in his own best interest. . . .

'This neighbourly love lends such warmth to our arguments that we finally begin to shake our man. Yet I have the conviction that he would not have turned around but for a happy event, to which we owe it that we did not become citizens of Memphis. As we were debating there on the bank, we heard an infernal music echoing in the forest; it was the noise of a drum, the whinnying of horses, the barking of dogs. There finally appeared a large troup of Indians, old men, women, children, belongings, all led by a European and steering toward the capital of our triangle. These Indians were Chactas (or Tchactaws), following the Indian pronounciation. *A propos* of that, I will tell you that M. de Chateaubriand has acted a little as did the monkey of La Fontaine; he hasn't taken the name of a harbour for a man, but he has given a man the name of a powerful nation of Southern America. However that may be, you no doubt want to know why these Indians had come and in what way they could be of service to us. Patience, I beg of you; to-day, having time and paper, I don't want to hurry. You shall know, then, that the Americans of the United States, who are reasonable and unprejudiced, and great philanthropists to boot, have taken it into their heads, as did the Spaniards, that God had given them the new world and its inhabitants in full ownership.

'They have discovered, furthermore, that, it being proved (listen well to this) that a square mile could nourish ten times as many civilized men as savages, reason indicated that wherever civilized men could establish themselves, the savages would have to move away. What a beautiful thing logic is. Consequently, whenever the Indians begin to find themselves a little too close to their white brothers, the President of the United States sends them a messenger, who represents to them that in their own best interest it would be well for them to retreat ever so little toward the West. The lands where they have lived for centuries belong to them, indubitably; no one refuses them this incontestable right; but these lands, after all, they are uncultivated wilderness, woods, swamps, a poor property truly. On the other side of the Mississip[p]i, on the contrary, are magnificent lands, where the game has never been disturbed by the sound of the *pioneer's* axe, where the Europeans will *never* come. They are more than 100 leagues away. Add to this some presents of inestimable price, waiting to reward their complaisance: hogsheads of brandy, necklaces of glass, earrings and mirrors: the whole backed up by the insinuation that if they refuse, it may perhaps be necessary to use force. What to do? The poor Indians take their old parents in their arms; the women load their children on their backs; the nation finally sets out, carrying with it its most precious possessions. It abandons for ever the soil on which, for a thousand years perhaps, its fathers have lived, to go establish itself in a wilderness where the whites will not leave them ten years in peace. Do you note the results of a high civilization? The Spaniards, like real brutes, throw their dogs on the Indians as if on ferocious beasts. They kill, burn, massacre, pillage the new world like a town taken by assault, without pity as without discernment. But one can't destroy everything; fury has its end. The remainder of the Indian populations ends by mingling with the conquerors, taking their customs, their religion; in several provinces they are to-day reigning over their former conquerors. The Americans of the United States, more humane, more moderate, more respectful of right and legality, never bloody, are more profoundly destructive; and it is impossible to doubt that before a hundred years [have passed] there will no longer be in North America, not just a single nation, but a single man belonging to the most remarkable of the Indian races. . . .

'But I don't remember at all where I was in my story. We were talking, I think, about the Chactas. The Chactas were a powerful nation living on the frontiers of the States of Alabama and Georgia. After long negotiations they finally, this year, succeeded in persuading them to leave their country and emigrate to the right bank of the Missip[p]i. Six to seven thousand Indians have already crossed the great river; those arriving in Memphis came there with the object of following their compatriots. The agent of the American government, who was accompanying them and was responsible for paying their passage, when he learned that a steamboat had just arrived, ran to the bank. The price that he offered for carrying the Indians sixty leagues further down * was the final touch that made up the captain's unsettled mind; the signal for all aboard was given. The prow was turned south, and we gaily mounted the ladder down which sadly came the poor passengers who, instead of going to Louisville, saw themselves obliged to await the thaw at Memphis. Thus goes the world.

'But we had not left yet: it was a question of embarking our exiled tribe, its horses and its dogs. Here began a scene which, in truth, had something lamentable about it. The Indians advanced mournfully toward the bank. First they had their horses go aboard; several of them, little accustomed to the forms of civilized life, took fright and plunged into the Missip[p]i, from which they could be pulled out only with difficulty. Then came the men who, according to ordinary habits, carried only their arms; then the women carrying their children attached to their backs or wrapped in the blankets they wore; they were, besides, burdened down with loads containing their whole wealth. Finally the old people were led on. Among them was a woman 110 years

---

* Just a month later, the *Boston Courier* published a letter from someone who said he was living on the road leading from the Choctaw nation to Memphis. The story thus spread before eastern readers was not very edifying. Apparently the Chickasaws who moved at the government's solicitation were not given lands 'as good' across the Mississippi, and those that stayed were not left lands enough. With the result that the Choctaws, who had been guaranteed undisturbed possession of the lands they retained, were now being asked to let the Chickasaws in. As for the removal business, it was a pitiful sight in the extreme cold. Apparently agents volunteered to accomplish the transporting at the rate of ten dollars a head (and made a profit!).

old. I have never seen a more appalling shape. She was naked save for a covering which left visible, at a thousand places, the most emaciated figure imaginable. She was escorted by two or three generations of grandchildren. To leave one's country at that age to seek one's fortune in a foreign land, what misery! Among the old people there was a young girl who had broken her arm a week before; for want of care the arm had been frozen below the fracture. Yet she had to follow the common journey. When everything was on board the dogs approached the bank; but they refused to enter the vessel and began howling frightfully. Their masters had to bring them on by force.

'In the whole scene there was an air of ruin and destruction, something which betrayed a final and irrevocable adieu; one couldn't watch without feeling one's heart wrung. The Indians were tranquil, but sombre and taciturn. There was one who could speak English and of whom I asked why the Chactas were leaving their country.—To be free, he answered,—I could never get any other reason out of him. We will set them down to-morrow in the solitudes of Arkansas.* One must confess that it is a singular fate that brought us to Memphis to watch the expulsion, one can say the dissolution, of one of the most celebrated and ancient American peoples.

'But that's enough about the savages. It's high time to come back to civilized men. Yet one word still about the Mississip[p]i which, in truth, hardly deserves attention. It's a great river, yellow, rolling gently enough through the most profound solitudes, in the midst of forests which it inundates in spring and fertilizes with its mud. You see not a single hill on the horizon but woods, more woods, and still more woods: reeds, tropical creepers; a perfect silence; no trace of man; not even the smoke of an Indian encampment.'

---

\* Beaumont counted between fifty and sixty Indians, all being carried on the open deck. His impression was that the old squaw was even more aged than Tocqueville said: 'The old are spared no more than the others. I have just seen on the boat deck an aged woman more than 120 years old. She is almost naked, and carries on her only a miserable woollen covering scarcely protecting her shoulders from the cold. She seemed to me the perfect image of old age (*vétusté*) and decrepitude. This unhappy woman is obviously at death's door, and she leaves the land where she has dwelt for 120 years to go into another country to begin a new life.

'We shall arrive to-morrow sometime during the day at the mouth of the White River where we shall set them down. They will be tossed on the bank as one tosses rabbits into a warren that one wishes to populate.'

The tragic scene was later to serve as material for Tocqueville, also, in his book: *Dém. en Am.*, II,305–6,311.

'We finally left Memphis this morning at five o'clock, and during the day we have made nearly forty leagues,' Beaumont that evening concluded his own account of their escape from Tennessee. 'The *Louisville* is a magnificent steamboat. The cabin in which I am writing you at this moment is vast and well decorated. One is as comfortable there as in a great salon, although there are forty passengers. Each one has his bed. Three meals are served. The cooking is bad, because in America there is no good cooking done (except in some private houses). Otherwise, as American cooking goes, it is excellent. . . .'

'At the instant of writing our boat is immobile; we are at anchor. It is nine o'clock in the evening; the weather is sombre; and it is dangerous to navigate the Mississip[p]i at night in the season in which we find ourselves. The waters are very low, because the northern rivers which feed the Mississip[p]i are all frozen. One runs the risk then of running aground, and furthermore there are in the river an unbelievable number of overturned trees (called snags in English) against which one is sure to stave in [the bottom]. These circumstances are the reason for our putting in 5 or 6 days in going to New Orleans. Besides, it's only from that city that I shall be able to send off my letter, and I shall not close it without telling you the incidents of the voyage, if any arise. . . .'

*

*     *

'If any arise.' . . . !

The letter stopped there. And apparently for one very good reason. A single glance at the date of Beaumont's sketch No. 36 * demonstrates that the very next evening an incident of the graver sort did arise. The *Louisville* ran aground on a sandbar! It was (counting since their departure from Pittsburgh) their third steamboat accident within the month. It was also the last straw. Tocqueville and Beaumont had seen too many disasters recently, interposing between them and the pursuit of their journey. This last threatened delay was more than they could bear. They ran to the captain to learn how long it would be before they could be got off. He referred them to the pilot, who was, of course, in charge. Looking down at them from the pilot house, as they hung on

* Here numbered 33. See the inscription.

the ladder, the pilot received them 'like a potentate,' blew smoke in their faces, and 'observed peacefully that the sands of the Mississip[p]i were like the French and could not stay a year in the same place.' *

The insulting audacity of the remark must have nearly knocked the Frenchmen off their ladder. Yet, in their awkward position, what could they do? Somewhat abashed, they climbed down again and re-signed themselves to await the efforts of the crew.

It was to be about two mortal days before they could be got off.†

The *Louisville* was a 'magnificent' steamboat, Beaumont had ob-served. The first day they had made 'forty leagues' between dawn and dark. Now that the motionless twenty-sixth had arrived, however, their admiration was suddenly a little cooled, and the offending vessel be-came the object of a new scrutiny. Beaumont could not refrain from comment about the cooking. And, in the normal course of events, Tocqueville once more found himself addressing a question to the cap-tain.

Their steamboat, the captain informed him, measured about 400 tons.[3] 'It cost,' Tocqueville noted in his diary, '50,000 dollars to build; it is to last only four years. The fresh water navigation, the *snags* and all the other dangers of the Mississip[p]i, reduce to this short space of time the life (on the average) of the vessels navigating this river.

'The cost of wood (average) on the banks of the Mississip[p]i is two dollars a cord. The vessels consume 30 cords a day, which makes the expense 60 dollars.

'The food and wages of the personnel, and [the maintenance] of the passengers amount to about the same sum, which bring to 120 dollars an operating day the expenses of a vessel of this size.'

So that was how this business of rapid communication (and pros-perity!) was handled on the Mississippi! Tocqueville and Beaumont had now seen about everything there was to see, experienced almost all the dangers, learned everything there was to learn about that extraordinary institution: the American river steamboat. They knew it could race, refuse to set passengers ashore, turn around in mid-voyage, explode, get caught in the ice, run aground, and sink. Sometimes it was the quickest way to suicide. Most generally it enabled you to cover unbelievable dis-

---

* For Tocqueville's complete description of the incident, see '*24 Heures à la Nouvelle Orléans*,' below, pp.619–20.

† Whether they were pulled off the bar by the second steamboat, shown in the back-ground of Beaumont's sketch, is not clear.

tances with a speed and comfort that excited admiration. But once in a while it held you like a prisoner, arrested your journey, and drove you almost crazy with impatience.

At such a time it was well to have one's resources.

Beaumont got out his pencil and his sketching album. And Tocqueville went to his trunk.

## XLVI

## TWO FAMOUS BOOKS—AND AN EXILE
## NAMED HOUSTON

ALL the way from New York, Alexis de Tocqueville had been carrying with him, whatever their weight might cost, two books. Each was a classic in its field, so he had gathered; and each was worth studying, particularly if one were interested in American government. So he had packed them along, hoping for an opportunity to look into them; yet never until this very moment had that opportunity arrived.

Now he got them out. The title of one was the *Federalist*. And the other was called Kent's *Commentaries on American Law*. It was the very same work that the cheerful and lively old Chancellor had presented to them almost on their first arrival in America.

Tocqueville opened them, read . . . and reached for his writing materials. He began to take notes.*

He was interested in American taxation and jotted down a pertinent observation or two. The patent and copyright laws claimed his attention for a moment. In the *Commentaries* he noted the swift alterations in the laws of Massachusetts and New York regarding slavery and religious tolerance. Kent also reported some very interesting things about Connecticut. It seemed that in that enlightened State the selectmen were so zealous in exercising their legal power to compel the education of every neglected child that illiteracy was almost unknown there. Chief Justice Reeve once told him, Kent wrote, that in his twenty-seven years of legal practice in that State he had met just one person who could not write.†

The power of the fathers, as heads of the family, was strangely miss-

---

* In 1930, in the Tocqueville château, was discovered a brief little notebook devoted almost exclusively to items taken from James Kent, *Commentaries on American Law* (4 v., 1826). Others of his reflections on the *Commentaries*, and on the *Federalist*, he placed in Cahier E (*papiers divers qui ne se classent point facilement*).
† Kent, *Commentaries*, edition cited, II,165 and note (Lecture XXIX). The next day Tocqueville composed for his friend, Chabrol, a brief and beautifully phrased essay

ing, on the other hand. '*La puissance paternelle,*' as Tocqueville phrased it,[1] 'which figured so heroically in the ancient republics that publicists have seen in it the source of their grandeur and long life, is almost reduced to nothing in American institutions.' Perhaps that was because paternalism was essentially an 'aristocratic' institution.* In any case, it accorded with the temper of the people. For Tocqueville could well recall Mayor Richards of Philadelphia saying that even in cases of elopement the sympathy of the public was almost always with the daughter and against the father.

All this, however, was random observation and beside the point. What Tocqueville was chiefly interested in was the political philosophy of the American Union and the basic principles underlying the Federal Constitution. For light on these fundamental but hitherto almost unexplored questions, Tocqueville turned next to the luminous and compelling essays in the *Federalist.*

His early notes showed him trying to distinguish American political institutions from the parent English Constitution, and from the old Common Law.

'. . . The generating principle of the English constitution,' Tocqueville very sagely noticed, 'is that Parliament is the source of all powers and can do what it wishes.

'The principle of the different American constitutions is diametrically opposed. In America the source of all powers is to be found in the Constitution, a law pre-existent to all others and which can only be changed by the authority from which it emanates, the people. The legislature [Congress], far from being the source of powers, is subjected like all the rest to this law, from which it can't deviate a single instant without violating the first of its duties.'

Here was an essential difference clearly distinguished and sensibly

---

on American education, pointing out the universal faith, the freedom enjoyed by private citizens in the founding of schools, the general vigilance exercised by New York State, the local control exercised throughout New England, etc. As for France, he still wasn't quite sure.

* In another speculation, confided to paper that same day (Port. III), Tocqueville remarked that perhaps it was the 'aristocratic character' of the English that accounted for the great difference between the two kindred peoples.

In thus suggesting that *démocratie* and *aristocratie* might each have its own set of institutions and social ways, Tocqueville was broaching the great question, the grand preoccupation that was one day to lead him to add to his book on America two more volumes dealing exclusively with the alteration of human social institutions under the irresistible weight of the equalitarian tendency. See *Dém. en Am.,* III,ch.3,etc. (1840).

stated. In America there were two orders of law, the constitutional and the legislative, and the former was fundamental. In this western continent the *constitutions*—the written, fixed constitutions—were the supreme laws of the land.*

Yet that raised a difficult question. The organization of the United States was federal: which was to say that the States had constitutions as well as the Union. In short, there must be a number of supreme laws. How reconcile them? Where did the supremacy lie? If in the State constitution, what had prevented the dissolution of the Union, like the federations of the past, under the strain of sectional jealousies? If the supremacy in all things lay, on the other hand, with the Federal Constitution, what of the Federal principle? Would not the United States long since have degenerated into a centralized despotism, with anæmia setting in throughout the provinces?

For the solution of this vital problem in American political science, Tocqueville could have chosen no better guide than the essays in the *Federalist*.

'. . . The great quality distinguishing the new American union from the old is this,' he noted in his diary:[2]

'The old union governed the *States*, and not *individuals*. It was shaped like a foreign power subjecting inferior powers to its laws.

'The new federal government is in real truth the government of the union in all that is within its jurisdiction; it applies not to the *States* but to *individuals* . . . and it has means of its own for forcing these individuals to obedience without resorting to any authority but its own. . . .'

By way of example Tocqueville analysed the question of taxation: showing how hard it was to compel a State, how easy to collect from individuals.

'. . . It's to ignorance of this principle that all the ancient and modern federations have owed their dissolution and their ruin,' Tocqueville concluded. That first principle he had now mastered.†

---

* In Cahier F, which Tocqueville reserved for notes on civil and criminal law in America, he now (31 Dec.) laid out some materials to aid his future understanding of the merits and demerits of the *Common*—or customary—Law, as distinguished from the written Roman—or Civil—Law. Again the inspiration, and much of the guidance, was provided by the *Commentaries* of Chancellor Kent.

† Tocqueville seems to have done considerable rapid reading in the *Federalist*, taking the example on taxation from No.XXI (also XXX?), by Hamilton; and the quotations (cited below) from Nos.XXIII and XII, by the same author. He particularly admired the skill with which Madison had handled the Greek experiments in confederation (No.XVIII).

Yet there remained, of course, the necessity of protecting the States from an all-centralizing, all-controlling National Government. How was that accomplished?

Apparently, and it was a curious and interesting invention, apparently by dividing sovereignty: by what the Americans called the doctrine of spheres.

'. . . It's an axiom of American public law that one must give each government full authority within its sphere, and so trace the sphere that it cannot go beyond. There's a great principle, and one worth meditating,' Tocqueville continued his note. And to substantiate his interpretation he copied into his diary, the next day, what Alexander Hamilton had said in the twenty-third *Federalist* paper.

' "If the circumstances of our country are such as to demand a compound, instead of a simple—a confederate, instead of a sole government, the essential point which will remain to be adjusted will be to discriminate *the objects*, as far as it can be done, which shall appertain to the different provinces or departments of power, allowing to each the most ample authority for fulfilling *those* which may be committed to its charge." '

Altogether, the more he reflected on this curious invention, on this hitherto unpractised *duality* in government, the more Tocqueville found himself forced to admire the political talents of the American people.

'What one can affirm is that only a very enlightened people could have invented the Federal Constitution of the United States; and only a very enlightened people, singularly habituated to representative forms, could make so complicated a machine work and know how to retain within their different spheres the various powers which, but for this continuous care, would not fail to collide violently.

'The Constitution of the United States is an admirable work, and yet it is to be believed that its founders would not have succeeded had not a past of 150 years given the different States of the Union *the taste and the habit of provincial governments*, and had not a high civilization at the same time prepared them *to support a central government that was strong though limited.*'

Already the young Frenchman was beginning to acquire an extraordinarily clear and masterful understanding of the American Constitution, and its political background.

'The Federal Constitution of the United States appears to me the best, perhaps the only, combination allowing of the establishment of a vast Republic. And yet an imitation of it is absolutely impracticable, wanting the pre-existing conditions of which I spoke above. . . .'

\*

\*   \*

'Sovereignty of the People.' The phrase kept returning with increasing frequency to Tocqueville's pen. However skilfully the fields of sovereignty might be portioned off between the governments, Federal and State, the sovereignty in question was always a delegated power. Essentially, as in principle, true sovereignty came from, or resided in, the people. Which was a philosophic way of saying that the active agents in American government, the ultimate and fundamental authority, remained always the people themselves.

What influence, then, did this irresistible trend toward complete equality and *self*-government have on the complicated political structure of the American Union?

For one thing, Tocqueville recalled, there were the 'Associations.' And not only did the American democrats band together privately in association and convention for the accomplishment of private ends and public improvements, but they had made use of the law to further such activities. Specifically, they had found the 'Corporation' device useful, and were now creating and multiplying these legal entities with a speed that seemed to frighten thoughtful men.

Chancellor Kent, for instance, had written in his book: 'We are multiplying in this country to an unparalleled extent the institution of corporations and giving them a flexibility and variety of purposes, unknown to the Roman and [or the] English law.' \*

On the other hand, thought Tocqueville, corporations were potential mass energy, actually released and organized for work. In that direction, at least, popular sovereignty resulted in activity and performance. But what about the unpleasant necessity of self-discipline? There, perhaps, was something altogether different.

'The principle of the sovereignty of the people often supplies the nations adopting it with an energy that the others lack. The people do not know, however, how to impose on themselves the sacrifices that are necessary,' Tocqueville reflected.

' "It is evident," says Hamilton in the *Federalist*, "from the state of

---

\* *Petit Cahier: Notes sur Kent.—Commentaries*, from the original, II,227; with further reference to page 219 (Lecture XXXIII).

the country, from the habits of the people, from the experience we have had on the point itself, that it is impractical to raise any very considerable sums by direct taxation: tax laws have in vain been multiplied; new methods to enforce the collection have in vain been tried; the public expectations have been uniformly disappointed, and the treasuries of the states have remained empty. . . ." '

And Tocqueville noted in his diary that he had already on numerous occasions noticed similar instances. 'It is hard to make disagreeable laws, even when they are useful.'

That entry was made on the twenty-seventh of December. That same day, or shortly after, Tocqueville added an interesting postscript:

'One can't know exactly what degree of energy or what power over itself American "Democracy" would find in itself at a time of crisis: it hasn't experienced any as yet.

'What's certain is that every time the central government wanted to establish direct taxes it failed, and that even with the ardour of political passion created by the Revolution it was never without the greatest trouble that they could get together men and money, and then always insufficiently.

'We must therefore await the time when the nation will have to resort to *conscription*, and to *heavy taxation*, before we can judge what sacrifices "Democracies" are capable of imposing on themselves.'

\*

\* \*

Meanwhile, one other unfortunate characteristic of popular sovereignty was already becoming only too obvious.

'We are travelling at this moment with an individual [named] Mr. Houston,' Tocqueville wrote after their vessel was at last off the sand bar.[3] This man was once Governor of Tennesse[e]. Since, he abandoned his wife after making her suffer, so they say, very ill treatment. He took refuge with the Indians, married among them, and has become one of their chiefs.

'I asked what could have recommended him to the choice of the people. His having come from the people, they told me, and risen "by his own exertions." '

One could not help but hear the echo of all those Baltimore and Ohio conversations. And Tocqueville was particularly reminded of an observation that he had made in Memphis the week before.

'When the right of suffrage is *universal*, and when the deputies are paid by the state, it's singular how low and how far wrong the people can go,' he had noted in his diary.[4]

'Two years ago the inhabitants of the district of which Memphis is the capital sent to the House of Representatives in Congress an individual named David Crockett, who has had no education, can read with difficulty, has no property, no fixed residence, but passes his life hunting, selling his game to live, and dwelling continuously in the woods.

'His competitor, a man of wealth and talent, failed.'

Now, here, on their steamboat, was a product of this system of universal suffrage in the flesh. Tocqueville evidently discussed the topic with his fellow passengers. 'Again to-day they assured me that in the new western States the people generally made very poor selections. Full of pride and ignorance, the electors want to be represented by people of their own kind. Moreover, to win their votes one has to descend to manœuvres that disgust distinguished men. You have to haunt the taverns and dispute with the populace: that's what they call *Electioneering* in America.'

Even Chancellor Kent himself had a word to say on the subject, Tocqueville now noted. ' "The fittest men," Kent says candidly, speaking of judges, "would probably have too much reservedness of manner[s] and severity of moral[s], to secure an Election resting on universal suffrage." ' *

\*

\*     \*

So Tocqueville and Beaumont had crossed the trail of the famous 'Davie' Crockett.

It really was extraordinary how little the two Frenchmen missed. Even a hundred years later, in the literature of American history and

---

* Kent, *Commentàries*, Lecture XIV (I,273). Looking into the second volume, Lecture XXIV (II,6), Tocqueville was startled to discover that 'in several Constitutions in the United States, recognition is given the voters' right to force their representatives to vote in a certain way. This principle is combatted by the best minds.'

Tocqueville was appalled at the thought of the direct mass government that such an extension of the democratic philosophy would produce, and without the slightest hesitation he joined the 'best minds' of the United States in denouncing the innovation. 'If it were adopted generally it would be a mortal blow to the representative system, that great discovery of modern times which seems called upon to exercise such a great influence on the destinies of humanity. It would then be the people itself which acted, the deputies becoming no more than passive agents.'

the lore of the Mississippi valley, Crockett would still be remembered: as a symbol—an extravagant type. Celebrated from Washington to the reaches of the frontier for his ignorance, his bad language, his lack of modesty, decorum, and respect for his elders, even in that day of back-woods democracy Crockett was considered a reproach to American politics. Not yet had the revolution broken out in Texas that was to enable this troublemaker to end a dubious career in heroism against the Mexicans at the Alamo. And even in the raw little frontier village of Memphis, the river front population could think him a little crude.

But who was this second *Tribune* of the people, this Mr. Houston, who had once been governor of Tennessee and then gone to live among the Indians? Could Tocqueville and Beaumont have seen into the future, they would have been struck dumb with astonishment. For his first name was Sam.

With their uncanny—sometimes it almost seemed their *providential* —knack of finding the men who among all others were doing, or would accomplish, the most in the America of their generation, the two young travellers had run into none other than the future general and president of the Republic of Texas.

Sam Houston's career in Tennessee had not been glorious. And of his doings among the Indians people said harsh things. 'Squaw man' was one of his nicknames, and sometimes he had been called 'Big Drunk.' But in a year or two he would be accomplishing unheard-of things in Mexico's northern province of Texas. Unabashed by his own past failures, he would lead the American settlers to arms, defeat Santa Anna at the battle of San Jacinto, and then crown his striking military achievements with a statesmanlike leadership that was to make him the unquestioned first citizen of the 'Lone Star' Republic. Eventually he would even lead his State into the Union, and so give the American people their greatest addition of territory since the Louisiana Purchase.

All this, of course, was still in the future. And practically nothing is now known of what Houston was about in the year 1831. Perhaps he had not even thought very much about Texas as yet. But, so far as can be ascertained, the truth is this: In December 1831, Houston was on his way to Washington. He was leaving the Indians and his Indian wife. He was going back into public life.* And Tocqueville and Beaumont

* According to Marquis James, Houston had left the Cherokee country in Arkansas, about 15 December, with a delegation of Cherokee Indians under Black Coat, the second chief. For the journey a venerable Creek chief had given Houston a hand-some buckskin coat with a beaver collar and a hunting knife to adorn the belt. The

had encountered him on the way—had met him, in other words, just at the dawn of one of the greatest careers that nineteenth-century America was to know!

At first they had noticed him as a phenomenon only: a bad example. There, they thought, stood one of the unpleasant consequences of popular sovereignty personified. And for three days no further remark about their fellow passenger found its way into Tocqueville's notes. But such a situation, obviously, was unnatural. With their curiosity, their extraordinary faculty for recognizing quality in a man, Tocqueville and Beaumont could not ignore Sam Houston for ever. On the thirty-first of December, therefore, on the last day before they would reach New Orleans, the inevitable happened. They fell into conversation with this Mr. Houston. And they began to ask him questions on a subject that they thought he would know something about.

'Indians' was the title Tocqueville subsequently gave his diary note.[5]

'Conversation with Mr. Houston,' he began. 'The past history of this man is very extraordinary. After a stormy and restless youth he had finally settled in the State of Tennesse[e]. There his natural abilities and doubtless also his obscure origin had won him the votes of the people and he had been elected governor of the State.

'At that moment trouble broke out in his family. He had reason to complain of his wife; others say that he acted very badly towards her. What's certain is that he left Tennesse[e], crossed the Mississip[p]i and retired among the Creeks * in the district of Arkansas. There he was adopted by one of the chiefs, and is said to have married his daughter. Since then he has been living in the middle of the wilderness, half European and half savage.

---

instructions of the Cherokee delegation, and their petition 'To Andrew Jackson, Great Father,' were in Houston's handwriting, though he himself was not an official member of the band. For 'he had then determined to end his exile and endeavour to reconstruct his life—in Texas if possible.'

Apparently it was on some sudden whim that he took the *Louisville* for New Orleans. On arrival he must immediately have boarded another steamboat to return up-river. For presently he was showing the Cherokee Indians through Nashville and President Jackson's place, The Hermitage. There he cut the famous hickory cane with which, the following April, he assaulted Representative Stanbery for an attack on his integrity in the House. Brought to sensational trial at its bar, he was finally sentenced to be reprimanded by the Speaker; but not before the proceedings had lifted his name from obscurity, and given Houston a national reputation. See M.James, *The Raven*, pp.162ff.

* Probably this should be *Cherokee*, with whom Houston's association was the closest, although he had made himself the friend and counsellor of all the tribes mentioned in the conversation that here follows.

'We encountered him the twenty-seventh of December at the mouth of White River, where we had stopped to set ashore the Chactas. He was riding a superb stallion, which had been caught on the prairies separating Mexico from the United States. These immense wastes are inhabited by innumerable herds of wild horses, a few of which fall into the hands of Spaniards or Indians. Their blood is Andalusian; the horse, as one knows, is not indigenous to America.

'Mr. Houston embarked on our vessel to go to New Orleans. Mr. H. is a man of about 45; the disappointments and labours of all kinds that have accompanied his existence have as yet left only a light trace on his features. His build is athletic; everything in his person indicates physical and moral energy.

'We asked him a great number of questions on the Indians, a few of which follow:

'*Q*. Have the Indians a religion?'

It must have seemed to Houston a rather unusual question. People did not often begin thus about the Indians. But he answered the query soberly and reasonably enough.

'A few do not believe in the immortality of the soul,' he said: 'but in general the Indians believe in the existence of a God who punishes or rewards in the other world the acts of this life.

'*Q*. Have they a cult?

'*A*. The Osages who live on the frontiers of Mexico pray each morning at sunrise. The Creeks have no regular worship; it's only in times of great calamity or when about to undertake some great enterprises that they devote themselves to a public practice of religion.*

'Have you often seen Christian Indians?' Tocqueville and Beaumont wanted to know.

'Seldom,' answered Houston. (Here was a question of policy on which something quite definite could be said): 'My opinion is that to send Missionaries among them is a very poor way to go about civilizing the Indians.†

---

* Obviously the double translation, from Houston's original words into Tocqueville's French and back again, does Houston an injustice. The flavour of his speech is gone. The sense, fortunately, remains unequivocal.
† In his life with the Cherokees, Houston had been stricken with malaria, and the Indian medicine men had nursed him according to their rites. He seemed to have no religious conviction himself, and was not always convinced that the missionaries were doing a good work. Generally, however, he did not allow himself to treat them otherwise than with consideration. For his conduct in this particular, see M. James, *The Raven*, pp. 118–120.

'Christianity is the religion of an enlightened and intellectual people; it's above the intelligence of a people so little advanced in civilization and so enslaved by material instincts only as the Indians. In my opinion one should first of all try to tear the Indians from their wandering life and encourage them to cultivate the earth.

'The introduction of the Christian religion would be the natural consequence of the alteration accomplished in their social state. I've noticed that only Catholicism was able to make a durable impression on the Indians. It strikes their senses and appeals to their imagination.

'*Q.* What kind of government have the Indians you have seen?

'*A.* In general, a patriarchal regime. Chiefs are made by birth. In the tribes enlightened by contact with the Europeans, they are elected.

'*Q.* Have they a [system of] justice?

'*A.* There is an idea deeply rooted in the minds of all Indians and which forms for many tribes their only penal code. It's that blood should be avenged by blood: in a word, the law of retaliation. (When therefore a man is killed, he [the murderer] is assigned to the vengeance of the relatives, to whom he is delivered.)

'*Q.* Does the law of compensation exist in the tribes you have seen?

'*A.* No. The Southern Indians would regard it as infamous to accept money as the price of their brother's life.

'*Q.* These notions of justice you speak of are very crude. They only apply to murder, anyhow. What happens in case of theft?

'*A.* Theft was absolutely unknown among the Indians before the Europeans introduced among them objects calculated to be a lively temptation to their cupidity.

'Since then laws have had to be made to punish stealing. Among the Creeks, who are beginning to civilize themselves and have a written penal code, stealing is punished by whipping. It's the chiefs who pronounce sentence.

'Adultery by the woman is punished in the same way; in addition they usually slit the nose and ears of the guilty. Creek law punishes fornication equally.

'*Q.* What is the position of women among the Indians?

'*A.* Complete servitude. The women are burdened with all the unpleasant jobs and live in great degradation.

'*Q.* Is polygamy allowed?

'*A.* Yes. You can have as many wives as you can feed. Divorce is likewise permitted.

'*Q*. Does it seem to you that the Indians have great natural intelligence?'

The questions about Indian women had been coming dangerously close to home. But here was something that could be answered in more than monosyllables. Apparently Houston entertained the highest regard for the natural intelligence of his life-long friends, the Indians.

'Yes, I don't believe they yield to any human race on this point,' he began.

'However, I am also of the opinion that it would be the same for the negroes; the difference you notice between the Indian and the negro seems to me to result solely from the different educations they have received.

'The Indian is born free; he makes use of that liberty from his very first steps in life. He is his own master as soon as he is capable; the paternal authority is even almost unfelt. Surrounded by dangers, hounded by needs, able to count on nobody, his mind has to be constantly on the alert to find the means of warding off such dangers and of sustaining life. This forced necessity gives the Indian's intelligence a degree of development and a sharpness that are often admirable. The common negro was a slave before being born, without pleasures as without needs, useless to himself [?]. The first notions that he receives from life show him that he is the property of someone else, that the care of his own future is not his concern, and that the very use of thought is for himself essentially a gift of providence.

'*Q*. Is it true that the Mississip[p]i valley shows traces of the passage of a race of men more civilized than those living here to-day?' (Tocqueville and Beaumont had not been a month in the Ohio and Mississippi valleys without hearing of the so-called Mound Builders.)

'*A*. Yes, I have often encountered fortified works giving clear evidence of the existence of a people risen to a pretty high degree of civilization. Where did this people come from? How did they disappear? There's the mystery. But it's impossible to doubt that they did exist; and there's nothing to indicate that the Indians of our days are remnants of them.

'The most likely opinion seems to me that they were Mexicans, come in former days to settle in the Mississip[p]i valley.'

So much for Tocqueville's first line of thought. The institutions, intelligence and past history of the American aborigines had all been touched on. Now the two Frenchmen pressed on to a problem which concerned them much more deeply: the future of this unhappy race.

The pitiful spectacle of the Choctaws at Memphis and on the *Louisville* was still so fresh in their minds.

'Can you give me some information about the conduct of the American government toward the Indian tribes?' Tocqueville asked.

'Yes,' volunteered Mr. Houston, 'very easily. There were, and are still, in the interior of southern United States several half-civilized Indian nations whose position in relation to the rulers of those States is very equivocal and who are slowing up the progress that this part of the Union is capable of. Congress, consequently, as much in the interest of the southern States as in that of the Indians also, has conceived the project of transporting them all with their consent into a country which would for ever remain essentially Indian. It chose the upper part of the district of Arkansas. The territory to be occupied by the Indian nations begins at an imaginary line that you can draw on the map from Louisiana to the Missouri, and stretches all the way to the frontiers of Mexico and to vast prairies inhabited by the hordes of wandering Osages. The United States have sworn, by the most solemn oaths, never to sell the lands contained within these limits, and never to allow the white race to work itself in by any means.*

'10,000 Indians are already to be found in the territory. I think that with time there will be 50,000 of them. The region is healthy and the land extremely fertile.'

Tocqueville and Beaumont must have been considerably surprised. Here, apparently, was a man of some intelligence, who had even lived in sympathy with the Indians; yet he seemed to believe in the good faith and the effectiveness of the government's policy.

'Do you believe that this device will prevent the Indian race from suffering that disappearance by which it seems menaced?' was their half-incredulous question. 'Do you think that this arrangement is not provisional and that the Indians will not soon be forced to retreat?'

'*A.* No, I believe that the Indian nations of the South will find a refuge and civilize themselves there, if the government wishes to take the trouble to encourage civilization among them. Notice that the isolated position in which the Indians will find themselves will permit the taking of effective measures to prevent the introduction of spir-

* 'Note. There is a law forbidding whites to buy lands of Indians. The United States permits the Indians to sell only in their capacity as a people and only when the buyer is the Union itself.'
   Materials from this conversation were later to be used by Tocqueville for his essay on 'The present state and probable future' of the Indian, *Dém. en Am.*, II,297ff.,305–306.

ituous liquors among them. Brandy is the great cause of destruction for the aborigines of America.

'*Q*. But aren't you afraid lest these nations, strangers to each other, make continual war on each other?

'*A*. The United States have a post in their midst to prevent it.

'*Q*. You believe, then, in the possibility of saving the Indians?

'*A*. Yes. Without question, 25 years of skilful handling by the government would certainly produce this result. Several of the southern nations are already half civilized.'

It was no use. Mr. Houston was too definite: they would get no confirmation of their point of view from him. They returned to his thought about the progress of the Indians toward white men's standards.

'What are the degrees of civilization among these peoples?' they asked.

'*A*. At the head of all are the *Cherokees*. The Cherokees live entirely by agriculture. They are the only Indian nation with a written language.

'After the *Cherokees* come the *Creeks*. The Creeks live by a combination of hunting and agriculture. They have positive penal laws and a form of government.

'Next I place the Chickasaw and Choctaw. It can't be said that they have begun to civilize themselves, but they have begun to lose many of the traits of their savage nature.

'The last of all are the Osages. They live in ever-wandering hordes, are almost naked, use fire-arms hardly at all, and are acquainted only with the fur traders among the Europeans.

'The Osages are the furthest tribe in the Southwest having a treaty with the United States.

'*Q*. But that Arkansas reserve we were speaking of just now is meant only for the Southern Indians. What have they decided to do with the Indians of the West and North?' Tocqueville and Beaumont could not forbear one parting shot at the conduct of the American people.

But Houston was not interested. 'The Indians of the West and North don't find themselves surrounded, like those of the South, by white populations,' he observed simply. 'They border the United States and are pushed back as advance is made.'

\*

\*　　\*

*'RETURNS OF THE LOUISIANA PLANTATIONS'*

'To-day, the 31st December, 1831, I visited a fine sugar plantation situated at 50 leagues from New Orleans on the Mississip[p]i. It contains 70 slaves. Its yearly income, I was told, is about five or six thousand dollars, all expenses paid. 25–30,000 francs.'

PART VIII: NEW ORLEANS TO WASHINGTON

# XLVII

## '24 HEURES À LA NOUVELLE ORLÉANS'

'You know, my dear friend,' Tocqueville began the story of his latest adventures very solemnly,* 'You know, my dear friend, that our intention was, on leaving Philadelphia, to go to New Orleans and pass two weeks there but, shipwrecked at Wheeling, stopped by the ice at Louisville, held back ten days in Memphis, we were a hundred times on the point of giving up the trip that we had undertaken. We were going to turn back on our steps when the — † of December (note well the dates, they are precious) a steamboat took us on board and offered to carry us down to Louisiana.

'After all our calculations were made there remained of our two weeks not more than three days to pass in New Orleans. What was there to do, however? We had to submit.

'We set out then: but you see the implacability of fortune. In the night of the 26–27 December, in the most beautiful moonlight that ever lit up the solitary banks of the Mississippi, our boat suddenly touched bottom and, after tottering a while like a drunken man, established herself tranquilly on the bar. To describe our despair at this affair would in truth be a difficult matter: we prayed to the heavens which said not a word, then to the captain who sent us to the pilot. As to the latter, he received us like a potentate. After having blown a cloud of smoke in our faces, he observed peacefully that the sands of the Mississippi were like the French and could not stay a year in the same place. The comparison, you will admit, was insolent enough to be chastised, but he was on his own ground and we were on a ladder; we therefore came down to await the efforts which the crew were going to make to get us out of the desperate condition in which we found our-

---

* Translation of '24 Heures' and 'Suite' by the late Paul Lambert White, who discovered the documents.
† Twenty-fifth.

selves. We stayed there two days. At the end of that time they finally succeeded in tearing us loose from the sand and the first of January 1832, the sun rising in a brilliant tropical sky revealed to us New Orleans across the masts of a thousand ships.

'We disembarked hastily, as you will readily conceive. There was no time to lose: to make the acquaintance of all those to whom we had been recommended, to enjoy the pleasures, so celebrated, of New Orleans, to study the laws, learn the usages, enter into the *mœurs*, to know the statistics and history of the country. Only 24 hours remained to us: I defy you to add a single minute, but don't go and judge us too harshly. Know that 24 hours usefully employed teach many things. I have this maxim from a young attaché of the French embassy with whom I talked the other day. He appeared to speak very pertinently of England. An Englishman present insisted that it was very impertinent but I, who saw that he was cutting into the quick at every stroke and that he had made up his mind about everything in that country, I began to be seized with admiration and I asked him that minute how long he had passed among our neighbours. One week, he replied.* I appeared surprised, I had not then my present experience. Seeing my astonishment he added with that air at the same time mysterious and engaging, deep and light—with a diplomatic air† in a word: one week, when one knows how to observe, is sufficient for many things. There's my excuse. If one week is indeed sufficient for a superior man to have an opinion upon the British Empire and all her colonies, it is clear that a man of an inferior capacity can still hope to learn something of New Orleans in 24 hours.

'Besides, we had no choice. After we had laid out our best clothes, therefore, we tried to introduce into our dress as much as possible a happy mixture of the Philosopher and the man of the world. We were under the necessity, without being able to return to our quarters during the whole course of a long day, of being alternately very deep and very amiable. We put on a black tie for the members of the legislature, a white vest (*gilet*) for the women, we took in our hand a little swagger stick to raise us into intimacy with the fashionable world, and, very

---

* Marginal note: '*Monsieur a sans doute habité longtemps chez nos voisins? il me t—et répondit: huit jours.*'
† Marginal note: '*qui distinguent tous les hommes d'une grande capacité et tous les-diplomats.*' Tocqueville must have been thinking of some of his acquaintances in high politics at home, possibly even of his lordly cousin Chateaubriand, though the allusion is not clear.

contented with ourselves, we descended the stairs. There the difficulty of putting order into our activities presented itself for the first time to our mind:

'We established ourselves on a kerbstone as a deliberating assembly and after a discussion which lasted an hour we adopted the following plan. We made an infinite number of classifications. We created principles of observation, then we made deductions from our principles, then deductions from our deductions; we discussed, classified, and unclassified for an hour and noon was smiling upon us when we finally adopted the following plan: You see that I possess indeed the style of *procès-verbal*:

'We resolved to consecrate two hours to an examination of the city, to knowing the external appearance, to seeing the character of its population, to studying the most apparent aspects of its morals and its customs.

'A short visit to our consul would bring us to three o'clock. There would then remain for us four hours of daylight during which we would visit all the celebrated men, legislators, publicists, lawyers, poets, and orators of New Orleans. Between these calls we would insert visits to the most beautiful women solely for the purpose of resting ourselves, I swear.

'At 7 o'clock we would go to the play. After the play would come the *bal*. At midnight we would go back to our lodgings to organize our notes. Has this plan your approbation? It received ours and we set out.

'*Coup d'œil de la Nouvelle Orléans . . .*'

*

*     *

The 'blow of an eye' at New Orleans Tocqueville never described. Apparently he was interrupted at this point in his writing and, when next he had an opportunity, resumed with a later part of their 24 hours. In the end he never returned to the middle portion of his sketch. It is wanting entirely.

What he and Beaumont saw, therefore, and particularly what they thought during the course of their hasty midday promenade through the streets of New Orleans, can only be surmised from two documents of an entirely different nature. The first is a sort of stenographic note on their whole day, evidently taken to recall the chief sights and their personal impressions: the second a comment buried in their prison notes.

'Fine houses, huts; streets muddy and unpaved. Spanish architecture, flat English roofs. Bricks, small French doorways, massive *portes-cochères*,' Tocqueville was to jot down at the end of a diary.[1]

'Population similarly mixed, faces of all shades of colour. Language French, English, Spanish, creole. General appearance French; and yet signs, commercial posters usually in English. Industrial and trading world, American. . . .'

That was all. Except that in their penitentiary report Tocqueville and Beaumont would one day write:[2]

'We would be unable to paint the dolorous impression that we received when, on examining the prison of New Orleans, we saw there men thrown in pell-mell with swine, in the midst of excrement and filth. In locking up criminals, no thought is given to making them better but simply to taming their wickedness; they are chained like wild beasts; they are not refined but brutalized.'

And in a footnote the two commissioners would insist: 'The place containing condemned criminals in New Orleans could not by any stretch of the imagination be called a prison: it's a frightful cesspool into which they are dumped and which is suitable only for those unclean animals one finds there with them. It is noteworthy that all those detained there are not slaves: it's the prison of free men. . . .' *

* * *

'The course of our observations,' Tocqueville resumed his interrupted narrative, 'had led us to the door of our consul whose name I am able to say: M. Guillemain.† We knocked. The negro who opened the door seemed completely surprised that we should wish to visit his

---

* Tocqueville and Beaumont must have talked to Governor André Bienvenu Roman about the situation, for their footnote concludes: 'It appears, however, that the necessity of reform in the prison regime is felt in Louisiana. The Governor of this state told us that he would immediately ask the legislature for a grant of funds for this purpose.' And next day, 2 January, the Governor's message to the legislature was in fact largely devoted to the subject—though without mentioning Tocqueville and Beaumont. It is interesting to note that the legislature acceded, and within the year authorized the construction of the penitentiary subsequently built at Baton Rouge.

† In his reports to his home government (*Ministère des Affaires Étrangères*), the consul signed himself: 'Guillemin.' After being identified for a short time with the consular service at Savannah and Baltimore, M. Guillemin had come to New Orleans, 23 Sept. 1816, on *ad interim* appointment.

master but what importance is it what goes on in a negro's head? We went in. M. Guillemain appeared in his turn surprised to see us enter his office, but he got possession of himself immediately and received us in the most polite manner. He wished first to speak with us about France, about our friends, our relatives—*C'était bien de cela en vérité qu'il s'agissait*: he believed that we had come to make a visit and that informal inquiries were in order. We, therefore, turned the conversation as decently as we could and by an adroit and well-managed circuit we led him back to N.O. Finally he began to speak of it and to speak very directly. He made us feel how important it was to France for French *mœurs*, customs, and habits to continue their sway in Louisiana. This has happened up to the present, he added, to such an extent that the other day the people, learning what had happened in the Church of St. Germain l'Auxerrois in Paris, remembered that a *curé* of the city had refused to bury a man who had committed suicide, and they ran to break his windows.* The consul then spoke to us of the prosperous state in which Louisiana found herself. In the 15 years I have been here, he said, the prosperity of this region has increased an hundred fold. I have seen the *quartiers* rear themselves in the midst of infested swamps, palaces replace cabins, the city increase in population in spite of the yellow fever. The same impulse is imprinted upon all the districts of the state. All are prospering, all are growing visibly, the future of Louisiana is wonderful. Ten states, in which will soon be found the strength and population of the Union, have as their only outlet the Mississip[p]i, and we hold the key to it. N.O. is the natural *entrepôt*.

'Thus spake M. Guillemain, and we kept very quiet, the reason being that we were occupied in registering in our mind every one of his words. M. Guillemain, moreover, had one of those egotistical intelligences which speaks but does not converse and which finds pleasure in the sight of its own thoughts.

'Meanwhile, the hour was passing, the time of the inquest was about over. I thought that we should in departing leave one of those outstanding and deep thoughts which remain in the mind of the listener and show him that every man who keeps quiet is not necessarily a fool.

* Cahier non-alphabétique III, under date of 1 January 1832, gives a detailed account of this conversation, with a friendly comment on the consul. 'M. Guillemain is certainly a man of *esprit* and, I believe, of means. The whole by exception, for incapacity seems to be the common right among French agents abroad.'

'I slid in, then, cleverly between two of his ideas and I said: the extreme prosperity of this region, of which you more than any one else have been the witness, Monsieur, commenced with the union of Louisiana with the United States. Such a coincidence tells more than all the theories in favour of republican institutions. Imagine my surprise when Mr. Guillemain, interrupting me, cried: ah Monsieur, one must live 15 years as I have done in the bosom of a small democratic republic such as this one to lose such ideas. Do you wish to have an idea of the public administration? Examine the streets of the city, what holes, what lack of order and alignment: the city, however, has more than a million of revenue. But into what hands it passes, God only knows. Do you want to have a clear-cut opinion about the wisdom of the deliberating bodies? Read the names of those who compose them, obscure people, lawyers of the third order, village intriguers. One would [be tempted to] say that [there is] a law preventing the choice of people of merit and talent. Nothing simpler. It is the lower classes of people who have the majority in the electoral colleges. They choose from their own kind. Open the acts of the sessions. It is a veritable Penelope's web. To make, unmake, remake, is the work of our legislators. The spirit not of party but of coterie absolutely directs the state. They suppress a position to ruin a man or create another to give a living to an honest friend persecuted by fortune. These, gentlemen, are the republican institutions which have made and still create every day the prosperity of Louisiana.* But I am mistaken, this government has one merit that one must not deny it. Without force as it is without skill (*habilité*); without plans as it is without energy, incapable of harm as it is incapable of good, powerless and passive, it lets society go its way (*marcher toute seule*) without trying to direct it. Well, in the present state of affairs America, in order to prosper, does not need either able leadership or deep-laid plans or great efforts, but liberty and still more liberty. The reason for that is that no one yet has any interest in abusing that liberty.

'I pray you to believe, my dear friend, that this tirade against republics had not in the least downed me, and I was going to reply

* Cahier non-alphabétique III: [M. Guillemin:] '. . . The destinies of New Orleans are immense. If they can conquer, or just reduce a good deal, the yellow fever scourge, New Orleans is certainly called to become the most vast city of the New World. In fifty years the mass of the American population will have moved into the valley of the Mississip[p]i, and we hold the gate of the river. . . .'

vigorously; but at the moment that I opened my mouth the clock struck four.

'We hastened to take our hats and we set out congratulating ourselves that France had not yet lost the right to be represented abroad by persons worthy of her.'

*

* *

### 'SUITE DE LA NELLE ORLÉANS'

'We had, if I am not mistaken, 71 letters * for New Orleans. It was a difficult task only to put in order this formidable correspondence and classify each letter according to the merit of the person to whom it was addressed. But we are, as you know, of the number of those who think that, no matter how hurried one is, one cannot sacrifice too much time in favour of logic. Order finally established, we directed ourselves toward the house of a M. Mazureau † who had been pointed out to us as the eagle of the New Orleans bar; furthermore as speaking French, an advantage which we had learned to appreciate in our travels. We had much trouble and lost much precious time in finding his home. The houses of N.O. have no numbers or the numbers do not run in sequence at all. Number 2 precedes 1, and 30 follows 70. It is an arithmetic peculiar to the corporation of N.O. with which we were not yet acquainted. This, *du reste*, ended by giving us a real consideration for our consul. How indeed can one imagine a good government in a city where strangers cannot find the way!

'We arrived at last: the negro who opened the door for us, and of whom we made our request to see M. Mazureau, at first regarded us fixedly without having the air of understanding us. He said to us finally: how, Massa, to-day?—"And Yes without doubt Butor [Butler?], why not?"

'There was some energy in our reply but of argument not a word. The slave, however, had the air of recognizing himself vanquished

---

* More probably: '21' (as in Cahier Portatif IV).

† Etienne Mazureau (1777–1849), after a childhood and revolutionary boyhood in France, had come to America on the seizure of power by Napoleon. Landing in New York, he had stayed for fifteen months in New Jersey, and then, March 1804, made his way to New Orleans. Established there in the law, his knowledge of French and Spanish had proven invaluable, he had become the partner of Edward Livingston, and was now known for his encyclopædic learning, and a legal income equalled only by his generosity and extravagance. Of a short and stout physique, his head appeared 'much too large for his body.'

and, bowing his head with a submissive air, he opened the door of the salon.

'The eagle of the N.O. bar, wrapped in the folds of a flowered dressing gown and seated tranquilly in the corner of what is called a French fireplace in Louisiana and an antique fireplace in France, was receiving at that very moment the homage of his assembled posterity.

'We saw there children, grandchildren, nephews, great-nephews, first cousins, distant cousins: * the family picture was complete. Joy seemed to shine in all the faces. Union reigned in all hearts. One is such good friends the day of New Year's gifts. I do not want to add a thing to this painting for fear of moving you too much. Know at least that at this sight there is not an 18th century Philosopher who would not have wept with sensibility and tenderness.

'As for us, we remained as though struck with stupor at this spectacle: a ray of light finally managed to penetrate our intelligence. We understood now the embarrassment of the consul, the astonishment of the negroes, of the good negroes we had treated as Butors. To set out with a letter of introduction on New Year's day! What a monstrous incongruity! Alas! Where is the happy time when I would rather have forgotten my name than the arrival of the first of January? At the sight of the two unwelcome visitors M. Mazureau rose brusquely and advanced toward the door enveloping in the folds of his dressing gown two small children who, lost in the midst of this obscure labyrinth, let out sharp cries. We on our part were hastening to go towards him, but our precipitation was fatal to several playthings which we crushed pitilessly in our course. We at last met our host in the middle of the salon and there we reciprocally assured each other of all the pleasure we had in meeting.'

*

*    *

At this delicate juncture, Tocqueville's sketch of their 24 hours in New Orleans broke off entirely. Certain diary notes, however, supplied the story for the rest of the day.

There was no headlong flight, to begin with, nor even apparently any attempt at a graceful retreat. Instead the determined young intruders showed signs of wishing to talk—and the eagle of the New Orleans bar suddenly found himself allowing his New Year's afternoon to be interrupted by quite a serious interrogation.

* '. . . bonbons, sweets and toys . . .' Cahier portatif IV.

'Before passing under American rule, did you possess some of the forms of a free government?' was the first question he was asked.[3]

The answer seemed simple. 'No,' said M. Mazureau.

'*Q*. Was the passage from complete subjection to entire liberty hard?'

Again the reply had to be in the negative. 'No,' he said, 'Congress was careful to conduct us by degrees to independence. At first it governed us in almost as absolute a way as our former governors. Then it gave us the government of a territory. Finally it put us into the Union as an independent state. We are doing as well in that role as the other provinces of the Union, even though the majority is still in the hands of the creoles. In my opinion, even, Congress could have dispensed with giving us an apprenticeship. A small state, placed as we were, is always capable of governing itself. Almost none of the evil consequences of popular sovereignty is to be feared in small societies.'

Tocqueville passed rapidly to another subject.

'*Q*. Do you believe that it would be possible in Louisiana for the whites to cultivate the land without slaves?

'*A*. I don't think so. Yet I was born in Europe; I came here with the ideas that you appear to have on this point; but experience has seemed to me to belie the theory. I don't believe the Europeans can work in the fields exposed to the tropical sun that we have. Our sunshine is always unhealthy, often mortal. It's not that I believe the impossibility of working complete. But the white, to avoid death, is obliged to labour in a fashion so restrained that he can scarcely gain his livelihood. We have an example of this in Arkansas. Some time ago Spain transported to this part of Louisiana some peasants from the Azores, who settled and remained there without slaves. These men farm the land, but so little, that they are the most miserable men of Louisiana.

'*Q*. But couldn't their poverty be attributed to want of industry rather than to climate?' Tocqueville was obviously reluctant to have one of his Tennessee theories so lightly upset. But M. Mazureau was adamant.

'In my opinion, the climate is the capital cause,' he answered.

Again Tocqueville vaulted swiftly to another topic.

'They say that in New Orleans is to be found a mixture of all the nations?'

'*A*. That's true; you see here a mingling of all races. Not a country in America or Europe but has sent us some representatives. New Orleans is a patch-work of peoples.

'*Q*. But in the midst of this confusion what race dominates and gives direction to all the rest?

'*A*. The French race, up to now. It's they who set the tone and shape the *mœurs*.' That was exactly what consul Guillemin had said, and Tocqueville was reminded of another item in their earlier conversation.

'*Q*. Is it true that yellow fever is as much of a scourge here as supposed?

'*A*. I think they exaggerate the evil. My experience has taught me that of ten foreigners who live wisely and allow themselves no excesses of any sort, but two die. I am speaking of people who do not have to work with their hands in order to live. Of the same number belonging to the working classes and passing the day in the open air, perhaps seven or eight succumb. Besides, you know that the yellow fever is confined to New Orleans. Two miles above or below, no one ever has it.

'*Q*. What is the lot of negroes in Louisiana?

'*A*. Mild enough. Harshness toward negroes is exceptional. The condition of negroes has altered singularly in the last twenty years. Before, they lived in miserable huts which did not, so to speak, protect them from the weather at all; their clothing consisted of a blanket, and for nourishment they were given a barrel of corn a month (about two bushels). Now they are in general sufficiently fed, completely clothed, and healthily lodged.

'*Q*. Does the law protect their life?

'*A*. Yes, I recall when I was Attorney General having a master condemned to death because he had killed his slave.'

\*

\*   \*

'Evening at the theatre. . . .' Tocqueville's skeleton notes for the day wound up.[4] 'Strange spectacle offered by the chamber. First stalls (*loge*) white, second grey, coloured women, very pretty, white ones among them, but a remainder of African blood. Third stalls black. Audience, we think ourselves in France, noisy, uproarious, turbulent, talkative, a thousand leagues away from the United States. We leave at ten. Quadroon ball. Strange sight: all the men white, all the women coloured, or at least of African blood. Single tie created by immorality between the two races. A sort of bazaar. The women vowed as it were by law to concubinage. Incredible laxity of morals. Mothers, young girls, children at the dance; still another harmful consequence of slavery.* Multitude of coloured people at New Orleans. Small number in the North. Why? Why, of all the European races, is the English race the one that has best preserved its purity of blood and mingled least with the natives?'

In the excitement of this intellectual puzzle, Tocqueville had begun to put in his verbs again, and was actually writing in complete sentences. And he thought he had a grasp on the answer. 'Besides the powerful reasons arising in national character,' he argued, 'there exists one particular cause of difference. Spanish America was peopled by adventurers drawn by the thirst for gold, who, planted alone on the other side of the Atlantic, found themselves in some sort forced to contract unions with the women of the country they lived in. The English colonies were settled by men fleeing their country for reasons of religious passion or whose object in coming to live in the new world was to cultivate the land. They came with women and children and were able to form a complete society on the spot.'

*

*    *

THE SECOND AND THIRD DAYS

Their '24 heures' were over. When a man knew how to observe, Tocqueville had been told, even the shortest time was sufficient to teach him many things.

But, after all! When they had spent two days on a sandbar in the Mississippi and a whole week in the deserted little village of Memphis! It was too much to ask. They had caught glimpses of too many shadows in Louisiana life. They had begun to sense fascinating aspects that even their vigilant curiosity had not divined. Naturally no single day, however industriously spent, could possibly satisfy them.

So Tocqueville and Beaumont changed their plans once more, and stayed, finally, not one day but three.

---

* Once again Tocqueville and Beaumont may be observed in the act of testing the hearsay evidence of a drawing-room conversation against the witness of their own eyes; and once again the fact coincided with the prediction. In this instance, it was ex-Senator James Brown, in Philadelphia, who had told them what the New Orleans balls were like.

One gathers that they saw the consul of France again, for further elucidation, in their own tongue, of the mysteries of Louisiana culture. Was there no bitterness arising out of the rivalries of the French population and the newly-arriving Americans from the North, for instance?

'They criticize each other mutually,' Guillemin admitted,[5] 'they see very little of each other, but at bottom there is no veritable enmity. The French are not, as in Canada, a vanquished people. On the contrary, they live on the footing of the most real and complete equality. Marriages are constantly being contracted between them and the Americans; finally the country is enjoying an immense prosperity, a prosperity that increases daily. . . .' *

Again Tocqueville mentioned a remark that he had heard. 'I am told that religion has little hold over souls here?' He could hardly have chosen a topic more in the line of the consul's special knowledge, for only a month or so before Guillemin had drawn up for his home government a long report on church affairs.†

'Religion hasn't much hold,' he answered, 'but I think that results partly from the bad priests sent us from Europe. We are inundated by Italians who have nothing in common with the population and whose morals are detestable. However, there is no political animosity of any kind against the ministers of the Catholic church, who on their part never concern themselves with [other] affairs. . . .'

On another occasion the acute M. Guillemin had remarked that he had 'never been able to understand how one could draw general deductions from American institutions, the position of America is so special.' But now, in the matter of Church and State, he seemed to think an exception might be made.

'. . . From what I see here and in the other American states,' he said with emphasis, 'I am profoundly convinced that in the interests of Religion one should make an absolute separation between the clergy and the state, and abandon Religion to the influence that it can generate for itself. . . .' ‡

Once again M. Guillemin was announcing an opinion of which

---

* 'I read to-day that in the course of the year 1828 there entered the port of New Orleans more than 1000 sailing vessels and 770 steamboats. The number increases each year.' Cahier portatif III.

† In the *Ministère des Affaires Étrangères* there still exists a long report on the state of the Catholic church in Louisiana, signed by Guillemin, and dated: 3 Sept. 1831.

‡ '*Q*. How are the priests paid in Louisiana? *A*. The State contributes nothing. But the *communes* generally have some lands set aside for this purpose; in addition there are the fees, the voluntary gifts, the pew rents. . . .'

Tocqueville had already been persuaded. The young investigator passed on, therefore, to an institution that had considerably exercised his indignation at the quadroon ball.

'They say that morals, particularly in the coloured population, are very bad?' he ventured.

'There exists, as a matter of fact, a great deal of immorality among the coloured people. But how could it be otherwise?' said M. Guillemin. 'The law destines, as it were, coloured women to debauchery. You've no doubt noticed, in the place reserved for mulattoes in the theatre and elsewhere, women as white as the most beautiful Europeans. *Eh bien*! For all that they belong to the proscribed race, because tradition makes it known that there is African blood in their veins. Yet these women, and many others who, without being as white, possess yet almost the tint and the graces of Europeans and have often received an excellent education, are forbidden by law to marry into the ruling and rich race of whites. If they wish to contract a legitimate union, they have to marry with the men of their caste, and partake their humiliation. For the men of colour don't even enjoy the shameful privilege accorded their women. Even did neither their colour nor education betray them, and that's often the case, they would not be the less condemned to perpetual indignities. Not a [illegible] white but has the right to maltreat the unhappy person in his way and to thrust him into the muck crying: "Get out of the way, mulatto!" At the head of legal documents the law makes him write: *homme de couleur*. Free, they can hope for nothing. Yet among them I know men of virtue and of means. It's in isolating itself thus obstinately from all the rest that the aristocracy of the whites (like all aristocracies in general) exposes itself to danger on the American continent and to almost certain destruction in the Antilles. If, without giving the negro rights, it had at least taken in those of the coloured men whose birth and education most nearly approximated its own, the latter would infallibly have been attached to its cause, for they are in reality much closer to the whites than to the blacks. Only brute force would have remained for the negroes. By repelling the mulattoes, however, the white aristocracy gives the slaves, on the contrary, the only weapon they need to become free: intelligence and leadership.

The whole problem fascinated and repelled the French visitors. What to do with the negro? They could see no satisfactory solution. Yet with some justice they now felt that they were at least fairly well acquainted with the subject and could talk with an air of authority about its inescapable features.

'When you meet people who tell you that climate has no influence on the character of peoples,' Tocqueville was soon writing to Chabrol,[6] 'assure them that they are mistaken. We have seen the French of Canada: they are a tranquil, moral, religious people. We are leaving in Louisiana other Frenchmen: restless, dissolute, lax in all things. Between them are fifteen degrees of latitude, which are truly the best reason that can be given for the difference.'

'What morals, my dear friend, are those of a region of the South into which slavery has been brought! The tableau confounds the imagination.'

\*

\* \*

On the second of January Tocqueville and Beaumont had a conversation with a lawyer (whose name they soon forgot). It revolved about the subject of the jury in civil cases. Their informant described the efforts that had been made by the Americans to introduce the system into Louisiana law, and the conflicts with French law that had resulted. Not yet had [trial by] jury entered into popular usage, apparently. People disliked being jurors. Lawsuits were held up, as a consequence. Cases were badly judged. In short, the jury system was not a great success in Louisiana. At least so they were told.[7]

But Tocqueville was not to be argued so lightly out of what had come to be one of his firmest political convictions. After a day's reflection he had the following comment to make in his diary:

'When an entire population proclaims an institution good; when all parties recognize its usefulness, and that not in one time or place but over a long series of centuries and in all parts of the world whither the fragments of this people go, and whatever the political laws they adopt; [when that happens] it is hard to admit that this institution can be vicious. That's what has happened in regard to the use of the jury for civil trials.'

Here, definitely, was a case where Tocqueville was ready to label his informant (and the majority of Louisianans) mistaken. But with the opinion of another lawyer, 'a very celebrated lawyer of New Orleans,' whom they had seen their first afternoon and whose name Tocqueville had likewise forgotten, they were thoroughly prepared to agree.

The eminent attorney had been elaborating. M. Guillemin's remarks about the legislature. 'When the legislature is in session, it can be said that the whole body of legislation is jeopardized,' he had affirmed.[8] 'Our houses are composed in large part of young lawyers, ignorant and fond of intrigue. (Every one here thinks he can be a member of the legislature.) They make, unmake, slice and cut up at random. Here's an instance: Since the cession to Spain, many points in our civil law have been regulated according to Spanish law. At the end of 1828, at the end of the session, a bill was passed unperceived which abrogated all the [these?] laws, in a body, without putting anything in their place. The next day, on waking up, the bar and bench learned with stupefaction the performance of the day before. But the deed had been done.

'*Q.* But why don't noteworthy men reach the legislature?

'*A.* I doubt whether the people would name them. Besides, little store is set by public office and the outstanding men don't solicit it. (This is at the same time what makes the state operate so badly and what prevents revolutions.)'

And Tocqueville had been reminded of 'another example of the same kind given by the consul. Three years ago the legislature, the last day of the session, passed, in such a way that it was not noticed and in an act having nothing to do with this object, a law decreeing that henceforth the tenth part of the goods belonging to foreigners dying in Louisiana should belong to the State. It was nothing less than the right of escheat. I made representations, said the consul; many of the members seemed to me themselves surprised at what they had done. The act was repealed the following session.'

Apparently it would be possible to go on with such instances *ad infinitum*. There was, fairness forced the young Frenchman to note, one counterbalancing bit of evidence: 'The present governor of Louisiana is a man of talent and character. The two senators from Louisiana, Mr. Johnson and Edward Livingston, are two of the leading men of the Union. Yet they are elected.' *

* André Bienvenu Roman (1795–1866), Governor 1831–1835 and 1839–1849 (the four year interval being required by law), had in earlier days often been Speaker of the lower house of the Louisiana Legislature, and would later be remembered as one of the State's ablest governors. Senator Josiah Stoddard Johnston (1784–1833), of Connecticut origins and a half-brother to (General) Albert Sidney Johnston, had made a reputation in both Kentucky and Louisiana, representing the latter in the Senate from the resignation of James Brown in 1823 until he was killed in a steamboat accident ten years later. In 1831 he had been re-elected by a legislature opposed to

The rule was not invariable, then. Yet clearly some tentative conclusions might already be stated. Tocqueville's first decision was interesting.

'Effect of elections, direct and indirect, in America,' he jotted in his diary the last day:[9] '[the latter] good; [the former] bad. . . .' In other words, Senators who were chosen by legislatures might prove able men. But the legislators themselves, being chosen directly by the people, were likely to be worse than mediocre.

Tocqueville's second decision was this: 'The bad choices in small republics result in part from the fact that distinguished men do not solicit the honours or enter politics. This inconvenience appears to me more than compensated by the absence of a great irritant or of revolutions born of ambition for power.' In two sentences, suddenly, he had summed up the lessons of a whole month: from the teaching of Timothy Walker of Cincinnati to the opinion of the celebrated lawyer of New Orleans. And now he came to his third conclusion, which turned out to be merely a rephrasing of something Consul Guillemin had said. As Tocqueville put it:

'The greatest merit of American government is to be *powerless* and *passive*. In the present state of things America needs, in order to prosper, neither skilful leadership nor profound plans, nor great efforts, but liberty and still more liberty. What a point of comparison between such a state of affairs and our own!'

---

him in political opinion. As to the abilities of Edward Livingston, who had resigned his Senate seat to become Jackson's Secretary of State the preceding November, no testimony is necessary. His successor, George Augustus Waggamann (1782–1843), seems to have been less distinguished.

## XLVIII

# FROM MOBILE TO THE CHESAPEAKE

THE next letters that Tocqueville and Beaumont found time to write home were dated the sixteenth of January, either at Norfolk, Virginia, or on the steamboat which they boarded the same day for the voyage up the Chesapeake to Washington. In twelve days they had crossed the whole South and were now on the threshold of their last objective: the Federal capital and the halls of Congress.

Originally, such had not been their intention. The dark belt, the cotton kingdom: there was a region worth studying. What might not the cities and the plantations of the old South tell them about slavery? the wild, uncleared fastnesses of the Creeks and Cherokees about the most nearly civilized of the aborigines in their last stand against the grasping whites? Tocqueville had even made a mileage chart,[1] showing that they would go from New Orleans to Mobile, from Mobile to Berkeley (13 miles), from Berkeley to Montgomery, the capital of Alabama (180 miles), from Montgomery to Fort Mitchell on the frontier (90 miles), thence to Mil[l]edgeville in Georgia (150), to Augusta (95), and finally Charleston in the State of South Carolina (another 150).

Charleston—old, half French, and thoroughly Southern—had been their particular objective. After that they had thought of visiting the venerable James Madison at his estate of Montpelier, before going on to Washington. Joseph Coolidge Jr. of Boston had given them a letter of introduction to the Father of the Constitution and co-author of the famous *Federalist.*

But just the prolongation of their stay at New Orleans had stolen two days. Then the overland journey by stage over the winter roads had brought them a recurrence of the same bad luck that had been dogging their footsteps ever since Philadelphia. At Mobile, for example, they had found the stage too crowded to take them. Momentarily the situation had been saved when two most courteous fellow passengers insisted on giving up their own places so that the French visitors might continue. But after that the elements had intervened, and delay had followed vexatious delay.

'I have just,' wrote Tocqueville from the Chesapeake,[2] 'I have just made a fascinating but very fatiguing journey, accompanied each day by the thousand annoyances that have been pursuing us for the last two months: carriages broken and overturned, bridges carried away, rivers swollen, no room in the stage; there are the ordinary events of our life. The fact is that to traverse the immense stretch of country that we have just covered, and to do it in so little time and in winter, was hardly practicable. But we were right because we succeeded: there's the moral of the story.'

They had had to give up Charleston, however; the visit to ex-President Madison also, as a matter of course. And even so they had had no time for letters and hardly any for their notebooks. As a result, they kept no record at all of their itinerary. They were at Mobile 4 January, reached Montgomery 6 January, passed through Knoxville [Georgia] 8 January, and stopped somewhere for quite a number of hours on 12 January. A chance note indicated, as well, that their road perhaps took them through Fayetteville, on their way to Norfolk.* But that was all.

'We have just completed a very long, most interesting, and very tiring journey,' was the abbreviated report Tocqueville sent his sister-in-law on the sixteenth.[3] 'After staying a little longer than we had planned at New Orleans, by which we could not have been better pleased, we realized that we had very little time left to get to Washington. All things considered, we then determined to abandon our plan of going to Charleston: we could have spent there only a very few days and almost all the distinguished men we wanted to see there are now absent at Congress, where we will catch them.

'We therefore left Charleston on our right and, passing successively across the States of Mississip[p]i, Alabama, Georgia, and the two

---

* The strong probability is that they followed a stage-coach route from Montgomery to Fort Mitchell, to Knoxville, to Macon, to Milledgeville, to Augusta, to Columbia, to Fayetteville, to Norfolk. Just east of Montgomery they must have passed through Creek country.

For this difficult journey, Tocqueville manufactured his fourth and fifth small pocket diaries (Cahiers portatifs IV & V), and kept his notes in pencil. These fugitive entries are very hard to decipher to-day.

Carolinas, we finally reached Norfolk yesterday. This morning we took a boat on the Chesapeak[e] to reach Washington, where we will arrive to-morrow and stay three weeks. But two days are needed to reach New-York from there.

'The journey from New Orleans to Norfolk was, as I said before, very interesting but very tough, several sections that we crossed being savage still.

'Yet, and here's the odd thing about it, for five or six years I have not been as well as during the two months just elapsed. I am, at the moment, the strength of the expedition; but I am expecting Beaumont to resume his advantage when we get back to France.*

'If ever I write a book of medicine, I undertake that it will not resemble those published every day. I shall argue and prove that in order to be well one must first dine on corn and pig, eat little, much, not at all, as opportunity offers; bed on the floor and sleep with one's clothes on; pass in a week from ice to heat and from heat to ice; put one's shoulder to the wheel or wake up in a ditch; above all not *think*, that's the main point; bury oneself in nature as much as possible; resemble, if one can, an oyster. I think it was Rousseau who said that the man who thought was a man depraved. In his place I should have said that the man who thinks is an animal who does not digest. Let's not think, then, dear sister, trust me; or if we have to, let it be only about our dinner (future, of course).

'I leave you to reflect on my last phrase, which is very profound, and I abandon you to put myself to bed. . . .'

*

*    *

To act and not to think! To travel in thoughtless and laborious stages toward a good digestion! There, no doubt, was a way of life meriting true devotion. But Tocqueville exaggerated his own constancy in the newly-discovered faith. Travel for twelve days without asking a question? With the furnace of his thoughts banked and slumbering within

---

* 'Here I am at the end of all my great American journeys and, *dieu merci*, I am as
well as when I set out,' Beaumont wrote his father from Norfolk, 16 January (BBlb).
   '. . . Our plan was to stop at Charleston, but on the way toward that city we
were held back en route by several accidents like overturned bridges, impassable roads
and smashed carriages, so that our advance was slowed down, and we calculated that
if we delayed any longer in getting to Washington we wouldn't reach it soon enough
to listen to the interesting discussions just now taking place in Congress. . . .'

him? The thing was not possible; even Tocqueville's own diaries betray the lapses of their master.

There had been the incident of the three races, for instance, almost at the beginning of their journey. 'Near Montgomery in the State of Alabama I witnessed a little scene that made me reflect,' Tocqueville artlessly contradicted himself: 'Near the house of a planter was a charming little white girl (his daughter) whom a young Indian girl was holding in her arms and showering with the most maternal caresses. By her side was a negress amusing the child. The latter, in its slightest gestures, showed a consciousness of the superiority which, according to its youthful experience, already raised it above the two companions, whose caresses and attentions it received with a sort of feudal condescension. Squatting before it, and spying out its slightest movements, the negress seemed curiously divided between the attachment, and the respectful fear, that her young mistress inspired. While even in the effusion and tenderness of the Indian girl there was visible something free, something a little savage, contrasting strangely with the submissive posture and humble gestures of her companion. Something I couldn't see having attracted her attention in the woods, she got up brusquely, pushed the child aside with some roughness, and plunged into the foliage.' It would not be wide of the mark to imagine the observer of the scene suddenly plunged into thought.

Again, there had been the mulatto question, the terrible problem of miscegenation. If Tocqueville and Beaumont had planned to ignore the sex relations between whites and blacks, they could not possibly, after their interview with the dying slaveholder. Years later Tocqueville would recall the incident in his book.

'I encountered in the Southern part of the Union an old man who formerly had lived in illegitimate commerce with one of his negresses,' Tocqueville was to point out to his readers in France. 'He had had by her several children who, on coming into the world, had become the slaves of their father. Several times the latter had thought of at least bequeathing them their liberty, but years had slipped by before he could clear the obstacles placed by the legislators in the way of manumission. During this time old age had come, and he was going to die. He pictured to himself, then, his sons dragged from market to market, and passing from paternal authority under the rod of a stranger. These horrible images threw his expiring imagination into delirium. I saw him the prey of the anguish of despair, and I understood then how nature could avenge the wounds given it by laws. . . .'*

Beaumont's whole future book was to be, in one sense, only a development of this last thought. In fact, despite the absence of specific notes in his own hand, it is safe to assert that the negroes of the South, their appearance, occupations, social status, legal position, and general misfortunes, must have been the object of his devoted and constant attention throughout the twelve days of their journey. For to Beaumont slavery had already become the grand preoccupation.† Tocqueville, however, almost from the beginning, had other interests plucking at his sleeve. He encountered, for instance—he could not very well help it—some fellow travellers. And companions led to conversation, conversation to questions, questions to notes. In Montgomery it was that he first got out his new pocket diary.

'Conversation with a lawyer of Montgomery (Alabama), 6 January 1832,' Tocqueville wrote.⁴ 'I've travelled two days with this young man. I've forgotten his name, which is an obscure one, anyhow. Yet I think I should make a record of his conversation. It is stamped with great practical common sense. What he says, furthermore, has been corroborated by a number of subsequent inquiries.

'Daily there is spreading more widely among us, said he, the erroneous opinion that the people (*peuple*) can do everything and can govern almost directly. Thence an unbelievable weakening of everything which might resemble executive power; there's the outstanding characteristic, and the capital defect, of our constitution, as it is that of the constitutions of all the new States of the southwest of the Union. The consequences of this are great. For instance, they didn't want to

---

* Tocqueville used both of these experiences to illustrate his discussion of the future of the three races in North America (*Dém. en Am.*, II,276–279,354–355). In the case of the Indian girl, the negress, and the white child, Tocqueville recalled that the spot was not far from Creek territory. Not wishing to disturb a pioneer family in their cabin, he had retired to rest by a near-by spring, when the trio approached, the Indian girl leading the child by the hand. From the nostrils and ears of the savage girl hung metal rings, and she still wore the shell collar of an unmarried girl of the tribe. Apparently it was Tocqueville's curiosity—for he had stepped closer to observe the scene—that displeased the savage and caused her flight.

† Curiously enough—so far as it is possible to judge—the two Frenchmen made one capital mistake: they never visited, or studied, a cotton plantation. In fact, their knowledge of the South would always be meagre. They would never begin to understand it as well as they knew New England and the Middle Atlantic region. Apparently they felt that the future would lie with the North; and a real study of the cotton states would require far more time than they could possibly spare. '. . . I have only a superficial idea of the South of the Union,' Tocqueville admitted to his family, 'but to know it as well as the North I would have had to stay there six months. . . .' Toc. to Édouard, Washington, 20 Jan. 1832 (TT).

give the governor in our State the right to appoint the judges, it was conferred on the legislature. What is the result? That the responsibility of selection is divided; that small coteries, that small local intrigues become all-powerful; that instead of drawing to our benches able men, they put there the small party chiefs, who run the elections in the districts, and whom the members of the legislature want to win over or recompense. Our magistracy is completely incapable, the mass of the people feel it as well as we. Thus no one is tempted to apply to regular justice. This condition of affairs, which is common to the States of Kentucky, Tennessee, Mississip[p]i and even Georgia, is in my opinion what contributes most to give the inhabitants of these States that ferocity of manners with which they are justly reproached.'

'Is it then true that the habits of the people of Alabama are as violent as we are told?' Tocqueville asked. Since leaving the Ohio he had made more than one observation on the prevalence of duelling in the South.

'Yes,' answered the young Alabaman, 'there is no one here who is not carrying arms under his coat (*habits*). In the smallest dispute, you pull out knife or pistol. This goes on all the time; it's a social state that is half barbarian.

'But when a man is killed in this fashion, isn't his assassin punished?

'He is always judged and always acquitted by the jury, provided there are no very aggravating circumstances. I don't recall a single man of the least note paying for such a crime with his life. This violence has entered the customs. Each juror feels that he himself may, on leaving the court, find himself in the same position as the accused, and he acquits. Notice that the jury is taken from among all the freeholders, however small their holding may be. The people are therefore judging themselves, and their prejudices in this matter stand in the way of common sense. Besides, added my interlocutor, in my own time I've been no wiser than the rest: look at the scars on my head. (Indeed, we saw the marks of four or five deep wounds.) Those are so many knife-cuts that I've had given me.

'But you lodged a complaint?

'My God! No. I tried to give back as good.'

The answer was emphatic. Obviously the barbarity of the Southern sense of honour would be a delicate matter to discuss among gentlemen so ready with their knives. Tocqueville returned to the topic of direct popular government.

'Do the people choose good representatives?' he asked.

'No,' answered the lawyer, 'generally they elect men of their own capacity, and flatterers. I haven't the slightest doubt of the advantage that would accrue from limiting the suffrage. The choices would certainly be much better. But it is in the nature of things, in a "democratic" state, that the qualifications be broadened steadily and irresistibly, until the whole world can vote, which is what has happened with us. I prophesy that in France you won't be able to arrest the movement indefinitely either.'

That was exactly what Tocqueville thought, himself. In fact, it had been this conviction above any other that had originally driven him and Beaumont away from home to discover, if possible, what the 'democratic' fates of the future held in store for France. Universal suffrage produced . . . what? Poor choices in elections, and mediocre representatives, the Western States had demonstrated. Was that consequence necessarily *fatal* to good government? Tocqueville thought he ought to try to find out.

'But there must result from these poor selections poor laws and a poor government,' he therefore suggested. The answer was a surprise:

'*A*. Not nearly to such an extent as one would at first believe. There are always, in our assemblies, some men of talent; from the first days [of the session] these overwhelm the others and dominate business entirely. It's really they who make and discuss the laws; the others vote blindly. We have had representatives who didn't know how to read or write.'

In democracies, in other words, the ignorant held office. But even under universal suffrage the influence of quality remained. It was a comforting thought . . . yet one that led straight to the curious anomaly of the planter aristocracy: a brilliant civilization founded— as it were—in social mud.

'*Q*. Do you personally find that there is a great difference between the state of society in the North and in the South?

'*A*. Immense. We men of the South, we have perhaps more natural ability than the Northerners, but we are very much less active and above all less persevering. Our education is very neglected. There is no regular system of schools, a third of our population cannot read. You don't see the same care given to all the requirements of society, or the same forethought for the future.'

Evidently, on this subject opinion tallied with observable facts.

Quickly Tocqueville turned the conversation toward an analysis of some of the fundamental institutions. He propounded, first, a question that he had once asked in the North.

'What strength has religious sentiment among you?

'*A.* There is infinitely less morality with us than in the North, but religious sentiment, properly so called, is perhaps more exalted. There is religion in the North, fanaticism here. The Methodist sect dominates.

'*Q.* What is the opinion of the majority in Alabama on the subject of the tariff?' Again Tocqueville had the opinion of New England in mind.

'The majority is very opposed to the tariff, but very attached to the Union. The Nullifiers of South Carolina have no support among us,' was the lawyer's answer. Tocqueville passed to a third institution with which New Englanders had seemed impressed:

'What do you think of the use of the jury?

'I think it useful in criminal justice [and] I believe it to be useful in civil cases when there's a question of facts clearly distinguished from law or appreciations of morality. For instance, I think that all suits for damages and slander should be judged by juries. But as for civil matters properly so-called, as for questions of law, of the examination of written instruments, I believe the jury detestable and I much prefer the judge alone. One of the inconveniences of our jury is that it is drawn from too small circumscriptions (the counties). The jurors are familiar with the matter before the argument. The case is judged before being heard, even into the taverns.'

'On arriving in Montgomery,' Tocqueville concluded his note, 'we learned that a man had been killed in the street by a pistol shot.' *

* 'Character of the southern States: institutions refined, *mœurs brutales.* . . . Population of southern adventurers one of the causes of the brutality of the customs in the new States of the South.' Port. IV.

# XLIX

## MR. POINSETT EXPLAINS

Six days later, 12 January (it must have been somewhere in the interior of South Carolina—perhaps at the edge of the broken country, at Columbia), Tocqueville and Beaumont made the second find of their journey.

They were apparently waiting at a tavern. An accident, a broken wheel or perhaps a washed-out bridge, had interrupted their progress. Suddenly a familiar face appeared—and they found themselves greeting their valued acquaintance, the distinguished world-traveller and ex-ambassador to Mexico, Joel Roberts Poinsett.

Mr. Poinsett, they recalled, had been introduced to them just at the end of their stay in Philadelphia; and on that occasion he had painted for them the fascinating westward movement of the American people. That illuminating word-picture Tocqueville still carried in his notes. Its faithfulness to the original had been obvious from their earlier experiences on the Great Lakes; and its accuracy with regard to conditions in the Ohio and Mississippi valleys had since been verified on innumerable occasions. Now Mr. Poinsett was himself on the road to Washington, was in fact to be their fellow passenger throughout the long journey to Norfolk and the Chesapeake.

Just how much Mr. Poinsett told his French acquaintances of his own recent activities is not clear. He may or he may not have confided in them what he was doing in South Carolina, told them perhaps that he was an active member of the Union or anti-nullification party in his State. Tocqueville and Beaumont knew that he was a member of the State legislature. But probably he concealed from the two Frenchmen, as from the rest of the world, the fact that he had returned to South Carolina in part as a personal agent of President Andrew Jackson, as well. In any case, while they had been travelling in the West, Joel Roberts Poinsett had been organizing the Unionist sentiment of the

State, had just sat at the session of the legislature as a representative of the conservative faction, and was now, the legislature having adjourned, on his way back to Washington, to continue the battle, and to report.* Like Sam Houston, on his way from the Indians to Texas, Mr. Poinsett was making history.

And for five days he and Tocqueville talked.[1]

'The future of the United States in maritime commerce is immense,' Poinsett said on the twelfth. 'We are surely called to become the first maritime power of the globe. This is the result partly of the produce of our soil. We have in this country a mass of raw goods that the whole world needs. We are the most natural carriers of it. Furthermore, our national genius calls us to become, like the English, the brokers of foreign nations. Look at what is happening already: there are hardly any but Americans that carry to Europe the products of America, and European products arrive in America on American ships. Our vessels fill the harbours of Le Havre and Liverpool, in our own we see hardly a French or English vessel.'

'They say that the Americans are the most economical navigators [Tocqueville was quoting their first American acquaintance, the New York merchant Peter Schermerhorn]; whence comes that?

'From intellectual qualities, not physical,' answered Mr. Poinsett.† 'The price of labour being very high in America, the vessels cost more to build and the wages of the crew are higher than in Europe. But the American sailor possesses an activity and an economical bent, he has an understanding of his own interests, unique with him. There

---

* In effect, Poinsett had been acting as one of the organizers of the anti-nullification sentiment in South Carolina since 1830; and he and his friends had actually been able to win a partial victory in the Charleston elections. Unfortunately, ill health had then forced Poinsett to take the summer of 1831 off for a rest and a sea voyage. And on his return in November, he had found the Nullifiers in the ascendant. Governor Hamilton had delivered a message condemning Jackson's interference in South Carolina politics, and Poinsett had been unable to secure an endorsement of the President for a second term from the majority of the legislature, which sat at Columbia. He and others were therefore now hurrying to Washington, to get if they could a revision of the tariff sufficiently broad to deprive the Nullifiers of legitimate grievance.

In this he was to fail. The next year would therefore see him organizing a semi-military resistance to the extremists in the State, and appealing to Jackson for military stores and for aid. The story may be followed in H.E.Putnam, *Joel Roberts Poinsett/a political biography*, 1935, pp.114–148; and in J. Fred Rippy, *Joel R. Poinsett/versatile American*, 1935, pp.134–149. Neither biographer of Poinsett seems to be aware of Poinsett's acquaintance with Tocqueville and Beaumont; and the fact that they travelled to Washington together is a hitherto unreported discovery.

† Compare *Dém. en Am.*, II,427ff.

is not an English or a French vessel crossing the ocean in as little time as ours, none that stays as short a time in port; in this fashion we make up and more than make up our handicaps. Furthermore, the American has a quality which, on sea as on land, makes him singularly apt to succeed and make money. He is very civilized, and he is thrown in a society which is just beginning and where the industries have not yet had the time to class themselves in a hard and fast way. It follows that with us every man knows a little of everything, has since childhood been habituated to doing a little of all. Our labourers make shoes, their wives cloth and rugs. There is a phrase constantly in our mouths at the sight of an obstacle: and it's a phrase that portrays us perfectly: "I will try." '

The phrase appealed to Tocqueville; it would stick in his mind. But meanwhile he had not exhausted his topic.

'*Q.* It is said that your ships generally don't last very long?

'*A.* One must distinguish between vessels built for sale and those for one's own use. There is in the North a ship-building industry. The vessels produced by it have in fact a short life. But when we want to make a ship that we can use as long as possible, we find in our building woods, and particularly in the Live Oak of the Floridas, the best materials in the world. What makes our ships last such a short time is the fact that our merchants often have little disposable capital at the beginning. It's a calculation on their part. Provided that the vessel lasts long enough to bring them in a certain sum, a surplus over the cost, the end is obtained. Besides, there is a general feeling among us that prevents our aiming at the durable in anything: there reigns in America a popular and universal faith in the progress of the human mind. They are always expecting that improvements will be discovered in everything, and in fact they are often right. For instance, a few years ago I asked the builders of steamboats for the North River why they made their vessels so fragile. They answered that, as it was, the boats would perhaps last too long because the art of steam navigation was making daily progress. As a matter of fact, the vessels, which steamed at 8 or 9 miles an hour, could no longer a short time afterwards sustain competition with others whose construction allowed them to make 12 to 15.

'*Q.* Don't you think that, when the mass of your population will have arrived in the Mississip[p]i valley, your maritime commerce will suffer? capital being directed chiefly toward industry and farming?'

Tocqueville was again quoting from conversations of more than seven months before. This time he was asking Joel Poinsett to comment on Albert Gallatin.

'*A.* I am positive of the contrary. It is as important for the peoples of the Mississip[p]i as for the Atlantic States that the Union have great maritime power, since the great outlet for their produce is across the seas. If we couldn't prevent our ports being blockaded, what would become of the cotton, corn, and sugar . . . growing on the banks of the Mississip[p]i, the Missouri and the Ohio, annually carried to South America and to Europe? That's what I emphasized to Mr. Clay in Congress. He was talking about the concessions made by the Western States to the commerce of the Atlantic States. I proved to him that what he called a concession was in the very interest of the West.

'*Q.* Don't you think that in the absence of coercing laws, such as impressment or the *inscription maritime,* it would be difficult for the Union to find sailors in time of war?' Again the opinion came from Gallatin; and again Joel Poinsett disagreed.

'No,' he said, 'the high wage scale will always keep us a mass of foreign sailors; and in addition commerce suffers in war time, and a great number of unemployed sailors ask nothing better than to go on the vessels of the state.

'*Q.* What are the principles of the Union in the matter of commerce and high seas rights?

'*A.* The most complete reciprocity in commerce. We've noticed that the special advantages that we got abroad in no way compensated for the injury resulting from the obligation of according privileges at home. Not only, then, do we never ask to be received on a special basis in foreign ports, but we positively refuse privileges. That was what happened when I was charged with negotiating a treaty of commerce with the peoples of South America. As for our maritime law, we maintain that the flag covers the merchandise. I believe that there we are wrong. I don't know in the first place whether this privilege really is contained in the law of nations. But what's certain is that the contrary principle is most useful to peoples who dominate the sea. Now we are destined, in a very short space of time, to find ourselves in that position.* We shall then have to disavow our prin-

---

* Apparently Poinsett convinced Tocqueville that Gallatin had been mistaken. 'How doubt that the Union will one day become (and the day approaches) the leading maritime power of the world?' he began a note on *Commerce* four days later.

Already the commerce was immense; and there waited the whole trade of South

ciples, an act that puts nations, like men, in the wrong always. The principle that the flag covers the merchandise is good only for nations who can't hope ever to dominate the seas. France is in that situation. France will always be a great maritime power, never the first. It doesn't even act in accordance with its own interests in trying to be.'

Perhaps Tocqueville was sensitive about France. At all events he brought the conversation back to American economy—and in so doing attacked the very problem that Poinsett had been wrestling with for months.

'What do you think of tariffs in general, and particularly of the United States tariffs?' was his direct question.

Mr. Poinsett assumed a judicious and non-partisan attitude. 'I am no partisan of tariffs,' he emphasized, 'I think they tend rather to retard than help trade. As for the United States tariff, I believe it's done neither great harm nor great good. Some disappointed ambitious men have taken it as a pretext. But I don't credit it with either the good or evil influence attributed to it. Friends say we owe to it the immense progress that our industries have made in the last fifteen years. I don't believe a word of it. What gave impetus to our manufactures was the war of 1812. Prohibitions are always insufficient in time of peace. Only war can truly close the approaches of a country. It was the war which forced us to become industrialists; the momentum would have maintained itself afterwards without the tariff. Even with the duties, the mass of English goods imported augments every year; * but we have on our soil, with or without tariffs, natural advantages that can't be taken away from us. The enemies of the tariff say that it ruins the South. I don't believe a word of that. The only effect that it produces on the South doesn't seem to me to have been discovered yet. Here it is: by refusing to goods manufactured in England entrance to our ports we are diminishing the fortune of the English manufacturer. In order not to lose in his business, he is forced to do one of two things: either diminish the cost of his labour or lower the price of the

---

America. 'This commercial activity will retard still further for America the moment of *crowding* which is so to be feared, and postpone the Century of Revolutions.' 16 January, Cahier E.

* This answer showed unusual insight, and understanding of the situation. With a hundred years of experience, with the cooling of passion that the passage of time brings, and with all the advantages that hindsight gives the modern economist, it would to-day be difficult to improve on Poinsett's analysis.

raw materials. Now, in England and even in all Europe, it is impossible to lower the wages of a worker without sending him to the hospital. He earns only just enough to live. The economy, then, has to be exercised on the raw materials. The result of the tariff has therefore been to diminish the value of our cotton. (*Note.* This seems to me to give the lie to the rest and prove that the tariff is useful to the North.) * I find the usefulness of tariffs in one thing only: moderate, they make a tax better based than many others.'

Tocqueville let the subject drop. There would be time enough to come back to it; and at the moment he was through with American economy. Economic factors moderated institutions, certainly. But in that respect were not morality and religion even more important? He had thought so on landing, he thought so still. So he asked again two of his earliest American questions.

'Are morals in America as good as they are said to be?' was the first.

'*A.* There is laxity in the lower classes of society, but morals are excellent everywhere else. I have never seen anything comparable in any of my travels. Nothing like it exists in England. The people and the upper classes are very disordered in their morals; morality exists only in the middle class. The marriage tie is so prodigiously respected with us that the lover of a married woman dishonours himself even more certainly than she who yields to him. The road of preferment is closed to him, even that of money-making becomes difficult; he should consider himself happy if he dies otherwise than by assassination, the relatives of the woman very often thinking themselves bound to avenge the family honour on him.

'*Q.* But how do you account for this extreme purity of morals? I tell you frankly that I am unable to regard you as a virtuous people.

'*A. I* don't believe either that we are more virtuous than many other peoples; the purity of our morals is the result rather of special circumstances and particularly of the total absence of a class of men having the time and means to attack the virtue of women. I believe, furthermore, that the race of women in America is very remarkable; I find them much above the men.

'*Q.* Do you think that this state of morals reacts on the political status of society?

---

* Tocqueville was correct in supposing such a situation to be injurious to the South. But what Poinsett clearly meant to say was that the tariff was slightly disadvantageous, rather than wholly ruinous, to the planting States.

'*A*. Certainly, a great deal. It gives us habits of order and morality that act as a powerful rein on political passions.'

Thus far Tocqueville and Poinsett were in perfect agreement. Now the French student asked his second question.

'*Q*. What is your opinion of the influence of religion on politics?

'*A*. I think that the religious situation in America is one of the things that help us most to bear our republican institutions. The religious feeling exercises a direct influence on religious passions, and an indirect one as well in forwarding morals. It's because many enlightened Americans are convinced of this truth that they not only conceal the doubts they may have of the verity of Christianity but even hesitate to adopt new sects like the Unitarian. They are afraid of arriving indirectly in this fashion at the destruction of the Christian religion, which would be an irreparable loss (*mal*) for humanity.'

*

* *

Their second day together Tocqueville finally tackled the political crisis in South Carolina.[2]

He had not previously given the tariff controversy much real attention, save only to wonder at the extraordinary use of conventions that Americans sometimes made.* Such free assemblages as the extralegal meetings, held in New York and Philadelphia the previous autumn by the friends and enemies of the tariff, had filled him with astonishment and forebodings. Regardless of the merits of the tariff question, the principle of free assemblage had seemed to him filled with dangers for an orderly government, and all the assurances and calm reasonings of sensible Philadelphians had not quite dispelled his doubts.

Now, however, the problem was more immediate. He and Beaumont had not travelled for five weeks in the South without hearing echoes of the grave dispute that was maturing between the State of South Carolina and the Federal Government. Here was a crisis, not for free government, but for the Union itself. At least, that was Tocqueville's impression. He thought he would ask Mr. Poinsett, who was a member of the South Carolina legislature, and should know something about it.

'What is meant by the system of nullification? This system seems to

---

* See J.Q.Adams and Ingersoll conversations, above, pp.418,480–82.

me to come down to the pure and simple annulment of the Union,' he began.

'That would be the indirect result, no doubt,' Mr. Poinsett replied; 'however, the *Nullifiers* deny the charge. They claim only that the individual States have the right to suspend the *laws* of Congress and to instigate the calling of a convention.

'*Q.* Does this doctrine make you apprehensive for the future of the Union?

'*A.* No. The Nullifiers are a party only in South Carolina; even there their majority is doubtful; and even if they had the whole State for them, what can the 700,000 [200,000?] whites living there do against the forces of the Union? Like so many others, this party owed its origins to the personal ambitions of a few citizens, particularly Mr. Calhoun and Mr. Duke [?]. The doctrine of nullification has been preached without conviction, now it has believers. . . .'

So Mr. Poinsett, in spite of his own Unionist activities, was no more apprehensive than the rest! Tocqueville was genuinely puzzled. Perhaps the tariff question was, after all, only an excuse. But, an excuse for what? Were there not, underlying this ephemeral dispute, certain fundamental, irreconcilable differences between the two sections that would one day prove fatal for the Union? Tocqueville thought a flank attack might elicit the true answer. He began with an apparent change of subject.

'Is there as real a difference as people say between social conditions in the South and in the North?' was his innocent question.

'*A.* Yes, the difference is obvious and all in favour of the North.

'*Q.* What are the reasons for this?

'*A.* The first cause is slavery, the second the climate. The South is actually progressing, but it appears to go backwards, the North and the West are going so fast. Every ten years the South loses a part of its representation, while the West and the Northwest on the contrary gain representatives. Power is rapidly leaving the old centres. Soon the thirteen original States will no longer have the majority in Congress.'

There was the opening Tocqueville had been working for. 'This state of affairs can't possibly fail to create a spirit of *jealousy* and suspicion in the South,' he suggested; 'the weak don't generally believe in the fairness of the strong.'

'That is true,' was all that Mr. Poinsett would say.

Tocqueville wanted to try one more avenue of approach. 'Has the South any ships to carry its produce?' he asked.

'*A*. Not one; it's the North that comes to pick up the products of the South and carry them all over the world.

'*Q*. What's the cause of this singular state of affairs?

'*A*. Partly the fact that in the South there is as yet no lower class. One wouldn't know where to find a population of sailors.

'*Q*. But why not employ the negroes?

'*A*. That would be to risk losing them: they would desert. Besides, enterprise (*industrie*) is wanting in the South.' All of which merely carried the argument back to Mr. Poinsett's original conviction: the South could not, and would not, abandon the North. Tocqueville at last abandoned the attack and turned to the even more intriguing problem of the blacks.

'*Q*. Do you see any way of getting rid of slaves?

'*A*. No. The plan which aims at buying them back at the expense of the State and transporting them elsewhere seems to me extravagant. The riches of the whole Union would not suffice. As the number of slaves diminished their price would become exorbitant. Besides, the need for them that would be discovered would lead to renewed importation of them by the slave trade. I don't share the fears for the safety of the white race that the multiplication of the blacks gives birth to. A slave revolt will never succeed. If they ever became enlightened enough to pool their resources and create a formidable league, they would be enlightened enough also to see that, placed as they are, no ultimate success can be hoped for.'

Again Mr. Poinsett was taking a wonderfully calm and optimistic view of things. If he thought Mr. Latrobe's colonization program hopeless, he was equally sure that white fears of race war and slave insurrection were likewise ill-founded. But Tocqueville was not quite satisfied. There remained the danger of the half-breeds.

'*Q*. Do the mulattoes make common cause with the blacks?

'*A*. No. They treat the blacks with arrogance, and the latter detest them.* They think themselves much closer to the whites than to the blacks. The men who are the most dangerous are the freedmen. Their presence disquiets the slaves and makes them want freedom. I believe

---

* 'There is one race that despises the blacks even more than the whites do: the mulatto. In this he acts like the lackeys of great lords, who call the populace *canaille*.' Toc. note, Port. V.

it indispensable to take away from the masters the power of freeing, and especially of freeing by will. Washington gave a very bad example in liberating his slaves at his death.'

Again Mr. Poinsett said: 'It's extraordinary how enlightened public opinion is becoming on the subject of slavery. The idea that it is a great evil and that we might be able to get along without it is gaining more and more. I hope that the natural course of events will disembarrass us of the slaves. I still know people who have seen slavery in New England. In our own time we have seen it abolished in the State of New-York, then in Pennsylvania; it has only the most precarious hold on life in Maryland; and in the legislature of Virginia speeches are already being made against it. The black race is steadily retiring into the South, pushed by the emigration of men belonging to the white race.

'*Q.* Do you believe that slaves are being brought by fraud into the territory of the Union?

'*A.* Hardly at all. But the slave trade nevertheless exists on a grand scale. Last year the House of Commons of England had an inquiry made into this point, and I myself read on its records that the number of blacks drawn from Africa each year reached 300,000.'

So much for one of the two oppressed races of America. The natural association of ideas led Tocqueville next to ask about the other.

'What is your attitude toward the Indians of the United States?' he wanted to know.

On this matter, the Southern statesman was dogmatic, and—like most of his fellow citizens—convinced of the justice of the white man's cause.

'I believe they are a race that will perish sooner than try to become civilized,' he said; 'success in that would be impossible without the aid of the *half-breed*. Aside from that, I think the civilized man has the right to take from the savage the land which the latter does not know how to use yet where the white man prospers and multiplies rapidly.' *

With such a conviction there was no use arguing, whatever Tocqueville might personally believe. In any case there were a number of other topics, some controversial and some more matter of fact, on which he desired information and light.

* Poinsett's later career as Secretary of War indicates that this opinion was characteristic of his thinking at this time.

'Do you think that the banking system in vigour in the United States has forwarded the prosperity of the country?

'*A*. Yes, in a country where there is as little capital as with us, banks are an immense utility; but I don't know whether the same reason would apply in France or England. Of all the government banks, that of New Orleans seems to me established on the most perfect plan.

'*Q*. Is it true that in the United States public opinion does not proscribe bankruptcy with the same severity as in Europe?' *

'*A*. Yes, so long as there is no evident fraud on the part of the business man, opinion has nothing against him. He may plunge into the most hazardous enterprises, begin without capital, risk in every way the money of his backers without materially damaging his reputation; to-morrow he will begin over again. Almost all our tradesmen play for doubles or quits, and that is taken as a matter of course. It must be admitted that the morality of our business is very different from the European.

'*Q*. How are roads made and repaired in America?

'*A*. It's a great constitutional question whether Congress has the right to make anything but military roads. Personally, I am convinced that the right exists; there being disagreement, however, practically no use, one might say, is made of it. It's the States that often undertake to open and keep up the roads traversing them. Most frequently these roads are at the expense of the counties. In general our roads are in very bad repair. We haven't the central authority to force the counties to do their duty. The inspection, being local, is biased and slack. Individuals, it is true, have the right to sue the communities which do not suitably repair their roads; but no one wants to have a suit with the local authority (*communes*). Only the *turn-pike* roads are passable. The turn-pike system of roads seems to me very good, but time is required for it to enter into the habits of the people. It must be made to compete with the free road system. If the turn-pike is much better or shorter than the other, travellers will soon feel that its use is an economy.

'*Q*. Does the nomination for President excite real political passions?

'*A*. No. It puts the interested parties into a grand commotion. It makes the newspapers make a lot of noise. But the mass of the people remain indifferent. The President has, in the last analysis, so little

* Compare with pp.49,55,71.

influence on their happiness! To tell you the truth, it's Congress that governs.'

About Congress Tocqueville would soon be in a position to form his own opinions. He had heard of Mr. Poinsett's career as ambassador, and he now asked about the country and people of Mexico.

'All that I saw in Mexico,' was the interesting reply, 'leads me to believe that the inhabitants of that beautiful country had reached, at the coming of the Spaniards, a state of civilization *at least* as advanced as the latter. But first a superiority in the art of war, and then oppression, destroyed everything.

'*Q*. How is the population of Mexico composed to-day?

'*A*. Of Spaniards, for whom a white skin is a kind of nobility; of Indians, poor and ignorant, cultivating the earth. In law they are free and the equals of the Spaniards, but in fact they count for nothing in the political balance. There are hardly any negroes or mulattoes.

'*Q*. What do you think of the future of this country?

'*A*. I hope that it will manage to get established on a solid basis. Certainly it is progressing. You mustn't judge the Spaniards of the New World too harshly. When the Revolution caught them, they were still in the sixteenth century, minus the savage virtues that the independence so widely enjoyed in that century often gave to the peoples of that time. That interpretation has often served me in business. I have often asked myself what men of the sixteenth century would have done in such and such a situation, what they would have thought. The answer to those questions enabled me to foresee the future almost with certainty. You can't conceive a more complete ignorance of all the discoveries of modern civilization. They began, as in South America, wanting to construct a great, undivided republic. They didn't succeed, and for my part I don't believe in the duration of a great republic unless it be a federation. The Mexicans finally adopted, save for some insignificant exceptions, the constitution of the United States, but they are not yet sufficiently advanced to make good use of it like us. It's a difficult and complicated instrument.

'*Q*. Don't you feel that the nations of Europe fell into a great blunder in supposing that the independence of the Spanish colonies would open vast markets to them?

'*A*. Yes, unquestionably. The needs which civilization brings have not yet made themselves felt in Spanish America. The time has not yet come, though it is coming.

'*Q*. What is the position of the clergy in Mexico?

'*A*. It is steadily losing the last of its influence. Already it has hardly any support among the people. You perceive that this state of affairs resembles not at all the conditions obtaining in Spain. The Mexican clergy still has its property, however. This is an immense wealth that one hasn't yet dared lay hand on. It's the clergy that began the Revolution in Mexico. It was afraid that the Cortes of Spain would confiscate its estates, and it aroused the people. Only a half-Revolution was desired but, the impetus given, it was impossible to stop.'

'I closed the conversation,' Tocqueville later concluded in his diary [it was curious how his ideas were always linked together], 'I closed the conversation by asking Mr. Poinsett what was the state of morals in Spanish America. He replied, laughing:

'That's not the fine side of the picture. I've spent a part of my life in Spanish America and I can say that, from Cape Horn to the 35th degree of latitude North, I have never known a woman faithful to her husband. The notions of right and wrong are so reversed in this matter that a woman thinks it a disgrace not to have a lover.'

# L

## 'WHAT MAKES A REPUBLIC BEARABLE'

It was Tocqueville's nature to philosophize. Never, for any consider-able stretch of days, was he without a grand thought. Some new *idée-mère*, some far-reaching generalization, was always in the process of formation within his brain. To live entirely in the world of facts and incidents was quite beyond his powers, as foreign to his wishes. He asked questions, he observed, he travelled, in order to reason. Adventure was beside the point.

So it happened that during his journey through the South he was not always listening to Mr. Poinsett, or watching the drab plantation landscapes roll by. Now and again, as delays or breakdowns offered opportunity, he would jot down an idea. And gradually he began to piece together the explanation of a problem that hitherto had always eluded his anxious comprehension.

The notes he took did not always seem to agree very well together. But essentially he was continually asking himself just one question. What was it that made Republicanism tolerable as a form of govern-ment to any given people?

He began, one day, at a tangent: with the parties that might make a Republic workable. '*Concerning Great and Small Parties*' was the title of his thought:[1]

'What I call great political parties, those that attach themselves to principles and not to results, to generalities and not to particular cases, to ideas and not to men, these parties generally have features more noble, passions more generous, convictions more real, and a way of acting that is more frank and bold. The private interests, which al-ways play a large role in political passions, are here able to hide them-selves more successfully under the cloak of public interest, and some-times are able even to conceal themselves from the eyes of the very men they motivate.

'Small parties, on the other hand, are generally without political faith; their whole character is stamped with an egoism which shows itself openly in their every act. They are always luke-warm (*s'échauffent toujours à froid*). Their language is violent, their conduct timid and uncertain. The means they employ are as miserable as the ends they propose. Great parties turn society upside down, small parties *pester* it more than they excite. The former often inspire one with pity for humanity, the latter with scorn. Both have one trait in common:

'They hardly ever use, in order to obtain their ends, means that the conscience completely approves. There are honest men in almost all the parties, but it can be said that there is no honest man's party (*parti honnête homme*).

'America has had great parties, but they no longer exist. In happiness she gained much from them, but as for morality, I have my doubts. I can't conceive of a sorrier spectacle in the world than that of the different coteries (they don't deserve the name of parties) which to-day divide the Union. You see operating in broad daylight in their bosoms all the small and shameful passions which are usually hidden with great care at the bottom of the human heart.

'As for the interest of the country, no one thinks of it; and if they talk about it, it's only for the form. The parties place it [the national interest] at the head of their platforms as our fathers once printed the King's licence on the first page of their books.

'It's pitiful to see what coarse insults, what small vilifications and what impudent calumnies fill the journals which serve them as party organs, and with what shameless scorn for all the social decencies they daily arraign before the bar of public opinion the honour of families and the secrets of the domestic hearth.'

This was hardly a very cheerful view of political parties in general or of the American political system in particular. On the face of it, too, Tocqueville's observation had apparently very little to do with the main point. But he had already hit on an illuminating fact: 'great parties,' he had discovered, 'turned society upside down,' while small parties, ignoble as they were, 'pester it more than they excite.' Already in his diary, he had elaborated on this significant distinction:

'There are, in the matter of political institutions,' he observed,[2] 'two kinds of instability which must not be confused. The one is to be found in the secondary laws, which change with the more or less variable desire of the legislator. This kind can exist in a regulated and quite stable society. It is even very often the necessary consequence of the political constitution of a people. The other kind of instability attaches itself to the very foundations of society, to the *generative principles* behind the laws. This kind cannot exist without trouble, without revolutions. The nation suffering them is in a violent and transitory condition.'

Tocqueville did not have far to go for illustrations. 'America offers an example of the former,' he continued. 'For the last forty years we have been tormented by the second. Because of confusing them, many people conceive exaggerated fears and hopes, and make inexact comparisons.

'I add that you don't see appearing the great political parties, the dangerous factions, save where the second exists. The first kind gives birth to coteries and not to parties, to discussions and not to quarrels, to noise and not to war.

'If you want to know whether a people is established, and whether or not it can count on its own future, examine it from this point of view.'

The conclusion was original and most interesting. Not every one would be willing to subscribe to so sweeping an indictment of political factions. But if they did it would not occur to them that they were demonstrating the strength of the American Union. To Tocqueville, however, 'coterie,' if it mean ignominy, signified also stability.

He was now ready to draw up a tentative statement on '*What makes a Republic bearable in the United States*':[3]

'There are a thousand causes contributing to make Republican liberty tolerable in the United States, but just a few are sufficient to explain the problem.

'In the United States, people say, society was constructed on a clean slate. You see neither victor nor vanquished, plebeian or noble, prejudices of birth or prejudices of profession.

'But all South America is in this state,* and Republicanism succeeds only in the United States.

'The territory of the Union offers an immense field for human activity, it provides inexhaustible supplies for industry and labour. The love of comfort and riches is constantly drawing off the politically ambitious on another scent.

'Yet in what part of the world does one find more fertile regions,

* This chance comparison was a little less than exact.

more admirable wildernesses, rivers more superb, riches more inexhaustible and untouched than in South America; and yet South America can't get on with a Republic.

'The division of the Union into small States reconciles interior prosperity and national strength; it multiplies political interests and weakens party spirit by dividing it.

'Yet Mexico is a federal Republic; it has adopted almost without alteration the constitution of the United States; yet Mexico is still very far from prospering.

'There is one great cause, which dominates all the others and which, after the rest have all been weighed, tips the balance by itself: The American people, taken by and large, is not only the most enlightened in the world but (and I place this well above the last-named advantage) it is the people whose practical political education is the most advanced.

'It's from this truth, in which I believe firmly, that arises in me the only hope I have for the future happiness of Europe.

'Yet there remains always a great insoluble question: the material and special advantages possessed by the United States would not suffice them without their high civilization and experience: but would that high civilization and that experience be enough alone?'

*
*   *

One ought to hope so. For in spite of the million petty deficiencies of self-governing peoples, the cause of political freedom was admirable. 'Political liberty is a food that is hard to digest,' Tocqueville was willing to allow.[4] 'Only the most robust constitutions can support it. But when it comes to pass, be it even with other [institutions], it gives to the whole social body a vigour and energy that surprise even those who were expecting the most from it.'

Yet was France ready? Were Tocqueville's own people robust enough in character and experience to undertake the Republican experiment? Had they the necessary institutions, or—if not—could they borrow what was needed from America?

Brought back to this ancient question, Tocqueville found himself still, as always before, a prey to doubts: 'Only a pretentious or weak mind could, after seeing America, maintain that in the present state of the world her political institutions could be applied to others. To be convinced of this one has but to glimpse the different ways in which the Republic is understood and applied in the different States of the Union, according to the different degrees of . . . [*lumières?*] and of experience to be found.'

On reading the above *dictum* over, Tocqueville realized that he had been too sweeping in his prohibition. 'When I say her institutions,' he amended, 'I speak of the whole structure in its entirety. There is not a people but could usefully appropriate some fragments.'

Very well. And what were some of these fragments? Wherein did the Americans order things better for the preservation of liberty than was done in France?

In a sense, any adequate answer to this question was impossible, at least without writing a book reviewing his whole American experience. Yet Tocqueville thought he could jot down a few ideas for future reference. One did not spend eight months in constant study without acquiring a few verities. Specifically, it now seemed to him that Americans showed an obvious and enviable superiority in local government, in constitutional practice, in the use of the jury.

'America created municipal liberty before political liberty,' he phrased his first thought; 'we have done and are doing the absolute opposite. Cause of all our ills. We want to raise a column by beginning at the capital, be masters before being apprentices.' *

The argument was familiar and perfectly plain. The advantages of an indigenous decentralization needed no new elaboration. Tocqueville took up the matter of constitutional theory.

The Americans, he noted,[5] made a great use of sworn oaths. So did the French. But the Americans required oaths of loyalty to the Constitution only from office-holders, and never from voters. For they recognized the right of the sovereign people to amend their Constitution, and had provided a specific and public process of amendment. 'As for imposing an oath of obedience to the Constitution on those who assemble to choose a constitutional convention, that's an absurdity that a logical people, that the American people, would reject with scorn.' Alas for the French nation! Not only were they uncertain as to where ultimate sovereignty (and the amending power) lay, but they exacted an oath of obedience to the law from the voter at the same moment that they allowed him to elect a representative who might legally modify

---

* 'Fatal influence on liberty of the military mind or classes. Americans possess not virtue but steadiness.'

or destroy that law. 'But the principles of liberty are still in their infancy with us, as ill understood by those who propose as by those who oppose them.'

There was, for instance, another item, another principle quite misunderstood in France: the proper use of witnesses in a jury system.*

'The Americans allow proof by witnesses in civil suits when not contrary to written evidence. The men of law I've seen maintain that [this practice?] does not produce here the abuses that might be feared. I should be tempted to believe them. In the entire confidence in law there is something that leads men not to abuse it. Respect for truth thus becomes a merit: a conviction of the first order and felt by all. But when the legislator classifies depositions in certain cases as presumable lies, he diminishes the value of depositions in all others. No better means exists of making men contemptible than to show contempt for them. I regard it as a very happy circumstance for a people if proof by witness be entered into its habits and customs. But it would be very dangerous to introduce it there where it had not always existed. It requires also the use of the jury in civil suits. The English owe the preservation of the proof by witnesses, as of so many other fine institutions, to the customary law, *common law.*'

Again Tocqueville wrote: 'The Jury is the most direct application of the principle of the sovereignty of the people. . . .' Yet neither Napoleon, nor Louis XVIII, nor even Louis Philippe, had given it to the French!

*
*  *

The more Tocqueville measured his own country against America, the more discouraged he sometimes became.

'We have had in France in the last 40 years every form of anarchy and despotism,' he lugubriously admitted,[6] 'but never anything resembling a Republic.' If the Royalists could only see into the machinery of an orderly Republic, he thought; if they could but glimpse the pro-

---

* Though converted in the matter of the jury, Tocqueville was apparently far from wishing to borrow American manhood suffrage. It had the advantage of reducing the number of the discontented, he felt, but required great enlightenment and long practice in self-government. In particular, it postulated a government built on the theory that sovereignty rises from the people; whereas in France sovereignty still descended in theory from the ruler to the ruled. Even in so favourable an environment as America, of course, manhood suffrage was not without its weaknesses and abuses. Toc. diary note, 16 January 1832, Cahier E.

found respect for rights, the power of law over the multitude, the real reign of the majority, the comfortable security of society, they would suddenly realize that they had never known what the hated name Republic really meant. And on the other side, the so-called Republicans of France would realize that what they had been proposing was a classical and obsolete monster. The wretchedness of the disputes since 1789 fired Tocqueville's anger:

'What matters it to me,' he exclaimed, 'what do I care whether tyranny be cloaked in the royal mantle or the toga of a tribunal, if I feel its hand weighing me down? When Danton had them cut the throats of the poor prisoners whose only crime was that of not thinking as he did, was that liberty? When, later on, Robespierre sent Danton to the scaffold for having shown himself his rival, that was justice doubtless, but was it liberty? When the majority in the convention proscribed the minority, when the arbitrary power of the proscribers took from the citizens their goods, their children, their lives, when [to hold] an opinion was a crime, and when a wish expressed in the sanctuary of the home, in the church, merited death, was that liberty? But I shall be running through all the bloody annals of tyranny. Let us pass by the Terror, with its *necessary* severities, will I see liberty reigning in the times when the Directory destroyed the journals and sent to die in the wildernesses of Guiana the members of the majority who were about to overturn it? When Bonaparte, consul, substituted the power, the tyranny of one man for the tyranny of factions, was that yet liberty? was that Republican? No; we have had in France every variety of anarchy and despotism, but nothing resembling a Republic.'*

It was true. And it was profoundly discouraging. France not only lacked some of the institutions that make a Republic bearable; she did not even know what freedom in government was. 'If ever I write anything on America,' Tocqueville scribbled at the bottom of the page, 'it will be extremely important to consecrate a chapter,' to this thought.†

* 'It suffices to see what a Republic is in this country to *prendre en horreur* the demagogic and revolutionary faction which usurps the name of republican in our country.' Toc. to Chabrol, Washington, 24 January 1832 (YT).
† Eventually, no such chapter was written. Instead, the assumption that Frenchmen were ignorant of true liberty and its institutions was to be one of the basic ideas underlying the whole exposition and commentary.

# WASHINGTON RECEIVES THE COMMISSIONERS

ON the twenty-third of January Monsieur Serurier was writing out a despatch to his home government. The minister of France was well on in years, a tried and experienced diplomat of *esprit* and genuine capacity.* He might claim to know America well, for he had represented his country once before in the same role in Washington, in the troubled bygone days when Napoleon was Emperor. It was his custom to report to his superiors on everything of importance and interest that occurred in Washington. Now he wrote: [1]

'Messrs. de Beaumont and de Tocqueville have just, Monsieur le Comte, arrived in Washington from New Orleans. On receipt of your Excellency's letter, particularly recommending them, I had made haste to write to our consuls to procure for them everywhere the reception and facilities that might facilitate their honourable mission. I am charmed to make the acquaintance of these interesting travellers, who are already being greeted here by every one with the same eagerness and enthusiasm that they have encountered wherever they have gone. During their stay here I shall endeavour to procure them all the kindnesses in my power. It is much to be wished that French travellers of their bearing and merit would come from time to time to visit this country, which is so different from all that is left behind on sailing. They would enlarge their views, and would leave here a most favourable impression of our young men of to-day. I have the honour to be . . . ,' etc., etc.

'I must tell you a little about our stay in Washington,' Beaumont wrote home on their third day in the Federal capital.[2] 'On our arrival

---

* Blessed with a sense of humour, Serurier regarded the earnest solemnity and the petty foibles of American politicians with an amused and kindly tolerance. Only the custom of innumerable toasts at public dinners bothered him. (See above, p.90.) As for his own profession, he could smile even at himself with a philosophical detachment. '*Les Diplomates, Monsieur, sont comme les vieilles filles, qui attendent toujours quelqu'un, ou quelque chose,*' he would write Edward Livingston, 9 Sept. 1832, Washington. Barton Collection, Boston Public Library.

we went first to see the Minister of France, Mr. Serrurier [*sic*], with whom we had been corresponding for several months and who treated us with especial kindness. The dear man is momentarily a little put out with the government of L.P. which has bethought itself of economizing on ambassadors' salaries. The truth is, they have reduced his salary in absurd fashion; he now gets only 40,000 francs. The veriest *chargé d'affaires* gets more, and it's unfortunate that the Minister of France should find himself in such a position of inferiority, above all in respect to the Minister of England, who gets 150,000.*

'Mr. Serrurier presented us yesterday evening to the President of the United States. The latter is General Jackson; he is an old man of 66 years, well preserved, and appears to have retained all the vigour of his body and spirit. He is not a man of genius. Formerly he was celebrated as a duellist and hot-head; his great merit is to have won in 1814 the battle of New Orleans against the English. That victory made him popular and brought it about that he was elected president, so true is it that in every country military glory has a prestige that the masses can't resist, even when the masses are composed of merchants and business men.

'The President of the United States occupies a palace that in Paris would be called a fine private residence. Its interior is decorated with taste but simply, the *salon* in which he receives is infinitely less brilliant than those of our ministers. He has no guards watching at the door, and if he has courtiers they are not very attentive to him, for when we entered the *salon* he was alone, though it was the day of public reception; and during our whole visit but two or three persons entered. We chatted of things that were insignificant enough. He made us drink a glass of Madeira wine, and we thanked him, using the word *Monsieur*, like the first comer. People in France have got an altogether false idea of the presidency of the United States. They see in it a sort of political sovereignty and compare it constantly with our constitutional monarchies. Of a certainty, the power of the King of France would be nil if it were modelled after the power of the President of the United States; and the authority of this President would be a thousand times too large, did it resemble that of the King of France.†

---

* To his government, Serurier pointed out that once he had received 80,000 francs: half that amount was not enough. The regular pay of 60,000 would be satisfactory.

† For the possible origins of Beaumont's opinion as to the relative power of President and Congress, see their stage-coach conversations, pp.639,654.

'I visited to-day the Senate and the Assembly of Representatives of the Union. These two political assemblies meet at the Capitol, a very fine palace and truly worthy of being cited as a magnificent monument. Even so the Americans exaggerate its merits greatly; they often ask foreigners candidly if there exists in Europe anything that can be compared to their Capitol. The aspect of the debates is grave and imposing; rarely do political passions intrude so as to make the debates disorderly. One of the great advantages of the government of the United States is to have as its seat a small town. Washington scarcely counts 20,000 souls. It was deliberately that the authors of the Constitution chose it as the seat of supreme authority. In a large city, where there is a numerous population and a great populace, political deliberations are never free. All the men I saw to-day discussed and deliberated with all the more sang-froid for all's being calm about them. We were introduced into the Senate and Legislature by Mr. Poinsett, a very distinguished man whose acquaintance we made in Philadelphia and whom we were delighted to find again in Washington. He has played in this country a very important political role; it was he who a few years ago plunged Mexico into revolution. . . .

'I don't know any one who has travelled as much as he; he has made the voyage from America to Europe and back 22 times. He is a man of curious discourse and most interesting conversation. We are finding again here many of the persons we encountered in our trip, and thus we are spared the difficulties one usually experiences on arriving in a town where one has to make new acquaintances. We are going to spend about a fortnight here as usefully as we can. The third or fourth of February we'll set out for New-York. We shall pass by Philadelphia, where we'll stay a day in order to see and say good-bye to certain persons; then we'll go directly to New-York, where we'll have two days to make our preparations for departure.

'This is already a long letter, dear Maman, yet I won't close it to-day, and, before sending it to New-York, whence it can't go before the first of February, I'll add a word or two to tell you how our time in Washington is passing.'

*
*   *

Apparently Andrew Jackson had received his young French callers with courtesy and simplicity, but with no great display of interest. He might have told them, had he chosen—or they might have asked him, had they dared—some very interesting things about national affairs. Tocqueville and Beaumont might even have learned from the hot-tempered general not to esteem the power of the Federal Executive quite so lightly. For, as President, Andrew Jackson had just consummated the sensational and unprecedented manœuvre of dismissing his entire Cabinet. He was at the moment deep in a personal and political struggle against Vice-President John C. Calhoun.* He was watching the campaign of the Second U.S. Bank, and the development of the nullification movement in South Carolina, like a hawk. Should the rebellious Southerners, or the friends of the Bank, come out in the open and challenge his authority, he would crush both factions ruthlessly. To students from France the duties and powers of the Presidency, as understood by so determined an incumbent as 'Old Hickory,' might well have been worth an investigation. But Tocqueville and Beaumont's visit was purely a social call. What might therefore have developed into a striking interview passed agreeably in platitudes, and ended with results of no moment whatsoever.

This was by no means an indication that the two friends would lack—or would fumble—other opportunities. The weather was fair and cold, Washington was in full season, society was giving entertainment after entertainment, and in the halls of Congress the nation's representatives were engaged in a series of important debates.†

'We are completely launched in Washington society,' Beaumont resumed his letter on the twenty-second. 'We spent a part of yesterday making calls, escorted by the first secretary of legation who introduced us.

'We traversed the city, therefore, in every direction. This town, whose population is inconsiderable, is yet immense in area. Distances

---

* 'I have no hesitation in saying that Calhoun is one of the most base and hypocritical and unprincipled villains in the United States,' the short-tempered but by no means helpless Executive wrote to a friend only two days later. '. . . This combination they know cannot effect me, but it is to bring Calhoun or Clay into the Presidency four years hence—a greater curse could not befall our country.' (J.S.Bassett, ed., *Correspondence of Andrew Jackson*, IV,400–403.)

As for the 'factious opposition' in the Senate, which was attacking both the President and his favourite Van Buren, Jackson could find no epithet to describe 'its blackguardism and demerit.' On the whole, he was of the opinion that the opposition Senators had degraded their 'august body, once the admiration of the world, lower than a Spanish inquisition.' Such was not to be Tocqueville's opinion, however.

† The Tariff (and nullification), the Second U.S. Bank, and Calhoun's attacks on Van Buren were occupying almost the entire attention of both houses, from 17 January to 8 February 1832.

are almost as great as in Paris. The consequence is that the houses are scattered here and there, without connection between them, without order and without symmetry. Outside of the fact that it makes a very ugly panorama, it's very annoying for those with visits to make.'

Tocqueville was particularly put out by the disappointing tableau presented by the Federal capital. 'If you would like to have an idea what power men possess to calculate the events of the future, you must visit Washington,' he wrote his Father, half in sorrow, half in scorn.[3] 'Forty years ago, when it was a question of building a capital for the Union, they looked, as reasonable men would, for the most favourable spot. On the banks of the Potomack was located a green plain, which they selected. The broad and deep river, at one end, was to bring to the new city the products of Europe; the fertile districts behind would provision the market and surround the spot with a numerous population. Washington, in twenty years, would be the centre of the domestic and foreign trade of the Union. A million inhabitants, arriving before very long, were predicted for it. In consequence they began to build public edifices that could match so vast a population; streets were laid out of enormous width; there was an especial hurry to cut down, as far as one could see, the trees that might hinder the building of houses. All that was but, on a large scale, the story of the *pot au lait*:

> Il était, quand je l'eus, de grosseur raisonable.
> J'aurai. . . .

'The peasant's wife and Congress reasoned in the same fashion. The population did not come; the vessels did not mount the Potomack. To-day, Washington offers the sight of an arid plain, burned by the sun, on which are scattered two or three sumptuous edifices and the five or six villages composing the town. Unless one is Alexander or Peter the Great, one must not meddle with creating the capital of an empire.'

Yet in America, even a disappointing cluster of villages might offer its features of interest, and first among these were the men. On the twenty-first, they had made a general round of visits, Beaumont had explained. And gathered now in the Federal capital they found most of the outstanding figures in the Union, their own friends and previous acquaintances included. That very evening Edward Everett, from Massachusetts, had called on them. The venerable Peter Duponceau from Philadelphia was in town.* Joseph Coolidge Jr. had not come himself but had given them a letter of introduction to Nicholas P. Trist, the Virginian, and recently followed this up with a letter to Trist himself asking after his two French friends. 'They are fine fellows!' he had written.†

'The evening [of the twenty-first],' Beaumont continued his account of their visits, 'I passed at the house of the Secretary of State, Mr. Edward Livingston, the most celebrated writer in America. He is a man of about sixty years, who is very kindly and speaks French wonderfully well. He is almost French in his ways because he was born and has spent most of his life in Louisiana. His *soirée* was charming. They play there *bad* music, because none other is made in America; but the concert didn't last long and soon they began to dance.—I mingled my square dances and waltzes with most interesting conversations with Mr. Livingston on the penitentiary system and especially on capital punishment, passing thus from the serious to the pleasant, from *Rigodon* to Syllogism.‡ That society, furthermore, has no peculiar char-

---

* Though not a member of Congress, or interested in politics, Duponceau was apparently trying to get a bill favouring a projected silk industry enacted into law. With his grandson, he had found comfortable lodgings, where good French soups and other dishes were served, the whole costing him 'only $25 a week.' Letter to William Short, 1 March 1832, William Short Papers, Library of Congress.

† '. . . Present me to them; say to them that their queries shall be answered and forwarded.' Joseph Coolidge Jr. to N.P.Trist, 5 January 1832, Trist Papers, Library of Congress.

Trist, a native of Virginia, after studying at West Point and under Thomas Jefferson, had entered the administrative service at Washington as a clerk in the State Department and become the warm friend of President Jackson. The most notable event of a rather disappointing diplomatic career was to be his errand as Peace Commissioner to Mexico in 1848.

‡ *Rigodon* was an eighteenth century measure or dance. The Livingston parties, graced by his daughter Cora, were famous in Washington; and, now that Peggy Eaton was gone, social life in Washington generally was beginning to recall 'the better days of the Republic.'

Beaumont was in error in supposing that the Secretary of State was of Louisiana origins. Born at Clermont, N.Y., and a graduate of Princeton in 1781, Livingston had been a lawyer, Congressman, District Attorney, and finally Mayor of New York City. It was while he held that latter post that a clerk in his office defaulted, and he had resigned and gone to New Orleans to found a new career. Such were his talents and industry that he soon not only paid off his debt of honour but published both a civil code and a plan for a penal code for Louisiana. The latter had failed of acceptance in his adopted State but was already widely read and admired in Europe.

Tocqueville and Beaumont recognized Mr. Livingston as the foremost penologist in the United States, and were interested to find that he favoured the Pennsylvania rather than the Auburn system. His writings and opinions they would refer to throughout their Report: *Du Syst. Pén.*, pp.16,270–273, 290 *et passim*.

acter; it's absolutely a European *salon*, and the reason is simple: all the members of the diplomatic corps gathered in Washington set the tone; French is the common language, and you would believe yourself in a Parisian *salon*.'

Meanwhile Edward Everett had received a note from the Minister of France, couched in French of the most diplomatic and flattering variety. 'Mr. Serurier,' the note began in the third person, 'Mr. Serurier, intending to dine to-morrow, *en famille et sans cérémonie*, two young French magistrates charged with an honourable mission to the United States, would like to add to the pleasures of this little reunion by having them meet one of the most distinguished men of this country; he requests Mr. Everett to do him the honour of coming to dine to-morrow with him, Mme Serurier, and these two gentlemen. He will be very flattered if Mr. Everett will be so good as to join him in putting aside, on this occasion, all etiquette and all formality.—Washington this Saturday morning. 21 January. Dinner at 5 o'clock.'

'Dined at the French Ministers in company with Messrs. de Tocqueville & Beaumont & Mr. Duponceau.—' Edward Everett noted in his diary the next day. The great Massachusetts Senator was given to being very terse—in his diary. It wasn't that he was uninterested in Tocqueville and Beaumont: while they remained in Washington he was to pay them the compliment of many attentions; and he obviously had enjoyed the Sunday dinner at the Seruriers.* Beaumont was a little more explicit.

'23 January—we dined yesterday with the Minister of France, who gave us an excellent dinner despite the reduction of his salary. His wife is pretty and very nice. We spoke long of France. . . .' And that was an absorbing topic. There was the Fall of the Restoration to discuss once more; there was the continuing weakness of the July Monarchy and the bitterness of the parties. On the one hand, news had just come of labour disturbances at Lyon. On the other, Tocqueville thought he could feel the wind 'beginning to blow quite strongly from the side of Royalism.' And always, like a shadow in the room, the fear of the cholera hung over the discussion. Apparently the dread Asiatic disease was speeding on its way toward the fairest portion of Europe. Irresistibly and fatally, it would visit France. 'We find it hard to hold

---

* See his papers, and the frequent mention of Tocqueville and Beaumont in his diary (No.145,pp.25–28), Massachusetts Historical Society.

ourselves in America, our feet are burning,' Tocqueville wrote.* But meanwhile it was at least good to talk with people who understood.

In four days they had met the President, been introduced into Congress, dined with the French Minister and attended a party at Edward Livingston's. And the entertainments for the two Frenchmen had only just begun. Celebrities came crowding with invitations, and Beaumont proudly drew up their calendar. 'In a couple of days they are going to give in our honour a great ball of 3–400 persons,' he announced to his family. 'All our week is going to be agreeably occupied. To-morrow we are passing the evening at Mr. Livingston's; Wednesday we have a dance at the house of Mr. Patterson, Commodore of the American navy;† Thursday, a great ministerial dinner at Mr. Livingston's; Friday, ball at the house of Mr. MacLane, Secretary of the Treasury;‡ we dine Saturday with Mr. Adams, ex-president of the United States. I am much afraid they will give us indigestion. All our evenings are taken, as you see. As for our days, we spend them almost entirely in the Senate and the Legislature. We have free passes, like the members of these assemblies themselves. I don't believe, however, that my stay in Washington will be as profitable as it might; in spite of all my efforts to fix my attention on the interesting objects all around, I am given over to one perpetual preoccupation: the idea of my return. So long as I had several months of absence before me, I was not without courage in bearing them; now that I have but a fortnight to spend far from you, I feel my strength failing. . . .'

* Once again Tocqueville was depressed, and full of discouragement when he thought about the future. 'I did not suppose that I could possibly return to my country with so much darkness in my soul,' he wrote to his brother Édouard, Washington, 20 Jan. 1832 (TT). See also Toc. to Chabrol, Washington, 24 January 1832 (YT).
† Daniel T. Patterson (1786–1839), was an able sailor who had had an exciting career afloat. A midshipman on the ill-fated *Philadelphia*, he had been captured by the Tripoli pirates in 1803, and held a prisoner for nineteen months. In 1813–1814, as Commander of the New Orleans Station, he had co-operated with Andrew Jackson against the English, and destroyed the forts of the pirate Jean Laffite on Barataria Bay. Captain of the *Constitution* in the Mediterranean, 1826–1828, he was now entering upon a four-year stretch as Commodore of the Mediterranean squadron.
‡ A native of Delaware, Louis McLane (1786–1857) had likewise begun as a midshipman in the United States navy. Switching to the study of the law under James A. Bayard, however, he had made politics his career, and had won a considerable prominence. After twelve years in Congress, he had been appointed Minister to England, and had now just returned to serve in Jackson's second cabinet. After three years successively in the posts of Treasury and State, he was to retire and devote his energies to managing the Baltimore and Ohio Railroad.
   Edward Everett, who was apparently in great demand, attended Commodore Patterson's dance, Mr. Livingston's dinner of 26 January, and what he described as 'Great party at Mr. McLane's in the Evening' (Friday, 27 January).

## LII

## FEDERAL STUDIES—AND THE RETURN

MIDWAY through that busy week, Tocqueville sat down to write a letter[1] that he told his father would 'perhaps be the last I shall write you from America. God be praised; we are counting on embarking the 10th or 20th of February from New-York; and thirty days being the average passage, we will arrive in France toward the 10th or 20th of March. . . .*

'. . . We have been here a week, and shall remain till the sixth of February. Our sojourn here is useful and agreeable. Washington contains at the moment the outstanding men of the entire Union. It's no longer a question for us of obtaining from them ideas about things we know nothing about: but we review, in our conversations with them, all that we knew already more or less exactly. We determine the doubtful points. It's a kind of counter-inquiry, which is very useful. . . .'

The evening of their dinner with the outstanding representative in the House, ex-president John Quincy Adams, for example, they had taken the opportunity to clarify their own minds about the role of the West. 'I asked Mr. Adams to-day,' Tocqueville noted,[2] 'why there was such a noticeable difference between the social conditions in the new western States and those in New England. He answered: That results

---

* Four days before, in a letter to his brother Édouard, Tocqueville had practised his last bit of benevolent deception in the interest of his family's peace of mind. Fearing that the date of their sailing would give rise to 'unreasonable terrors,' he had pointed out that he would arrive before the Equinox and that, in any case, the American packets weathered the worst storms. In the last ten years—such were the figures, he said—a vessel had sailed each week for Liverpool, and two others every ten days for Havre and London respectively. Yet in all that time not one had been lost.

   That these statistics did not quite accord with the facts, Tocqueville's family probably had no way of knowing. (To Chabrol, Tocqueville admitted that there had been two exceptions: one vessel lost, and one wrecked on the coast of France, both in the month of March.) In any case, Tocqueville triumphantly insisted, the American steamboats had been a hundred times more dangerous. In their first six weeks in the United States alone, 30 had either exploded or sunk. 'We got off one three hours before the event,' he said: 'another time we were smashed like a nutshell on a rock.'

almost [entirely?] from the point of departure. New England was peopled by a race of very enlightened and profoundly religious men. The West is being populated by all the adventurers to be found in the Union, people for the most part without principles or morality, who have been driven out of the old States by misery or bad conduct or who know only the passion to get rich.'

Here might be only the bitterness of a declining section, expressing itself through one of its most drastic spokesmen, but from their own experiences in the West Tocqueville could not smother the uncomfortable conviction that Mr. Adams was at least in part correct. And if that were so, there obtruded itself once more the unpleasant problem of the durability of the American federation. '*Future of the Union*,' Tocqueville began a reflection in one of his diaries.[3]

'One of the greatest dangers run by the Union appears to arise from its very prosperity.

'The rapidity with which the new nations are arising in the West and Southwest certainly subjects it to a rude test.

'The first result of this disproportionate growth is a violent change in the equilibrium of power and political influence. Powerful States become weak, territories without a name become States with preponderant influence. Wealth, like population, is displaced. These changes cannot take place without injuring interests, without exciting violent passions. The rapidity with which they operate renders them yet a hundred times more dangerous.*

'That's not all. A society of nations, like a society of individuals, is a thing difficult to maintain. The more members there are, the harder it becomes, the more necessary it is that each one bring moderation and wisdom to the common councils.

'Now, not only do the new States of the Union increase, by their very existence, the difficulty of maintaining the federal tie, but in addition they offer far fewer guarantees of wisdom and moderation than the old. The new States are in general composed of adventurers; social progress is so rapid, one might say so impetuous, that everything is still in disorder. Nothing in the customs, ideas, or laws gives the impression of order or stability. In short they possess the half-savage and uncultivated spirit characteristic of the first inhabitants in a wilderness together with the power which ordinarily belongs only to old societies.'

Of course such a state of affairs was in part only transitory, and not

---

* See Poinsett conversation, above p.650,

in any case conclusive. 'One of the things militating singularly in favour of the Union,' he noted on the other hand, 'is the fact that all the powerful men and all the great political passions are interested in maintaining it.'

Two other questions arose in Tocqueville's mind. The United States were obviously not only a federation, but also a democracy, and dependent as such very largely on the *tendencies* and *qualities* of their leadership. Any failure in one or the other might also lead toward destruction. Whatever the size—or the western membership—of the Union, it depended for its very existence on the propensities and abilities of the men in Washington.

> The Empire of Democracy does not always perish from weakness and inability to act.
>
> It's not in the nature of a democratic power to lack material means, but rather moral force, stability, and skill.
>
> Two ways for a government to perish.
>
> 1. Default of power (like the first Union, for instance).
> 2. Bad use of power, as with all the tyrannies.
>
> It's through this second evil that the American republics will perish.
>
> The first way more rapid and spectacular than the second [which is?] none the less sure.[4]

Tocqueville was back on an old thought, and one that he was to emphasize very strongly in his book. Democracy might lead to tyranny quite as directly as might any of the so-called 'less free' types of government. One day he would insist on this danger, much to the mental discomfort of his American readers. And now, if tyranny was a tendency, what of the leadership?

The leaders were lawyers, it was true. And lawyers were by training and habits conservative. 'Mr. Everett (Edward) said to me to-day: that among the members of Congress nine-tenths belonged to the legal profession. Landholders have gained entrance in very small numbers.'[5]

But where, in all Washington, were the giants, the statesmen of other days? Tocqueville was impressed by the kindness and general intelligence of the men he was being introduced to, but had there not been a change?

'*Id.* Mr. Serrurier, who was Minister of France to the United States twenty years ago, said to me that on his return he had found that a great change had taken place. The men had grown smaller; one no longer saw great political talents,'

And on the same twenty-fourth of January, their indefatigable guide Nicholas Trist, 'employed in the administration [and] a Virginian of such *esprit,* said to me to-day that Virginia was now only the shadow of its former self; that the great men, and even the noteworthy men, had disappeared; and that one no longer saw men of that kind rising to take their place.'

Here was indeed a serious weakening in the American system, and one perhaps not very clearly realized abroad. 'Great men of the early times of the Republic. Their understanding. Their true patriotism. Their high character.

'Convention that made the Federal Constitution. Few prejudices gaining admission; constant struggle against provincial prejudices. Love, science of republican liberty; on the other hand a courageous and constant struggle against the evil passions of the people.*

'Character of Washington. Still more admirable for his courage in fighting against popular passions than for what he did on behalf of liberty!

'*Les Dieux s'en vont*!

'A separate chapter on Washington. Washington has been admired for not having wanted to assume a dictatorship, for having withdrawn into the crowd. . . . Ignorance of the true state of affairs, historical memories badly applied.

'Cincinnatus. Washington could not reasonably presume to dominate. Yet *admirable* in his resistance to the exaggerations of popular opinion. There's his superiority, his culminating achievement.

'Washington could not raise himself by force of arms (absurd) but by popular favour. And he did not seek that a moment.

'Why has Washington, whom the majority finally deserted while he was alive, why has Washington become a superman since his death?'

Tocqueville was puzzled, and no little concerned. Nine months before he had come to America in a very dubious frame of mind about the durability of the American experiment. An increasing equality was the irresistible tendency of the modern world, he had felt, but whether a Federal Republic could succeed and, succeeding, endure: that was an

---

* Tocqueville had been reading the *Federalist* again. The larger the political assemblies, apparently, 'the more opportunity they give to the oligarchic control by a few members.' And Congress was still small. Yet where were the men in 1832 who could have written the *Federalist*? Where now were presidents like the great Washington? See 'Paquet 21,' *O.C.,*VIII,299.

entirely different question. And in spite of all that he had seen to praise, in spite of all the pleasant surprises that the United States had given him, still he was not reassured.

'At this moment I am turning over a great many ideas about America,' he wrote his father.[6] 'Many are still in my head; quite a number are thrown, in embryo and without order, on paper, or are spread through the conversations written up in the evening on returning to my lodgings. All these preparations will pass under your eyes; you will find nothing interesting in itself; but will be able to judge whether I can make some use of them. During the last six weeks of travelling, when my body was more tired and my mind more tranquil than for a long time past, I have thought a good deal about what might be written about America. To try to present a complete picture of the Union would be an enterprise absolutely impracticable for a man who has passed but a year in this immense country. I believe, moreover, that such a work would be as boring as it would be instructive. One might be able, on the other hand, by selecting the topics, to present only those subjects having a more or less direct relation to our social and political state. In this way the work might have at the same time a permanent and an immediate interest. There's the plan: but will I have the time and discover in myself the ability to carry it out? That's the question. There is, besides, one consideration always present in my mind; I shall write what I think, or nothing; and all truth is not palatable (*bonne à dire*). In two months at the latest, I hope, we will be able to talk about all that at our ease. . . .'

And again he wrote: 'You say in one of your letters, dear Father, that you are counting on me to do something worth while in the world. I want to justify your expectation even more for your sake, I swear, than for my own.'

*

*   *

Their visit to Washington was closing, and in the early days of February Tocqueville and Beaumont got ready for the voyage home. They had attended the debates in Congress with unflagging attention; they had taken all the time that the judicious Edward Livingston could spare them.* With the aid of Nicholas Trist they had collected a mass

---

* Edward Livingston was the only American to whom Tocqueville would render public acknowledgment in his *Démocratie* for services and assistance rendered during their study of the United States. The reason for so ungenerous a policy was really

of printed matter on the operation and history of the Federal Government.\* They had talked again with Joel Poinsett and tried to persuade him to make his twenty-third trip abroad in their company.† From Edward Everett, and others, they had promises of letters and essays on various phases of American political and social life.‡ It was hard to break away, for many of their friends and acquaintances wanted to keep them longer in Washington.

Yet France was calling and they felt they had to go. Serurier asked Tocqueville whether he would be willing to carry a despatch that he

---

the delicate one of protecting his many American hosts from the disappointment or embarrassment of being quoted or contradicted or held up to ridicule as a result of his own breach of confidence. 'I would rather injure the success of my recitals than add my name to the list of those travellers who send back chagrin and embarrassment in return for the generous hospitality that they have received.'

With Mr. Livingston, however, Tocqueville thought he might make a graceful exception, the reason being that the noted Secretary had in the interval left his post to become the Minister Plenipotentiary of the United States at Paris. 'Among the American officials who have thus favored my researches,' Tocqueville's book was to proclaim, 'I shall cite above all M. Edward Livingston. . . . During my sojourn at the seat of Congress, M. Livingston was so good as to see that I was supplied with the greater part of the documents now in my possession relating to the Federal government. M. Livingston is one of those rare men whom one [learns to] love by reading their books, whom one admires and honours even before meeting, and to whom one is happy to owe a debt of gratitude.' *Dém. en Am.*, I,xxii–xxiii.

\* Apparently it was Trist who actually supplied the assistance (and the Federal documents) for which Livingston could not spare the time. Happily, Mr. Trist could speak French fluently. But to find even a few books and records was no easy matter. 'Mr. Trist, a high official in the State Department, said to me to-day: Everything is public in this country; yet there is perhaps no country in the world where it is harder to gather together documents bearing on events already past. As nothing is stable, neither men nor things, in the administrations, the papers disappear with incredible rapidity. Nothing is harder, for instance, than to procure the debates of Congress in sequence. Latterly Virginia wished to have printed the sessions of its legislature since the Revolution; yet never were they able to get hold of a complete copy of the debates. The enterprise had to be given up.' Toc. diary note, 27 Jan. 1832 (Non-Alph. III).[7]

† Apparently Tocqueville and Beaumont had grown fond of Poinsett, and superstitious about the Southerner's lucky star in travelling; for on reaching New York, and finding no boat ready to sail, Tocqueville wrote to say that good luck had deserted them. He hoped the American would not forget them, sent Poinsett a couple of documents from France, and forwarded his own address in Paris, in the hope that Poinsett would soon follow them to Europe. Draft of a letter (BIE).

‡ On their last Sunday in Washington, despite 'a violent storm of snow & hail,' Edward Everett called on them. He was at the moment investigating a reservation question arising out of a Chickasaw Treaty; and Beaumont took advantage of the opportunity to exact from the Massachusetts Senator a promise of some printed documents on the subject of the American Indian.

Possibly the two commissioners also made the acquaintance of John Marshall, the Chief Justice. They later thought of sending him a copy of their prison report; and Tocqueville was to refer to his *Life of Washington* in *Dém. en Am.*, I,31,41.

was sending to his government.* One last day, 2 February, they spent in the Senate. That evening at five o'clock they called on Nicholas Trist, to say good-bye.[8] And next morning, before it was light, they were off. The stage took them to Philadelphia, where they spent a day, making a round of farewell visits and reminding the Recorder of the city that he had not yet sent them the essays on the legal and judiciary system of Pennsylvania that he had promised them.[9] Another journey, and they were once again in New York, hastily gathering up and packing the bundles of documents that had been left there in October, together with the fresh accumulation of letters and essays that had since come flocking in through the mails.[10]

There was, at the last minute, an unexpected disappointment. The boat for Havre, that was to have put out on the tenth, postponed its sailing until the twentieth.† So Tocqueville and Beaumont found they had ten days to wait. The delay, however, was not without its compensations and *agréments*, for all their New York friends came crowding in with greetings and invitations.[11] Thus it was that on the sixteenth they once more found themselves dining at James Gore King's, and chatting with the charming Philip Hone.[12] That same evening, they encountered their New England *Nestor* Jared Sparks, just down from Boston, and had an opportunity to thank him in person for his 'Essay on Town Government.' ‡ Robert Emmet sent them 'a copy of the Comptroller's

---

* Actually, Serurier seems to have sent the despatch after them to New York. In it he said of them that they had left in Washington 'the highest opinion of their mission and of their abilities (*personnes*). They have employed the six months [*sic*] passed in this country very advantageously, have come to understand it very well, and will be able to offer your Excellency the most up-to-date observations, which they have been in a position to make, from one end of the Union to the other, in so far as such information may seem of use. The President, his cabinet, and particularly Mr. Livingston, have received them with all the distinction that such interesting travellers, presented by His Majesty's Minister, deserve.' 6 February 1832, *États-Unis*, vol.86,p.51, *Ministère des Affaires Étrangères*.

† Apparently the incoming packet, the *Charlemagne*, had failed to put in an appearance, though already 71 days at sea; and the service was thrown off schedule. Originally, Tocqueville and Beaumont had intended to sail home by way of England and the English prisons, but the cholera and the impatience of the government had made them decide to sail straight for France. *National Gazette*, 9 February 1832.

‡ Philip Hone recorded that the evening party was 'at Mrs. Davis's (quite too large for the occasion) to witness the Rehearsal for the last Soirée of the musical club.'
   In his journal for the same day, Sparks wrote: 'At seven in the morning went on board the Steamboat for New York, & arrived at 5 in the afternoon. Put up at Bunker's, Broadway. Evening at a musical party, at Mrs. Davis's.—Genl. Santander from Colombia was there; also M. Tocqueville & M. Beaumont, whom I was glad to meet, as I feared they had already sailed for France.' Sparks Papers, Widener Library, Harvard.

account of our City Expenses for the last year,' and tried to prolong their stay. And on the very eve of their sailing Recorder Riker took the trouble to write them a note of elephantine gracefulness, assuring them of his 'sincere regard' and 'unfeigned' good wishes for their voyage home.*

On the twentieth day of February 1832, the *Havre* finally set sail. It was the very same vessel on which they had first embarked on their momentous undertaking, ten long months before. But this time no mismanagement, no untoward accidents seem to have marred their passage. They were becalmed one day in the Channel, within sight of the shores of France, and for the last time Beaumont took out his sketchbook. But the rest of the voyage they seem to have relaxed and rested. They were suddenly so tired—and both of them so overwhelmingly eager to be home.

What they would do when they got there, what use they would make of their new-found knowledge, even whether their great adventure had been worth while, they did not know.

'I leave America after having employed my time there usefully and agreeably,' Tocqueville had written his brother from Washington. '. . . In general, two years are necessary to get a complete and exact picture of the United States. Yet I hope I have not wasted my time. . . .'

---

* In Sparks' Journal, 19 Feb.: 'Evening at Mr. Charles King's, & Mr. Brooks's, with Mr. Blunt. Bid adieu to Messrs. Tocqueville & Beaumont, who are to sail to-morrow.'

# PART IX: THE INTERPRETATION OF AN EXPERIENCE

## LIII

## 1832–1840

## THROUGH DISGRACE AND DISILLUSION

THEY had spent nine months in America, trying to spy out the future for France, planning thereby also to establish their careers, trusting in the end that they had not wasted their time. Nine months.

It would be nine years before Tocqueville would finish his commentary, or either of them would be able to take so much as a single stride into the field of politics.

For the France to which they were returning seemed ill: a country stricken with an intermittent, debilitating disease. And they themselves, despite all their planning, were shortly to find themselves more disoriented than ever.*

The two friends reached Paris toward the latter part of March. Already the dreaded cholera had anticipated them and was beginning to stalk in the city. They called at the Ministry, but failed to secure an interview. The journals noticed the return of prison commissioners from America, but the government—rather sullenly—refused to be interested. After vainly waiting a week, Beaumont reported the successful completion of their mission by letter, and went home to the Sarthe to see his family. It was the beginning of April, and the plague was now taking its hundreds in a day. But Tocqueville stayed on in Paris, both to be near his own family and to begin the organization of notes for their

---

* A sketch of political developments under the July Monarchy in the years 1832–1836, and again in the period 1836–1840, will not be attempted here. Suffice it to say that both the government and the various groups of the opposition seemed to Tocqueville to be pursuing the wrong objects, by an unscrupulous conduct. He found himself sympathizing as little with the ardent Bourbons, and their conspiracies for a restoration, as with the factious Republicans and the extremists of the left. And as for the weakness, jealousy, suspicion, and petty tyrannies of the successive ministries under Louis Philippe, for such administration he had only the profoundest contempt. Most discouraging of all, from his point of view, was the increasing materialism of private and public life.

prison report. He was worried and disgusted, and more than ever before he found himself suffering from emotional instability. After a year of travel an extraordinary restlessness had hold of him. Tired as he was, he could not relax. Yet when he tried the discipline and routine of composition, his mind refused its function.

'You would laugh with all your heart,' he wrote to Beaumont after a few days,[1] 'if you could see how I direct my intellectual labours in the mornings. I get up and at once plump into the vast armchair that my father was so imprudent as to give me. By one side I place a chair, and on the chair an ink stand. On my knees I have a notebook, a great copy-book of paper, and nearby a pile of books.

'Thus prepared I lean back and, eyes half closed, wait for the genius of the penitentiary system to appear before me.

'I finally grew tired of this manner of *working* because I noticed that I was thinking of everything except of prisons. I judged that, cost what it might, it was necessary to emerge from this culpable inertia. I therefore picked up your letter and read it through twice, without stopping to breathe. But, having observed that once at the end I could not recall a single word that it contained, I prepared a great sheet of paper and wrote at the head of it in large and legible characters: WHAT I HAVE TO DO BEFORE BEAUMONT'S RETURN.

'There follows an enumeration. So far we have reached number II, I am proud to tell you.

'This first labour accomplished, I felt the holy enthusiasm beginning to come to me and I at once began to attack the number I, being decided not to reverse the order for fear of getting mixed up. It's thus that Richemond [*sic*] and Baltimore have already been passed in review. . . .

'I feel overwhelmed by the responsibility you leave me. I might still have been capable of following your instructions word for word; but, if you abandon me to myself, I am lost. The fact is that I sincerely hope, for the honour of the American Penitentiary System, that you have felt more inspired the last week than I.

'I almost forgot to give you the single even moderately interesting piece of news that I have for you. Two days ago I went in the morning to talk to cousin d'Aunay. He received me, as he always does, with open arms, more enthusiastically even than usually. There was an indescribable something about his conduct that betrayed the fact that our journey was having the same effect on his brain as on the brain of many others. Furthermore, I was bringing him the American documents that we had promised him and for which he seemed very grateful (I made it quite clear, of course, that this was only a loan).

'We then chatted, feet cocked up, for more than an hour. He first spoke about our position. He advised me earnestly not to hurry, seeming to take a lively interest in the success of our *mémoire*. As to its composition, he gave me many counsels, of which a number I believe are very good, and the whole of which was received by me as such. I haven't time to explain them all to you. Roughly, his thought is to be positive and practical in what concerns America, more general and tentative for France.

' "You are both of you very young," he said; "you have before you a great future. Don't tie yourself to one idea, in such a way as to fall irrevocably with it."

'There's something worth thinking over in that. But I am too hurried at this moment to tell you all that, practically, these words suggested to me. My instinct tells me that he is right.

'We then, or rather, he then tackled the subject of politics. I could have wished that you had been there, my dear friend. It was the oddest *séance* that I have had in some time. If you could have heard him speak of the state of France, of the ministry, of the chambers, of the man they have put at the head [of the government], and even of *la glorieuse* [*sic*] as a whole, you would have been stupefied at the path travelled by opinion in the last year. One conversation of that stripe teaches you more about revolutions than all the histories of the world. You would have smiled inwardly on observing with what admirable ease the leaders of the liberalism of 1828, those makers of 1830, serenely put to the sword the same first principles of civil liberty that we others, we old royalists, would never abandon at any price.

'Truly, the world of politics is a foul pit. . . .'*

Indeed it was. But just how malodorous, the two friends were a long way from suspecting. The blow was to come out of a clear sky, only a few weeks later.

As commissioners, and men of ambition, both Tocqueville and Beaumont were convinced that—whatever line they adopted—a thoroughgoing, written report on their prison investigation was immediately in order. Yet if they were to make any comparison whatever between the

---

* 'I am afflicted, disgusted, almost *honteux* at the state I find my country in,' Tocqueville confessed to his friend E.Stoffels (St. Germain, 22 April 1832, fragment, copy YT).

penitentiaries of America and the old-fashioned prisons of France, one further detail of investigation now seemed prerequisite. They understood the *maisons centrales* from experience and observations before sailing. But they had never studied the *bagnes*, the hulks, the famous prison ships of France. While Beaumont therefore undertook the shaping of the main body of their report, Tocqueville, glad of the slightest excuse for action, leaped from the ancestral armchair and set out for Toulon.

He had been there only a few days when he read in a journal that Beaumont had been dismissed from his post in the government courts! It was tyrannical, it was incomprehensible.

Yet perhaps not so incomprehensible. Apparently certain malevolent superiors were at last getting even with the young noble who had forced their hands over the prison mission. They had not been able to prevent his getting the leave of absence. But they had managed to recall him ahead of the agreed time. And now, as a measure of discipline and to test his loyalty, they had been inspired to require him to handle a case for the government that they knew would be odious to him. It concerned a suit for slander by a *protégé* of the administration, a certain Baronne de Feuchères, against the Prince de Rohan. Beaumont was to make the concluding plea on behalf of the prosecution. The case was not before his own division at Paris, and it was scandalous. Beaumont had begged to be excused, alleging ignorance of the circumstances. The government had persisted. In point of fact, even his curtailed leave had not expired, and Beaumont had not yet reported for duty to his court. Again he had asked to be excused. Thereupon his superiors took the step that they must have had in mind from the beginning. They cashiered the independent-minded prosecutor, and announced his dismissal in the press. Just, as Beaumont put it in a letter to his friend, at the very moment that he was using his full literary capacity in the government's service.*

Tocqueville was terribly angry. Without a moment's hesitation, he decided to resign his own gratuitous post. 'I have only this day,' he wrote to his *Procureur Général* on the twenty-first,[2] 'learned from the Moniteur of 16 May of the rigorous and, I venture to say, sovereignly

---

* Beaumont must have had premonitions of trouble, for on 1 May he had written to Edward Everett that they were delighted to have an 'occupation that is serious, interesting, and has nothing to do with the political debates in which France is engaged. Present circumstances are so powerful as to crush men, and no one is capable of struggling against them to advantage.' Everett Papers, Mass. Historical Society.

unjust decree with which *M. le Garde des Sceaux* has struck M. G. de Beaumont.

'Long bound by intimate friendship to the man who has thus just been discharged, whose opinions I share and of whose conduct I approve, I feel bound to associate myself voluntarily with his fate, and abandon with him a career where service and uprightness are unable to forestall an undeserved disgrace.

'I have the honour to request you, *M. le Procureur Général*, to be so good as to lay before *M. le Garde des Sceaux* my resignation as *juge suppléant* at the Versailles court. I have the honour . . .'

*
*   *

So, after two short months at home Tocqueville and Beaumont found themselves farther than ever removed from political office or any prospect of a career. The conscientious labours of a year had won them, not honours but an official disgrace.

By the same untoward circumstance, of course, they had now unexpectedly regained their freedom, and a complete command of their own time. By industrious effort, therefore, they would be able to complete their extensive prison report and have it in the hands of a printer by November, to be published early in 1833. This duty honourably concluded, each man would then set to work on his American masterpiece. Beaumont would work at his novel in the country. And Tocqueville would secrete himself in a little city garret, '*mansardé* under the roof,' to compose the first part of his *Démocratie*. The two years to follow thus promised to become (and were even at a later day said to have been) the happiest interval of Tocqueville's life.

Unfortunately, the young author was not fated to escape so easily. For already a second unlooked-for development, shattering the momentary calm of politics, had broken in upon his private thoughts. The extremists among the Bourbon royalists were rising in revolt.

The menacing shadow of revolution had never ceased to haunt Alexis de Tocqueville. And it happened that, at the very moment of their return from America, an ultra-royalist conspiracy had been brewing. Some minor figures, plotting to kidnap the King and his family, had already been arrested at a banquet in the *rue des Prouvaires*. And now, through the whole remainder of the year, the restlessness and bitter dissatisfaction of the legitimist Bourbon following began to detonate, in a series of futile uprisings. Tocqueville was at once touched on the raw. It was not that he approved any such ventures. Quite the reverse. If the July Monarchy were upset, it would not be in favour of the Bourbons, he protested, but of 'Republicanism' or worse.* To make the situation even more intolerable, the very men who were gambling so disastrously were of his own class, many of them known to his own family. One, even, was his own intimate friend, high-strung and passionate Louis de Kergolay.

Poor Kergolay had been caught right at the start. Implicated in the miserable fiasco of an unsuccessful landing in the South of France, he had been thrown into prison at Marseilles and was now threatened with a drastic condemnation. Dropping his prison inspection at Toulon, Tocqueville at once went to see him. The visit wrung his heart.

'Ah! what tragic times we live in,' he exclaimed, 'when right, courage, and honour have such difficulty in marching together!' And to the English girl whom he was later to marry, he confided his melancholy premonitions:[4]

'. . . I am filled with sadness and foreboding, Marie. Just as I had foreseen and predicted to you a few days ago, civil war has broken out in the West. The royalists will perhaps have some momentary successes, but I predict again that they will be utterly crushed. How much loyal and honourable blood will flow! I have already read in the papers the name of a fine young man whom I knew. He has just been killed like a wretch. Tell me why in all ages honour and folly seem to have gone hand in hand. What more courageous, more loyal and, at the same time, more clumsy and more unfortunate than your Jacobites? Our French royalists follow exactly in their path. . . .' †

Worse was not long in following. Not only was the badly-managed

---

* Of all the forms of government that the inexperienced people of France ought to fear, a direct experiment with mass rule would be the worst, Tocqueville was convinced. How little they had studied—or understood—the safeguards that popular government required, it was his earnest intention to point out in his book. As for 'Republicanism,' the champions of that cause did not even know the true meaning of the word. What they had in mind was a return to '91, and so perhaps to '93, with its massacres.

Sometimes it almost seemed as if France were caught in a vicious spiral: Monarchy—Revolution—Tyranny—Restoration—more Revolution—and so on without end. 'The Revolution has not stopped,' he said. 'It no longer, indeed, brings to light any great novelties, but it still keeps everything afloat. The mighty wheel turns and brings nothing up, but it seems that it will turn for ever.'[3]

† Compare these despairing exclamations with the stern indictment of the errors and tragic stupidity of the aristocracy of France, that Tocqueville was soon to insert in his famous 'Introduction.'

uprising in the Vendée suppressed. But the Duchesse de Berry, widow of the eldest son of Charles X—she whose romantic imagination and mysterious appearances and disappearances had inspired the sputtering revolt—was betrayed to the Minister of the Interior, Adolphe Thiers. Located at her hiding place in Nantes, she was captured, and held by the government without trial. Stung with rage and despair, the legitimists deafened the air. Let the Duchesse be released, they howled. Her detention was illegal, monstrous. Minister Thiers was overwhelmed with insults and threats. A number of 'Reclamations' contre la captivité de la Desse de Berry were got up.

To one of these documents both Tocqueville and Beaumont asked to be allowed to add their names.

The gesture was not a happy one. Each young lawyer thought it owing to his dignity to state his independent reason for adhering to a protest from the legitimists. And each adduced to the support of an action essentially emotional reasons that were based in principle and in law. The Duchesse de Berry was not a prisoner of war, said Tocqueville; she should therefore be tried. What trial she had received, said Beaumont, was illegal, her imprisonment equally so.* In later years the instinctive action was to lay both of the aspiring statesmen open to awkward charges of conspiracy and legitimism. And at the moment the protest could not help the Duchesse de Berry. For shortly Minister Thiers discovered that she had been indiscreet: that she was with child, as a result of contracting a secret marriage with an Italian below her station. For the cause of Charles X and of the Bourbons, for honour, possibly even for the hope of good government in France, it was complete disaster.†

Meanwhile the trial of Louis de Kergolay came on, in March 1833, and Tocqueville prepared to appear before the Assizes of Montbrison. The indiscreet and scornful young Louis was making things no easier for himself. He refused to recognize the government of Louis Philippe, its competence or authority, and therefore would not plead. Another

---

* Tocqueville also wrote out his father's protest, a Petition aux Deux Chambres, published in Paris in 1833. Comte Hervé's argument was much longer. He pointed out the danger for France, declared the two Chambers incompetent to judge the captive princess, and suggested that all France might perhaps act as jury. Alexis either rephrased his father's ideas or, more probably, took the old prefect's statement by dictation. Cf. portrait, p.18.

† There is no record of what the two critical lawyers thought of this incredible dénouement. Certainly the performance of the Duchesse de Berry can hardly have strengthened Tocqueville's confidence in the older leadership.

lawyer entered an argument in defence. But it remained for Tocqueville to secure his friend's acquittal. Seizing upon the charge that Louis de Kergolay was disloyal and dangerous to France, Tocqueville launched into an eloquent and feeling speech. He exposed his own friendship for the accused. He elaborated Kergolay's patriotism, his past services to the Bourbons and to France. Louis de Kergolay had always been devoted to liberty, in the highest sense of that abused word. If Tocqueville was interrupted by cries and applause, if he even allowed a faint personal contempt for the spineless and persecuting conduct of the Orleanist administration to become perceptible, could he help it? His words had a deep effect upon the jury: opened the gate of prison for his friend. No matter how his action might later be interpreted by his enemies, or by the small, venomous politicians of lower Normandy, he would never be able to regret his speech or treat his accusers in the matter with anything but withering scorn.*

Spring drifted into summer, the menace of the Vendée subsided, and once again this passionate and sensitive aristocrat—a sort of French Sir Philip Sydney he was to seem to his new friends across the Channel— set out on an unforeseen journey. Postponing his book for the third or fourth time in favour of a new project, in the early days of August he sailed from Cherbourg for the coasts of England. He had letters for the aristocracy of London.

What his intention was, is not altogether clear. Possibly he hoped in old England to find the roots of new America: examine, as it were, into the ancestry of the peculiar society and government about which he intended to write. If so, he was astonished, disappointed, even led astray. 'I rediscover our America,' he wrote to Beaumont, 'nowhere.'

The fact was, on his arrival in the 'vast metropolis' of London, he had been overwhelmed by a feeling of helplessness and inferiority. 'We

---

* 'Eh! since when has it been a crime for a lawyer to lend the support of his plea to a political prisoner?' he protested to the electors of Valognes in 1842. 'Since when have people reproached him for what, in the exercise of his profession, he has said to get his client acquitted? In our most violent civil discords, it is without precedent for an accused man not to find, even in the ranks of a party not his own, lawyers ready to defend him with as much courage and fire as if they had been themselves attached to the same cause. That is one of the glories of our fatherland. The eloquent defence of political prisoners has always seemed to the French Bar the first of its duties, and, far from excusing myself for having bowed to this noble duty, I declare that I take honour in it. . . .

'This man, whom I am accused of having snatched from capital punishment, this man was my childhood friend. . . .' Quoted, Marcel, *Essai politique sur Alexis de Tocqueville*, p.291, note 2.

were something in America. We don't amount to much at Paris. But you have to go below zero and take what the mathematicians call negative numbers to compute what I am here. This is owing to two causes: first to the immensity of the city, which surpasses anything that Paris can suggest; secondly, to the position which the aristocracy here occupies, something of which, it seems to me, I didn't have the faintest idea. . . .' All the customs of England betrayed an aristocratic flavour. 'The aristocratic spirit seems to me to have descended into all classes.'[5]

This first impression grew stronger with every hour. August was the dead season in London, and the majority of the ruling class were unapproachable, being absent at their country estates. But already at the first moment of landing, he had caught a glimpse of the parks and country houses, the magnificent equipages, lackeys and horses, on the roads near Southampton. In London, now, as once in new-world Boston, he attended a meeting on behalf of the Poles. The meeting was presided over by a Lord. Finding that the Prison Report was already known to some members of Parliament, he received a very flattering reception, and was present at a penitentiary dinner attended by the Bishop of Dublin. He visited the House of Lords, and was struck by the Duke of Wellington's clumsiness and hesitation in debate. The tall conqueror of Napoleon didn't seem to know what to do with his hands or his feet, but kept buttoning and unbuttoning his breeches, and stumbled through his remarks like a small boy reciting his lesson. Lord Brougham had a monstrous, powdered wig. And most of the listening Lords were lolling on the cushions, and seemed very carelessly attired. Nevertheless, to the young Frenchman this club of leisurely gentlemen in boots exhaled—as he put it—the very *parfum d'aristocratie*.[6]

Had there only been time, Tocqueville wrote his father, he would like to have seen the Liverpool Railroad. As it was, he was going to Oxford. Did he mean by this to suggest that an interest in the material and educational institutions of modern society was at last being awakened in him? Apparently not. For what actually struck him most forcibly about Oxford (aside from the indigestion he got from overeating with the Fellows) was the university's antiquity and decay. The curriculum of classic languages was medieval, the sciences were hardly, or badly, taught, and the ancient endowments were fallen into abuse. One had but to enter the side streets to walk again in a Gothic town of the fourteenth century.

Then, one memorable day, he achieved his ambition of visiting Warwick and Kenilworth, which had been described to him as the 'most magnificent remains of the feudal age.' The two great castles were beyond all expectation. At Warwick he saw the portraits of Henry VIII and Anne Boleyn, the giant fireplaces; inhaled the 'wild grandeur' of feudalism. And that same evening, on horseback, he found Kenilworth—bathed in the moonlight—and walked through its ruins in enchanted reverie. It was, as he wrote his father, 'a veritable *feudal intoxication.*' Certainly he must have been dreaming, 'for the day of the cavaliers is gone long since, and that of all kinds of aristocracy is rapidly slipping away.' [7]

Here, then, was a first and very strong impression. Of all the lands that he had visited or heard about, England was still the most aristocratic. The rule of the best and the well-born, so swiftly sinking to an inexorable doom under the universal onslaughts of revolution and equalitarianism, had here in England still a stronghold. If he would study the past that was going, the point of departure that so many peoples had already irrevocably left behind, he could find no better spot. It was an idea—an illusion almost—that was to stick in Tocqueville's mind until he died.

His second idea was more pragmatic. England might still cherish her feudal families; but these same families composed a thoroughly modern and accessible ruling class in several ways. In the first place, they were now an aristocracy of wealth quite as much as of birth. Tocqueville was stunned by the prosperity visible everywhere, and much impressed to note how surely wealth gave entry to power and social consideration. As a result, no drastic French exclusiveness was possible—and no real class hatred. The commoner was inspired to emulate, not goaded to destroy. And the ruling nobility had ready an alliance and a defence for the future: they had made a compact with commerce and the industrial age. The new lords of business would in time become Lords indeed. And 'Gentlemen,' he thought, would still be ruling in England when he himself was dead. But it would be a different, broader class of 'gentlemen.' The definition of the word itself was changing.*

---

* 'During the centuries,' Tocqueville later wrote, 'the sense of the word "gentleman" has completely altered in England. Even by the year 1664, when Molière wrote the line in *Tartufe*, "*Et tel que l'on le voit, il est bon gentilhomme*," it would have been impossible to translate this literally into English. If you seek another application of the science of language to that of history, trace through time and space the destiny of the word "gentleman," which sprang from the French "*gentilhomme.*" You will see its meaning spreading in England in proportion as social classes approximate. With successive centuries, it is used of men standing a little lower in the social scale.

This prospect led Tocqueville to admit that he had been altogether mistaken in one other particular of his expectations. England was still destined for *démocratie* in his opinion; not even the House of Lords could make the young visitor believe these English capable of escaping the universal levelling law that was sweeping the modern world. Nevertheless an accessible aristocracy *did* make a difference. Contrary to the experience of France, the transition in old England would be slow, easy, and natural.*

'I came to England,' he confessed, 'persuaded that this country was on the point of being precipitated into the miseries of a violent revolution: my opinion is partly changed in this particular.

'If you denominate revolution all capital change introduced into the laws, all social transformation, all substitution of one regulating principle for another, England is assuredly in a status of revolution, for the aristocratic principle, which was the vital principle of its constitution, is each day losing strength; and it is certain that the "democratic" principle is tending to take its place. But if by revolution you mean a violent and brusque change, England does not seem to me ripe for such a development; and I even perceive many reasons for doubting that it ever will be.'

Again, for his own future guidance, he noted: '. . . if things follow their natural course, I do not believe that this revolution will come, and I see many chances of the English being able to modify their political and social status, no doubt with great discomfort, but without convulsion and without civil war.'[8]

It must have seemed to Tocqueville that he now had this phenomenon of 'equality' in his grasp. He had, at least, studied each of the three stages of transit from the old regime to the new. In America the people had already arrived at the social equilibrium of the future. In France a transitional society was still stumbling blindly and headlong down the perilous road. In England an inherited but supple aristocracy could be discerned just making ready for the journey.†

---

But in France the word *gentilhomme* always remained strictly confined to its original meaning. The word was preserved intact as serving to indicate the members of a caste, because the caste itself had been preserved, as much separated from all others as it ever was.' Quoted, André Maurois, *The Miracle of England*, p.357. For the first perception of this idea, see *O.C.*,VIII,328.

* Tocqueville recorded, as further evidence, his observation that the English generally still believed in large landed estates, and hardly questioned such aristocratic inheritance laws as entail and primogeniture.

† For the influence of his English experiences on Tocqueville's thinking, see also below, pp.693,763.

In October 1833, with these fresh items added to his intellectual baggage, Tocqueville was back in France. At last he felt content to begin the composition of his book. He set to work with an almost savage intensity. And in January 1835, simultaneously with the publication of Beaumont's *Marie*, there appeared the first two volumes of his *Démocratie*.

\*

\*    \*

The applause which greeted Beaumont's novel, and the almost thunderous acclaim rewarding Tocqueville's five-year effort, did much to soothe and pacify two restless spirits. Each author also followed his literary debut with a happy marriage.\*

Yet neither was, for more than an instant, even remotely content. *'Il n'y a pas à dire, c'est l'homme politique qu'il faut faire en nous,'* Tocqueville had once exhorted Beaumont.[9] And this ambition to become leaders rather than simply counsellors now burned with a mounting flame. Yet how achieve a real entrance into politics? The old and exasperating problem seemed farther than ever from a solution.

Each of the pair felt himself partly handicapped by the desire to crown his literary career by an additional achievement before withdrawing entirely from this field of initial venture. Beaumont was therefore to spend a considerable time in Ireland, in order to do for that unhappy land, in all seriousness, what Tocqueville had done for the United States. And Tocqueville himself, after a second visit to Eng-

---

\* Beaumont, in 1836, married his cousin, Clémentine de Lafayette. She was the granddaughter of Lafayette, the 'Hero of Two Worlds,' through his son Georges Washington Lafayette. The celebrated old revolutionary, however, had passed away in 1834; and Clémentine's great charm and serenity of mind more than reconciled Beaumont to the connection.

In 1835, Tocqueville had already taken Marie Mottley, an Englishwoman of no fortune and no particular family, as his bride. Apparently he had met her some six or seven years before at Versailles, where she had been staying with the aunt who had brought her up, a Mrs. Belam. The latter was an undistinguished woman, said to have been the widow of a pharmacist of Portsmouth. At least one of Marie Mottley's brothers was in the British navy. She herself was homely, and some years older than Tocqueville. Her serene disposition and her intellectual tastes, however, had appealed to the young noble, and he had been in love with her since before the American trip. Now he ignored the much more 'brilliant' and wealthy matches that he might have made, and forced his family's reluctant consent. Marie Mottley was never to win their whole-hearted affection, but Tocqueville himself was never to regret his *'mésalliance.'* 'Dieu, que cela m'a réussi!' he later said. They were to have no children. (For Tocqueville's own explanation of his marriage, see his letter to Charles Stoffels, Paris, 18 Oct. 1835, in possession of Mlle Stoffels d'Hautefort. For an unfavourable description of her character, and of the life of the couple together in Normandy, see A.Redier, *Comme disait M. de Tocqueville...* , pp.122ff.)

land, and an unsatisfactory pursuit after health through Germany and
Switzerland, determined that he still had much to say about America
and about *démocratie*.* Specifically, having analysed the political institutions of an equalitarian nation, he now wanted to describe the social
and cultural effects of *démocratie* that to him seemed already visible,
or shortly to be expected, in European society.

The consequence was another four-year agony of research, interruption, and composition.

First in Tocqueville's company, then alone, Beaumont visited the miserable Irishmen, in their poverty and squalor. It wasn't long before he
learned the difference between the Protestant minister—with his fine
park, rich chapel, and no parishioners—and the devoted Catholic priest,
cherishing the whole countryside on no income at all. He early learned
to distinguish between the well-to-do peasant, and the poor tenant with

* By 1836 the two friends had made an amicable arrangement whereby they divided
their literary spoils into two separate spheres of opportunity. Henceforth Beaumont
was to have the exploitation of England and Ireland to himself, while Tocqueville
was to be free to do whatever further writing about America he chose.

This partition, of course, did not stop Tocqueville from using the ideas about
*démocratie* that his English experiences suggested to him. It is, accordingly, worth
noting that during his second visit to his wife's country he paid particular attention
to commerce and to industry. Inspired in part, no doubt, by the obvious and increasing materialism in France, this time he actually visited Birmingham and Man-
chester, studied the investment by the wealthy in trade rather than in land, and
remarked (though apparently without being reminded of the United States) how feverish was the pursuit of money, and what power money brought. By contrast, the
poverty that he now encountered was so appalling as to drive Tocqueville to an
anxious study of poor-law legislation, and to the uneasy conviction that his friend
Nassau William Senior was a little too complacent in the matter. In political custom,
what struck Tocqueville most forcibly (again apparently without American connota-
tion) was English localism and decentralization. Might there not be some curious
connection between local self-government and liberty, he wondered; and in turn
between freedom of action and commercial prosperity?

On the whole, though his emphasis on English aristocracy was now a little less
pronounced, Tocqueville was for the second time impressed with the differences between England and the United States rather than by any similarities. This interpretation—which was to handicap his work—was due both to an over simplification in
his mind of the America that he once had known and to a failure to understand
England nearly so well as he perhaps should have. Tocqueville himself admitted that
six months was too brief a study: 'A year has always seemed to me too short a
time to enable one decently to appreciate the United States; and it is infinitely easier
to acquire clear concepts and precise ideas on the American Union than on Great
Britain. In America, all the laws originate, so to speak, in the same thought. All
society is founded on a single fact; everything deduces from a single principle.
America might be compared to a great forest pierced by a multitude of straight roads
all ending at the same place. It's only a question of discovering the hub of the wheel
(*le rond-point*), and everything is visible at a glance. But in England the paths cross,
and it's only by following each one of them that a clear idea of the whole may be
gained.' *O.C.*,VIII,135.

no pig whatever to share his smoky interior. He followed the assizes, studied the land question, attended an election, and probed into the bitterness of the religious conflict. The English, apparently, got everything: land, wealth, power. The Irishmen cultivated their native soil for foreigners—and starved. Beaumont did not foresee the potato famine. But 'what a volcano!' was his thought, as he gathered in his documents for one more case-study of injustice and tyranny. The subject was magnificent. Yet inwardly Beaumont cherished no great illusions. When his new work * was received with enthusiasm by the journals, and even compared with Tocqueville's *Démocratie*, Gustave entered an immediate disclaimer. He himself, he modestly said, would rather have written one half of the *Démocratie* than two *Irlandes*. Their penitentiary report was a good book not widely read; *L'Irlande* was read, but might be worthless. If the journals persisted in their comparison it was only to belittle Tocqueville, or because they were honestly in error. He, himself, he rather pathetically confessed, was conscious of some merit; but that merit he knew to be—as the future would surely acknowledge—inferior to Tocqueville's. It could hardly be said that his literary efforts had brought to Gustave de Beaumont any complete or enduring satisfaction.

Strangely enough, the same sense of failure was in large measure shared by Tocqueville. His first two volumes had brought him the *Légion d'Honneur* and a seat in the *Académie des Sciences morales et politiques*; but a decoration from the government he would gladly have avoided if he could, and the 'promotion' to the *Académie française* itself still eluded him.† To disturb his author's hard-won peace of mind now came also the first real doubts about his work. The first two volumes had been relatively specific, descriptive, and to the point. The second two seemed to many of the reviewers a little too generalized; and he himself, all through the period of composition, had been painfully afraid that he was losing his anchorage in fact and drifting too far into the fog of philosophical deductions.‡

---

* *L'Irlande sociale, politique et religieuse*, 2 vols., 1839. Before the end of 1840, it reached its fourth edition.

† Tocqueville's private correspondence, particularly with Beaumont, contains innumerable evidences of this ambition, with calculations on his chances, and bulletins on the declining health of members who might conveniently pass on.

In studying Tocqueville's mood at this period, it is worth noting that for satisfaction and self-esteem he was practically driven to seek such public recognition. For his marriage had deprived him of social contacts and the semi-private recognition accorded by the *salons*.

‡ For an explanation on this point, see below, pp.757–60.

The exasperating part about the whole work was the fact that even when he was specific, and plain to the point of baldness, his readers insisted on mistaking his meaning. What he had intended as a manual on the grand strategy of self-government, many of his readers interpreted as campaign oratory, on one side or the other of the partisan disputes of the day.

'They absolutely insist on making of me a party man, and I am nothing of the sort. They give me passions where I have but opinions; or, rather, I have but one passion, the love of liberty and of the dignity of man. All the governmental forms are in my eyes merely the means, more or less perfect, of satisfying this holy and legitimate human passion. . . . I came into the world,' Tocqueville explained his own detachment, 'I came into the world at the end of a long revolution which, after having destroyed the ancient state, had created nothing durable. The aristocracy was already dead when I began to live, and *démocratie* was not yet in existence. My instinct could not therefore draw me blindly either toward one or toward the other. . . . In a word, I was so nicely balanced between the past and the future, that I was not naturally or instinctively drawn toward either; and it has not required great efforts on my part to cast tranquil glances at both sides.'[10]

Tranquillity, however, was hard to maintain in the face of misrepresentation. Already in 1837 the campaign to appropriate his book—or to discredit the author himself by imputing to him 'democratic or aristocratic prejudices' that he did not possess—was in full blast. To the ambitious young author-politician it even seemed as if his few friends in the government were trying to damage his prospects with labels.

For it was in this same year that he ventured to make his first effort to reach the Chamber of Deputies, and the result proved an ignominious disaster.*

---

* Parenthetically, it should be noted that this was not quite his first attempt to take a hand in national politics. For in 1833–1834 he and Beaumont, and two or three others, had entertained the romantic idea of making themselves influential by founding a new Review. They had set the price of membership at a thousand francs, had planned to secure great names to advertise the venture, and had even begun the search for collaborators (among others, Kergolay and Chabrol were approached). According to Tocqueville, the Review was to adopt a very decided *tone*. The Orleanist regime was to be accepted as a *fait accompli*; this was not to be a dynastic sheet. Instead the object would be to combat the materialistic tendencies of the day, to emphasize the importance of morality in the search for happiness and prosperity, to bring back into politics the spiritual qualities. These last were to be made popular by demonstration of their utility (!). The same was to be done for the sciences and the arts.

How did Tocqueville propose to accomplish these noble ends? By limiting his journal to reviews! There would be no original articles and the reviews would all be anony-

The occasion was the national election of 1837. By a family arrangement Alexis had been given the ancient seat of the Clerels, the weather-
rotted and untenanted little château at Tocqueville. The village and
estate of Tocqueville lay not far from the sea, between Cherbourg and
Barfleur on the channel peninsula of lower Normandy. As a child, he
was told, he had once been carried there, horseback and slung in a
*panier*, for there were no roads. And even yet the muddy paths, winding through the lush green country, were too narrow for carriages. At
first such a remote and soundless solitude had not appealed to him. He
had revisited the old Norman mansion on his way to England in 1833.
And 'the life of a potato,' that it offered, was not to the taste of his restless 28 years. Gradually, however, as he saw that his family was known
and respected in the region, there had come to him the idea of founding '*une influence*' some day in that part of the country. He had accepted
the château as his part of a family partition, with Marie he had busily
set about repairing it, and in 1837 he allowed some friends to put him
up for election at near-by Valognes.

Calamity! The government of Minister Molé was supporting him.
Tocqueville wanted none of such support. His whole idea had been to
arrive in the Chamber on his own merits and without engagements.
To Molé, who was his personal friend, he wrote a rather sharp and
insulting protest. Piqued in his turn, Molé pointed out to his young
critic that the administration had made no demands on Tocqueville.
In politics, moreover, there could be no neutrals; one had to be either
for the government or against, and arrive under obligations either to
its friends or to its enemies. In literature one might balance in the nice
equilibrium of a cool and lofty detachment. In the Chamber, no.

The comment was reasonable and just; it accorded with reality. But
it hardly relieved Tocqueville's feelings. And now, since he would have
none of its support, he had the government's stern opposition. To make
the situation even more exasperating, his fortunate but unscrupulous
rival was inspired to appeal to class prejudice. 'Look out! He'll bring
the pigeons back on you,' was the cry. M. de Tocqueville was an aristocrat, and as such to be feared by all good citizens of Normandy. It

---

mous! In this fashion they would not have to pay so much for their authors, and
would retain a better control! He would rather be consistent, and less brilliant. So
said Tocqueville.

How this scheme survived for so long as a year is still a mystery. For a man who
wanted to play a role in France, however, this step was hardly auspicious.[11]

made no difference that the individual thus accused had just written a famous book on Democracy, and laboured with his whole soul to stand above prejudice. The old ruling class didn't change its spots: 'cats will hunt mice,' was the phrase. And Tocqueville found himself being greeted by the stout Normandy farmers, for whom he was already beginning to entertain an affectionate regard, with cries of '*pas de nobles.*' It was disheartening.

He lost the election.*

In 1839 he ran again, and won. It happened that he had grown fond of his little 'towered' château, reconciled to the quiet of country life, and genuinely interested in the peasants and tenant-farmers of that remote corner of France. He set no store by his title; and it was his unaffected way to treat each man, even to the humblest, so as not to offend that individual's dignity. The result was that this considerate 'aristocrat' had so captured the hearts of the local people that no intrigue could avail against him, and a seat in the Chamber was assured to him for as long as he cared to run. By 1840, then, his period of trial and disappointment seemed over. Beaumont had joined him in the Chamber; the first great obstacle was at last surmounted. Once more the future beckoned invitingly.

Yet even in his first days as a deputy Tocqueville learned that he had now undertaken a task for which he perhaps was not made. To his chagrin, the new work overwhelmed and exhausted him. Debating wracked his nerves. From literary habit he found it impossible to speak extempore, and even after fatiguing preparations he was awkward in delivery and more than ill at ease. As for those other legislative arts—the willingness to compromise, the agility of seizing an advantage on the wing, the force of personality to dominate a chaotic assembly,—those gifts he simply did not have. If high principle and unswerving idealism could accomplish anything for France, his life might yet serve the long-planned purpose, fulfil the grand design. But already both he and Beaumont were beginning to entertain fresh doubts.

*

*     *

---

* Beaumont was likewise defeated, in the Sarthe. His peculiar difficulty had been the family affiliations. If given their way his parents and relatives would have brought in all the unconverted legitimists to see him, and hopelessly compromised his position and his case before the electors. As a consequence, he had not even dared go home, or let himself be seen in the Sarthe, until a week before the voting.

The nine years following their return from America, then, became for both of the ambitious political scientists a period of singular disillusionment. Neither conditions in France, nor their own personal fortunes, seemed to make the progress on which they had so anxiously counted. In national politics a certain pacification and a greater unity were indeed achieved. But the peace had been won only by the curtailment of liberty of the press and of assembly, and by the increasing suppression of recalcitrant minorities. And the unity was the product of political frustration and economic profits. Few, if any, of the basic problems had been settled. On the one hand an ambitious King had been working to increase his personal power, while the leading statesmen pulled at cross-purposes. On the other, it appeared simply that the government and an amazing number of the people of France were going in for industrial improvements and momentarily sinking their differences in a degrading materialism. To Tocqueville and Beaumont the crisis was not passed; it had merely been postponed. The factious men were helpless and the greedy men were feasting; but they would all quarrel again. And meanwhile their own personal careers, like their idealistic hopes for France, had suffered terribly. For a while it had seemed that they were actually going backwards, and thereafter, whenever they thought that they were really making progress, it turned out to be progress only to ever-fresh disappointment.

'I shall never be happy, Marie, that is certain,' Tocqueville had written in 1834.[12] 'Nothing is in agreement within me. With a limited and incomplete capacity, I have immense desires; with delicate health, an inexpressible need of activity and emotion; with the taste for the good, passions which lead me astray; with enough intelligence to see what I ought to desire, enough folly to wish the contrary. I am of mediocre strength and mind, at the extremity in my passions and my weakness.

'For a man thus organized there is not the slightest chance ever, no matter what he does, of reaching a durable happiness. What is happening to me, of course, has happened to a thousand others before me. No one is happy in this world—or nearly so—save the truly superior man, or the fool. The first executes the wonderful things he meditates, and the second imagines nothing above the small things that he does.'

Their own aim was perhaps a little selfishly imagined: he and Beaumont wanted the almost exclusive privilege of saving France. Perhaps they were fools. Yet there was something superior, almost heroic about their dedication. For they were acting not for personal glory, not to establish two names, not even really to achieve contentment and happiness, but simply and sincerely under the lash of an overwhelming anxiety. Their interest was consuming, their concern really desperate. If the government treated them badly, if the people refused to do justice to their intentions, that did not really matter. What mattered—as Tocqueville said—was the fact that once their forefathers had possessed the ability to accomplish serious things with lightness and gaiety, while now the people of France were pursuing folly with a desperate seriousness.

That was why they had engaged in so long a preparation for statesmanship: why they had gone to America in the first place, why through the nine bitter years that followed they had worked so hard, why—even in the face of almost certain misunderstanding—they had never doubted but that it was imperative to publish their books.

'There is,' said Tocqueville, 'but one great goal that merits the efforts of man: that is the good of humanity.'

LIV

## THE PRISON REPORT AND A PRISON CRUSADE

BOTH Tocqueville and Beaumont were given to looking ahead. As embryo statesmen it was their pleasure, as self-conscious humanitarians their solemn duty, to translate experience into counsel and intuition into warning. In the process of composing their books, it even became an accepted part of their literary routine to study the future, and to prophesy. The measurement of the present against some anticipated portrait of the future made telling argument.

But Tocqueville and Beaumont did not always guess right, either about the future or even about themselves. In their prison investigations, for example, they were a long way from suspecting the changes that time would bring. In fact, it is not too much to insist that could the two friends have had a true vision of the future, could someone have told them exactly what was to happen to the penitentiary question in the United States, or to their own opinions and prison program in France, they would have been stunned, incredulous, and more than a little angry.

\*

\* \*

To begin at the American end, and from the vantage point of the twentieth century: Could Tocqueville and Beaumont have returned to the United States in 1933—that is to say: could the two commissioners, one hundred years after the publication of their prison report, have come back to visit Sing Sing, or Auburn, or Charlestown, or Wethersfield; examine again the philanthropic theories and the great penal institutions about which they had once written with such confidence and humanitarian persuasiveness—what would they have found?

In 1933 the famous names would still have greeted them, and the great prisons that they had known. These last, of course, would seem to have grown larger and ever larger with the years. Everywhere, too, new penitentiaries and reformatories and houses of detention, a 'classification' idea and indeterminate sentences and the parole system, con-

vict colonies and prison farms and asylums for the insane would testify
to the growth and invention of a century. Necessarily, to the old trunk
they would have found grafted certain 'improvements.' Yet at Auburn,
on the old site at the bottom of the slope, precisely where Beaumont
had sketched it with the highway running by, a prison would still be
standing. And Sing Sing, carved only a little farther into its river
bank, would still be doing grim service. Even the original long cell-
block of damp stone—which Elam Lynds, the martinet, had erected
out of the sweat of frightened convicts, and where they themselves
had toiled in midsummer heat—even after 107 years it would still be
carrying its human freight. If at Wethersfield the great, square enclosure by the bend in the Connecticut had in the interval become
choked with newer buildings (and the old cell-block been converted
into concert hall), nevertheless, the cells, the tiers, the grates, the walls,
the shops, the very shape of the cell-blocks themselves would have been
easily recognizable. And still, as once under Warden Pillsbury, the
punishment for fractious prisoners would be 'solitary,' with no bed-
ding and a diet reduced to water and bread.

Apparently, then, the Auburn system was still in vogue? For the
nation that had quadrupled in population and overrun the continent,
for the democracy that was said to be no longer quite so law-abiding,
did this great penitentiary idea still hold good? Had the vision of
Louis Dwight and the hard sense of Elam Lynds sufficed for one hundred years? And was their own book still a good description of a
practice and of philosophic principles that had triumphantly been generalized for the benefit of all North America?

A second glance would have been more disquieting. Strangely, some
important items would stand out conspicuously by their absence. What
about the whip, for instance? What about that cruel discipline by the
lash and counted stripe, at which the philanthropists of France had so
long balked but which Captain Lynds had considered so indispensable?
It was gone! No more whipping in the prisons! But how maintain the
absolute and necessary silence during the day, when the men were so
tempted, working together? Tocqueville and Beaumont would at once
have asked. Absolute silence?—no doubt would have been the unmoved answer of the twentieth century—we hardly bother with that
any more. You know it's impossible to keep men from communicating
with each other a little, they have so many ingenious ways. Besides, so
long as they don't make any trouble. . . . You see, we even have a

football team: keeps them out of mischief. . . . Contamination? Of course there's contamination to a certain extent. But then, there isn't much chance of any of these repeaters being exactly innocent in the first place. Besides, we've got too many of them. We're too busy keeping them in line—and trying to find work that the law will let them do—to bother much with reform. They're hardened. It isn't the job of the penitentiaries to reform criminals; we *put them away* for a certain time, that's all.

So the very meaning of the word *penitentiary*—the absolute kernel of the great idea—had been forgotten! No hope in the system any more, no human salvage! There were even riots . . . ! Tocqueville and Beaumont would have reminded themselves that they always had had their suspicions of the Auburn plan. Too mercenary and too dangerous: they had said so themselves. No doubt at Philadelphia, where complete solitude and the pure theory of penitence had always come first . . .

At Philadelphia they would have rejoiced to find the Quaker Prison Society still in existence. They would have smiled in indulgent recollection at the famous crenellated façade of the Eastern State. There would be more spokes inside the old wheel, of course; but not a sound. Did Beaumont remember how he had interviewed the prisoners one by one, and then lost his notes?

It is hard to image what Tocqueville and Beaumont's feelings would have been on walking to the gate of the first cell and discovering *three* prisoners inside.

No solitude, no silence, no penitence, no reform! Instead, this fine old institution, this monument to American hope and philanthropy, given up to sheer housing. Because there were so many convicts, so very many, and the public wasn't interested.

How much the American people had forgotten in a hundred years! Was it possible that they had discovered some terrible defect in the penitentiary idea? Or had they simply lost interest, and with their interest the secret? Whatever the answer, there could be no dodging one fact. In the field of the great prisons, and of prison reform, America had degenerated.* Nowhere in all the United States would Tocqueville and

---

* The writer feels somewhat strongly on this subject. Without pretending to be an expert penologist, and without wishing to criticize any particular prison administration, it seems to him clear that the American people have lost both interest and skill in the treatment of the social problems presented by crime. Not only are the prisons terribly overcrowded (which may or may not be the fault of society), but

Beaumont have been able to find either an adequate substitute, or even a fair copy of the magnificent penitentiaries of the century before. And as for evidence to corroborate their own theories and prove perhaps that their recommendations to the French people had been good, they would have hunted in vain.

For in 1933 such institutions and such evidence would exist only in France.

\*

\*    \*

---

the wardens and prison administrations are almost all either political time-servers, or corrupt, or shining examples of mediocrity. Nowhere can one find any slightest excuse for optimism. Apparently intelligence and ability are not being applied to this critical problem on any comparable scale, or with anything like the enthusiasm or conscientiousness of the earnest philanthropists whom Tocqueville and Beaumont knew. The solutions of the 1830's may have been over-simple and American hopes a little naïve, but the proposals and remedies of the 1930's are either infantile or the products of hopelessness and despair.

If this seems strong language, let the reader apply one of two tests.

Let him compare the prison literature of to-day with the energetic and scholarly pamphlets that Tocqueville and Beaumont read. Those pamphlets were written by able and purposeful reformers, by men of training and cultivation and standing in their communities, by Senator Francis Calley Gray and by Judge Gershom Powers, by Roberts Vaux and Louis Dwight and Francis Lieber. A statesman of the calibre of Edward Livingston could owe a part of his world-wide reputation to the composition of a penal code. Today, by contrast, we are instructed by aldermen, or drink in the wisdom of the wardens of Sing Sing and of Alcatraz.

Or let the reader apply a second test. Let him make a personal tour of the prisons that Tocqueville and Beaumont saw, and interview the wardens and the chaplains as the Frenchmen did. The present writer, in the course of trailing the two commissioners and running down this problem, has been in more prisons (he trusts) than have all his ancestors put together. He has been in Auburn, and he has interviewed Lewis Lawes. He has studied the records and discipline of Massachusetts State. He has seen Wethersfield, inside and out, from cell-block to shop to execution chamber, from librarian to warden to parole officer to inspector. After a 'penitential' lunch with the officers, there was a visit to the 'solitary' section, where three convicts were being given the special punishment already described. One of them was singing. Another had thrown his bread out, in rage, upon the floor. Finally, an inspection of the Eastern State (now inside Philadelphia) completed the disillusionment. Isolation and reform? Let the reader visit the cigar-making shop, or the basket workers. In the rest period the convicts were playing ball in the yards. At night the unusual size of the original Pennsylvania cells makes possible a convenient doubling or tripling in the allocation.

It would be unjust to the many sincere and philanthropic individuals who have assisted me in this investigation to deny the existence of many intelligent campaigns and experiments being carried on to-day. The fact nevertheless remains that, by and large, the former optimism and energy have disappeared. Warden Lawes probably represents the new leadership and its disillusioned point of view very well. In a lecture at Yale University, he said: 'If you keep a man in a cell long enough you will destroy everything there is in him that goes to make up a man.' The adequate substitute for solitary, however, does not yet seem to have been found. (As a third test, the reader might consult B.McKelvey, *American Prisons, a study in American social history prior to 1915*, 1936.

Perhaps, in the beginning, Tocqueville and Beaumont had not been so very serious about this matter of prison reform. Conditions in the *maisons centrales* were bad enough, yet the prison investigation, after all, had been merely an accident in their careers, an invented excuse. The penitentiary idea being new and attractive—in fact one of the many reform theories just churned to the surface of politics by the July Revolution,—a mission to investigate the latest American improvements had seemed to Tocqueville and Beaumont a natural ladder up from the cellar of suspicion to the daylight of recognition and prominence. That it was wise in this new day to make oneself master of some humanitarian reform was a conviction fairly widely shared. More important still, of course, this particular mission had provided the opportunity to see the United States and study the coming *démocratie* there. In its origins, to repeat, the whole affair had been a device, rather than an absorbing campaign: a means to a personal end, rather than a genuine crusade.

Before they got through, however, both Beaumont and Tocqueville were to become honest humanitarians, and the convinced if often disappointed leaders of a vigorous prison crusade.

They began very modestly and in a dubitative tone, as became young men and scholars who knew the facts about America, yet hesitated to dogmatize in favour of a specific program for France. Under the gentle guidance of D'Aunay,* they even swallowed their pride and made overtures to the Minister of Commerce and Public Works, to the Minister of the Interior, to the Minister of Justice. In October 1832, they submitted their manuscript report to the government, and with it 127 precious documents, the whole comprising six volumes of newly stitched pamphlets, letters, tables, and statistics, all brought in their trunk from America to support their own conclusions and to aid the government in its researches. Finally, they even presented one of the first copies of their manuscript, as printed for the public of France, to none other than the *Garde des Sceaux*. D'Aunay was delighted; the

---

* See Toc. to Bt., 4 April 1832, quoted above, p.682; also letters from Le Peletier d'Aunay of 19 October and 1 November 1832 (BB). From Washington, Serurier also wrote to Beaumont to offer a bit of fatherly advice. He expected a lot from their book, he said. They should strive to be truthful and impartial. It was the custom of English travellers to show violent prejudice against the United States. He would hope that a French author, by contrast, would take delight in praising, and blame only with regret. Serurier to Bt., 1 Oct. 1832 (BB).

administration seemed mollified;* and their long report itself was at once seen to be of no little interest.

The title that they gave their work was suggestive. *Du Système Pénitentiaire aux États-Unis et de son application en France; suivi d'un appendice sur les colonies pénales et de notes statistiques*—an unexpectedly thick volume of 440 pages—seemed to promise a feast of penological information and recommendations. Yet half the fascination and variety in the document still awaited the reader's investigation. For in the first place, aside from the main text and the advertised essay on penal colonies, there were unannounced appendices on prison farms; on American education, poor laws, imprisonment for debt, and temperance societies; there was the plan for a prison for 500 by Judge Martin Welles, and a letter from Gabriel Barrett, the kindly chaplain of Wethersfield; there were Tocqueville's unique and appealing conversations with the solitary prisoners of Philadelphia; there was the striking conversation that the two authors had had with Elam Lynds at Syracuse; and there were innumerable citations, quotations and notes. Warden Wood and Louis Dwight and Joseph Tuckerman and Recorder Riker were described, and their opinions quoted. The writings of Edward Livingston and Roberts Vaux and J.C. Spencer and innumerable others were cited. The financial history of the American penitentiaries was condensed into most usable tables. In fact, the notes that Tocqueville had put together turned out to be a small encyclopædia of information and surprises.†

The main text of their report Beaumont had likewise filled with the whole stuff of their experience. Their long and painstaking prison visits, however tedious they had once seemed, had given the two friends an extraordinary grasp of the past history and present character of American long-term prisons, which institutions were now described

---

* The Ministry of Commerce and Public Works delayed acknowledging receipt of their manuscripts for a whole month. But there is some evidence to indicate that the administration of Justice tried to get Beaumont to accept official employment in the government courts again (BB).

† These notes occupied more than 200 pages in all. Their provenance, together with that of the 127 listed *pièces justificatives*, will be clear to any reader who has followed the two commissioners through their tour of American prisons. It should be said that, by way of good measure, they added five special charts at the end of the volume, to wit: a plan of the 'new prison' at Wethersfield, a plan of the wheel-like prison of Philadelphia, a plan and elevation of the first great cell-block of Sing Sing, a plan of a model prison by Gershom Powers, and, finally, a reproduction of Beaumont's sketch of the famous Gothic façade of the Eastern State Penitentiary.

with all their defects or promising implications. In addition, Beaumont included a striking study of the so-called Houses of Refuge for juvenile delinquents; and this was a phase of the new reform that was coming to excite a very general interest in France. Altogether, an experienced penologist would have been hard pressed to name a single phase of the American penitentiary development that had been left out.

As for recommendations, however, both Beaumont and Tocqueville gave evidence of an heroic restraint. There was, first of all, the delicate question of preference between the two American penitentiary systems. To which would they award the palm of superiority? Would it be to Auburn, with its lower first costs, its higher cash returns from prison labour, its social training and discipline through the device of co-operative production? Or should the advantages of complete solitude and a less brutal discipline win for the Pennsylvania Quakers the recognition and imitation of Europe? Tocqueville and Beaumont did not clearly decide. Partly this was because they had not been able to make up their own minds; * partly they hesitated to be dogmatic on a subject over which a number of influential men were already becoming partisan. What the two friends did, instead, was to give a thorough and impartial description of each system, with careful notes on its advantages and disadvantages, then in the end leave the reader to decide for himself.

The title of their report, however, mentioned a possible application in France. Was the copying of the American penitentiaries really practicable? And, if so, would the commissioners dare say what they really thought?

The problem was a thorny one, and admirably resolved. As to the general comparison between the prisons of the United States and of their own country, candour compelled them to state that there could be no real doubt or comparison. The most superficial acquaintance with the regimes in vogue in the two countries compelled even a patriot reluctantly to condemn the prisons of France. The indiscriminate herding together of the convicts, the vice and corruption that such confinement produced, the mercenary *cantine* system with its corollary of the outside contractor, the total lack of a programme aiming at penitence, or reform or even social training: all were vicious and in need

* The tremendous cost of construction of a Philadelphia-style prison was undoubtedly the chief stumbling block in the way of their recommending the Pennsylvania system. Perhaps the difficulty of giving so many convicts individually the desired education and religious instruction was another obstacle.

of immediate attention. Over the primary decision, then, Tocqueville and Beaumont felt that there could be no honest hesitation.

The words in which this opinion was conveyed, nevertheless, were modest, non-partisan, and persuasive. Tocqueville and Beaumont condemned the principles of the French system, not its administration. Some form of solitary confinement, with labour, really ought to be attempted, they suggested. But as to the particular system or the exact degree of imitation, they felt it beyond their capacity to decide. That decision would be of the greatest importance for France, and should therefore be left to wiser heads:—such was the artful implication. No question but what there were weighty obstacles. Tocqueville and Beaumont even undertook to specify the particular difficulties, that any sensible man could see, in the shape of different laws, different customs, and the staggering initial costs.

'We have pointed out what difficulties the penitentiary system would encounter in France, and we have not disguised their gravity,' they then remarked in conclusion.[1] 'We do not dissimulate the fact that we perceive very great obstacles in the way of the establishment of this system among us, such as it exists in the United States and with like environing circumstances. Yet we are far from thinking that there is nothing that can be done for the amelioration of our prisons. . . .

'Let us not declare incurable an evil that others have known how to cure: Let us not condemn the *régime* of our prisons: let us labour to reform them.'

*

*  *

Somewhat to Tocqueville and Beaumont's surprise, this first scholarly venture into humanitarianism immediately began to receive the recognition that its importance and non-partisan character merited. The reviews were interesting and very flattering.[2] The *Académie française* awarded it the *Prix Monthyon*. In England, where their American mission had already been heard of, a partial translation was attempted.[3] In Prussia the learned Dr. Julius translated the whole work into German.[4] And in the United States their friend Francis Lieber, now residing in Philadelphia, got out an annotated translation the same year.[5]

There followed an even more flattering demonstration by the governments of three of the major countries of Europe. For in the course of the next twenty-four months a procession of similar missions went

708 THE INTERPRETATION OF AN EXPERIENCE

across to the United States to study the penitentiary systems that Beaumont and Tocqueville had so admirably described.* Each of the missions returned with a heightened opinion of *Du Système Pénitentiaire* and with reports that confirmed its major conclusions. The book had apparently touched off a great campaign in Europe for the liberalization of prison practices. The movement that John Howard had once worked so hard to start was at last under way.

'Our book, which is hardly selling at all, is nevertheless growing in reputation,' Tocqueville was able to write to his collaborator in November 1833. 'I have received Lieber's English translation, and the German one of Julius accompanied by a very kind and amusingly Germanic letter from the aforementioned. Lieber hasn't written, perhaps his letter was addressed to you. It happens that I have not been completely satisfied with his translation. He has loaded it down with notes in which, in his capacity as a foreigner, he feels himself obliged to contradict the smallest truths that we utter about America. It's clear that he is singularly afraid of centralization. The whole of his work has led me to believe that the Americans haven't felt themselves even yet well enough treated by us. Those people there have an incorrigible conceit. In other respects it appears that our book has made a great reputation in America, according to what Sparks tells me. Harris has told me the same thing. . . .'

Tocqueville was approximately correct on both counts. American society as a whole recalled with pleasure the enthusiasm of the two visitors of 1831, and now seemed delighted with the flattering content of their report. At the same time, however, there were not wanting certain signs of dissatisfaction, particularly in the neighbourhood of

---

* From England came Sir William Crawford with a companion: he was particularly impressed with Tocqueville and Beaumont's thoroughness at Sing Sing (see above, p.105). From Prussia came the great translator and authority, Dr. Julius, who proceeded to spend an unconscionable time at Richmond, not because the old prison at Richmond was worth visiting, but simply because Tocqueville and Beaumont had missed it. The investigation of the American penitentiaries in 1834, by a Canadian mission composed of their two friends Mondelet and Neilson, has already been mentioned (above, p.317). Finally, by 1837, France had sent out Demetz and Blouet, with the apparent object of verifying Tocqueville and Beaumont and of reporting on developments since 1832. Demetz was the penologist, Blouet the architect of this team. They returned with a shorter report, confirming the fact that the houses of detention and the short term prisons were terrible, but deciding in favour of the Pennsylvania system for the penitentiaries. Apparently, Demetz accepted without question the health and insanity evidence of Dr. Franklin Bache, grandson of Franklin, so dear to the French (!). Blouet, with his detailed plans of the different prisons, discovered that an Auburn penitentiary cost but half as much; yet he also came back a partisan of the Philadelphia idea.[6]

Philadelphia and among the advocates of the Pennsylvania system. For if Tocqueville and Beaumont really perceived the superior moral philosophy underlying the principle of complete solitude—and the two authors certainly seemed to—why did they not pronounce unhesitatingly in favour of the Pennsylvania idea? The confident philanthropists of Philadelphia were puzzled and disappointed, and the pro-Auburn enthusiasts of Boston and New York were proportionately pleased. That was why Lieber, who had now moved to Philadelphia, and who was a strong believer in the superiorities of the Pennsylvania system, had felt it so necessary to correct certain misapprehensions of his French friends with learned arguments in favour of the one true penitentiary faith, in the footnotes to his translation. And that was also why, once this translated and corrected version by Lieber was in print, the champions of Auburn lost some of their enthusiasm, and the Pennsylvanians themselves tended to forget the reservations of the two Frenchmen and to regard their book instead as testimony for the Pennsylvania idea. The approbation of the reading public, then, was general but it was not unanimous. Practically, also, their report would never have the effect of settling the great dispute and uniting both camps on the contented advocacy of one or the other of the two penitentiary theories. Conceit and partisanship would stand in the way until both systems died. For more than twenty years the hot arguing would go on, with the protagonists alternately praising or depreciating the famous French report, depending on the point under dispute at the moment.[7] Then theories, penitentiaries and French masterpiece would start together for oblivion.

In France, likewise, the praises of their work soon gave way to a lively and not always very friendly argument. To a young Sedgwick from America, Victor Cousin said that 'he tho't the attention paid to prisons was beginning at the wrong end—that he wished very much for accurate information about our common schools.'[*] Apparently the great Cousin (who was not above riding a hobby himself!) felt critical of Tocqueville and Beaumont's method of becoming liberal leaders. A newspaper article, no doubt inspired by someone in the government, protested against a mission, at taxpayer's expense, which resulted only in praise of American prisons and condemnation of the French.[8]

The real critic of their work, however, stepped out from the ranks of the administration. It was no less than the Inspector General of the

* Diary of Theodore Sedgwick 3rd, 28 October 1833, in the Massachusetts Historical Society. For Sedgwick's connection with Tocqueville, see below, p.731.

*Maisons de Détention*, M. de La Ville de Mirmont, with some 'Observations' to make.*

He began with a word of praise for the commissioners' exposition of the rival American systems. To any imitation of the American penitentiaries, however, he was strongly opposed. Indeed the whole body of his argument betrayed the fact that—tactful as Tocqueville and Beaumont had tried to be—their criticisms of the regime, over which he himself had presided for the past sixteen years, had touched this administrator on the raw.† All regimes had their defects, he admitted, and the French system did suffer from changes in personnel and from political interference. But the Pennsylvania system was impossibly expensive and impractical, despite certain apparent advantages. And as for the prisons on the model of Auburn, they were no better than the dormitories of the *Maisons Centrales*, where silence and discipline could even more effectively be enforced. Furthermore, it seemed a little foolish to go to the considerable expense of installing cells for the sole purpose of bringing in the barbaric punishment of the whip. Finally, in the institutions of the *cantine* and the outside *entrepreneur*, he saw nothing wrong.

Having thus disposed of Beaumont and Tocqueville's major recommendations, La Ville de Mirmont went on to make some suggestions of his own. Certain improvements, he thought, could be installed without going to the expense of borrowing the Pennsylvania plan. He named the better classification of prisoners, by the study of character and the use of psychology (an experiment on which only bare beginnings had so far been made). He liked the American idea of educating the prisoners, and agreed also with the commissioners in their approval of preventive Houses of Refuge for the young. Finally, he brought up the possibility of using a parole system to keep first offenders from becoming repeaters. As far as adopting American ideas on any wholesale scale, however, it was clear from what he said that the government had no such reform in mind.

Tocqueville and Beaumont were disappointed and angry. Some reply to the obstructionist officials would have to be made. In 1836, therefore, they got out a second edition of their work, revised to include a few of Lieber's less obnoxious footnotes, some comments of Dr. Julius,

* *Observations sur les maisons centrales de détention, à l'occasion de l'ouvrage de MM. de Beaumont et de Tocqueville,* 1833.

† Mirmont even had the ill grace to suggest that the two commissioners had not visited enough prisons, or studied them thoroughly enough!

and a long introduction or answer of their own to the various attacks that had been made.* They began with an account of how the penitentiary ideas had been spreading in the United States, since the date of their visit, and cited the English experience with New South Wales in support of their arguments against penal colonies as a solution. Then they took up the case of France. What was needed, they thought, was local initiative, for the stationary national administration was apparently afraid to try out new ideas. Certainly the *cantines* were bad, and the free communication of prisoners with each other produced nothing but vice and corruption. After rehearsing all the obvious arguments again, they next proceeded to take up the personal suggestions of La Ville de Mirmont in detail. The classification of prisoners, whatever its advantages, seemed to them contrary in its essence to the whole principle of solitude, penitence, and reform. The reluctant proposal of the government to try out the cellular idea by building just one such prison for the very worst offenders in all France was an obvious attempt to kill the whole programme by an experiment conducted under the worst possible circumstances. If a gradual beginning was indeed necessary, let the experiment be made with those who most needed protection from contamination: with those who had just been arrested and were being held for trial. Not having been condemned, they were, under law, presumed to be innocent. Let them be kept so. There, at least, would be a start. As it was, in the four years since they had reported back from America, the government had accomplished practically nothing.

The whole tone of Beaumont and Tocqueville's new Introduction was one of righteous indignation, and before they knew it they were trying to achieve practical results. Having been drawn out of their position of scholarly detachment, they were entering upon a campaign of propaganda. The fact that prison reform had been only a device, an excuse, was forgotten in the heat of their resentment. They were not going to be *salon* philanthropists but real humanitarians, the artisans of a practical and lasting reform.

Thus it was that by 1839, when the two friends at last reached the Chamber of Deputies, they found themselves plunging immediately into a bitter, three-cornered contest.

On one side were certain administrative officials, the dead hand of

* *Système Pénitentiaire . . . seconde édition entièrement refondue et augmentée d'une introduction, etc.,* in two volumes of 763 pages, Charles Gosselin, 1836.

the past, the forces of obstruction and delay. On the other were the two schools of penitentiary philosophy: the Auburn and the Pennsylvania. It was almost as if the whole American rivalry had been transferred bodily to France.

Where did Tocqueville and Beaumont stand? And what, finally, did they accomplish? The future was to tell a depressing and ironic story.

It happened that their old *bête-noire* Charles Lucas—the same reformer and prison *fonctionnaire* who had anticipated them in the American field and whom Tocqueville so despised*—was becoming convinced that the Pennsylvanians were wrong. He distrusted their extreme idealism, the ultimate beneficence of complete solitude, and in particular their statistics on mental and bodily health. In a word, the Pennsylvania system seemed to Lucas to conduct society toward bankruptcy and the convicts to insanity. There was a practical streak in this reformer, and the more limited claims of the Auburn school seemed to him more susceptible of practical realization.

Apparently, this decision by Lucas was enough for Tocqueville. He and Beaumont had always felt more kindly disposed toward the Philadelphia system: there was something about the Quaker idealists and their concern for the moral welfare of the prisoners that warmed the heart, while the cold-blooded and brutal practicality of Auburn had from the first subconsciously repelled them. Had it not been for the appalling costs of the Eastern State Penitentiary—and a personal necessity of reserving judgment—they might even have pronounced for the Pennsylvania system right at the start. Now, however, Tocqueville was pushed by personal prejudice. He made his decision. He became the champion—and in the Chamber of Deputies the outspoken advocate—of the Pennsylvania system.[9]

When Lucas, therefore, proposed the adoption of a greatly modified Auburn plan, Tocqueville took up the challenge and began a debate that was to extend throughout his parliamentary career. Lucas would point out that (by 1844) twenty-one states in America had decided for the Auburn system, and only two for the Pennsylvania. Tocqueville would reply that all the commissioners of Europe, who had studied both systems in operation on the spot, had reported in favour of the latter, which was now the only system being imitated in Europe.†

---

* See above, p.213, and note.
† Tocqueville wrote Charles Sumner that he deeply regretted finding that the Boston Prison Discipline Society had reversed the path of intelligent Europeans and gone

Lucas would cite the statistics of Auburn and question—with considerable reason—the veracity of the mortality and insanity statistics issued by the partisan Dr. Franklin Bache on behalf of the Eastern State. To Tocqueville, on the contrary, these misleading figures seemed the ultimate in reliability. And he continued to push for the Pennsylvania principle of solitude day and night, with energy and obstinacy. Once he had been a scholar; but now he was frankly partisan.

To Francis Lieber, and to the confiding Roberts Vaux, whom Tocqueville had once so cruelly disappointed by his impartiality, the conversion of the famous 'Criminalist'* must have seemed a good omen for the success of their theories in France—particularly as Tocqueville was visibly superior in eloquence. The hopes of neither side, however, were destined for complete realization.

After considerable Parliamentary agitation, the Government opened the question in 1839–1840 by bringing in a project for penitentiary building according to the Auburn plan. Partly through Tocqueville's leadership, the Chamber rejected this proposal.[10] The administration then brought in a compromise bill which sought to combine the best features of both systems: that is to say, the Pennsylvania principle of complete solitude day and night was to apply to all prisoners, up through the first twelve years; thereafter the convicts were to be returned to congregate prisons of the Auburn type.† This proposal was accepted by the deputies but only after the Pennsylvania confinement period had been reduced to ten years, with transportation substituted for the Auburn prisons thereafter. The project finally went to the Chamber of Peers which, after four years of study, decided in favour of the straight Pennsylvania system throughout the term of imprisonment. Before this parliamentary triumph could be translated into fact, however, the Revolution of 1848, and the *coups d'état* of 1851–1852, intervened.

---

over to the Auburn camp (6 Aug. 1847, in Sumner, *Works*, I,530). The charge was hardly fair, for Louis Dwight had made his decision against complete solitude long before Tocqueville had become an active champion of the Pennsylvania idea. Beaumont, of course, had sided with Tocqueville from the very beginning.

* Francis Lieber, in his translation, had employed a number of new words, such as 'criminalist' and 'bureaucracy.' Whether Lieber was likewise responsible for introducing them into the English language on this occasion is not certain. But such was Chancellor Kent's statement and the impression of at least one later student. See Lieber Papers, Johns Hopkins University Library.

† In general, French opinion seems to have considered complete solitude too severe a punishment for ordinary men to withstand over a prolonged period. Lucas would have limited its application to the first eight months of the sentence at the outside.

Meanwhile, the practical accomplishment had been discouragingly small. Under the pressure of public opinion, and with the connivance of the two Chambers, the government had indeed undertaken the building of a few cellular prisons, despite the failure of the said Chambers to pass the required legal authorization. An experiment or two had also been tried with the isolation of juvenile delinquents; and this first effort had been abetted by the founding of a number of 'refuges' under private initiative. The Revolution of 1848 itself was favourable to reform. For under the Second Republic the construction of cellular prisons was continued, until in 1852 forty-five such penitentiaries, with some faint connection to the Pennsylvania idea, had been established in the Departments.

Then came disaster. In 1853 the government of Napoleon III stopped all further cellular building, even destroyed some prisons already so modelled, and instead adopted as its program a third alternative: the appealing but ultimately hopeless solution of exile and transportation. This English colonizing device—which harmonized so well with certain Empire aspirations—had been rejected by Tocqueville and Beaumont as early as their youthful visit to French Canada. It had been the subject of the most important and dogmatic appendix in their report of 1833. It had been attacked again in the Introduction to the second edition of 1836; and its defects, as an honest solution for the problem of the criminal class, had been subjected to more than one searching and unfriendly analysis in Tocqueville's work for the Chamber of Deputies.

But already the two reformers had been forewarned what to expect. For Louis Napoleon had given them personally a cruel and humiliating experience. It was almost as if the new tyrant of France was not content merely to arrest the liberals of France, and so drive them out of politics. Apparently he wanted also to hold up their most cherished humanitarian ideals to ridicule and scorn. Certainly, whether by intention or not, he had underlined for Tocqueville and Beaumont the futility of their whole liberal careers, and brought their penitentiary ambitions in particular to an ironic close.

The occasion had been the first Napoleonic seizure of power. It was the night of 2 December 1851, and the two friends had gone to join the dissatisfied Deputies, at their meeting in the Tenth *Arrondissement* in Paris, to protest the *coup d'état*. It was the last night of their political careers. To the protesting Deputies, in their helpless uncertainty, had come the soldiers of Napoleon III, to arrest and cart them away. Tocqueville and Beaumont were led out with the others, and found the police wagons waiting.

The wagons were cellular carriages. . . .

Before the idea of isolation—so as to prevent contamination among the guilty—would have the honour of being used again, Tocqueville and Beaumont would both be dead.

*

* *

In 1870, with the fall of the Second Empire, this unnatural interruption itself came to an end. And thereafter, at last, definite results began to be achieved. As a consequence of complete restudy, the original Compromise of 1840 was finally adopted, modified, and gradually put into operation. In the France of the Third Republic, then, there was visible the curious phenomenon of the borrowing and rejuvenation of two ideas that in the United States, the country of their origin, were already beginning to die. Specifically, the ultimate arrangements provided for the use of a perfected Pennsylvania system for some of the convicts in the first months or years of their confinement, with return to congregate prisons, some of which were cellular and some of which were still the *maisons centrales* that Tocqueville and Beaumont had known, for the completion of their terms.*

Could the two commissioners have returned to the scene of their humanitarian labours in the twentieth century, therefore, they would not have felt completely frustrated and forgotten. For, however far the American people had departed from the true path of reform, the French had remembered. In fact they had even raised a sort of monument to Tocqueville and Beaumont (and to Charles Lucas) in the shape of the great 'model' prison of Fresnes. There a certain number of prisoners would have been found undergoing an almost complete isolation, with work, in large cells. The architecture itself would have reminded the two commissioners of a building that they had once seen; for here again were the interior corridors, a sort of *rond-point*, and the elementary spokes of a wheel. There would be no outdoor yards for exercise attached to each cell, for this twentieth-century prison was

* Because of the supposed severity of total isolation, convicts subjected to the Pennsylvania punishment were to have their sentences reduced by a certain fraction. In the short term prisons and jails, for those awaiting trials, cells are now in general use: a fact which of itself testifies to the influence of the reform crusade.

several stories high.* But by way of compensation an ingenious device had been imagined to improve the once limited educational possibilities of the Quaker system. An auditorium had been built, with seats so enclosed that the inmates could see only the stage or the speaker's stand. From down in front the appearance was even a little ludicrous: one seemed to see row on row of old-fashioned bathhouses rising in tiers into the background, each with a side-door, a plank seat, and the one small opening focussed on the stage. However, the plan was said to work. At a given signal all the convicts would slip pillow cases over their heads and, thus blinded, stand by the gates of their cells. When the keepers unlocked the bars, the convicts would step out, turn, and—in single file with one hand on the shoulder of the anonymous man ahead—march to the auditorium. Once inside his cage, each man would then remove his hood, lean back against the seat and await the beginning of the service or lecture from the stage. Finally, the hour of edification completed—but the solitude still unbroken—the pillow cases would go on again, and the convicts in their darkness would march back to their cells. For a prison administration that could afford to hire no surplus of chaplains and teachers, the whole arrangement was a happy idea. It combined so neatly the needs of economy with the requirements of religion and reform. Perhaps the isolation was not quite so perfect as a true Pennsylvanian would have desired; perhaps Roberts Vaux would even have rejected the ingenious improvement. Yet there was something so artless and confiding in this idealistic compromise, that Tocqueville and Beaumont would have smiled in recognition. If not Philadelphian, the idea nevertheless 'belonged.' If not practical, it was just the same so eminently philanthropic.

*
*    *

Where, then, in the vast movement of nineteenth century prison reform, did Tocqueville and Beaumont stand?

A disillusioned critic, with good show of justice, might accuse them of impracticality and of failure. They had entered the field by accident, and had emerged as narrow partisans. Conscientious as their American investigation had been, they had never really got to the bottom of the matter. Misled by biased statistics, unable to get under the hides of

* As a consequence, the high surrounding wall is of real necessity. It has been made double, with a deep alley between, into which fierce dogs are liberated at night.

convicts, and themselves not sufficiently aware that the principle of
solitude was just one among many hopeful possibilities in the treatment
and cure of the growing convict population, they had become champions of a one-sided and defective reform.* In a word, they had been
blinded by the very enthusiasm for American penitentiary philanthropy, 1830 brand, that they themselves had helped to create. And
even their compromise program had perished in their own lifetime,
defeated like its authors, and in disgrace. As for the longer view, and
a possible immortality of influence, there too, Tocqueville and Beaumont came close to absolute failure. For never would the Pennsylvania idea achieve in France a completely successful realization.

On the other hand, it must be allowed that Tocqueville and Beaumont had indeed contributed to a humanitarian cause. The reform
of the overcrowded, pestilential jails of Europe was desperately
needed; for the rapid industrialization of the Continent was beginning
to build up cities and slums that would be so many plague spots for
the democracies of the future. It was no small achievement just to have
pioneered, and to have aroused the concern of all European society
for its own self-preservation under a rule of law. It was perhaps an
even greater achievement to have rescued the penitentiary idea for a
day when they themselves—and the American enthusiasm that had
lighted the path—would both be gone. They had caught the torch, and
they had passed it on.

Ultimately, one ventures to believe, it is on their book, rather than
on their careers as reformers, that their fame must rest. For, whatever
their failures of vision and whatever their inadequacies as practical
reformers, *Du Système Pénitentiaire* remains to this day—as it was in
1833—probably the outstanding study and description of the two great
American penitentiary systems to which the world owes so much.

---

* It should be said for Tocqueville that his interviews with the poor convicts of Philadelphia represented one of the few genuine attempts to see the prison question from
the malefactor's point of view. Nevertheless, it does not escape notice that Tocqueville never really saw crime as an evidence of anything but moral maladjustment.
He neglected the educational and industrial approaches, rejected the promising 'Classification' idea, and seemed never to have considered the parole system, in spite of the
fact that an experiment or two with that useful device had already been undertaken.
As for the American systems themselves, he always seemed to believe that the silence
was perfectly observed. That this was really the case the present writer finds it hard
to credit.

# LIX

## THE MATERIALS FOR TOCQUEVILLE'S BOOK *

THE study of ideas, their origins and influence, is a provocative but difficult pursuit. Masterpieces of literature, in particular, lend themselves but stiffly to analysis, especially when the author—like Tocqueville—seems to possess so 'intuitive and individualistic a personality.' When, in addition to originality of opinion, the author is also master of an extraordinary talent for generalization, and a vision of things to

---

* Beaumont's *Marie* has already been described, and so thoroughly analysed (see above, ch.XXXVIII), that only three further remarks seem in place here.

The first concerns a suggestion, made to me by Professor Gilbert Chinard, that Beaumont was perhaps indebted to Victor Hugo for the theme of his novel. In 1820 Hugo had published a romance of the Santo Domingo insurrection—called *Bug-Jargal* —in which a black man, named Bug, loved a white woman who bore the same name as Beaumont's heroine, Marie. Both books obviously revolved about the evils of racial tyranny, and advanced the same theory of negro nobility. A borrowing, therefore, is more than possible. On the other hand, this belief in the essential nobility of the negro slave was one of the commonplaces of romantic literature—and Beaumont was much more affected by the Romanticism of the period than Tocqueville. Furthermore, in Hugo's tale the sexes are just reversed; and only the blacks are admired, the mulattoes being held up to scorn. The present writer is therefore inclined to regard the resemblance between the two novels as accidental.

In any case, Beaumont's *Marie* achieved a curious sort of popularity. Like his own later *L'Irlande*, it was awarded a medal by the *Académie* and it sold into a number of editions. Because of its theme, it was in the literary fashion of the day and appealed to the reformer temperament. Because it painted a dark picture of the United States, moreover, it won as well the praises of those conservatives who could not stomach talk of following the American example of democracy.

Its most striking defect, of course, was evident to every one. Louis Blanc accused Beaumont of having 'framed his science in a rather poor novel, treating his century like children who are taught to read with toys.' (*Revue Républicaine*, V,115-116.) The criticism hurt, but it was deserved. In justice it might even be said that there was something fatally impractical about the whole of Beaumont's literary statesmanship. For where Tocqueville laboured to preserve the personal liberty of Frenchmen by an intelligent defence against mass government, Beaumont could hear only the cries of the oppressed. And what poor subject peoples had he selected to champion against their tyrant overlords? The criminals, the Negroes, the Indians and the Irish! The heart of Gustave de Beaumont sometimes overbalanced the head. For a short study of Beaumont and his career, see G.W.Pierson, 'Gustave de Beaumont: Liberal,' *Franco-American Review*, Spring 1937, I,307ff.

come that approaches second sight, even the most devoted scholars are discouraged. Accordingly, the attempt to discover the origins—or even to trace the youthful development—of Tocqueville's ideas has seemed to his countrymen of its very nature a presumptuous and hopeless proceeding.

To-day, happily, a more intimate approach is possible. For with the new materials of this study at hand, that which was cryptic and dark with mystery has now become luminous. And almost visibly, through the pages of this famous commentary, flash familiar faces and familiar thoughts. In fact, it is probably not too much to say that most of the elements that went into the making of *De la Démocratie en Amérique* are now at length clearly recognizable. With only a little further analysis, it will be evident that the book was composed (1) out of a known experience (or body of information), (2) by an ascertainable method, and (3) under the compulsion of a very definite purpose.*

\*

\*   \*

Of fundamental importance—it has been suggested—was the factor of personal experience. Actually, in the fall of 1833, when Tocqueville finally sat down to compose the first two volumes of his book, it almost seems as if he must have begun by reviewing his own life. No doubt the process was largely subconscious. Yet somehow most of the adventures and experiences of a troubled youth were made to tell: all the fragments of information gathered on three continents, and each small increment of wisdom that a youth passed amidst scenes of revolution and class struggle had yielded, were sorted out and laid ready to hand.

As a small boy, for instance, he had been told stories of the Revolution, and of the happier golden days of the aristocracy that had pre-

---

\* Perhaps the list of elements or component factors should really be expanded to five, For Tocqueville's information will be found to have been drawn, not only from his personal experiences, but from certain books about America, and also from the special aid of some Americans who were living in Paris at the time. The table of factors—or key to the genealogy of his commentary—would then stand as follows:

> *Information*: 1. Tocqueville's experiences in America (and elsewhere)
> 2. Books on the subject of the United States
> 3. Outside suggestions and assistance
> *Method*: 4. Tocqueville's mental habits, philosophic approach, literary style
> *Purpose*: 5. Tocqueville's fundamental convictions, or doctrine
>
> Of these the first three will now be investigated.

ceded. A sense of time and sadness had been born in him. Again, as a student on his travels in Sicily, he had stumbled on the ruins of an ancient city, and been overwhelmed with the transitoriness of things. Like the sad songs his mother used to sing, these deserted temples of the Mediterranean had taught him that whole peoples and even glorious civilizations could perish. And so it had continued. The confident masterpieces of the eighteenth century *philosophes*, once dear to Malesherbes but now so forlorn in their betrayed futility; the visit to Oxford, and the great ruins of Warwick that commented so strangely on the portrait of Henry VIII; the very château of Tocqueville, in its dilapidation and decay; all testified to a past that was now gone, and to the devastating force of time. Even in his own life and career in Paris, it seemed as if he had been chained to the deathbed of a once powerful society, forced, as it were, to watch the destructive process, and contemplate the agony of ultimate decay. In the fine time of youth, in years of normal exuberance and optimism, then, Tocqueville had become acutely aware of the past, and even more acutely aware of change. It was against such a background of irresistible and not necessarily happy evolution that his whole American tableau would be thrown.

Again, he had the tools of comparison. At least he was not, like most of the 'Republicans' of France, dependent upon hearsay, or the optimism of a Lafayette, or the preachings of the '1688 school' of liberals after the manner of England. Intelligent enough to be dissatisfied with any such easy parallels for France, he and Beaumont had taken the pains to study the history of the English, and they had personally visited the scene, to measure the lag in the insular development. In the search for republican parallels, Tocqueville was even to look at Switzerland, review the history of the Greek experiments, and read about the city states of Italy.[1] If not the accomplished student of comparative government that James Madison had once been, he was at least no utter novice. In addition to momentum, he was aware of perspective.

Most important of all, however, his personal experience had given him an intimate acquaintance with what he might have called direction or destination. For he had himself seen that predestined, self-governing, and equalitarian society which all Europe was approaching: he had studied the appearance and character of the United States. The nine months spent on the other side of the Atlantic had given him undreamed-of ideas and information; and the diary notes, and sketches, and essays, and letters home were now the raw substance of a large part of Tocqueville's book. In manuscript form, and on the bright canvas of his memory, he already had the outline and much of the detail of what he wanted to say.

How important these documents were for the shape and contents of Tocqueville's commentary perhaps only those admirers of his book who have also troubled to read the foregoing account of their American journey can fully appreciate. In any event, a skeleton recapitulation may not be out of place. What did the American experiences, that Tocqueville had so carefully recorded, now yield him in the way of literary material?

It would, of course, be necessary to say something about the physical scene. The geography of the United States he knew at first hand, with its rough grandeur, and its incredible distances. In person he had suffered more than one striking encounter with its variable and brilliant climate, that touched the extremes of heat and cold so easily. Its mountains he had traversed in the snow, its great rivers and lakes in the fabulous, collapsible steamboats. As for the vast and interminable forests of the New World, he felt he knew them by heart: they were so clear in his mind that he was even a little angry at his cousin Chateaubriand for having described them so badly.[2] Yet his experience went deeper than that. For in the forests he had come across—talked to—lived with—the American pioneer. He had a first-hand knowledge and an unusual understanding of the frontier. He had studied the westward movement of the population; seen the first emigrants come; watched the despairing Indians retreat; noticed the building of the roads, the sale of land and the organization of a territory; in Ohio he had even been able, as it were, to reconstruct the whole manufacture of an American State. Again, his journeys had made him acquainted with American regionalism, with its vivid contrasts, its racial problems and economic rivalries, its scarcely concealed menaces for the future of the federation. For any discussion of the physical background of American democracy, Tocqueville was not badly prepared.

The same was true in a closely related and important field. On landing in New York, it will be recalled, Tocqueville and Beaumont had immediately been struck by the shop-keeping habits, the commercial turn, and the money-chasing proclivities of the Americans. This crass materialism of New World society had not made the happiest first impression. It had not taken Tocqueville long to realize, however, that the wealth and opportunities offered by so empty and rich a continent might have a beneficent influence on the problems of government.

Specifically, he had made up his mind that the American people were too industrial, too busy conquering their land, too tempted (after failure) to start life over again in the West, to bother seriously about politics, or to disturb the state. Opportunity was too free: there was no suppressed discontent.

This reflection had led the young political philosopher to a discovery —which only America had been able to suggest to him—that there was no absolute value in political institutions. The usefulness of a given constitution depended on the physical environment, and on the inherited characteristics of the society to which it was applied, even more perhaps than on its own nice handling of the problem of sovereignty. There might, in law as in personal relationships, be such a thing as maladjustment. Certainly no government would be perfect everywhere. His own judgments in the field of political science would obviously have to be relative. A good American institution might be recommended to his own people if it fitted—but not otherwise. Complete self-government might work in the United States, but the question was: would the French be able to tolerate it?

Very well. What was there then about the origins of the American people that made them able to tolerate, and even prosper under, that very difficult and dangerous type of government called democracy? Had he learned anything, in his nine months' prison tour, about the inherited attitudes or special inventions of the Americans that would help to explain their peculiar success with unrestrained self-rule?

Assuredly, he had. Tocqueville had not escaped out of the hands of Jared Sparks and Henry Gilpin without hearing about the English heritage, and the long practice of colonial times. More than one landholder, like old Carroll of Carrollton and John Livingston of the patroons, had explained about the defeat of the Tories in the American Revolution, and traced the decline of the aristocracy under the Republic. Dozens of lawyers had contributed their comments on the broadening of the suffrage. The value of American religion—both because of its emphasis on morality and because of the republican characteristics inherent in Protestantism—had been mentioned again and again. About the necessity of separating Church from State Tocqueville had been lectured until he had become a complete convert. And as for education, even Tocqueville's French prejudices had finally had to yield a little before the unanimous faith and enthusiasm of these enlightened democrats. From his American experiences, then, Tocqueville had drawn some useful conclusions. The Americans were able to tolerate democracy (so much more easily than the French (because they were English, because they were Protestant, because of their continental opportunities, because they were intelligent, and most of all because long practice had taught them how.

In particular, there seemed to exist in the United States certain habits, certain institutional practices, that increased the good effects obtainable from self-government at the same time that they mitigated or even altogether eliminated the dangers inherent in mass control. The greatest of these inventions, for example, was decentralization. Distinguished Americans without number, from President Quincy to Senator Everett, from minister Tuckerman to Mayor Richards, from J.C.Spencer to Jared Sparks, had sung the praises of political localism, both as a training school for citizenship and as a device to keep even the humbler and less intelligent citizens interested in their government and happily occupied in its service and perpetuation. Of almost comparable importance, Tocqueville had decided, was the Federal principle, which managed to give such play to the ideas of popular sovereignty and home rule, yet establish an interstate or national government of sufficient force in the fields where such government was clearly required. The carving of sovereignty into spheres was not easy to understand. But how impressed he had been with the beauty and cleverness of American statesmanship, when first his reading in Kent and the *Federalist* had made this unprecedented dualism clear to him!

Then there were also, of course, the special institutions and all the ancillary practices that contributed to 'make the republic bearable.' First among these vital safeguards stood the independent judiciary, protecting the rights of the individual citizens, handing down the precious heritage of the common law, and teaching all men, through the beautiful device of jury duty, the art of decision, a respect for law, and the full nature of their own responsibilities. After Curtis and Gilpin had lectured, McIlvaine had written his treatises, and Beaumont and he had personally attended trials in five different cities, Tocqueville's knowledge of American judicial institutions was decidedly above the amateur.* And the same was true in connection with the other aids to freedom and good government that he had discovered operating in

---

* One whole diary, Cahier F, was entitled 'Civil and Criminal Law in America.' A certain number of undated items in Cahier E, and elsewhere, dealt with the same field of investigation.

America. He had but to recall what Gallatin and Everett had said about the conservative nature of the American bar, what Spencer had told him about the characteristics of a free press, and the necessity of two chambers in a legislature; he had but to look up his own notes on the difference between small coteries and great parties, on the effects of frequent elections of officeholders, and on what Ingersoll had said in favour of conventions: in a word, he had but to glance through his recorded American experiences, and at once, and almost without further reflection, he would be able to list and to expound for his own people the safeguards that in the United States seemed to make democratic government tolerable.

This is not to say that his visit had turned Tocqueville into an enthusiast and a champion. On the contrary, about many aspects of popular self-government he remained, as before, extremely dubious; and he was still resolved on a warning letter to France. Only he was now less fearful than he had been at first about the whole American experiment, and for the first time he knew exactly where the weaknesses of democracy lay. If he had carried some prejudices to America, the fact was that the Americans themselves had again and again supplied the corroborating information. It had been Ohio and New Orleans—not his own aristocratic training—that had taught him the specific defects in manhood suffrage. It had been Andrew Jackson, and the Congress of the United States itself, that had driven home to him the vulgarity and mediocrity of American leadership. The anti-tariff men and South Carolina had underlined the dangers of free assembly; and it had been none other than Jared Sparks who had first uttered the tell-tale words: 'tyranny by the majority.' As for the differences and antagonism between North and South, as for the problems of the Indian and the negro slave, Tocqueville now saw them, not through the romantic haze of a tale by Chateaubriand, but in terms of personal contact and experience.

What of the future? People were so dogmatic and partisan in France, both *pro* and *con*, that some estimate as to the probable duration of the Union would obviously have to be made. On shipboard Peter Schermerhorn had seemed not in the least apprehensive for the near future, but thought that the division of the Union might come some day, 'by and by.' In New England, also, there had been confidence as to the present but some doubt—at least so ex-President Adams had implied—about the more distant future. In Cincinnati, Timothy Walker had emphasized the tremendous growth of the Union and the consequent strains; and in the South Poinsett had allowed the dawning menace of the slavery dispute to become perceptible.* In the last pages of his second volume Tocqueville was to give his answer. He could not, he thought, pretend to tear aside the veil of the future. But of two things he did feel reasonably certain. The first was that the opponents of American democracy were 'premature' in their predictions of disaster. The second was that, in the Federal Republic, it was the federalism that was menaced more than the republicanism or practice of local self-government. If anything failed, it would be the ties of union. The conquest of the continent might make the United States too large, the bitterness of regional jealousy might split the Union into sections. Yet even this was not to be anticipated with certainty, or in the immediate future. At most disunion would come only after many years, or by and by.†

The readers of Tocqueville's *Démocratie* will not find repeated in his book all of the impressions and views of his American tour precisely in the wording of their first preception, or even in the order here outlined. But the general plan of what he meant to say had been clear to him as early as his departure from New York for Albany and the West. And it was from his American experiences more than from any other source that he was to draw his inspiration and his materials. Even his errors in observation and his misapprehensions would be reproduced.‡ In fact, one may without exaggeration insist that there is not a single chapter in the first two volumes of his commentary§ that did not draw most of its basic ideas and many illustrative

* On 30 August 1833, in a characteristic opinion, Sparks wrote to Tocqueville that the Nullifiers of South Carolina had caused alarm, but had been beaten because the voice of the nation was strong for union. 'Any attempts at disunion, from whatever quarter, will be met with an overwhelming opposition. What will be effected by time, it is difficult to foresee; but, for many years to come, the Union of the States will remain firmly established.' (Copy, YT.)

† This instance is cited, not as evidence of Tocqueville's prophetic abilities, but to show the source of one of Tocqueville's opinions. As a matter of fact, Tocqueville also made a third guess in this field, and guessed just exactly wrong. He thought that the tendency of the American federation was centrifugal: that the strength of the administration at Washington was slowly but surely declining. The source of this erroneous impression seems to have lain in his failure to take sufficient account of the growth of a national economy. See below, pp.764–65.

‡ See below, pp.764–67.

§ If further evidence is desired, let the reader glance through the chapters in question. The very topics discussed will be old friends. For convenient reference a list of Tocqueville and Beaumont's American acquaintances, with indications of relative indebtedness, is appended below, Appendix B.

There is in existence, also, a special manuscript index constructed by Tocqueville

details directly from the study that he and Beaumont had made, personally, in the United States, on the spot.

\*

\*    \*

It is, by now, well known that Tocqueville found it hard to use the assistance of others. He had to think things through for himself, and he wanted no disturbing guidance. In fact, so delicate was the balance of his nerves that an outside suggestion before he had made up his own mind—or a contradictory opinion expressed after his mind was made up—would often upset him, throw all his meditations awry, and make him desperately unhappy for days.

For that reason he rarely consulted any but the most intimate friends while in the process of composition, and he even adopted the extraordinary course of never reading contemporary books or articles on his own immediate subject. When Beaumont mentioned Harriet Martineau's travel book, he did not read it. There is no record of his having consulted Capt. Hall, or Mrs. Trollope. The appearance of Chevalier's first letters from the United States made him uncomfortable, but he did not alter his procedure. Because he was afraid of being influenced, of having his thoughts jolted from the path of strict logic and rigorous deduction, he thus denied himself a very material assistance that might have been his.\*

In another fashion, however, and with a rare intelligence, the author

---

to give him ready access to the materials in his fourteen diaries. In this index sixty topics are listed, with more than three hundred page references to actual American experiences.

\* 'Blosseville informed me the other day that Chevalier's book had appeared,' Tocqueville wrote to Beaumont in 1836. 'You realize that I am always on the *qui vive* where America is concerned. Yet I will not read Chevalier's work; you know that it's a principle with me. Have you glanced at it and, in that case, what do you think of it? What is its tone? What is its object? Also, what impression is it making in the world? And in what way might it be prejudicial to the philosophico-political work that I am preparing? If, without *distracting yourself*, you can reply to these questions, you will do me pleasure.' Toc. to Bt., Baugy, 4 Nov. 1836 (BB).

Again, in 1837, he wrote to the same friend: 'What you tell me about Miss Martineau's book makes me uncomfortable. You appreciate that on such subjects I am what the English call *touchy*. Every time that I hear America spoken of, and well spoken of, I experience a veritable uneasiness. I realize perfectly that I ought to publish soon. But what am I to do? I am incapable of publishing things with which I would be dissatisfied. It's better to arrive too late than to utter *pauvretés*.' Tocqueville, 9 July 1837 (TT).

Beaumont subscribed to the *National Intelligencer* in 1833, but Tocqueville apparently relied on the almanacs to keep him abreast of American affairs.

of *De la Démocratie en Amérique* did make a notable use both of books on America and of personal aid in the course of his writing.

To begin with Tocqueville found that, however much his American experiences and notes now gave him, he was still in need of detail. The major aspects of American democracy were clear enough, but the precise facts needed verification. What, actually, *was* the law of Massachusetts in a certain matter? Precisely what was the wording and the meaning of a particular section of the Constitution? Even when Tocqueville felt reasonably certain of the contemporary custom or institution, the colonial origins and the long background of development had never been made clear to him. What he needed was history, law, statistics. And this information no single year in the United States could possibly have supplied.

So he turned to the Royal Library. He borrowed books from whatever Americans in Paris he knew and from the American legation. A number of the legal treatises and statute collections he and Beaumont had themselves brought back from America; and Francis Lieber now sent him the new edition of Joseph Story's *Commentaries*. He drew up lists of works—descriptive, ethnological, statistical, legal, historical, and documentary. He explored the resources of the Institute. He read, in translation, Jefferson's *Notes on Virginia* and Warden's *Description of the United States*. He consulted Humboldt and the narratives of Major Long. To bolster his knowledge of the American Indians, he used Heckewelder, Tanner, and some legislative documents supplied by Edward Everett. He studied the Revised Statutes and the voluminous almanacs, and consulted the collections of documents made by Pitkin and Ebenezer Hazard. He read a translation of John Marshall's *Life of Washington*; and in the field of law and government his constant guides were de Lolme, Blackstone, the *Federalist*, Kent, and Story. Finally, he explored the histories, from Morton's *New England Memorial* to Hutchinson, from the *Magnalia* of Cotton Mather to Trumbull's *Connecticut* and the appealing volumes of Jeremy Belknap on New Hampshire. In all he was to cite over seventy individual items in the footnotes and appendix of his *Démocratie*,—and there is some reason to believe that he must have consulted some twenty or thirty more.*

---

* Untrained in scholarship though Tocqueville was, his list of authorities is impressive. One doubts whether a single Frenchman of his day could have matched his literary range in the two fields of American law and history.

Below is given a composite bibliography for *De la Démocratie en Amérique*. It is made up from the footnotes of the commentary itself, from two manuscript catalogues

Not that these literary sources in any way supplanted the materials of experience. That would have been impossible—and for two reasons. On their visits to Albany and Boston and Washington, Beaumont and he had been appalled to discover how seldom and how badly official records and statistics were kept in the United States. As a sub-

---

found in the Tocqueville papers, and from the library of Alexis de Tocqueville as it exists to-day. Those works which Tocqueville found most valuable, and from which he quoted extensively, are here capitalized. Omitted from this compilation are a few titles which it has been impossible to identify, a number of items which Tocqueville probably never used, and also the many pamphlets collected in America, of which Tocqueville must have made some use but to which reference has already been made.

### Description

W.Darby, *View of the United States, historical, geographical, and statistical*, etc., 1828

D.B.Warden, *Description statistique, historique et politique des États-Unis*, etc., 5 vols., Paris, 1820

Major S.H.Long, *Account of an Expedition from Pittsburgh to the Rocky Mountains*, etc., 2 vols., 1823

Major S.H.Long, *Narrative of an Expedition to the Source of St. Peter's River*, etc., 2 vols., 1824

C.Malte-Brun, *Annales de Voyages*

M.E.Descourtilz, *Voyages d'un naturaliste*, 3 vols.

Volney, *Tableau du Climat et du Sol des États-Unis*

La Rochefoucauld-Liancourt, *Voyage dans les États-Unis d'Amérique fait en 1795, 1796, et 1797*, Paris, 8 vols.

### Indians

A. von Humboldt, (title uncertain)

Fisher, *Conjecture sur l'origine des Américains* (?)

J. Adair, *History of the American Indians*

Heckewelder and Duponceau Correspondence, in *Transactions of the Historical and Literary Committee of the American Philosophical Society*, 3 vols.

JEFFERSON, *NOTES SUR LA VIRGINIE*

Le Page du Pratz, *Histoire de la Louisiane*

Charlevoix, *Histoire et description générale de la Nouvelle France*

Gookin on Indians, in *Collections* of Mass. Historical Society, ed. of 1806

John Tanner, *Narrative of Captivity and adventures*, 1831 (bought [?] by Toc. from author)

Schoolcraft, *Travels in the Central portion of the Mississippi valley*

J.H.McCulloch Jr., *Researches . . . concerning the aboriginal history of America*, 1829

U.S. Congress, *Legislative Documents*, 20th, 21st, 22nd Congresses.

### History

E.Hazard, *Historical Collections*, etc.

T.Pitkin, *A Political and Civil History of the United States*, 2 vols., 1828

A.Scheffer, *Histoire des États-Unis de l'Amérique septentrionale*, Paris, 1825

Capt. John Smith, *Generall Historie of Virginia and New-England*

William Stith, *History . . . of Virginia*

Beverly, *History of Virginia*

John Lawson, *History of* (Description of North?) *Carolina*

N.MORTON, *NEW ENGLAND'S MEMORIAL*, ed. of 1826

C.MATHER, *MAGNALIA CHRISTI AMERICANA*

T.Hutchinson, *History of Colony of Massachusetts-Bay*

stitute for the real thing, Hazard and Pitkin and the almanacs were hopelessly inadequate. And even in the field of their own history the Americans had as yet produced no broad survey, nor any single work of the first class. It would, therefore, have been utterly impossible for Tocqueville to have made up his commentary wholly, or even largely,

---

B.Trumbull, *Complete History of Connecticut*, etc., 2 vols., 1818
Jeremy Belknap, *History of New Hampshire*
S.Williams, *Natural and Civil History of Vermont*
William Smith, *History of the Late Province of New-York, from its discovery to 1762*
R.Proud, *History of Pennsylvania*, etc., 2 vols., 1797–1798
JOHN MARSHALL, *VIE DE WASHINGTON*, 5 vols., 1807
D.Hosack, *Memoir of De Witt Clinton*
R.Vaux, *Memoirs of life of Anthony Benezet*
Joseph Blunt, *Historical Sketch of the Formation of the Confederacy*, etc., 1825
Works of William Penn
Works of Benjamin Franklin

*Legal Commentary*

Montesquieu
Blackstone
J.L. de Lolme, *The Constitution of England*
J.STORY, *COMMENTARIES ON THE CONSTITUTION OF THE UNITED STATES*, 3 vols., 1833
J.KENT, *COMMENTARIES ON AMERICAN LAW*, 4 vols.
THE *FEDERALIST*
L.P.CONSEIL (ed.), *MÉLANGES POLITIQUES ET PHILOSOPHIQUES EXTRAITS DES MÉMOIRES DE THOMAS JEFFERSON, PRÉCÉDÉS D'UN ESSAI SUR LES PRINCIPES DE L'ÉCOLE AMÉRICAIN ET D'UNE TRADUCTION DE LA CONSTITUTION DES ÉTATS–UNIS, AVEC UN COMMENTAIRE TIRÉ, POUR LA PLUS GRANDE PARTIE, DE L'OUVRAGE PUBLIÉE, SUR CETTE CON- STITUTION, PAR WILLIAM RAWLE LL.D.*, 2 vols., Paris, 1833
Th. Sergeant, *Constitutional Law, being a view of the practice and jurisdiction of the Courts of the United States*, etc.
W.A.Duer, *Outlines of the Constitutional Jurisprudence of the United States*, 1833 (sent by author at Duponceau's suggestion)
*Annual Law Register of the United States*, 2 vols., 1821–1822
W.Sullivan, *Political Class Book*
*Traité sur les règles des actions civiles*, New Orleans, 1830

*Documents Legal and Political*

U.S. Constitution
Articles of Confederation
A collection of the laws of the United States
U.S. Congress, Senate & House *Documents*, 18th, 19th, 20th, 21st, 22nd Congresses
Washington's Farewell Address
Jackson's Message on Internal Improvements (procured from Ed. Livingston)
Annual *Reports* of Secretary of Treasury, 1823–1832
I.G.Worcester, *The Town Officer*, 1827
Massachusetts, 'Historical Collection of State Papers'
General Laws of Massachusetts, 3 vols., 1823
Connecticut, 'Constitution of 1638'
Connecticut, 'Code of 1650'
*Revised Statutes* of New York
*Rules and Orders* (N.Y. State) 1832

out of second-hand materials, assuming that he so desired. That was the first reason. And the second was even stronger. To put it baldly, it never occurred to him to become a mere compiler. His whole plan was to rely on books about America only for information and corroboration, and then only for those sections in his own work where the emphasis was to be on description and detailed analysis. To be exact, he was to make an extensive use of such printed assistance only for the second, fifth, and eighth chapters of his first volume, and for the eighth and tenth chapters of volume two. When, for example, he wanted the history of colonial development (what he called the *point de départ*), or the minutiæ of town organization and government, or the specific constitutional powers of President and Congress, or the state laws in the matter of the jury, or the text of treaties with the Indians, or statistics and literature on the negro question, then he indeed turned, scholar-fashion, to books and Senate documents. And these he read to such purpose, and digested so well—particularly in the field where the Americans stood pre-eminent: the field of legal commentary and political treatise—that he was even by one disgruntled American jurist accused of having borrowed too much without giving credit.

The accuser in this instance was no less a person than the noted

---

Miscellaneous Reports of Officers of New York City and New York State
Digests or Collections of Laws of: Pennsylvania, Ohio, Tennessee, South Carolina
Constitutions of: Maine, New Hampshire, Vermont, Massachusetts, Connecticut, New
    York, Ohio, Illinois, Virginia, North Carolina, South Carolina, Georgia, Tennessee,
    Alabama, Mississippi, Louisiana (also Mexican Constitution of 1824)

### Other Documents and Statistics

Williams, *New York Annual Register*, 1831, 1832
*American Almanac*, 1831, 1832, 1834
*National Calendar*, 1833
*Companion to the Almanac*, London, 1834
Emerson (?), *Medical Statistics*
*Niles' Weekly Register*
'Elliot's Pocket Almanac of the Federal Government, 1832'

### Miscellaneous

M.Carey, *Letters on the Colonization Society*, 1833
*Encyclopedia Americana*, 7 vols.
W.E.Channing, *Discourses, Reviews and Miscellanies*, 1830
'Morrison's Mental Diseases'
J.F.Cooper, *The Travelling Bachelor*
'The Fashionable Tour'
E.Bates, *The Doctrine of Friends*
D.Hosack, *Essays on Various Subjects of Medical Science*, 3 vols.
The American Medical and Philosophical Register
'Fisher's Pauperism and Crime'

Associate Justice of the Supreme Court, Joseph Story, whose able *Commentaries* Tocqueville had cited again and again, with frequent quotation. Wrote Story to Francis Lieber:[3]

'The work of De Tocqueville has a great reputation abroad, partly founded on their ignorance that he has borrowed the greater part of his reflections from American works, and little from his own observations. The main body of his materials will be found in the Federalist, and in Story's Commentaries on the Constitution; *sic vos non vobis.* You know ten times as much as he does of the actual workings of our system and of its true theory.'

This charge is so serious that it merits some consideration. How had the famous Massachusetts Justice come to level such an accusation?

It has been suggested that Story was bitter because Tocqueville was so slow in getting him elected to the *Académie.* Perhaps there was indeed some feeling of irritation and disappointment lurking in the great jurist's breast. In this instance, however, it does not seem necessary to call Joseph Story's character or vanity too strongly into question. For Tocqueville had in effect done several things that might make it seem as if he had been a borrower, rather than an observer in his own right.

The facts are these. When Tocqueville was first getting together his collection of American authorities, he realized at once that to read and digest them all would be beyond his power. It would take too hopelessly long. He therefore hit upon the device of getting a second kind of outside aid. He went around to the American legation and asked where he would find some 'educated and intelligent' young American to help him. He found two.

The first was Theodore Sedgwick 3rd, a young and able scion of the Sedgwick clan, whom he had once seen at Stockbridge on the occasion of his visit to that Berkshire town in search of an American authoress.* Sedgwick was staying in Paris for a time, and Tocqueville found him a likeable and intelligent youth, ever ready to discuss the questions that were on his mind, and to assist him at the legation in finding the most useful books. As a result, the two became fast friends, and Tocqueville seems to have used the opportunity to clear up his own doubts and regiment his ideas by trying them out on Sedgwick.† In this

---

* See above, p.349, and note.
† See Sedgwick's third diary. Massachusetts Historical Society, pp.29ff., for 1833–1834. It is not possible to give the full quotations here, but the following extracts will perhaps indicate the nature of their relationship:

fashion, precisely as in the case of his original American conversations, and just as with the essays of Sparks and Coolidge and Joseph McIlvaine which he was now reviewing, Tocqueville made a direct contact with the current of educated thought in America. That is to say, he was exploring the thought of those who had themselves been brought up on the *Federalist* and on Kent or Story, who had followed Webster's career and read his great debate with Hayne. Tocqueville, himself, was to cite the Dartmouth College Case in a note. As a matter of fact it would have been extraordinary if, after such intimate contact with American lawyers and college graduates, some fertilizing waters from the clear, cool stream of American legal philosophy had not seeped into his *Démocratie*.

In the case of the second young American, Tocqueville proceeded somewhat differently, and the connection with Story and the *Federalist* was much more direct. On inquiry at the Legation, he had been given the address of a 22-year-old graduate of Brown, named Francis J. Lippitt. Finding that Lippitt was able to read and write French with ease, Tocqueville set him to work digesting American pamphlets and treatises into brief notes in French. With the intention of keeping Lippitt completely unbiased, however, Tocqueville never told him what the work was for, or that he was himself preparing a book on the United States. The young college graduate never even knew that Tocqueville could read and speak English, for their whole conversation was in French. The connection began and ended in reticence.

Sixty-three years later, when a very old man, General Lippitt was to write out with some pride all that he could remember about his own inadvertent share in the composition of *Democracy in America*.*

'Saturday 4th Jan'y 1833[1834]—about 12 called on M. Tocqueville . . . He said that all the Administrative system was founded under Napoleon & that it is essentially inconsistent with the representative & free order of things. . . . To the Legation to look for some books about the Indians that Tocqueville wanted.'

'Monday 20 Jan: 1834 . . . Tocqueville came about ½ past 11 & staid till 1— talking partly about the work he is to publish on our Country & partly about France —He says that as regards the religious spirit—Paris is an exception to the rest of France, . . . He says that the *manners* of the nations have changed entirely within 50 years . . . the salon is no longer the same. . . . He said that he believed the social spirit of equality must sooner or later create the republic—He is right—The Republic is the inevitable system to which all tends. . . . Murat's plan of federalising France he regarded as absurd and impracticable. . . . Russia & the United States were the only powers wh. presented an avenir. . . .'

'Saturday 8th Feb: 1834 Tocqueville called about 11 for some information about the Etats Unis—while I was breakfasting—'

* I am indebted to the late J. Franklin Jameson for my first knowledge of this incident. Dr. Jameson had heard General Lippitt tell the story at the 1901 Brown Commence-

'I can tell you very little about M. de Tocqueville himself,' his letter was to confess; 'our intercourse being confined to our joint labors— if I may call them so—in his study. I shall first state certain particulars which are not wholly mal-à-propos. (1) My knowledge of French began in my early childhood; and when I first met M. de Tocqueville I spoke it fluently, and wrote it with tolerable correctness. (2) In my senior year in college, we had Rawle on the Constitution, for six months.* (3) Before the arrival of Mr. Livingston, our new minister, with his secretaries and attachés, I had been attaché for several months to our Legation in Paris.

'Some time in 1834 I was called on by a stranger who informed me that he was desirous to have the assistance of an American gentleman "of education," and that I had been recommended to him by the American Legation. I accepted at once the terms he offered me, and I was to commence at once in his study at his father's hotel in the Faubourg St. Germain. His physique was not at all striking. He was slightly built, and his height did not exceed five feet six inches. His age was apparently somewhere between twenty-five and thirty. There was certainly nothing about the contour of his head or the expression of his face that indicated him to be a man of more than ordinary intelligence. His manner was quiet and dignified, but somewhat cold. I afterwards learned that he had lately returned from the United States . . . and that he was a son of the Comte de Tocqueville, of the old noblesse. My connection with him lasted some three or four months. His treatment of me was always very kind and appreciative. My daily attendance in his study was from 9 a.m. to about 5 p.m.

'A few words will describe the nature of my duties. Many shelves in his study were filled with books and pamphlets he had brought

---

ment, the substance of his remarks on that occasion being included later in his *Reminiscences*. The version here quoted is from a letter that Lippitt wrote in 1897 to Daniel C. Gilman, President of Johns Hopkins University, as reproduced in the latter's article on 'Alexis de Tocqueville and his Book on America.—Sixty years after,' *Century Magazine*, Sept. 1898, vol.LVI,p.707.

By a curious coincidence, the young Lippitt had been arrested on a walk from Marseilles to Paris, having been taken for Tocqueville's friend, the Vicomte de Kergolay. The latter, who was wanted for his connection with the Duchesse de Berry and the Carlo-Alberto affair, had the same appearance, and apparently talked French intentionally with an English accent. As has already been suggested, Kergolay was caught elsewhere; and Lippitt was released, to arrive in Paris penniless.

\* Before this, Lippitt had read the *Federalist* with deep interest. Rawle's *A View of the Constitution of the United States of America* was an expository analysis, which the the author himself described as an 'elementary treatise for students' and a guide for foreigners. Its chief virtue was a frequent citation of Supreme Court decisions.

with him from America. What he desired of me was to write out summary statements of our political organizations, both State and Federal; and those books were chiefly statutes of the different States of the United States.*

'The statutes of the new western States were still unbound. And when even these were wanting there were newspaper slips containing sheriffs' and other official notices, so that the materials furnished me were amply sufficient to enable me to write out for him all the particulars he desired. He usually came in about 3 p.m. to read over the mémoirs I had been preparing for him, and to get my oral explanation on certain points that interested him. Our interviews throughout were simply of questions on his part and answers on mine. You will easily believe that his questions indicated a most penetrating intellect.

'He was the most reticent man I ever met. Only twice, so far as I can remember, did he ever volunteer a remark: once when he corrected a certain idiomatic blunder in my mémoire, and clearly explained the rule to me; and at another time, when we had been talking about town meetings, he exclaimed with a kindling eye (usually quite expressionless), "Mais, c'est la commune!"

'I think it was then that I received the impression that he deemed such meetings to have been the root of our Anglo-Saxon liberties and capacity for self-government. But it is possible that this impression did not come to me until after reading his book. From the *ensemble* of our conversations I certainly did carry away with me an impression that his political views and sympathies were not favorable to democracy. I knew nothing of his intention to write a book until after my return to America in 1835, . . .'

Once again, it is clear, Tocqueville had drawn large drafts from the same living springs of constitutional interpretation. Supposing, apparently, that he was getting an entirely fresh analysis through the uncoloured mind of a college student, he actually received instead a further translation from Story and Kent and the *Federalist*, as propounded in a college text and as conveyed through the lectures of a New England professor.

The net result was that either Justice Story or Kent, the old chancellor, might indeed have felt that Tocqueville had borrowed a good deal

* 'But such a wilderness of books was of very little use to him, and what made his task an easy one was the mastery of general principles he had acquired in his senior year at Brown, where he made a thorough study for six months under Professor Goddard of "Rawle on the Constitution."' Lippitt, *Reminiscences*, p.37.

from them for the pages of his *Democracy*. For what the young Frenchman had actually done was to consult again and again and again with
the Americans who had read their books and who constituted their intellectual clientele. Tocqueville had borrowed directly and indirectly, both. Better still, he had gone to the same sources that they had
consulted, felt the influence of the same great tide of opinion that had
given birth to the interpretations they advanced, read for himself the
riddles of American Constitutional law, and come out with a similar
answer. In addition to direct and indirect borrowing, therefore, there
had been independent judgment. Having looked at the United States
for himself, he found the *Federalist* and the two great commentaries
not only accurate, but full of wisdom and suggestiveness. That he
agreed with them often, and used them occasionally, was therefore
no derogation to his own integrity or intelligence.* He would have
been foolish not to have used them. And, in the end, his own performance more than justified his course. For in his *Democracy* he succeeded
in restating the best American opinion on their constitutional development perhaps better even than the ablest American authors had done.
What had been clear before became under his masterful grasp as transparent as crystal. That was one reason why Americans were to use his
own commentary as a text in their schools for two generations.

That was also the reason, however, why a second and equally serious
charge was one day to be laid at Tocqueville's door. This second accusation was to come from some of the more belligerent Jacksonian democrats, who found themselves disappointed by Tocqueville's comments
on their idolized leader, and on certain of Andrew Jackson's principles
and policies.

In 1851 Thomas Hart Benton, for example, stout champion of the
newer forces in American politics that he had always been, was shocked
to discover the general tendency of Tocqueville's remarks and particularly distressed by what the Frenchman had said about Jackson's character and banking policies. As he was himself just writing his *Thirty
years' view; or, A history of the working of American government for
thirty years, from 1820 to 1850*, he wrote to Van Buren in some consternation to ask whether Van Buren had read 'de Tocqueville.' He was
himself going to devote a chapter to the Frenchman's 'errors.' Not

---

* Furthermore, Tocqueville declared his intellectual baggage. If he refused to name his
personal informants, so as to save them from possible obloquy, he cited his printed
authorities, chapter and page.

that he accused 'Mons. de Tocqueville' of having written in bad faith. On the contrary, in his book the noted Senator would call the correction 'a piece of respect which I do not extend to the riffraff of European writers who come here to pick up the gossip of the highways, to sell it in Europe for American history, and to requite with defamation the hospitalities of our houses. He is not of that class: he is above it; he is evidently not intentionally unjust. But he is the victim of the company which he kept while among us; and his book must pay the penalty of the impositions practised upon him.' Again, in private to Van Buren, Senator Benton insisted that 'De Tocqueville . . . must have kept bad company when in the U.S.'

'Bad company'? Did Benton know what he was talking about? He thought he did. The Frenchman must have 'written his essay on our democracy from what he read in the B.U.S. [Bank of the United States] and federal papers, and what he heard in their talk.' And as for his opinions of Jackson, 'a majority of those classes which Mons. de Tocqueville would chiefly see in the cities, and along the highways— bankers, brokers, jobbers, contractors, politicians and speculators— were certainly against him.'

So Tocqueville had consorted exclusively with Federalists and the eastern money interests! In his observations and in his reading, both, he had been imposed upon. Benton was genuinely concerned. For Tocqueville was 'authority on American democracy in Europe, & with the federalists here, & will be with our posterity if they know nothing but what the federalists write.' 'Read it all,' he urged Van Buren, 'and see what a figure we are to make if we do not write for ourselves.'[4]

Benton was exactly right. Or, rather, he hit the nail on the head in just two particulars. Tocqueville was indeed to be 'authority' with American posterity. And the reason was perhaps partly as stated: because those many westerners of the Jacksonian persuasion had neglected to write their own law commentaries from their newly developed 'democratic' point of view. The charge that Tocqueville had consorted exclusively with one class of men was, of course, ridiculous. He had visited and heard them all, from the Eastern bankers and lawyers (there were precious few 'federalists' left) to the Ohio settlers and the Michigan pioneers.* In the field of history and constitutional in-

* Among the Americans, outstanding in public life, whom Tocqueville and Beaumont had not consulted were Madison, Benton, Henry Clay, John C. Calhoun, Van Buren,

terpretation, however, it was only the Easterners who had got their views into enduring print. Though the Federalist party had passed from the scene long before the time of the Frenchman's visit to the United States, it was true that in the field of political science and legal philosophy—if not at the polls—their views in some sort survived. Perhaps the explanation was that the quality of the thinking in the *Federalist Papers*, and in the great law commentaries, simply would not down. At all events, though a section of the American people was enthusiastic to try an experiment with *direct* democracy, the jurists and the lawyers and the substantial men still clung to the theory of *representative* democracy and a federal government of divided branches and powers. And Tocqueville agreed with them. He was 'imposed upon,' yes. But he was imposed upon by what, after long and independent study, he considered the clearest and most brilliant thinking in the field of the theory of government that he had perhaps ever encountered.

Was it then true that Tocqueville was *predisposed* to accept the Federalist interpretation? Was he, instead, the victim of himself, and his book the product of personal prejudice and bias?

Benton made no such charge. Yet actually an instinctive sympathy with aristocracy and an equally unconquerable repugnance for the masses * were indelibly stamped on the Frenchman's character. It will not have escaped the reader, for instance, that Tocqueville intuitively believed that good government could come only from religion and training and elevation of character: i.e. from an aristocracy of intelligence and tradition and morality. He never in his life brought himself to think of democracy as the ultimate in desirability. Complete self-government might work well in a given situation; but it was by no means the panacea for all situations. As a consequence, while in the United States, Tocqueville clearly looked harder for Federalist arguments than for Jacksonian justifications. He even seemed to feel that there was more to be learned in Boston than in Ohio. And he was definitely more persistent in ferreting out the weaknesses of the American system than in discovering its virtues.

Nevertheless, he did expose himself to both sides of the question again and again and again. Neither his own scrupulous honesty nor

---

John Marshall, and John Tyler. Madison, however, was a very old man; John Marshall they had apparently met; the same was true for Henry Clay; and they must have watched Benton and Calhoun at work in the Senate. Any list of important men not seen would, apparently, have to be a very short one.

* See next chapter.

the enthusiasm of his hosts allowed him to do otherwise. He heard (and carefully set down!) pro-democratic evidence of the strongest kind; he chewed over and adopted unexpectedly favourable opinions on practices that at first glance had seemed like pure demagoguery or the last word in vulgarity and irresponsibility. Frequently he had acknowledged his original impressions mistaken. And since he wanted to reconcile conservatives in France to their inevitable fate, he now reviewed the rewards and compensations of popular self-government with perseverance and fidelity. All of which brought him back to his American notebooks. By instinct and training he had been predisposed to see the Federalist point of view: that much was undeniable. But to accuse Alexis de Tocqueville of having gone no deeper was to underestimate the man and misunderstand his book.

The nub of the matter really was that, out of the materials of his personal experience, supplemented and in some cases modified by his reading in the classics of American political science, he had got the raw substance of a book that in its range and really extraordinary impartiality would exactly please no school of partisans.

# LVI

# THE DESIGN OF THE *DÉMOCRATIE*

It may, perhaps, be conceded that as an observer and a scholar Tocqueville had great abilities. Yet he was more than a mere literary carpenter, plying a skilful tool and choosing his materials with a nice eye to quality and durability. For, fundamentally, his forte was architecture. He meant the masterpiece that was to grow out of his craftsmanship to have *style* and *purpose*, as well as sound materials. Like a medieval cathedral rising under the eye of some building bishop, it should be built according to method and law, and in the end be filled with meaning. Only so could it overtop the petty monuments of the day and stand for the uncertain peoples of the world, like some enduring pyramid, perpetually pointing to the stars.

### TOCQUEVILLE'S LITERARY PRINCIPLES AND STYLE

With Tocqueville, it so happened, the matter of literary attitude and style was fundamentally less the product of choice than of a pre-existent, in-born necessity. For the simple fact was that he could tolerate neither inactivity nor a haphazard performance. An approximation outraged his sensibilities, just as intellectual laziness was antipathetic to his whole nature.

He had, as Beaumont truly said, a 'steam-engine' of a mind, for ever turning and turning. Never for an instant were his thoughts still. In the phrase of a later French critic, 'for him intellectual activity was an intimate, imperious necessity, an incessant craving of his being.'[1]

Yet because he was also of a scrupulous, logical, and exacting temperament, his thoughts did not scatter. Once on a subject, he stuck to it with a single-minded intensity that was appalling.[2] When a new idea came to him, he was scarcely ever satisfied with it in its original dress,

739

but must turn it and word it again.* When he had an unfinished chapter on his hands, only sheer physical exhaustion could make him rest. 'You would excuse me,' he once wrote to J.S.Mill in apology for a delayed article,[3] 'you would excuse me if you knew what difficulty I have in satisfying myself, and my total inability to leave things incomplete. I have always believed that the public had the right to ask authors to go to the limits of their powers, and that's a requirement to which, for my part, I try to submit myself.' On another occasion he gave it as his conviction that an author should never appear in undress. For himself, he was incapable of letting a thing go until persuaded that he 'could do not better.' By personal taste and by a sort of nervous compulsion, both, he invited the tortures of the perfectionist.

It followed that he required solitude and time. His very handwriting betrayed the fact that his constitution was merely a bundle of raw nerves; and untoward disturbance or interruption would sometimes upset him as much as extreme fatigue. He had to have a refuge, therefore, some place where he could hide and work in peace, while the ideas ripened and his attentive mind still-hunted the elusive phrase.

This requirement led to an amusing series of experiments, which eventually produced a change in his manner of living, which in turn helped modify one feature of his literary technique.

He began with the thought that city life was the thing. Shut up in some hidden room during the day, he could work until his powers were exhausted, then emerge from his cocoon to attend some *salon*, mingle with society, and from the stimulus of metropolitan life draw refreshment and inspiration.† The possibility of living in the country hardly occurred to him. That was the place for cows, not thinking human beings.

So in 1833 he found in Paris a little secret garret, high up under a mansard roof, and threw himself with such fury into what he called his 'American monomania' that his health began to suffer.

In the summer of 1834, with the major part of his first two volumes behind him, he visited Gustave de Beaumont at his friend's home in

---

* Beaumont later told Senior that he had 'known him to re-cast a sentence twenty times over.' Senior, *Conversations with Thiers*, etc., II,351.

† It must be added that, in actual practice, Marie Mottley rather took the place of metropolitan society as the provider of stimulation. 'From morning to dinner I lead a life *tout de tête*, and in the evening I go to see Marie,' Tocqueville wrote Kergolay (13 Nov. 1833, copy YT). 'Since my return from England, my book and Marie are my whole life.'

the small, rolling country of the Sarthe. The place was a retreat. Tocqueville had not dreamed that such a corner of peace existed in all nineteenth-century France.* But he was puzzled rather than converted. Prior to that summer, he confessed to Kergolay, he had not spent six weeks in the country since the age of nine; and he thought he would rather 'leave for China, or enlist as a soldier, or risk my life in any other ill-considered enterprise, than condemn myself to leading the life of a potato.'[4]

Already, however, his conversion was under way. For he was imperceptibly growing very fond of the old *gentilhommière* at Tocqueville, where he and Marie Mottley were to spend so many happy years. In 1833 the decayed Norman farm, with its heavy stone towers and vast, windy chimneys, had rather depressed him. By 1837, however, it was his own property, his bride was having workmen restore the interior, and he had a large room—a library—all to himself. The windows were high, so he perched a small writing desk on a table, procured a high thatched chair, and set to work. Where once he had been afraid of the silence, he now came to crave it. So the square of farm buildings forming the château court was opened up, and Tocqueville moved the old stone gate more than a hundred yards down the avenue, in order to shut out the world even more effectively. It is a family tradition that he also had all the cattle put down on farms well removed from the house, so as not to have the delicate train of his thoughts broken in upon. Even against the inclement climate, of which he was with reason somewhat afraid, he had a protection arranged. For just outside his library door, Marie built him a special corridor (with panels after the English fashion) where he could take his exercise.

In this old two-towered château, therefore, Tocqueville finally found, even better than in his Paris attic, the leisure and the solitude and the undisturbed tranquillity that he needed so badly for his writing. Conversely, also, the peaceful remoteness of his Norman countryside intensified the very quality of thoughtfulness and reflection that had played so large a part in his creative efforts from the beginning. For the fact was that his books *might* be the product of information, but

* For a description of the *Château de la Borde*, and the—to Tocqueville—incomprehensible interest of the Beaumont family in such homely matters as the hatching of a brood of chickens, see Toc. to Marie Mottley, 23 Aug. 1834, copy TT; also above, p.21, note; and G.W.Pierson, 'Gustave de Beaumont: Liberal,' *Franco-American Review*, Spring 1937.

742 THE INTERPRETATION OF AN EXPERIENCE

they *had* to be the product of thought. He was not only a scholar, and conscientious; he went a step further, he meditated.

Practically, this meant that, in the process of composition, the contents of his head were put through a sort of refining process. One reason why the influence of Tocqueville's American experiences on his *Démocratie* has never been adequately recognized is to be found just here. He refused to use even the best materials raw, but tossed ideas, facts, surmises, all into the revolving furnace of his mind, from which they did not again emerge until they had been purified of dross and fused into an organic, homogeneous whole. It was true in his Paris attic, where he had all his notes and facts to hand. It was even more true at Tocqueville, where he undertook to continue the study of '*démocratie*,' but with no fresh documentation. Hence, again, the difference between the first and second parts of his work. In both parts he employed his brains to describe and to analyse equalitarianism. But in the first the emphasis was on a fresh and obstinate illustration: on the description and analysis of that peculiar sample of equalitarianism known as the United States. By the time that he came to write the second, on the other hand, he had abandoned notes and documents, and superficial details of observation, in favour of a further analysis and an advanced deduction. Assuming a type society, a normal equalitarianism, he tried by sheer power of undisturbed thought to discover what its characteristics and natural tendencies would be.\* Neither half of his commentary, accordingly, would in the least resemble photography; but the second would be one step still further removed from surface description. As a consequence of this mental process it might perhaps be added that in the first two volumes he translated the matter-of-fact statements of American lawyers into trenchant and thoughtful French; in volumes three and four, into the still higher language of philosophy.

The intense and single-minded concentration of which he was capable also enabled Tocqueville to labour over his verbal style, an item to which he gave unsparing attention. The manuscript drafts for his *Démocratie*, for example, reveal his use of an ingenious mechanical device to assist himself toward clearer statement. Apparently it was his custom to divide his page by a line into two vertical columns. Into the column on the right then went the first statement, the rough draft—leaving the column on the left for revision, change of

\* For further analysis of volumes III and IV see also above, p.694; below pp.758–61.

order and rephrasing. Sometimes three or even four columns were necessary before he had the passage to his satisfaction.*

What he was aiming at was clarity, brevity, and dignity of style— nothing more. Perhaps his ear also passed judgment on the product, for his best passages attained a cadence and a musical balance that were to haunt his readers. Primarily, however, he tried to say what he had to say exactly, and in the fewest possible words. He was not an accomplished stylist, unless the possession of a distinctly individual manner and an almost classic simplicity earned him the title. Certainly he wrote in a fashion that had become almost outmoded in his day. For all around him seethed and bubbled the heady wine of the new Romanticism. Chateaubriand and Victor Hugo, with their titanic tragedies, their unbridled imaginations, their purple passages, were the acknowledged literary demigods of the period. But Tocqueville wrote as if Romanticism had never even been born.† He read Pascal instead, Pascal and Montesquieu. And then, in his leisure moments in the country, with no Paris diversions to distract, he plunged into an enchanting study of the great masterpieces of world literature. He read Plato and Aristotle, Plutarch and the Koran and Machiavelli, Rabelais, Cervantes, and Rousseau. By Aristotle, Machiavelli, and the Koran he

---

* It should be added that, before he sent his manuscript to the printer, Tocqueville submitted it to his father, his brothers, and to Beaumont, and showed his Introduction to Louis de Kergolay as well.

The result was a thoroughgoing criticism. They read and commented his treatise page by page, paragraph by paragraph, word by word. In general they did not try to dispute his main propositions, but contented themselves with trying to make what he did say more effective. To that end, no criticism was too minute. Citing chapter and page, they set down on paper all repetitions, or exaggerations, or awkward passages, or unhappy comparisons. They marked passages that they thought would needlessly offend the government, or the adherents of some religion; they suggested alternative phrasings; they endeavoured to restrain him from expressions that seemed too partisan or too absolute; they advised as to the excision or retention of dubious paragraphs. Before he published, therefore, Tocqueville had the advantage of three hundred pages of detailed criticism, in longhand.

What he did with these suggestions is not so easy to determine. Sometimes he preferred the original reading and kept it. Occasionally, he adopted the change verbatim. In the vast majority of instances, however, he seems to have accepted the idea behind the criticism and then gone on to find his own new wording. See '*Observations critiques de mon père, mes frères et Beaumont sur mon ouvrage—Notes de Louis sur l'avant-propos*' (TT, marked CIIIb). For literary exaggerations that Tocqueville kept in his text, see C.Cestre, in *Revue des Cours et Conférences*, 1934,I,520–521.

† Save only for his melancholy introspection. A preoccupation with the '*moi*' was one of the distinguishing characteristics of a young Romantic; and in his gloomy forebodings, his wrestlings with doubt, his distrust of his own powers, Tocqueville clearly shared the *mal de siècle*. For this suggestion, as for many others, I am indebted to Professor John M. S. Allison.

admitted that he was repelled. On the other hand Plato, with his idealism, and the great prose writers of the age of Louis XIV, with their
classic simplicity, appealed to him most. To survive, he concluded, a
writer needed great ideas: preferably, as with Plato, some aspiration
after the beautiful or the good. Yet even such ideas were not a certain
guarantee.

'Buffon certainly said something false when he pretended that style
was the whole man,' Tocqueville counselled a young friend in an illuminating letter; [5] 'yet, of a certainty, style does make a large fraction
of the man. Show me the books which have remained, having as their
sole merit the ideas contained in them. They are in small number. I
don't even know any examples to cite unless it be a few whose style
was of extreme simplicity, a negative defect which did not absolutely
repel the reader like the opposite vice.' And he mentioned Pascal. What
kind of style was desirable, then? Tocqueville thought that the foundations must lie in reason and common sense. 'Without myself possessing a style which satisfies me in the least, I have yet studied and
meditated the style of others a great deal, and I am convinced of what
I am going to say to you: There is in the great French writers, whatever the period you find them in, a certain characteristic turn of
thought, a certain way of seizing the attention of readers which is
proper to each one of them. I believe that one is born with this individual
stamp; or at least I confess that I see no means of acquiring it. . . .
But there is a quality common to all the great writers; it serves in a
fashion as the foundation for their style; it's on this base that each one
then lays his own colour. This quality is, very simply, *good sense.* . . .
What, then, is good sense applied to style? . . . It is care in presenting
ideas in the simplest order and the most easily comprehended. It is
taking precaution never to present the reader at a single instant with
more than a simple and clear point of view, whatever the diversity
of the objects treated by the book, so that the mind does not, as it were,
light simultaneously on two ideas. It is taking pains to use words in
their true sense, and so far as possible in their most limited and certain
meaning, so that the reader is always sure what object or image you
want to offer him. I know some clever persons who, if you cavil with
them over the meaning of a phrase, substitute another meaning on
the spot without actually changing a single word, each of them being
approximately suited for the matter. Persons of that kind may be good
diplomats, but they will never be good writers. . . .'

Such was Tocqueville's literary creed. He did not always live up to it himself.* But his failures were not owing to any want of method or perseverance. Steadily, remorselessly, he forced his mind to master the variegated materials of his experience, sort them out, organize them, and give them back in the most sensible, logical, and straightforward order.†

The particular stamp or *cachet* of his own writing? What was it gave his exposition its recognizable individuality? For Tocqueville must certainly have superimposed on *le bon sens* his own colours as a man and as a prophet.

Perhaps the first 'quality' of his writing, in fact, was that same intense and almost mournful seriousness that ruled his own life. Few writers, as few men, have been so passionate, so devoted to the truth, and yet so entirely modest and forgetful of self in that exacting pursuit. When he had an unpalatable discovery to announce, he did not flinch. Yet he took no pleasure in criticism. He wrote what he had to, often reluctantly and as if under some outside compulsion. There was a flavour of fatalistic abnegation, of warning and of prophecy, of sadness mixed with the most sympathetic concern for the suffering humanity for whom he wrote.

Again there was another peculiarity about his style. His exposition was 'logical' and 'philosophic' to a degree. He used the inductive and deductive methods both,‡ and never let whimsy obstruct the rigorous development of the argument. For like the classicists and like the great *philosophes* whom his family now scorned, he instinctively believed in reason and in the sovereign capacity of man's intelligence. His own experience seemed to justify this faith; for when he sat down to develop a given topic, he never finished the chapter without, through the strait exercise of thought, seeing it grow in importance and in implications.

The immediate effect of such ratiocination was, of course, synthesis and the development of general ideas. And these ultimate generalizations, when they emerged, often came clothed with a deeper meaning and a wider application than the author himself had at first thought pos-

---

* Notably in his use of the word *démocratie*, and in his constant balancing between the United States and France (see below, pp.757–58).
† ' "*La forme*" was his ruler, almost his tyrant. "No idea," he used to say, "ought to be produced *en déshabille*. To be received it must be presented in the fewest words consistent with clearness." ' Senior, *Conversations with Thiers*, II,362.
‡ For the defects in this reasoning technique, see below, pp.759–64.

sible. The whole process of composition, certainly, reposed on a rigorous method, under the severest self-discipline. For the French people Tocqueville reported not only what he had found, but what he was forced—after the longest and most conscientious meditation—to conclude about his findings.

Once he had scorned the solitude and monotony of country life. No bovine existence for him. Yet already he had become—as one of his English friends observed—himself a *ruminating* animal.[6]

*De la Démocratie en Amérique* was the product of his American experiences, but only after this secondary digestion. What he had cropped in the United States, he now rechewed at home.

### TOCQUEVILLE'S 'DOCTRINE'

The greatest singularity of Tocqueville as an author—his doctrine—remains to be described.

If he was an observer of extraordinary perseverance and intelligence, a scholar of good judgment, and a philosopher with a meditative turn of mind, nevertheless his outstanding distinction lay elsewhere. At least it seems clear that part of his genius was a matter of faith and of purpose, rather than of literary performance. Specifically he held a certain belief as to the destination of mankind. And, because he held that striking and pessimistic belief, he was driven first to find and then to advocate a special program of social insurance. Together, this foreboding conviction and these precautionary warnings constituted what might be called the *doctrine* of Alexis de Tocqueville. Without that doctrine he would never have written, and but for it he would hardly to-day be remembered in France.

The pessimistic faith or conviction, underlying Tocqueville's whole performance, was of course that famous—and by now familiar—belief of his about the foredestined levelling down of conditions that was to overtake all the peoples of the civilized world. It was his specific creed that the progressive elimination of privilege and inequality had been the unperceived but fundamental law of the past, as it would continue to be the great gravitational principle of the future, for at least another century to come. The momentum, certainly, was too strong to be resisted. All societies of which he had any knowledge were now going toward, and would sooner or later arrive at, an almost complete equality. The word that he used was *démocratie*, but by *démocratie* he did not mean what the English-speaking world sometimes supposed. The distinction is important. For when they translated his word into *Democracy*, they failed to note that what he really was predicting was *equality*; equality in social and economic conditions as well as in political: equal privileges in government, equal civil rights before the law, equal economic benefits, equal intellectual training, no classes of any kind, even the disappearance of distinctions in fashion and 'society.'

On the first page of his 'Introduction,' Tocqueville informed his readers that he had encountered this law, this levelling tendency, in the United States, where it seemed to have run almost its full course already. Certainly its influence was visible everywhere; it was the basic, original cause to which his observations had led him back again and again; only by recognizing this underlying levelling tendency could one understand the distinctive features of American society.* He had come back home. At once he had noticed something similar in the spectacle that France presented. Conditions were not yet so equal on the Continent, but each day they were approaching nearer and nearer to that unlimited quality with which he was now familiar. 'It appears to me beyond question that sooner or later we shall arrive, like the Americans, at an almost complete equality of conditions.'

It will not escape the student that Tocqueville had just reversed the sequence of his perceptions. For literary purposes he implied that he had discovered his great natural law of modern societies in America. Actually, this idea had been the product of his youthful experiences at home. The sad history of the old aristocracy, the fate of the Restoration Monarchy, the suggestive lectures of Professor Guizot, the pronouncements of certain statesmen of France: all had seemed to Tocqueville to indicate that the process of levelling down had been going on for a long time and could not now be stopped. His discoveries abroad, therefore, had but confirmed a conviction that he had already begun to entertain—with the further result that now he felt justified in applying his law to the whole modern world. Such was the article of faith, the fatalistic belief, the *idée-mère* which ruled his thinking.

It happened, in the second place, that Tocqueville felt also a deep sense of obligation to society. It followed that he would have to find the medium of speech. Some description, some tangible and realistic image would have to be presented, if his own vision were to be trans-

* Cf. above, pp.164–66.

lated into terms that his countrymen could understand. The vehicle that offered itself was the United States. Some of his countrymen preferred to look down the road that England had taken. But to Tocqueville the Americans seemed to be further advanced. In the United States, better and more completely than anywhere else in the world, the fate of mankind had already been realized. If he wished to paint a picture for France, he could choose no better model.

Out of the fundamental article in Tocqueville's creed, therefore, came not only the original necessity of writing but the very title and subject of his book. He elected to devote his masterpiece to the United States, not out of admiration for American society, not even primarily because he felt that this New World country was interesting for itself, but simply because it presented his object lesson for him. He described America because he had decided to preach to the French. As he himself confessed to J.S.Mill, 'America was only my framework, *démocratie* was the subject.' *

Yet Tocqueville took no pleasure in prophesying for its own sake. The role of Cassandra held too little appeal for him. As a matter of fact, even if he had been able to paint an exact likeness of the society that was to come, he would never have undertaken the task, unless he had felt that some use could be made of the picture once it had been presented. In a word, it was only because some thread of optimism was mingled with Tocqueville's pessimism that he bothered to write. Despite his fatalistic premonitions, perhaps something *could* be done about the future. In addition to a conviction and a pat illustration, then, it should be recognized that he had an ulterior incentive, a third purpose. *De la Démocratie en Amérique* was composed, partly because he foresaw, partly because he wanted to foretell, but partly also because he wanted to forewarn, and to forewarn in time.

If there was paradox, or contradiction, in first announcing an unavoidable fate and then proposing to do something about it, Tocqueville did not let so small an inconsistency interfere with his efforts. In any case, he stood rather in the position of a weather forecaster, who predicts the weather, realizes that nothing can stop the coming storm, yet trusts that the people may profit by his advance information to take shelter. As Tocqueville himself put it, the coming equality might take

* As late as November 1839, Tocqueville planned to use the word *égalité* rather than *démocratie* in the title of his second pair of volumes. See his letters to J.S.Mill, *O.C.*,VI,67,94.

several forms, ranging in desirability from a happy democratic republic to the dead-level uniformity of universal slavery under some despot or tyrant. Was it *impossible* to choose the former? Tocqueville thought not. For 'I cannot believe that God has for several centuries been pushing two or three hundred million men toward equality just to make them wind up under a Tiberian or a Claudian despotism. Verily, that wouldn't be worth the trouble. Why he is drawing us toward *la Démocratie*, I don't know; but, embarked on a vessel that I did not build, I am at least trying to use it to gain the nearest port.'[7]

But how reach the happy landfall on so dangerous a coast? Did this self-elected pilot have any suggestions for the other passengers on board? He did. And his first counsel was one of moderation. The enthusiasts should not try to get there too quickly, nor the reluctant try to prevent the landing altogether. Neither by crowding on sail, nor by dropping anchor, would the ship of state come safely into port. In a letter just after the appearance of his first two volumes, he stated this idea in striking terms.[8]

'I wanted to show what an equalitarian people is in our day, and, by this rigorously exact painting, I have aimed to produce a twofold effect on the minds of men in our times.

'To those who have made for themselves an ideal *démocratie*, a brilliant dream, which they believe it easy to realize, I have undertaken to demonstrate that they have clothed their tableau in false colours; that the "democratic" government which they extol, if it produces real benefits for the men who are able to bear it, does not possess the high traits that their imaginations attribute to it; that this government, besides, can only be maintained by means of certain conditions of enlightenment, of private morality, of *croyances* that we do not possess, and that we must labour to obtain before drawing from it its political consequences.

'To the men for whom the word *démocratie* is the synonym for disorder, anarchy, spoliation, murder, I have tried to demonstrate that *démocratie* [the population as a whole?] could manage to govern society while respecting fortunes, recognizing rights, sparing liberty, and honouring religious beliefs; that if "democratic" government developed, less than some other, certain grand faculties of the human soul, it yet had its beauty and its greatness; and that perhaps, after all, it was God's wish to spread a mediocre happiness throughout mankind, and not to concentrate a great amount of happiness on a few and bring a small number near to perfection. I have presumed to show them that, whatever their opinion in this matter, the time for deliberation was past; that society was marching, and dragging them along each day, toward the equality of conditions; that all that was left was to choose between evils henceforth inevitable; that the question was not one of finding out whether aristocracy or "democracy" might be obtained, but whether one was to have an equalitarian society progressing without poetry or grandeur, yet with order and morality, or a "democratic" society disordered and depraved, delivered up to frenzied furies or bowed under a yoke heavier than any that have weighed on men since the fall of the Roman Empire.

'I have wanted to diminish the ardour of the former and, without discouraging them, show them the only path to take.

'I have tried to decrease the terrors of the latter and bend their wills to an inevitable future, in such a way that, the former having less impetuosity and the latter offering less resistance, society could advance more peacefully toward the necessary accomplishment of its destiny. There you have the *idée mère* of the work, the idea which links all the other ideas into a single system.'

Tocqueville wrote, then, not just because he foresaw, and had a fine example, but because he wished to counsel moderation. If the tide was strong, let there at least be peace on board this vessel. There must be a concerted effort to reach the better harbour. He himself was neither an ardent democrat nor a reactionary. If anything, his sympathies were with the *ancien régime* and with the ideal of aristocracy.[9] But his reason told him that any resurrection of that cause was hopeless. 'You judge "democracy,"' Guizot wrote to him in 1835, 'like an aristocrat who has been vanquished, and is convinced that his conqueror is right.' And later Sainte-Beuve's shrewd intelligence divined the fact that Tocqueville's whole doctrine had been 'a marriage of reason and necessity, not at all of inclination.'[10] In sober conviction, on the other hand, Tocqueville resembled the republicans more nearly than he did the absolutists. Yet he was a very reluctant republican at best. And this personal disharmony, this spiritual debate within himself, naturally prevented his becoming an extremist—led him instead to adopt the role of peacemaker.*

---

* What form of government Tocqueville would have elected, could he have had an absolutely free choice, one cannot be sure. For he was persuaded that no such free-

There was also another reason for counselling harmony. For it seemed to Tocqueville that each side championed certain qualities that needed to be preserved. 'What has always struck me in my country, but principally in the last few years,' he explained to a friend,[11] 'has been to see ranged on one side the men who prized morality, religion, order; and on the other those who love liberty, [and] the equality of men before the law. This spectacle has struck me as the most extraordinary and the most deplorable ever offered to the eyes of man; for all these things that we thus separate are, I am certain of it, indissolubly united in the sight of God. They are all *holy* things, if I may so express myself, because the grandeur and happiness of man in this world can come only from the reunion of all these together.'

Tocqueville's purpose, then, went beyond mere peacemaking. He proposed to be a mediator, unquestionably, but he mediated only because he wanted to rescue certain ideals from destruction. Resignation—the counsel of resignation to the future and to each other—was certainly a part of his program. But it was morality, order, religion, personal liberty, and the equality of all human beings before the law—rather than peace—that he was really interested in.

The growing materialism of nineteenth-century France worried him. The irreligion of the pro-republican lower classes seemed to him a deplorable error. Why should morality be divorced from equity, and order from liberty? To reconcile these ideals in the public mind appealed to Tocqueville as 'one of the grandest enterprises of our times.'

Most of all he was concerned for liberty and personal freedom. The dignity and value of the individual seemed to him the finest, rarest product of the old aristocracy, and he was desperately anxious not to lose it. Yet if the 'levellers' were to be encouraged in their present tendencies, they would in their effort to cut down disparities between individuals perhaps destroy individual freedom and personal initiative altogether. Rather than have one man worth more than another, they threatened to regiment all society and destroy the individual personality entirely. To Tocqueville, on the other hand, society was nothing if it suppressed the human soul. He was profoundly convinced, therefore, that it was the mission of all enlightened Frenchmen to counteract equalitarianism 'with the genuine love and practice of freedom.' As he

---

dom of choice existed any longer; and in any case he was more interested in the manner of governing than in the name of the governor. Nevertheless, if pressed, he would apparently have cast his vote for a *constitutional*, hereditary monarchy.

was to proclaim again in his fourth volume: 'it is not in the least a question of reconstructing an aristocratic society, but *de faire sortir* liberty from the bosom of the "democratic" society in which God makes us to live.'[12]

What Tocqueville was most afraid of, as he insisted again and again, was tyranny.* For once all outstanding classes had been eliminated, all disparities banished, the societies of the future would be terribly defenceless against all forms of oppression. Whether the tyranny took the form of tyranny by the majority over the minority, or came by the tyranny of a single despot, seemed to him to make little difference. It was tyranny, and oppression of the individual, whatever the source. As he wrote to Kergolay on beginning volumes three and four, 'To indicate to men, if it is possible, what they must do in order to escape from tyranny and degeneration while becoming *equalitarian*, such is, I think, the general idea which epitomizes my book and which will appear on every page of the one that I am writing. To labour in this direction is in my eyes a *sainte* occupation, and one in which one must spare neither one's money, nor one's time, nor one's life.'[13]

But what must men do in order to save the best, and avoid the worst, as Tocqueville counselled? As to that, the young author again had a pertinent proposition or two. He was prepared to be a little less dogmatic, in fact he saw no panacea, when it came to prescribing practical remedies. But certainly force had to be avoided. And, almost as certainly, the United States offered some useful suggestions.

Again, in other words, his American experiences were to be put to use. Only this time American society was to serve as an example of conduct to be followed quite as much as the idealized portrait of what all Europe would be like in the future. Specifically, he meant to tell his fellow-countrymen that in the United States there had been discovered, and were now being practised, certain very useful precautions against the aberrations of the masses in a complete democracy.

Tocqueville could by no means pretend to recommend the whole American example. In fact, there were a number of particulars in which the American people erred, a number of devices which it would not be safe for a continental nation to imitate. Now, at long last, however, he was finally prepared to assert that in four or five essentials the American example was indeed worth the careful study and prayerful imitation of Europe.

* See below, pp.766,771.

What these good points were, the reader will already have learned. On this section of Tocqueville's doctrine the briefest recapitulation will, therefore, suffice. For the successful practice of popular self-government, Tocqueville recommended: (1) *religion* (i.e. a Church separated from the State, and a faith that taught morality and respect for law and order); (2) *experience and practice* in self-control; (3) the maximum *decentralization* compatible with the exposed position of the French nation in a crowded and hostile Europe.*

In addition to these three great principles, Tocqueville ventured to recommend some lesser aids to the practice of successful self-government. From the American juridical institutions might be borrowed, he thought, (4) the idea of an independent judiciary as a check on the excesses of popular legislatures, and (5) the wonderful political device of the American jury system. The French people ought also to give careful study to the problem of leadership. He did not believe in complete manhood suffrage or in the direct control of the government by the whole people. His own experiences in the United States had taught him that direct democracy was vicious in its tendencies. Instead, he recommended (6) indirect election of important officers and a representative democracy only.†

In sum, the proper objectives of French statesmanship seemed to Tocqueville recognizable and clear. 'To define for the power of the government limits that are wide, yet visible and fixed; to give to individuals certain rights, and guarantee them in the undisputed enjoyment of the same; to save for the individual the little of independence,

---

* As to this third recommendation, Tocqueville did not mean to advocate so weak a Federation as their isolation in the new world enabled the Americans to tolerate. On the contrary, 'it is both necessary and desirable that the central power directing a "democratic" nation be active and powerful. It is not a question of making it feeble and indolent, but only of preventing it from abusing its agility and strength.' (*Dém. en Am.*, IV,323.) Also, it was a part of Tocqueville's thought to borrow at least some of the many wonderful advantages that local self-government had produced for the Americans. Something of the energy in self-improvement, something of the training in citizenship that the local administration of their own affairs yielded to the men of a New England town, seemed to Alexis de Tocqueville distinctly desirable. What he suggested, therefore, was a sort of compromise. He would borrow the American idea of spheres, but simply divide the spheres a little less evenly. Let the national government make all the great laws, but administer only those functions of government where uniformity was absolutely necessary. Let the *communes*, on the other hand, be developed and invigorated to administer the rest. Legally, let France continue to be centralized. Administratively, however, let a beneficent home rule be encouraged in the *pays*. (*O.C.*,V,436–437.)

   For the influence and importance of this suggestion, see below, pp.771–72.

† Further suggestions included (7) a free press, (8) two chambers, and (9) a constitution sufficiently elastic to allow for its own peaceful amendment.

power, originality remaining to him; to raise him up by the side of society as a whole and sustain him against it: such appears to me to be the first object of the legislator, in the age that we are now entering.'[14]

Such, in any case, was Tocqueville's ultimate purpose in writing the four volumes of his book. If in the first two, published in 1835, he concentrated almost entirely on the United States, and made only occasional allusion to France, that was due simply to a double accident: to the accident, first of all, that America was both his illustration and his example; to the unforeseen accident, secondly, that it had charmed him and intrigued him far more than he had originally planned that it should. In fact, in certain particulars, democracy in the United States had enlisted not just his thought, but his reluctant admiration.

Into the manufacture of his commentary, therefore, Tocqueville put information, method, and beliefs, all three. To his American readers the information and description—the careful analysis and the occasional approval of volumes one and two—would be the most interesting. But to Alexis de Tocqueville his conviction and his warning were what really mattered.

## LVII

## TOCQUEVILLE'S WORK IN RETROSPECT:
## ITS DEFECTS

ABOUT this same body of philosophic doctrine, on which Alexis de Tocqueville was so insistent, Sainte-Beuve was one day to make an un-kind remark. Tocqueville had, he said, begun to reason before acquir-ing his information: *il a commencé à penser avant d'avoir rien appris*.[1] The comment was sharp; in some ways it was even quite unfair. Yet it serves to call to mind a fact which ought not to be overlooked.

In the United States, after the appearance of *Democracy in America*, Justice Story and some of the more militant democrats were not entirely satisfied. In England the reviewers, and even a few of Tocqueville's de-voted friends, expressed a reservation or two when they had finished reading. And it is of course well known that a prophet is never without his critics in France.

At the very start, then, *De la Démocratie en Amérique* was not ac-cepted as pure gospel, or swallowed whole. Everywhere there was at least some discontent, and here and there a protesting voice was raised. Whether in partisanship or in reluctant disagreement, faults were pointed out. One man was not satisfied with the author's approach. An-other quarrelled with his doctrine. Still others listed the errors in logic or in observation that they claimed to have found. And so it continued throughout the long and generally glorious career of the celebrated commentary. The book remained an acknowledged landmark in nine-teenth century thought: no educated man could possibly ignore it. Yet, equally, the masterpiece contained a number of imperfections. And Tocqueville himself was sometimes roundly criticized. As the years passed, therefore, and the astonishing treatise was studied and studied again, an indistinct body of criticism and reservation was gradually for-mulated. And over against an accepted admiration there came to stand an accepted critique.

To the present writer this conduct seems entirely just. For Tocqueville's treatise merited a searching criticism. It was not only imperfect, as all human works must be: it contained some really serious faults. On thoughtful analysis, for example, it will be clear that the doctrine of his commentary was tendencious, and in certain respects pretty thoroughly misleading. Again, the description of the United States that it supplied left much to be desired, both as a piece of contemporary observation and as a vision of world conditions to come. Finally, Tocqueville's *method* itself—his style of writing, his way of research, his prevailing habit of thought—was vulnerability itself. In fact it was his philosophical method that, more than any other factor, gave birth to errors in his thinking and injected into his classic the strong dose of mortality that it undoubtedly contains.

In the interest of balancing our *dossier* on Tocqueville, therefore, let us consider the defects of his *De la Démocratie en Amérique* unsparingly, and in detail.*

## 1. THE DEFICIENCIES IN TOCQUEVILLE'S PHILOSOPHIC METHOD

It has been pointed out again and again—and with justice—that Tocqueville was neither a historian nor a scientist but a philosopher, and a philosopher whose concepts and whose habits of thought were not well calculated, if he wanted, rigorously, to find the truth.

Certainly Tocqueville was not, in practice or in intention, a real historian. For an untrained amateur—or even in comparison with some of the acknowledged historians of that day—he made an exceptionally intelligent use of original documents and of secondary works. But he was not interested in recording the past; and he so thoroughly slighted the backgrounds of his subject that in seeking explanations he came to mislead himself.

Lord Acton once intimated that Tocqueville's knowledge of the colonial period of American development was decidedly weak. And innumerable readers have noticed with surprise how little was said about the inheritance from England. Despite hints from Jared Sparks and Alexander Everett, Tocqueville never fully grasped the significance of the English connection. Despite his access to the best materials on American colonial history then in print, he also failed to understand or to develop some of the most important characteristics and peculiarities

* After a century of comment, of course, no critique of Alexis de Tocqueville can be altogether original or all-inclusive. The following analysis, however, pretends to co-ordinate, in brief compass and in logical form, the most telling criticisms that have been, or can be, advanced against Tocqueville's book.

of the early settlements. The influence of the climate and a niggardly soil on the formation of New England character escaped his notice. The vital role played in the Revolution by class quarrels and regional antagonism had been in part disguised from his penetrating glance by the Fourth of July patriotism and the anti-British legends of Jacksonian America.

And as for American 'democracy,' he never bothered to trace its rise. It was almost as if he had surprised it in America, perfect, matured, full-grown: an absolute type without a significant past.*

At the beginning of his sojourn in the United States, he had indeed started a promising exploration into the factors of environment and previous history. But that beginning he had never followed up, and the further his American experiences slipped into the background, the further Tocqueville himself had receded from the historian's point of view. The spectacle that on the spot had seemed to have limitless depth, in retrospect had flattened out into an ideal picture, without sufficient perspective.

Again, it has been said that Tocqueville was unscientific. Both as a student of politics and as a reasoner on his observations, he has been accused of being decidedly inaccurate. Certainly he was not precise in his use of terms, despite his conviction that such precision was necessary. One word alone was enough to convict him on this charge. As a matter of fact, how he ever allowed himself to use *démocratie* in seven or eight different senses is still something of a mystery.† It was his key word. To *démocratie*, if to anything in his book, he should have given a precise meaning. Yet he did not. The result was that it held out false promises to men of all parties and beliefs. To Americans the word might mean representative self-government; to the French Republicans, manhood suffrage and the destruction of privilege; to the conservatives, the violences and aberrations of the populace; to the socialists the charms of a regulated commonwealth. And each of these antagonistic groups would be able to cite chapter and verse in the new gospel for proof. Perhaps Tocqueville was persuaded that the levelling tendency or law embraced all these possibilities, as special manifestations. If so, how-

---

* This statement (see also above, pp.163–66) needs one reservation. Tocqueville did see the roots of a democratic tendency in the colonial charters, the town meetings, and in dissenting Protestantism. But he tended to exaggerate the germs of equalitarianism in early Massachusetts, and he never bothered to trace their slow development during the next two hundred years. In effect, he made one dubious and sweeping generalization, and then let the matter go.

† See above, pp.158,165.

ever, he was forgetting the mutual incompatibilities of the variant readings. So vague and general a term was indefensible. If generously used, it could only lead to multitudinous contradictions, as indeed it did.

Once more, Tocqueville was unscientific in his use of, or rather in his failure to use, contemporary literature. For not only did he deliberately avoid other books immediately on his own subject, but he never did do enough scattered, general, careless, miscellaneous reading. As a result, he sometimes seemed to come to subjects as to an undiscovered country. Not having the guidance of other explorers, he found it hard to start in; and in the end he often had the air of announcing a new discovery, when actually he had but restated conclusions already reached by others. In one or two instances, he slighted, or even missed altogether, what others considered a salient feature of his subject. The method had this to recommend it, that it enabled Tocqueville to dodge the ruts and that it gave his writing a tone of originality and appealing sincerity. But it was hardly scientific.

The same was true of his choice of subject, which was far too large for any exact analysis. To describe the political institutions of a foreign people—as in his first two volumes—was quite hard enough. But when he elected to compare America to France, a known to an unknown, the difficulty was immensely increased. Tocqueville himself was essentially 'binocular'; he seemed to have the power to bring two widely separated objects into one field of vision. Even when he was most successful in making this comparison clear, however, the reader found the constant switching back and forth a fatiguing business.* And when he then proceeded to include in his field the even larger topic of equality in Europe—as he tried to do in volumes three and four—the strain on the reader, and on his own extraordinary powers of condensation, was visibly too great. In effect, he was analysing the whole of modern civilization, yet trying to explain it all by the development of one great idea. Obviously, such an effort could be scientific neither in method nor in result.

Yet Tocqueville personally believed that he was using a scientific method, and the most rigorous accuracy. For he had a clearly developed approach, and he governed his thinking by a most exacting law. On any given topic, his research was painstakingly pushed through the same pre-determined—and to him scientific—series of steps. He would be-

---

* As has been pointed out by more than one critic, America was for ever getting in his way when he wanted to speak of equality, and his preconceptions about *démocratie* were for ever interfering with his specific descriptions of the United States.

gin, as in New York, by a conscientious search for document and information; his first step was always—eliminating prejudice—to establish the ordinary and visible facts. To Tocqueville, however, mere fact meant nothing. It did not explain. His second step was therefore inductive and interpretative. He would study the phenomena he had noted, analyse them for points of similarity, ponder their probable origins, and thus seek to read into them a message. In a word, he would *induce* into his materials their real character: find the basic idea or ideas of which they were all an expression: squeeze from them their hidden meaning. That done, he had the key. And rigorous, logical thought would *deduce* from the fundamental force that he had now discovered all the consequences that it held for the given society. By linking observation, induction, and deduction, in that order, Tocqueville made bold to think that a scientific explanation could be produced.*

The trouble was that Tocqueville overreached himself on the second and third steps. He was too logical, too mathematical, too intellectual—and not sufficiently inquisitive. He relied too much on induction, and then too much on deduction. Once he had found the 'true explanation,' for example, he ceased to be interested in gathering facts, or, rather, he tended to gather only those facts that fitted his theory.†And once his theory or thesis was fairly stated, then his preoccupation became the discovery of all its myriad consequences. On these he would ponder and ponder until he was satisfied; and he was rarely satisfied before he had somehow and in some fashion related almost every observable phenomenon to his great central Law or primary cause. ‡

---

* For the development of this method, see above, pp.77–80. By nature Tocqueville had such a horror of any kind of uncertainty, that one is almost tempted to see in this dialectic primarily an elaborate mechanism against doubt.

† See his remark during his Great Lakes tour, above, p.302. It should be noted that his tendency to 'select' his evidence was increased by the fundamental purpose of the book. What he was seeking was not always the whole truth but useful *'renseignments'* for France.

‡ 'He probes every subject to the quick. He sounds every depth to the bottom. He critically inspects every side of a question, while from one demonstrated point he is capable of deducing a thousand corollaries with all the relentless exactitude of a mathematician, until, in sheer despair, the reader cries, Hold, enough!' W.C.Robinson, in *The Catholic World*, Nov. 1880.

The method derived, of course, from the classic writers of the eighteenth century. 'To follow in all research, with all confidence, without either reserve or precaution, the method of the mathematicians; exact, circumscribe, isolate a few very simple and very general notions; then, abandoning experience, to compare them, combine them, and, from the artificial composite thus obtained, to deduce by pure reasoning all the consequences therein contained: such is the natural procedure of the *esprit classique*.' Taine, *L'Ancien Régime*, 1887, pp.262–263.

Sometimes the intensive meditation that Tocqueville practised led him to the most unexpected and illuminating discoveries. On other occasions, however, he could be detected drawing from the same origin the most contradictory conclusions. And in any case, the tendency was to over-simplify, to explain too much by too little, to substitute a universal man for particular men, to fuse all causes and all origins into the single law.

The vice of Tocqueville's method, therefore, was precisely its *unscientific* quality. And the vice grew on him. In his first two volumes he showed himself an observer of precision and amazing insight. As his American experiences receded, however, his dependence on his reasoning powers and his dialectic increased proportionately. He became an exponent of the *a priori* method.* He did not check his thesis—which had now assumed the status of an inveterate prejudice—against fresh observation. His reasonings became more and more abstract. He began to write sections on the influence of *démocratie* on American intellectual life, or on American morals; and chapters on the sources of poetry, or the proclivities of standing armies in equalitarian societies.†
The tendency of the eighteenth century classicists, or even of writers of his own day, to express themselves in sounding generalizations, Tocqueville unaffectedly denounced. Yet he himself came to resort more and more to sweeping statements and all-inclusive final phrases. He happened to be a master at the art of condensing thought; and some of his pages were so closely packed with ideas as to require the slowest, most painstaking digestion. Generally, the reward for the reader was proportionately great: it was as if Tocqueville had lifted himself onto some high mountain, and thence in one swift glance comprehended a majestic countryside. Yet all too often, on the other hand, his thoughts seemed to have spun out into pure theory. The process of

* Again and again Tocqueville reminds one of Professor Guizot. In his sixth lecture on the history of civilization in Europe, after some broad statements as to the general tendencies of European development, Guizot had made the following interesting remark: 'Nous avons maintenant à contrôler nos assertions par les faits, à vérifier par l'histoire ce que nous avons déduit de la nature même et de la situation de la société. . . .' That was precisely what Tocqueville was always doing.
† In his obsession with *démocratie*, Tocqueville even puts one in mind of Mme de Staël, who is said to have been so impressed with the sovereign importance of the forms of government and the names of political institutions that, 'in a book on Passions (1796), she gave separate treatment to love under *constitutional monarchies*, love under *absolute monarchies*, and love in *republics*.' (Michel, *L'Idée de l'État*, p.289, note 2.)
  Needless to say, such topics as those mentioned above did not make up the whole content of Tocqueville's last two volumes.

deduction from deduction had been carried so far that all connection with fact and reality had been left behind; and in effect a rational process had wound up in purest nonsense. Where once, in the United States, he had observed, now, back in France, he had become a ruminating animal, and taken to expressing himself.

He was acutely aware of the danger, and struggled against it.[2] But essentially it was his belief that truth could be found by taking thought.

### 2. A CRITIQUE OF PURE DOCTRINE

With this philosophic approach, it was natural and perhaps inevitable that Tocqueville should have evolved a faith or fundamental doctrine that only partly corresponded to reality. When he deliberately withdrew from the confusion of the contemporary scene, and ceased to expose himself to the variegated and hopelessly contradictory features of American civilization, but set to work instead to apply to a selected body of evidence the processes of pure reason, the result would necessarily be an over-simplification of his subject. And when his over-logical mind was constantly driven ahead by a fearful and foreboding soul, the product of such ratiocination was almost bound to be tendencious: a one-sided doctrine unconsciously pushed to the point of propaganda.

Essentially, Tocqueville's whole personal philosophy revolved around four very simple ideas. The first was a belief in *necessity* or inevitability: the concept of predestination translated into the field of social evolution. He shared this faith in natural law with Guizot and Mignet and many of his contemporaries.* In his second idea, however, he was

---

* What were Tocqueville's philosophical debts? At the risk of seeming to slight an essential aspect of his work, the present writer has deliberately avoided a frontal attack on this question. The reason seems a good one: Tocqueville had affiliations, not debts. Undoubtedly he must have borrowed at least a few of his ideas and attitudes, in some fashion or other. But if and when he did so, it was entirely unconsciously, it was even against his will. For few men have ever made a greater effort to stand on their own intellectual feet. As a consequence it is not only safer, it is more accurate, to say that Tocqueville *shared* an idea, rather than that he borrowed it. One can *locate* Tocqueville on the intellectual map of his day, but one can only rarely name his obligations.

Students wishing to pursue this matter further may perhaps find suggestions in the following outline or chart of

TOCQUEVILLE'S INTELLECTUAL AFFILIATIONS

—*Problem of Individual in Society*
　Eighteenth century concern—duty to society—faith in human worth
—*Idea of 'Necessity'* (at least three schools)
　　1. Savigny, Hegel, Guizot, Mignet, Royer-Collard: what past has made—gradual evolution—'necessity of things'

more original. Where some believed in divine law, and others in the law of economic progress, Tocqueville felt sure that the *levelling tendency*—the progressive equalization of conditions—was what was fundamental and in the long run unavoidable. His third idea was an immediate product of this assumption. If progress was toward equality, it must be away from inequality: that is, away from privileges, class divisions, and distinction of all kinds. In his mind, therefore, Tocqueville created a stuffed image of the past and labelled it *aristocratie*, just as he had already made a dummy model of the future with the cognomen of *démocratie*. Finally, his fourth idea was a belief in the superior desirability and effectiveness of moral forces, as distinguished from forces of a military or an economic or a mechanical order.

This last predilection led Tocqueville to emphasize, in fact to exaggerate, the role of religion and of personal morality and of law in the maintenance of good government. It led him also to champion the individual—or man as a moral entity—against both the claims of the State and the destructive regimentation of some mass Utopia. What he wanted to preserve was freedom and human dignity. If equality had to come, let there at least remain some opportunity for free thought and free action: in a word, for the realization of the highest capacities of man. Comfort? Physical comfort, and wealth, and economic happiness? Tocqueville hardly considered such alternatives. On any comparative basis they stood beneath his contempt. In fact, the weakness of Tocqueville's fourth belief lay exactly on its negative side. He was not interested in material progress. He was so little interested, indeed, that he had never seriously considered the industrial revolution! In England he had been struck by what had seemed a feverish commercialism. But in the United States he had neglected entirely the one great factor that was going to transform his chosen civilization almost over-

---

2. de Maistre, Bonald: divine laws
3. St. Simon: mechanical, unmoral 'progress'
—*'Democracy' as the thing necessary*
    NOT 'representative' government of Royer-Collard, or 'capacités' of Guizot, or 'Rule of Reason' of Rémusat . . .
    Closer to de Serre, 'La démocratie . . . coule à pleins bords'; also to Guizot's idea of the rise of the third estate
—*America as the place to study it*
    Of school of Lafayette, La Rochefoucauld-Liancourt, Destutt de Tracy
    Opposed to Mme de Staël, Guizot, Doctrinaire, '1688 school'
—*Special Affiliations*:
    —With Benjamin Constant on danger of tyranny by majority, on decentralization. . . .

night. Chevalier was to be guilty of no such oversight; but perhaps Chevalier was less interested in moral values. At all events, Tocqueville had spent nine months in America, and now ventured to predict the future of many American institutions, without once giving any adequate consideration to what was already becoming the most potent factor in nineteenth century American development: the industrial exploitation of the continent, with the transformation of an agrarian population into an entirely different order of economic society. The penalty for so one-sided an assumption would of course have to be paid some day.*

As for his third idea—the belief in a vanishing *aristocratie*—that did him less harm. It stood in the way of his really understanding the English, of course. But England was not the object of his study; and his idealized concept interfered with his commentary to but a minor degree.† Its chief effect was visible in his mood; it made him sad. Standing between an old way of life, which he knew was doomed but which aroused his instinctive sympathy, and a new way of life which filled him—as he said—with a kind of *religious terror*, he felt there could be no choice. He had to face the facts, and go forward. At the same time, however, he could not help it if the choice also made him melancholy. All his life he was to be haunted by his vision of what might have been. The witty Sainte-Beuve diagnosed the malady at once, and was reminded of a classic parallel. 'As for me, I immediately compared him in his search for the *démocratie* of the future, toward which he was progressing but with so pensive and sad a face, to pious Aenaeas setting out to found the city of Rome, though still weeping for Dido. *Mens immota manet, lacrymae volvuntur inanes.*'[3]

Without real question, of course, it was his second idea—his belief in an inevitable *démocratie*—that constituted his most debatable proposition and the weakest link in the chain of his philosophy. For, aside from his questionable definition of the word, he tended—as is now abundantly clear—to assimilate all visible forces and phenomena under the one master head. What Tocqueville attributed to the operation of *démocratie* in England, for example, John Stuart Mill believed to be due to the normal activities of a commercial middle class. The qualities

* See below.
† It prevented useful comparison between the two English-speaking countries, or any adequate recognition of the possibility that many American peculiarities might be racial in origin. In certain respects Tocqueville understood the English people better at Saginaw than he did in London.

of envy and jealousy and impatient individualism, to which Tocqueville pointed with triumphant finger in France, have since seemed to André Siegfried definitely less equalitarian than racial in origins, not democratic but characteristically French. Even the Americans were to find Tocqueville transforming their representative democracy into an example of pure equalitarianism. What such an interpretation did to the other factors of environment, of inheritance, and of accident, is of course already obvious. In a word, even granting that Tocqueville had divined the most important influence that was to operate on the civilization of the western world, he made his explanation too narrow and too simple. In neglecting (or misinterpreting) the other, almost equally important, influences, he falsified his interpretation.

### 3. THE ERRORS IN OBSERVATION

It now remains to point out the particular errors of Tocqueville as an observer of conditions in the United States. Some of these have already been referred to in the course of this work. Others have been brought out by that later commentator and keen student of Tocqueville's books, James Bryce; or given a more recent listing and analysis by Charles Cestre, in a course of public lectures at the Sorbonne.[4] That there would be a number of minor slips and misapprehensions, of course, the very nature of Tocqueville's enterprise made inevitable. That he in the end managed to make at least several serious blunders, as well, the following brief recapitulation will make only too clear.

Tocqueville's first error, from the point of view both of logic and of damage, was probably his misreading of the American inheritance laws.*

The second, in the mind of the present writer, was his neglect of American material development. Some critics would call this Tocqueville's greatest blind spot. At all events, the omission was very damaging. Even moral and intellectual conditions may be altered by economic change; and in the field of political institutions the connection was certainly much closer than Tocqueville allowed himself to suppose. As one result, he entirely failed to do justice to the nationalizing influence of American commerce, and therefore underestimated the centralizing tendency in American politics, and the durability of the Federal Union. As another consequence he neglected to study the growing towns, and failed to foresee the tremendous cities of the fu-

* This point needs no further elaboration. See pp. 126–28.

ture, with all the strains that they would put on American institutions of local self-government. Again, he failed to realize that the institutions of 1787 were essentially agrarian, whereas the nation that was using them would soon be pretty thoroughly industrialized. Most tragic of all, perhaps, he called on the people of the world to recognize the paramount importance of political science at precisely the moment when the Americans themselves—and Europeans with them—were turning instead to a pursuit of happiness by economic means. For the next hundred years, at least, the western world was to concentrate its energies on material progress, while theories of government would gradually fall into neglect. By the accident of character and the irony of fate, Tocqueville had chosen to plead a cause in which the world was losing interest, in a philosophic language that was no longer being spoken.

Tocqueville's third major failing as an observer lay in his lack of perspective: in his attempt to read the character of American institutions without first obtaining a sufficient knowledge of their historical background. The young Frenchman cannot fairly be criticized simply because he eschewed the role of historian—or even because he presented to his readers only certain carefully selected aspects of contemporary American society.[5] For Tocqueville's purpose was not an encyclopædic comprehension of American development, but the education of the people of France in the science of politics and the difficult art of self-government. When, however, he was guilty of errors in this work of edification, and when these mistakes of observation or understanding were due directly to ignorance of history, then his methods and his description may justly be called into question. In such a fashion he misread the inheritance laws. From similar causes he undertook to discuss the slavery dispute, and the bitterness between North and South, without once taking into account the rivalry for western land, or the Missouri Compromise. He discussed the right of assembly without much knowledge of how conventions had been used in the past. And he described the characteristics of legislatures in a democracy, without noting how much of their business was beginning to be done in committee.

In the field of political science, itself, Tocqueville made two considerable errors of omission. He failed to notice the growth of a two-party system, based upon patronage and spoils. And, as has already been noticed, he neglected the intermediate unit in American government, the State, with its significant possibilities as a balancing force and an experimental laboratory. Both of these mistakes can be traced to his visit to Albany, and his failures of observation there.

A few more significant errors may be listed, and the table will be almost complete. Tocqueville never allowed to education the beneficent possibilities that the American people still see in it. He missed the rising abolitionist movement. He failed to give adequate credit to American enthusiasm for liberty and freedom, as distinguished from jealousy of privilege. Owing to his experiences with Andrew Jackson and Governor Throop, he underestimated the power of the executive branch in American government. And he perhaps overestimated the tendency of democracy, at least as practised in the United States, to degenerate into tyranny by the majority.

As to this last pronouncement or warning, Tocqueville's American readers were once almost unanimously of one mind. The conscientious Frenchman was entirely wrong. Majorities changed too rapidly; and, anyhow, there could be no tyranny in the United States. Even fifty years later, considering this prophecy in retrospect, James Bryce failed to detect any such tyranny as Tocqueville had spoken of—at least in peace time. When called upon to name the one outstanding mistake in this great commentary, therefore, nineteenth century Americans generally pointed to his remarks about tyranny by the majority. Neither theory nor experience justified the charge. So it was said.

To-day, with the Civil War, the World War, the 'Red Scare,' and the 'Depression' in retrospect, one cannot afford to be quite so complacent. Perhaps a suppression of individual or minority rights *is* possible, and even in times of peace. Perhaps, therefore, before many more years have passed, what was once a grievous error may have to be listed instead as one more example of Tocqueville's uncanny perspicacity.

Yet meanwhile a very curious omission on Tocqueville's part requires notice. In all his talk of tyranny, in all his warnings as to the dangers inherent in equalitarian government, Tocqueville never pointed to the one kind of tyranny that nineteenth century Americans actually did come to experience, to their hurt and later regret.

For where did he mention *tyranny by a minority?* * Strange as it

* I am indebted to Cestre and to Professor H.S.Commager for emphasis on this point. Tocqueville did foresee the possibility of tyranny by plutocracy, but never developed the theme sufficiently. In his chapter on 'how aristocracy could emerge from industry' (*Dém. en Am.*, III) he said: 'All things considered, I believe that the manu-

might sound, the majority in a democracy could become victim quite as easily as bully. One ought not to trust too blindly to the logic of numbers. In spite of manhood suffrage, the field was still open to the powerful or the dishonest. Might not the minority of wealth or industrial control perhaps misuse their power, even to the point of securing legal sanctions for oppression? And what, for example, was to stand in the way of unscrupulous 'machines'? Might not some ring of venal politicians so twist the democratic processes as almost openly to cheat the voting millions? In short, was not the innocence and carelessness of the masses even more to be feared in a democracy than their malevolence or positive tyranny?

Somehow—and it is to be regretted—Tocqueville never adequately grasped this possibility. With his fears of the mob, and his concern for the atom individual, he did not enough allow for the ingenuity of the designing few, the potential indifference of the many. Whatever the justice of his remarks about tyranny by the majority, therefore, the emphasis of this prophecy was hardly warranted.

---

facturing aristocracy rising under our eyes is one of the harshest ever to appear on earth; but at the same time it is one of the most restricted and least dangerous.

'Nevertheless, it's in this direction that the friends of *démocratie* should continually be turning an anxious eye; for, if ever a permanent inequality of conditions and an aristocracy again enter the world, one may predict that they will enter by this gate.'

## LVIII

## TOCQUEVILLE'S WORK IN RETROSPECT: CERTAIN ENDURING QUALITIES

If it be granted that Tocqueville's philosophic method was too scholastic and theoretical, his interpretation of the nineteenth century too narrow, his portrait of the United States defective, and even his style too condensed and old-fashioned—if we recognize, in a word, that his commentary left so much to be desired—wherein, then, did his distinction as an author lie?

The question cannot be avoided, for Tocqueville was universally admired. Judges so hard to please as Guizot and Chateaubriand, or Faguet and Sainte-Beuve; personalities so diverse as Royer-Collard and Ampère, George Ticknor and Charles Sumner; reviewers of such eminence as Lord Acton and Henry Reeve: all acknowledged the charm and the extraordinary distinction of Tocqueville's book. The *De la Démocratie en Amérique* discussed a subject which, during the next hundred years, was to receive many serious treatments; Tocqueville would even have to compete with such outstanding craftsmen in the field of political philosophy as J.S.Mill and Auguste Comte, Karl Marx * and Viscount Bryce. Yet in spite of this handicap, and its own obvious defects, his treatise would in several respects compete with notable success. In originality, intelligence and elevation, at least, *De la Démocratie en Amérique* was generally and long conceded to be the pre-eminent work of its kind.

Unquestionably, the first reason for this was personality and character. Royer-Collard was mistaken when he proclaimed his young follower a second Montesquieu. For the resemblance was really super-

---

* There is more than one curious similarity between Tocqueville and Karl Marx. The most obvious is probably their common belief in the gradual and necessary evolution of human societies toward a class-less equalitarianism. Only, the increasing equality of conditions, that Tocqueville saw as a political (and social) phenomenon, Marx translated into the field of economics.

768

ficial.* Tocqueville did not owe his greatness to any Olympian disinterestedness, still less to an adroit inspiration and a beguiling humour. As an observer he was able enough, but he could not remain aloof. Rather, his own commentary was solid, passionate, a little prejudiced, and very humble. One could not read a single page without being impressed with his sincerity and utter unselfishness. His every paragraph breathed a transparent honesty and an overwhelming desire to be right. Even when he was in error, therefore, he remained, as Lord Acton confessed, the 'hardest to find fault with.' And when he criticized, one could not feel resentment. For it was clear that he had tried to put his 'whole dose of intelligence' into his work, and had begun by purging himself of wilful prejudice under the most austere and ascetic self-discipline. Other writers might lay claim to honourable intentions. But with Tocqueville morality and high principle were an absorbing cult. His very anxiety made an impression on his readers. And by his humility, his concern for humanity, and his devotion to the truth, he won their undying respect.

Furthermore, Tocqueville startled and interested his readers by his peculiar approach. For if he was no true historian of the past, and if his technique of observation and analysis did not in fact measure up to that employed in the physical sciences, he did possess a novel and extraordinary virtue. He was a *sociologist*—and very nearly the first sociologist in French experience. Not until many years later would it become common for men to examine into the basic laws of human association, in order to find out—as one might study the gravitational movements of the stars—what makes societies act the way they do. If Tocqueville was not interested in the 'events' of history, the unpredictable accidents, the military victories or the casual revolutions, it was precisely because he thought such 'history' superficial. What he was looking for were the underlying and enduring influences, the forces perpetually at work, the customs, moral habits and basic institutions guiding the evolution of human groups, over long stretches of years.[1] From the point of view of society, that kind of history alone seemed real. As one admiring critic put it: 'He was possessed, one

* Both seemed to treat the fundamental problems of human government and society from the vantage point of a calm and lofty detachment. And Tocqueville also appeared to have copied Montesquieu's device of dividing his discussion into short chapter essays or treatises, each essay being given a general topic title preceded by the modifying preposition *De*: 'of, or concerning.' The implication was that he, too, was going to discuss rather than describe.

might almost say haunted, by the desire to know the causes of events and the sources of human action.'[2] To use a modern term, he was a psychologist, and a psychologist whose subject was not the individual human but all humankind, not the people of Paris but the societies of the contemporary world, not even civilization as it was but civilization as it was becoming. Like some observant mariner who, beneath the meaningless swells of a boundless and storm-tossed waste, discovers a steadily moving tide, some great Gulf Stream irresistibly bearing him on, Tocqueville was sounding for subterranean currents. If he could find them, he would know in what direction society was moving, and how fast. Meanwhile, he could afford to ignore the contradictory winds and the accidental lurches of 'history,' for he intended to make himself the historian of institutions and of long-range societal development. And that was *fort nouveau* at the time when he undertook the task.

Tocqueville's third quality—or appeal to the readers of the nineteenth century—arose directly out of this ambition. For in his self-imposed role of pioneer he managed to make a number of real discoveries, both about the present and about the future. Despite a faulty technique and a series of errors in observation and in judgment, he proved himself an able and intelligent explorer. What he reported about the always present characteristics of human societies arrested the attention of his contemporaries; and what he ventured to offer in the way of prediction opened new vistas to their startled gaze.

It was Tocqueville more than any one else, for example, who persuaded the liberals of the nineteenth century that aristocracy could not be revived, and that a greater equality of conditions was the destiny of Europe.

Again it was Tocqueville who pointed out that democratic self-government was not necessarily the perfect government, or even perhaps a desirable state of affairs. For he never let his readers forget that the raising of the underprivileged to a share in power and responsibility would bring dangers as well as opportunities. It would mean a jealous levelling down as well as an idealistic grading up. And once classes and privileged groups were gone, the obstacles to anarchy or to despotism would also be removed.

At its best—so ran Tocqueville's teaching—self-government would make possible a phenomenal release of initiative and energy, an unprecedented prosperity, a peaceful non-interfering government, a self-respecting citizenry, and a happy nation. Yet the price that would have to be paid was high. Only by long practice, constant vigilance, and high moral standards could so difficult and complicated a mechanism be maintained. Let the 'Republicans' make no mistake! All the romance, the glories and the outstanding distinctions, all the inspired leadership of the old regime, would be a part of the sacrifice. For the new leaders would be smaller, undistinguished men; and statesmanship under the future democracies would consist in the unimaginative performance of mediocre things. At best the approach to equalitarian government would mean the sacrifice of individual distinction and of national glory to a generalized well-being.

At its worst, on the other hand, *démocratie* could degenerate into unspeakable tyranny. And for the student-politicians of the nineteenth century it was again Tocqueville who specified the dangers. Others might warn, as their prejudices or apprehensions suggested. But Tocqueville alone seemed to have thought the matter through, and to know exactly what he was talking about and where the risks lay.* He even had a program for diminishing those risks, or perhaps avoiding them altogether.

It was Tocqueville, for instance, who first made the intelligent politicians realize the benefits that, ideally, could be drawn from localism or decentralization. Surprisingly enough, he even had a suggestion as to how some of those benefits could actually be achieved without sacrificing the national strength and unity so vital to France, surrounded as she was by a hostile Europe. Let the laws continue to be national, but let the administration of those laws be decentralized. If citizens could be encouraged, and locally trained, to take a larger share in their own communal government and its affairs, the result would be, not a loss of unity, but a tremendous increase in energy, satisfaction and stability. In the same fashion, let group institutions be encouraged. In fact, let everything possible be done to encourage and bolster the individual and the small local group against the crushing weight, and the annihilating philosophy, of a superior State.

Once again, it was Alexis de Tocqueville who made clear for Europeans the distinction between *representative* and *direct* democracies, and indicated what was to be expected from the latter. In his *Auto-*

---

* Subject, of course, to the reservations already listed. Tocqueville may have drawn both of his alternative portraits in too sombre colours, with too deep a pessimism. But as to that, it seems dangerous to be dogmatic.

*biography*, John Stuart Mill later confessed his own philosophic debt on this point. It had been the young Tocqueville, he said, who had first taught him the disadvantages of direct mass rule, and showed him the points to be guarded against. In similar fashion, the famous Englishman owed his rescue from a thoughtless belief in centralization to Tocqueville's book. Had it not been for *Democracy in America* he might have followed the majority of reformers in all times, he admitted, and worked for a strong and thoroughgoing administration. It was so tempting; the necessary reforms could so swiftly and competently be put into effect. But Tocqueville had made him realize the dangers, in time.[3]

In fact, as early as 1840, in a very able analysis written for the *Edinburgh Review*, Mill stated it as his considered opinion that Alexis de Tocqueville had done more to ascertain the properties of democracies than any successor would ever be able to add.[4] And that was likewise the verdict of most of those Europeans whose intellectual distinction gave their opinions weight.

When, then, to that conviction was added the obvious fact that Tocqueville's inquiry dealt, 'not with the past but with the present, not with the reconstruction of the life of by-gone times but with the foremost question of the day: the onward march of Democracy'; when it was realized, in short, that Tocqueville's book was essentially not one of abstract philosophical speculations but one of the most immediate and practical politics, the surprise and interest and enthusiasm of the European reading public could not be contained. And with the years a popularity that had been captured overnight matured into an enduring reputation.

Whatever his shortcomings or deficiencies, the simple fact was this: Alexis de Tocqueville had taken one of the great enthusiasms of the century, and given it a magistral analysis.

\*

\* \*

As for the American part of Tocqueville's book, and the description that he had devoted to the peculiar institutions of the United States, enough has already been said to indicate the reason for the admiration and gratitude of the American people when they discovered his treatise in translation. Perhaps two retrospective comments, however, may not be out of place.

The first was supplied in 1887 by a young Englishman, James Bryce. At the time Bryce was just fitting himself to become the second foreign visitor and student to give the American people a thoroughgoing commentary. By temperament the Englishman was himself more pragmatic and pedestrian, more interested in fact and in detail than Tocqueville had been. His book, *The American Commonwealth*, would therefore be descriptive rather than prophetic, an analysis of institutions as they were rather than a guess as to what they might some day be. Just the same, Bryce did not intend his own approach to stand as a repudiation or reproach to his illustrious predecessor. In fact he paid *Democracy in America* the compliment of an exhaustive study.[5] And when he had listed Tocqueville's prophecies, and compared the predictions with what in the intervening fifty years had actually come to pass, he found that in no less than eight separate and important instances Tocqueville had been right! The Frenchman had also been mistaken on occasion, and these bad guesses were intermingled with the good.* Nevertheless, his record of successful prophecy was such as to call for admiration and astonishment. 'More than any other man he had possessed,' as one French critic put it,[6] 'the intuition of the modern world, of what it was and of what it was to be.' And in his study of the strange Americans he had been most successful of all. At least, as a young traveller in exile, he had early given evidence of a seeing eye and a divining soul. And in the humblest and most scrupulous fashion he had then gone home to make himself into a prophet, a prophet of whom even the American people would not need to feel ashamed.

The second comment is of to-day, and is suggested by what has happened in the last period of fifty years. It deals not with prophecy but with analysis, not with the foreseeing eye but with the understanding mind. It is concerned with what Tocqueville said about the enduring problems of self-government.

Tocqueville's descriptions, it should be prefaced, are now completely outdated. After the passage of a century, neither Federal government nor New England town bears much resemblance to the units that Tocqueville saw. In size, and even in character, American political institutions have changed almost beyond recognition.

* Bryce likened the dangers, of which Tocqueville warned, to clouds. 'Of these clouds one rose till it covered the whole sky, broke in a thunderstorm and disappeared. Some have silently melted into the blue. Some still hang on the horizon, darkening large parts of the landscape.'

In another respect, however, a large part of what Tocqueville wrote is still valid. As a sociologist he was sometimes primitive, and as a political scientist inexperienced, so that he made numerous mistakes. Yet more than any other writer, more even than Bryce himself, he had the gift, the extraordinary faculty, of understanding the essential problems of self-government. What the tendencies of democracy were, what its risks and dangers might be, what steps should be taken to exorcise the evils and preserve the good, he saw and carefully set down.

It was not given to him to foresee all of the political problems of the twentieth century. The overwhelming importance of interstate commerce and its regulation was not provided for in Tocqueville's calculations. Chancellor Kent had indeed suggested that the corporation device might be abused. Yet the excessive power of giant companies and their careless inhumanity, the growth out of industry of an irresponsible plutocracy, the organization of a self-conscious and belligerent labouring class: such were not the burning problems of his day. The possibility of steady starvation and unemployment, or the inexorable drying up of economic opportunity, were hardly the worry of Jacksonian Americans. And Tocqueville had never even heard of such a thing as a minority lobby or 'pressure group.'

Yet of certain enduring political truths the Frenchman was absolutely certain. Without undertaking to supply the solutions for unimagined possibilities, he nevertheless argued that to survive societies must operate according to principle and law; and he made it his business to discover what those laws of government or social organization might be.

He realized the necessity for experiment, of course, and change seemed to him the very condition of existence. Yet at the same time he knew and said that training and intelligence and understanding were needed for self-government. Only by experience and long practice could citizens qualify to govern, or the beneficence of institutions be tested. And only when the new devices had been measured in the mind against the devices of the past, and the best available knowledge of human nature and group psychology, could such changes safely be attempted. Not lightly or suddenly or in a passion ought a legislature or a governor to act. Above all not with good intentions only. For the first prerequisite to good government was intelligence, not warmth of heart. Only through knowledge of human nature, experience of the workings of government, and understanding of the character of the inherited institutions could excellent administration be achieved.*

The warning seems obvious enough. It must have been almost a truism when Tocqueville uttered it. Yet truisms are sometimes forgotten, and may usefully be revived. There is also another remark by Tocqueville on which the citizen voters of the two major parties, and even more the leaders of minority parties of reform, might with benefit meditate. After long study, Tocqueville gave it as his serious and considered opinion that direct democracy did not produce either able leadership, or stable conduct, or even the maximum of liberty. He was a convinced adherent of *representative* government, as distinguished from the choice by the whole populace of all the legislators and officers of administration. The closer the control by the masses, he insisted, the more mediocre the legislation would be, the more picayune the legislation, the less stable and solid the government. Had he lived to see the day, he would no doubt have felt unalterably opposed to the initiative, referendum, and recall. He actually did say in his book that judges should not be elected; for an independent judiciary was an essential bulwark, and one of the few remaining, against *démocratie* in its worst moments: against the aberrations of the masses—the passions of the moment—the tyranny of some victorious majority.

This opinion was not lightly hazarded, and—whether erroneous or not—ought not to be scorned or lightly rejected, even to-day.† Certainly Tocqueville did not intend to be partisan or anti-democratic. He merely insisted that not all democracy was excellent, and that one ought to distinguish between the bad features and the good. He did not even condemn direct democracy, or its worst features, in any absolute terms. So long as there was the unsettled continent, so long as no strong neighbours threatened, so long as opportunity beckoned to every man and the best interest of the individual really did serve the best interest of society as a whole, the American people could do very happily with an imperfect government, or even with no real government at all. Once let the continent fill up, however, once let the competition become destructive and the pressure of population upon resources begin to resemble that of many European countries, and the

* To-day this restatement of Tocqueville's philosophy seems faintly partisan. It is not so intended. Or, rather, the intention is to be partisan only to the extent of agreeing with Tocqueville that experience is better than inexperience, knowledge than ignorance, wisdom than good intentions or popularity.

† On the issue of representative *versus* direct democracy, I do not altogether agree with Tocqueville. Whatever one's opinion, however, Tocqueville's analysis of the weaknesses of direct democracy is worth careful study.

acid test would come. Then, for the first time, real difficulties would confront American democracy. How the political institutions of the United States would fare under such pressure, Tocqueville was not sure. Or, rather, he was humbly and solemnly persuaded that, in proportion as the American people had encouraged the bad features of democracy, in proportion as they had allowed such abuses as inexperience and direct mass control to insinuate themselves, precisely in that proportion would American society suddenly begin to do rather badly.

With a philosophy thus reasoned, it is easy to quarrel, yet no longer so easy as once it was. In the nineteenth century, of course, most Americans were proud of their political institutions, even sure that they had found the ultimate answer to the age-old problem of human governance. They had reconciled order with liberty, opportunity with justice for all. Most of them, as a consequence, were inclined to discount the warnings that Tocqueville had so earnestly given. In the twentieth century, by contrast, the scene is no longer the same, and the very mood of America's millions has undergone a change. To-day it would be a bold man who would assert that our political institutions are still so well adjusted and our democracy so successful. And it would be a wise man, indeed, who would not be stimulated and informed—and perhaps warned—by reading Tocqueville again.

One further proposition from *De la Démocratie en Amérique* may perhaps serve as a pertinent remainder. It was Tocqueville's belief that in their political *dualism*, that is to say, in their happy reconciliation of local self-rule with national government, the Americans had stumbled on one of the greatest inventions known to political science. The benefits that American citizens drew from a contented participation in their own local affairs, in his mind far outweighed such loss of unity or regularity as a divided sovereignty might entail. Centralization might mean efficiency, but certainly it was not liberty. Nor would it ever be.

To-day this thought is still worth pondering. No doubt under the Industrial Revolution conditions have altered irrevocably. Perhaps, therefore, an effective localism is no longer possible. Many of us even question whether the old dualism could—or wisely should—be reconstructed. Probably it would be futility itself to try to recapture the spirit and practices of Tocqueville's day. Yet still the kernel of his thought is sound. Granting the inevitability of the change, what of the loss involved? If we can no longer tolerate the semi-independent localism that contributed so much in the early nineteenth century, have we a substitute? Ought there not to be some other institution or set of practices, some comparable inventions, to take its place? Can we, in fact, afford to do without some equivalent for those prodigious social aids that Tocqueville would tell us we have lost?

Tocqueville was not always right. And what he would say, could he return to-day, no man can guess. But what he once did write is still worth reading.

*

*     *

*De la Démocratie en Amérique*, it may reasonably be concluded, has merited its immortality. For, in the pages of this humble commentary, Tocqueville treated a great topic with the grasp of a master and a prophetic instinct hardly short of providential.

By character, Tocqueville himself belonged to the race of thinkers, not of actors. In his later political career he would find himself unable to translate either his political philosophy or his humanitarian impulses into enduring legislation. He would therefore have to be content with the role of those who enunciate great ideas, and then watch others use or misapply them. To his own chagrin, he had the insight but not the practical abilities, the compassionate humanitarianism of a great statesman but no opportunistic talents. Like Hamilton in his fire, and like Jefferson in his social idealism, he was not even to have the success of the scholarly and hesitant James Madison in actual performance. From the point of view of political achievement, accordingly, his life would end in disillusion and in bitter disappointment.

Yet he had written well, and on the mind of the world he had left his enduring mark. Not for his scorn, not for a towering personality would he be remembered. But because he was humble, because he was wise, because he had tried to be, so far as his frail tortured nature would allow, as just as Aristides.

His was a mind that fell just short of genius. But he had used it to pioneer. And as a pioneer he would be followed and long honoured. And this would be true despite his foreboding anxiety and his failure to comprehend the whole thought of his time.

He had 'performed the task with the air of a half-awakened man marching in the insufficient light of the first dawn.' But he had gone ahead.

# APPENDIX A

## ACKNOWLEDGMENTS

THESE Tocqueville investigations have met with such universal help-fulness and with so many individual kindnesses both here and in France that I am afraid that it is now physically impossible to make adequate acknowledgment of my debts.

It was Paul Lambert White, the Yale instructor in history to whom this book is dedicated, who first discovered the existence of unpublished Tocqueville manuscripts. Finding himself in France after the War, White's love of the French people and his training as an historian suggested an inquiry into Tocqueville's visit to the United States. He located the Tocqueville and Beaumont châteaux, began the copying of the Tocqueville diaries, and was just organizing his plans for a book, when he suddenly died. A Memorial Fund was created by his friends to complete the transcription of the documents that he had seen, and to aid in the publication of his discoveries. I hardly need say that without these beginnings, and without material assistance from this fund, my own discoveries and book might never have been possible.

I wish to express my deep gratitude, also, to the present members of the Tocqueville and Beaumont families, without whose interest and friendly help, in the first instance, this study could not have been continued. For their hospitality, their personal encouragement, and their unfailing generosity in providing access to the family papers, I am particularly indebted to Comtesse de Tocqueville and to her son, the great-grandnephew of Alexis de Tocqueville, Comte (Jean) de Tocqueville, *Inspecteur des Finances*. For the manuscripts of the Château de la Borde, as well as for untold acts of friendship and consideration, the writer will always stand indebted to the granddaughter of Gustave de Beaumont, Madame de Beaumont-Hennocque, and to his great-granddaughter, Madame de Larminat of Paris, I wish to acknowledge the kindnesses of the late Vicomte de Romanet and of Madame de

Langavant in allowing reproduction of Beaumont documents in their possession, and to thank Mademoiselle Stoffels d'Hautefort for the use of a group of Tocqueville letters to the Stoffels family.

Acknowledgment is due to the French Government, and to the other authorities concerned, for access to archival material in the *Archives Nationales*, the *Ministère des Affaires Étrangères*, the *Bibliothèque Nationale*, the Wallace Collection in the American Embassy in Paris, and the Division of Manuscripts of the Library of Congress. I also wish to express my appreciation for the privilege of using manuscripts in the possession of the Huntington Library, the Widener Library of Harvard University, the Massachusetts Historical Society, the Historical Society of Pennsylvania, and the Johns Hopkins University.

I am indebted to the editors of the *Franco-American Review* for permission given to reproduce the story of Tocqueville in New Orleans; to the editors of the *Yale Review* for their kindness in permitting new use of materials originally published by Paul Lambert White (copyright, Yale University Press); and to Professor Henry Steele Commager for his intelligent reading and criticisms. The grant of Yale College and Sterling Fellowships during the course of graduate work originally made possible a study of Tocqueville, with adequate research abroad. I am also under sensible obligations to Professors Charles M. Andrews, Ralph H. Gabriel, Leonard W. Labaree and Sherman Kent— as well as to the other members of the Department of History of Yale University—for advice and encouragement most generously given. The facilities and unselfish assistance provided by the staff of the Yale University Library have been invaluable; and without the faithful secretarial aid of Mrs. Esther Davison and of three bursary students of Davenport College—Messrs. David Dwight Bloomfield '38, Harry Bennett Anderson '39, and Paul Trowbridge Gillespie '40—this study could not have been completed. Most of all, for the original opportunity, for countless suggestions, and for the never-failing stimulus of his friendship, I am indebted to Professor John M.S.Allison.

Of all those others—of the historians, of the librarians, of the countless descendants of Tocqueville and Beaumont's American acquaintances whose aid was asked and so seldom refused—indulgence is craved. If space forbids the listing of their names, their generosity has not been forgotten.

G.W.P.

Davenport College, January 1938.

The first thirteen chapters of this work, in somewhat extended form, were accepted in partial fulfillment of the requirements for the degree of Doctor of Philosophy in Yale University, and were awarded the John Addison Porter Prize, June 1933.

# APPENDIX B

## AMERICAN ACQUAINTANCES *

of Tocqueville and Beaumont
April 1831–Jan. 1835

### ON SHIPBOARD (2 April to 10 May 1831)

Captain E.L.Keen
Mr. & Mrs. PETER SCHERMER-
HORN
J.J.Schermerhorn
P.A.Schermerhorn
C.N.Palmer (English traveller)
Miss (?) Edwards
Rev. William Creighton (N.Y.)
Mr. & Mrs. Samuel L. Breese
A.L.Montaut (Phila.)

Samuel P. Long (Portsmouth,
N.H.)
Fortier (New Orleans)
Édouard Schérer (France)
Douant (St. Malo)
Dance (France)
L.F.Steiger & Family (Switzerland)
N.Hernandez (Havana)
A.Coutan(t) & family

### NEW YORK CITY
(11–29 May, 7–30 June, 8–11 Oct. 1831; 7?–20 Feb. 1832)

NATHANIEL PRIME
RICHARD RIKER
ALBERT GALLATIN
JAMES KENT
Schermerhorn family
Jones Family (related to Schermer-
horns)
John R. Livingston Jr. & family
Henry D. Sedgwick
James Gore King
John Duer

William Alexander Duer
William W. Campbell
Robert Emmet
James O. Morse
Rev. John Power
Enos T. Throop
Rev. Jonathan Mayhew Wainwright
Hugh Maxwell
Ogden Hoffman
Nicholas Fish
David Hosack

---

* The names of those individuals who contributed most to their understanding of the
United States are given in capitals.

Philip Hone
Joseph Blunt
Miss Julia Fulton
Mrs. (?) Davis
N.C.Hart

John O. Woodruff (Blackwell's Island)
Walter Bowne
Durant St. André (French Consul)
Pessac (French Consul)

(also Palmer, Miss Edwards, Rev. Creighton & others from shipboard)

NEW YORK STATE

(29 May–7 June; 30 June–18 July; 17–20 Aug.; 4–7 Sept. 1831)

JOHN CANFIELD SPENCER & family
ELAM LYNDS
AZARIAH C. FLAGG
Enos T. Throop (Auburn)
C.C.Cambreleng (Albany)
Reuben Hyde Walworth (Albany)
Edward Cornelius Delavan (Albany)
Livingston family (near Yonkers)
Rev. James Richards (Auburn)
Rob. Wiltse (Sing Sing)

George W. Cartwright (Sing Sing)
Rev. (?) Prince (Sing Sing)
Mrs. & Miss MacHedge (?) (Sing Sing)
* * *, Sing Sing landlady
E.P.Livingston (Albany)
J.B.VanSchaick (Albany)
Isaiah Townsend (?) (Albany)
E.C.Genet (?) (Greenbush)
S.Warren (?) (Troy)
Rev.B.C.Smith (Auburn)
Clark, Auburn Prison clerk

(also Oneida fishwife, Oneida & Seneca Indians, etc.)

GREAT LAKES & CANADA

(18 July–4 Sept.)

John Tanner (on Lake Erie)
Major John Biddle (Detroit)
Rev. Gabriel Richard (Detroit)
Mrs. Moderl (?) (Detroit)
Amasa Bagley (Pontiac)
Oliver Williams (Indian Trader)
Dr. Burns (Pontiac)
John & "Aunt Polly" Todd (Flint River)
G.D. (or E.S.) Williams (Saginaw)
Rev. James I. Mullon (on *Superior*)
G.T.Vigne (English traveller)
Miss Clemens (Englishwoman)
Miss Thompson (on *Superior*)
Misses Macomb (on *Superior*)

* * * (Lucius Smith?) Episcopal Minister
* * *, Presbyterian Minister
Samuel Abbott (Michilimackinac)
Mme Framboise (Michilimackinac)
Major Lamard (?) (Green Bay)
Dominique Mondelet (Montreal)
Charles J.E. Mondelet (Montreal)
Joseph-Vincent Quiblier (Montreal)
JOHN NEILSON
Jean Thomas Tascherau (Quebec)
(D.B.?) Viger (Quebec)
* * *, Quebec Merchant

(also Chippewa & Menominee Indians, fur traders, *habitants*)

## MASSACHUSETTS
(9 Sept.–3 Oct.)

Sedgwick family (Stockbridge)
FRANCIS LIEBER
JARED SPARKS
JOSEPH COOLIDGE Jr.
FRANCIS CALLEY GRAY
EDWARD EVERETT
J.Q.ADAMS
Josiah Quincy
Rev. William Ellery Channing
Rev. Joseph Tuckerman
William Sullivan
Alexander Everett
Charles P. Curtis
Tappan brothers
Daniel Webster
David Sears

George Ticknor
H.G.Otis family
R.Fletcher
* * *, a judge
(?) Clay, Southern planter
Nathan Hale
LOUIS DWIGHT
E.M.P.Wells
Samuel A. Eliot
William Austin
Charles Lincoln Jr.
Rev. Jared Curtis
Charles Wells
Sherman Leland
George Rogers (?)
Piquet (French Consul)

## CONNECTICUT
(4–8 Oct.)

Samuel H. Huntington
Robert C. Winthrop (of Mass.)
William C. Woodbridge (?)
Laurent Clerc
Prof. Gregorio Perdicaris

* * *, Hartford judge
Martin Welles
Rev. G. Barrett
Amos Pillsbury
Julia Brace

## PENNSYLVANIA
(13 Oct.–22 Nov. 1831; 4 Feb. 1832)

JOSEPH McILVAINE
BENJAMIN W. RICHARDS
ROBERT WALSH
HENRY D. GILPIN
Ch. J. Ingersoll
Roberts Vaux
Peter S. Duponceau
Samuel R. Wood
George Washington Smith
J.J.Smith
James J. Barclay
Nicholas Biddle

James Brown
Charles S. Coxe
Samuel L. Southard (New Jersey)
John Vaughan
Joel Roberts Poinsett
E.S.Burd
Job R. Tyson
Rev. William H. DeLancey
George M. Dallas
John Sergeant
Thomas L. McKenney
William Short

M.Carey
Thomas Bradford
Dr. Franklin Bache
John Bacon
William H. Hood

* * *, House of Refuge Supt.
Dannery (French Consul)
Choiseul (French Consul)
John Patterson (Pittsburgh)

(also the prisoners of the Eastern State Penitentiary)

## BALTIMORE
(28 Oct.–5 Nov. 1831)

J.H.B.LATROBE
Ebenezer L. Finley
Charles Carroll of Carrollton
James Carrol(l?)
Dr. Richard S. Stewart
Richard W. Gill
George Howard
William Howard
Peter H. Cruse

Nicholas Brice (?)
Rev. * * * (St. Mary's Seminary)
George Henry Calvert
Z.H.Miller
Archibald (?) Stirling
John McEvoy
Mary Randolph (?)
Cte Jules de Menou
(?) Williamson

## OHIO VALLEY AND SOUTH
(24 Nov. 1831–18 Jan. 1832)

TIMOTHY WALKER (Cincin-
nati)
John McLean (Cincinnati)
Salmon P. Chase (Cincinnati)
Bellamy Storer (Cincinnati)
Dr. Daniel Drake (Cincinnati)
D. Van Matre (Cincinnati)
(B.R.?) McIlvaine (Louisville)
Harris Family (Sandy Bridge)
* * *, Memphis family

Sam Houston
* * *, Capt. of *Louisville*
Étienne Mazureau (New Orleans)
Guillemin (French Consul)
A.B.Roman (New Orleans)
Josiah Stoddard Johnston (New
Orleans)
* * *, Montgomery lawyer
JOEL ROBERTS POINSETT

(also miscellaneous settlers, travellers, Chickasaw and Choctaw Indians)

## WASHINGTON
(18 Jan.–3 Feb. 1832)

EDWARD LIVINGSTON
Nicholas P. Trist
Andrew Jackson
Joel Roberts Poinsett
Roger B. Taney

Louis McLane
John Marshall (?)
Daniel T. Patterson
Edward Everett
Serurier (French Minister)

(also many Senators and Representatives, etc.)

PARIS
(1831–1835)

D.B.Warden
J.C.Rives                          Francis J. Lippitt
Theodore Sedgwick III              Edward Livingston

# APPENDIX C

## TABLE OF ABBREVIATIONS

TT  The manuscripts and papers of Alexis de Tocqueville (now collected and arranged according to date and subject matter) in *chartrier* of the Château de Tocqueville, Tocqueville, Manche.

TBT  Tocqueville's writings, in Beaumont's hand, at Tocqueville. These are usually copies by Beaumont from originals which have since been lost.

YT  The Yale Tocqueville collection.

BB  The manuscripts and papers of Gustave de Beaumont in the library of the Château de la Borde, Beaumont-la-Chartre, Sarthe.

BBlb  Beaumont's letter-book, copied from the letters which he wrote to his family from America, at Beaumont-la-Chartre.

*Du Syst. Pén.* *Du Système Pénitentiaire aux États-Unis et de son application en France, suivi d'un appendice sur les colonies pénales et de notes statistiques.* Par MM.G. de Beaumont et A.de Tocqueville, avocats à la Cour royale de Paris, membres de la société historique de Pennsylvanie. Paris H.Fournier Jeune . . . 1833 (First edition).

*Dém. en Am.* *De la Démocratie en Amérique,* Par Alexis de Tocqueville, avocat à la Cour royale de Paris, L'un des auteurs du livre intitulé: Du Système pénitentiaire aux États-Unis. Orné d'une carte d'Amérique, Librairie de Charles Gosselin . . . , vols. I and II, 1835; vols. III and IV, 1840 (First edition).

*Marie* *Marie, ou l'Esclavage aux États-Unis, Tableau de Mœurs Américaines;* par Gustave de Beaumont, l'un des auteurs de l'ouvrage intitulé: Du Système pénitentiaire aux États-Unis. 2 v., Paris, Librairie de Charles Gosselin . . . M DCCC XXXV (First edition).

O.C.      *Œuvres Complètes d'Alexis de Tocqueville,* publiées par Madame de Tocqueville, 9 v., Michel Levy frères . . . , 1861–1865. This is the memorial publication, edited by Gustave de Beaumont from Tocqueville's writings and manuscripts, which eventually reached nine volumes. Beaumont got out a new edition of *Dém. en Am.* for the first three; republished Tocqueville's famous *L'Ancien Régime et la Révolution* (1st ed. 1856) for the fourth; and collected a number of his political addresses and reports for the ninth and last. The other four (with the dates of the editions cited in the present work) were:

O.C.,V,VI      *Œuvres et Correspondance inédites d'Alexis de Tocqueville,* publiées et précédées d'une Notice par Gustave de Beaumont, membre de l'Institut. 2 v. 1861 (First edition).

O.C.,VII      *Nouvelle Correspondance, entièrement inédite de Alexis de Tocqueville,* 1866 edition. (First edition 1865.)

O.C.,VIII      *Mélanges, Fragments Historiques et Notes sur L'Ancien Régime et L'Empire, Voyages—Pensées, entièrement inédits, par Alexis de Tocqueville,* 1865.

# APPENDIX D

## CHAPTER NOTES

### I

#### A Celebrated Book

*Materials on Tocqueville's 'Democracy'*: The literature on Alexis de Tocqueville and on his *De la Démocratie en Amérique* is so extensive, that it will be impossible, within brief limits, to do more than cite a few of the outstanding books and articles which will serve as useful guides to the reader who wishes to explore.

Exclusive of Tocqueville's own letters (*O.C.*,V,VI,VII), probably the most comprehensive and illuminating works will be found to be the four major biographical and philosophical studies of the man: E. d'Eichthal, *Alexis de Tocqueville et la Démocratie libérale* . . . , (Paris, 1897); R. Pierre Marcel, *Essai politique sur Alexis de Tocqueville* . . . , (Paris, 1910); Antoine Redier, *Comme disait Monsieur de Tocqueville...*, (Paris, 1925); and von Helmut Göring, *Tocqueville und die Demokratie* (München and Berlin, 1928). Of these, each has its virtues and its marked defects. Eichthal's is an old-fashioned political biography, conservative and unoriginal, which yet has considerable usefulness and charm. The second and last, as their titles imply, are more methodical and scholarly attempts to analyse Tocqueville's work and assign him rank as a political philosopher by breaking up his thought into its logical elements, and by tracing the influence of his teachings on his own and subsequent generations. The reader will find, however, that both are badly written, and that Marcel's study, in particular, crammed though it is with documents and new information, lacks all sense of continuity and development. Quite otherwise is it with Redier's book. In conversational tone, and in a fascinating and supple style, he carries the story of certain of Tocqueville's ideas all the way from the ancient Clerels of Normandy down to the philosopher's death. Unfortunately, the narrative is marred by carelessness and inaccuracies, and the reader has constantly to be on his guard against Redier's *partis pris*, especially his strong anti-republican bias.

After these four works, the reviews of *De la Démocratie en Amérique* in the periodicals, and certain of the articles and essays first published on Tocqueville's death and later printed in more permanent form, will be found valuable and informing. In addition to the French reviews cited in the footnotes below, the most intelligent and interesting were: Léon Faucher, 'De la Démocratie aux États-Unis,' in *Le Courier français*, 24 Dec. 1834 (before Tocqueville's treatise was off the press); Sainte-Beuve's article in *Le Temps*, 7 April 1835 (republished in *Premiers Lundis*); F.de Corcelle's essay 'De la Démocratie américaine,' *Revue des deux Mondes*, 15 June 1835; Villemain's review of the third and fourth volumes of *Démocratie* in *Journal des Savants*, May 1840; Rossi on the same, *Revue des deux Mondes*, 15 Sept. 1840; and another excellent and moderate article by Léon Faucher in *Le Courier français*, 20 Jan. 1841.

Of the later publications, in addition to Laboulaye's essays in the *Journal des Débats*, 30 Sept.–4 Oct. 1859 (reprinted in *L'État et ses Limites*, 1863), the best written and most illuminating are: Sainte-Beuve's articles in the *Moniteur*, 31 Dec. 1860, 7 Jan. 1861 (reproduced in *Causeries de Lundi*); Lacordaire et Guizot, *Discours de Réception à l'Académie française*, 24 Jan. 1861; P.Janet, 'Alexis de Tocqueville et la Science politique,' *Revue des deux Mondes*, 1 July 1861 (*Problèmes du dix-neuvième Siècle*, I); Ch.de Rémusat, 'De l'Esprit de Réaction, Royer-Collard et Tocqueville,' *Revue des deux Mondes*, 15 Oct. 1861; Prévost-Paradol's article from the *Journal des Débats* in his *Essaie de Politique et de Littérature*, II, 1863; Mignet's 'Notice' before the Academy (1866) reproduced in his *Nouveaux Éloges historiques*, 1877; and finally the most intelligent analysis and criticism of E.Faguet, first published in *Revue des deux Mondes*, 1 Feb. 1894, then reprinted in *Politiques et Moralistes du dix-neuvième Siècle*, 3<sup>e</sup> série. In addition, H.Michel's *Idée de l'État*, 1896, while less striking on Tocqueville himself, provides an excellent background for a study of his place in the development of French political thought.

In England, the best reviews of the first part of *De la Démocratie en Amérique* were those of: J.S.Mill, *London Review*, July 1835; the flattering article in the *Monthly Review*, Nov. 1835; and Lockhart in the *Quarterly Review*, 7 Sept. 1836. Of the last two volumes of Tocqueville's treatise, English thinkers entertained a far less favorable opinion, as was shown by the striking critique printed in *Tait's Edinburgh Magazine*, Aug. 1840; and by the review in *Blackwood's Magazine*, Oct. 1840. J.S.Mill, on the other hand, in his powerful analysis in the *Edinburgh Review*, Oct. 1840 (reprinted, *Dissertations and Discussions*, II, 1859), brought out the strong points of Tocqueville's argument in arresting fashion. Of the later publications, H.Reeve's 'Remains of Alexis de Tocqueville,' *Edinburgh Review*, April 1861 (reproduced in *Royal and Republican France*, II, 1872), proved to be an excellent and original review of Tocqueville's life; while other notable articles appeared from the pens of A.V.Dicey, in the *National Review*, Aug. 1893, and D.Woodruff in the *Dublin Review*, April 1928. In addition, there are a number of interesting references to Tocqueville to be gleaned in Acton's essays; in J.K.Laughton, *Memoirs of the Life and Correspondence of Henry Reeve*, 2 v., 1898; and in C.S.Parker, *Sir Robert Peel from his Private Papers*, 3 v., 1899.

Probably the first article to appear in the United States on *Democracy in America* was the essay in the *North American Review*, July 1836, which is attributed to Edward Everett and which announced: 'We regard this work now before us, as by far the most philosophical, ingenious and instructive, which has been produced in Europe on the subject of America.' This was immediately followed by a reprint in Littell's *Museum of Foreign Literature*, 1836, of a most flattering article originally published in the *British and Foreign Review*, Jan. 1836. Then, with the issue of Spencer's American edition in 1838, laudatory reviews began to multiply. Among others, the *Democratic Review* devoted nearly forty pages in its first two volumes (Oct. 1837, July 1838) to what it called 'the best summary account of our institutions now in print.' The *Knickerbocker Magazine*, Sept. 1838, began a 'notice' of his work with the statement that 'M. de Tocqueville is a philosopher. He comprehends men, things, and even the Americans.' And in 1840, *Hunt's Merchants' Magazine* (III,343ff.), continued the pæan with the remark that, 'In our deliberate judgment, it is the most original, comprehensive, and profound treatise that has ever appeared regarding our republic, a treatise which is destined to live and take rank with the master works of former ages.' As the years passed, naturally, the reviews become somewhat more balanced and critical; and Heilprin, H.B.Adams and Gilman began to investigate the origins and background of the commentary. But the respect and admiration of the thinking public continued. In 1861, Ch. R. Norton published an article honouring Tocqueville's life and memory: *Atlantic Monthly,* VIII,551ff. In 1880, W.C. Robinson's essay in the *Catholic World,* XXXII,157ff., recalled the democratic philosopher and the man. And in 1889, after the appearance of Bryce's *American Commonwealth,* no less a prophet of democracy than Woodrow Wilson intimated that he preferred Tocqueville's method and philosophy, in a review of Bryce's masterpiece in *Political Science Quarterly,* IV,153ff.

One interval, one lapse in the sustained interest in Tocqueville's book remains to be recorded. As the nineteenth century passed away in America, and the nationalized, industrialized era of the twentieth century came in, swiftly to sweep away the traces of the farmer democracy that Tocqueville had known, it seemed a little as if Tocqueville and his thoughts were at length outmoded. In the United States one no longer read his book in school. Apparently, even with scholars, *Democracy in America* was at last fading out of the content of political thought.

Yet now, suddenly, the interest in Tocqueville, and in what he once said, is alive again. A hundred years after, not only the celebration of the centenary of his great commentary in 1935, but a revived anxiety over democracy, a re-opening of all the questions of government once thought so happily settled, has drawn scholar and statesman back to a serious re-study of nineteenth century thought. And the result has been a fresh series of articles, both in America and abroad. In France, Professor Charles Cestre has delivered a course of public lectures on 'Alexis de Tocqueville, témoin et juge de la civilisation américaine' (*Revue des Cours et Conférences,* XXXIV, vols. I and II); Robert G. Mahieu has analysed the work of *Les Enquêteurs Français aux États-Unis de 1830 à 1837,* with special emphasis on '*L'Influence américaine sur l'évolution démocratique en France*' (1934); and MM. Firmin Roz, Fortunat Strowski, and André Chevrillon have reviewed the work of Alexis de Tocqueville in the light of a hundred years of fame. Meanwhile in America the centenary, especially celebrated in Washington and New Haven, and widely observed by notices in the press, was marked by Gilbert Chinard's address to the American Association of Teachers of French (*The French Review,* Dec. 1935), and by the notable study by Albert Salomon of 'Tocqueville, Moralist and Sociologist' (*Social Research,* II, 405–427); and has led the writer to recall Tocqueville's trip through the United States, and the timeless value of his political thought, by a group of three studies preliminary to the present work: 'On the Centenary of Tocqueville's *Democracy in America*,' *Yale Library Gazette*, Oct. 1935; 'Alexis de Tocqueville in New Orleans, January 1-3, 1832,' *Franco-American Review*, June 1936; and 'Alexis de Tocqueville in America' (prepared for publication in France). In England, H.J.Laski's essay on 'Alexis de Tocqueville and Democracy,' in *The Social and Political Ideas of some Representative Thinkers of the Victorian Age* (ed. F.J.C.Hearnshaw, 1933), should also be mentioned.

1. Toc. to E. Stoffels, Paris, 16 Feb. 1835, in *O.C.*,V,426 [for abbreviations, see Table C in the Appendix]; also Bt. 'Notice' (*O.C.*,V,39); and R.P.Marcel, *Essai politique sur Alexis de Tocqueville*, p. 88 and note.

2. Louis Blanc's articles appeared in the *Revue Républicaine* (V,114-116,129-163); Salvandy's in the *Journal des Débats* (23 March, 2 May 1835). Odilon Barrot wrote the author a most enthusiastic letter (quoted in Marcel, *Essai politique sur Alexis de Tocqueville*, p.100, note 3); and for Lamartine, Chateaubriand, Molé, Thiers, etc., see also *O.C.*,V,38-39,426; Redier, *Comme disait Monsieur de Tocqueville...*, p.132; and *Correspondance de Lamartine*, III,357-358.

3. Toc. to Bt., 1 April 1835 (*O.C.*,VI,28-29). For a sparkling description of the joint salon of Chateaubriand and Mme Récamier at this time, see Funck Brentano, 'Salons et Cénacles romantiques,' in *La Vie parisienne à l'Époque romantique* (Conférences du Musée Carnavalet, 1930).

4. Toc. to Bt., Paris, 14 July 1834 (BB, quoted *O.C.*,VI,27); Bt. 'Notice' (*O.C.*,V,39).

5. Toc. to E.Stoffels, Paris, 16 Feb. 1835 (*O.C.*,V,426-427).

6. See Toc. to N.W.Senior, Paris, 21 Feb. 1835 (*O.C.*,VI,30-33, and later letters in the same volume).

7. See Bibliographical Essay, Appendix E.

8. Documents in TT; Marcel, *Essai politique sur Alexis de Tocqueville*, p.292; Bt. 'Notice' (*O.C.*,V,42-43).

9. Referred to in J.S.Mill's article in the October 1840 issue of the *Edinburgh Review* (LXXII,2-3).

10. Tocqueville's article, translated by Mill, appeared in April 1836.

11. *Democracy in America* [*in relation to Political Institutions*] by Alexis de Tocqueville . . . translated by Henry Reeve, Esq., adapted for the use of schools and district libraries by John C. Spencer, counsellor at law. . . . New York, 1845.

12. Bryce, 'The United States Constitution as Seen in the Past,' *Studies in History and Jurisprudence*, I,320. See the rest of this essay (enlarged and revised from the same author's 'Predictions of Hamilton and de Tocqueville,' *Johns Hopkins University Studies*, V,329ff.).

13. *Moniteur*, 19 Aug. 1836.

14. J.R.Bellot, *Journal d'un Voyage aux Mers polaires*, quoted by L. de Loménie in 'Publicistes Modernes,' *Revue des deux Mondes*, 15 May 1859.


## II

### THE EDUCATION OF AN ARISTOCRAT

THERE are in all four chief sources of information on Tocqueville's background, youth, and education.

The first are the *Mémoires* of Hervé de Tocqueville (in the *chartrier* at the Château de Tocqueville), of which only a first fragment has been published, under the title *Épisodes de la Terreur, extraits des mémoires du Comte de Tocqueville, ancien Paire de France, suivis d'une lettre inédite de Louis XVI et d'une lettre inédite de M. de Malesherbes, extrait du Contemporain, Revue d'Économie chrétienne, numéro de janvier 1867*, Compiègne, 1901. The Revolutionary 'Episodes' compose the most fascinating section of these *cahiers* of manuscripts; but the later and unedited volumes yield a rare insight into the duties and activities of a prefect and friend of the Court during the troubled years of the Restoration.

The second and largest group of documents is made up of the youthful papers of Alexis de Tocqueville himself (TT): his early letters, his school-books, his law thesis and legal papers, his travel records, lecture notes, and the miscellaneous manuscripts revealing his attempts to re-educate himself for a career of statesmanship and service. The third group is that collected and largely published by Antoine Redier on the family history of the Norman Clerels and Tocquevilles before Alexis was born—together with a document or two of value for a study of Tocqueville's youth as well—(see first four chapters, *Comme disait Monsieur de Tocqueville...*). Finally, we have the two small but important groups of manuscripts of the year 1830: Beaumont's notes, and correspondence over the prison mission; and the letters of Tocqueville to Ch. Stoffels (in the possession of Mlle Stoffels d'Hautefort).

1. Toc. to Lady Theresa Lewis, Paris, 6 May 1857 (*O.C.*,VI,383-384).

2. Toc. to Louis de Kergolay, Versailles, 23 July 1827 (TT, published, *O.C.*,V,301).

3. See Toc. to Bt., Gray, 29 Oct. 1829 (*O.C.*,VI,18).

4. Toc. to Kergolay, Amiens, 'ce 29,' 1824 (TT fragment, quoted *O.C.*,V,297–299).

5. Toc. to Alexis Stoffels, Tocqueville, 4 Jan. 1856 (*O.C.*,V,469).

6. *Souvenirs d'Alexis de Tocqueville* (1893), p.93; Toc. to E. Stoffels, Philadelphia, 18 Oct. 1831 (*O.C.*,V,417ff.).

7. Memoir and notes on experiences during the July Days (BB).

## III

### THE DECISION TO VISIT AMERICA—AND A GOOD EXCUSE

MUCH that is false, much that is only partly true, has been written to account for Tocqueville's interest in America. Upon the publication of *De la Démocratie en Amérique*, four and a half years after the events just described, certain facts came to the attention of the public. It appeared that early in 1831, or about eight months after the July Revolution, the government of Louis Philippe had commissioned M. de Tocqueville, together with a friend Gustave de Beaumont, to make a study of the penitentiary systems and other penal reforms lately developed in the United States. The two young men had sailed for America and, apparently, made a thorough investigation. At all events, upon their return they had together published an able Report, containing a great mass of detailed information on American prison conditions.

The government mission had, then, been Tocqueville's reason for visiting America? Hardly. People came to realize at a fairly early date that this prison investigation had been only the excuse, only provided the opportunity for an excursion which Tocqueville had desired to make on other counts.[1] Careless readers, Americans in particular, have therefore tended to assume that it had been an enthusiasm for 'free' institutions, particularly an admiration for the type of government so successfully practised in the United States, that had caused the intelligent Frenchman to cross the Atlantic and make a first-hand study of American democracy. But this, likewise, hardly seemed a reasonable explanation. Most readers have recognized, for instance, that Tocqueville was far from feeling an unqualified enthusiasm for democratic institutions. Of certain features of American civilization he obviously disapproved, certain tendencies of republican self-government he actually seemed to fear. Tocqueville, himself, stated in his introduction that his whole book had been 'written under the impression of a kind of religious terror' at the sight of the irresistible progress that equality was making in Europe, and particularly in France. 'I confess that, in America, I saw more than America,' they read;[2] 'I sought there the image of equality (*démocratie*) itself, with its inclinations, its character, its prejudices, and its passions, were it only to learn what we have to fear or to hope from its progress.' *De la Démocratie en Amérique* had been prepared, then, not for Americans but for Frenchmen: not aimlessly or even calmly, but as an urgent message and a warning.

Of these speculations as to Tocqueville's purpose in visiting America, the last alone approximates a part of the truth. And this interpretation, itself, is neither exact nor sufficiently inclusive. For it accepts—as Tocqueville's motives for visiting the United States in 1831—the reasons he was to give, in 1835, for writing his book. It assumes that the purpose, so sombrely to be stated at the later date, was as clear and resolute in the author's mind at the moment of his departure from France. Furthermore, this interpretation completely leaves out of consideration certain other factors that exercised an unmistakable influence on Tocqueville's conduct.

1. Cf. Bt. 'Notice' (*O.C.*,V,16).

2. *Dém. en Am.*, I,vii,xxi.

3. Toc. to Marie Mottley, 17 Aug. 1830 (from copy in TT, quoted, Redier, *Comme disait M. de Tocqueville...*, pp.85–86).

4. There is a series of four unpublished letters (those of Tocqueville in rough draft) which throw much light on the attitude of certain of his friends. The above quotations are from the first two: Kergolay to Toc., 25 Sept. 1830; Toc. to Kergolay, 17 Oct. 1830; Kergolay to Toc., 25 Oct. 1830; and Toc. to Kergolay, 19 Nov. 1830 (TT).

5. See Toc. to his brother Hippolyte, Versailles, 18 Aug. 1830 (*O.C.*, VI,7); and Toc. to Ch. Stoffels, 26 Aug. 1830 (YT from copy in possession of Mlle Stoffels d'Hautefort); also *Souvenirs, 1785–1870, du feu Duc de Broglie* (1866) IV, *passim*.

6. Tocqueville's letters to Ch. Stoffels (Versailles, 26 Aug.; Paris, 4 Nov. 1830—copies in possession of Mlle Stoffels d'Hautefort) are a mine of information on his hopes and plans during this critical period. See also E.Stoffels to Toc., 2 March 1831 (TT).

7. Drafts of this request, submitted 31 Oct. 1831, are to be found among the Tocqueville papers, and the request itself, in Beaumont's

hand, is in the *Archives Nationales,* BB¹⁸1323. The rest of the correspondence on the subject of the mission, about thirty-five pieces in all, is to be found in the same category, or among the Beaumont manuscripts.

8. See especially Robert G. Mahieu, *Les Enquêteurs français aux États-Unis de 1830 à 1837* . . . , Paris, 1934. Also P.Cuche, *Traité de Science et de Législation pénitentiaire* (1905), p.340; M.Bérenger, *De la Répression pénale, de ses formes et de ses effets* (1855), pp.246–247; Marcel, *Essai politique sur Alexis de Tocqueville,* p.289 and note.

9. Toc. to Ch. Stoffels, Paris, 4 Nov. 1830 (copy in possession of Mlle Stoffels d'Hautefort).

10. E.Stoffels to Toc., 2 March 1831 (TT).

11. Toc. to Ch. Stoffels, Versailles, 26 Aug. 1830 (copy in possession of Mlle Stoffels d'Hautefort).

12. Toc. to Ch. Stoffels, Paris, 4 Nov. 1830 (copy in possession of Mlle Stoffels d'Hautefort).

13. Toc. to E.Stoffels, Paris, 21 Feb. 1831 (*O.C.,*V,414).

14. Bt. 'Notice' (*O.C.,*V,16).

## IV

### PREPARATIONS FOR ESCAPE

1. Bt. to his father, on board the *Havre,* 25 April 1831 (BBlb).
2. From bills in TT.

## V

### HAVRE TO NEW YORK—38 DAYS

1. Toc. to his mother, on board the *Havre,* 26 April 1831 (YT, quoted, *O.C.,*VII,1–12). The materials for this, the opening episode of their American trip, are taken from the letter above and the opening paragraph of Beaumont's first letter home (Bt. to his father, on board the *Havre,* 25 April, BBlb).

2. Quoted, Redier, *Comme disait Monsieur de Tocqueville...,* p.88.

3. Toc. to his mother, on board the *Havre,* continued, New-York, 14 May 1831 (cited above).

4. Toc. to Bt., Versailles, 8 May 1830 (*O.C.,*VI,23).

5. Toc. to E.Stoffels, New-York, 28 June 1831 (YT).

6. This statement is to be found in the concluding paragraph of Mrs. Schermerhorn's Diary of her family's tour in Europe. (The unpublished diary is now in the possession of A.Coster Schermerhorn of New York.)

7. Bt. to his mother, New-York, 14 May 1831 (BBlb).

8. Toc. to his mother, continued New-York, 14 May 1831 (cited above).

## VI

### RECEPTION IN NEW YORK

1. New-York, 14 May 1831 (BBlb).

2. Serurier to Tocqueville and Beaumont, Washington, 17 May 1831 (BB).

3. 'The early reports attracted so much attention and were so valuable that they were reprinted several times, partly at public expense.' Channing, *History of the United States,* V,201. Among the authors and philanthropists who had already carried their views before the public in the form of pamphlets or open letters in the press, should be mentioned Edward Livingston (author of the Louisiana code), William Roscoe of Great Britain, and Roberts Vaux, George W. Smith, Samuel R. Wood, and Dr. Franklin Bache of Philadelphia. Of the publications that came directly from the prisons, Judge Gershom Powers' *Brief Account . . . of the New York State Prison at Auburn* was a notable example.

4. Geo. W. Cartwright to consul St. André for Tocqueville and Beaumont, Mount Pleasant, 18 May 1831 (BB).

5. See 'Beaumont and Tocqueville to Rev. Barret, Boston, 12 Sept. 1831.' In Simon Gratz Collection, 'French Authors,' Historical Society of Pennsylvania; pub. by R.L.Hawkins, *Romanic Review*, XX,351.

6. Wm. W. Campbell to 'Cocqueville' and Beaumont, New York, 20 May; same, 24 May 1831 (BB).

7. 16 May 1831.

8. Lossing, *History of New York City*, I,239–242.

## VII

### FIRST IMPRESSIONS OF THE AMERICANS

1. New-York, 14 May 1831 (YT).

2. New-York, 16 May 1831 (BBlb).

3. New-York, 18 May 1831 (YT).

4. Toc. to E. Stoffels, New-York, 28 June 1831 (YT, quoted, *O.C.,*- V,415–419).

5. Toc. to his mother, New-York, 14 May 1831 (YT).

6. Toc. to his brother Édouard, New-York, 28 May 1831 (YT, quoted, *O.C.,*VII,8–14).

## VIII

### SOCIETY AND THE CITY AUTHORITIES

1. Bt. to his brother Jules, New-York, 26 May 1831 (BBlb).

2. *New-York Evening Post,* 14 May 1831.

3. Serurier despatch, *Ministère des Affaires Étrangères, États-Unis,* 1832,vol.86.

4. Toc. to abbé Lesueur, New-York, 28 May 1831 (YT, quoted in part, *O.C.,*VII,14–19).

## IX

### SING SING—THE PRISON

1. Channing, *History of the United States,* V,184. For a brief introduction to the history of the American prison reform movement, see the ensuing pages, with notes, and the index under 'crime' in vols. I & II.

2. See particularly H.E.Barnes, *The Evolution of Penology in Pennsylvania* (1927), pp.31–35.

3. The influence of Howard and Bentham and Beccaria on prison reforms in the United States need not be discussed here. (See Barnes, *Evolution of Penology in Pennsylvania,* pp.75ff.,92ff.) On the American penitentiary movement, the best authorities in English are still: Frederick H. Wines, *Punishment and Reform* (rev. and enlarged by W.D.Lane, 1919); Bt. & Toc., *On the Penitentiary System in the United States, and its application in France* (trans. by Francis Lieber, 1833); the early *Reports* of the Boston Prison Discipline Society; and Barnes, op.cit., also 'A History of the Penal . . . Institutions . . . of New Jersey,' vol.II of *Report of Prison Inquiry Commission, State of New Jersey* (1917). See also B.McKelvey, *American Prisons,* 1936.

4. I am indebted to M. Bernard Faÿ for suggesting how widespread this interest was in France. See: Cte. de Mirabeau, *Observations d'un Voyageur anglois, avec une lettre de Benjamin Franklin* (1788) and

other works cited in Faÿ's *Bibliographie critique des ouvrages français relatifs aux États-Unis, 1770–1800* (1925), in particular, *Des Prisons de Philadelphie, Par un Européen* (La Rochefoucauld-Liancourt, pub. by Moreau de St. Méry, 1796).

5. See *Du Syst. Pén.*, pp.13–14,20 and note.
6. *Du Syst. Pén.*,p.341, note. This famous anecdote is retold, with modification, by Warden Lewis E. Lawes, *Cell 202—Sing Sing*, pp.109–110.
7. New-York, 7 June 1831 (BBlb).
8. Diary note, Sing-Sing, 29 May 1831 (Alph.A,TT).
9. *Du Syst. Pén.*, p.275, note q.
10. *Du Syst. Pén.*, p.279, note t.
11. New-York, 7 June 1831 (BBlb).
12. *Du Syst. Pén.*, p.99, note.
13. 7 June 1831 (Punctuation somewhat lightened).
14. Bt. to his mother, New-York, 7 June 1831 (BBlb).

## X

### Sing Sing—Reflections on American Society

1. Toc. to his father, Sing-Sing, 3 June 1831 (TBT, quoted in *O.C.*,VII,19–25).
2. Bt. to his mother, New-York, 7 June 1831 (BBlb).
3. 3 June 1831, cited above.
4. Diary note, Sing-Sing, 29 May 1831 (Alph.A,TT, quoted *O.C.*,VIII,228–229).
5. 3 June 1831, cited above.
6. Bt. to his mother, New-York, 7 June 1831 (BBlb).
7. Toc. diary note. Conversation with Mr. Livingston at Greenburgh on Hudson, 7 June 1831 (Non-Alph.I,TT).
8. So dated in *O.C.*,VIII,231. Not dated in the original (Alph.A).

## XI

### Finding a Philosophy—and Losing It

1. Toc. to Édouard, New-York, 20 June 1831 (YT).
2. Redier, *Comme disait M. de Tocqueville...*, pp.96–97.
3. Toc. to Chabrol, New-York, 9 June 1831 (YT, quoted in large part in Redier, *Comme disait M. de Tocqueville...*, pp.96–101).

## XII

### June in New York

1. Toc. to Chabrol, New-York, 20 June 1831 (YT).

2. Bt. to his brother Achille, New-York, 18 June 1831 (original in hands of Mme de Langavant of St. Malo).

3. Toc. diary note 9 (?) June 1831 (Alph.A).

4. Bt. to his brother Achille, New-York, 18 June 1831 (cited above).

5. Toc. to his sister-in-law Émilie (Mme Hippolyte), New-York, 9 June 1831 (TBT, quoted *O.C.*,VII,25–28).

6. Bt. to his brother Achille, New-York, 18 June 1831 (cited above).

7. Toc. to his sister-in-law Alexandrine (Mme Édouard), New-York, 20 June 1831 (TBT, quoted *O.C.*,VII,29–32).

8. Toc. to Chabrol, New-York, 20 June 1831 (YT, quoted in part by White, 'American Manners in 1830; de Tocqueville's letters and diary,' *Yale Review*, Oct. 1922).

9. Bt. to his father, New-York, 29 June 1831 (BBlb).

10. Toc. to Lesueur, New-York, 30 June 1831 (YT).

11. Fragment of above letter, apparently suppressed before sending (TT).

12. New-York, 19 June 1831 (YT).

13. Toc. to his brother Édouard, New-York, 28 May 1831 (YT); to Alexandrine (Mme Édouard), New-York, 28 May 1831 (YT); to Lesueur, New-York, 28 May 1831 (YT, quoted, *O.C.*,VII,15–16); to Lesueur, New-York, 30 June 1831 (YT). See also Bt. to his father, New-York, 29 June 1831 (BBlb).

## XIII

### Taking Stock of Impressions

1. Extracted from letter: Bt. to his brother Jules, Albany, 4 July 1831 (BBlb).

2. New-York, 20 June 1831 (YT).

## XIV

### To Albany by Sloop and Steam

1. Bt. to his brother Jules, Albany, 4 July 1831 (BBlb). For the Livingstons, see above, pp.111, 116–18[?].

2. Toc. to his mother, Auburn, 17 July 1831 (quoted, *O.C.*,VII,32-38).

3. Bt. to his brother Jules, Albany, 4 July 1831 (BBlb).

4. Toc. to his father, Albany, 4 July 1831 (YT).

5. Bt. to his sister Eugénie, 14 July 1831 (BBlb). Cf. *Marie*, II,203ff.

6. Bt. to his sister Eugénie, 14 July 1831 (BBlb).

## XV

### A State without a Government?

1. Toc. to Chabrol, Auburn, 16 July 1831 (YT).

2. Toc. to his father, Albany, 4 July 1831 (YT).

3. Toc. to Chabrol, Auburn, 16 July 1831 (YT).

4. Bt. to his sister Eugénie, 14 July 1831 (BBlb).

## XVI

### Where Once the Iroquois . . .

1. Auburn, 17 [?] July 1831 (YT, quoted, *O.C.*,VII,36-38).

2. Bt. to his brother Jules, Utica, 6 July 1831 (BBlb).

3. Cahier Port.I, 6 July 1831 (quoted in part, *O.C.*,VIII,234-236).

4. Bt. to his sister Eugénie, 14 July 1831 (BBlb).

5. Cf. Chateaubriand's *Mémoires d'Outre-tombe*.

## XVII

### The Exile of Lake Oneida

1. Among the early visitors were: Elkanah Watson in 1791, Van der Kemp in 1792, Baron de Zeng in 1793, La Rochefoucauld-Liancourt in 1795, and De Witt Clinton in 1810; among the historians have been Clark in his history of Onondaga County, Johnston and Churchill in their histories of Oswego County, Beauchamp in *Past and Present of Syracuse and Onondaga County*, and W.S.Cee in the *Syracuse Journal* (?), 6 July 1895.

2. For the following résumé, and for much additional information on the subject, I am indebted to Mr. Harry F. Landon of Watertown, N.Y.

3. For the Van der Kemp papers, see *Buffalo Historical Society Publications*, II,33ff.

4. Quoted by Beauchamp, *Past and Present of Syracuse and Onondaga County.*

5. La Rochefoucauld-Liancourt, *Voyage dans les États-Unis d'Amerique, fait en 1795, 1796, et 1797,* Paris, 1799,II,252–261.

6. Again I am indebted to Mr. Landon for the information given.

7. *Cours au lac Oneida.*

## XVIII

### AUBURN

#### WHERE HUMANITY MEANT THE WHIP

1. Cahier Non-Alph.I.
2. *Du Syst. Pén.,* p.49.
3. Auburn, 16 July 1831.
4. On board the Ohio on Lake Erie, 24 [?] July 1831 (BBlb).

## XIX

### ENCOUNTER WITH A GOVERNOR, A SQUIRREL, AND A JURIST

1. Auburn, 17 [?] July 1831.
2. Beaumont was later to attribute this remark to 'Mr. S . . . , an obscure lawyer residing at Sing-Sing.' (*O.C.*,V,229.)
3. Bt. to his mother, 22 [?] July 1831 (BBlb).
4. 17 and 18 July 1831.
5. See especially *Dém. en Am.*, I,ch.5 (near end); II,ch.3.
6. Toc. to his sister-in-law Alexandrine, Batavia, 25 [18] July (*O.C.*,VII,39–45). For the stories of Red Jacket, see *O.C.*,VIII,239–242.

## XX

### FORTNIGHT IN THE WILDERNESS

1. The documents bearing on their visit to Buffalo, and their change of plans, are: Bt. to Chabrol, on board the *Ohio* on Lake Erie, 24 [?] July 1831 (BBlb); to his father, Detroit, 1 August 1831 (Michigan) (BBlb); Bt. to Chabrol, 2 August on board the *Superior* on Lake Huron (BBlb); Toc. to Lesueur, Detroit (Michigan), 3 [?] August 1831 (*O.C.*,VII,46); Toc. to his father, on Lake Huron, 14 August 1831 (*O.C.*,VII,47); Toc. to Chabrol, Buffalo, 17 August 1831 (TT); and Bt.'s 'Notice' on Toc. (*O.C.*,V,22–25).

In addition to the above letters, the following diaries contain references to the Michigan expedition that ensued: Port.II (daily); Alph.A (for July 22,23,30).

2. So stated in the Buffalo papers.

3. *O.C.*,V,25.

4. It was Senator Charles Sumner who reminded Mrs. Davis and the Michigan antiquaries of Tocqueville's visit to Michigan, when the peninsula was still a territory. The occasion was Sumner's speech in Pontiac (7 October 1867) when he came to lecture on his favourite topic 'Prophetic Voices concerning America.' (Cf. Edward L. Pierce, *Memoirs and Letters of Charles Sumner*, IV,334 and note.) For later reference by Michigan writers to Tocqueville's 'Fortnight in the Wilderness,' see: G.N.Fuller, *Economic and Social Beginnings of Michigan*, I,369–370; also *Pioneer Collections*, II,39;VIII,132;XXVI,532–533.

## XXI
### FORTNIGHT IN THE WILDERNESS (*Cont.*)

1. Cf. Bt., *Marie*,II,332.

2. On Gabriel Richard, 1764–1832, the authorities are Rev.Dr.E.J. Hickey and Rev.Dr.G.W.Paré, Sacred Heart Seminary, Detroit.

3. Bt. to Chabrol, 2 August, on board the *Superior* on Lake Huron (BBlb).

4. Toc. diary note, 22 July.

5. Bt. to Chabrol, 2 August, on board the *Superior* on Lake Huron (BBlb).

6. Cf. Bt., *Marie*,II,330.

7. Bt. to Chabrol, 2 August, on board the *Superior* on Lake Huron (BBlb).

8. Cf. G.M.Fuller, *Economic and Social Beginnings of Michigan*, p.136.

9. *Allgemeine Zeitung*, 12 Mai 1861.

## XXII
### ON THE UPPER LAKES

1. Bt. to his brother Achille, on board the *Superior*, Lake Michigan, 11 August 1831 (BBlb).

2. *Detroit Courier*, 21 July 1831.

3. Tocqueville's story of their excursion is contained in: Cahiers Port.II, Alph.A, Non-Alph.I (which Bt. later reproduced in part, *O.C.*,VIII,242–251); also in Toc. to his father, 14 August 1831 (TT, quoted, *O.C.*,VII,47–50); Toc. to Mme Hippolyte, Albany, 7 September 1831 (YT); and Toc. to his cousin, Mme de Grancey, New-York, 10 October 1831 (*O.C.*,VII,73–76).

4. Toc. to his father, 14 August 1831 (cited above).

5. Diary note, 6 August 1831.

6. *Detroit Courier*, 1 September 1831.

7. It has not been possible to identify the officer in question. 'Major Lamard' may possibly have been either Col. William Lawrence, who resigned his post at Fort Howard in 1831, or Joseph H. La Motte, stationed at Fort Crawford, Wisconsin.

8. *Six Months in America*, II,120–121.

9. *Detroit Courier*, 1 September 1831.


## XXIII

### THUNDER OF WATERS

1. Toc. to his mother, 21 August 1831, on Lake Ontario (quoted in part, *O.C.*,VII,51–54).

2. Draft of letter, Toc. to Dalmanny, August 1831 (TT).

3. Toc. to his mother, 21 August 1831, on Lake Ontario (cited above).

4. Bt. to his father, Lake Ontario, on board the vessel *Great Britain,* 21 August 1831 (BBlb).


## XXIV

### LOWER CANADA: A LOST EMPIRE?

1. Albany, 7 September 1831 (quoted, *O.C.*,VII,54–58). The manuscript sources for this chapter, in addition to the sketches and documents cited in the text, include: Toc. to Lesueur (above); Toc. to Mme Hippolyte, Albany, 7 September 1831 (YT); Bt. to his father, Albany, 5 September 1831 (BBlb); and Cahiers: Non-Alph.I (24,26,27 August); Alph.A (25,27–31 August); 'Canada' (27 August, 1–2 September)— these being quoted in part, *O.C.*,VIII,252–267.

2. Toc. diary note [24] August 1831.

3. Toc. diary note, 24 August 1831.

4. Bt. to his father, Albany, 5 September 1831.

5. Toc. diary note, 25 August 1831 (quoted with some changes, *O.C.*,VIII,252–253).

6. See list of sources, note 1.

7. Toc. diary note, 27 August 1831.

8. Quoted, *O.C.*,VIII,253–254.

9. Conversation with Mr. ***** at Quebec (Merchant)—26 August 1831.

10. 'Visit to one of the civil tribunals of Quebec.' Toc. diary note (dated the 26th by Bt., *O.C.*,V,255, but apparently belonging to the 27th). G.T.Vigne's account (*Six Months in America*, II,171) identifies the court and makes it evident that he and the French commissioners must have gone there together. Vigne had passed straight through Montreal without stopping, and so preceded Tocqueville and Beaumont to Quebec.

11. Jean Baptiste Denisart (1713–1765), *Collection de Décisions nouvelles et de notions relatives à la jurisprudence actuelle* (various editions).

12. 'My dear Sir,                    Montreal, 24 August 1831

Allow me to procure you the advantage of knowing Messrs. de Beaumont and de Tocqueville, whom their merit, and the mission with which they are charged by the French government, sufficiently recommend. I can do no better than to address these two gentlemen, who are travelling to know the country and its inhabitants, to a man like you who will certainly be able to give them some interesting and useful information.

Please believe me, with much esteem, your very hble & obt. servt.

Charles Mondelet'

(Trans. from French, Neilson Papers, Public Archives of Canada.)

13. Toc. diary note, 27 August 1831 (quoted in part, with some changes, *O.C.*,VIII,257–260).

14. Toc. to Mme Hippolyte, Albany, 7 September 1831 (YT).

15. Toc. diary note, 29 August 1831.

16. Toc. diary note, 2 September 1831.

17. Quoted in part, *O.C.*,VIII,262–264.

18. These remarks are included in a diary note of 2 September 1831.

19. Toc. diary note, 2 September 1831 (quoted, *O.C.*,VIII,265–267).

## XXV

### To Stockbridge, Boston, and Bad News

1. Bt. to his brother Jules, Boston, 16 September 1831 (BBlb).
2. Toc. diary note (Alph.A, dated 19 September in *O.C.*,VIII,272).
3. We know this from the letter which Beaumont and Tocqueville sent to the Rev. Mr. Barrett at Wethersfield, three days later (Simon Gratz Collection, 'French Authors,' Historical Society of Pennsylvania). R.L.Hawkins has included this interesting document in his 'Unpublished Letters of Alexis de Tocqueville' (*Romanic Review*, XX,351), with the remark that it is the earliest missive from Tocqueville to an American yet published.
4. Toc. to his cousin, Mme de Grancey, New-York, 10 October 1831 (YT, quoted, *O.C.*,VII,69–77).
5. Bt. to his brother Jules, Boston, 16 September 1831 (BBlb).
6. 17 September 1831 (YT).

## XXVI

### The Chilliness of Boston—and the Poles

1. Bt. to his brother Jules, Boston, 16 September 1831 (BBlb).
2. Toc. to his cousin, Mme de Grancey, New-York, 10 October 1831 (cited above).
3. *Essex Register*, 15 September 1831.
4. 13 September 1831.
5. 13 September 1831.

## XXVII

### The Aristocrats Unbend

1. Ellen W. Coolidge to Mrs.N.P.Trist, Boston, 20 November 1831 (Joseph Coolidge Jr. Papers, lately in possession of Mr. Harold Jefferson Coolidge).
2. Bt. to his brother Jules, Boston, 16 September 1831 (BBlb).
3. Toc. diary note, 20 September 1831 (Alph.A). For Boston his notes are contained in Cahiers Alph.A,Alph.B,Non-Alph.I,Non-Alph.II (reproduced in small part, *O.C.*,VIII,273–283).

4. Bt. to his brother Achille, 25 September 1831 (Boston) (fragment in possession of Mme de Langavant, of St. Malo).

5. Toc. diary note, 17 September 1831.

6. Bt. to his brother Jules, Boston, 16 September 1831 (BBlb).

7. Toc. diary note, 18 September 1831.


## XXVIII

### Boston *(Cont.)*

#### Social Observations and Lesson on the Jury

1. Bt. to his brother Achille, 25 September 1831 (cited above).

2. Toc. diary note.

3. Diary note.

4. Bt. to his brother Achille, 25 September 1831 (cited above).

5. This particular plan Lieber was never to carry out, except in so far as his *Manual of Political Ethics* (1838) and *Civil Liberty and Self-Government* (1852) touched on the subject. For more complete accounts of Francis Lieber, the reader is referred to Th.S.Perry, *Life and Letters of Francis Lieber* (1882); and to the work which Ch.B.Robson, of the University of North Carolina, is shortly to bring out.

6. See below; also Perry, op.cit.,91.

7. Bt. to his brother Achille, 25 September 1831 (cited above).

8. *The Stranger in America; or, Letters to a Gentleman in Germany: comprising Sketches of the Manners, Society, and National Peculiarities of the United States* (1835), p.34.

9. Toc. diary note.

10. Toc. diary note, 21 September 1831.

11. Curtis' conversation on American legal institutions Tocqueville preserved in the special diary devoted to such matters: Cahier F.

12. *Dém. en Am.*, II,ch.8.


## XXIX

### With the Leaders of Church and State . . .

1. Toc. to his cousin, Mme de Grancey, New-York, 10 October 1831 (YT, *O.C.*,VII,69–77).

2. Bt. to his mother, Harford (Conneticut) 7 October 1831 [*sic*] (BBlb).

3. Ellen W. Coolidge to her mother, Mrs. Randolph, 25 September 1831, Boston (lately in possession of Harold Jefferson Coolidge).

4. Francis Lieber to Bt., 14 February 1832, Boston (BB): 'A propos, M. de Beaumont's très-aimable Mad. Otis must be by this time in Washington. Has he not quite revived since his eyes can behold her once more, except if she stay too late, and he must accompany her?'

Later still when, back in France, Beaumont was trying to induce Lieber to come to Europe, he returned the compliment: 'My whole fear is lest you be detained at Boston by the charms of Mrs. Otis,' he teased. 'Is she still furiously fond of waltzes and square-dances? That's all I have to reproach her. For otherwise she's the best woman in the world. Why the devil have I spoken of her? There are at Boston a crowd of young and pretty ladies, the recollection of whom is altogether agreeable, and whom you, happy inhabitant of Massachusetts, see every day. There's the lady whose enchantress influence for you I fear. . . .' Bt. to F. Lieber, Paris, 16 November 1832 (Lieber Papers, Huntington Library).

5. Bt. to his brother Achille, 25 September (Boston) cited above.

6. Bt. to his mother, Harford (Conneticut) 7 October 1831 (BBlb).

7. Lieber to G.S.Hillard, December 1852, in T.S.Perry, *The Life and Letters of Francis Lieber*, p.256.

8. *Du Syst. Pén.*, p.284, note (z).

9. Toc. diary note (Alph.B).

## XXX

### Sparks—and Local Self–Government

1. Diary, Edward Everett Papers, Massachusetts Historical Society.

2. Toc. diary note (Non-Alph.II).

3. This Sparks conversation has been reconstructed from a Tocqueville diary note (Non-Alph.II) and from Beaumont's single surviving record of like character.

4. Bt. to his mother, Harford (Conneticut), 7 October 1831 (BBlb).

5. Information gathered from a collection of printed pamphlets at Tocqueville, and from certain MSS. references at Beaumont.

6. Hartford, this 7 October 1831 (YT).

7. Toc. to Blosseville, New-York, this 10 October 1831. Through Chabrol and Elie de Beaumont, Tocqueville got several other friends

to draw up for him some clarifying questions on the poor and insane, an essay on the Ministry of Justice in France, etc. (*O.C.*,VII,66–68).

8. Hartford, 7 October 1831 (YT).

9. Letters received from Gray, 27 September 1831; from Sullivan, 30 September 1831 (BB). It is doubtful whether Hale, who had married Edward Everett's sister, was managing Boston's first daily newspaper, and was deeply interested in politics and the new railroad improvements, ever found the time to fulfil his rash promise (see Toc. to Sparks, Cincinnati, 2 December 1831, in Sparks Papers, Widener Library, Harvard).

10. The reader who wishes to analyse these four essays in complete detail is referred to: YT, CIIIA, 'Paquet No. 16'; and to the Sparks Papers, Widener Library, Harvard. Sparks' essay is also reproduced with approximate accuracy by Herbert B. Adams, in 'Jared Sparks and Alexis de Tocqueville,' *Johns Hopkins Univ. Studies in Historical and Political Science*, XVI,No.12 (Dec. 1898), pp.579–600.

11. Herbert B. Adams, 'Jared Sparks and Alexis de Tocqueville,' in *Johns Hopkins Univ. Studies in Historical and Political Science*, XVI, No.12, p.570. For Sparks' attitude in writing the essay, see his Journal for January 20, 1832, quoted ibid.

12. *Dém en Am.*, I,129.

13. *Dém. en Am.*, I,137–138.

14. Diary note (Port. III).

15. Toc. diary note, Boston, 30 September 1831 (Cahier F).


## XXXI

### Mr. Adams and Dr. Channing

1. Edward Everett Papers (No.144, p.127), Massachusetts Historical Society.

2. Letter to Alexander Everett, 18 September 1831, J.Q.Adams Papers, Library of Congress.

3. Diary (Non-Alph.V.); Letter from 'J.Tuckerman,' 1 October 1831 (BB). Being unable to go out, Mr. Tuckerman offered to send one of his children to 'go with you as far as Dr. Ch's.'

4. Bt. to his brother Achille, 25 September (Boston), fragment in possession of Mme de Langavant of St. Malo.

## XXXII

### Two Massachusetts Prisons

1. Toc. to his cousin, Mme de Grancey, New-York 10 Oct. 1831 (YT, quoted, *O.C.*,VII,69–77).
2. *Du Syst. Pén.*, pp.53–54.
3. *Du Syst. Pén.*, pp.267–268.
4. *Du Syst. Pén.*, p.192.
5. *On the Penitentiary System in the United States and its application in France with an appendix on Penal Colonies and also Statistical Notes* by G. de Beaumont and A. de Tocqueville, Counsellors in the Royal Court of Paris, and members of the Historical Society of Pennsylvania. Translated from the French with an introduction, notes and additions by Francis Lieber (Philadelphia: Carey, Lee and Blanchard, 1833), p.121.
6. For the analysis that follows, see *Du Syst. Pén.*, pp.192–210.
7. Bt. to his brother Jules, Boston, 16 Sept. 1831 (BBlb).

## XXXIII

### Seen (and Not Seen) in Connecticut

1. Toc. diary (Port. III, quoted, *O.C.*,VIII,283).
2. *Du Syst. Pén.*, pp.75–77.
3. *Du Syst. Pén.*, pp.342–349. See also pp.136 and note, 349–359.
4. *Du Syst. Pén.*, pp.368–369.
5. Bt. to his mother, Harford (Conneticut), 7 Oct. 1831 (BBlb). Beaumont, himself, drafted a twenty-page report to the *Procureur Général* (BB) while Tocqueville composed a long essay embracing not only the great penitentiaries they had seen, but the Houses of Refuge, the police stations, and the short-term prisons as well. Of the Houses of Refuge he said that New York had the better system, Boston the better man. The short term prisons and the places where the newly arrested were detained for trial he found awful, their chief effect being contamination, not reform. As to the penitentiaries, there the interest was alive, the personnel excellent, and contamination really prevented, he thought. *Archives Nationales*, BB[18] 1323.

To his father, Tocqueville had already written: 'This establishment of Wethersfield, by its pecuniary results, offers the strongest argument in favour of American prisons. Before its reform it cost the State annually 30,000 fr.; to-day it brings in 40,000: these are not theories, but figures proved and supported by documents.

'In spite of all, however, it is probable that on our return you will find us less decisive on the Penitentiary System than when we left France. You know that it is *de règle* never to speak with more assurance or certainty than when one knows something imperfectly. Now that we are beginning to get our affair pretty well in hand we are no longer certain but of two things: the first, that the American system is more economical than ours; the second, that the men subjected to it never become worse in the prisons than they were on entering. But do they really reform themselves? I know no more here about that than you do at the corner of your hearth. What's certain is that I would never confide my purse to those honest people.' (Harford, 7 Oct. 1831, YT.)

## XXXIV

### Connecticut Afterthought

1. For this anecdote I am indebted to George Dudley Seymour (*Captain Nathan Hale / Major John Palsgrave Wyllys / a Digressive History*, p.284) and Donald G. Wing of the Yale University Library. They found the quotation in Wm. Chauncey Fowler, *The Ministers of Connecticut in the Revolution / The Report of the Committee appointed by the General Association of Connecticut*, pp.143–144.

2. Toc. diary (Port.III).

3. Erroneously dated by Beaumont: New-York, 15 Oct. 1831 ('Paquet 17,' TT; *O.C.*,VIII, 283).

4. Toc. to Bouchitté, 29 Oct. 1831 (YT, erroneously dated by Beaumont 11 Oct., *O.C.*,VII, 77).

5. Toc. diary, Alph.A, no date.

6. For further confirmation, see esp. *Dém en Am.*, ch.I, p.37; and *Dy Syst. Pén.*, p.304 and note.

## XXXV

### The Heavenly Prison of the Philanthropists

1. Toc. to his sister-in-law, Mme Édouard, Philadelphia, this 18 Oct. 1831 (YT).

2. Bt. to his father, 16 Oct. 1831, Philadelphia (BBlb).

3. Minute Book of the Society, II, entry for 13 Oct. 1831. A copy of the resolutions was forwarded to Tocqueville and Beaumont (BB). For the report on the discharge of the committee's mission, see entry in Minute Book for 11 Nov.

4. Non-Alph.II, 13 Oct.

5. *Du Syst. Pén.*, pp.viii,369–371. The conversation with the Director of the House of Refuge apparently did not take place till November.

6. *Du Syst. Pén.*, p.131.

7. *O.C.*,V,18.

8. *Du Syst. Pén.*, pp.329–332.

9. *O.C.*,V,19.

10. *Du Syst. Pén.*, p.44.

11. *Du Syst. Pén.*, p.73.

12. *National Gazette*, Tues., 22 Nov. 1831.

13. *United States Gazette for the Country*, 18 Nov. 1831.

14. Toc. to Chabrol, Philadelphia, this 19 Nov. 1831 (YT).

## XXXVI

### SOUNDING THE PENNSYLVANIA MIND

1. Bt. to his sister Eugénie, Cincinnati (Ohio), 1 December 1831 (BBlb).

2. Toc. diary note (Port.III).

3. Bt. to his father, 16 Oct. 1831, Philadelphia (BBlb).

4. *Marie*, I,393.

5. Toc. to his mother, Philadelphia, 24 Oct. 1831 (YT, quoted, *O.C.*,VII,84–86).

6. Bt. to Félicie (Mme Jules), Philadelphia, 26 Oct. 1831 (BBlb).

7. Alph.B, 10 Oct. 1831.

8. *Du Syst. Pén.*,pp.316–318.

9. Toc. diary note (Alph.B).

10. Toc. diary note, 27 Oct. 1831 (Non-Alph.II).

11. Toc. diary note, 25 Oct. 1831 (Port.III).

12. Toc. diary note, 14 Oct. 1831 (Alph.B).

13. Toc. diary note, 27 Oct. 1831 (Non-Alph.II).

14. Toc. diary note, 14 Oct. 1831 (Port.III).

15. Toc. diary note, 24 Oct. 1831 (Port.III).

16. Toc. diary note (Non-Alph.II).

17. Toc. diary note (Non-Alph.II, *O.C.*,VIII,285–286).

## XXXVII

### BALTIMORE

1. Bt. to his brother Achille, Philadelphia, 8 Nov. 1831 (BBlb).
2. Toc. diary note, 29 Oct. 1831 (Port.III).
3. In their report, Tocqueville and Beaumont were to approve the payment of the convicts, but deplore the breakdown of the isolation theory: 'At Baltimore the experiment of work without isolation is at the moment being tried, and that trial does not seem to be a happy one.' See *Du Syst. Pén.*, pp.v–viii,43,70–71,434.
4. Non-Alph.II (quoted in part, *O.C.*,VIII,287–288).
5. Non-Alph.III.
6. Toc. diary note, 3 Nov. 1831 (Port.III).
7. Non-Alph.II.
8. Toc. diary note (Non-Alph.III, *O.C.*,VIII,289–291).
9. Toc. diary note (Non-Alph.III).
10. Port.III.
11. 'Paquet 17,' TT, dated by Bt. 29 Oct. (*O.C.*,VIII,286).
12. Toc. diary note (Port.III).

## XXXVIII

### BEAUMONT'S *Marie*

1. For the conversations that resulted, see particularly Tocqueville's many notes in Port.III, Alph.B, and Non-Alph.II.
2. Bt. to his brother Achille, Philadelphia, 8 Nov. 1831 (BBlb).

## XXXIX

### PHILADELPHIA AGAIN

1. Bt. to his sister Eugénie, Cincinnati (Ohio), 1st Dec. 1831 (BBlb).
2. Bt. to his sister-in-law Félicie, Philadelphia, 26 Oct. 1831 (BBlb).
3. Toc. to Chabrol, Philadelphia, this 26 Oct. 1831 (YT).
4. Toc. to Charles Stoffels, 22 Oct. 1831 (*O.C.*,VII,81–82).
5. Toc. diary note (Port.III).
6. Bt. to his father, Philadelphia, 17 November (BBlb).
7. Toc. to Mme Édouard, Philadelphia, this 18 Oct. 1831; rough drafts of a letter to ?, Philadelphia, 8 Nov. 1831; Toc. to Chabrol, Philadelphia, this 26 Oct. 1831 (YT).

8. See Cahier F, and Tocqueville papers under heading BIc. A conversation with an unidentified lawyer, 27 October, had touched on the subjects of party politics and bankruptcy (Toc. diaries, Alph.A, Non-Alph.II).

9. Toc. diary note, Philadelphia, 18 Nov. 1831 (Non-Alph.III).

10. Non-Alph.III.

11. Bt. to his sister Eugénie, Cincinnati (Ohio), 1st Dec. 1831 (BBlb).

12. From the *Philadelphia Gazette*.

## XL

### JOURNEY TO THE OHIO: THE HAZARDS OF STAGE AND STEAM

1. Bt. to Eugénie, Cincinnati (Ohio), 1st Dec. 1831 (BBlb).

2. 25 Nov. 1831 (Port.III). The name of the steamboat is erroneously given as *Ohio*.

3. Toc. to Chabrol, on board the *4th July*, on the Ohio, 26 Nov. 1831, (continued) 28 Nov. (YT).

4. *Marie*,I,390–391.

5. 30 Nov. 1831 (Cahier E).

## XLI

### CINCINNATI

1. Bt. to his sister Eugénie, Cincinnati (Ohio), 1st Dec. 1831 (BBlb).

2. Cahier E.

3. Bt. to his brother Jules, 1831 (on the Ohio) 4 December (BBlb).

4. Toc. dairy notes (Non-Alph.III).

5. Toc. diary note (Non-Alph.III).

6. Toc. diary note (Non-Alph.III).

7. See Cahier F.

8. Toc. diary note (Non-Alph.III).

9. Toc. diary note (Non-Alph.III).

## XLII

### OHIO—OR REFLECTIONS ON THE MANUFACTURE OF AN AMERICAN STATE

1. Toc. to his mother, Louisville, 6 Dec. 1831 (*O.C.*,VII,90).

2. Cahier E; Bt. to his brother Jules, 1831 (on the Ohio) 4 December (BBlb).

## XLIII

### The Winter Road to Memphis

1. Bt. to Eugénie, Cincinnati (Ohio), 1st Dec. 1831 (BBlb).
2. Bt. to his mother, Sandy bridge, 15 December 1831 (BBlb).
3. The corrected story that follows has been pieced together from the following documents: Toc. to Chabrol, Louisville this 6 December, 1831 (YT); Beaumont's 'Notice' (*O.C.*,V,29–33); Toc. to his father, Memphis, 20 Dec. 1831 (*O.C.*,VII,93–98).
4. *O.C.*,V,22,25.
5. *Nashville Republican and State Gazette*, 15 Dec., 17 Dec., 1831.
6. Nichol to A. Jackson, Nashville, 30th December 1831, Jackson Papers, Library of Congress.
7. Hone diary, New York Historical Society.

## XLIV

### Tennessee Reflections

1. Bt. to his mother (cont.), Memphis, 18 December (BBlb).
2. Toc. diary note, 9 Dec. 1831 (Non-Alph.III).
3. Cahier E.
4. Toc. diary note, 15 Dec. 1831 (Non-Alph.III, quoted, *O.C.*,VIII, 293–294).
5. Cahier E.

## XLV

### Encounter with Choctaw Indians—and an Accident

1. Toc. to his mother, 25 December (YT, quoted, *O.C.*,VII,99–106).
2. Bt. to Achille, 25 Dec. 1831 (on board the steamboat *Louisville*, on the Mississippi) (BBlb).
3. Toc. note, 26 Dec. 1831 (Cahier E).

## XLVI

### Two Famous Books—and an Exile Named Houston

1. Cahier E.
2. 'Union: Central Government,' 28 Dec. 1831 (Cahier E).

3. On the Mississip[p]i, 27 Dec. 1831 (Cahier E).
4. Memphis, 20 Dec. 1831 (Cahier E).
5. 31 Dec. 1831 (Cahier E).


## XLVII

### *'24 Heures à la Nouvelle Orléans'*

1. Port.III.
2. *Du Syst. Pén.*, p.27.
3. Toc. diary note, Non-Alph.III: '1 January 1832. Conversation with Mr. Mazureau, one of the foremost lawyers of Louisiana.' (Quoted in part, *O.C.*,VIII,294.)
4. Port.III.
5. Toc. diary note (Non-Alph.III, quoted in part, *O.C.*,VIII,296).
6. Letter dated 'Chesapeak Bay, 16 January 1832' (YT).
7. Toc. diary note (Port.III).
8. Toc. diary note (Non-Alph.III, quoted, *O.C.*,VIII,296–297).
9. 4 January (Port.III).


## XLVIII

### FROM MOBILE TO THE CHESAPEAKE

1. Toc. diary note (Port.IV).
2. Toc. to Chabrol, from Chesapeak bay, 16 January 1832 (YT).
3. Toc. to Alexandrine, in Chesapeak Bay, 16 Jan. 1832 (TT, quoted, *O.C.*,VII,107–109).
4. Toc. diary note (Port.IV, quoted in part, *O.C.*,VIII,297–298).
5. Non-Alph.III (from Port.IV).


## XLIX

### MR. POINSETT EXPLAINS

1. 'Conversations with Mr. Poinsett, from the twelfth to the seventeenth of January 1832.' Toc. diary note (Non-Alph.III, fragment quoted, *O.C.*,VIII,298–299).
2. Rough notes on the topics discussed 13, 14, 15 January may be found in Port.V.

## L

### 'WHAT MAKES A REPUBLIC BEARABLE'

1. 14 January 1832 (Cahier E).
2. Knoxville, 8 January 1832 (Port.IV).
3. 14 January 1832 (Cahier E).
4. Toc. diary note (Port.V).
5. Toc. diary note (Port.IV).
6. Toc. diary note (Port.V).

## LI

### WASHINGTON RECEIVES THE COMMISSIONERS

1. 23 Jan. 1832, *Ministère des Affaires Étrangères, États-Unis*, 1832, volume 86,p.31.
2. Bt. to his mother, Washington, 20 January 1832 (BBlb).
3. Toc. to his father, Washington, 24 January 1832 (*O.C.*,VII,109).

## LII

### FEDERAL STUDIES—AND THE RETURN

1. Toc. to his father, Washington, 24 January 1832 (*O.C.*,VII,109).
2. Non-Alph.III.
3. 31 January 1832 (Cahier E).
4. 'Paquet 21,' erroneously dated 15 January (TT).
5. 24 January 1832 (Non-Alph.III).
6. Washington, 24 January 1832 (*O.C.*,VII,109).
7. '. . . Sometime since Mr. Beaumont wrote to me that he was indebted to you for many kindnesses at Washington: *Mille graces de ma part.*' Jos. Coolidge Jr. to N.P.Trist, Boston, 15 Feb'y [1832], Trist Papers, Library of Congress.
8. See the very grateful letters from Beaumont, 2 February and 16 February 1832, Trist Papers, Library of Congress (Copies, BIc, YT).
9. On 7 February 1832, Henry D. Gilpin wrote to Edward Livingston: '. . . I saw Messrs. Beaumont and Tocqueville who expressed great pleasure at having seen you, though they s$^d$ you were so much occupied that they had much less conversation than they desired. They

only remained one day here. . . .' Gilpin Papers, Historical Society of Pennsylvania.

10. Among these last were: three communications from Mayor Richards (covering the topics of Philadelphia finances, Philadelphia government, and county administration in Pennsylvania); a letter for Beaumont from Th. L. McKenney on the subject of the American Indians; S.L.Southard's essay on New Jersey criminal law; and Sparks' invaluable essay on Town Government in New England. There reached them, also, in the ten days while they were waiting to sail: Statistics from Gill in Maryland and Riker in New York on crime in their respective States, with observations thereon; the three monumental essays from Recorder McIlvaine; and a set of answers from Joseph Coolidge Jr., in response to some further questions forwarded to him from New Orleans. In addition, William Short sent Tocqueville a letter for his friend Hyde de Neuville in France. (See BIc,YT.)

11. It is not improbable that Tocqueville and Beaumont attended a public dinner given on 9 February for General Santander. Philip Hone, Charles King, and Albert Gallatin were among the hosts, and thirteen toasts were given. The general spoke in Spanish for fifteen minutes, and few in the company understood him. When a translation of his remarks was read, however, they were 'received with 9 cheers.' *New York American*, Feb. 10.

12. See mention of 'De Bourmont & De Tocqueville' in Hone's diary for 16 February, New York Historical Society.

## LIII

### 1832–1840:

#### THROUGH DISGRACE AND DISILLUSION

1. The materials for this study of Tocqueville's and Beaumont's careers upon their return to France are taken from Tocqueville's notes and correspondence, published in *Œuvres Complètes* (V,35–58, 319–359,423–444;VI,19–96;VII,112–178;VIII,301–474); from *Correspondence & Conversations of Alexis de Tocqueville with Nassau William Senior from 1834 to 1859* (I,Preface,1–25ff.); and Henry Reeve's biographical notice of Tocqueville, printed in the 1889 London edition of his translation of Tocqueville's Commentary. Also from a number

of unpublished notes and manuscripts (TT,YT), notably a series of letters from Beaumont to Tocqueville, and another group from Tocqueville to his family and intimate friends. The letter to Beaumont, here quoted, is dated Paris, 4 April 1832.

2. Quoted from a copy of this letter in Beaumont's hand to the *Procureur Général* in whose jurisdiction lay the sectional court of Versailles.

3. Quoted by Reeve (cited above), p.xxiii.

4. Toc. to Marie Mottley, fragmentary copies in the latter's hand, 18 May and 3 June 1832 (TT).

5. *O.C.*,VI,25–26.

6. *O.C.*,VIII,301–303.

7. Paris, 16 Sept. 1833 (TT).

8. *O.C.*,VIII,327,337.

9. Toc. to Bt., Gray, 29 October 1829 (*O.C.*,VII,16).

10. Toc. to Henry Reeve, Paris, 22 March 1837 (*O.C.*,VI,70–71).

11. Toc. to Bt., 13 Aug. 1833; Toc. to Kergolay, 21 Sept., 28 Sept. 1834 (TT).

12. 23 Aug. 1834, copy by Marie Mottley (TT).


## LIV

### The Prison Report and a Prison Crusade

1. *Du Syst. Pén.*, pp.183,187.

2. See, for example, the citations and quotations given in the second edition, *Système Pénitentiaire*, II,358–372.

3. W.B.S.Taylor, *Origin and Outline of the Penitentiary System, translated from the French Official Report of MM. Gustave de Beaumont and Alexis de Tocqueville*, 1833.

4. *Amerika's Besserungs-System, und dessen Anwendung auf Europa, mit einem Anhange über Straf-Ansiedelungen und zwei und zwanzig Beilagen . . . nebst Erweiterungen und Zusatzen von Dr.N.H.Julius*, Berlin, 1833.

5. *On the Penitentiary System in the United States, and its Application in France; with an appendix on penal colonies, and also, Statistical notes.* By Gustave de Beaumont and Alexis de Tocqueville, counsellors in the Royal Courts of Paris and members of the Historical Society of Pennsylvania. Translated from the French, with an introduction, notes

and additions. By Francis Lieber. Philadelphia: Carey, Lea & Blanchard, 1833.

6. The literature and progress of this movement may be reviewed in Robert G. Mahieu, *Les Enquêteurs français aux États-Unis de 1830 à 1837*, Paris, 1934; Ed. Ducpétiaux, *Des Progrès et de l'état actuel de la réforme pénitentiaire* . . . , Brussels, 1837; *Edinburgh Review*, January 1837. See also Demetz et Blouet, *Rapports* . . . *sur les Pénitenciers des États-Unis*, 1837; Bérenger, *De la Repression Pénale*, 1855; and the very informing Paul Cuche, *Traité de Science et de Législation pénitentiaire*, 1905.

7. In addition to Lieber's interleaved copy of his translation, to be found in the Johns Hopkins University Library, see also: the eighth and ninth *Reports* of the Boston Prison Discipline Society; Lieber's correspondence with Beaumont and Tocqueville (letters of 19 Nov. 1832 and 7 Jan. 1833 at Beaumont; letter of 10 Nov. 1832 at Huntington Library); *Christian Examiner*, July 1836; *North American Review*, July 1839; F.C.Gray, *Prison Discipline in America*, 1849 (these three pro-Auburn); also *Letters on the Comparative Merits of the Pennsylvania and New York Systems of Penitentiary Discipline*, by a Massachusetts man, 1836; *A Vindication of the Separate System of Prison Discipline from the Misrepresentations of the North American Review*, 1839; and *An Inquiry into the Alleged Tendency of the Separation of Convicts, One from the Other, to Produce Disease and Derangement*, by a Citizen of Philadelphia, 1849 (these being replies from the Pennsylvania point of view).

The bickering of zealots, happily, has not obscured for modern scholars and sociologists the value of Beaumont and Tocqueville's report. See F.H.Wines, *Punishment and Reformation, a study of the Pentientiary System*, rev. ed. 1923; and the statement of Harry Elmer Barnes (in his *Evolution of Penology in Pennsylvania*, pp.173–174) that their book is 'a most calm and judicious document . . . not at all marred by partisanship. . . . One of the chief sources for the early history of American penology.'

8. *Le Blaisois*, 20 Nov. 1833 (copy by Bt., BB).

9. For Tocqueville's adoption of the Pennsylvania philosophy and the later development of his views, see Ed.L.Pierce, *Memoirs and Letters of Charles Sumner*, III,79,95note,534; also the third edition of the *Système Pénitentiaire, augmentée du Rapport de M. de Tocqueville sur le projet de réforme des prisons et du Texte de la loi adoptée par la*

*Chambre des Députés*, 1845; and Charles Lucas, *Exposé de l'État de la Question pénitentiaire en Europe et aux États-Unis*, 1844.

10. See note 9, above, and also P.Cuche, *Traité de Science et de Législation pénitentiaire*, 1905.

## LV

### THE MATERIALS FOR TOCQUEVILLE'S BOOK

1. In so doing, Tocqueville made the acquaintance of Machiavelli as a historian. See *O.C.*,VIII,437–474.

2. *O.C.*,VI,173–174.

3. 9 May 1840, quoted in William W. Story, *Life and Letters of Joseph Story*, II,330. See also comments by R.L.Hawkins, *Romanic Review*, XX,355.

4. Benton to Van Buren, 25 Sept. 1851, 28 Sept. 1851, Van Buren Papers, Library of Congress; Benton, *Thirty Years' View*, I,113,114,226.

## LVI

### THE DESIGN OF THE *Démocratie*

1. Faguet, *Politiques et Moralistes du dix-neuvième siècle*, III,68.

2. This seems to have been the chief reason why Tocqueville never went very far with the project for their Review. See Toc. to Bt., 13 August and 1 Nov. 1833 (BB).

3. *O.C.*,VI,56–57,69.

4. Toc. to Kergolay, Paris, 25 June 1834 (*O.C.*,V,322).

5. Toc. to Charles Stoffels, 31 July 1834 (from copy in possession of Mlle Stoffels d'Hautefort).

6. Greg, *Literary and Social Judgments*, 1873, p.257.

7. See fragments of a very striking letter, without date or address, but written in answer to the protests of some friend (TT, in section labelled CIc).

8. *O.C.*,V,427–429.

9. The present writer has not himself seen the document, *mon instinct, mes opinions*, published by Redier (*Comme disait M. de Tocqueville...*, pp.45–49); and it seems to him perfectly clear that Redier exaggerates Tocqueville's aristocratic tendencies. Nevertheless, Tocqueville's sympathies did lie with quality rather than with quantity. He

shared the highest ideals of honour and duty known to the *ancien régime*, he feared the masses, and he scorned vulgarity.

10. Quoted by Marcel, *Essai politique sur Alexis de Tocqueville*, pp.67–68.

11. *O.C.*,V,432.

12. *Dém. en Am.*, IV,322.

13. *O.C.*,V,341.

14. *Dém. en Am.*, IV,335. See also the fine paragraph next following about the foolishness of trying to make an energetic nation out of citizens who are individually weak and pusillanimous.

## LVII

### Tocqueville's Work in Retrospect:

### Its Defects

1. Quoted, Marcel, *Essai politique sur Alexis de Tocqueville*, p.89. For the literature on which this chapter is in part based, see the Bibliography, with particular attention to the articles of Faucher, Mill, Sainte-Beuve, and Faguet.

2. See Toc. to Bt., Baugy, 22 Nov. 1836 (BB); also the numerous references in Tocqueville's correspondence to the 'nightmare' of his second two volumes: *O.C.*,VI,67,109;VII,149,164,175–176.

3. *Moniteur*, 31 Dec. 1860.

4. Charles Cestre, 'Alexis de Tocqueville, témoin et juge de la civilisation américaine,' *Revue des Cours et Conférences*, 1932–1933, XXXIV, vols. I and II.

5. In this matter it seems to the present writer that Professor Cestre's detailed critique is somewhat too emphatic. Tocqueville, as a historian, was unquestionably guilty of a number of omissions; and he would have been the first to confess the fact himself. For he was not writing a history; he had a quite different purpose in mind. Equally, it seems a little unfair to measure Tocqueville's knowledge of the American past against the best or most fashionable historiography of almost a century later (in this case: the brand of 1920–1932). When Cestre criticizes Tocqueville for not reaching the frontier interpretation of the Revolution, or Beard's philosophy on the Federal Convention, or a Jacksonian-Rooseveltian view of the Supreme Court, the charge has been carried too far.

## LVIII

### TOCQUEVILLE'S WORK IN RETROSPECT:

### CERTAIN ENDURING QUALITIES

1. For an excellent statement of Tocqueville's point of view toward history, see Faguet, *Politiques et Moralists du dix-neuvième siècle*, III,75.

2. A.V.Dicey, *National Review*, XXI,774.

3. J.S.Mill, *Autobiography*, edited by J.J.Coss, Columbia Univ. Press, 1924, pp.134–136.

4. *Edinburgh Review*, Oct. 1840, pp.1–47.

5. 'The Predictions of Hamilton and De Tocqueville,' Johns Hopkins University *Studies in Historical and Political Science*, 1887, pp.329–381.

6. E.Faguet, *Revue des deux Mondes*, Feb. 1894, p.672.

# APPENDIX E

## BIBLIOGRAPHY

THE literature on Tocqueville's celebrated commentary and the documentary sources available for a study of his youth and education have already been listed (see Chapter Notes, Chapters I and II). Only the materials on Tocqueville and Beaumont's American experiences and on the writing of their books remain to be analysed. Reference has already been made to all of these manuscript and printed sources, but their history and general character require a special word of explanation.

### HISTORY AND NATURE OF THE AMERICAN MATERIALS

It is recorded that occasionally, in after years, Alexis de Tocqueville would regale the circle of his intimate friends at dinner with anecdotes of his and Beaumont's travel adventures in America, particularly among the Indians. And it is now known that he was careful to preserve, among his private papers, his share of the manuscripts and documents resulting from their visit. But during his lifetime he never published anything on their experiences in the United States after his *De la Démocratie en Amérique*; and in the Introduction to the first volume of that work, he wrote:

'In support of what I advance, I could often have cited the authority of names which are known, or which at least are worthy to be known; but I have taken care not to do so. The stranger often learns, at the fireside of his host, important truths which the latter would perhaps conceal from a friend. With a stranger people relieve themselves of their enforced silence; his indiscretion is not feared, because he is only a passer-by. Each of these confidences was recorded by me as soon as received; and they will never leave my portfolio. I would rather injure the success of my recital than add my name to the list of those travellers who send back chagrin and embarrassment in return for the generous hospitality that they have received.'

Needless to repeat, Tocqueville kept his word. As a result, even the identity of his American friends and acquaintances was concealed from the reader. And of course the philosophic and analytical nature of the commentary precluded the author's giving any description of his travels or adventures while investigating the penitentiaries of the United States and gathering materials for his work. As a matter of fact, the very documents from which such a story might have been written—the letters, the sketches, the essays and diary notes: unpublished and still only partly used—were put away, when he had finished writing, in a cabinet of his library in the remote Norman Château de Tocqueville. And there, during his lifetime, they remained. In 1859 when he came to die, therefore, he left to Mme de Tocqueville (among his voluminous papers) a group of American manuscripts whose existence was known only to his near friends, and whose possibilities were still unexploited.

### MANUSCRIPT SOURCES

First in number and importance, therefore, among the documents cited or quoted in the present volume are the American manuscripts (TT and TBT, copies in YT) to be found among the papers of Alexis de Tocqueville at the Château de Tocqueville, in Normandy. These include diaries, letters, essays, rough drafts, and a quantity of miscellaneous notes, nearly all actually written in the United States. Of greatest interest among these original materials are Tocqueville's fourteen *cahiers* or pocket diaries, most of them manufactured by Tocqueville himself out of folded sheets of paper, and all crammed by him with the record of his impressions and reflections, with conversations that he and Beaumont had with prominent Americans, and with accounts of their activities and travels through the various sections of the Union. Next in interest is the romantic fragment called *Quinze Jours au Désert*, a long descriptive account of their expedition into the Michigan wilderness that Beaumont first edited (see Chapters XX, XXI). Scarcely less important are the letters, these including copies (TBT) of eighteen that Tocqueville wrote home to his family and that Beaumont later published, and the originals of a number that he and Beaumont received, while in the United States, from their families and friends in France. Three of the last-named take the form of essays on judicial and administrative practices in France, written for purposes of comparison at Tocqueville's special request by his father, Chabrol, and E. de Blosseville (see Chapter XXX). In addition, Tocqueville's papers include a mass of unclassified notes and miscellaneous documents, all collected by Beaumont and himself in the course of their investigations in the United States, and brought back for use in the composition of his book. Finally, the collection contains whole *dossiers* of manuscript left over from the writing of *De la Démocratie en Amérique* during the years 1832–1840: outlines and rough drafts, sheaves of unused fragments, lastly, the original manuscript of the famous commentary itself.

Next in importance unquestionably—from the point of view of the student—is the Yale collection (YT) in the keeping of the University Library. Though consisting largely of copies and practically devoid of original manuscripts, this collection now contains the most comprehensive and one of the most valuable groups of documents, on the American trip of the two Frenchmen, anywhere available. It includes, first of all, the faithful and legible copies made for the Library by M. Bonnel (*Instituteur*, and secretary to the *Marie*, of Tocqueville) of all but the last of the above-mentioned American manuscripts in the Tocqueville collection. Secondly, it contains copies or reproductions made by the present writer of almost all of Beaumont's letters and American documents (listed below). Thirdly, it boasts photostats and reproductions of a number of the more interesting items discovered in the course of the present writer's investigation in this country. And finally, it contains as well certain papers that are now unique. Here a word of explanation is necessary. At the time when Paul White began his researches in France, a number of the original American manuscripts from the Tocqueville collection were in the temporary possession of M. Antoine Redier, who was then engaged in writing his life of the famous liberal aristocrat. Among these were forty-eight unpublished letters home, Tocqueville's amusing account of his stay in New Orleans, and a number of lengthy notes and important essays on legal and governmental topics, written at the particular demand of the young Frenchmen by certain well-informed citizens of Boston and Philadelphia. Appreciating the importance of these documents, White first catalogued them and then had them copied by the secretaries of M. Abel Doysié of Paris. Thereupon these copies were brought to Yale, where they have since been kept. Meanwhile, however, the originals, the Tocqueville manuscripts themselves, have somehow been mislaid and lost, with the consequence that the Yale reproductions are to-day the only records of these documents remaining.*

* These copies, like those of M.Bonnel, are unusually legible and accurate. As a result, the writer has been able to use the Yale collection in making his translations and

The third group of manuscripts is the small but important collection of papers, already referred to, to be found in the library of the Château de la Borde at Beaumont-la-Chartre. This group includes, in addition to the notes for their Prison Report and for Beaumont's *Marie*, a letter-book (BBlb) reproducing twenty-nine letters written home to his family; an album of about thirty original pencil and ink sketches of American scenes; a package of more than a score of letters received from Americans during their expedition; and almost the whole correspondence relative to their request for—their execution of—and their recall from—the prison mission.

In addition, there are one or two more items of considerable interest in private hands in France. The family of Romanet, descended from Jules de Beaumont, is in possession at the Château du Guillets (par Courgeoût, Orne) of the important second album of Gustave de Beaumont's pencil and ink and wash sketches made during his American travels. Mme de Langavant of St. Malo has four of Beaumont's original letters home to his other brother Achille. And Mlle Stoffels d'Hautefort of Versailles has a series of three most revealing letters written by Tocqueville to Charles Stoffels of Metz during the critical months just before and after the July Revolution.

Finally, there are a few original Tocqueville and Beaumont letters— as well as a number of unpublished items referring to them—to be found in the manuscript collections in this country, notably in the Library of Congress (Trist, Short, Warden Papers), the Massachusetts Historical Society (Edward Everett and Norton Papers), the Widener Library at Harvard (Papers of Sparks and Charles Sumner), the Historical Society of Pennsylvania (Gilpin Papers), and the Huntington and Johns Hopkins University Libraries (Francis Lieber Papers). Of these documents, the essay on New England town government, written for Tocqueville by Jared Sparks, is probably the most significant.

### Supplementary Documents

The Tocqueville and Beaumont manuscripts tell the story of their American visit in voluminous fashion and considerable detail. For the

---

excerpts for the present work. In addition to the above-mentioned letters and essays, two other groups of documents now seem to be missing. The first are the letters that Tocqueville wrote to his future wife from America; the second the 'journal' that Beaumont claimed to have kept during their travels, and from which he even published an extract (see above, pp.596–97).

background of their expedition, however, and for many of the sidelights on their experiences and adventures in the United States and
Canada, the public and private archives, here and abroad, must be
consulted.

In the *Archives Nationales* in Paris, under the heading BB[18]1323,
are to be found the correspondence between the different Ministries
over the appointment of Tocqueville and Beaumont to their mission,
some of the documents and reports that the two young magistrates
sent their superiors from America, and the papers relating to their
recall. In the *Ministère des Affaires Étrangères* (*États-Unis*, 1832, v.86)
are two interesting letters from Serurier, Minister to Washington,
commenting on the character and activities of the visiting commissioners, as they came within his view. And in the modern prisons of
France, as well as in the French prison literature of the past century, a
vivid impression of the successes and failures of Tocqueville and Beaumont as prison reformers may be gathered (see Chapter LIV).

In the United States, the published and unpublished literature on
Tocqueville and Beaumont's mission and Report is even more extensive. The wardens' Journals at the Charlestown and Eastern State
Penitentiaries contain numerous references to the visits and investigations of the French commissioners; as do also the 1831–1832 reports
of the state prison inspectors of Massachusetts, Connecticut and Pennsylvania, the publications of the Boston Prison Discipline Society,
and the Minute Book of the Philadelphia Society for the Alleviation
of the Miseries of the Public Prisons. Of interest in this connection also
are the manuscripts of Francis Lieber (Huntington and Johns Hopkins University Libraries), his notes and additions in the translation
that he made of their report, and his own interleaved copy of that
work (at Johns Hopkins). In addition to the standard histories of punishment and reform, there are also still extant a few examples of two
special groups of publications which almost always referred to Tocqueville and Beaumont's visit and to their Report: the controversial
pamphlets and the findings of special legislative commissions of inquiry (see Chapter XXXII).

From one other source, the newspapers of the day in the larger
towns which Tocqueville and Beaumont visited, much incidental information of interest and value for this study has been obtained. Generally speaking, the American press in 1831 was preoccupied with politics and business, and few, even among the most widely subscribed

journals of the metropolitan centres, could boast a large staff of reporters or an efficient system for gathering news. In a surprising number of instances, however, these much-read periodicals noticed the arrival of Tocqueville and Beaumont in town, and contrived to announce the purposes and first results of their diligent inquiries. Moreover, even when they neglected to mention the presence of the distinguished foreigners within their gates, they frequently reported the ceremonies and occasions in which the commissioners took part, thus preserving for the modern reader the scenes through which Tocqueville and Beaumont passed.

## PUBLISHED MATERIALS

The published writings of Tocqueville, Beaumont, and others on the subject of their American trip are, as has been intimated more than once, extremely disappointing.

Of the three works that the two friends published shortly after their return from the United States, Tocqueville's *Démocratie* was too delicate of American feelings and too impersonal and philosophic in approach, to yield any picture whatever of their travels. Beaumont's *Marie* likewise concentrated on its tragic romance and on its weighty notes to such an extent that only a reader of unusual acuteness would suspect how many of its adventures and incidents and opinions had been drawn directly from their own experiences. The earliest book, their Prison Report, was really specific and illuminating. Its text and its voluminous notes contained minute and circumstantial accounts of many phases of their penitentiary inquiries. It was reticent neither as to names, places, nor opinions. Whom Tocqueville and Beaumont had met and from whom they had drawn their documents and opinions was made perfectly plain. Their methods of investigation stood out on every page. Accordingly, a comparison of this book with parallel statements in their manuscripts (and in the wardens' journals) has made it possible to reconstruct in unusual detail what happened in each of the prisons that they visited.

But that revelation covered only their penitentiary investigation. About their other activities and manifold experiences in the United States Tocqueville, at least, published no more until he died.

It was, as is known to close students of Tocqueville, the memorial edition of Tocqueville's writings, got out by Gustave de Beaumont in the years 1861–1866, that first revealed something of the true character of their American excursion and of the investigations that had preceded the making of *De la Démocratie en Amérique*. Into this edition, with the permission of Mme de Tocqueville, Gustave de Beaumont inserted a carefully limited number of Tocqueville's American Manuscripts. In addition to a biographical 'Notice' that he wrote himself, he placed the two sketches of Oneida and Michigan in volume V, a score of Tocqueville's letters home in volume VII, and in volume VIII about seventy pages quoted from his diaries, including the record of one or two rather illuminating conversations.*

Even this unexpected publication, however, presented no clear and satisfactory picture. The trouble was, the American documents were so fragmentary, so poorly distributed through the edition, and in each case so overwhelmed by the sheer mass of the other new materials presented simultaneously, that the unity and continuity that they should have had was lost. For the student of to-day, moreover, there is a second reason why these volumes, giving Tocqueville's American manuscripts the only real publicity that they have enjoyed to date, are less than satisfactory. Beaumont did not always reproduce Tocqueville's papers exactly as he found them. This is particularly true of his edition of Tocqueville's American letters, where—without warning to the reader—individual words are changed, and whole passages are omitted, or telescoped, or even materially altered from the original. To call Beaumont an unscrupulous editor would be somewhat unjust. For anxious as this devoted companion was, in his old age, to avoid giving offence to Tocqueville's American friends or to his fellow-countrymen, he nevertheless did not knowingly alter the es-

---

* The *Œuvres Complètes* have been reproduced, in whole or in part, both in England and in the United States. With certain additions, the individual volumes were translated and published in England as soon as they appeared, beginning with *Memoirs, Letters and Remains of Alexis de Tocqueville,* translated from the French by the translator of Napoleon's correspondence with King Joseph, 2 v., 1861. These two volumes were brought out in Boston as well, in 1862. The narrative *Quinze Jours au Désert* had already been published by Beaumont, apparently as a sort of trial balloon, in the *Revue des deux Mondes,* 1 Dec. 1860, under the title 'Quinze Jours au Désert, souvenirs d'un voyage en Amérique, papiers posthumes, par M. Alexis de Tocqueville, de l'Académie française.' Subsequently this fragment, together with extracts from his Sicilian notes, was republished in England as an example of fine French, in a text-book edited by J.E.Mansion, 'Quinze Jours au Désert and Voyage en Sicile by Alexis de Tocqueville,' *Oxford Modern French Series,* 1904. And five years later R. Clyde Ford reproduced the narrative together with extracts from some of Tocqueville's letters, as a text for the schools of Michigan: *De Tocqueville's Voyage en Amérique,* edited with introduction, notes and vocabulary, Boston, 1909. In 1897, again, Beaumont's *Notice sur Alexis de Tocqueville* was republished in Paris. But in none of these cases was there a fresh resort to the original manuscripts.

sential meaning of a document. Simply, he made it a practice to tone
down the acerbity of a statement, omit a sentence that might wound,
amend the awkward construction of another, leave out what seemed
to him insignificant:—in a word, he thought it his task to contrive
that Tocqueville's works should preserve him for the world in the
most attractive light. One characteristic instance of this procedure has
been pointed out in the foregoing chapters: Beaumont's toning down of
Tocqueville's sharp remarks about the singing of American women
(Chapter XII). A great many others could have been cited, as well,
for not all of which are Beaumont's motives so easily discernible. When
we find him omitting the names of most of their fellow-passengers on
the *Havre*, we can guess at the reason; but why for example he should
have felt it necessary to cut out the part of Tocqueville's letter to
Lesueur (28 May, Chapter VIII) describing the mayor's dinner, it is
harder to understand. Fortunately, except in occasional instances, the
student is now no longer forced to rely on Beaumont's version and can
get his copy or translation, as the present writer has done, either straight
from the original manuscripts themselves, or from the copies in the
Yale collection.

As for all the reviews, articles, essays, and books, published both
while Alexis de Tocqueville was still alive and in the seventy-nine
years since his death, they will be found to contain but little of value
or interest on the American trip. In France, among the biographers,
only Antoine Redier succeeded in digging up and printing any new
materials relative to his voyage; and among the political philosophers
only Édouard Laboulaye's *L'État et ses Limites* (1863) is worth con-
sulting in this respect. Among Englishmen, James Bryce made a careful and most illuminating analysis of Tocqueville's study of America
(revised and republished as 'United States Constitution as Seen in the
Past' [*Studies in History and Jurisprudence*, I,311–358]); but that was
all. The subject of Tocqueville's visit has therefore been left almost entirely to American reviewers and commentators; and their success
has been limited by their lack of materials. In 1865, M.Heilprin, reviewing Tocqueville's *Œuvres Complètes* in the *Nation* (I,247–249),
called attention to the similarity of the opinions expressed by J.C.Spen-
cer in a conversation with Tocqueville (*O.C.*,VIII,236–238) to certain
passages in Tocqueville's great book. He also inaugurated the attempt
to trace the prison commissioners' itinerary through the various sections of the country and through Canada, by culling incidental bits of

information from the letters, sketches, and diary notes scattered through Tocqueville's works.* In 1898, then, D.C.Gilman, in his introduction to a new edition of *Democracy in America* (2 v., Century Co.), wrote what was probably the best review yet published on Tocqueville in America. Using the above-named materials, he sketched their visit in 1831–1832, and then went on to give a description of the writing of the famous treatise and a critical analysis of its contents. In 1898 again, H.B.Adams made public his important discovery of Tocqueville's indebtedness to Jared Sparks for his picture of New England town government (*Johns Hopkins University Studies*, XVI,12ff.). And in 1928–1929, R.L.Hawkins published two articles in the *Romanic Review* (XIX,195ff.,XX,151ff.) on Tocqueville's trip and on his subsequent relations with Americans, basing these on Tocqueville's published works and on the discovery of a dozen new Tocqueville letters in the Widener and Historical Society of Pennsylvania manuscript collections. Finally, there should be mentioned the article in which Paul L. White, from the manuscript sources enumerated earlier in this bibliography, anticipated the present study: 'American Manners in 1830; de Tocqueville's Letters and Diary' (*Yale Review,* Oct. 1922); and the series of articles by the present author (listed in Chapter Notes, Chapter I).

* R. Clyde Ford, in the introduction and text of *De Tocqueville's Voyage en Amérique* (cited above) managed to put together some of the fragments of the story.

# INDEX

ABBOTT, Mr. and Mrs. Samuel, 783.
abolition, 61,554 note,766; progress, 652.
accidents, steamboat wreck, 546–8; to stage-coach 574,579; steamboat caught in ice, 574–7; steamboat aground, 599–601,619–20; in South, 635–7; 671 note.
Acton, Lord, 756,768–9.
Adams, H.B., 833.
Adams, John, 301,360.
Adams, John Quincy, 417–421,649 note, 670–2; appearance, 417–8; on political conventions, 418; on the South, 418–20; on French Revolutionary influences, 420; on Union, 724.
Alabama, 635–42.
Albany, 176–88,345,766.
*Albany Argus,* 180–4.
'Albany Regency,' 177,186.
Allegheny Mountains, 543.
Allison, John M.S., 743 note,780.
Almshouse, Baltimore, story of the crazed negro, 516–7,519.
American character, overweening interest in money, 49,55,70,81–2,131,239,261; commercial ingenuity, 49–50 note,614–5; susceptibility to flattery, 59–60,112, 402; sensitive to criticisms of English travellers, 60; interest in penitentiaries, 61–3,182; humanitarian interests, 61–3,177–8,391,459–60,463; democratic equality in social relationships, 65–6, 118,373–4,379–80,417–8; national conceit, 68,69,73,80–1; small town attitude, 69; belief in religion, 69,73,124, 364; middle-class characteristics, 69–70,82,117,483; high morality, 71–2, 125,131,139–40,154,374–5,378,453, 487,648; lack of fine arts, 73,150; hankering for titles, 73,91–2; feverish activity, 76,150; few refinements, 81, 117,150,478; diverse origins, 114,123, 129; faith in education, 114,124–5, 153,365; restlessness, 118–9,123,130; lack of standards, 119,131; optimism, belief in progress, 119,123,153,645; faith in republican self-government,

152; respect for law, 161; tranquillity under physical discomforts, 189,243, 547–8; curiosity, 246–51; high level of intelligence, 452; *see also* North, South, West, plutocracy, suffrage, etc.
American Philosophical Society, 476.
Ames, C.F., 184.
Ampère, 5,768.
Anderson, Harry Bennett, 780.
Andrews, Professor Charles McLean, on Sparks, 410,780.
'Antony's Nose,' 172.
Apprentices Society, Albany, 181.
Arbre-Croché, 298–9.
*Archives Nationales,* 780.
aristocracy, disappearance of, in U.S., 118,127,152,158–9,160,355–6; in New York, 63,91–2; in Boston, 363–5,371, 390–1; in East, 483; in Maryland, 494–7,503,506–8; in South, 567,569, 582,585–6; paternalism, 602–3; English 'aristocracy' *vs.* American 'democracy,' 603 note; as dominant characteristic of English society, 688–90,763; of wealth, 690–1,766–7 note; decline in world, 722,762–3, 770; Tocqueville's instinctive sympathy for, 737–8,750; *see also* equalitarianism, American character.
Aristotle, 743.
Arkansas, 611,614.
army, want of one in U.S., 71–2,82,130; frontier posts, 305.
articles, on Tocqueville and on Beaumont, *see* footnotes, chapter notes, and bibliography. Sources are not listed in this Index.
Assembly of Lower Canada, 317 note,331, 335 note.
assembly, right of, *see* conventions.
Association of Printers and Albany Typographical Society, 180.
Atala, an Indian heroine, out of Chateaubriand, 305–6; *see* Indians, Tocqueville on.
Athenæum, Boston, 391.